FUNDAMENTALS OF CURRICULUM

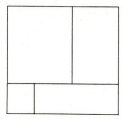

Decker Walker

Stanford University

HARCOURT BRACE JOVANOVICH, PUBLISHERS

San Diego   New York   Chicago   Austin   Washington, D.C.
London   Sydney   Tokyo   Toronto

Illustration Credits

Fig. 1–1: Reproduced with permission of the National Council for Educational Technology; **Fig. 1–2:** V. K. Weigand. "A Study of Subordinate Skills in Science Problem Solving." *Basic Studies of Learning Hierarchies in School Subjects.* © 1970 UC Press; **Fig. 1–3:** Benjamin Bloom. *Taxonomy of Educational Objectives: The Classification of Educational Objectives.* © 1956 McKay Pub.; **Fig. 1–4:** Arizona Art Education Association. "Art in Elementary Education that the Law Requires." *InPerspective.* © 1982; Fig. 1–5; Ralph Tyler. *Basic Principles of Curriculum and Instruction.* © 1949 University of Chicago Press; **Page 43:** Culver Pictures; **Page 53:** Courtesy of the Harvard Archives; **Fig. 2–1:** Culver Pictures; **Fig. 2–7a:** HBJ Collection; **Fig. 2–7b:** Smithsonian Institute; **Pages 64 and 75:** The University of Chicago Archives; **Fig. 3–1:** Roger Viollet; **Page 100:** Special Collections, Millbank Memorial Library, Teachers' College, Columbia University; **Page 101:** Dartmouth College Library. Photo by Mary Morris; **Page 102 and 103:** Courtesy of the Harvard University Archives; **Pages 104 and 105:** Office of War Information, Library of Congress; **Page 106:** © 1940 by the Schauer Printing Studio, Inc. Santa Barbara, CA; **Page 111:** The Ohio State University Archives; **Page 162:** The University of Chicago Archives.

Requests for permission to make copies of any part of the work should be mailed to: Copyrights and Permissions Department, Harcourt Brace Jovanovich, Publishers, Orlando, Florida 32887.

ISBN: 0-15-529434-2
Library of Congress Catalog Card Number: 89-84684

Printed in the United States of America

To Glenn, David, and Decker, Jr.

Writing a book is an adventure: to begin with it is a toy and an amusement, and then it becomes a mistress, and then it becomes a master, and then it becomes a tyrant, and the last phase is that just as you are about to be reconciled to your servitude, you kill the monster and fling him about to the public.

Winston Churchill

PREFACE

I still remember my astonishment when I learned more about waves in one day of helping high school physics students do experiments in a ripple tank than I had in several years of college physics. These ripple tank experiments were part of a newly developed course in high school physics—one of the first of the "new curricula" created in the late 1950s and early 1960s. It was the pedagogical elegance and power of this course, and a few others like it, that attracted me to curriculum making.

I began to read about curriculum making and soon became fascinated—and perplexed—with the sometimes surprising and often conflicting ideas. Curriculum developers who relied on Jerome Bruner's ideas about the structure of knowledge and discovery learning, for instance, designed different curricula than did developers who used B. F. Skinner's ideas about reinforcement and conditioned responses. I knew I liked one set of ideas more, but I could find no generally accepted principles that would show that one set of ideas would lead to a better curriculum. The more I read, the less consensus I found. Although I still have not found a consensus, I have gradually come to see the profound diversity of ideas about curriculum as a legitimate reflection of diversity in American life and thought.

The events that unfolded before me during this time of discovery also shaped my opinions of curriculum. In the 1960s at Stanford, as on many other campuses, students established "free universities" that offered courses on anything students wanted to learn, and did away with grades, diplomas, requirements, records, and everything else associated with formal institutions of learning. At about the same time, a bill was introduced in the California legislature to outlaw the teaching of the "new math" in California public schools. In a city less than 100 miles from where I grew up, angry parents blasted the door off a schoolhouse to protest the books their children were required to read. The United States Congress, responding to widespread public criticism, investigated the government's role in funding national curriculum projects, and eventually cut off funds for projects like the physics curriculum that had first attracted me to the subject. Such incidents taught me that curriculum materials development was not the whole story of curriculum making. I began to realize that the curriculum of American public schools was shaped by open conflict among various interests, public and private, professional and lay. This idea was not in the books I was reading.

Why Study Curriculum?

Everyone with a serious interest in education should be vitally concerned about curriculum matters. The most basic and important issues in education are addressed in the fundamental questions of curriculum study:

What educational goals should schools ask students and teachers to pursue?

What content should schools present to students?

How should schools organize the components of their educational programs?

Over the past three decades, the American educational system has been challenged by a grim parade of curricular crises that seems now to have degenerated into a chronic state of emergency. Today neoconservatives criticize cafeteria-style elective curricula. Controversies still simmer over compensatory education, bilingual education, and multicultural education. The nation is concerned about its economic competitiveness. Tests indicate that American children are not performing as well as their peers in other industrialized countries, and each new test result renews the sense of crisis.

By almost any measure, the American school system as a whole has failed to resolve satisfactorily any of the major curriculum crises that have befallen it since World War II. Achievement test scores have not improved significantly. Respected public figures still launch flaming criticisms at the nation's schools, and public confidence in the schools remains low. Government leaders repeatedly demonstrate their lack of confidence in the schools by intervening, and yet their actions have not yet had a noticeable impact, either. Despite the hundreds of millions of dollars federal agencies have spent on national education reforms, and even greater expenditures by state and local agencies, the declines, the criticisms, and the crises continue.

Educators today need to study curriculum so that they can act more intelligently and effectively to do their part to resolve these chronic crises. The analysis of curriculum determination offered in this book, for example, shows why curricular crises have occurred so frequently in the United States since World War II and suggests how we might cope with them more effectively. This book deals comprehensively with the many-faceted problems of curriculum, rather than looking at piecemeal situations. Such an overview of curriculum can help decision-makers to understand what they and others will need to do in order to achieve lasting and substantial curriculum improvement on a large scale.

The Plan of the Book

The book is designed to be used as a textbook for an introductory graduate level curriculum course. It is divided into four major parts. Part I introduces curriculum, providing definitions and an orientation to the entire subject, a brief history of the curriculum of American schools and of the forces that have shaped them, and an introduction to the main ideas people have used to think about curriculum questions.

Part II examines the place of theory in curriculum work, reaches the conclusion that curriculum is fundamentally a practical discipline, and works out the implications of this perspective for curriculum work.

Part III considers in detail how curricula operate in three crucial types of settings: classrooms, schools and local school districts, and state and national education systems. These chapters elaborate on the insight that the curriculum children actually encounter is strongly influenced by norms and conditions in the settings in which they occur.

Part IV shows how the ideas and perspectives presented earlier in the book can be applied to four main types of curriculum work: realizing a curriculum in a classroom, managing a curriculum in a school or local school system, curriculum policy-making, and the development of curriculum plans and materials.

In order to avoid overwhelming students with detail and complexity, it is essential that the material in Part I be understood before approaching the remaining chapters. In Part II, it is vital that students have a solid understanding of at least one curriculum theory of the mainstream type. It is also vital that students understand the practical perspective and the different role that theory plays in resolving curriculum questions in a practical, as contrasted with a theoretical, approach. Chapter 10, on the curriculum in the classroom, should be read before later chapters. Beyond these few guidelines, chapters can be covered in any order and with any degree of detail.

ACKNOWLEDGMENTS

I am grateful for the many ways my colleagues Edwin Bridges, Larry Cuban, Elliot Eisner, Michael Kirst, and David Tyack at the Stanford School of Education have been helpful. Former Dean J. Myron Atkin and current Dean Marshall Smith were extremely understanding and supportive throughout the period in which this text was written. For their helpful comments and suggestions, I would like to thank Michael Apple, University of Wisconsin; Jack Fraenkel, San Francisco State University; Gary Griffin, University of Texas at Austin; Herbert Kliebard, University of Wisconsin, Madison; Edmund Short, Pennsylvania State University; Ian Westbury, University of Illinois, Urbana-Champaign. I owe more than I can say to the many students in my classes who suffered through my gropings toward understanding and my early efforts at expressing what I only dimly understood. I wish especially to thank those who worked with me as research assistants: David Bergin, Sue Griffiths, and Liora Bresler.

I thank the staff of Harcourt Brace Jovanovich: Julia Berrisford, Acquisitions Editor; Debbie Hardin, Manuscript Editor; Cheryl Hauser, Production Editor; Linda Wild and Martha Gilman, Designers; Paulette Russo, Art Editor; Sarah Randall, Production Manager. I also thank my secretary of many years, Dorothy Brink, for her helpful contributions.

Finally, I would not have had the peace of mind to complete this work without the love and support of my family. Many good times we might have had were spent writing this book. Such losses can never be made up, but I hope they will be able to take pride in the results their sacrifices helped produce. In any event, I ask them to please accept this book as a token of my love and my gratitude for all that they have given me.

—Decker Walker

CONTENTS

PART I
Orientation

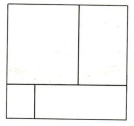

For the creation of a democratic society we need an educational system where the process of moral–intellectual development is in practice as well as in theory a cooperative transaction of inquiry engaged in by free, independent human beings who treat ideas and the heritage of the past as means and methods for the further enrichment of life, quantitatively and qualitatively, who use the good attained for the discovery and establishment of something better.

John Dewey
American philosopher and educator, 1952

STUDYING CURRICULUM

Mankind are by no means agreed about the things to be taught, whether we look to virtue or the best life. Neither is it clear whether education is more concerned with intellectual or with moral virtue. The existing practice is perplexing; no one knows on what principle we should proceed—should the useful in life, or should virtue, or should the highest knowledge be the aim of our training; all three opinions have been entertained.

Aristotle. *Politics.*
Greece, Fourth Century B.C.

PURPOSE OF THE CHAPTER

- to explain the varied meanings people give to the term curriculum and why they disagree on these meanings
- to define the term in a way that provides a sound foundation for future study of the subject and to interpret the key concepts in that definition
- to describe curriculum as a field of professional work and study and to show what there is to be learned about it
- to explain why it is important for those concerned with education to study and learn about curriculum

OUTLINE

What Is Curriculum?

Fundamental Concepts of Curriculum

The Importance of Curriculum Decisions and Actions

Curriculum As a Field of Professional Practice

Curriculum As a Field of Study

Studying Curriculum: A Personal View

WHAT IS CURRICULUM?

Since nearly everyone has been a student at one time or another, nearly everyone has some experience with a curriculum. Those who have also been teachers will have direct experience using a curriculum and perhaps even have participated in developing one. This familiarity is helpful to the student just beginning to take curriculum as a course of study, but it can also be misleading. Individuals performing in varying roles will generally have quite different associations to the word *curriculum* and will therefore approach the study of the subject with quite different ideas and expectations. A beginning teacher who has been presented with a bundle of papers and told "This is our curriculum for 6th grade Language Arts" is likely to form quite a different idea of what curriculum is than a principal concerned about the quality of her school's writing curriculum. The teacher in that situation is likely to think of the curriculum as some sort of plan spelled out on paper, made by others; he will probably also think of it as a constraint on his academic freedom, and perhaps even as an insult to his professional judgment. The principal, on the other hand, is likely to think of the curriculum as the actual program of the school, presented by teachers in their classrooms but determined by formal procedures prescribed by school authorities, and functioning as school policy that she is expected to maintain.

Differences in educational values also lead to different ideas about curriculum. A person who believes deeply that education is the introduction of the young to the treasures of the past will look at a school curriculum in a different light than someone who believes that the primary purpose of education is to foster the development of each individual child. Box 1-1 presents a number of definitions of curriculum from a variety of sources. Sharp differences of opinion about what curriculum actually is arise from such varied experiences and values. Box 1-2 presents five distinct concepts of curriculum that underlie many definitions such as those in Box 1-1. Each of these concepts is fervently espoused by large and influential communities of educators.

Diversity of experience and values makes it difficult to achieve wide public or professional consensus. The resulting controversy extends even to definitions of the most basic terms. The pervasiveness of controversy is in itself an important lesson to learn about curriculum. Box 1-3 suggests why such controversy is likely to continue.

Those beginning the systematic study of curriculum need a conception of the subject that is basically sound and inclusive enough to accommodate most points of view. A partisan definition that intentionally defines the subject in a way that is biased toward one point of view or value system makes an open-minded

■

BOX 1-1   Conflicting Definitions of Curriculum

The definitions below are quoted from various sources published in the last half-century.

- the planned learning activities sponsored by the school (Tanner and Tanner 1977, 406)

- the content pupils are expected to learn (Smith and Orlovsky 1978, 3)

- the contrived activity and experience—organized, focused, systematic—that life, unaided, would not provide (Musgrave 1968, 6)

- a set of events, either proposed, occurring, or having occurred, which has the potential for reconstructing human experience (Duncan and Frymier 1967, 181)

- situations or activities arranged and brought into play by the teacher to effect student learning (Shaver and Berlak 1968, 9)

- that *series of things* which children and youth must do and experience by way of developing abilities to do the things well that make up the affairs of adult life (Bobbitt 1918, 42)

- the total effort of the school to bring about desired outcomes in school and out-of-school situations (Saylor and Alexander 1954, 3)

- a sequence of potential experiences set up in school for the purpose of disciplining children and youth in group ways of thinking and acting (Smith, Stanley, and Shores 1957, 3)

- a set of abstractions from actual industries, arts, professions, and civic activities, and these abstractions are brought into the school-box and taught (Goodman 1963, 159)

- the offering of socially valued knowledge, skills, and attitudes made available to students through a variety of arrangements during the time they are at school, college, or university (Bell 1971, 9)

consideration of the merits of different points of view more difficult. Scholarly ideals demand that while a point of view may be rejected for good reasons it should not be *defined* away. Furthermore, those who work with the curriculum must work together with others whose experience and values will inevitably differ. In an open, democratic society, such differences should be valued and must be respected. A conception of the subject that is so limited that it excludes views held by many others is a poor basis for cooperation or even for constructive dialogue.

The following definition of a curriculum will serve as the starting point for this book:

A **curriculum** consists of those matters:
  (a)   that teachers and students *attend to together,*
  (b)   that students, teachers, and others concerned generally recognize as *important to study and learn,* as indicated particularly by

BOX 1-2   Five Concepts of Curriculum

Subjects Offered for Study

English, social studies, mathematics, science, foreign languages, visual arts, physical education, and vocational subjects, for example. Or, in more detail, courses or course descriptions.

Educational Activities

What students do in school and in the classroom that is intended to foster learning, such as reading, writing, discussing, practicing, doing library research, conducting laboratory experiments, or carrying out projects.

Intended Learning

What students are supposed to learn, variously expressed as purposes, aims, goals, objectives, or the like.

Students' Experiences

What students *actually* experience under the guidance and direction of the school.

Learning Outcomes

What students *actually* learn. The results actually achieved with students, including subject matter learning, such as arithmetic, as well as ancillary learning, such as attitudes toward mathematics, beliefs about their mathematical ability, or attitudes toward authority.

using them as a basis for judging the success of both school and scholar,

(c) *the manner in which these matters are organized* in relationship to one another, in relationship to the other elements in the immediate educational situation and in time and space.

The same definition may be abbreviated as follows:

The curriculum refers to the *content* and *purpose* of an educational program together with their *organization*.

This definition does not construe the curriculum in terms of particular kinds of objects or events, such as subjects, activities, intentions, experiences, or outcomes, but rather as *whatever* students and teachers attend to and consider important to study and learn. It defines curriculum in terms of the actions and attitudes of those engaged in teaching and learning. The activities that students and teachers engage in would certainly be among those matters they attend to and consider important. Subjects are ways of organizing these matters. The student's experience may or may not be a part of the curriculum depending upon whether students and teachers attend to it together and consider it important to study and learn. If it is not, we

■ **BOX 1-3   Sources of Controversy over Definitions**

You might hope that eventually people will reach a consensus on a definition of curriculum and related basic terms in the field. This has not happened in nearly a century and it is not likely to happen soon. The fundamental obstacle is not the complexity of the underlying phenomenon, but differences of values and priorities.

Seen in the broadest perspective, disputes about definitions are struggles over ideals and values. The parties that dispute how to define curriculum hope to come a step closer to realizing their own educational ideals by gaining acceptance for a definition in harmony with those ideals. So long as people disagree about what kind of education is best for humanity, they will prefer different definitions of curriculum. Thus, fundamental disagreements about what is important permeate curriculum discussion to its very core—since even the meaning of the term itself is disputed.

But arguing about definitions is seldom constructive. When people disagree about educational ideals, they should engage in a dialogue about those ideals and their implications, not about how to define terms. When the parties in dispute want to understand one another's views, they can reach tentative agreement on working definitions, or they can agree that each side will use the terms they prefer and both will translate what the others say. In this way they can discuss matters of substance without stumbling over definitions.

As a general rule, disagreement about definitions so persistent that it blocks discussion of substantive issues simply indicates that one party does not want to hear the other's views or to have them heard by others. This usually means that the reluctant party fears that the other's views would be persuasive, and thus indicates a lack of confidence in the soundness or appeal of their own position. It can also mean that one party stands to gain more support by promoting their own position than by debating the opposition.

could still speak of the student's private, unexpressed experiences as "the curriculum as experienced by the student."

Four features of the definition are worthy of special notice: abstractness, complexity, essential subjectivity, and relative neutrality.

Abstractness The definition above defines curriculum in terms of a series of abstractions that must be inferred from what we observe in any particular situation. We can observe students and teachers when they are using textbooks, viewing films, visiting a zoo on a field trip, or over an extended period while they are studying some school subject, but we cannot directly observe *what they are attending to* during these activities. We can only infer what matters they are attending to from what they say and do. Similarly, the abstract phrase "study and learn" that appears in our definition encompasses such diverse activities as listening, reading, writing, discussing, and silently thinking. Defining curriculum in terms of abstractions rather than of things that are directly observable makes it harder to explain the term to a person unacquainted with curriculum, but gives the serious student of the subject a more flexible and powerful concept. For example, note that this abstract definition can be applied to *any* teaching and learning situation. A definition of curriculum as merely the subjects studied does not apply to a classroom in which students do projects that spill over the boundaries of many subjects. A definition of curriculum as classroom activities would cover the case of project teaching, but it misses the point in conventional classrooms where students' activities in nearly all subjects consist mainly of sitting, listening, reading, and writing. Therefore, as a result of its abstractness, the definition we have been considering applies equally well to both situations.

Complexity The definition of curriculum we are using is in three-parts, and we need all three parts. No simpler definition of curriculum will be adequate to the complexity of the subject. A story from Indian folklore illustrates how oversimplifications can lead to controversy and misunderstanding. In this story several blind men came across an elephant for the first time. Each of them explored the elephant by touch. After the elephant left, they fell into a discussion of the animal, whereupon great controversy arose. One man claimed that the elephant was long and round and flexible like a large snake. Another claimed that it was tall, cylindrical, and rigid like a tree. A third claimed that it was broad and nearly flat like a great wall. When people have limited experience with something, or experience with only parts of the whole, their impressions of it are often oversimplified and when their experiences differ, so do their conceptions. What we call the curriculum is a multifaceted whole made up of the relationships between content, purpose, time, and individual and institutional actions as perceived and interpreted by various parties. We experience this complex as a whole, rather than as a collection of independent parts. If we begin to consider one part of it, we find ourselves necessarily dealing with the other parts sooner or later. For example, when a high school English department is developing its literature curriculum, it may decide to include Shakespeare's *Macbeth*. But this decision only begins their curriculum planning. They still need to decide what educational purposes they will try to achieve through the study of *Macbeth*. Will students memorize key passages verbatim in order to internalize the rhythms of the language? Will they master facts about the plot and characters so that they can be culturally literate? Will they discuss the theme of guilt so that they can learn how literature can help us understand our humanity more deeply? In preparation for the SAT will they analyze how the structure of this play compares to the structure of classical Greek tragedy as described by Aristotle? Or, will they strive to understand the art with which the playwright has blended subject, form, and language into a powerful aesthetic whole? These are very different curricula. It is the whole, this complex entity comprised of content, purpose, and organization, that is the elephant we are all describing differently from our limited experiences with its parts.

No matter how we define the curriculum, if we are to make it work, improve it, and engage in constructive dialogue with others about it, we will have to attend to a wide range of interrelated processes. No matter what we choose as the central, critical, defining part of the entire process by which a curriculum works and has its impact on students, we will need at some point and in some way to consider the other essential processes as well.

Essential Subjectivity Curriculum must be looked at in terms of real events, rather than plans or intentions, as understood by teachers, students, and other interested persons. The notions of attention and of considering something to be important point not only to the physical reality, but also to the meanings people find in or bring to these events. To discover whether people consider something *important to study and learn* requires one to make a complex judgment that could be based on the actions of students and teachers, their plans, or their statements, among other signs, but that ultimately rests upon meaning as well as behavior. Such judgments are therefore essentially subjective.

Relative Neutrality The definition of curriculum is not designed to favor any one of the many contending philosophical orientations toward curriculum issues, but rather to be useful to all of them. This does not mean that it is neutral on all value issues. No definition can be completely neutral, but this one does not go out spoiling for a fight. It should be widely useful and relatively uncontroversial. *Generally recognized* allows room for differences of opinion about what should be studied and learned. Those who need to work with people who adamantly insist on using their own definition will need to learn to use other definitions as well. This definition seeks a common ground.

FUNDAMENTAL CONCEPTS OF CURRICULUM

Content

At one level the content of a school curriculum can be represented by course titles or, in an elementary school, by the subjects taught. These broad categories of content—mathematics, English, social studies, science, the arts, and physical education, for example—are descended from ancient traditions. Mathematics is a human enterprise almost as old as civilization. The practice of literature and the systematic study of language are both far older even than the invention of writing. Signs of the visual and performing arts accompany fossils of the earliest remains of homo sapiens. Social studies is a modern term, but history and studies very much like what we now call geography and anthropology were well established among the ancient Greeks. Physical education, too, whether for sport, as preparation for combat, or as an element of general culture, was prominent in the education of ancient Greece. Science is a relative newcomer as a named, self-conscious enterprise, dating from only the seventeenth century, though the works of various

Greeks and nameless predecessors in other cultures are often cited as precursors. Works and ideas from these ancient traditions are the ultimate sources of the content of the academic subjects in schools in all developed countries and give meaning to the subjects taught today.

Other building blocks have been proposed for school curricula, as we shall see in later chapters, but no other single alternative to these traditional academic subjects has achieved widespread acceptance. Practical subjects, such as job training, preparation for home and family living, and citizenship education, have been the nearest competitors, and this competition continues.

When we look at the content of an academic subject in more detail, we find that it has its own components organized in its own way. For centuries Euclid's *Elements* defined the content and purpose of the study of geometry and organized them in a tight, logical structure of axioms, postulates, and theorems that has been an ideal of clarity and coherence for scholars ever since. English courses, at the other extreme, have for centuries been loose assemblages of varied elements of language and literature. Language study often includes grammar, spelling, and composition. Literature involves reading classic works and writing about them in various ways.

The academic subjects have been so familiar for so many generations that they might tend to seem more works of nature than of humanity. In the logical near-perfection of Euclid's geometry we believe we have glimpsed some eternal truths about our world or at least about our minds—not something arbitrary, not a creation of a particular individual in a particular culture, but a timeless truth that just happened to have been discovered by a Greek in the third century, B.C. Mathematics, we may feel, *is* what it *is*—and not even mathematicians can change it except by new and revolutionary discoveries that transform our understanding of the field. Even among the arts, we have a sense that music is music and must simply be accepted as such. So, a course in music must cover certain topics in order to be a course in music.

However, despite our own conceptions of the inevitability of such concepts of studies, other cultures define and order the content of mathematics or music quite differently. For centuries, the mathematics of cultures on the Indian subcontinent developed in its own path, quite distinct from that of the Greeks and Romans producing wonderful inventions, among them the concept of zero that the West appropriated. The role of Arab and Persian mathematicians in preserving and continuing the Greek tradition gets a mere mention in most of our history books, but it was a glorious scholarly tradition that lasted far longer than the history of European civilization on North America and produced much remarkable mathematics, including our present system of numerals and many of the arithmetic algorithms we teach today. Also, conceptions of content have changed through history. Music was once taught as one of the seven liberal arts in Europe during the middle ages. To educated people of that time it felt natural to think of music as a study of abstract patterns, like mathematics and astronomy, with which they grouped it. These similarities are not apparent to most people today. Centuries earlier, in ancient Greece, music included poetry and was taught primarily to inspire young warriors to noble and heroic action.

Is content, then, a given? Is it something that, like the laws of gravity, we discover about the world? Or, is content rather a product of social and cultural enterprises that could well be defined differently, a product that may already be defined differently elsewhere, and one that is almost certain to be defined differently by generations to come? If we consider the content of the classic academic disciplines to be the closest humanity has yet come to knowledge of eternal truth, then clearly it is important for teachers and students to study and learn them. The responsibility of curriculum makers would then be to identify those items of knowledge from the various traditions that are most fundamental and important and to ensure that they are included in the curriculum. On the other hand, if the content of the academic disciplines represents merely one way of viewing the world, a particular human social invention inevitably colored by the purposes and interests of those who invented it and its present defenders, then we also have the tasks of critically analyzing that knowledge and its origins and asking whether other social enterprises may not have an equally valid claim to a place in the curriculum. This is one of the enduring curriculum issues that has been debated since the beginnings of philosophy and remains under discussion today.

In practice, those who make and use curricula need ways of representing content and of illustrating internal relationships among items of content. A number of techniques have been developed. One, the concept map, is illustrated in Figure 1-1. Box 1-4 talks about some of the most important recurring issues centered on content and its organization. These are among the most fundamental curriculum issues. We will be considering them throughout this book.

Although our ideas about content have ancient roots, they have been, until recently, poorly integrated with twentieth century thought. In ordinary usage the term *content* refers to the sum and substance of a message, its main points. But scholars who have attempted to locate the content in the message have run into a dead end. The very idea of the content of a message as being somehow in the message itself turns out to be a conceptual mistake. The content of a message is an interpretation a person offers of the import or significance of the message as a whole. People often find it difficult to make a summary or abstract of the main point of a message. To program computers to carry this out once seemed a relatively straightforward task, but it has proven to be unexpectedly difficult and has not yet been accomplished. To identify the content of even simple sentences from the meanings of the individual words and the rules of grammar turns out to require an immense amount of knowledge about the world and much active inference-making. Terms such as *topics, themes, concepts,* and the like, do not refer to material entities at all, but to abstractions people have invented and named. Behaviorism and logical positivism, influential schools of thought early in this century, rejected such mentalistic terms as unscientific. As a result, ideas related to content have until recently floated somewhere beyond the pale of contemporary social and psychological disciplines. With the advent of computers and the concept

■ FIGURE 1-1   A Concept Map of Educational Technology

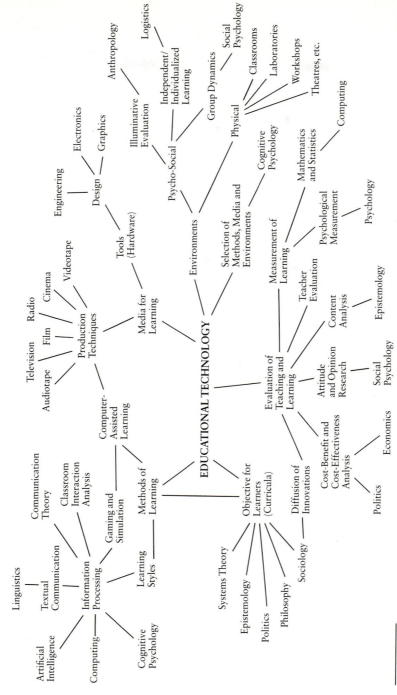

SOURCE: Hawridge, David. 1981. The Telesis of Educational Technology. *British Journal of Educational Technology* 12:4–18.

BOX 1-4   Some Recurring Questions about Curriculum Content and Its Organization

- What are the major bodies of human knowledge?

- How can we determine which content from the whole corpus of human knowledge is most important for students to learn?

- What content should be presented in schools, K–12? Should the content of education be drawn entirely from academic disciplines, or should the curriculum also include content from other sources, such as the knowledge and skill required for everyday life or for particular occupations?

- How can the content of the school curriculum be kept up-to-date as knowledge expands?

- What should happen to the content of the curriculum when an item of content becomes controversial? Should schools avoid controversial topics, take sides, or present all sides?

Organization of Content

- Should the content of school programs be divided into separate school subjects, or should the curriculum be unified, integrated, or inter-disciplinary?

- Should the same content be presented to all students or should content be tailored to particular students?

- Should the subjects offered in school reflect the academic disciplines? If so, how many academic disciplines are there, and what are they? If not, how should the content of school programs be categorized?

- In what sequential order should content be presented to students? Which subjects, units, topics, and concepts should be presented earlier and which later?

- At what ages should specific bodies of content be presented to students?

---

of information, psychology gained a conceptual framework with which to study these ideas in ways that are scientifically acceptable.

The concept of *attention,* which appears in our definition of curriculum, is an established concept of modern psychology, yet also a mentalistic term. The entities to which students and teachers attend are what we mean by content. It is clear from careful studies that people can and do attend to words, to their own thoughts, to mental images, and to patterns and orders of various kinds, as well as to stimuli perceived through their senses. The content of a school curriculum is no more mysterious than the thoughts, images, and plans cognitive scientists study routinely. This recently opened door between psychology and curriculum is already leading to exciting advances in the study of how both experts and beginners represent curriculum content, how ideas can be presented to students more effectively, and how the learning of some ideas promotes or inhibits the learning of others.

Purpose

The issue of what should be the aims or ends of education has been a perennial topic in civilized discourse. Aristotle's conclusion that "mankind are by no means agreed about the things to be taught" applies today as well as to the Golden Age of Greece. In this century in the United States debates about the aims of education have swirled around three competing categories of aims: intellectual, social, and personal (Walker and Soltis 1986). Those who give primacy to intellectual aims argue that schooling is first and foremost a way to bring the next generation into possession of humanity's accumulated store of knowledge and to equip them to preserve it and add to it. Formal schooling was originally designed for this purpose, its proponents argue, and remains the one contemporary institution dedicated primarily to it.

Those who maintain that social aims should come first argue that schools are social institutions created and sustained by the social order to serve whatever ends it sees fit. They point out that the education of scholars has always been a minor purpose of schooling, having less importance than preparation for more valued social roles, such as warriors, priests, government officials, or simply cultivated ladies and gentlemen. A modern society needs citizens prepared to participate in democratic self-government, to assume lawful and constructive roles in society, and to support themselves and others materially by being economically productive. The purpose of schooling, advocates of this position maintain, is to prepare such citizens.

Those who urge that priority be given to personal aims argue that all human beings are unique individuals and deserve an education that utilizes each individual's unique potential. Education, they argue, is not to serve the social order. Rather, the social order exists to enable individual human beings to fulfill their potential.

All but the most fanatical advocates acknowledge that each of these categories of aims has some merit. Typically, those who put a higher priority on one aim maintain that achieving this one will achieve the others as well. For example, it has been argued that knowledge of the truth about oneself and others is the best route to personal fulfillment and that fulfilled persons will naturally associate with one another in healthy ways that foster social welfare. A strong society is comprised of strong, healthy, independent individuals, all following their own paths. Others maintain that a strong and vibrant society is the best environment for individual growth and development. Advocates abound for all sorts of other blendings of these three main aims.

Various constellations of these aims come in and go out of style each decade reflecting events, trends, and moods in the public and the education professions. Educational reform movements typically endorse aims that their members feel have been neglected and need greater emphasis. Currently one reads a great deal about *at-risk* students, a group whose needs are not being met, it is claimed, by schools bent on raising academic standards. Little more than a decade ago, advocates of more emphasis on academics by schools were complaining that the educational programs of the Great Society had neglected that priority in favor of social equality and human potential.

The most fundamental issue about purpose, then, is simply the priority to be put on the various aims valued in this society. Throughout the last century, one weak, temporary consensus has succeeded another, bringing with it a new series of reforms. Is this process leading gradually toward an established social compact on educational priorities, is it leading toward open confrontation, or is it simply a continuing process of adjustment and change in response to circumstances and ideas?

We often suppose that actions reveal purpose, but the relation between purpose and action is complex at best. The same action can serve many purposes depending on its context, how it is done, and how those involved interpret it. Teaching a second language in elementary school, for instance, can be interpreted as promoting traditional academic goals. But it can be equally well interpreted as furthering cultural pluralism or enhancing economic competitiveness in global markets.

Stated purposes are not always reliable indicators of either actions or genuine purposes. The philosopher's purposes, quoted in the school system's statement of educational aims, may not coincide with the school board's priorities as reflected in the budget. The principal's goals for the school for the year may be different still, not entirely contradictory, perhaps, but with a different emphasis. The teacher's objectives may take still another tack. And who knows what purposes the students may pursue? In this welter of purposes, does it make sense to speak of *the* purposes of an educational program?

Problems of purpose arise continually in curriculum work. A common problem is how to divide a major purpose into smaller subpurposes and then recombine the subordinate purposes so that the student achieves the larger purpose. Figure 1-2 shows an example of one method of handling this problem: establishing a hierarchy of purposes. Another vexing problem of purpose encountered in everyday curriculum practice is the tendency to emphasize simple, readily attained purposes over more complex and difficult ones. In an effort to counter this tendency, Benjamin Bloom and collaborators developed a taxonomy of educational objectives (Krathwohl, Bloom, and Masia 1964) that has come into widespread use. The Bloom Taxonomy identifies six levels of educational objectives in the Cognitive Domain and five distinct levels in the Affective Domain, as shown in Figure 1-3.

These and similar issues related to the purpose of educational programs stated in Box 1-5 are central concerns of those who plan and use curricula and of those who study them.

As with content, purpose has been a vexing notion for scholars. Some of the most fundamental and controversial themes in Western thought are associated with the concept of purpose: free will versus determinism, the existence of the soul, causality. It is not clear, philosophically or scientifically, what we mean when we speak of a person as having a particular purpose. How would we verify such a statement? We cannot see or weigh a purpose. We can only infer it from what

FIGURE 1-2 A Hierarchy of Educational Purposes

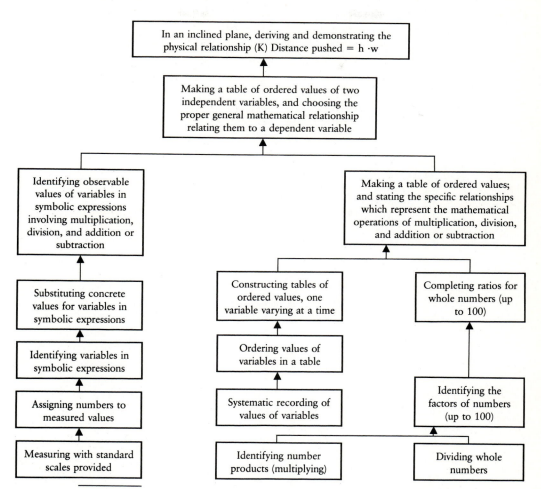

SOURCE: Weigand, V. K. 1970. A Study of Subordinate Skills in Science Problem Solving, (Robert M. Gagne, ed.) *Basic Studies of Learning Hierarchies in School Subjects*. Berkeley: University of California.

people say or do or from observable states of their body. The tradition of humanistic thought from which modern education has taken shape takes the existence of free will in human beings as a given of experience. It is one of the traits that separates humans from lower forms of life. That we cannot explain it philosophically or scientifically simply shows how inadequate our philosophy and science are. Behaviorists and logical positivists, on the other hand, argue that all we

FIGURE 1-3   **The Categories in the Bloom Taxonomy**

COGNITIVE DOMAIN

1.0 KNOWLEDGE
   1.1 Knowledge of specifics
   1.2 Knowledge of ways and means of dealing with specifics
   1.3 Knowledge of universals and abstractions in a field
2.0 COMPREHENSION
   2.1 Translation
   2.2 Interpretation
   2.3 Extrapolation
3.0 APPLICATION
4.0 ANALYSIS
   4.1 Analysis of elements
   4.2 Analysis of relationships
   4.3 Analysis of organizational principles
5.0 SYNTHESIS
   5.1 Production of a unique communication
   5.2 Production of a plan or a proposed set of operations
   5.3 Derivation of a set of abstract relations
6.0 EVALUATION
   6.1 Judgment in terms of intended evidence
   6.2 Judgment in terms of external criteria

AFFECTIVE DOMAIN

1.0 RECEIVING (attending)
   1.1 Awareness
   1.2 Willingness to receive
   1.3 Controlled or selected attention
2.0 RESPONDING
   2.1 Acquiescence in responding
   2.2 Willingness to respond
   2.3 Satisfaction in response
3.0 VALUING
   3.1 Acceptance of a value
   3.2 Preference for a value
   3.3 Commitment
4.0 ORGANIZATION
   4.1 Conceptualization of a value
   4.2 Organization of a value system
5.0 CHARACTERIZATION BY A VALUE OR VALUE COMPLEX
   5.1 Generalized set
   5.2 Characterization

SOURCE: Bloom, Benjamin S. 1956. *Taxonomy of Educational Objectives: The Classification of Educational Goals. Handbook 1: Cognitive domain.* N.Y.: McKay.

BOX 1-5   Some Recurring Questions about Curricular Purpose and Its Organization

- What should be the purposes of public education, K–12? What should be the priority among these?

- Who should decide the purposes of schools and through what process? What should be the roles of students, teachers, parents, school officials, and others?

- Should the purposes of education change in step with changes in students, in human knowledge, and in the world outside schools? Or should they reflect more enduring traditions that change little over a child's school career?

- How should controversies about the purposes of education be resolved?

- How can teachers and students be brought to embrace common school goals and pursue them as their own?

- How do we monitor, assess or evaluate progress toward attainment of the purposes of the school?

Organization of Purposes

- Should all students pursue the same purposes, or should purposes be tailored to individuals somehow?

- How should responsibility for achieving various purposes be allocated among persons and occasions within the school program?

- Should we attempt to plan for the attainment of specific purposes on certain planned occasions, or should teachers decide when the time is ripe for their students to work on a given purpose?

- Should purposes be organized in a hierarchy leading from simpler, less sophisticated lower order ones to more complex, higher-order ones?

---

can ever really know about another person is what we can observe. We cannot observe purposes, therefore they do not exist. Purposes are epiphenomena explainable in terms of patterns of genuinely observable phenomena.

Curiously, the greatest contemporary challenge to the common sense notion of purpose in education comes not from methodological objections of scientists or philosophers of science but from political and social doctrines, specifically from the dialectical materialism of Hegel and Marx and their followers. They argue that people's actions reflect their material *interests* and that expressions of purpose are only used to hide their true motives of self-interest. In their deterministic forms, these doctrines assert that people *cannot* transcend their interests, even if they genuinely want to and try. Naturally, a follower of these doctrines would not expect to find a school's true educational purposes by looking at the words written in official documents, nor even at what the principal or teachers say, but rather at what they actually do and at the actual results. A consistent materialist would assume that individuals would seek to hide their true motives from others and perhaps even from themselves, so that discovering their true purposes requires real detective work. A materialist would look at the economic, social, and political interests of all those involved and would favor the assumption that everyone's actions are designed to protect and advance their most fundamental interests.

Some of the most searching debates about educational purpose today have been provoked by the criticisms of prevailing curricula made by materialists following this line of thought. It will be interesting to see how the insights that emerge from this debate may influence how we pose and settle questions of curricular purpose in the future.

Organization

Learning is cumulative. Having learned to speak and listen, children can begin to learn to read and write. Having learned to read and write, they can begin to study other subjects from books and to externalize and objectify their thoughts. Last year's learning forms the basis for this year's, and high levels of educational attainment demand years of study. Curricula, therefore, extend over years of time and may require the coordinated action of thousands of teachers and principals in schools throughout a city, county, state, or nation. Achieving such coordination is a gigantic logistical challenge. It is remarkable that schools do as well as they do.

As we have just seen, when they are considered separately, certain organizational questions are associated with content and purpose. Content is organized into concepts, themes, topics, and subjects. Purposes may be expressed in terms of hierarchically organized chains of objectives or loosely grouped categories of aims. In any real curriculum, content, purpose, and organization form one whole, the curriculum itself, which may be more or less elaborately organized. The aspects of curricular organization that traditionally receive the most attention are:

scope: inclusion of content and purpose
sequence: the order of presentation over time
schedule: allocation of content and purpose to occasions
content × behavior grids: how content and purpose are related
curriculum design: overall plan for the organization of a curriculum.

Figure 1-4 shows a scope and sequence chart for one concept in a discipline-based art education program for the elementary grades. A scope and sequence chart lists the main items of content in their order of presentation and often indicates the emphasis to be placed on each item by suggesting an amount or percentage of time that should be spent on each. It shows many of the main organizational features of a curriculum at a glance, but it does not make plain how content and behavior are related. An alternative mode of representation, the

■
FIGURE 1-4   A Scope and Sequence Chart in Elementary School Art

This chart lists objectives grouped in three broad domains (productive, critical/appreciative, and cultural/historical) and indicates when each is to be taught.

COLOR

Definition:
    Color is our perception of light wavelengths when light is refracted by a prism or reflected from a surface. Color has three dimensions: hue (the color name), value (lightness or darkness), and intensity (saturation or purity).

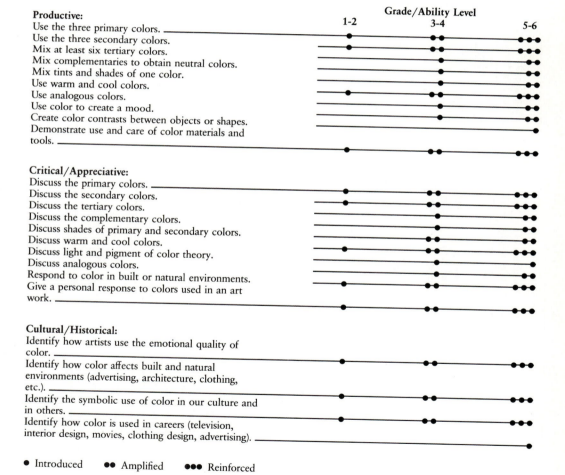

	Grade/Ability Level		
Productive:	1-2	3-4	5-6
Use the three primary colors.	•	••	•••
Use the three secondary colors.	•	••	•••
Mix at least six tertiary colors.		••	•••
Mix complementaries to obtain neutral colors.		•	•••
Mix tints and shades of one color.		•	•••
Use warm and cool colors.		•	•••
Use analogous colors.	•	••	•••
Use color to create a mood.		•	•••
Create color contrasts between objects or shapes.		•	•••
Demonstrate use and care of color materials and tools.	•	••	•••

Critical/Appreciative:			
Discuss the primary colors.	•	••	•••
Discuss the secondary colors.		••	•••
Discuss the tertiary colors.		••	•••
Discuss the complementary colors.		•	•••
Discuss shades of primary and secondary colors.		•	•••
Discuss warm and cool colors.		•	•••
Discuss light and pigment of color theory.		•	•••
Discuss analogous colors.		•	•••
Respond to color in built or natural environments.	•	••	•••
Give a personal response to colors used in an art work.	•	••	•••

Cultural/Historical:			
Identify how artists use the emotional quality of color.	•	••	•••
Identify how color affects built and natural environments (advertising, architecture, clothing, etc.).	•	••	•••
Identify the symbolic use of color in our culture and in others.	•	••	•••
Identify how color is used in careers (television, interior design, movies, clothing design, advertising).	•	••	•••

• Introduced   •• Amplified   ••• Reinforced

SOURCE: Arizona Art Education Association, 1982, Fall. Art in Elementary Education: What the Law Requires, *InPerspective, The Journal of the Arizona Art Education Association* 1:6–24,

FIGURE 1-5   A Content x Behavior Grid for High School Biology

Illustration of the Use of a Two-Dimensional Chart in Stating
Objectives for a High School Course in Biological Science

	Behavioral Aspect of the Objectives						
	1. Understanding of important facts and principles	2. Familiarity with dependable sources of information	3. Ability to interpret data	4. Ability to apply principles	5. Ability to study and report results of study	6. Broad and mature interests	7. Social attitudes
A. Functions of Human Organisms							
1. Nutrition	X	X	X	X	X	X	X
2. Digestion	X		X	X	X	X	
3. Circulation	X		X	X	X	X	
4. Respiration	X		X	X	X	X	
5. Reproduction	X	X	X	X	X	X	X
B. Use of Plant and Animal Resources							
1. Energy relationships	X		X	X	X	X	X
2. Environmental factors conditioning plant and animal growth	X	X	X	X	X	X	X
3. Heredity and genetics	X	X	X	X	X	X	X
4. Land utilization	X	X	X	X	X	X	X
C. Evolution and Development	X	X	X	X	X	X	X

SOURCE: Tyler, Ralph. 1949. *Basic Principles of Curriculum and Instruction*. Chicago: University of Chicago Press.

content × behavior grid (Figure 1-5) emphasizes this aspect of curricular organization. It is used to show which types or levels of performance will be expected for each major item of content and thus relates content and purpose to one another. Box 1-6 sketches an overall curriculum design, in this case, a core curriculum.

Issues of curriculum organization are of more than merely technical interest. For instance, British scholar Basil Bernstein (1971) argues that the strength of a curriculum's organizational features is related to the strength of its impact on students and teachers, and is therefore an indication of the extent to which the curriculum is used as an instrument of control. The more tightly organized a curriculum, the more students and teachers are constrained in their classroom decisions and actions. A school district with a detailed and strictly enforced sequential mathematics curriculum from kindergarten through grade 12 constrains

---

BOX 1-6   The Curriculum Design for the Horace Mann Junior High School

This distinguished private day school in New York was one of thirty secondary schools participating in the Eight Year Study from 1933–1941. The purpose of the study was to examine the processes and effects of innovative school programs developed by the schools themselves. In *Thirty Schools Tell Their Story* the Junior High program is described as follows.

"The framework finally decided upon to initiate this new type of program into the junior high school was embodied in the theme 'The Story of Man Through the Ages.' . . . The content framework from which experiences are drawn . . . is:

First year (seventh grade). Prehistoric man; river valley civilizations of the Nile, Tigris, and Euphrates; cultural contributions of Greece and Rome.

Second Year (eighth grade). Life in the Middle Ages; the Renaissance.

Third Year (ninth grade). Modern age (Reformation; the commercial, agricultural, and industrial revolution) through the present.

"With the introduction of the new program the school day was divided into large time-blocks of from two to three class hours each. One time-block, or approximately one-third of the day, is devoted to the coordinated program of each grade, and is in charge of a coordinating teacher. Working in close cooperation with the large-theme teachers are teachers of fine arts, science, industrial and household arts, music, mathematics, and the languages. . . .

"The coordinating teacher in each grade . . . is the home room teacher. She and the children together discuss the problems they wish to study. Then she has conferences with participating teachers to help to delimit the phases of the work to be developed and to determine a tentative time for participation."

SOURCE: Progressive Education Association. 1943. *Thirty Schools Tell Their Story*. N.Y.: Harper and Brothers.

every teacher of mathematics in its schools to follow a common schedule. By contrast, a curriculum in art or literature that is a loosely organized aggregation of topics to be covered in any order gives teachers and students maximum freedom in planning their classroom activities.

THE IMPORTANCE OF CURRICULUM DECISIONS AND ACTIONS

Some people find curriculum matters fascinating enough to study them for their own sake. Those whose careers involve specific responsibility for making curriculum decisions obviously need to learn about the subject. But because curriculum decisions and actions are so central to the educational enterprise and participation in curriculum work so widely distributed, everyone involved in education needs to study this subject.

Responsibility for curriculum decisions and actions is more widely shared than is the case with any other aspect of education. Instruction is primarily the teacher's responsibility, shared in small measure with district supervisors and in-service education specialists. School administration is the responsibility of principals and their staffs, shared with district officials. But everyone who has a stake in an educational program wants a voice in shaping the curriculum.

Responsibility for curriculum decisions and actions is dispersed very widely among school personnel, parents, public officials, professional organizations, and a host of voluntary groups pursuing public and private interests. In this welter of overlapping and competing influences, no single agency is preeminent in curriculum decisions. Strictly speaking, there are no curriculum decision-makers, in the sense that an individual has both the power and the authority to make curriculum decisions that are binding on those who must carry out the decisions. All that you get now with a position of authority over curriculum decisions is a seat at the "game" of curricular influence—and you have to parlay that position into influence over what happens in schools and classrooms. To do this you have to know where the floating crap game is today, what the current rules of the game are, who are the other players, what's at stake, and how to play the game. To act intelligently in such an environment requires an understanding of how the game is played. Because all of us involved in education help to shape the curriculum and all of us must also live with the results of everyone's efforts, we must all understand it and the processes that sustain it if we are to govern education intelligently.

Curriculum improvement offers an opportunity to enhance the lives of many thousands of students, teachers, and communities. The matters we ask children to learn in their formative years make as much of a difference in their lives as an open, democratic society allows itself to make with its formal institutions. If we teach homemaking to girls and wood shop to boys, they learn different things than if we teach both subjects to both sexes. It makes a difference whether we teach them a second language, personal health and fitness, parenting, art, economics, or statistics. They will learn different values and become different people pursuing different careers and making different use of their leisure time. They will even form a different conception of themselves, of their abilities and interests. It makes a difference whether we teach arithmetic by rote or teach mathematical concepts for real understanding. Students will come away from their study of mathematics with a different idea of what mathematics is, with different levels of mathematical skill and knowledge, and with different conceptions of their own mathematical abilities. Students have different attitudes toward their country and government when they are taught its history fully and accurately than when they are merely fed names, dates, and historical myths. *What children study and learn in school makes a difference in their lives.*

The curriculum of elementary and secondary education is also an important factor in shaping our national culture. A people has a common heritage only if the content of that heritage is relearned successively by every new generation. It is no accident that schools in the most authoritarian countries have the most rigid programs of study and the most rigid standards of conduct for students, while in the most open societies students are given the most choice in their studies and the greatest latitude in conduct. Similarly, it is no accident that every student in French schools is taught to draw at least passably or that every student in Russian schools studies mathematics every year they are in school. These curricular emphases reflect the cultural traditions of those countries. In some countries, all children are taught science systematically from the early elementary grades through the completion of high school. We should not be surprised that those countries graduate more engineers and scientists than the United States, where science is much less widely taught. The curriculum of early schooling determines the distribution of various forms and levels of skill and knowledge within a society and therefore affects nearly all aspects of society, including national character, politics, and national economic competitiveness.

The need for curriculum improvement in American elementary and secondary education during the remainder of this century is, in my judgment, as great as at any time since the early decades of this century. Immigration and differential birth rates are reemphasizing the multiethnic character of American society, adding large numbers of Asians and Hispanics to the social mix. Together with large existing populations of Americans of African and Hispanic descent, these "minorities" are becoming a majority in the schools of many states. The American economy is undergoing a far-reaching transformation from predominantly industrial produc- tion to predominantly information and services, and from a world of limited competition among developed countries to a truly global economy with strong economic centers outside the West. Various forms of technology are transforming the workplace and making new demands on workers for more sophisticated knowledge and skill. These changes in the economy will affect people's perceptions of the preparatory value of various school subjects and these perceptions will affect the school curriculum, though exactly how is hard to foresee.

Other American institutions are also changing. Radio, television, and opinion polls have become the primary channels of communication between citizens and government. The ability to raise money for access to these channels has become a major determinant of political power. Traditional institutions of government have become overloaded—the courts are overloaded with cases, legislatures are overloaded with bills, the executive branch is overloaded with making and implementing policies, and every agency is overloaded with budget preparations and paperwork. The public's confidence in its public institutions is at a new low. How long can schools continue to teach civics and government as if all this had not happened? Will schools not be expected to play a role in strengthening young people's identification with their governmental institutions? What changes in the teaching of the social studies, say, or in school government or in extra-curricular activities would be helpful?

Also, families are changing. Increasingly both parents work. Divorce and remarriage shuffle children about. Parent-child relations are affected. Bonds between the generations may be weakened. Children seem to rely more on their peers for emotional stability and support, and schools are the focus of peer contacts. Should relations in school also change between students (more cooperation), between school and family (more evening extracurricular programs, more frequent parent-teacher contact) or between teacher and students (more supportive, more personal)? Should students remain with one teacher for several years, for example, to provide more social stability?

Leisure activities have expanded and taken on more important roles in personal and family life. Television, video recording, and computers have made many households information-rich, highly entertaining, electronic environments. As a result, children come to school more prepared in some ways—if they have watched Sesame Street, for example, they will know their numbers and letters—and less prepared in others—they may not have the ability to sit and concentrate in a quiet environment, for example, or the ability to take turns. Likewise, students' standards have risen. The traditional second grade unit on weather, based on pictures cut from magazines and a few pages of a textbook, just does not measure up to television weather segments that show satellite photographs of global cloud patterns, films of actual tornadoes, hurricanes viewed from planes flying inside the eye, and time-lapse studies of cloud formation.

Knowledge is still exploding. Major breakthroughs in the sciences that require us to revise what we believe about our world come almost annually. We now know that continents move. Protons, neutrons, and electrons are no longer the fundamental particles of physics. Newly deciphered protein molecules are described in newspaper headlines while their commercial applications are explored on the business pages. Mathematics has become the basis of our technological economy, but it is a different mathematics than we have been teaching, a discrete mathematics, for one thing, rather than a continuous one, and a mathematics of inquiry, problem-solving, discovery, and proof rather than one of numerical computation. Now anyone can buy calculators to do most of the mathematics taught in the first eight grades of school. Soon anyone will be able to buy computer programs that will diagram sentences and check spelling and grammar well enough to pass senior English. Already students can rent videotapes of filmed versions of the classic novels assigned in English class.

The needs for curriculum improvement, then, remain immense, but our means for meeting these needs have not measured up to the challenge. Schools have never before been able to change their curricula at anything like the pace required to keep up with these expanding frontiers of knowledge. When Americans have tried to bring about major changes in the curricula of schools nationwide, the efforts have been costly, controversial, and generally disappointing. On the other hand, can schools maintain their credibility with students and the public if they continue to teach nineteenth century content in a twenty-first century world?

Despite our best efforts at curriculum improvement, dissatisfaction persists among both public and professionals from nearly all shades of the spectrum of political opinion. Rates of illiteracy remain unacceptably high. Test scores in school subjects are either down or at best up only slightly. Problems of school age children, such as suicide, drug use, early pregnancy, and delinquency, are becoming more frequent and serious. Calls for curricular reform are at least as frequent and shrill now as ever. Enrollments in private schools are rising. Proposals for restructuring public education by issuing vouchers that entitle parents to choose any school, public or private, are now receiving serious consideration by practical politicians. Steadily more radical measures will be forced upon schools unless and until they demonstrate an ability to deliver programs that satisfy the public. There is clearly plenty of curriculum work to be done.

CURRICULUM AS A FIELD OF PROFESSIONAL PRACTICE

Curriculum is, first and foremost, a field of professional practice. Like other professional fields, such as medicine, law, business, architecture, journalism, agriculture, and social work, people study curriculum primarily so that they can do a difficult and important job better. The field of study associated with a profession typically draws material from several disciplines, including whatever most enables a person to do the job better. To understand curriculum as a field of study, therefore, we must first understand curriculum as a field of professional practice. In characterizing curriculum as a field of practice we will look at the seven traits listed in Box 1-7.

Cultural artifact: Every curriculum is created and is thus an artifact, a work of human ingenuity, not a fact of life imposed on us by nature like the law of gravity. What one human can perceive can in principle be communicated to another. Therefore, in a fundamental sense, curriculum is an idea. Any curriculum in widespread use for a decade or more must be sustained by some extended group

---

■
BOX 1-7   Seven Important Characteristics of Curriculum Practice

1. The curriculum is a cultural artifact.
2. The curriculum takes on a multiplicity of forms.
3. What happens in the classroom is the primary focus of curriculum work.
4. The curriculum is deeply embedded in several contexts.
5. The responsibility for curriculum practice is shared widely.
6. Those responsible for curriculum practice are distributed widely in a loose network of persons and organizations.
7. All curriculum work favors some human values at the expense of others.

---

of people who share traditions, language, and ways of life. A curriculum is thus a product of some form of collective choice, often extended over decades of time and spreading gradually and differentially throughout a culture. It could be other than it is if the cultural group behaved differently than it does, but widespread, substantial, sustained curriculum change requires cultural change, either as cause, cofactor, or consequence. Because it is a cultural artifact, curriculum needs to be interpreted. The meaning a curricular artifact holds for those in a culture must be discovered by interpretation; meaning is not written on the face of curriculum documents, nor is it there to be discovered by the purely objective methods of the natural sciences. Furthermore, the meaning of curricular artifacts usually depends on the context in which they appear. Magnet schools designed to promote racial integration may have a different meaning in the rural South than in a midwestern suburb, for example. To understand curricula, then, we must interpret them in context.

Multiplicity of forms: We commonly speak of the curriculum as if it were written down somewhere, or at least capable in principle of being wirtten down. But the written documents that are commonly thought to embody the curriculum—curriculum guides, courses of study, syllabi, teachers' guides and the like—are, at best, one influence on what happens in classrooms. Other things and events that can shape the classroom curriculum at least as much include: textbooks, workbooks, tests, and other curriculum materials; in-service education of teachers; district policies, especially budget policies, policies of the school principal, department chair, or other school leaders; and even the policies of distant agencies such as employers and colleges. When these various influences are consistent with one another and with the written documents, then the documents may be said to fairly represent the curriculum. But is is a grave error to suppose that changing the documents will, by itself, change the curriculum students experience.

Classroom as the focus: The curriculum work that affects students directly is the most fundamental. The school classroom remains the place in which most students encounter a curriculum, and the work teachers do there must be the main focus of all curriculum practice. Of course, students are affected by their experiences elsewhere, both in and out of school, often in ways that are more profoundly educative, or miseducative, than what they experience in classrooms. When these other activities are informal, as they usually are, the concept of curriculum is seldom helpful in understanding them. But when family members make explicit efforts extended over some time to educate one another, it is reasonable to speak of the curriculum of the home. Similarly, the concept of curriculum could be extended to community organizations, museums, the mass media, and a host of other influences if and when they adopt an explicit educational purpose. In each case, the focus of curriculum practice would be on what happens in the setting in which students encounter the educational program.

Embedded in contexts: The school curriculum is deeply intertwined with several contexts, including the classroom, the school and community, the state, the nation, and the entire global international context. The curriculum is ingrained in the routines of teachers: the books they use, the tests they give, the report cards they fill out, their academic calendar, and their schedule. It is part of teachers' professional background and identity, their certification, and even their right to practice their profession. The school schedule is built around the curriculum. The assignment of teachers and students to classes is typically by subject. Often a portion of the school's budget is allocated to different subjects. Many schools are organized in departments that reflect curricular boundaries. School curricula affect and are affected by state laws and policies, as well as national trends and innovations. They are part of a global network of information about education that includes international comparisons of educational achievement, for example. Every curriculum must function in close and constant interaction with these contexts. One reason why so many efforts at curriculum reform fail or go awry is that planners give too little thought to how the innovative curriculum will fit into all these contexts.

Shared responsibility: Every curriculum is a collective, corporate work. Even if a single individual makes the plans, others must collaborate in order to carry them out. Furthermore, that lone curriculum developer must rely on the work of countless generations of predecessors who developed the subject and its pedagogy. To focus on the individual or the group that makes the plans slights those who realize the curriculum through their dealings with students, as well as those whose support makes sustaining the curriculum possible financially, politically, intellectually, and otherwise. In contemporary American society, at least, the responsibility for curriculum practice is widely shared. As a consequence, curriculum practice always involves social interaction, communication, and coordination of efforts—in a word, collaboration. Many of those involved in curriculum work belong to organizations, and they represent and are represented by that corporate entity in their curriculum work. Shared responsibility can be turbulent. Collaboration among people whose opinions differ can lead to open conflict that requires negotiation or other forms of conflict resolution.

Distributed network: The work associated with creating, maintaining, evaluating, and changing school curricula is not concentrated in the hands of certain identifiable individuals at particular times and places, but is widely distributed in space and time and among individuals and organizations. This means that collaboration and resolution of conflict must often be carried out at a distance. Consequently, inconsistent trends can be at work in different parts of the network for some time before some unforeseen event precipitates a direct encounter between their respective advocates. Before the advent of mass media of communication, professional meetings and publications were the primary channels through which those involved in the distributed network learned about what was happening elsewhere, formed alliances with friends, and battled foes. Today, the mass media of communication are the most efficient channels for transmitting information throughout the network and therefore they often become the main meeting place, organizing hall, negotiating table, and battle ground for those who champion curricular ideas on different branches of the network.

Value-laden: One cannot take a step in the field of curriculum without trampling on some value. A decision to offer a statistics course as an elective in the high school mathematics curriculum threatens enrollment in other elective courses and also raises questions of equity, since the new offering will likely serve mainly more academically able students. The values at issue may sometimes seem minor, but there are always those to whom even the most trivial issue will loom large. While there is a loose consensus in contemporary American society on broadly stated educational aims, such as mastery of fundamental academic skills, fostering individual growth, and social progress, Americans are sharply divided on priorities between and within these broad aims and on the best curricular means to achieve them. Consequently, controversy lurks everywhere behind the thin veil that hides the future directions of curriculum stability and change from us.

CURRICULUM AS A FIELD OF STUDY

What studies might help a person learn to do better the various kinds of work associated with a curriculum? Traditionally the curriculum field has offered three answers: curriculum theory, curriculum development, and the comprehensive survey course. Curriculum theory introduces students to the major traditions of thought about pivotal curriculum issues and to the great works in the field and their authors. Such a course, together with studies in philosophy, psychology, and the social sciences, provides an extremely important part of a sound foundation for handling curriculum issues. One must learn about the ideas that guide people's thinking about curriculum issues in order to use these ideas oneself to critically assess the adequacy of these ideas, and even simply to read contemporary works with understanding. Too often, though, courses in curriculum theory slight questions of curriculum practice. Practical questions are often presented as mere occasions for applying theory, as in "How would a Deweyan approach this problem?" Sometimes practical curriculum questions are treated as if they were not worthy of discussion, or, more kindly but with the same results, as if they were to be taken up in a later course. As a result, students often leave a first course in curriculum theory with the impression that the field of curriculum is idealistic, abstract, naive, and impractical.

Courses in curriculum development, by contrast, are eminently practical. They consider the questions teachers, principals, and school district officials face every day in planning, maintaining, and revising curricula. Such courses typically present step-by-step procedures for accomplishing each of the important kinds of tasks, such as setting objectives, selecting textbooks and curriculum materials, and implementing curricular innovations. Specific information about how to do important curriculum work is clearly important, but all too often these courses fail to make clear how practices are or should be grounded in ideas and values. They slight ideas by failing to explain why the procedures proposed are appropriate and better than others. Furthermore, such courses usually give far too little attention to the contexts of practice. Many times procedures are proposed without mention of the situations for which they are more or less appropriate.

The comprehensive course, often titled Introduction to Curriculum, surveys ideas and methods and thus provides a broader, more complete foundation than the other two types of courses. Often comprehensive introductory courses are organized historically. Alternatively, they may be organized around major curricular orientations, such as behavioral, humanistic, or pragmatist, or around an assortment of important topics, such as development, implementation, the hidden curriculum, the school subjects, and so on.

STUDYING CURRICULUM: A PERSONAL VIEW

In my opinion a good comprehensive introduction provides the best foundation for both practice and further study of curriculum. The key to a good comprehensive introduction, however, lies in its organization and structure. A poorly structured introduction leaves students with little more than a confused blur of details. Such a course strikes a beginning student as a jumble of philosophical doctrines, broad approaches to curriculum practice, how-to-do-its, descriptions of school practice, historical accounts of important trends and events, analyses by social scientists of the social processes underlying curriculum, and critiques of the prevailing school curriculum. To be effective, a comprehensive introductory course must cumulate into a clearer and deeper understanding of a subject so that the student can begin to see it as a coherent whole.

The fundamental purpose of curriculum study, in my view, is to foster better curriculum practice—in other words, wiser, more thoughtful, better grounded curriculum decisions and actions. A secondary purpose is to prepare students to make their own contributions to the evolving body of knowledge and lore in the field. The most important bodies of content for the student of curriculum are 1) the ideas and terms people have created for thinking and talking about curriculum problems; 2) typical and notable curricula, their origins and impact; 3) the methods, approaches, procedures, and techniques people have devised for coping with curricular problems; and 4) perspectives on curricula and the people, phenomena, and processes associated with them.

The following principles should guide the organization of these purposes and this content for a comprehensive introduction to the subject. 1) Since students probably come with varied prior experience, begin with an overview of key ideas, people, and events as an orientation and to provide a certain common ground for later work. 2) Show how knowledge of various kinds can be brought to bear on curriculum decisions and actions. This process of thought should pervade their future studies and therefore should be introduced at the earliest possible moment. It also offers a pattern for using the knowledge they have gained in their orientation and the knowledge to come and thus makes an important contribution to coherence. 3) Show curricula at work in their various contexts, presenting analytical frameworks and value perspectives when appropriate and constantly referring back to the key ideas and events as orientation, and repeatedly applying the pattern of thought presented earlier. 4) When this foundation has been laid, offer opportunities to address questions of improving curriculum practice directly. Throughout, there should be a constant traffic between concrete actions and abstract ideas. The plan of this book reflects these priorities and organizing principles.

QUESTIONS FOR STUDY

1. Refer back to Box 1-2, and identify which of the five concepts of curriculum underlies each of the definitions in Box 1-1. Which definitions seem more value-free or neutral? Which seem most slanted toward some particular point of view?

2. Which of the definitions of curriculum presented in this chapter appeals most to you? Why? Which appeals least? Why? Is the least appealing definition totally useless, in your opinion, or can you think of circumstances under which it, too, would be useful?

3. Find the definition from Box 1-1 that seems most practical and the one that seems least practical. Find the one which reflects the most distant, detached attitude and the one that reflects the most involved, committed attitude. Which one most favors change and which one most favors tradition? Which values are most prominent in the definition you favor most?

4. Two friends are arguing about whether a school needs a curriculum. One claims that it is possible and may even be desirable to have a school with no

curriculum, one in which teachers and students decide what they will do each day or week, following no advance plan. The other thinks that such a school would be a bad idea, and, more importantly, that it *would* have a curriculum anyway, just a different kind of curriculum. They begin to argue about what a curriculum really is. Help them to settle their argument.

5. Apply the definition of curriculum presented in this chapter to the curriculum you know best. Does it fit? Do you find any respects in which the definition is constraining or inappropriate?

6. Comment on the accuracy and usefulness of the following analogies.

> A curriculum works like a jazz group. All the musicians play in the same key, they play the same song, and the score for that song can be written down. But jazz musicians treat the score as a starting point for improvisation, so that the song never plays the same way twice.

> A curriculum works like a skeleton. It orders, arranges, and supports the entire educational program the way a skeleton orders, arranges, and supports all of the body's organs. It is an individual organ with its own parts to play, in creating red blood cells, for example. Yet it is an integral part of the educational program and can no more be separated from the functioning program than a skeleton can be separated from a living body.

In what ways are the analogies accurate and helpful, and in what ways are they limited or misleading?

7. Explore the limits of the definition of curriculum presented here. Does it apply to an entire school program? Does it apply to the schools of a state or nation? By this definition, does "Sesame Street" have a curriculum? Does a library? Museum? Scouting? A summer camp? A family? A movie like *Star Wars*?

8. Using the definition of curriculum as content, purpose, and organization, is it appropriate to speak of a curriculum as being developed or built? Is it appropriate to speak of a curriculum's effects or impact? Of its being adopted by a teacher or a school?

9. Imagine that you have been asked to visit three classrooms in your subject in a grade familiar to you, and to describe their curricula in writing. Using the definition presented here, list what things you would look for or ask about during your visit.

10. Identify the assumptions or presuppositions that are implied by the definition of curriculum in terms of content, purpose, and organization. Does the definition, for example, presume anything about consensus, compulsion, or control in education? Is it desirable to eliminate such presuppositions? Can a definition be formulated that makes no presuppositions?

11. Choose a school subject you know well. List some of the main items of content in that subject. Compare your list with others' lists in the same and other subjects. Have you used many of the same terms? Is there a consensus among you on the content of school subjects?

12. Consider how to describe the organization of content and purpose in the subject you examined in question 5. Compare your description with others' descriptions of the same and other subjects.

13. Completing the following incomplete statements may help you to discover your own or someone else's priorities among educational purposes.

The single most important thing society needs from its schools is . . .

The single most important way schools help to preserve and enhance our culture is . . .

The single most important thing a school can do for students is . . .

14. Reflect on the curriculum you received in grades K–12. How important an influence do you think it was on your life? How would you compare it to the influence of your family? Of peers? Of teachers as persons? Of religious organizations? Suppose these other influences on your childhood remained the same, only what you were taught in school changed radically. For example, suppose every school child had spent a period in fields or factories learning about life from a worker's perspective. Do you think this would have made a major difference in your life?

RECOMMENDED READING

On the forms of verbal conflict and the futility of arguing about definitions, Anatol Rapoport's *Fights, Games, and Debates* (1960) remains educative and interesting. D. Bob Gowin's *Educating* (1981) is the best recent general treatment of the subject of content I have seen. Any recent introduction to cognitive science will illustrate the developing techniques for representing content and studying individuals' cognitive representations. My favorite works in this genre are David Perkins's *The Mind's Best Work* (1981) and Alan Schoenfeld's *Mathematical Problem-Solving* (1986). Mary Louise Seguel (1966) gives an historical overview of the development of curriculum as a field of study. William Schubert's *Curriculum Books* is an essential reference work for anyone who plans to continue their studies in the field of curriculum.

REFERENCES

Arizona Art Education Association. 1982. Art in Elementary Education: What the Law Requires. *In Perspective, The Journal of the Arizona Art Education Association* 1:6–24.

Bell, Robert. 1971. *Thinking about the Curriculum*. Bletchley, England: The Open University Press.

Bernstein, Basil. 1971. On the Classification and Framing of Educational Knowledge. *Knowledge and Control* (Michael F. D. Young, ed.) London: Collier-Macmillan Publishers.

Bloom, Benjamin S. 1956. *Taxonomy of Educational Objectives: The Classification of Educational Goals. Handbook 1: Cognitive Domain*. New York: McKay.

Bobbitt, Franklin. 1918. *The Curriculum*. Boston: Houghton Mifflin.

Duncan, James K. and Jack R. Frymier. Oct. 1967. Exploration in the Systematic Study of Curriculum. *Theory Into Practice VI*: 4.

Goodman, Paul. 1967. Why Go to School? *Readings on the School in Society*. (Patricia C. Sexton, ed.) Englewood Cliffs, N.J.: Prentice Hall.

Gowin, D. Bob. 1981. *Educating*. Ithaca, N.Y.: Cornell University Press.

Hawridge, David. 1981. The Telesis of Educational Technology. *British Journal of Educational Technology* 12:4–18.

Krathwohl, David R., Benjamin S. Bloom, and Bertram B. Masia. 1964. *Taxonomy of Educational Objectives: The Classification of Educational Goals: Handbook 2: Affective Domain*. New York: McKay.

Musgrave, Phillip W. 1968. *The School as an Organisation*. London: Macmillan.

Perkins, David. 1981. *The Mind's Best Work*. Cambridge, MA: Harvard University Press.

Progressive Education Association. 1943. *Thirty Schools Tell Their Story*. New York: Harper and Brothers.

Rapoport, Anatol. 1960. *Fights, Games, and Debates*. Ann Arbor, MI: University of Michigan Press.

Saylor, J. Galen and William Alexander. 1954. *Curriculum Planning for Better Teaching and Learning*. New York: Holt, Rinehart, and Winston.

Schoenfeld, Alan. 1986. *Mathematical Problem-Solving*. Berkeley: University of California Press.

Schubert, William. 1980. *Curriculum Books*. Washington, D.C.: University Press of America.

Seguel, Mary Lou. 1966. *The Curriculum Field: Its Formative Years*. New York: Teachers College Press.

Shaver, James and Harold Berlak. 1968. *Democracy, Pluralism, and the Social Studies*. Boston: Houghton Mifflin.

Smith, B. O. and Daniel Orlovsky. 1978. *Curriculum Development*. Chicago: Rand McNally.

Smith, B. O., William Stanley, and Harlan Shores. 1957. *Fundamentals of Curriculum Development*. New York: Harcourt, Brace, and World.

Tanner, Daniel and Laurel N. Tanner. 1980. *Curriculum Development*. New York: Macmillan.

Tyler, Ralph W. 1950. *Basic Principles of Curriculum and Instruction*. Chicago: University of Chicago Press.

Walker, Decker and Jonas Soltis. 1986. *Curriculum and Aims*. N.Y.: Teachers College Press.

Weigand, V. K. 1970. A Study of Subordinate Skills in Science Problem Solving. (Robert M. Gagne, ed.) *Basic Studies of Learning Hierarchies in School Subjects*. Berkeley: University of California.

LANDMARKS OF AMERICAN CURRICULUM HISTORY

Anyone concerned with cultural progress must necessarily make use of the historical possibilities of the age in which he lives.

Werner Heisenberg. *Physics and Beyond*, 1971

PURPOSE OF THE CHAPTER

- to present an account of the principal continuities and changes in the curricula offered in American schools from colonial times to the present decade

- to show the complicated and changing relationship between what has happened to the curriculum and concurrent happenings in the society outside schools

- to show the shifting tides of ideas that have influenced curriculum trends and events.

- to explain the important part that knowledge of history can and should play in responsible curriculum decision-making.

OUTLINE

The Importance of History in Curriculum Studies

The American School Curriculum before 1890

The Progressive Transformation of the School: 1890–1930

The Decline and Fall of the Classics

Curriculum Making by National Committee

The School Survey

City-Wide Curriculum Revision

Curriculum Development in Laboratory Schools

Objective Studies As a Basis for Curriculum Change

Curriculum Reform by Direct Political Action

Professionalization of Curriculum Making, 1930–1960

Experiments with New Ways of Organizing the Curriculum

Ideological Issues Affecting Curriculum

The Professionalization of Curriculum Reform

Recent Years, 1960–Present

Some Lessons of Curriculum History

Using History in Making Curriculum Decisions

THE IMPORTANCE OF HISTORY IN CURRICULUM STUDIES

A knowledge of history is essential to making responsible curriculum decisions. Teachers who champion curriculum reforms in ignorance of what happened to earlier reforms take a needless step in the dark, shoulder unnecessary risks, and expose their students, their profession, and their community to needless danger. The more momentous the decision, the more imperative it is that decision-makers know the relevant history.

A few examples of how history can come in handy follow.

- Knowing what happened before can help us make better judgments about what might happen today or tomorrow under similar circumstances. For instance, historian Larry Cuban studied what happened when attempts were made to introduce radio, films, and television into American schools. What he found and reported in *Teachers and Machines: The Classroom Use of Technology Since 1920* (1986) can help us anticipate what might happen with computers or videocassette recorders.

- Studying the past can remind us to ask questions about the present that we may have overlooked. For instance, Americans often assume that schools are a force for change in society, an instrument of progress. Yet historian Ruth Miller Elson in *Guardians of Tradition* concluded from her studies of nineteenth-century school books that what was taught in school lagged behind changes in public attitudes and behavior. This discovery about the nineteenth century suggested to her that schools might still be behind the times.

- Sometimes we discover that people who lived before us created something we can use today. The scientists who created the Physical Science Study Committee course in high school physics in the late 1950s believed that physics students needed to learn about wave motion because it had become fundamental to all modern physics. But the teaching of wave motion involves mathematics more advanced than that taught in high school. The scientists involved searched for a way to make the study of waves accessible to students who lacked the mathematics used in college courses, and found a demonstration device, the ripple tank, that had been widely used by college physics teachers nearly a hundred years earlier but that had been neglected and nearly forgotten. They were then able to build a major part of their course around studies of waves in ripple tanks.

- We always understand our present practices more deeply and appreciate their implications more keenly when we learn the circumstances under which they originated and the manner in which they came down to us. Can you guess why biology books always show the anatomy of worms and frogs? You might be tempted to think that these organisms have some special biological significance, but my colleague, science educator Paul DeHart Hurd, tells me that these animals were introduced into school biology books in the nineteenth century by English authors who used them because they were widely available in the British Isles. This story illuminates an important aspect of the curriculum change process: a successful innovation can persist for generations with only minor changes and can cross fairly substantial cultural, historical, and geographic boundaries.

- We always learn from studying history what meanings people credit to past actions and, in turn, this helps us to understand meanings people may impute to present or future practices. For example, what made the New Math so significant to so many in the 1960s that they organized political campaigns to drive it out of their schools? Surely there is nothing inherent in the topics of sets, proof, inequalities, and number systems in bases other than ten to provoke such a reaction. What, then, did people see in this reform that was so threatening? And what does this suggest about how today's or tomorrow's reforms may be received?

- The study of curriculum history can help us develop more constructive attitudes toward the present. It can give us hope by demonstrating that constructive curriculum change has taken place and at the same time give us a realistic appreciation of the difficulties we must face to achieve lasting, significant curriculum change. It can help us see the present as a human creation by making us aware of alternative visions that were put forth and subsequently lost. It can give us a healthy skepticism about the extent to which sweeping generalizations can adequately cover the intricate individuality of circumstances, and thus instill in us sound judgment about the appropriate levels of generality and abstraction in principles proposed for use in making various kinds of curriculum decisions.

- History has special significance for curriculum because it is the closest we come to a laboratory for studying the phenomena and processes underlying curriculum practice. We cannot learn about the effect of schools on society by making the schools in some communities guardians of tradition and those in other communities builders of new social orders just to see what happens. But we can find records of communities where schools played these contrasting roles and study what happened. History is an imperfect laboratory since we cannot know for certain what factors were at work and we cannot control their interactions. But it remains the only means we have for studying many important curriculum questions, such as the relation of curriculum practices to social conditions.

This chapter provides an historical backdrop for events that will occupy center stage later in the book and it shows how historical thinking can be used responsibly in making contemporary curriculum decisions.

The history presented is divided into four periods, with increasing attention given to more recent years:

- before 1890
- the Progressive era, 1890–1930
- the period of professionalization, 1930–1960
- recent times, 1960–Present

THE AMERICAN SCHOOL CURRICULUM BEFORE 1890

Literacy and moral training were the twin foci of formal schooling from the colonial period to roughly the 1830s. The curriculum most Americans encountered in their six years or so of formal schooling consisted of reading, writing, and arithmetic, taught by letter perfect memorization and permeated with religion, nationalism, moral virtue, and strict discipline. Noah Webster, the Republic's foremost educator and first lexicographer, described his purpose in writing his pioneering reader, *An American Selection of Lessons in Reading and Speaking* (1789), as "to refine and establish our language, to facilitate the acquisition of grammatical knowledge and diffuse the principles of virtue and patriotism."

The great bulk of the population lived in rural areas. The people had to make substantial sacrifices to provide schools. It was not uncommon for a rural classroom to contain only a few books, and it was a rare classroom in which every child had a copy of the same textbook (See Figure 2-1). Therefore, most schoolwork was oral. Children also copied letters from a book onto their slate—chalkboards did not begin to be used until late in the nineteenth century. The first books children used were spellers and arithmetics. Spellers presented the alphabet and a list of syllables to be memorized, followed by lists of words and, eventually, sentences (See Figure 2-2). These early books do not look childish to modern eyes; they contained all the words adults used and no special effort was made to move gradually from simple ones to complex ones. The authors of the

FIGURE 2-1   Selections from The New England Primer (1727)

A.
In *Adam's* Fall,
We sinned all.

B.
This *Book* attend,
Thy Life to mend.

C.
The *Cat* doth play,
And after slay.

D.
The *Dog* doth bite
A Thief at Night.

E.
An *Eagle's* flight
Is out of sight.

F.
The Idle *Fool*,
Is whipt at School.

G.
As runs the *Glass*,
Man's Life doth pass.

H.
My Book and *Heart*
Shall never part.

I.
Jesus did dye,
For thee and I.

K.
King Charles the
Good,
No man of Blood.

W.
Whales in the Sea
God's voice obey.

X.
Xerxes the Great did die,
And so must you and I.

L.
The *Lyon* bold,
The *Lamb* doth hold.

M.
The *Moon* gives
Light,
In time of Night.

N.
Nightingales sing,
In time of Spring.

O.
The Royal *Oak* our
King did save,
From fatal stroke of
Rebel Slave.

P.
Peter denies
His Lord, and cries.

Q.
Queen Esther came
in Royal State,
To save the Jews
from dismal fate.

R.
Rachel doth mourn
For her first-born.

S.
Samuel anoints
Whom God appoints.

T.
Time cuts down all,
Both great and small.

U.
Uriah's beauteous
Wife,
Made David seek his
Life.

Y.
Youth's forward slips
Death soonest nips.

Z.
Zaccheus, he
Did climb the Tree,
His Lord to see.

SOURCE: From *The New England Primer* (1727).

FIGURE 2-2   **Lessons from an Early American Speller (1831)**

LESSONS OF EASY WORDS, TO TEACH CHILDREN TO READ,
AND TO KNOW THEIR DUTY

Lesson I

No man may put off the law of God:
My joy is in his law all the day.
O may I not go in the way of sin!
Let me not go in the way of ill men.

II

A bad man is a foe to the law:
It is his joy to do ill.
All men go out of the way.
Who can say he has no sin?

III

The way of man is ill.
My son, do as you are bid:
But if you are bid, do no ill.
See not my sin, and let me not go to the pit.

IV

Rest in the Lord, and mind his word.
My son, hold fast the law that is good.
You must not tell a lie, nor do hurt.
We must let no man hurt us.

SOURCE: From Noah Webster. *The American Spelling Book,* 1831.

books included such abstract words as *heresy, popery, republic,* and *kingdom,* and
seem to have made little effort to focus students' and teachers' attention on easy
and familiar words. Arithmetics consisted of introductions to numbers—addition,
subtraction, multiplication, and division—and of problems drawn from economic
life. The problems presented to students contained all the numerical difficulties and
complexities that their parents would encounter on the farm, in business, in the
household, or in the shop. They were not simplified, but they were slightly
graduated in difficulty. Although American education was closer to practical life
than its European counterparts, actual preparation for trades and occupations took

place mainly out of school, informally and in the home or community or through apprenticeship arrangements between parents and tradespeople.

This was a very basic and elementary curriculum, indeed. About all that can be said of the students who completed it is that they were literate and had been instilled with God-fearing and patriotic attitudes. This was enough for most Americans. Yet the curriculum was quite demanding, since students were required to memorize large quantities of complex verbal material and to make intricate arithmetic calculations.

Decisions about schools, including decisions about the curriculum, were made directly by local citizens as were nearly all other decisions of significance about the school. In private schools, decisions were made by the parents whose fees supported the schools. In some cases a schoolmaster or schoolmistress attained such standing in the community that his or her judgment was accepted by the local community without question. In many cases, though, the schoolmaster or mistress and teachers served at the pleasure of the parents and local citizenry and were replaced when their work or conduct failed to satisfy the parents or minister. Parents formed their impressions of the quality of schoolwork by listening at home to the children's recitals of what they had learned and by attending formal recitals at school.

Figure 2-3 and Figure 2-4 show typical school artifacts, lessons, and textbooks of this period. Figure 2-5 shows excerpts of Benjamin Franklin's proposal to establish an Academy; it later became a model for private, voluntary secondary schools in the nineteenth century.

· After 1830 American education entered a period of expansion and far-reaching change. The main concerns of educational reformers prior to 1830 had been to strengthen the infrastructure of schooling: to expand enrollments, to lengthen the years of schooling, to increase expenditures and to make them more dependable, and to upgrade the qualifications of teachers. The big story of the period between 1830 and the Civil War was the success of the crusade for universal free public education. Due in large part to the tireless efforts of Horace Mann, Henry Barnard, and their followers, free public schools were established in Massachusetts (1827), Pennsylvania (1834), and later in the other states. Massachusetts was also the first state to enact a compulsory school attendance law in 1852. By 1860, a majority of the states had established public school systems, and a majority of the nation's children were receiving some formal education. In Massachusetts, New York, and Pennsylvania, the notion of free public education expanded to include secondary schools, and in Michigan and Wisconsin the public school system was capped by a state university (Cremin 1961, 13).

Many early American educational leaders shared Noah Webster's desire to combat the influence of European ideas by teaching American political and social ideals, but otherwise curricular reforms were gradual and little noticed before 1830. After 1830, concurrent with the expansion of public schooling, several significant pedagogical reforms appeared and spread. Spellers with their syllabaries were replaced by readers that taught children to sound out words presented in

---

FIGURE 2-3   The Program of a New England Academy (1790)

(The certificate of graduation of Phillips Exeter Academy describes the attainment of one of its graduates . . .)

> *Be it therefore known that _____ has been a member of the (Phillips Andover) Academy seven years, and appears on examination to have acquired the principles of the English, French, Latin and Greek languages, Geography, Arithmetic and practical Geometry; that he has made very valuable progress in the study of Rhetoric, History, Natural and Moral Philosophy, Logic, Astronomy and Natural Law; and that he has sustained a good moral character during said term . . .*

SOURCE: Cited in Crosbie, Laurence M. *The Phillips Exeter Academy: A History,* 1924.

meaningful sentences. Readers began to include more material familiar to the child. Geography and history were increasingly taught along with the three R's. Reformers began to discuss how teachers could become better prepared—their education heretofore often consisted only of completing the highest grade they were teaching.

FIGURE 2-4   A Selection from McGuffey's Reader

---

news′pa per	cold	or′der	seem	through
stock′ings	chat	sto′ry	light	Har′ry
branch′es	kiss	burns	Mrs.	e vents′
an oth′er	Mr.	stool	lamp	mends

Evening at Home

1. It is winter. The cold wind whistles through the branches of the trees.

2. Mr. Brown has done his day's work, and his children, Harry and Kate, have come home from school. They learned their lessons well to-day, and both feel happy.

3. Tea is over. Mrs. Brown has put the little sittingroom in order. The fire burns brightly. One lamp gives light enough for all. On the stool is a basket of fine apples. They seem to say, "Won't you have one?"

4. Harry and Kate read a story in a new book. The father reads his newspaper, and the mother mends Harry's stockings. . . ."

SOURCE: From William Holmes McGuffey, *McGuffey's Second Eclectic Reader,* 1879, pp. 11–12.

■ **FIGURE 2-5**   **Excerpts from Franklin's Proposal for an Academy (1749)**

*N*otice is hereby given. That the trustees of the ACADEMY of Philadelphia, intend (God willing) to open the same on the first Monday of January next: wherein Youth will be taught the Latin, Greek, English, French, and German Languages, together with History, Geography, Chronology, Logic, and Rhetoric; also Writing, Arithmetic, Merchants Accounts, Geometry, Algebra, Surveying, Gauging, Navigation, Astronomy, Drawing in Perspective, and other mathematical Sciences; with natural and mechanical Philosophy, &c. agreeable to the Constitutions heretofore published, at the Rate of Four Pounds per annum, and Twenty Shillings entrance.

SOURCE: Robert F. Seybolt, 1925. *Source Studies in American Colonial Education. The Private School.* Urbana, IL: 1925

A few American schoolmen were beginning to look to Europe for models of better education. Calvin Stowe and Horace Mann made a much-publicized tour of the new state-run school system in Prussia that provided free, compulsory, universal, basic education to all children. They, like many other American educators who went abroad for advanced degrees in the last half of the nineteenth century, were impressed with the radical new pedagogical ideas they also found in Europe, especially with those of disciples of the kindly Swiss schoolmaster Johann Pestalozzi (1746–1824). Pestalozzians opposed strict discipline, verbalism, and memorization and favored a more experiential style of teaching. Influential editors of American education journals, such as William Woodbridge, Horace Mann, and Henry Barnard, publicized the European models and ideas and calls began to be heard for similar reforms in American schools.

Historian Lawrence Cremin identifies William Torrey Harris as the leading figure in education in post-civil war America. The curriculum reforms he advocated eventually came to be prevailing practice in American schools. As Superintendent of Schools in St. Louis from 1868–1880, and United States Commissioner of Education from 1889 to 1906, Harris "rationalized the institution of the public school" and "professionalized the art of school administration" (Cremin 1961, 15). Harris believed that the curriculum should serve to bring the child into possession of the best of the civilization through orderly, systematic study of subjects that provide children with ideas about the world in which they live. Following the German philosopher Georg Hegel, Harris looked on institutions as enabling mankind to attain its highest development. In his pedagogical creed, Harris attacked Rousseau's belief that children should be freed from arbitrary adult authority as "the greatest heresy in educational doctrine" (Cremin 1961, 37). Civilized life, Harris wrote, was "a life of order, self-discipline, civic loyalty, and respect for private property" (Cremin 1961, 17). The following passage from Harris' *Compulsory Education in Relation to Crime and Social Morals* (1885) conveys the tone and central message of his educational doctrines.

William Torrey Harris, 1835–1909

The great object, then, of education is the preparation of the individual for a life in institutions, the preparation of each individual for social combination. . . .

The ordinary type of school—the so-called "common school"—receives the child from the family at the age of five or six years. It receives him into a social body (for the school is a community) and educates him by "discipline" and "instruction" as they are technically called. By "discipline" is meant the training in behavior, a training of the will, moral training. It consists in imposing upon the child a set of forms of behavior rendered necessary in order to secure concert of action,—such forms as regularity, punctuality, silence, and industry. These are the four cardinal duties of the school pupil. Without them, the school cannot act as a unit, instruction cannot be given in classes, and no good result achieved. . . . (Harris 1885, 2–3)

The program Harris recommended for the common or elementary school included the conventional three R's, plus geography, hisotry, natural history, literature, and drawing. The program for the high school included algebra, geometry, plane trigonometry, analytical geometry, natural philosophy, chemistry, physical geography, astronomy, botany, zoology, physiology, Latin, Greek, French or German, history, Constitution of the United States, rhetoric, English literature, and mental and moral philosophy. These subjects were taught by textbooks. The teacher conducted oral recitations on assigned lessons to make certain students had read and mastered the assignment. Pupils would be assigned into grades by achievement, not age. They would be promoted from one grade to the next only when they had passed written tests on the skills and knowledge required for that grade.

Harris's plan came to be an accurate description of the schools in America's fast-growing cities and towns by 1890. There was, to be sure, enormous variety, especially in the secondary schools of the country's regions. Generally, New England led the nation in educational sophistication, though the upper midwest and middle-Atlantic states could also claim leadership in some areas. The South, the West and rural areas lagged behind. But schooling was largely verbal and academic, permeated by strict discipline, and conducted within a rigid, highly structured institutional framework of grades, textbooks, and examinations.

During the last quarter of the nineteenth century the curriculum and pedagogy advocated so ably by Harris came under increasing criticism from both lay and professional leaders. The most frequent criticisms were that the content was irrelevant for the majority of American youth, that the emphasis on order and discipline was deadening and excessive, that schoolmasters were often cruel to children in the name of discipline, and that the system was inefficient because so many children failed and were retained in earlier grades. Many reformers thought that the new European pedagogical ideas offered ways of overcoming the problems of the prevailing system, and some of the more innovative American educational leaders began to experiment with alternatives.

The experience of one such leader, a young superintendent of schools in Oswego, New York, epitomizes the experience of many such innovators. Edward Sheldon, had been an ardent advocate of strict order and discipline until the 1850s, when he began to experiment with methods based on the work of Pestalozzi. He was soon converted to the gentler, more natural Pestalozzian methods, in which instruction followed the child's interest and sought to appeal to constructive motives within the child rather than to impose discipline from without by force or coercion. Once converted, Sheldon was an equally ardent advocate of the new methods. His success can be judged from this report of the Examining Committee appointed annually by the Board of Education at Oswego to report on the condition of the schools.

> The Examining Committee . . . have taken special pains to observe carefully the results of this [school] system in awakening mind, quickening thought, perception, and all the early faculties of the child, and they return the most flattering reports of its success as a means of mental development.
> Wherever the teachers have caught the spirit of the plan, and have made a practical application of it, the effect is very marked in the awakened and quickened faculties of the children. It was never our pleasure before to witness so much interest in any class exercise. There was no dull routine of questions and monosyllabic answers, no mere recitation of dry and

stereotyped formulas, no apparent unloading of the memory, but we seemed as in the presence of so many youthful adventurers fresh from their voyages of discovery, each eager to recount the story of his successes. In their explorations, the fields, the wood, the garden, and the old house, from the cellar to the garret, will testify to their vigilance. The knowledge both of the parents and the teacher is often put to the severest test. They are continually plied with questions too difficult for them to answer.

Teachers say to us now, "We have no longer any dull pupils." All are wide awake. The children say it is "real fun" to go to school now. It is not that the work of the schoolroom is less real and earnest, but that it is better adapted to child nature, and meeting the demands of their young life energies. This is what we call education, in its true spirit and purpose. (Annual Report of the Board of Education, Oswego, New York, for the Year Ending March 31, 1861, quoted in Cubberley 1934, 343–345.)

Sheldon's "object teaching" became the heart of the Oswego movement that challenged the hold of textbooks and memorization on the curriculum of the post-war era, promoted pupil activity in contrast to the passive, receptive role allotted to them in prevailing school practice, and emphasized observation of the real world in place of books. The Oswego movement, together with the introduction of kindergartens to America and the introduction of manual training, established an alternative pedagogy in some American schools. The kindergarten's emphasis on the educative value of play contrasted as sharply as anything could with Harris' insistence that discipline be imposed upon the student. Manual training, built on the assumption that working with one's hands develops both mind and body and builds moral character, challenged the preeminence of verbal learning in school.

Among the public, many merchants and industrialists of the period were dissatisfied with the products of the schools. A rapidly expanding industrial economy needed a large supply of skilled workers, many more than were trained by apprenticeship. They looked to the schools to provide vocational training. Calvin Woodward's Manual Training School, established in St. Louis in 1879, was the kind of school they wanted. It provided a three-year program equally divided between mental and manual labor, mental labor consisting of practically-oriented versions of the conventional academic subjects and manual labor consisting of explicit training in school workshops. This was a program designed to prepare young men to earn a living in an industrial society. By 1890 most major cities offered private manual training schools on this model, often sponsored by businessmen. Many within industry and labor saw a great need for "practicalizing" the public schools, too.

Business and labor were supported in this aim by agrarian interests. As early as 1874 the Grange, the principal organization representing farmers, had advocated the teaching of practical agriculture and domestic arts and sciences. In 1876 the Grange established a standing committee on education to formulate its educational policies and to guide state Granges in local actions (Cremin 1961, 42). Cremin quotes one agricultural opinion leader of the time on the frustrations of those who sought a place for agriculture in their children's education.

> . . . as it was 60 years ago in our boyhood, so it is today in 99 out of every 100 schools. Not a grain of progress that will help the country boy to a better understanding of the problems of agriculture. (Cremin 1961, 45)

The educational system of the late nineteenth century was also criticized by a new breed of social reformers for not ministering to children's most pressing life problems, particularly those of immigrants and city slum dwellers. In the 1890s there was an increasing awareness of the urban poor by socially concerned Americans. The sufferings of tenement dwellers were dramatized in popular journals. Activist reformers refused to accept the pat conclusions that the poor would always be with us, that it was their own fault for drinking and immoral living, and that nothing could be done for the sufferers. The most valuable expression of this awakening of conscience were the settlement houses. The most famous of these was Hull House, established in Chicago by Jane Addams and Ellen Gates Starr in 1889. Others were established in almost every major city by 1900. From the beginning, settlements found themselves involved with education. They established kindergartens and nurseries, taught working men and women to read, established playgrounds and vacation centers for city children in the summer, set up drama and choral groups, and taught nutrition, English for immigrants, child care, millinery, dressmaking, and dozens of trades and crafts. The conception of socialized education that emerged from the work of the settlements stood in sharp contrast with the narrowly academic emphasis of secondary schools. Many reformers thought it set a pattern the schools should follow.

By 1890 the prevailing pattern of school governance was the locally appointed or elected public school board, which was an arm of city, township, or county government. In cities, school board members were elected or appointed to represent particular wards. All appointments of school employees, including superintendents, principals, teachers, and janitors, were made by the board. Most personnel served on one-year contracts, and many superintendents and teachers found themselves without jobs on little or no notice because of changes in the composition of the board of education, because they had displeased one or more board members, or because a friend or relative of a board member needed a job.

Meanwhile, teaching and school administration had become steadily more professional. Normal schools designed to prepare elementary teachers beyond high school had multiplied. Professional journals of educational theory and practice were established. The National Education Association was founded in 1857. Increasingly, leaders of educational organizations and the opinion leaders among all those concerned with education were being drawn from the ranks of professionally trained educators. These leaders were going abroad to study, chiefly to Germany, where many received Ph.D.s. It was more than coincidental that the chief educational leader of the period, William Torrey Harris, was a professional educator, in contrast to earlier educational leaders such as Mann, Barnard, and

Webster, a politician, an editor, and a publisher, respectively. By 1890 the most influential educational leaders were professional schoolmen who saw themselves as part of a national network of professionals trained and equipped for leadership on questions of education. This, of course, put them in direct competition with boards of education composed of laymen.

Thus, many currents of discontent were running in the post-Civil War decades. By the 1890s these currents had become "a nationwide torrent of criticism, innovation, and reform that soon took on all the earmarks of a social movement" (Cremin 1961, 22). This was the atmosphere in 1892 when a New York monthly, *The Forum,* published a series of articles on American schools by a young New York pediatrician, Joseph Mayer Rice. Rice's muckraking articles were based on a six month tour of 36 cities, during which he talked with some 1200 teachers. Historian Lawrence Cremin describes what Rice found:

> In city after city public apathy, political interference, corruption, and incompetence were conspiring to ruin the schools. . . . with alarming frequency the story was the same: political hacks hiring untrained teachers who blindly led their innocent charges in singsong drill, rote repetition, and meaningless verbiage. (Cremin 1961, 4–5)

Rice's series provoked intense debate about education. It reinforced a widespread concern among a newly emerging generation of American leaders about corruption and inefficiency in all areas of government. It marked the beginning of the most fundamental wave of reform in theory and practice American education has yet known—Progressive Education.

THE PROGRESSIVE TRANSFORMATION OF THE SCHOOL: 1890–1930

By 1890 changes in American society left William T. Harris' curriculum out of step with the most vital, expanding, and influential sectors of the society. America was becoming a wealthy, industrial society, not a poor but virtuous agricultural republic. To many Americans the deeds of Rockefeller, Gould, Morgan, Carnegie, and other captains of industry outshone those of the ancient heros of Greece and Rome. The scientific discoveries of Newton and Pasteur and the inventions of James Watt, Guglielmo Marconi, and Thomas Alva Edison impressed many Americans as being more important to the progress of civilization than the writings of Aristotle, Plato, Horace, and Cicero. Modern science and technology seemed to many to hold out promise of a qualitatively new world as unknown to the ancients as the Americas themselves. Many Americans who traveled to Europe found the old world, as they called it, to be moribund. Progress had passed it by. The news was being made here at home. The traditional curriculum with its staid moralism, reverence for ancient languages and cultures, and emphasis on rote verbal learning came to seem old-fashioned and backward-looking.

Probably the most fundamental change in American education between 1890 and 1930 was the sheer growth of the educational enterprise. Official government statistics show that in 1889 less than 14 million students, barely 50% of the school age population, were enrolled in elementary and secondary schools (public and private) in the United States. By 1930 the same source records nearly 28 million enrolled, over 70% of the school age population. In 1890, less than 5% of American 17 year olds were high school graduates; by 1930 nearly 30% were. In 1900 less than 20 baccalaureate degrees per 1000 could be found among 23 year-olds; by 1930 there were nearly 60 baccalaureates per 1000. More students were in school, they were staying longer, and even the school day and school year were lengthening. School was becoming the normal place for American children to grow up.

This development affected the schools in many far-reaching ways. New, modern schools became the center of community life in many small towns and cities (See Figure 2-6). More teachers were needed quickly, so normal school enrollment expanded and departments and schools of education were created in colleges and universities. Rapid growth in these institutions stimulated the professionalization of education and, since the institutions of higher education were less tied to local governance, encouraged national uniformity and standardization. The sudden appearance in local schools of many young, idealistic, and often ambitious teachers and principals created an atmosphere favoring innovation. It became a period of great ferment, deserving the designation given it by historian Lawrence Cremin in the title of his history—*The Transformation of the School: Progressivism in American Education; 1876–1957* (1961).

Some of the most fundamental and far-reaching curriculum changes associated with the Progressive transformation were:

- broadened aims of elementary schooling,
- decline of the classics,
- expansion of vocational education,
- reorganization of secondary courses,
- redesign of textbooks, and diversification of curriculum materials.

A brief look at each of these developments illustrates the variety of substance and method found in the curriculum innovations of the Progressive period.

Broadened Aims and Content of Elementary Schools

The American public's image of a good and proper education at the turn of the century is well expressed in the lyrics of the nostalgic "Bicycle Built for Two," a popular song of the turn of the century:

> *Readin' and 'ritin' and 'rithmetic,*
> *Sung to the tune of a hik'ry stick, . . .*

FIGURE 2-6 **One-Room School**

SOURCE: Exterior and Interior of the New School in the Same District
Modernization of schools in the 1920s.

To go to school meant to sit quietly in neat rows of desks, to read, to memorize, to do arithmetic problems at the board and at one's desk, or to recite orally—in short, to undergo a rigorous, no-nonsense program of literacy training and discipline. Other content that might be included—geography, natural history, ancient or American history—would generally be confined to memorization of names and facts.

Here, for contrast, is an account, published in 1900, of a visit by the mother of a prospective student to John Dewey's Laboratory School at the University of Chicago.

> None of the children seemed to have any books as they came up [to the school]. I didn't see even a geography or a reader among the older children. One little girl had a live alligator in a box; a small boy was carrying a large Indian blanket in from a carriage; one child had a basket of fruit, and another a package which I had heard him tell the teacher contained "sandwiches". . . . I concluded that this must be an off day with the school; but thought that I might as well stay and see them start,—they seemed to be having such a good time. . . .
>
> I followed the children to the gymnasium, where seats were arranged for the morning exercises, which consisted chiefly of singing. One or two groups of children were asked to sing their "Group Song." Upon inquiry I was told that the charming melody and the words of the song I heard were composed by the children who sang them. . . . Upstairs I found a group of children about ten years old engaged in setting up electric bells. . . . A group of younger children had a sheepskin from which they were taking wool. . . . Everywhere the children were busy, but the morning was half gone and I had heard nothing that reminded me of a school except a class talking Latin as I passed. (Runyon 1900, 590–91)

Pioneering teachers in major centers of educational innovation around the country were developing innovative classroom activities. At Lincoln School in New York City, for example, students actually built a play city in the first and second grades. Daily life in homes, neighborhoods, shops, stores, factories, farms, towns, and cities became objects of study, along with words and numbers. Progressive schools broadened the traditional concern for discipline to include a concern for social development in general. Teachers organized activities to give students practice in cooperation, leadership, and service to others. They patterned classrooms on families and made the social relationships an explicit focus of attention. They established formal governance arrangements for schools and classrooms, and students participated in making rules and establishing penalties for breaking them, in choosing activities and planning and carrying them out.

Such experiments were a mere drop in the bucket of American elementary education, but they caught the imagination of a generation of teachers and of young parents ready for a change from the rigid, formal, traditional elementary school curriculum. Gradually, elements of the new programs found their way into traditional classrooms and the curriculum of elementary schools was thus greatly broadened. The content subjects—history, geography, science—had been considered too difficult for young children when they had to be studied from books, but they became more accessible when teachers began to employ a wider range of pedagogical strategies. Soon literacy became merely the backbone of the elementary curriculum, not its entirety.

Redesigning Textbooks and Curriculum Materials

By 1930 textbooks were larger, more colorful, and easier to read and use. Beginning readers offered colorful scenes illustrating simple stories about familiar happenings in familiar surroundings. Vocabulary was strictly controlled to include only the simplest, most familiar words. Words were always included in meaningful sentences of the simplest possible structure. New words were repeated many times. Textbooks for older children were full of activities to do in the classroom— "Things to Do," "Questions for Discussion," and the like. The most difficult problems and exercises, along with the most difficult words and phrases, were gone. In their place was a much greater number of simpler, beginning exercises, giving students more opportunity to practice the most rudimentary but most fundamental skills. The progress from familiar to new and from simple to complex was much more carefully graduated and controlled than it had been. And the textbooks had help from a whole battery of newly developed supplementary educational materials—workbooks, teachers' guides, and standardized tests and performance scales.

These changes were a result of a new philosophy and a new technique. The new philosophy required textbook authors to respect children's natural impulses and use them to help children learn, rather than to thwart them as a means of disciplining the child. So, publishers who espoused this philosophy made books as easy and attractive as possible rather than purposely austere and difficult. The new technique used to redesign textbooks was empirical research. Faculties of education and psychology in leading universities carried out detailed scientific investigations of children's responses to textbooks. Psychologist Edward L. Thorndike of Teachers College, Columbia University, was the most distinguished of these pedagogical researchers. He studied words used in American publications and compiled a dictionary based on actual usage (Thorndike and Lorge 1938). He published lists of the most frequently used words and publishers used these lists to revise their textbooks. Thorndike also studied the difficulties children encountered in learning arithmetic and algebra and consulted with publishers in revising textbooks in these subjects.

A whole generation of educators and psychologists joined Thorndike in studying and redesigning textbooks and curriculum materials. As a result of their efforts, the textbooks of 1930 were an altogether new creation, as different from those of 1890 as these were from colonial spellers and arithmetics.

THE DECLINE AND FALL OF THE CLASSICS

In 1890 only a small fraction of youthful Americans attended secondary schools, and everyone assumed they came to prepare for college. Since Latin, Greek, and ancient history—the classics—were prerequisites for entrance into college, these subjects were the backbone of the secondary school curriculum. The classics had long been suspect in America. Benjamin Franklin's Academy was founded on the principle of preference for the useful over the ornamental, and classics were considered ornamental. It was perhaps to be expected that leaders of business and industry would oppose the teaching of classics, but many leaders of cultural life, including many university professors and college presidents also opposed requiring all undergraduates to study the classics. Early in the nineteenth century the classics faculty of Yale had felt so threatened by opposition from within and without that they issued a report in 1828 describing the value of learning the classics. The Yale Report, which remained a center of controversy for nearly a century, set the terms of the debate over the classics. The essence of the report's message was that the function of a college education should be to discipline the mind, to furnish the mind, to expand its powers, and store it with knowledge. The various subjects each contributed to this purpose in a unique fashion by training a different set of mental faculties. Mathematics disciplined deductive reasoning. Physical sciences disciplined induction, probable reasoning, and use of facts. Classics, unique among subjects, were said to discipline all the mental faculties: taste, memory, reasoning, ethical judgment, copiousness and accuracy of expression—the whole lot. Thus, the classics deserved their dominant place in the undergraduate curriculum and therefore in the secondary curriculum.

Opponents of the classics seized upon the doctrine of mental discipline—that mental powers exist as independent faculties that can be strengthened with practice—and ignored other justifications for study of the classics. In the first two decades of the twentieth century, psychologists, feeling the power of their emerging science, subjected the claims for mental discipline to extensive and rigorous laboratory tests that eventually discredited the concept of mental discipline. The most direct and damaging blow to the teaching of classics came from a series of studies published by Edward L. Thorndike in 1924 under the title, "Mental Discipline in High School Studies." He compared the intelligence test scores of two groups of pupils, otherwise as nearly identical as could be arranged, one group who had taken mathematics, in comparison with another who had taken stenography or cooking instead. The gains in intelligence were the same for the two groups of pupils; studying mathematics did not improve intelligence as measured on these tests. Subsequent studies confirmed the startling finding that studying more demanding classical subjects thought to foster the development of mental faculties, did not improve intelligence scores any more than studying other subjects. Henceforth, anyone who argued for the inherent superiority of one subject over another for developing mental faculties had to contend with a large body of very

Charles W. Eliot, 1834–1926

good evidence to the contrary. Few of the studies were directly relevant to the claims made for the educational value of studying the classics, but the doctrine of mental discipline suffered a fatal blow and the rationale for the classics given in the Yale Report fell with it.

Defenders of the classics had a much harder job than convincing faculties and trustees of colleges, however. They had to convince students. Many otherwise qualified students did not attend college, going directly into business instead or into preparation for careers that did not require undergraduate degrees. They tried everything to attract more students: lowering entrance requirements, sponsoring preparatory schools on campus where interested prospective students could study to meet entrance requirements, even part-time, non-degree programs. Some dropped required study of the classics. In particular, the land grant colleges, founded under the Morrill Act of 1862 that ceded federal land to states for the purpose of founding colleges of the mechanical and agricultural arts and sciences, soon made it possible to earn a bachelor's degree without studying the classics. The land grant colleges proved immediately successful in attracting students and soon the more established colleges and universities in the East and South followed their lead and made the classics elective subjects. As early as 1886, under President Charles W. Eliot's leadership, Harvard began to accept advanced mathematics and physics in place of Greek as an admission requirement. By 1903 Greek was no longer required at Yale. Historian Frederick Rudolph describes the final fall of the classics from dominance in the undergraduate curriculum this way:

> By 1915 fewer than fifteen major colleges still required four years of Latin for the B.A. degree. In 1919 Yale accepted students without admission Latin and enrolled them as candidates for the Ph.D. degree. Four years later the faculty voted to abolish Latin as a requirement for admission or for the B.A. degree, but they were overruled by the Yale Corporation, one member of which, William Howard Taft, exclaimed: "Over my dead body!" Taft died in 1930. Latin went in 1931. (Rudolph 1977, 214)

High school enrollments in Greek dropped precipitously once it ceased to be a requirement for college entrance. By 1910, in the words of historian Edward A. Krug (1964), "Greek had been surrendered as a hopeless cause" (p. 336). Government statistics for 1924–1925 showed only 11,000 students nationwide enrolled in secondary school Greek. Enrollments in Latin, however, continued to rise, although the proportions of students enrolled in Latin declined steadily from 50.6% in 1900 to 37.3% in 1915 to 27.5% in 1923–1924. Latin remained a popular subject, although it ceased being the pillar of the academic curriculum and became merely another elective like art, music, or typewriting. We see that, in the curriculum as in civilization, the mighty can fall.

Reorganizing the Secondary School Studies

In 1890 both college entrance requirements and course offerings of secondary schools varied to an extent that many found confusing and alarming. In the 1890s leaders in the colleges and secondary schools cooperated in reorganizing both entrance requirements and secondary school programs, with the result that by 1930 high schools around the country offered a uniform, sequential, departmentally organized academic curriculum. Box 2-1 contrasts typical secondary school course offerings before and after the reorganization.

Two famous national committees played pivotal roles in this reorganization of the secondary school curriculum. The Committee of Ten, whose official name was The Committee on Secondary School Studies, was appointed by the National Education Association in 1892 and charged to bring order into the scattered and chaotic program of studies in secondary schools. Its membership included both college and secondary school faculty, though the colleges were dominant both in numbers and influence. Charles W. Eliot, President of Harvard University, chaired the committee. The Committee's report proposed four college preparatory curricula: classical, latin-scientific, modern languages, and English. Any student who completed one of these four programs should be admissable to college, the committee declared. All of the subjects taken were considered as having equal value toward college preparation.

BOX 2-1   Typical Secondary School Course Offerings in 1890 and 1930

<table>
<tr><td align="center">1890</td><td align="center">1930</td></tr>
</table>

English

1890	1930
rhetoric, logic, etymology, reading, English literature, recitation, composition, and grammar	four years of a subject called English

Mathematics

1890	1930
advanced arithmetic with logarithms, algebra, geometry, trigonometry, surveying, navigation	general math, business math, algebra I and II, geometry, and trigonometry

Social Studies

1890	1930
The Constitution of the United States, moral philosophy, mental philosophy, ancient history, European history, political economy, and American history	social studies, American history, problems of American democracy, civics

Science

1890	1930
anatomy, physiology, botany, astronomy, chemistry, navigation, and surveying, physical geography, natural philosophy and geology	general science, biology, physical science, chemistry, and physics

Additions of other subjects between 1890 and 1930

home economics, consumer education, business education, agricultural education, and other vocational subjects

---

The bulk of the Committee's report was taken up by the recommendations of five separate subject committees for the classics, science, English, mathematics, and social studies. Practical and vocational subjects were omitted, as were the arts. Courses and course content for these recommended programs were further specified some years later by the Committee on College Entrance Requirements, appointed by the NEA in 1896 to propose ways to implement the recommendations of the Committee of Ten regarding the articulation of high school and college.

This Committee reported in 1899, giving detailed recommendations about course content, time allotments, and modes of instruction.

In science, for example, the Committee of Ten had organized three subject matter conferences: 1) Physics, chemistry, and astronomy; 2) Natural history, including nature study, botany, zoology, and human physiology; and 3) Geography, including geology and meteorology. Each of these groups recommended required courses in their subdivision of science. At a joint session they resolved that one-quarter of the time of the high school grades should be given over to science and that this amount of work should be required for college entrance. When the Committee on College Entrance Requirements considered science requirements a few years later, they recommended that botany, zoology, and human physiology be combined into a single biology course. The committee proposed that secondary schools offer a standard science sequence of three science courses: biology, chemistry, and physics. Later, in 1918, the Committee on the Reorganization of Science in Secondary Schools, appointed by the NEA, recommended the addition of a course in general science as the first course normally taken in high school. The histories of the other school subjects were similar. The term *social studies* was first used in a truly public, national context when a Committee on the Reorganization of the Social Studies was appointed by the NEA in 1917. Although English had been recognized by the Committee of Ten as a subject category as early as 1892, opposition to considering it as a school subject in its own right continued well into the twentieth century. Woodrow Wilson, then a professor at Princeton, opposed it in a speech to the Middle States Association in 1907, saying that "English should not be taught as a subject, but should pervade the teaching of all subjects." (Krug 1964, 354) Nevertheless, the National Council of Teachers of English was founded in 1911 and its president chaired the English committee of the Committee on the Reorganization of Secondary Education in 1917. The content of English courses, right down to the works of literature read and studied, had been largely determined by college entrance requirements, specifically by list of books to be examined by the College Entrance Examination Board, formed in 1911. Even though most students did not attend college, the lists of works recommended by the CEEB defined the content of English courses in high schools throughout the country.

By 1930 the academic curriculum of secondary schools in the United States attained essentially the form it has today. As high schools grew, they assumed a departmental organization along the subject matter lines laid out by the Committee of Ten. The academic curriculum that resulted has been one of the most lasting curriculum reforms in our history and one of the most substantial in its impact on all parts and phases of the educational system.

The Rise of Vocational Education

Vocational subjects were the main curricular beneficiaries of the decline in classics and the expansion of the school population. A variety of vocational subjects, including manual training, agriculture, home economics, trade and industrial education, bookkeeping, shorthand, and other commercial, industrial, and domestic studies, had been taught for decades in many public high schools in major cities. But these courses enrolled only a few students who elected them in addition to the academic requirements for the high school diploma. By 1910 the number of high schools offering distinct vocational programs of study had risen into the hundreds (Venn 1964, 50). By 1922 vocational courses enrolled a larger fraction of students (42%) than Latin (Krug 1964, 376). The great increases in number and percentage of students enrolled in vocational programs (to 9.0 million or 26.3% of the age group in 1970–1971) took place after 1917, the year in which one of the great political campaigns in curricular history ended in the enactment of a law authorizing federal aid to vocational education. This story is important for the light it casts on the role of politics in curriculum decisions.

In spite of decades of calls from influential national figures for a more practical form of education, advocates could point to few changes in schools by 1900. For example, the report of the prestigious Committee of Ten in 1896 outlined four curricular patterns for the high school, none of which included any "vocational" or "industrial" components. Advocates assumed, with reason, that leaders of traditional schools were simply deaf to their pleas for industrial education, and many urged separate vocational high schools, a proposal that encountered strong resistance from defenders of traditional schools and from those who believed that separation would be undemocratic.

Advocates of industrial education began to pursue their aims politically. They could count on many more sympathetic ears in legislative halls than among school leaders. In 1906 they achieved a political victory in Massachusetts that attracted national attention. The Douglas Commission, appointed by the governor to study the question of industrial and technical education in that state, called for the creation of independent industrial schools throughout the state and for the introduction of day or evening industrial courses in the regular high schools. The report seemed to ignite the smoldering sentiment for more practical education and calls for similar reforms began to fill editorial pages in newspapers and professional publications around the country. Also in 1906 the National Society for the Promotion of Industrial Education (NSPIE) was founded in New York "to bring to public attention the importance of industrial education", and "to promote the establishment of institutions for industrial training." (NSPIE 1907, 10) By 1910 the NSPIE had grown from a small band of educators and educational reformers to a powerful political coalition supporting vocational education. The organization was supported by labor, business, education, and agriculture. This remarkable political coalition was active in campaigns in dozens of states between 1906 and 1917, ringing up many impressive political victories in the form of laws establishing publicly supported programs of industrial education, sometimes as separate schools and sometimes as programs within the existing public schools.

Early successes roused resistance in other states, making each battle more difficult than the last. In 1910 the NSPIE began to work toward federal support for vocational education. Education had always been a jealously guarded prerogative of the states, and numerous attempts to secure federal support for educational initiatives had all failed, including attempts to found a national university. To seek federal support for vocational education was a bold move. In 1914 the first step was taken in the House of Representatives. A Commission on National Aid to Vocational Education was formed. The report the Commissioners produced in record time later that year recommended federal aid to vocational education and outlined a plan in considerable detail. It took three long years of politicking, but in 1917 the Smith-Hughes Act was passed and federal aid to vocational education became the first federally financed program in American public education. The act required states to prepare plans for statewide vocational education programs and specified criteria and guidelines in great detail. While in theory states were free to meet these guidelines with plans of their own, in fact few states were in a position to devote as much care to planning as the Commission recommended and so most followed in detail the specimen programs provided. The Act also specified separate arrangements for governing vocational education within local school districts. The vocational program was to be administratively separate from the academic program, the so-called dual administration scheme designed to protect vocational education from subversion by unsympathetic local school officials. Thus, vocational education entered American high schools with federal support and with a license entitling it to an autonomy not vouchsafed to the rest of the curriculum.

Within three years of passage of the Smith-Hughes Act enrollment in vocational programs doubled and total expenditures for vocational education quadrupled (Venn 1964, 63). In 1918 the total enrollment in vocational programs was 164,000, including 15,000 in agriculture programs, 118,000 in trade and industrial programs, and 31,000 in home economics programs. By 1944 total enrollment was 2,600,000 and the corresponding figures for the separate vocational areas were 610,000 for agriculture, 850,000 for trade and industrial, and 954,000 for home economics (Struck 1945, 14). By 1970–1971, 9,000,000 students, some 26.3% of the age group in secondary schools, were enrolled in vocational programs. The shift from classical and academic high school courses in 1890 to the comprehensive high school with its substantial enrollments and offerings in a multitude of vocational areas is the most striking and far-reaching transformation the American high school curriculum has yet seen.

Invention of Procedures for Planned Curriculum Change

In the process of transforming the curriculum of American schools, the Progressive reformers invented new ways of going about curriculum reform. Horace Mann and his fellow crusaders for the common school had relied largely on their own personal efforts to bring about the changes they sought. They traveled widely, speaking to whatever groups or individuals would listen; they wrote articles for professional journals as well as for newspapers and popular magazines, and they used their personal influence with the wealthy and well-placed. A generation later, William T. Harris had been able to move schools away from the oral recitation toward written examinations and textbooks largely by oratory and campaigning directed toward educational leaders. Reform movements of various kinds continued to be a major way to advocate curriculum change, but by 1930 curriculum reformers had available to them a veritable tool kit of other procedures for curriculum revision. Among the more important items in this kit:

> national committees
> school surveys
> city-wide curriculum revision projects
> research studies: of students, of life outside the school, of errors and difficulties
>   in learning
> field experiments in laboratory schools
> direct appeals to lawmakers and politicians.

Curriculum-making was becoming, if not a science, at least an area of professional expertise.

CURRICULUM MAKING BY NATIONAL COMMITTEE

The Committee of Ten on Secondary School Studies, appointed in 1892 at the annual meeting of the National Council of Education of the NEA, was the first great success in curriculum making by national committee. It is still unclear whether the Committee's report blazed a trail or simply publicized practices already widely in use. But the Report was extensively discussed, its recommendations came to pass, and this was enough for educational leaders to regard it as a success and to imitate it in future reform efforts.

Only seven months after the appointment of the Committee of Ten, the Department of Superintendence of the NEA appointed a new national committee, the Committee of Fifteen on Elementary Education. This committee became famous for fiery debates between representatives of established educational thought and practice. It was headed by William T. Harris, who also chaired the Committee, along with proponents of the new education who advocated less formal, less verbal, more experiential elementary education. Other influential committees appointed by the NEA included:

- The Committee on Economy of Time in Education, appointed in 1903 to consider how many years of schooling ought to be standard in each of the levels, elementary, secondary, and college,
- The Committee of Nine on the Articulation of High School and College, appointed in 1911,
- The Commission on the Reorganization of Secondary Education, appointed in 1913, whose 1918 Report *Cardinal Principles of Secondary Education*

(National Education Association 1918) outlined the platform of Progressive education for reform of the public schools.

The early committees featured collaboration between school and university leaders and struggled to standardize divergent practices. As we saw earlier, they were remarkably successful in negotiating a series of compromises that were widely accepted by colleges, high schools, and the public. Although voices were raised in opposition to their recommendations, the national committees possessed a visibility and legitimacy that their critics never approached. This unique standing resulted from the evident and nearly unanimous support of respected educational leaders at all levels, including Presidents of Harvard and the University of Michigan; distinguished professors from Oberlin, Wisconsin, and Columbia; and Commissioners of Education appointed by the President. Still, their success was remarkable, especially in view of the fact that they had no official standing in law or governance and no official authority over so much as one school or teacher.

The national committees appointed later did not pursue standardization and compromise, but advocated Progressive reforms. Their membership consisted for the most part of professional educators from school systems and teacher education institutions. Their successes, though striking in the short term, did not last.

THE SCHOOL SURVEY

The practice of conducting school surveys began about 1910 with surveys in Boise, Idaho, Montclair and East Orange, New Jersey, and Baltimore, Maryland, and spread rapidly to city school systems throughout the country. Surveys were commissioned by school superintendents, boards of education, or lay and civic groups. Newly appointed city superintendents could capitalize on the authority of their professional expertise by sponsoring a thorough study of the system and bringing recommendations to their board with the support of an impartial study. Reformist boards could overcome entrenched opposition by mobilizing progressive local opinion through highly publicized studies of the deficiencies of the present school system.

Surveys might be conducted by a single person, by a commission, or by departments or bureaus of research when these were established in large city systems and in universities beginning in 1913. Somewhere at the center of every school survey, though, a professor of education could be found. Jesse Sears, George Strayer, Charles Judd, Leonard P. Ayres, and Franklin Bobbitt were among the most active surveyists. A survey might consist of anything from a one-man, six week exercise using questionnaire and interview data to evaluate a single issue, to a comprehensive inquiry lasting several years and looking into every nook and cranny of a school system's operations. The more massive surveys were funded by the Carnegie Foundation for the Advancement of Teaching, the Russell Sage Foundation, the General Education Board, and the Commonwealth Fund.

The net effect of surveys was generally to question existing practices and to promote reform. Typically a survey attempted to identify educational needs among students and community, to anticipate future needs, and to propose programs and practices accordingly. The survey's chief attraction and the feature that distinguished it from earlier efforts by commissions of various sorts was the collection and use of a wide range of qualitative and quantitative data. Typical sources of data included: observations made during school visits or field trips into the community, analysis of existing records in the school district or other agencies, interviews, checklists and scorecards of various kinds, and results of standard tests. Surveys were intended to reveal problems in critical areas of the school system's operations, including curriculum, finance, school buildings and facilities, training of teachers, teacher salaries, student enrollment and pupil promotion and retention policies. Often, though, surveys collected so much raw data about so many aspects of the school system's operations and produced such massive, detailed reports, that readers could draw any conclusions, or none at all. Clients often had to appoint several committees to interpret the survey report and to make recommendations for changes.

A number of investigative techniques were pioneered by the surveyists: studies of the local cost of living were done to determine appropriate salary levels for teachers, methods of population forecasting were employed to anticipate enrollments and to plan for growth, various studies of building design, illumination, ventilation, and so on were conducted, studies were made of various sources of tax revenue and the suitability of each for school finance, and various sorts of tests, scales, and measurement devices were invented and used to assess students' achievement. Eventually textbooks were written and courses were taught on survey methods in schools and colleges of education.

The survey movement lost steam by the 1920s, however, for several reasons. First, it was no longer new; other educational problems and innovations took the spotlight of public attention. As the number and variety of scientific studies of education grew, it became increasingly difficult to say just what was a survey. Techniques of educational research were developed to a refinement that made the scattergun fact-collecting of the school survey obsolete. Finally, as it became clear to thoughtful educational leaders that a survey had limited usefulness for certain purposes but was not a cure-all for school problems, its status reverted to that of just another administrative tool for school reform, one that produced some successes, some failures, and no miracles.

CITY-WIDE CURRICULUM REVISION

Ambitious school superintendents, strengthened by reforms in governance that prevented the local board of education from interfering in strictly professional matters, fired with enthusiasm for the new educational ideas they encountered in their graduate work and at professional meetings, and faced with institutional growing pains, soon hit upon the idea of doing their own system-wide curriculum revision. Some called on experts from the universities to guide the revision. In other districts, superintendents themselves assumed leadership.

The pattern in these city wide revisions was to establish committees to develop district-wide goals and philosophy. These committees generally consisted of board members or other influential lay leaders, administrators, often the superintendent, and sometimes teachers appointed by the superintendent. Once the overall aims and guidelines were accepted by the board, committees of teachers and administrators would be formed to work out the details and put them into practice. The members of these committees met after school and on weekends, donating their services in the interests of school improvement.

In 1902, in one of the earliest widely publicized city-wide curriculum reforms, Superintendent Louis Soldan of St. Louis drafted a plan for the curriculum of the city's public schools. He appointed a committee of eight teachers, principals, and supervisors to revise the draft and circulated the resulting tentative course of study to more than 1,000 teachers for their suggestions. He then appointed a committee of teachers and administrators to draw up detailed plans for implementing the program. This was a notorious example of the one-person rule method of curriculum-making later caricaturized by the NEA in the 1930s when it campaigned for more teacher participation in curriculum revision.

According to Cremin (1961, 295) Carleton Washburne, superintendent in Winnetka, Illinois in 1919, "typifies the particular brand of progressive education that developed in numbers of small, high-income suburban districts scattered across the country. . . ." He divided the curriculum into the "tool subjects"—the three R's, social studies, sciences—also called "common essentials," and the rest, subjects regarded as providing opportunities for self-expression and for development of the individual's own interests and talents. The common essentials were individualized. Each pupil was permitted to advance at his or her own pace through a graded sequence of curriculum units in the tool subjects. School days were divided into periods of individual work and periods of group activity. Teachers provided assistance on an individual basis and managed the complex flow of work necessitated by the individualized system. Washburne's reforms were accomplished with the active assistance of a staff of administrators hand-picked to support these ideas, and with the voluntary participation of interested teachers on their own time. The work was financed entirely by the Winnetka Board of Education.

Beginning in 1922, Superintendent Jesse Newlon of Denver created a set of district-wide curriculum committees in every school subject. Membership in these committees consisted almost exclusively of classroom teachers, reflecting Newlon's belief that "No program of studies will operate that has not evolved to some extent out of the thinking of the teachers who are to apply it." (Cremin 1961, 299). The committees were initially given a broad assignment: to study and discuss the professional literature and to think deeply about what curriculum revisions were needed in Denver. After this initial phase, Newlon requested and received from the Denver Board of Education $35,500 to provide substitutes so that teachers who were committee members could be released to meet during school hours and to secure the services of curriculum specialists as consultants. Working steadily, the committees produced course syllabi that were published by the Denver Public Schools and purchased by the thousands for use in other districts throughout the country and abroad. These syllabi were eclectic compendia of progressive classroom practices, long on practicality and philosophy, but short on unity and organization, as might be expected from creations of committees.

As a means of effecting curriculum change, these city-wide reforms had many advantages and some limitations. City-wide reforms were close to the action: the teachers, students, and communities affected were located right there, and could be consulted, studied and even invited to participate. A strong superintendent supported by a progressive board had the authority to organize the planning and implementation of reforms, and the financial backing to put the reform into practice. Ideas could be tried and the ones that did not work out could be revised or discarded. The same individuals were involved in both planning and implementation, so that accountability was direct. On the other hand, the reforms were often not-so-subtle impositions of the superintendent's ideas, carried into practice by hand-picked subordinates. The products of committee work often lacked not only coherence but any leading idea, reflecting instead whatever was in fashion. And the courses of study produced were only pieces of paper, unless teachers made changes in their classrooms. Precious hours could be wasted wrangling over words of doubtful significance in the educational process.

CURRICULUM DEVELOPMENT IN LABORATORY SCHOOLS

It had long been customary for teacher training institutions to maintain practice or demonstration schools in which budding teachers could observe master teachers and try their own wings under close supervision. Professor John Dewey enrolled his son in the first grade of the Cook County Normal School's practice school when he moved to Chicago in 1894. In 1896 the Deweys opened their own school at the University of Chicago; Professor Dewey's wife Evelyn was principal, Dewey himself director. They called it The Laboratory School because it was to be used to test new educational ideas, and it became the pattern for literally hundreds of other schools founded by, with, and around departments, schools, and universities across the country. Here a generation of professional educational reformers worked out their ideas in close association with teachers and students in real, if not typical, classroom situations.

Dewey's Laboratory School was organized roughly according to the ages of the children, with the youngest children being four- and five-year-olds. Their schoolwork was designed to be a natural extension of the home. Activities included stories, songs, games, simple types of constructive work, and conversations or discussions. They made field trips to farms, to stores, to city buildings and streets. Resourceful teachers made use of the children's experiences to lay the groundwork

John Dewey, 1859–1952.

for reading, writing, and other formal school subjects to come. The six-year-olds studied occupations serving the home. They planted wheat, harvested it, and baked bread. Older children worked on projects dealing with science, invention and discovery, history, and other theme activities, interwoven with specific lessons in language, arithmetic, science, music, art, history, and geography.

Dewey viewed the work of the Laboratory School as an opportunity to learn how to conduct education, not as a source of detailed plans for others to follow. As a result, the work there was constantly evolving and no attempt was made to capture it on paper for dissemination to others. Still, it attracted enormous world-wide interest and had a constant stream of visitors. Written accounts of the work of the school were eagerly read, and countless teachers and educational reformers drew inspiration from it.

Lincoln School, affiliated with Teachers College, Columbia, was founded in New York City in 1917 by Abraham Flexner, famous for reshaping medical education. He wanted the School to be "a laboratory from which would issue scientific studies of educational problems—a laboratory". . . which would test and evaluate critically the fundamental propositions on which it is itself based, and the results as they are obtained." (Flexner 1923, 120). The School's motto became "Try anything once and see if it works." In addition to running an excellent innovative school, the staff produced an array of curriculum guides, textbooks, workbooks, and tests that were widely purchased and copied. The School worked on the basis of units, each of which occupied several weeks of class work for several hours each day. Students worked together on the unit, each student taking major responsibility for some tasks and helping on others. Teachers worked to integrate basic skills and academic subject matter into the unit naturally.

Scores of laboratory schools were created between 1900 and 1930 in cities around the country. Most were associated with a college or university. They produced a formidable array of curriculum plans and materials that often found their way into the mainstream of public school practice and into commercial textbooks and curriculum materials. They gave gifted and imaginative teachers an opportunity to experiment in collaboration with specialists and scholars in search of practices that could be shown to work in the classroom. Unfortunately, the experimental classrooms were not typical; they usually enrolled children of college faculty and wealthy professionals in concentrations far higher than their proportions of the local population. Even John Dewey's Laboratory School soon became an exclusive private school for children of University of Chicago faculty. It proved nearly impossible to balance the often competing demands of experimentation and innovation with maintaining the quality of the school in the eyes of parents. A principal who stood for imaginative if risky experimentation often lost parental support in favor of one who put higher priority on maintaining quality in conventional terms. And surprisingly, laboratory schools did little in the way of formal, rigorous evaluation. They functioned in fact more to develop practices and materials based on new ideas than to test either the ideas or the practices.

OBJECTIVE STUDIES AS A BASIS FOR CURRICULUM CHANGE

The most innovative curriculum revision procedure employed in this period was known then as "the objective study." Joseph Mayer Rice, a Boston physician passionately interested in education, conducted a study of education in 1892 in the course of writing a series of muck-raking articles on education for the Atlantic Monthly. He visited classrooms in thirty-six cities, talked with teachers, attended school board meetings, and interviewed administrators and parents. He was not happy with his reports of the sad state of American education, however. As Rice saw it, in spite of all his research, critics could dismiss his study as subjective and biased. He planned another study, published in 1897 under the provocative title "The Futility of the Spelling Grind," which could not be so easily dismissed. Rice developed a standard list of spelling words that he carried with him to several major cities. He personally administered identical spelling tests in classrooms in every city, and scored them on a common scoring system. His results showed that students in schools that allocated more time to spelling did no better on his tests then students from schools that allocated less time. The results set off a furor of controversy among educators and the public.

In the next three decades thousands of such studies were conducted. Studies were done to compare different ways of teaching and learning spelling, to determine, for example, whether a small amount of practice daily produced better results than the same amount of practice concentrated on fewer days; to determine whether explicit practice was better than learning to spell a word incidentally in the course of writing; to determine whether practice on pronunciation improved spelling; and so on. Every factor that might influence spelling instruction was investigated and its impact evaluated. Standardized achievement tests were constructed and scaled so that any youngster's performance could be compared with others of similar age and grade. Similar objective studies were carried out in arithmetic, reading, and handwriting. In the content subjects—science, history, geography—studies were made of children's informal knowledge, including misconceptions they may have had, of their interest in various topics, of the number and importance of applications of various concepts in daily life, of the difficulty children encountered in learning different concepts, and so on. Again, revisions were made in courses of study, textbooks, workbooks, and other curriculum materials on the basis of the findings of such objective studies.

Objective studies as a basis for curriculum revisions were an integral part of a self-proclaimed movement toward a "Science of Education" in the early decades of the twentieth century. The outstanding curricular success of this movement was the overthrow of mental discipline and the consequent undermining of claims for the classics. The lesson of the struggle over classics seemed clear: claims that could not be verified scientifically would be discredited, no matter how prestigious or powerful their advocates might be. Soon every claim on behalf of traditional studies was being studied, measured, and evaluated. Claims of the arts, the humanities, and the crafts were also called into question. The purer and more academic topics were called to judgment to justify their claims to a place in the school curriculum. Before long the new science of education was making questionable claims of objectivity and omniscience, there was a backlash, and the excesses of the scientific movement in education were, in their turn, ridiculed and displaced.

In spite of the many powerful advantages of objective studies as aids to curriculum work, it soon became apparent that formal studies were expensive, time consuming, and usually equivocal. Subsequent research on transfer of training, for example, showed that transfer was indeed possible and was, in fact, vitally important educationally. But it was necessary to teach explicitly for transfer. Study of Latin *could* help students increase their English vocabularies, *if* they were taught how to analyze the Latin derivations of English words. Transfer did not occur automatically, but it could be made to occur and, when it was systematically sought, important educational results ensued. With experience, educators learned that objective studies alone rarely resolve important educational disputes. Every study rests on assumptions that are not tested by that study. If these are false, the study's results may be worthless. Extending results of laboratory studies to the classroom may give misleading results. Further studies are needed to confirm and test the limits of the generalization, but action cannot always wait years for definitive results to emerge from a series of studies.

CURRICULUM REFORM BY DIRECT POLITICAL ACTION

Proponents of agricultural and industrial education received a cool reception in prestigious national councils, school district offices, and university laboratories, but they were welcomed at meetings of farmers and industrialists and, as they soon discovered, in legislative chambers. Business leaders were worried about foreign competition, immigrant workers, shortages of skilled workmen, and anti-business attitudes among young people studying the so-called higher subjects. Farmers were worried about keeping their children on the farm and about preparing them to use more scientific farming methods. They saw to it that their legislators worried about these things, too. This translated into a great deal of political support for vocational education, an idea that had not been well received in the circles of professional educators and lay educational leaders.

In 1910 the National Society for the Promotion of Industrial Education surveyed the states and ascertained that twenty-nine states had passed laws making some provision for industrial education. Ten provided for technical high schools, eighteen provided manual training, nineteen agricultural training, and eleven industrial and trade courses. Twenty-five of these states had enacted their laws since 1900. The society's report concluded: "No other educational movement calling for large expenditures and involving sweeping changes in curriculum and method has received such prompt legislative recognition." (Cremin 1961, 51) Advocates of vocational education had discovered that political methods could be used to bring about curriculum change.

The NSPIE demonstrated the remarkable political feat of getting labor, business, agriculture, and educational organizations to work together for a sustained period on nationwide campaigns on behalf of a legislatively sponsored curricular reform. The lessons of their success in the Smith-Hughes Act of 1917 that created a nationally financed system of vocational education, and prior successes with state legislatures, were not lost on proponents of other educational reforms. Proponents of physical education, American history, and biology were notably successful in securing the enactment of state legislation mandating a place in the secondary curriculum for their subject. Forty years were to pass before another major success was to be scored in Congress, but a pattern was set. Henceforth any group desiring admission for their subject to the public school curriculum established local, state, and national organizations and began lobbying.

Legislation seems a particularly effective route to quick, large-scale curriculum reforms. A vote, a flourish of the pen, and the matter is settled with the full force of the law behind the decision. Yet educators soon discovered that laws were not a royal road to curriculum improvement. Legislation did not provide trained teachers. Students did not necessarily elect the subjects legislators required schools to offer. Legislation proved most successful where money was appropriated to fund new programs. Even then, local officials could often thwart the intent of the legislation, though the Smith-Hughes Act was remarkably free of loopholes and extraordinarily successful in its purpose. In some cases legislative mandates have been successfully challenged in the courts on the grounds that they interfered with rights of free speech or religious belief. Also, the security afforded by legislation is only as great as the continuing political support; laws can always be repealed.

PROFESSIONALIZATION OF CURRICULUM MAKING, 1930–1960

The three decades from 1930 to 1950 encompassed the Great Depression, World War II, the Cold War, and the Korean conflict. Throughout these years national agenda were filled with life and death issues, and, except for the issue of funding schools, the public left educational reform to local school leaders and national professional associations. This, too, was a time of burgeoning school enrollments. Early in the period, lack of work on farms and in idle factories kept more youths in school longer. Later, the post-war baby boom accelerated enrollments. Buildings could hardly be erected fast enough to house expanded school populations and schools were chronically short of qualified teachers. Local budgets for schools increased steadily throughout the period, especially in the post-War economic expansion, yet were barely sufficient to meet the rising costs of building and staffing new schools.

No dramatic new developments of ideas, substance, or method emerged in this period. The main story was of attempts by professional leaders to realize the promises of Progressive education. Superintendents, principals and teachers exposed to Progressive ideas in professional training took the lead in experimenting with a variety of basically Progressive reforms emphasizing the characteristic Progressive values of democracy and practicality. Democracy was not only pursued in the social studies, but in something new—student government—and even in curriculum development itself, where teachers were involved in teacher-led, democratic procedures for curriculum revision. Curriculum reform became bureaucratized as procedures and personnel were incorporated into the expanding administrative and governance structure of increasingly larger schools and school systems. These reforms were not without their critics, and some bruising political battles were fought over education, especially early in the period over the issue of whether schools should be agencies of social reform. But, on balance, the period was one of relative peace and continuity compared to the euphoria of the Progressive period and the frantic reforms in the decades to follow. Let us consider some of these developments in more detail.

Content to Meet the Needs of Youth

By 1930 many young Americans who formerly would have left school by age 16 stayed in, not always willingly. Some stayed because they could not find work, some because local officials began, under pressure from adults who feared job competition, to enforce compulsory attendance laws, and some because they could not find any other way to grow up in an increasingly industrialized society. This new category of students created many problems for the schools. One of the most serious was failing marks. A 1927 survey of 300 high schools found that "30 percent of first year students failed at least one subject, with corresponding figures of 29 percent, 24 percent, and 11 percent for the second, third, and fourth years" (Krug 1964, 141). In Pennsylvania high schools, probably not very different from the nation as a whole, Latin was the subject most often failed (16.9%), followed by algebra (16.1%), ancient history (11.5%) and first year English (10.3%).

Another serious problem was these students' lack of interest in the curriculum offered by the schools. A 1938 report of the American Council on Education entitled *Youth Tell Their Story* reported that lack of interest in school was the second most common reason young people gave for dropping out (24.6%), following only economic reasons (54%). More immediate problems for the teacher were the disruptions and behavior problems fomented by unhappy youths unwillingly attending school. The combination of problems spelled trouble for everyone. Many educators felt that the school curriculum must change if schools were to serve these children and to realize the dream of a truly universal and democratic educational system.

Efforts were made to ease the problems by changing the content and aims of the school program. Vocational programs already existed, of course, and enrollments in these increased faster than enrollments in academic programs. But many students and their parents refused to enroll in vocational programs even though they were discontented with the academic program. For these students many schools developed a general education program that was not as academically demanding as the traditional academic curriculum, and was not narrowly focused on vocational preparation, either.

Programs of general education omitted some of the more difficult subjects that so many students failed, such as languages and abstract mathematics. More elementary courses in reading and practical arithmetic were designed to build skills that had formerly been assumed to have been mastered in elementary school. Other academic courses were modified to make them less demanding and more appealing to students. For example, English courses were designed to focus on developing practical communication skills such as conversing, telephoning, discussing, reading to find information, reading to secure directions for action, and writing letters. Social studies courses were developed to deal with social functions—such as production of goods and services, communication, expression of aesthetic impulses—and social problems—such as crime, poverty, war—instead of with ancient, European, and American history. General mathematics courses and general science courses were developed that dealt with broad practical themes such as how energy helps man, using machines to change the earth, how counting helps in everyday situations, and using percentages. Credit toward high school graduation began to be awarded for courses in physical education, art, and music, subjects that formerly had not counted toward completion of the 16 units of high school work typically required.

The rationale for these changes was well-expressed in a 1947 report of the Education Policies Commission, the influential voice of the leadership of the National Education Association, then the one organization representing all professional educators. The report, entitled "The Imperative Needs of Youth of Secondary School Age," listed the needs of youth that should serve as a basis for curriculum reform.

1. All youth need to develop saleable skills and those understandings and attitudes that make the worker an intelligent and productive participant in economic life.
2. All youth need to develop and maintain good health and physical fitness.
3. All youth need to understand the rights and duties of the citizens of a democratic society.
4. All youth need to understand the significance of the family.
5. All youth need to know how to purchase and use goods and services intelligently.
6. All youth need to understand the methods of science.
7. All youth need opportunities to develop their capacities to appreciate beauty.
8. All youth need to be able to use their leisure time well.
9. All youth need to develop respect for other persons.
10. All youth need to grow in their ability to think rationally, to express their thoughts clearly, and to read and listen with understanding. (Education Policies Commission, 1947)

Such lists, obviously extensions of the 1918 *Cardinal Principles of Secondary Education,* still appealed to many educators who believed that the academic secondary school curriculum forged in the Progressive era was not serving all young people adequately. Spurred on by such beliefs, school systems reformulated their course offerings, teachers planned new classroom activities, and publishers revised curriculum materials in ways they thought would help all American youth to profit from the school experience. The comprehensive high school emerged from these efforts. Designed to meet the needs of all, rather than only the needs of the academically inclined and the college-bound, the comprehensive school offered a smorgasbord of courses, with academic content ranging from the rigor envisioned by the Committee of Ten to the relevance of life adjustment education—truly something for everybody.

EXPERIMENTS WITH NEW WAYS OF ORGANIZING THE CURRICULUM

The subject organization of the secondary curriculum achieved at the turn of the century, was now challenged as too rigid and too remote from the needs of youth. Some secondary schools now began to experiment with flexible, integrated organizational patterns similar to those of elementary schools, where a single teacher taught all subjects to the same children all day long. Some of the prominent organizational innovations were: core curriculum, unit plan, Dalton plan, contract plan, project method, and activity curriculum. Also adopted from the elementary school was the homeroom, a sort of vestigial elementary school classroom in that many of the organizational, extracurricular, and school-wide activities took place and where all students rubbed elbows in a miniature democracy.

The central idea of a core curriculum was a block of work, the core, common to all students. In some schools, half of the curriculum time was allotted for electives, the other half for core classes. In one particularly innovative school the core time was divided among four areas of study: health, community living, leisure, and vocation (Krug 1964, 262). In other, milder versions, the core might consist of a combined English and social studies class common to all the pupils in a given grade. Work in the core was supposed to be centered around the needs of youth rather than the structure of the subject.

Other innovative organizational schemes relied upon individually assigned units of work for each pupil. Subject matter was divided into small blocks and assigned to individual students or to small groups with similar needs and abilities. Pupils reported regularly to a teacher, who monitored their progress but did not conduct formal group lessons. Often this individual work took place in the core portion of a core curriculum; otherwise it would be in various subjects. The Dalton Plan, organized in the high school in Dalton, Massachusetts in 1918–1919, involved fairly lengthy and complex individual assignments occupying a week or more of students' time and requiring use of the library, and sometimes other outside resources. Such units culminated in written or oral reports and sometimes in class discussions. Variations on the Dalton formula were innumerable.

Another form of curriculum organization that became popular in the 1920s was known as the project method. Originally this was a teaching method intended for use in any subject. In the project method a group of students worked together on a project related to their coursework. William H. Kilpatrick, Professor at Teachers College, developed an elaborate theory to justify the project method, beginning with the assumption that learning was most effective when it resulted from a purposeful act on the part of the learner. Therefore, subject matter set out in advance by teacher or textbooks was less likely to lead to effective learning than projects chosen by the student. Following this line of thought, teachers organized courses consisting of a series of projects punctuated by brief periods of formal study of subject matter. Projects were often made the center of work in a core curriculum organization. Much less often an entire grade or school might be involved in a large common project. Projects could also be undertaken by individual pupils and thus incorporated within individualized curricula.

Efforts to break the high school curriculum out of the subject straitjacket, as reformers saw it, were at best only partially successful. The chief roadblocks were logistical. Coordinating the work of different classes and teachers proved burdensome and time-consuming. Integrating the content of formal subjects with the topics of projects was also difficult. The burden of organizing the work and monitoring progress fell fully on the teacher, making teaching more difficult. Testing was not really compatible with project methods. Students in individualized programs showed wider variations in achievement than students in conventional programs, making it more difficult to keep track of students' progress. Partly as a result, tensions developed between such reforms and college entrance requirements, reformers claiming the colleges were stifling innovation while the colleges feared the reforms neglected academics.

In an effort to convince the colleges of the value of innovative secondary school programs, the Progressive Education Association sponsored an extensive study, called the Eight-Year Study, begun in 1933, in which graduates of an experimental group of progressive secondary schools were to be admitted to college solely on the basis of the records of their high school work and faculty recommendations. Their performance in college was to be monitored and compared with the performance of matched students from similar non-experimental schools. The results, published in 1942, showed the students from the experimental schools to be fully comparable in academic achievement and superior in such extracurricular and cocurricular activities as class offices, student newspaper, and other voluntary student activities. By the time these results were available, however, attention had shifted from education to the problems of the war. When public and professional attention was once again free, other issues took priority. The reforms of this period survived only in isolated places and as the seeds of further reforms.

IDEOLOGICAL ISSUES AFFECTING CURRICULUM

The period was marked by a series of intense, emotional debates about fundamental political and economic issues. In the depression of the 1930s prominent educators were among the voices calling for social, political, and economic reform. George S. Counts was one of the most outspoken.

> Our Progressive schools therefore cannot rest content with giving children an opportunity to study contemporary society in all of its aspects. This of course must be done, but I am convinced that they should go much farther. If the schools are to be really effective, they must become centers for the building, and not merely the contemplation, of our civilization. (Counts 1932, 12)

The very title of Counts' essay, *Dare the School Build a New Social Order,* was challenging. William H. Kilpatrick, another member of the group that styled themselves as social reconstructionists, was equally blunt.

> The school as we know it must be remade to a more social point of view. Now the aim is too often so to equip each pupil that he may the better get ahead of others. . . . As far as the age of the pupils will permit they must become intelligently critical of our, and their, social life and institutions. (Kilpatrick 1932, 79)

While the proposal that the schools lead the way to a new and better social order found many eager listeners in the scary depths of the Depression, it also found staunch opposition from two quarters: patriotic organizations and those school people who felt that citizens in their communities were not all that unhappy with their country's economic and political institutions. Organized political conservatives soon gained the upper hand politically. They responded to educators' challenges to the existing social order with demands for teacher loyalty oaths, and with publicity campaigns against people and practices they found subversive and un-American. One of the victims of such campaigns was Professor Harold O. Rugg of Teachers College, who had worked for more than a decade to create a social studies textbook series that would enable students to build an intelligently independent viewpoint on social issues. The series had attained wide use and popularity by the mid-thirties when it became a specific object of attack by William Randolph Hearst, owner of a chain of newspapers and self-appointed watchdog against left-wing movements. Largely as a result of the attacks and local pressures from organizations sympathetic to Hearst's views, districts avoided controversy by not adopting and purchasing the books, so that sales declined rapidly and the books went out of print soon thereafter.

Opposition to the social reconstructionists also came from practical school people who argued that schools could not take the lead in social change, that schools had to follow the wishes of the prevailing society. Krug quotes one educator's trenchant comment:

> Those of us who have not taken leave of our senses know that the schools and schoolmasters are not generally going to be permitted to take the lead in changing the social order, nor in conducting experiments likely to lead to a radical redefinition of the aims of that order. (Krug 1964, 239)

Schools and schoolmasters *were* permitted to take the lead, however, in instilling respect for democratic ideals against the challenges of fascism and communism.

The idea that schools should encourage criticism of our social order and its institutions began to seem disloyal. No one wanted to be seen as undermining the nation in the face of threats from enemies. Calls were made for schools to stop teaching what's wrong with America and start teaching what's right with it. Debunking of cherished myths of American history, a practice that had enjoyed a heyday in the depression, fell into disfavor. Articles began to appear in the professional journals outlining programs of patriotic music, celebrations of patriotic events, flag ceremonies, and extracurricular and homeroom activities with a patriotic focus as well as less jingoistic proposals—such as one for serious comparative study of the merits of democracy as compared to other forms of government. Programs of student government also received a boost from the widespread desire to prepare citizens who were aware of democratic processes and able to participate in them intelligently and to willingly support them. Much was written about citizenship education, and about the development of democratic values, understandings, attitudes, and skills.

THE PROFESSIONALIZATION OF CURRICULUM REFORM

The reformers who led movements for curriculum change prior to 1900 included both professionally trained educators and untrained members of the interested public. Joseph Mayer Rice had been a pediatrician, John Dewey a philosopher, and Charles W. Eliot a chemist and university president. Those earlier reformers who had been professional educators—William T. Harris and Colonel Francis Parker, for example—were individualists whose leadership flowed from their personal characteristics of energy, eloquence, and persistence. Like evangelical religious leaders, educational reformers exercised their influence with words in rousing speeches as well as with deeds that set examples for the faithful. Their immediate target was local education authorities. It was assumed that if leaders could be persuaded to fight for a reform, they would be apt to implement the reforms in schools and classrooms.

In the 1920s superintendents of schools in some cities began to launch curriculum reforms in a new pattern. They assembled administrative staffs to carry out the recommendations of prestigious outside consultants, who prepared surveys or did other analyses of the local situation and prepared lists of recommended changes. Local committees of teachers worked under the supervision of the administrative staff to prepare the necessary classroom plans and teaching/learning materials to translate the superintendent's report into a classroom program. Conditions and curricula changed so rapidly that schools found they had to maintain committees in service more or less continually. Many superintendents decided that a truly professional approach to curriculum revision required a continuing program of systematic curriculum revision with a permanent professionally trained staff. In a large city, one or two subjects or grades each year would

Francis W. Parker, 1837–1902

be made the focus of curriculum revision. Committees of teachers and administrators would be formed and assigned the task of studying the situation, and then the task of recommending actions to the superintendent, who would then authorize the formation of other committees to produce the plans and materials needed to implement the superintendent's recommendations. Curriculum development was gradually incorporated into the operations of the school system. Directors of curriculum were appointed to serve the superintendent by managing curriculum revision in the district. Other supporting roles were Supervisor of _____ (school subject), Assistant or Associate Superintendent for Curriculum (or Curriculum and Instruction), or Curriculum Associate. Various laboratories, bureaus, and offices were established to house these persons, both physically and organizationally. Thus, curriculum revision was institutionalized, built into the day-to-day operations of school districts—some would say, bureaucratized.

RECENT YEARS, 1960–PRESENT

In October of 1957 the Russians launched the first artificial earth-orbiting satellite, *Sputnik I*. Americans were profoundly shocked. They had seen their nuclear lead over the Soviet Union erased in less than a decade, and now they faced the prospect of scientific and technological inferiority. In searching for a remedy, public attention soon focused on the public schools. The schools, critics charged, had pursued the goals of life adjustment and had neglected the teaching of science and mathematics. The efforts to remedy the educational deficiencies exposed in the wake of *Sputnik* launched a new era in American curriculum-making. University scholars—physicists, mathematicians, biologists, psychologists—interrupted their academic careers to develop curriculum plans and materials for use in the public schools. Originally intended as mere content updating of science, math, and language courses, these projects developed into major nationwide, federally funded curriculum reforms. Later, in the 1960s and 1970s when other urgent national concerns arose and displaced concern about technological preparedness, major federally-sponsored curriculum reforms were again mounted, but for quite different reasons and in substantially different ways. This section presents the highlights of this most recent period.

The Post-*Sputnik* Curriculum Projects

Many commentators laid at least part of the blame for American technological and scientific decline at the door of American schools. Admiral Hyman G. Rickover, for example, pioneer of the nuclear navy, spoke of education as "America's first line of defense." He recounted how, in his efforts to develop nuclear propulsion, he had searched vainly for experienced engineers "of independent mind and venturesome spirit" and how he was led to conclude that the schools were not producing any.

> Our schools are the greatest "cultural lag" we have today. When I read official publications put out by the men who run our educational system—booklets such as *Life Adjustment Education for Every Youth* or *Education for All Youth*—I have the strange feeling of reading about another world, a world long since departed if it ever existed at all. I sense the kindly spirit, the desire to make every child happy, the earnest determination to give advice on every problem any young person might ever meet in life—and with so complete a misunderstanding of the needs of young people in today's world that it frightens me. . . . I am worried about the chances which young people, so poorly equipped to deal with modern life, will have when things become more complex and difficult, as they surely will before very long. (Rickover 1959, 20–24)

James B. Conant, also a President of Harvard and, like his illustrious predecessor Charles W. Eliot, vitally interested in American public education, conducted a study published in 1959 under the title *The American High School Today*. He visited 55 high schools in all regions of the country and his report was basically supportive of the American comprehensive high school except on one point.

> If the fifty-five schools I have visited . . . are at all representative of American high schools, I think one general criticism would be in order: *The*

*academically talented student as a rule, is not being sufficiently
challenged, does not work hard enough, and his program of academic
subjects is not of sufficient range.* The able boys too often specialize in
mathematics and science to the exclusion of foreign languages and to the
neglect of English and social studies. The able girls, on the other hand, too
often avoid mathematics and science as well as the foreign languages.
(Conant 1959, 40)

Conant and Rickover were among the more temperate critics. Albert Lynd's article,
"Quackery in the Public Schools" took a more strident tone and did not hesitate to
point the finger of blame.

Next to the minister, the high school principal of thirty years ago was the
most learned fellow in town. Today you may find your local high school in
charge of a brisk Kiwanian whose "professional" training has been free of
the elements of traditional culture. His teaching experience may have had
nothing to do with letters or science; it may have been in auto driving or
basketball or pattern-making or "guidance". . . . He may wear the splendid
title of Doctor, earned through researches into the theory and function of
school cafeteria. He may not be able to decipher the Latin date on the
cornerstone of his own school building, or to read a single word in any
other foreign language, living or dead, or even to write a decently turned
paragraph in English, but he can lead an enraptured class discussion in A
Democratic Solution to Our Traffic Problem. (Lynd 1950, 33)

The responses to *Sputnik* and the criticisms that followed were vigorous.
Curricular leadership was wrested from professional educators. Scientists and
mathematicians organized special curriculum development projects to revise
and modernize school textbooks and curriculum materials in the sciences and
mathematics. A few outstanding teachers were included, but the projects were
dominated by subject-matter specialists. The best known of these projects were
known to the public as "the New Math," but eventually projects were launched in
all academic subjects. In 1959 Congress enacted the National Defense Education
Act, intended to strengthen the nation's defenses by creating a greater pool of more
qualified scientific manpower. The Act funded projects designed to update content
and curriculum materials in science, mathematics, and foreign languages, and to
train teachers in the new content. It created a national agenda of curriculum reform
for the first time since the Smith-Hughes act of 1919 had established a national
system of vocational education.

Almost as abruptly as it began, the post-*Sputnik* era of national curriculum
reform ended. By 1965, the major post-*Sputnik* projects had completed their
curriculum materials, but teacher training was still scanty and implementation in
schools and classrooms was spotty. With these reforms well under way but by no
means complete, the spotlight of national attention turned to a new series of
shocks: poverty, racism, and inequality. Michael Harrington's *The Other America*
and a spate of subsequent books had brought to public attention the existence of

poverty in the midst of a society of unprecedented affluence. President Kennedy was assassinated and succeeded by President Johnson, who had ambitious, activist plans for social programs in the tradition of the New Deal. But the most dramatic news events were the Civil Rights demonstrations in the South and urban riots in northern black ghettos. Almost overnight, it seemed, society demanded a new imperative for schools—to ameliorate and compensate for social inequities.

Again, the approach was direct. Congress enacted the Elementary and Secondary Education Act in 1965, just a year after the landmark Civil Rights Act of 1964. The focus of ESEA was equalization of educational opportunity by improving the educational programs for disadvantaged children. This legislation helped to fund several programs, including Project Head Start, a curriculum designed to remedy early deficits in the education of "disadvantaged" children; Teacher Corps, to retrain teachers to deal with the problems of the disadvantaged child; and thousands of local programs directed to the same end. These educational programs of the Great Society established that the power of the federal purse could be used not only for national defense, but also to implement national social policies. Significantly, the Great Society programs did not challenge local and professional control over curriculum, as the post-*Sputnik* reforms had done, but rather provided funds and assistance for local authorities to use to implement new programs.

Before these programs had reached full maturity, the public mood had changed again. This time the stimulus was domestic unrest fomented by the Vietnam war and by backlashes against the social reforms of the Great Society program. Commissioner of Education Sidney P. Marland, appointed by President Nixon, set as the top national priority something called *career education*. The idea was to offer something more practical and directly useful to the majority of youngsters who were not well served by either the college preparatory program or the vocational program. The goal was set to provide every youngster who leaves high school, whether or not by graduating, with a suitable skill. Federal funds appropriated for various other educational programs were reallocated to career education.

At the beginning of this period, in the late fifties and early sixties, most of the fifty states had demonstrated little concern over curriculum questions, which were left as decisions for local school systems. But gradually more states began to assume active roles in curriculum matters. Federal funds for education were funneled through the states to local districts, so state departments developed experience in administering statewide programs. The new federalism of the Nixon and Ford presidencies distributed funds to states by formula and left them with the responsibility for deciding how the funds should be spent. Leaders of several populous and progressive states—Illinois, New York, Florida, California, and others—had earlier perceived a threat to their authority from the new federal presence in education, and had set about establishing a stronger presence of their own.

Competency based education was one of the first popular state initiatives. The idea here was to hold schools accountable for producing measurable results in the achievement of their graduates. Schools in several states were required by state law to state objectives that could be measured and to determine at critical points in each child's schooling whether these objectives had been met. This policy was seen by many legislators as a means of bringing the educational bureaucracy in their state back under control of the political system that in theory should govern it. Later curriculum initiatives in the states included moves back to the basics—emphasis on the three R's and on discipline; career education, in which state and federal funds were combined; and mainstreaming, in which handicapped youngsters were reintegrated into the regular school program.

From their earliest beginnings these large-scale state and federal programs had been criticized by conservatives suspicious of centralized programs on the grounds that they would be ineffective and would waste taxpayers' money. Critics and defenders joined together to attach riders to the various bills in Congress calling for evaluation of the impact of the programs, each convinced that results would prove them right. The move for curriculum evaluation came too late to have much effect on the post-*Sputnik* projects, but, even so, a number of the most sophisticated evaluations yet seen were carried out then—for example, the National Longitudinal Study of Mathematical Abilities certainly stands out as a high water mark. Head Start evaluations showed that students in the programs performed almost on a par with their advantaged peers until 3rd or 4th grade, at which time the gap widened again. A new program, Follow Through, was established to maintain the gains. But, by and large, the results of evaluations of large scale programs showed no significant differences. Debate raged in academia about whether it was the evaluations or the programs that were at fault, but the message received by the public was that not only new programs, but schools as a whole, were having little impact on children. It began to be fashionable to question the efficacy of schooling, to look toward television, community agencies, and private schools for truly effective education.

An astute observer might have predicted that in this pluralistic society, even the social changes favored by a clear majority of Americans would nevertheless be opposed by substantial minorities. In this case, opposition was most heated in the South, especially among those opposed to integration and among religious fundamentalists, and among conservative and traditional groups in all sectors of the society. In one of the more dramatic protests, angry West Virginians bombed a schoolhouse door to show their opposition to "godless" and "sinful" textbooks. The books in question quoted prominent black spokesmen using explicit street language. But a fundamentalist minister who acted as spokesman for the dissidents also objected to the teaching of evolution, to omission of God and prayer from the schools, and in general to the teaching of secular values.

Objections by religious people to the teaching of a modern, scientific, secular world view have a long history in the United States. In Tennessee's famous "monkey trial" of 1921, a biology teacher, John Scopes, was charged with teaching evolution in violation of a Tennessee statute forbidding it. The trial attracted worldwide attention and is generally remembered as a victory for academic freedom, but the state won the case and the teaching of evolution was banned by state law in Tennessee for several more decades. Today, the issues are in some ways similar—the banning of books from school libraries, the black-listing of textbooks expressing unacceptable views, admission of religious worship and prayer to the public schools, the teaching of traditional religious beliefs about the creation and about humanity's place in the universe. The fundamental and inescapable curriculum dilemma is the same: one curriculum cannot satisfy everyone. Not even an individualized or differentiated curriculum will satisfy *every*one. Fundamentalists would not tolerate an atheistic program, even if their children were not required to study atheism, nor would liberals be content with a school program openly espousing racial segregation.

More recently still, curricula are being affected by international comparisons of school achievement, by controversy about test score declines, by declines in the school age population, and by moves to restrict funds for public education. The first International Study of Educational Achievement (IEA) was in mathematics. Thirteen countries participated, including advanced industrialized countries—Japan, the United States, France, and others, and developing countries—Iran, Israel, Nigeria, and others. Test items were carefully translated into the various languages and administered in each country to a representative sample of youngsters in the grades corresponding to the ages being studied. The results showed enormous differences between countries. Students in industrialized countries outscored their peers in developing countries by a wide margin. Another interpretation is that rich countries, those with high per capita income, outscored poor countries. The United States ranked last among the advanced nations in average achievement, though it retained a far larger proportion of children in school than practically any country, so direct comparisons are not wholly fair. Still, latent concern about how well our children are doing in an increasingly international world was activated by the results. Subsequent IEA studies have been carried out in other school subjects, with a similar pattern of results, leading to a national storm of concern in the public. So far, the most pervasive effect of the IEA studies appears to be in convincing professionals and policy makers that a) more effective school systems are possible, since they exist already in other countries; but b) the effectiveness of a school system depends in substantial part on the culture served by the school—a cultural environment that supports school achievement permits the school to be more effective than an environment that is indifferent, ambivalent, or even hostile.

The public appears to be troubled by evidence that the test performance of American young people has declined over the past decade. For the first thirty years of data that made comparing standardized tests meaningful year-to-year (roughly from the 1930s to the 1960s), the scores of American youngsters on standardized tests of educational attainment increased. Each generation was learning more (at least as measured by these tests) than its predecessors. There were slight downward fluctuations occasionally, but the trend over any period as long as five years was clearly upward. In the 1960s, a decline in test scores began to be noticed. The College Entrance Examination Board announced that scores on the Scholastic Aptitude Test (SAT), the most widely used college entrance exam, had declined slightly but significantly over the last few years. Some states experienced more of a decline than others, but the declining trend was widespread. Many explanations were advanced. Some of these could be refuted. It was argued, for example, that retention of more low income and minority children in schools during this period lowered the overall rates of achievement. But careful examination of the scores showed declines among abler students as well as among low scorers. Also, there were declines in areas with a very low percentage of disadvantaged racial minorities. A commission was established to look into the causes; it found many and was unable to settle on one or a few as most likely. For this reason, perhaps, widespread public concern about the decline has yet to be reflected in a concerted campaign of reform.

One line of thought still brewing interprets the decline as a result of a watering down of the curriculum. Students, it is claimed, have chosen less demanding courses as electives and hence have not developed their abilities as much as previously. Also, the content even of basic courses has subtly become less demanding—reading levels of texts have been adjusted downward, more difficult content has been trimmed, easier problems and exercises included, teachers have lowered their standards of acceptable performance, and the school has protected students against failure to such an extent that students no longer see poor performance as having important consequences. This line of thought explaining the downward trend in student test scores appears to be gaining wide acceptance, and supports the movement to strengthen the academic rigor of the curriculum.

During the 1970s declining enrollments and declining funds forced many schools to eliminate courses and teachers. These cuts appear to have been deepest in elective subjects, especially those generally perceived as frills, most especially the arts and other nonacademic electives and advanced courses with small enrollments. School equipment and supplies budgets were reduced or eliminated, making the teaching of laboratory sciences more difficult, and adding further pressures to slight the arts. Now, spurred by renewed concerens about academic quality in order to foster international economic competitiveness, advanced academic courses have once again attained a high priority.

During this last quarter century, then, American schools were swept by a rapid succession of nationally funded and nationally directed curriculum reforms. These were massive efforts with far-reaching and profound aims. In each case, schools were subjected to intense public criticism; reformers took direct action by intervening in the ordinary processes of curriculum revision; new programs were created to implement the aims of the reforms; new people were recruited into the ranks of teachers, administrators, and policy-makers whose views reflected those of the reforms; and intense efforts were undertaken to disseminate these programs widely. Established leaders of curriculum reform—local school boards, superintendents, central office staff, associations of professional educators, professors of education in colleges and universities—found themselves bypassed in favor of a new cadre of lay reformers—college professors of school subjects, legislators and legislative aides fresh out of college or graduate school, psychologists, sociologists, and advocates for disadvantaged groups.

These reforms were traumatic for the schools that attempted them. Each required a major reorientation and realignment of efforts. And before the first of these could be implemented and digested, along came the second, and then the third. Now it seems that the effort may have exhausted itself, at least temporarily, from lack of funds. Some claim the national curriculum reform movements have been complete flops; no one claims complete success, but a good case can be made for very substantial accomplishments. My own guess is that these efforts will seem more significant and more successful in the future than they seem to us now. But it is quite clear as a result of these events that large-scale curriculum change is a long, difficult, and risky proposition. Americans' first halting tries at centrally directed curriculum reform have not been resounding successes.

SOME LESSONS OF CURRICULUM HISTORY

History does not tell us what to do today or tomorrow, but we can learn from it, nevertheless. We can learn what kinds of things have happened, with what frequency, and in what relationships to other events, and from such knowledge we can learn important lessons about the nature of the phenomenon we are addressing—curriculum, in our case. From this brief summary of landmark developments in the history of the American school curriculum, we can learn such lessons as the following.

1. The content, purpose, and structure of American schools have changed substantially over more than 200 years.

- Actual curriculum practice has not changed as much as have ideas about what the curriculum should be.
- The school curriculum has generally reflected the prevailing views of the more educated segments of American society, and thus has seldom been either in the vanguard of change or among its opponents.

2. Curriculum change, even planned change, has often come in response to pressures generated outside the educational system, including pressures from:

- dramatic events such as wars, economic booms and panics, political upheavals, and religious awakenings,

- gradual trends, such as industrialization, immigration, population growth, economic growth, and increasing social pluralism.

3. Important curriculum changes are often associated with and strongly influenced by major changes in the educational system, such as in the number and types of students enrolled, how and by whom educational institutions are governed, and the type and extent of teacher preparation.

4. Excitement about ideas regarded as new and momentous usually accompanies major episodes of curriculum reform

- Reforms arouse widespread optimism, excitement, and fervor among advocates and implementors.

5. The methods and procedures employed in curriculum change have varied. Often they have been improvised to suit a particular situation and then subsequently the improvisation has been developed into a general method. Reforms rarely achieve the curriculum changes reformers propose.

- Many proposed changes are never realized except in a few experimental sites.
- Those that are realized widely never entirely displace earlier practices and seldom come to prevail, but they often find secure niches for themselves within a diverse, decentralized school system.

6. Lessons of history such as these give us valuable perspective on contemporary curriculum problems and help us to act wisely in attempting to resolve them. Sometimes history can also be of help in a more focused and direct way.

USING HISTORY IN MAKING CURRICULUM DECISIONS

In addition to giving a general perspective on events, history also provides specific historical analogies and specific historical knowledge, and all three of these may play key roles in current decisions. For instance, many observers today see strong similarities between the current movement for academic excellence and the post-*Sputnik* reforms. In both cases, the curriculum problem was poor achievement in academic subjects. In both cases advocates and the public perceived a strong external threat if our able students did not learn more in school. Here, then, is an historical analogy that may be used to guide actions in a current controversy. Accepting the two as analogous leads us to wonder what we can learn from the earlier episode. The post-*Sputnik* reforms are widely regarded as having failed in their purpose, since the evidence available indicates that American science and mathematics achievement did not increase in the decade or so after these reforms. In fact, test scores declined. Many blame the failure of the earlier reforms on their use of an ineffective mechanism—the federally sponsored curriculum development project. The case against projects is that they failed to bring about change in classrooms, that teachers, having not been involved in the development of the new curricula, were reluctant to try them. This line of reasoning has undoubtedly influenced current reformers in their decision not to press for curriculum development projects today. Here is a specific historical generalization that plays an important role in determining our national response to a current curriculum problem.

Historical reasoning such as this comes into play in virtually all important curriculum decisions. Wider, deeper knowledge of history strengthens our arguments and decisions, but certain skills of historical reasoning are also important. Developing your ability to use history wisely is an important part of learning to be good at curriculum decision-making. Usual practice in curriculum decision-making fits uncomfortably well with public policy decision-making generally as described by historians Richard Neustadt and Ernest May.

> "Usual" practice, we fear, has six ingredients: a plunge toward action; overdependence on fuzzy analogies . . . ; inattention to an issue's own past; failure to think a second time . . . about key presumptions; stereotyped suppositions about persons or organizations . . . ; and little or no effort to see choices as part of any historical sequence. (Neustadt and May 1986, 32–33)

They suggest that the staffs who advise decision-makers learn how to draw on history to frame sharper questions and examine proposed answers more critically. The first step is to describe the current situation well.

BOX 2-2   How to Use History to Make Better Decisions (Based on Neustadt and May 1986)

1. Study the issue's history.
   Create a timeline. Start the story as far back as it properly goes and plot the main events and trends.
   Ask the journalist's questions: Who, what, why, when, where, how?
2. Place critical organizations and key individuals on the timeline. Try to infer what their life histories mean for how they interpret this situation.
3. List possibly analogous situations and for each note likenesses and differences with the present situation.
4. Array your options.
   Try to judge feasibility in light of historical experience with similar projects.
   Ask yourself if you would bet real money on an option. What odds would you give?
   Ask what fresh data would cause you to revise or reverse your judgment?

> Faced with a situation prompting action, the first step in good staff work is to grasp its manifestations. What goes on here? . . . If there is a problem to be solved (or lived with), what is it? And whose is it? . . . Ask "What's the story?" How did these concerns develop? (Neustadt and May 1986, 234–236)

They suggest that this examination be done by listing key elements of the immediate situation in three columns: **known, unclear,** and **presumed.** Then, historical information becomes potentially useful. Box 2-2 summarizes Neustadt's and May's suggestions for making good use of the available historical knowledge.

QUESTIONS FOR STUDY

1. In what ways was the curriculum of a typical nineteenth century school functional for that time and place? In what way was it non-functional or harmful?

2. The nineteenth century school curriculum is presented by historian Ruth Miller Elson as replete with myths, such as the belief that hard work and virtue would lead to material success. She calls it "a world of fantasy." Might this same judgement be made of the curriculum of schools today by a writer of the twenty-first century? What would such a writer identify as myths that we perpetuated in our schools? Are such myths necessarily bad? Are they avoidable?

3. If you were a parent in the nineteenth century who did not believe in the myths being taught in the schools, what could you do? What options were open to you, and what do you think the consequences would be of your exercising each of those options? How do these options and their consequences compare with those open to a contemporary parent in the same position?

4. Find among the landmarks of curriculum history any instances where the school curriculum has functioned to hasten or foster social change or to guard tradition against the inroads of change. What can you say from reflection on these instances about the role school curricula play in social change?

5. Find among the landmarks of curriculum history any instances in which curriculum changes have been pressed by the public against prevailing opinion among professional educators. Find instances where professionals have pressed changes against the wishes of powerful sectors of the public. What do your inquiries suggest about the relationship of public and lay leadership in curriculum reform?

6. Why do you think both educators and the public seem regularly to get so excited about curriculum issues? Why do they seem to ignore curriculum

issues in the intervening years? Are other educational issues (such as the quality of teaching or school budgets) any different in this respect?

7. Many observers comment on the coming and going of curricular fads in recent years. Do you see evidence for fads in the recent history of the school curriculum? If so, when did the phenomenon of faddism begin? What might account for the beginning and continuation of curricular fads? If not, what mistakes are those who see fads making? In either case, do you think the phenomenon is good or bad for American education?

8. What generalizations about curriculum stability and change do you think are warranted by the history of these landmark developments?

9. It has been argued that the reason such widespread and lasting curriculum changes took place in the decades between 1890 and 1930 was that the schools were growing. How would growth in the school system facilitate curriculum change?

10. Follow the procedure recommended by Neustadt and May for the case of the problems identified in *A Nation At Risk*. Assume you were acting as a consultant to the Secretary of Education to recommend federal actions to solve these problems. Locate the closest historical analogies you can find among these landmark developments. Analyze their appropriateness as analogies.

11. Two of the most substantial deviations from America's historic posture of federal nonintervention with local schools were the Smith-Hughes Act establishing vocational education and the post-*Sputnik* federally sponsored curriculum projects. Compare the two cases systematically in the manner recommended by Neustadt and May. What generalizations about federal intervention in curriculum matters seem plausible in light of your analysis?

12. Compare the historical development of curriculum in the United States with that of another country over a similar period. See the bibliographical essay at the end of this chapter for histories of developments in the English-speaking world. List similarities and differences. What do these tell you about the two school systems? The two cultures? How confident are you of your conclusions?

13. Read "Moral Majorities and the School Curriculum: Historical Perspectives on the Legalization of Virtue," by Tyack and James (*Teachers College Record* 86:513–537, Summer, 1985), or another article by a professional historian drawing historical parallels to a contemporary event. Before you read, write down the historical parallels you know already. Then, compare your informal use of history with the authors' formal use of a greater historical knowledge. Have you learned anything from the historical analysis? Compare how the authors go about using history to the procedures suggested by Neustadt and May.

RECOMMENDED READING

The two volumes of Lawrence A. Cremin's *American Education* published so far, *The Colonial Experience, 1607–1783* (1970) and *The National Experience, 1783–1876* (1980) are indispensable sources. Cremin's histories take an extremely broad view of education, covering newspapers, religious organizations, and libraries in addition to schools. His histories are organized by theme rather than strictly by period. Readers especially interested in curriculum issues must look carefully for relevant material and must read actively in order to follow the continuing connections among curriculum issues emphasized here. But the effort is well worth it. Cremin's (1971) article "Curriculum-Making in the United States" makes up for the scattered treatment of the subject in his larger histories and has influenced my thinking on the subject a great deal. Ruth Miller Elson's *Guardians of Tradition* (1964) is full of delicious detail of curriculum and textbooks in nineteenth century schools. Frederick Rudolph's *Curriculum: A History of the American Undergraduate Course of Study Since 1636* (1977) is the single most useful source I have found on the history of college and university curricula.

For those who want to start their historical study even earlier than colonial America, Werner Jaeger's *Paideia* (1939) and H.I. Marrou's *History of Education in Antiquity* (1956) are particularly valuable histories of education in ancient Greece and Rome. Foster Watson's *The Beginnings of the Teaching of Modern Subjects* (1909) is an indispensable source for developments in curriculum of European schools.

Lawrence A. Cremin's *The Transformation of the School: Progressivism in American Education, 1876–1957* (1961) is still the definitive history of Progressivism in education, and still a delightful reading experience. Herbert Kleibard's *The Struggle for the American Curriculum* (1986) argues that no unified Progressive Education movement existed; rather the label was given to all those who advocated alternatives to the nineteenth-century school program. His account is rich in anecdotes, photographs, and other details of great interest. Edward Krug's two-volume work, *The Shaping of the American High School* (1964, 1972) is a more straightforward account of the people and events told in essentially chronological order. Krug focuses more sharply on schools and on the issues that captured the attention of the school people of the time. Theodore Sizer's *Secondary Schools at the Turn of the Century* (1964) is particularly useful for the light it sheds on the Committee of Ten and its successors. Harold Rugg's own account of his work in the education, *That Men May Understand* (1941) makes fascinating reading. The historical sketch of vocational education by Grant Venn in *Man, Education, and Work* (1964) has been a particularly useful source on that subject. William F. Connell's *A History of American Education in the Twentieth Century World* is a remarkably detailed account focusing on schools, containing many excellent photographs and illustrations. Sol Cohen's *American Education: A Documentary History* is a ready source of many important original documents. Larry Cuban's *How Teachers Taught: Constancy and Change in American Classrooms 1890–1980* (1984) is a crucial source for understanding what actually happened in classrooms, as contrasted with what was advocated, during nearly a century of virtually constant reform efforts.

None of the aforementioned histories gives enough attention to what strikes me as the remarkable resemblance of American Progressive curricular and pedagogical reforms to earlier British and contemporaneous Australian reforms. The stories of these reforms are admirably retold in Stewart and McCann's *The Educational Innovators, 1750–1880* (1967), Brian Simon's *Studies in the History of Education, 1780–1870* (1960), and R. J. W. Selleck's *The New Education, 1870–1914* (1968).

References

American Council on Education. 1938. *Youth Tell Their Story*. Washington, D.C.: The Council.

Cohen, Sol. 1974. *American Education: A Documentary History*. N.Y.: Random House

Commission on the Reorganization of Secondary Education. 1918. *Cardinal Principles of Secondary Education*. Washington, D.C. National Education Association.

Conant, James. 1959. *The American High School Today*. N.Y.: McGraw-Hill.

Connell, William F. 1980. *A History of American Education in the Twentieth Century World*. N.Y.: Teachers College Press.

Counts, George S. 1932. *Dare the School Build a New Social Order?* N.Y.: The John Day Co.

Cremin, Lawrence A. 1961. *The Transformation of the School: Progressivism in American Education, 1876–1957*. N.Y.: Knopf.

Cremin, Lawrence A. 1970. *American Education: The Colonial Experience, 1607–1783*. N.Y.: Harper and Row.

Cremin, Lawrence A. Dec. 1971. Curriculum-Making in the United States. *Teachers College Record* 73:207–220.

Cremin, Lawrence A. 1980. *American Education: The National Experience, 1783–1876*. N.Y.: Harper and Row.

Crosbie, Laurence M. 1923. *The Phillips Exeter Academy: A History*. Exeter, N.H.: The Academy.

Cuban, Larry. 1984. *How Teachers Taught: Constancy and Change in American Classrooms 1890–1980*. N.Y.: Longmans.

Cuban, Larry. 1986. *Teachers and Machines: The Classroom Use of Technology Since 1920*. N.Y.: Teachers College Press.

Cubberley, Ellwood P. (ed.) 1934. *Readings in Public Education in the United States*. Boston: Houghton Mifflin.

Education Policies Commission. March 1947. The Imperative Needs of Youth of Secondary School Age. *Bulletin of the National Association of Secondary School Principals*. 31: 145.

Elson, Ruth Miller. 1964. *Guardians of Tradition*. Lincoln: University of Nebraska Press.

Flexner, Abraham. 1923. *A Modern College and a Modern School*. Garden City, N.Y.: Doubleday, Page and Co.

Harrington, Michael. 1964. *The Other American*. N.Y.: Macmillan.

Harris, William Torrey. 1885. "Compulsory education in relation to crime and social morals". Address delivered at the 12th Annual Conference of Charities and Convents", cited in Kurt F. Leidecker. 1946. *Yankee Teacher: The Life of William T. Harris*. N.Y.: The Philosophical Library.

Jaeger, Werner. 1939. *Paideia: The Ideals of Greek Culture, Volume 1*. Oxford: Oxford University Press.

Kandel, Isaac L. 1926. *Twenty-Five Years of American Education*. N.Y.: Macmillan.

Kilpatrick, William S. 1932. *Education and the Social Crisis: A Proposed Program*. N.Y.: Liveright.

Krug, Edward. 1964. *The Shaping of the American High School, 1880–1920,* N.Y.: Harper and Row.

Krug, Edward. 1972. *The Shaping of the American High School, 1920–1941*. Madison: The University of Wisconsin Press.

Lynd, Albert. 1950. Quackery in the Public Schools. *The Atlantic.* 175.

Marrou, H.I. 1956. *History of Education in Antiquity.* N.Y.: New American Library.

McGuffey, William Holmes. 1879. *McGuffey's New Second Eclectic Reader.* Cincinnati: Wilson and Hinkle.

National Education Association. 1918. *Cardinal Principles of Secondary Education.* Washington, D.C.: NEA.

National Society for the Promotion of Industrial Education. 1907. "Constitution". Bulletin Number 1. Washington, D.C.: The Society.

Neustadt, Richard E. and Ernest R. May. 1986. *Thinking in Time, The Uses of History for Decision-Makers.* N.Y.: The Free Press.

Rice, Joseph Mayer. 1897. The Futility of the Spelling Grind. *The Forum* 23: 163–72.

Rickover, Hyman G. 1959. *Education and Freedom.* N.Y.: Dutton.

Rudolph, Frederick. 1977. *Curriculum: A History of the American Undergraduate Course of Study Since 1636.* San Francisco: Jossey-Bass.

Rugg, Harold. 1941. *That Men May Understand.* N.Y.: Doubleday, Doran and Co.

Runyon, Laura L. 1900. A Day with the New Education. *Chautaquan.* 590–91.

Selleck, R. J. W. 1968. *The New Education, 1870–1914* London: Sir Isaac Pitman and Sons.

Simon, Brian. 1960. *Studies in the History of Education, 1780–1870.* London: Lawrence and Wishart.

Sizer, Theodore R. 1964. *Secondary Schools at the Turn of the Century.* New Haven: Yale University Press.

Stewart, W. A. C., and W. P. McCann. 1967. *The Educational Innovators, 1750–1880.* London: Macmillan.

Struck, F. Theodore. 1945. *Vocational Education for a Changing World.* N.Y.: Wiley.

Thorndike, Edward L. 1924. Mental Discipline in High School Studies. *Journal of Educational Psychology* 15: 1–22, 83–98.

Thorndike, Edward L. and Irving Lorge. 1938. *A Semantic Count of English Words.* N.Y.: The Institute of Educational Research, Teachers College, Columbia University.

Tyack, David and Thomas James. Summer 1985. Moral Majorities and the School Curriculum: Historical Perspectives on the Legalization of Virtue. *Teachers College Record* 86:513–537.

Venn, Grant. 1964. *Man, Education, and Work.* Washington, D.C.: American Council on Education.

Watson, Foster. 1909. *The Beginnings of the Teaching of Modern Subjects.* London: Sir I. Pitman and Sons.

Webster, Noah. 1789. *An American Selection of Lessons in Reading and Spelling.* Various printers, including Boston: I. Thomas and E. T. Andrews, reissued by Arno Press of NY in 1974.

Webster, Noah. 1831. *The American Spelling Book.* N.Y.: George F. Cooledge.

AN INTRODUCTION TO CURRICULUM THOUGHT

Here is the beginning of philosophy, a recognition of the conflicts between men, a search for their cause, a condemnation of mere opinion, and the discovery of a standard of judgment.

Epictetus
Greece, Fourth Century, B.C.

PURPOSE OF THE CHAPTER

- to describe in general terms the historical development of curriculum thought and to sketch the main outlines of a few historically important works

- to introduce the major forms of contemporary curriculum thought: theory, methods, criticism, metatheory, and explanatory theory, and to describe briefly a few outstanding examples of each type

- to provide a basis for later understanding of curricular discourse and for comprehending and appreciating the ideas that support different perspectives people adopt on curricular matters

OUTLINE

Philosophical Writing about Curriculum Questions

Progressivism and the Emergence of Curriculum Theory

Contemporary Curriculum Thought

Contemporary Writing in the Mainline Tradition

Other Forms of Contemporary Curriculum Thought

Analytic Tools

A Taxonomy of Educational Objectives

Metatheory

Curriculum Criticism

Explanatory Curriculum Theory

PHILOSOPHICAL WRITING ABOUT CURRICULUM QUESTIONS

The ideas people have developed over the centuries to help them handle curriculum matters are the most valuable things anyone can learn from the study of curriculum. The techniques, methods, and procedures people have developed are useful in particular situations, but the ideas are essential as a vocabulary for thinking and communicating about curriculum matters. These ideas have helped to shape the history of the school curriculum, and they continue to be important today. This entire book is only a bare introduction to these ideas. This chapter supplies an orientation to the larger body of ideas by briefly describing a few selected highlights of curricular thought, works that are typical in form and content, exemplary in quality of thought and expression, and historically important.

For most of recorded history, questions about the purpose, content, and structure of educational programs have been considered a special case of the grand question of how life should be lived. Common people sought the advice of the wise—philosophers, theologians, cultural leaders, and commentators of all kinds. Since "What should be taught and learned?" has always been an important question, most authors with pretensions to wisdom addressed it. For example, it is addressed directly and indirectly in passages throughout the Bible, in the great philosophical texts of Ancient Greece, in the writings of the medieval church fathers, by great scholars of the Renaissance and the Enlightenment, and by many modern philosophers. The trail of commentary on curriculum matters can be traced right down the center of the Western intellectual tradition to the present day. These works are claimed by philosophers of education, but their ideas on curriculum are fundamental to curricular thought and practice, too.

Plato's Curricular Ideas

More than 2,000 years ago the ancient Athenian Greek philosopher Plato (427?-347 B.C.) produced what is generally regarded as the first full, theoretical, coherent treatise on government and education, *The Republic*. Plato's *Republic* describes a utopian society, one in which education plays a central role. The educational system Plato invented arose from a consideration of some of the most fundamental questions in education: What should be the relation of education to society? Who should be educated? What should be the purposes of the educations provided to various individuals? What subjects should they study? In what order? How should formal study be related to educative experience in life outside school? Plato's answers to these questions were radical in the Athens of his day and they have remained radical for almost two millennia. Nevertheless, *The Republic* has had a profound influence on Western educational thought, shaping debate by posing the questions, often stimulating dissent, but still challenging dissenters to show that their answers are better than Plato's.

In Plato's *Republic,* early childhood education would consist of gymnastics for the body and of music for the soul including reciting literature and poetry to musical accompaniment. This was the prevailing practice in Athenian education, so Plato's proposal was conventional, except for one feature: Plato would have the songs sung to children selected so as to instill in them desirable adult qualities. Since as adults they should be brave, children should not be told terrifying stories. Since as adults they should be reasonable, they should not be told that the gods quarreled, plotted, and fought against one another.

Other teaching young people received was to be done through play rather than as part of a compulsory regimen, since play is natural to children and what they are made to learn rarely stays with them, according to Plato. Plato suggested that through games and play a foundation could be laid for later study of subjects such as arithmetic, geometry, and astronomy. But children were to be forbidden to engage in philosophical speculation—dialectic, argumentation—lest they develop a superficial fluency, a tendency toward idle and aimless contention, and a disrespect for thought.

During early education children should be closely watched for signs of excellence in health, in athletics, in memory, in their sense of rhythm, harmony, and aesthetics, in their conduct, and in their moral qualities. They should be exposed to stresses and temptations of various kinds—pains, pleasures, frightening experiences, challenges to their wit, skill, and character. Those who emerged from these tests whole, unspoiled, and excellent would be selected for further training leading toward leadership responsibilities within the state. Those who failed these tests were to be apprenticed to various trades and crafts depending on their talents and inclinations.

After their compulsory three-year basic military training (Plato's vision did not extend to women or slaves), young soldiers were to be taught arithmetic, geometry, and astronomy. Plato deemed these subjects to be useful to soldiers but, more importantly, they would encourage them toward pure thought, toward use of the highest human faculties, toward the search for truth. During their military service some of the soldier-students would prove to be more intelligent, courageous, enterprising, and able than others. The best would be selected at age 30 to undertake further study of the higher branches of arithmetic, geometry, and astronomy and also to begin study of the highest discipline of all—dialectics, or philosophy itself, reasoning about the good for man, contemplation of pure, eternal truth. During this period, the soldiers were to live in an austere, frugal style. They were to have no property other than a few personal possessions. They were to live communally, sharing everything with their peers. Their needs would be provided for by the community as the wages of their military service. They would not farm, trade, or engage in any way in the mundane affairs of ordinary men. After five years of study, they would return to active life, holding commands in war, holding public offices, and serving in other leadership capacities.

At the age of fifty those who had withstood all these tests and grown wise from study and experience would be appointed guardians of the state, empowered to make its laws and to govern it. The prohibitions on ownership of private property by the guardians would continue so as to ensure against corruption. They would oversee the affairs of the state and ensure that it continued to support and encourage the highest and best sort of life among its citizens.

Plato was convinced that the highest, noblest, most powerful, and indeed most characteristically human of mankind's capabilities was abstract thought. Thought alone could determine which of the many ends people sought were worthy. The capacity for thought would distinguish mankind from the beasts. The man of thought perceived eternal truth, the forms of things, their essence, while ordinary mortals dealt with the changeable, contingent appearances of things. Thought was the light that would enable men to see the truth. Only thought, the light of reason, could reveal to man his true condition. Obviously, then, the training of the guardians of the state must include those studies most conducive to pure, abstract thought. As enlightened leaders, they would see to it that the community moved steadily toward greater awareness of the truth and toward a life compatible with that awareness.

Plato's steadfast focus on formal knowledge as the highest aim of education, an aim to be attained only in maturity and only by a few, and his conception of government by an elite of talent, experience, and education have been fundamental elements of European education ever since. The progressive strain in contemporary American educational thought owes much to Plato's ideas about early education.

Rousseau's Writings about Curriculum

Jean Jacques Rousseau (1712–1778) was a social philosopher whose ideas prepared the way for the French Revolution of 1789. He maintained that "Man is born free and everywhere he is in chains." In a state of nature, a person is not subject to any government, nor to the norms of any society and is thus free. Trouble starts when society imposes its arbitrary demands. Man is naturally good; society makes him bad. The solution was a return to nature. This applied particularly to child-rearing and education. In *Émile* Rousseau described the details of the rearing and education of a fictional child (Figure 3-1). It was an upbringing that he believed would help achieve a return to a state of nature.

Title page of Rousseau's *Émile*.

Rousseau insisted that the education of a human being begins at birth. People learn most of what they know when they are very young, he maintained, so early education was fundamental. Rousseau urged that well-to-do mothers nurse their own children, rather than using wet nurses, that parents spend time with their children and develop a rich and lively domestic life, rather than living primarily for public gatherings in the highly formal society of the time, and that adults value childhood in its own right, as deserving of happiness in its own terms, rather than sacrificing it always to preparation for entry into adult society. Children should not be constrained by early artificial habits. They should eat when hungry, sleep when tired, and play freely, so that they might enjoy and appreciate their freedom from the earliest possible moment. Children should be treated kindly, not severely, with a tender regard, they should be indulged in their diversions and pleasures, as befit their innocent, harmless natures.

When the child grew beyond infancy it should be coaxed, guided and stimulated to learn, but not taught directly. Verbal instruction should be minimized where it could not be avoided altogether. Instead, experiences were to be arranged, where necessary, or simply allowed to happen, that would motivate the youngster to seek whatever instruction might be necessary. Children reason very well, Rousseau argued, when it comes to matters within their childish experience, but they fail when they try to reason abstractly about things of which they have no direct, sensory experience. Yet all the studies normally imposed on children in school concern things entirely foreign to children: reading, writing, arithmetic. Émile was to be taught to read by his parents sending him written invitations to dinners and festive occasions. If he could not decipher the writing or get someone to do it for him, he would miss the event, so his motivation to learn could be counted on. Desire to learn counted for more than all the refined methods of instruction imaginable.

Rousseau urged educators to cultivate children's curiosity, ask them leading questions, and respond subtly to their questions, lest their curiosity be quenched too readily. Follow the child's interest—don't expect the child to follow adult interests. Children should be active. Instead of sitting quietly reading books, they should be in the workshop building things and out in the field observing and experimenting. Children should be busied with useful activities. Later, the youngster, even the aristocrat, should learn a trade so that he would be independent, capable of living on his own and supporting himself. Above all, Rousseau sought to educate Émile in a way that would foster his freedom and independence, acting in ways that reflected his original nature and his own freely chosen path. He should not follow the dictates of society or of civilization. Education was cultivation of natural potential, not the impression of preset form on the child.

Rousseau's ideas, like Plato's, were sharply at odds with prevailing practices. But whereas Plato's differences with the educational practices of his time were greatest at the later, adult end, Rousseau's were greatest at the earlier, childhood end. Once the child reached the age of reason, Rousseau was essentially finished with his education, whereas Plato had hardly begun. Both Plato and Rousseau sought a greater excellence in people's lives. Both saw the nature of society as critical in determining the character of the individuals reared within it. Their visions of the ideal society are utterly different. Rousseau's chief concern was individual freedom and independence, whereas Plato's was the search for truth. Rousseau tried to free children from the impositions of society, while Plato tried to use social institutions to shape young peoples' values and conduct. Yet, strangely, the methods they advocated are similar: games, play, music, kindness, and indirection.

PROGRESSIVISM AND THE EMERGENCE OF CURRICULUM THEORY

The term *curriculum theory* came into use in the United States in the 1920s to describe the writings of a few dozen men and women participating in the progressive education movement. Curriculum theory arose as an attempt by these reformers to convince themselves, one another, and the world that a new curriculum would be better than the traditional one found in most schools. Even those who supported the traditional curriculum were challenged by the reformers' zeal to explain and defend their views. The result was a rich outpouring of ideas about the curriculum, ideas that continue to influence reformers and traditionalists alike, ideas that are indispensable to understanding modern writing about the curriculum.

No one author represents either progressive or traditional views on all curricular questions, and no brief summary can do justice to the issues debated. Individual progressives actually held quite a variety of positions on curriculum matters. Some, for example, proposed that individual teachers plan their own curriculum; others advocated joint curriculum planning by whole school staffs; still others urged that the entire community participate in curriculum planning. Yet, the progressives' various proposals had more in common with each other than they did with the traditional curriculum, and so the curricular debates of the era centered around the conflict of traditional and progressive views. The brief passages quoted in Boxes 3-1, 3-2, and 3-3 convey merely broad tendencies of thought of a number of central curriculum issues debated between progressives and traditionalists.

As the labels imply, the fundamental value difference between traditional and progressive views is the attitude each takes toward social and historical change. The differences in their views on curriculum arise from differences of belief and value inherent in the two perspectives. Progressives view change as inevitable, pervasive, and good. They welcome it and enlist themselves in the cause of shaping a better future. Progressives align themselves with the young, who are untrammelled by the prejudices of the past, and stand against the entrenched powers. Youth is seen as likely to be good; evil as likelier to arise in age. Freedom is more important to progressives than discipline or order, since only original exploration can discover the directions we should take toward a better future. Actual experiences of people

BOX 3-1

PROGRESSIVE

Learning of the right kind helps one to live better. In the last analysis we concern ourselves about education and learning because we wish our pupils to live fuller and better than they otherwise would. It is living that fundamentally concerns us. (William H. Kilpatrick, in Rugg 1927, 121)

The drawing out of the child's inner capacities for self-expression constitutes only one of the two great goals of the new school. (Harold Rugg and Ann Shumaker 1928, 8)

The first of these articles of faith [to which all child-centered schools subscribe] is freedom. "Free the legs, the arms, the larynx of a child," say the advocates of the new education, "and you have taken the first step toward freeing his mind and spirit." (Rugg and Shoemaker 1928, 55)

TRADITIONAL

The general public has a very high regard for literacy, both numerical and linguistic. This, of course, is only a highbrow method of saying that the general public desires, first of all, that the elementary school teach the three R's passing well. It may be added that the adult world apparently retains a firm faith in certain one-time virtues now generally discredited by our profession—notably "thoroughness" and "discipline." (William C. Bagley in Rugg 1927, 36)

It is said that pupils should be adopted as the guides to the educational process because the natural unfolding of their interests and desires will lead them forward to that stage of maturity which is to be desired as the end of life. The view here defended is based on a categorical denial of the assumption that the individual unfolds because of inner impulses into a civilized being. Civilization is a social product. It requires cooperation for its maintenance exactly as it required cooperation for its evolution. Even Shakespeare did not create the English language. No child can evolve the English language. (Charles H. Judd in Rugg 1927, 114–115)

BOX 3-2

PROGRESSIVE	TRADITIONAL
Since its all-controlling purpose is educational and since it is relieved from these pressing demands of the moment which commonly dominate other institutions, [the school] may become a peculiarly effective instrument for giving expression to social foresight and wisdom. In fact, the school is about the only instrument of this kind that society possesses. The mature generation is always the victim of its own past. At any moment society is so caught in the meshes of its folkways that its behavior lags behind its knowledge. . . . The school is an instrument for doing the difficult educational tasks, for anticipating the problems of the future, and for directing the course of social behavior. (George S. Counts, in Rugg 1927, 85)	What is the primary function of the public school system in American democracy? It is, as I see things, the training of minds and the dissemination of knowledge. . . . There are many . . . who look to the school to correct all the ills of humanity. Society creates conditions that foster crime; the schools must serve as crime prevention agencies. Society sends undernourished, ill-clad, and sick children to school; teachers must feed and nurse the unfortunate. . . . It is right and proper, of course, that any individual teacher may feel bound to assume the obligations of the soldier, propagandist or politician. In this case let the teacher take up the profession with which such obligations are properly associated. (Charles A. Beard 1936, 278)
The content of the school must be constructed out of the very materials of American life— not from academic relics of Victorian precedents. The curriculum must bring children to close grip with the roar and steely clang of industry, with the great integrated structure of American business, and must prepare them in sympathy and	The large groups of elementary, or "fundamental," materials seem to be fairly well stabilized. The basic language-arts and the basic arts of computation and measurement occupy the place of major importance in universal education. This is true of the elementary schools of all civilized countries. . . .

(continued)

■
BOX 3-2 continued

PROGRESSIVE	TRADITIONAL
tolerance to confront the underlying forces of political and economic life. . . . We must discover a sane method by which useless subject matter can be discarded from the school curriculum and, instead, major problems, institutions, and modes of living that are of social importance utilized and taught. (Rugg 1927, 149)	Universal literacy is clearly the first and most fundamental objective of mass-education. (William C. Bagley, in Rugg 1927, 29)

in the present are a surer guide than the inherited wisdom of a past quite different from our present. Progressives place great importance on helping individuals to learn to think for themselves. Such independent learning counters the tendency of societies to control opinion by the tyranny of currently dominant views, which are usually the views favored by those in power, who are, in turn, supported by traditional ideas and practices. Creative individuals with original ideas must be

■
BOX 3-3

PROGRESSIVE	TRADITIONAL
We must invent a new synthesis of knowledge and make it the basis of the entire school curriculum. The conventional barriers between the existing subjects must be ignored in curriculum making. The *starting points* shall be the social institution, or the political and economic problem, and the capacities of children —not the subject. (Rugg 1927, 155)	Knowledge will always have to by systematized and arranged in coherent subjects. . . . The materials of instruction need to be amplified and arranged and organized. . . . [but this] statement is not an invitation to plunge into intellectual chaos or to follow the caprice of untrained or immature minds. (Charles H. Judd, in Rugg, 1927, 116–117)

William Heard Kilpatrick, 1871–1965

nurtured, for they enable us to adapt intelligently to changing conditions. Progressives seldom worry about preserving what is valuable from the past because they see a tremendous inertia in human affairs that more than adequately protects our inheritance from the past. As for the notion of surviving the test of time, the true progressive regards every day as a new test, independent of all those that have gone before, just as likely to topple the old giant of the forest as the young seedling. In fact, the true progressive takes pleasure in the passing of the oldest traditions, since these leave room for something new to emerge, something more adapted to current and future circumstances.

Traditionalists, by contrast, value continuity with the past. They view the accumulated wisdom of humanity, as embodied in the culture transmitted from one generation to the next, as a supreme value, the source of nearly all that is highest and best in life. They view nature itself as favoring continuity and very gradual change. Most innovations, they figure, like most mutations, are unsuccessful. Those ideas and practices that have survived the test of time are far more likely to be of enduring value than today's inventions. Traditionalists align themselves with the wisdom and skill of maturity and view the young as a precious human resource to be developed, but callow, unformed, and potentially barbarous if not properly initiated into civilized ways.

The traditional-progressive debate continues to influence curriculum thought and practice. Its influence is so strong, in fact, that virtually all newly proposed reforms seem to fall into one or the other camp, just as most political proposals seem to be either conservative or liberal, left or right.

Harold O. Rugg, 1886–1960

PROGRESSIVE ROLE IN FOUNDING CURRICULUM THEORY

In addition to its continuing influence on curriculum thought, the progressive-traditional debate is important because of its formative influence on the enterprise of curriculum theory. The theories that emerged from debates between advocates of progressive and of traditional education early in this century became the prototype of curriculum theory. They were not philosophical speculations, but practical proposals grounded in ideas. Progressives rejected tradition as a legitimate justification for present action, but they also rejected the arbitrary prejudices of any group, even the progressives themselves. Arbitrary authority was a tactic of the entrenched interests viewed as the enemy by progressives. So, many progressives sought to ground their proposals in reason, not traditional scholastic reason, but twentieth-century reason, of which modern science was the prime example. Progressives came to view it as a matter of the utmost practical importance that their proposals for change be grounded as firmly as possible in a consistent system of modern ideas.

Progressives placed high priority on values of social progress, democracy, and the realization of individual potential. They viewed science as the method by which these values could best be realized in modern life. Progressive educators viewed education as an essential institutional instrument for realizing these values. This meant that new educational purposes, content, and structures would need to be

George S. Counts, 1889–1974

developed and the schools transformed. The process of transformation would itself need to be consistent with progressive values, as well. Therefore, reform proposals would have to be openly advocated before the people in democratic forums. Reforms would also have to be scientifically defensible. Curriculum theory emerged as a method of systematically grounding reform proposal in ideas that would appeal to the public and to scientists and philosophers as well. Progressive educators believed that if their proposed reforms were solidly grounded in these beliefs and values, they would command the support of all reasonable people of good will who were sincerely interested in improving the educational system. With this support the reformers would be able to overcome the entrenched powers supporting prevailing practices.

During the progressive era in education, curriculum attained the status of a field of professional work and study. The content of the new discipline was taken mainly from seminal works of curriculum theory produced between 1900 and 1940 by its founders. Some of the most important figures and the works of curriculum theory from this period include,

John Dewey   *The School and Society* (1900)
                    The Child and the Curriculum (1902)
                    Democracy and Education (1916)
                    Experience and Education (1938)

William C. Bagley, 1874–1946

Franklin Bobbitt	*The Curriculum* (1918) *How to Make a Curriculum* (1924)
William H. Kilpatrick	*The Project Method* (1918) *Foundations of Method* (1926) *Remaking the Curriculum* (1936)
George S. Counts	*The Senior High School Curriculum* (1926) *Dare the School Build a New Social Order?* (1932)

Harold Rugg	*The Child-Centered School* (1928) (with Ann Shumaker)
	Foundations and Technique of Curriculum-Making.
	    Twenty-sixth Yearbook of the National Society for
	    the Study of Education (1927)
	American Life and the School Curriculum
	    (1936) (with Axtelle, Caswell, and Counts)

William W. Charters	*Curriculum Construction* (1923)
Boyd H. Bode	*Modern Educational Theories* (1927)
L. Thomas Hopkins	*Curriculum Principles & Practices* (1929) *Integration: Its Meaning and Application* (1937) *Pupil-Teacher Learning* (1938)

An example of a traditional classroom: New York City Elementary School, Fourth Grade Class, 1943.

The inclination to look to theory when faced with a perplexing curriculum problem owes a great deal to the continuing influence of progressive ideas and values.

CONTEMPORARY CURRICULUM THOUGHT

Introduction

The progressive era was a high water mark for curriculum theory. Although curriculum 'theory of the sort characteristic of this period continues to be produced, as does philosophical writing in the earlier tradition, curriculum writing has turned in new directions in the three decades or so of the post-Progressive era of American education. Conflicting tendencies which coexisted uneasily in the comprehensive theories favored by Progressives seem to be going their separate ways. For example, a type of theory has emerged that quite frankly pursues the scholarly aim of explaining curricular phenomena and makes no pretense at telling

Another traditional classroom: Washington, D.C. Woodrow Wilson High School, White, Algebra Lesson, 1943.

us what kind of curriculum we should have. Another type of writing also abandons the search for a direct answer to the curriculum question and seeks instead methods, procedures, and tools for curriculum improvement. A type of metatheory has emerged that examines curriculum thought in somewhat the way philosophers and historians of science examine scientific thought. Let us consider some examples of this contemporary diversity of curriculum thought, beginning with contemporary continuations of the mainline tradition of theory as a rationalized plan of action.

CONTEMPORARY WRITING IN THE MAINLINE TRADITION

The Writing of G. H. Bantock

According to the English author G. H. Bantock, until the coming of industrialization late in the last century, Western civilization supported two cultures, a *high* culture confined largely to the upper classes and based on an ability to read and

A progressive classroom: Santa Barbara, circa 1930.

write and a *folk* culture based largely on traditions of oral communication. Folk cultures were not uniformly less sophisticated and were often more direct and powerful than the corresponding high cultures. The arts of high culture were often refinements of popular arts, rather than completely independent or antagonistic creations. High culture could not have maintained itself without a vital popular culture.

Bantock maintains that industrialization impoverished the everyday life of working people and undermined folk culture. Work that had offered innumerable sensory and emotional satisfactions and had furnished the materials for folk art was transformed into machine-governed routines with far less aesthetic and emotional potential. The efficient, mechanical organization of work replaced the organic, personal, natural human exchange found on the farm and in the shop or home.

The universal literacy training fostered by free, compulsory elementary schools in the late 1800s imposed on the working class majority of Europeans the rudiments of the high literary culture of the upper classes and ruthlessly destroyed the remnants of folk culture. In school, culture meant the culture of the educated minority, "the best that has been thought and said." There was no room for the nonliterate, oral tradition or for the nonliterary arts—dancing, singing, handcrafts, performing arts, and the like—that constituted the popular culture of the day.

The results of this new literacy training for children of the working class were alienation from the only living culture open to them, along with a failure to induct them fully into the high culture. The bits and scraps of literacy conveyed in the few short years of elementary education were poor preparation for a rewarding, satisfying life in any adult community. The school stood for abstraction, for a purely mental life, whereas the authentic traditions from which the children came were based on direct contact and immediate participation, on the senses and the feelings. Thus school was then and remains a failure for a substantial proportion of the populace.

According to Bantock, today we have another popular culture built around the mass media. It is not a folk culture because it is not created by the folk, but rather consumed by them. But it is still largely nonliterate and appeals directly to the senses and to the feelings. Thus the school is still in the position of offering the remains of a high, literate culture to a population of children whose lives at home are built around a completely different culture. "The world implicit in work of the school variety is the stubborn, irreducible real world; that contained in pop culture is one manufactured out of floating emotions and aspirations exploited by clever men who thus feed rather than check the dreams of unreality" (Bantock 1968, 65). Bantock believes this is the chief dilemma facing those in education in the twentieth century.

> The culture of the people, then, is one which, generally speaking, appeals to the emotions. I have tried to show that, all too often, it is a cheap and tawdry culture, likely to betray one's sense of emotional reality, erecting "images" of no substance between the individual and his attempts to grapple with the real world of relationships, inhibiting true empathy or fostering a debilitating sentimentality.
>
> Yet this too has to be said. This culture is enormously appealing, in the emotionally undereducated environment we inhabit. It clearly "gets" young people to an extent that school achieves but rarely. . . . (Bantock 1968, 71)

What sort of curriculum will enable schools to come to grips with this dilemma? First, it is important to note that no one curriculum will be satisfactory for both children of the elite, literary culture and children of the popular culture. The traditional literary-historical curriculum does quite a good job of fitting some youngsters for later participation in the high culture into which they were born. For them, the chief problem with schooling is the erosive effect of the introduction of science and technical subjects, engendering skepticism, emphasizing the material while denigrating the spiritual, the emotional, and the aesthetic concerns that lie close to the heart of literary-historical high culture. In Bantock's view, this development has gone too far and needs to be corrected.

Bantock maintains that the curriculum for children of the lower classes needs to be wholly redesigned. For them, education needs to unite thought and feeling, to use these children's natural propensities toward direct participation, toward sensing, toward feeling, but to use them to the ultimate end of induction into higher, more serious, more refined, more encompassingly truthful and satisfying ways of dealing with reality. The central aim of elementary education, particularly, must be education of the emotions. This involves both becoming aware of one's emotions and also being able to experience emotion in new, subtler, more articulated forms.

The methods and concerns of the arts lie at the heart of the alternative curriculum Bantock proposes. He suggests movement education as the soundest starting point. In movement education children are involved in exploring space in a disciplined way as well as in expressing their feelings. Children are stimulated to think how they can position themselves in space and move through space in order to achieve given effects or in order to communicate their feelings. Dramatic sequences of movement and gesture can convey narrative. Gesture leads to symbol and hence to language. The path from movement to drama and the other performing arts leads in a natural way to the popular art forms of the twentieth century—radio, film, and television. Through participation in and study of these forms of expression children can develop a heightened awareness of the major media of communication they experience in their lives outside school.

In addition, schools for children not academically inclined should attend to home and family life and to vocational and technical education, following the principle of learning by direct contact and participation. Throughout this curriculum every effort should be made to elevate and refine emotional, aesthetic, and intellectual abilities using the materials of a culture familiar to the students, a culture in which they will live once their schooling is over.

Americans, like many Europeans, may find Bantock's proposal for separate curricula unacceptable on political and ideological grounds. But he makes his proposal in full awareness of the claims of democracy and egalitarianism. Responding in advance to the charge that he is merely trying to make the lower classes happy in their subordination, Bantock replies by asking what sort of life school presently holds out for them. He answers "repetitive work in a factory of the soul-destroying type." By contrast, the curriculum he proposes would offer, he claims, preparation for all sorts of work in the applied arts, communication, design, and so on, with at least as much promise of material reward and greater promise of personal satisfaction. "The prospect of an elite prestige job held out to youngsters presently as the reward for school completion is an illusion for all but a tiny fraction of them" (Bantock 1980, 99).

A Comprehensive Curriculum for American Secondary Schools

Harry S. Broudy, B. Othanel Smith, and Joe R. Burnett, authors of a comprehensive curriculum for American secondary schools, were professors of education at the University of Illinois, Smith a curriculum specialist and Broudy and Burnett philosophers of education. Their chief concern in *Democracy and Excellence in American Secondary Education* (1963) was to reconcile the demands for academic excellence, which had risen to a crescendo in the wake of *Sputnik,* with the ideals of education in and for a democratic society. Progressives had not been primarily concerned with academic excellence. Yes, it was important, particularly for some children whose talents veered in that direction. But the primary goals of individual and social welfare could often be attained with only a modicum of academic learning. Progressives believed it was important that schools offer an education for all American youth, not just for the academically talented. They believed they had fought and won this battle at the turn of the century when they defeated the recommendations of the college-dominated Committee of Ten with their own less academic and more egalitarian programs. Then, after *Sputnik*, inheritors of progressive ideals found themselves having to battle once more against demands for academic excellence as the chief goal of secondary education.

Broudy, Smith, and Burnett profess a commitment to education for democracy. "The American ethos affirms that the technological resources of modern society can and should be exploited to enhance the excellence and significance of all, rather than an elite. . . ." (Broudy, Smith, and Burnett 1963, 6). They proceed to work out a program for secondary education to bring about this reconciliation. They argue that secondary schools should offer a common curriculum, basically the same for all. This curriculum should contain "those central skills, ideas, and evaluations which can be most significantly and widely used in order to deal with life in our times" (Broudy, Smith, and Burnett 1963, 10). They criticize the curriculum existing at the time on several grounds: they claimed that it was too diverse and fragmented; that too much emphasis was put on immediate experience and behavior as contrasted with flexible responses based on understanding and intelligence; that values were neglected; that too little emphasis was placed on the more difficult but more powerful applications of knowledge, and too little on verbal behavior. The authors outline and justify a program to remedy these shortcomings.

The book is a masterful example of rational justification for a comprehensive program of education. It begins with an analysis of the curricular demands of modern mass society: citizenship, vocational competence, and self-cultivation. The emergence of a highly technological society held together by mass media of communication and mass patterns of production and consumption imposes new demands on school programs in each of these three areas. Every person must have a specialist's command of some area of knowledge to be vocationally competent and a generalist's knowledge of others to fulfill the demands of citizenship. Specialists and nonspecialists make different demands on the same knowledge base. Specialists need to master the rigorous application of knowledge to the field of practical or professional problems with which they deal. Nonspecialists have to learn to construct and use relatively simple but powerful cognitive and valuative maps so that they can bring what knowledge they have to bear on the problems they face. Only occasionally does a person need to use an item of knowledge in exactly the way it was learned. More often, the item must be transformed in order to be applied to a new and unfamiliar situation. This transformation involves both cognitive interpretation and a valuative orientation.

To realize this conception for all students the authors propose a program with the following components:

Symbolics of information (languages and mathematics)
Basic sciences
Developmental studies (evolution of the cosmos, of social institutions, and
   of culture)
Exemplars (the arts)
Molar problems (typical social problems)   (Broudy, Smith, and Burnett
   1963, 247)

Each of these areas should be studied by every student but to varying depth and in varying ways, depending on whether that student wants and needs a specialist's or generalist's knowledge of that area. The authors recommend that the secondary school not be divided into grades to be completed one year at a time, but that students be free to proceed at their own pace through the studies offered. Work within each component should progress in complexity, with each component having, they suggest, about five levels from the introductory level to the most sophisticated. Thus every student will be provided with a common program of general education.

Observations on Contemporary Curriculum Writing in the Mainline Tradition

The pioneering curriculum theorists of the progressive era believed that they could reason their way to, if not an ideal curriculum, at least a better one. They created many promising plans based on a variety of ideas and perspectives, but in the end, all these theories were found to be limited, if not actually faulty. As each new theory joined the others in the modest status of an interesting perspective, professional students of curriculum gradually lost faith in the power of theory to give definitive answers to curriculum problems. The experience of the pioneers chastened the next generation. Curriculum theory of this original sort, theory that sets out to discover the best curriculum and to show that it is the best, is more commonly written by nonprofessionals today. Professional students of the curriculum more often write theoretical pieces that take other forms, generally with a more limited and practical purpose. Theorizing in the grand manner seems more and more out of place in the writings of professional curriculum specialists.

OTHER FORMS OF CONTEMPORARY CURRICULUM THOUGHT

Methods for Curriculum Development

Contemporary theories in the mainline tradition still have as their primary purpose the rational grounding or justification of some curricular course of action. Another type of theory approaches the same problems less directly, by proposing

Ralph Tyler, 1902

and rationally justifying methods or procedures for arriving at a course of action, rather than the course of action itself. The first work clearly in this vein was Franklin Bobbitt's *How to Make a Curriculum* (1919). Bobbitt was a champion of scientific management and a practitioner of time-and-motion study. His method was essentially an extension to education of the methods the new efficiency experts were applying to business and industry. However, the classic work in this tradition is Ralph Tyler's *Basic Principles of Curriculum and Instruction*.

The Tyler Rationale

Ralph Tyler has had as much influence on the thought and practice of twentieth-century American education as any other individual, with the possible exception of John Dewey. A substantial part of his influence in curriculum matters is traceable to a slight monograph published as a syllabus for Education 360—Basic Principles of Curriculum and Instruction—at the University of Chicago. Tyler refers to it as a "rationale" and says "it is not a manual for curriculum construction since it does not describe and outline in detail the steps to be taken by a given school or college that seeks to build a curriculum" (Tyler 1950, 1). Rather, he says, it outlines a way of viewing the program of an educational institution. Although they may be loosely and flexibly described, Tyler's recommendations can only be interpreted as procedures to be followed in curriculum-making and they have, indeed, been quite widely used in this way.

Tyler organizes his rationale around four fundamental questions that he says must be answered in developing any curriculum.

1. What educational purposes should the school seek to attain?
2. What educational experiences can be provided that are likely to attain these purposes?
3. How can these educational experiences be effectively organized?
4. How can we determine whether these purposes are being attained? (Tyler 1950, 1–2)

One chapter is then devoted to each of these questions, with an additional brief closing chapter on how the rationale could be used by schools or colleges in curriculum building.

Unlike the curriculum theorists we have so far considered, Tyler does not himself suggest what purposes the school should seek to attain. Rather, he suggests that each school should determine its own purposes. He recommends that those involved in the determination of purposes seek guidance from objective studies relevant to the local situation—studies of the student as a learner, studies of contemporary life outside the school, and studies of the various subjects. Suggestions derived from these inquiries should then be screened and reduced to a smaller number of "consistent, highly important objectives."

Tyler proposes that a school develop a statement of educational philosophy and that the school's philosophy should then be used as a set of standards to screen the objectives in order to ensure that each is in harmony with the school's philosophy. He suggests that what is known about the psychology of learning provides another screen, enabling us to determine what can be learned and what cannot, which goals are practicable for schools and which take too long or cannot be attained by students at that age level, and so on. Since learning theories sometimes differ among themselves, a school may need to select its psychology of learning to harmonize with its philosophy. Finally, when objectives have been determined, they should be stated in such a way that they specify precisely and unambiguously just what is supposed to be learned. Objectives should specify the changes to be brought about in the student specifically enough to provide a way to judge through evaluation whether the student has really attained the objectives.

Once objectives have been stated, it becomes possible to determine which sorts of learning experiences might lead to the attainment of these objectives. Tyler suggests that this process is a creative one in which the teacher "begins to form in his mind a series of possibilities of things that might be done" (Tyler 1950, 53). These possibilities are written down, elaborated on, and then checked against the objectives to see whether they give students the opportunity to acquire the behavior stated in the objective. They can also be checked to determine if they are likely to lead to the effect for which they are intended. And they should be screened for economy. Those experiences that meet these tests are ready for the next step—organization.

If learning experiences are to produce a cumulative and growing impact on students, they must be organized so that experiences in one class or subject are in harmony with experiences in others, and so that experiences from month-to-month and from year-to-year result in steady growth. Important objectives need to be addressed time and time again in different ways, so that they are learned thoroughly—the principle of continuity. Successive learning experiences should build on one another, taking the student more deeply into the subject each time—the principle of sequence. And the various learning experiences the student encounters in school ought to be coherently and constructively related to one another—the principle of integration. An education is more than a collection of unrelated skills and knowledge.

Tyler recommends that curriculum developers select a type of organizing element appropriate to their task and then use each element to build continuity, sequence, and integration into the curriculum. For example, he suggests that concepts and skills have been important types of organizing elements in mathematics. Social studies curricula often include values as well as concepts and skills among their organizing elements. On a larger scale, the entire school program needs an organizing structure. In secondary schools the organizing structure is usually subject matter fitted into a daily schedule of courses. In elementary schools the organizing structure is often more flexible, sometimes nongraded, usually under the immediate direction of a teacher or team who is free to schedule the days and weeks of the year as they see fit within broad limits. Each school should decide on an organizing structure that suits it best.

Evaluation is a process for determining whether the curriculum is achieving the desired results. Through evaluation the assumptions and hypotheses on which the program has been built are checked, as well as the efficacy of the particular means chosen to put the program into effect. Evaluation involves an appraisal of the students' actual behavior. Furthermore, it requires an appraisal at several times to secure evidence on the permanence of the learning. A variety of methods may be used—tests, work samples, questionnaires, records, and so on. Sampling is a technique for reducing the quantity of information that must be obtained in evaluation without unduly limiting the conclusions we may draw from the evaluation. Evaluation instruments should be tailored to the school's objectives. The instruments should be objective, in the sense that different individuals administering a given instrument to the same students should receive the same results. Results of evaluations should be used to indicate strengths and weaknesses in the school program and to plan for revision.

Clearly, Tyler's rationale concentrates on the *how* of curriculum making, not the *what* of the curriculum itself. Tyler assumes that curricula will vary from one school to another and, indeed, that they should vary. The curriculum that is good for a school in rural Illinois may not be good for a school in New York city. What can be and should be somewhat the same are the methods followed to arrive at the curriculum in each case.

Paulo Freire's Method for Curriculum Development

Paulo Freire is a Brazilian educator who developed a method for teaching illiterate adults in the backward Northeastern region of Brazil. In 1964 he was forced to leave Brazil because his work was considered subversive. His book, *Pedagogy of the Oppressed* (1970), presents his political and philosophical ideas as well as the pedagogical practices he has developed. Here we shall be concerned mainly with the method he describes for developing a curriculum whose main purpose is to stimulate and sustain critical consciousness.

Freire's fundamental concern is the domination of poor, powerless, and ignorant people by wealthy, powerful, and sophisticated ones. The struggle of these people for liberation from their oppressors Freire sees as the fundamental theme of our epoch. An oppressive construction of social reality is imposed by the dominant groups on the oppressed, making it impossible for them even to perceive and assess their situation. This version of social reality is inculcated through words, images, customs, myths, popular culture, and in countless other obvious and not-so-obvious ways. The oppressed accept this version of social reality as truth and are psychologically devastated by it. They come to think of themselves as worthless, helpless, and inferior. They therefore acquire the personality traits (fatalism, self-depreciation, and emotional dependence) characteristic of oppressed people.

The primary task of education is to overcome these attitudes and replace them with traits of active freedom and responsibility. This cannot be done by treating the oppressed as *objects* to be transformed by the educator. Rather, they must be treated as *subjects,* as active human agents to be led and guided toward their own liberation. They must be awakened to see themselves as people "engaged in the ontological and historical vocation of becoming more fully human" (Freire 1970, 52). This is to be accomplished through dialogue. The task of the educator is "posing of the problems of men in their relations with the world" (Freire 1970, 66). The students and their teachers must become collaborators, coinvestigators developing together their consciousness of reality and their images of a possibly better reality. This ability to perceive the world critically, even in the midst of pervasive, powerful, subtle forces tending to distort and oppress, is critical consciousness.

So how does one develop a curriculum to foster critical consciousness? Freire proposes that a team of educators work with the people of a given locality to develop *generative themes* based on and taken from the ways of life found in that place. First, the team members meet with representatives of the people who are to be educated to discuss their plans and to secure their permission and cooperation. Members of the team visit the locality and observe how the people live—how they behave at home, at work, at church, at play; the language they use; their postures; their dress; their relationships. Observers look for anything and everything that indicates how the people construe their situation.

Preliminary findings of these local investigations are presented in a series of evaluation meetings held in the locality, involving members of the team and volunteers from the community. As an observer reports on an incident, the group discusses various ways this incident might be interpreted, ways it might be related to other aspects of people's lives. From these discussions emerge the contradictions that, if clearly perceived, would reveal to the people their oppressed state. These become the initial themes to be used in discussion and in literacy training for these people.

The investigators, having identified the themes and collected specific materials from the local community related to them, then return to the community to present them to the people to be educated in a series of "thematic investigation circles." In these meetings, the people discuss the concrete materials presented to them. The coordinator of the team elicits views and challenges speakers to reflect on the relationship of their views to those of others. Freire uses the example of alcoholism. Instead of railing against drinking, participants are encouraged to express their views about specific incidents. In the course of discussion, comments are made that reveal dimly perceived relationships with other matters. "He's got to do something to blow off steam" leads to acknowledgement of stresses centered around work—no job security, low wages, feelings of exploitation.

Based on the work of the thematic investigation circles, an interdisciplinary team of psychologists, sociologists, educators, as well as nonprofessional volunteers identifies the generative themes to be used in the actual instruction and develops concrete materials—readings, tapes, visuals, and so on—related to each theme that can be used by the teachers who will work in the next phase, "culture circles."

These concrete materials are presented to the culture circles as a focus for discussion. Sometimes these are dramatized. Always they are presented as problems, not as answers. Thus the people's own lives are reflected back to them, but this time in ways that encourage critical awareness of their situation, not passive acceptance of an oppressive interpretation.

ANALYTIC TOOLS

Not all theories that emphasize methods develop a comprehensive procedure for all aspects of curriculum development. Some create a set of analytic tools that help with some part of the curriculum development task. Below are two examples.

A Typology of the Uses of Schooling

In their book, *Democracy and Excellence in American Secondary Education*, Broudy, Smith, and Burnett develop a set of four "uses of knowledge": replicative, associative, applicative, and interpretive. This typology offers a powerful analytic tool for examining what is taught in a curriculum. Simply listing the topics covered does not reveal whether the material has been memorized and can only be recalled verbatim or whether it has been learned in a way that enables students to solve unfamiliar problems by applying what they have learned in a flexible way.

Knowledge is used replicatively when students merely repeat it in the form in which they learned it. Reciting a list of French equivalents of English words is a replicative use. Knowledge is used associatively when we connect it with other things we already know, so that mention of one thing calls to mind the others. Hearing a news report of a *"coup,"* the student of French may be reminded of the phrase *"coup d'etat"* and its French signification. Such an association requires going beyond the original form in which the material was first learned, but not very far beyond.

In applicative uses of knowledge students apply what they have learned in a new context, that is, they recognize that the basic principle applies to a new situation and proceed to apply it to analyze or to solve the new problem. Listening to a radio broadcast in French involves such applicative uses of the language because the broadcast may use words or phrases in new and unfamiliar ways that require students to extend what they have learned. Knowledge is used interpretively when it colors our modes of experiencing, when it influences the way we perceive, think, and feel. For some students, learning French helps them to experience the world in subtly but importantly different ways. The student learns that there are other ways of greeting people, of expressing such basic facts as one's degree of comfort with the temperature, of projecting masculinity and femininity into one's world, and generally that there are other ways of interpreting the world through language.

Each of these uses of knowledge is legitimate, indeed, necessary. The nonspecialist most often needs to use knowledge interpretively and associatively. The specialist also needs to use it applicatively and sometimes replicatively. Unfortunately, replicative uses are all too often the main focus of school work. A good curriculum should permit students to practice all these uses for their knowledge.

A TAXONOMY OF EDUCATIONAL OBJECTIVES

Professor Benjamin Bloom and his co-workers developed *A Taxonomy of Educational Objectives: Handbook I: The Cognitive Domain* (1956) to help developers and evaluators to distinguish the cognitive level of educational objectives. A criticism frequently made of the use of behavioral objectives is that the objectives are too elementary and require too little thought. The authors concede that this is in fact a problem. Objectives to "Name this" or "Select the one that . . ." or "Define that" all too often call for the student simply to recall an isolated fact. Yet writing more sophisticated objectives is a difficult skill. Bloom's Taxonomy is a tool intended to make this job easier and to foster greater use of higher-order objectives.

A Taxonomy of Educational Objectives is arranged in six main levels. Each level is assumed to involve responses that are more complex and abstract than the levels that follow. The first level, knowledge, includes objectives that call for straightforward recall from memory of facts, methods, or patterns. The second level, comprehension, requires the student to relate two or more items of knowledge so as to make sense of the whole. Some of the types of mental operations that fall into this category are translation, interpretation, and extrapolation. The typical comprehension objective requires a paraphrase of a passage or asks questions not directly answered in the passage but inferable from it.

The third level is application. It requires students to apply some concept or principle to a new and unfamiliar situation. Since the item to be applied must be remembered and since the student must understand the new context to which it is being applied, application generally involves both earlier levels. The fourth level is analysis and the fifth level is synthesis. Respectively, they cover objectives in which students must logically break down a complex into its constituents or build it up from those constituents. The complexes may be arguments, theories, or other works. The sixth and highest level is evaluation. It consists of objectives that call for qualitative or quantitative judgments about the extent to which given complex entities satisfy appropriate criteria.

A *Taxonomy*, along with its companions in the affective and psychomotor domains, can be used to analyze a curriculum to determine whether all the various levels are represented in appropriate proportions. It can also be used in development to plan for an appropriate balance, in implementation to determine whether the balance is being preserved in the field, and in evaluation to develop an appropriate bank of test items.

METATHEORY

When any activity reaches a certain level of development and of historical continuity, its practitioners become conscious of working within a tradition and begin to examine that tradition. This self-conscious examination of the field extends beyond distant historical figures to include one's peers presently at work, one's own work, the tools and procedures one uses, and so on. In the case of theory, one result of this self-examination is metatheory—*theory about theory*. The metatheorist asks such questions as: What are the important outstanding problems in this field? What methods are available to address these problems? What are the fundamental concepts in terms of which the phenomena of the field can be best understood? How should the field be organized to address its problems most effectively?

Dwayne Huebner: The Tasks of the Curriculum Theorist

Dwayne Huebner is an example of a contemporary metatheorist. He observes that confusion is widespread about exactly what curriculum theory is, but he believes that "the possibilities of being led astray are increased" by efforts to begin with a definition of theory (Huebner 1975). Instead, he believes one should begin with an analysis of the three types of activities in which theory is used: practice, research, and language (writing and talking).

Huebner notes that curriculum talk and writing contain a diversity of types of language. He distinguishes six: descriptive, explanatory, controlling, legitimating, prescriptive, and affiliative. "One of the tasks of the curricular theorist is to articulate the uses of language within the curricular domain, and to . . . critique the language forms used in curricular discourse" (Huebner 1975, 256–257). He remarks that "curricularists have drawn freely from philosophy, theology, psychology, and other behavioral sciences, sometimes various humanities and technologies and often the commonsense language of nondisciplined people" and recommends "a historical search for our language sources" so that we may be more aware of the subtler implications of the words we use. "Another task of the curricular theorist is to articulate the history of the languages used by curricularists" (Huebner 1975, 257–259).

The practice of curriculum is concerned with the creation and maintenance of an educative environment, a material environment as well as an environment of symbols and an environment of human resources. Huebner maintains that one of the tasks of the curricular theorist is to focus his attention on the characteristics of the educative environment, which involves the development of a descriptive language for this purpose and the study of the history of our attempts to create such environments. Curricular theorists should create conceptual systems that will articulate the intricacies of the human relationships and human interactions possible and desirable in education.

In research, the theorist works to uncover new phenomena and to create new forms of language. Research is essential for the continued revitalization of curricular practices and institutions.

In summary, the theorist should help us to be aware of the history of the man-made forms we use in curriculum practices, research, and discourse, to subject them to criticism and thereby help us improve them. "All educators attempt to shape the world; theorists should call attention to the tools used for the shaping in order that the world being shaped can be more beautiful and just" (Huebner 1975, 269).

CURRICULUM CRITICISM

Curriculum criticism considers and weighs the merits of some given set of proposals or ideas from some point of view. Sometimes recommendations for improvement emerge from criticism, making it a kind of amendment to the theory being criticized, if the changes required are minor, or a substitute proposal if the changes are major. Other criticisms lead to the conclusion that the original program or theory should be abandoned altogether, never mind that the critic has not proposed a viable alternative. Thus criticism is in one sense easier than theory in the mainline tradition. It is reactive rather than originative, but it is, nevertheless, important; it reminds us of places where improvements are needed and it indicates directions we might explore to improve theory and practice.

In curriculum criticism writers strive to make us aware of significant features of a curriculum and to appraise their value. Curriculum criticism became a self-consciously identified genre in the 1960s. The widely read criticisms of schools by talented writers such as Paul Goodman in *Compulsory Miseducation* (1964) and John Holt in *How Children Fail* (1966) were influential models, but curriculum critics also draw on various scholarly traditions. Elliot Eisner (1982) and Elizabeth Vallance (1977) take art criticism as a model for their curriculum criticism. Maxine Greene (1988) and Madeline Grumet (1988) use the language and methods literary criticism. Michael Apple (1979) follows in the tradition of social criticism. William Pinar (1974) seeks to understand the personal feelings and perspectives of students and teachers much as clinical psychologists do.

Kliebard's Critique of the Tyler Rationale

Professor Herbert Kliebard's (1970) critique of the famous and influential Tyler rationale summarized earlier in this chapter offers an excellent illustration of the form of curricular criticism that has become a staple of curriculum thought since the early 1960s. Kliebard draws the concepts and methods he uses from many humanistic disciplines. For example, he uses historical scholarship to show that Tyler erroneously characterizes the Committee of Ten Report as recommending a program for the college bound. Kliebard notes that the Committee specifically stated that it proposed one program for all secondary school students regardless of their likely future careers. He suggests that Tyler's misunderstanding of the Committee's position reveals a bias against subjects as ends in themselves and in favor of content with social or personal relevance.

Kliebard's criticism of Tyler's use of the concept of needs to justify selection of objectives draws on philosophical analyses of the concept that show that appeal to need is a way of seeming to provide factual grounding for what is essentially and necessarily a value judgment. To claim that a survey of student reading habits that reveals a high proportion of comic books shows a *need* for developing broader and deeper reading interests is simply a way of cloaking a value judgment about different types of reading matter in the appearance of scientific objectivity. He also draws on philosophy in criticizing Tyler's notion that a philosophy of education can be used as a screen for choosing among objectives generated by studies of various kinds. This amounts, Kliebard argues, to nothing more than the statement that ultimately one must choose in light of one's values, an obvious, nearly vacuous truism.

Much of Kliebard's critique relies on his knowledge of curriculum theory and his experience with curriculum problems. For example, he asks how learning experiences can be "selected," as Tyler's rationale requires, when the student's experience is a unique and not wholly predictable *interaction* with the environment provided by the teacher. Kliebard also questions the wisdom of an evaluation that merely checks on the attainment of previously stated objectives. He quotes John Dewey's claim that the aim of an action is not necessarily even the most important of its consequences.

Having pointed out so many flaws, Kliebard is left with a responsibility to explain how the Tyler rationale has exerted so great an influence on American curricular thought and practice. Kliebard suggests that its success is due to the moderation and wisdom Tyler has shown in applying the ideas and to the way the ideas themselves "skirt the pitfalls to which the doctrinaire are subject" and strike "compromises between warring extremes. . . . It is an eminently reasonable framework for developing a curriculum," but it is "not *the* universal model of curriculum development," and a new model is "long overdue" (Kliebard 1970, 270).

Michael Apple: A Neomarxist Critique of Modern Schooling

Michael Apple (1979) is concerned with the role of schooling in reproducing the social order. According to Apple, the social order of the United States, like that of other capitalist countries, is dominated by the interests of capital, that is, of corporations and businesses. These dominant interests exert hegemony over individuals in the society through subtle but powerful mechanisms of domination in which the school plays an important part.

According to Apple, schooling functions to reproduce and maintain this unjust, inequitable, and inhumane distribution of power. It does this, in part, by purveying a selective version of history, of tradition, and of knowledge. A partial and biased set of facts is given as the complete, neutral, objective truth. Also, the structure of the school as an institution acts subtly to sustain control. The work is divided up and parcelled out in such a way as to discourage concerted inquiries into the fundamental forces at work. Teachers and students are busied with details, enmeshed in bureaucratic rules, and required to follow the dictates of plans and materials externally imposed on them. Students with an inclination to question or challenge their role and status within the school are subjected to disciplinary action.

Apple argues that knowledge is a form of cultural capital. The school legitimizes certain kinds of knowledge by including them in the formal curriculum. By defining the knowledge everyone is expected to have, schools confer special status on items of knowledge important to dominant interests while denying such status to knowledge equally as important, or even more important, to other segments of the society. This explains why schools place higher value on science and technology than on the arts. In teaching history and social studies, harmony and consensus are emphasized and conflict minimized, thus conveying the impression of a society where people are basically content and happy. In this way school plays a pivotal role in the preservation of the cultural capital of the dominant cultural and economic forces.

Another important aspect of Apple's criticism is that the school controls through a hidden curriculum. In analyzing children's first school experiences in kindergarten, Apple notes that "the four most important skills that the [kindergarten] teacher expected the children to learn during those opening weeks were [not academic but social—] to share, to listen, to put things away, and to follow the classroom routine" (Apple 1979, 53). Children had no part in choosing their classroom activities. While attractive materials were present for play, the teacher's structuring of time and activities made them effectively unavailable. Such socialization training as this, although not considered by many a formal part of the curriculum, functions powerfully to produce attitudes and habits that sustain the currently dominant cultural and economic order.

Apple's curricular ideas spring from a commitment to a set of moral and political ideals, "a framework that continually seeks to be self-critical and places both one person's responsibility to treat another person ethically and justly and the search for a set of economic and cultural institutions that make such collective responsibility possible at the center of its deliberations" (Apple 1979, 162).

Theory and research are therefore tools for exposing and thereby undermining the deceptive foundations of the prevailing order and for guiding the construction of a new one.

Curriculists must take an advocacy position on a number of critical fronts, both in and outside of education" (Apple 1979, 163). Apple suggests that these fronts should include students' rights, teachers' rights, and the rights of oppressed minorities. He urges those in curriculum work to stand back from the prevailing ideology and institutions and to work to better them through the education system.

EXPLANATORY CURRICULUM THEORY

The final type of contemporary curriculum theory we shall consider takes as its aim the explanation of curricular phenomena and their relationships with one another and with other phenomena. This type of theory is frankly academic and scholarly in orientation. Its practitioners do not attempt to resolve the curriculum problems people face in schools. Rather, they try to understand the elements and events that constitute a curriculum and how these are related to one another and to elements and events outside the curriculum. With such an understanding, presumably, it will be possible for others to design better curricula. However, it is also possible that a thorough understanding will disclose inherent limits to our ability to control curricular phenomena and to produce results we want. If so, we can at least avoid wasting our energy in fruitless efforts to do the impossible and turn instead to those matters where some success is possible.

Walter Ong: The Curriculum and Dominant Modes of Expression

Walter Ong's *Rhetoric, Romance, and Technology* (1971) consists of a series of historical essays that the author aptly labels "Studies in the Interaction of Expression and Culture." Ong sees mastery of the dominant medium of expression as an important determinant of power in any culture. Prior to the widespread introduction of print, Western cultures were based on oral traditions and speech was the dominant medium of expression. During this time schools prepared their students to use this medium skillfully. They emphasized memorization, essential when written notes were time-consuming and could not always be consulted when the occasion for speaking arose. Schools taught mnemonic techniques—rhyming and metrical patterns, visualization strategies, fixed rhetorical forms. When students recited or wrote essays, they were taught to use "the commonplaces," lists of topics conventionally agreed to be relevant and important. (Our who-what-why-when-where-how questions are a holdover of the commonplace tradition.)

> Practice of one sort or another in the use of the commonplaces . . . helped form virtually all the poetry and other literature in the Western world from Homer through neoclassicism. This practice was a residue . . . of the oral heritage, which must place a premium on fixity. (Ong 1971, 264)

When printing became widespread it was no longer as necessary to insist on adherence to fixed literary forms. Both authors and readers could pause to reflect on a difficult passage or read it again—luxuries not provided by speech.

> Any culture knows only what it can recall. An oral culture, by and large, could recall only what was held in mnemonically serviceable formulas. In formulas thought lived and moved and had its being. (Ong 1971, 275)

But,

> When print locked information into exactly the same place upon the page in thousands of copies of the same book in type far more legible than any handwriting, knowledge came suddenly to the fingertips. With knowledge fastened down in visually processed space, man acquired an intellectual security never known before. . . . It was precisely at this point that romanticism could and did take hold. For man could face into the unknown with courage or at least equanimity as never before. (Ong 1971, 277–278)

Schooling changed under the influence of the newly dominant medium of print. Mass literacy became important. Textbooks and tests replaced the oral recitation. Memorization declined in importance. As public speaking and ability in debate had been crucial accomplishments in earlier days, reading and writing skills became vital to success in the new cultural milieu. Now, as electronic media rise in importance, still other abilities become important and schools are already undergoing changes necessary for them to help students acquire newly important skills.

Pierre Bourdieu: Schooling and Intellectual Culture

Pierre Bourdieu in "Systems of Education and Systems of Thought" (Young 1971) studies the mutual interaction of intellectual culture and schooling. On the one hand, the early experience of schooling profoundly shapes the mental skills and habits of those who later contribute the products of their creativity to the culture. On the other hand, the intellectual and cultural resources from which the school selects what it teaches and the value system which guides this choice are substantially governed by culture. In Bourdieu's words:

> The relationship which an intellectual maintains of necessity with the school and his educational past is a determining weight in the system of his most unconscious choices. Men formed by a certain school have in common a certain cast of mind. (Young 1971, 182–183)

> Whatever the form [of a society], a plurality of social forces almost always exists in all societies, sometimes in competition, sometimes co-ordinated, which by reason of their political or economic power or the institutional guarantees they dispose of, are in a position to impose their cultural norms on a larger or smaller area of the institutional field. (Young 1971, 174–175)

Within a given culture, say modern French culture, there are at any one time several schools of thought competing within a common intellectual style or system of thought. This encompassing common mindset is largely shaped by schooling. Bourdieu says "Every individual owes to the type of schooling he has received a set of basic, deeply interiorized master-patterns on the basis of which he subsequently acquires other patterns" (Young 1971, 174–175). "Specialized education, imparting specific types of knowledge . . . is liable to produce as many 'intellectual clans' as there are specialized schools" (Young 1971, 198). In particular, provision of different schools for children of an elite "separates those receiving it from the rest of society by a whole series of systematic differences" (Young 1971, 200).

On the other hand, commonalities in schooling enforce a national intellectual style. "To account for such traits as the fondness for abstraction or the cult of brilliance and distinguished performance that are commonly regarded as part of the 'intellectual make-up' of the French, we must surely relate them to the specific traditions of the French educational system" (Young 1971, 201). Bourdieu does precisely this, showing how specific events and trends in French history favored the control of French schooling by a classical literary elite, and favored forms of teaching that emphasized a good show delivered to a general audience rather than sustained instruction to specialized students. He contrasts these events and trends with German history, which favored a very different style of intellectual work.

Urban Dahllof: A Macromodel for the Curriculum Process

In the late 1960s, when *comprehensivization* was being urged for Sweden's traditionally ability-streamed secondary schools, Dahllof became concerned about the impact of ability grouping on academic achievement. After reviewing existing studies of ability grouping that found no statistically significant differences between achievement test results for students taught in mixed-ability classes and those taught in ability-grouped classes, Dahllof (1971) looked in more detail at the processes actually at work in the classrooms to see if he could get a clearer view of the results. He reanalyzed the data from three studies. He began by sorting items from the achievement tests into categories corresponding to the units of the curriculum. He found fewer test items for units occurring late in the year, which meant that this curriculum content was weighted less heavily in the findings of no significant differences in achievement. He discovered that high ability classes spent less time on nearly all units than classes of mixed ability; hence high ability students were at least moving more slowly through the material in mixed-ability classes than their counterparts in ability-grouped classes. And the data showed modest positive correlations—from .09 to .50 in six comparisons—between classroom time actually spent on a unit and achievement on that unit for students in high-ability classes. Apparently, the reason for the findings was that high ability youngsters in mixed-ability classes were making slightly higher scores on the many items covering units appearing early in the course, while their counterparts in ability grouped classes were covering more units but gaining only a few points on test scores because these units were underrepresented among the test items.

These investigations led Dahllof to construct his "Outline of a Macromodel for the Curriculum Process." The central idea of the macromodel is that, other things being equal, the scores of a group of students on an achievement test that covers material they were taught is a function of 1) the group's general intelligence and initial achievement, 2) whether the objective was advanced or elementary, and 3) the time students actually spend studying the material. In traditional classroom instruction, the method of grouping youngsters determines the value of the first variable in Dahllof's model. The other two variables are determined by the teacher, in principle, but in fact are also affected by a variety of factors in the school environment that define and constrain the work of students and teachers, such as the school schedule, course syllabi, class size, length of school year, and so on. Dahllof called these variables *frame factors.*

Acting within these frames, the teacher controlled time allotments of students to different curriculum units and the level of objective that would be sought and expected. Dahllof theorized that teachers set the pace of a class's progress through the course material, depending on the performance of some subset of the class. He guessed this subset would be students achieving below the average. He called this group the *criterion steering group*. If students in the criterion steering group seemed ready to move on to the next unit, the teacher would move on. In high-ability classes, of course, the steering group would be able to move at a faster pace than in mixed-ability classes where students in the criterion steering group would have lower absolute ability.

Dahllof's model generates testable hypotheses about the curricular determinants of achievement. He does not advocate either ability-grouped or mixed-ability classes, but suggests principles that would help determine the trade-offs involved in the choice.

Summary

Today's writing about curriculum questions belongs to a tradition of serious thought about the purpose, content, and structure of education dating back to the dawn of Western civilization. These writings are a great conversation among some of the most seminal thinkers of every era. This work shows continuous historical development in response to changing social conditions and diverse values and perspectives. Many ideas treated as common sense today originated in one or another of these works, and many of today's proposals have their roots in them. We can understand today's and tomorrow's ideas and practices and their implications better if we are familiar with the originals. The brief summaries given here are absolutely no substitute for reading the original works, but they offer a foretaste that, I hope, will make you want to read them, and an overview that will enable you to guide your reading more intelligently. The continuing vitality of this body of work is remarkable testimony to continuing faith in the effort to bring the resources of the human mind to bear on curriculum problems.

QUESTIONS FOR STUDY

1. Make a diagram showing the similarities of the various theorists mentioned in the chapter. Put the names of the writers on small pieces of paper. Begin by placing any one writer in the center of a large blank page. Then choose a second writer at random and decide how compatible the second writer's work is with the first. Then, place a third writer in relation to *both* the other two. Proceed in this way until you have placed all or nearly all of the writers. Examine the clusters on your paper and give them simple labels. Reflect on why these clusters emerged from your classification of the writers. What do the clusters reveal about curriculum theory? About your own curriculum ideas and perspectives? Look at the writers who are central and those who are peripheral to various clusters and reflect on why they might occupy these

positions. When you have difficulty in placing some writers, reflect on what this might reveal.

2. Based on what you know now about curriculum thought, do you think it shows progress over time (the way the sciences and some scholarly fields such as logic or mathematics do) or does it circle around the same themes and issues in slightly different form down through the ages (as is characteristic of literature and the arts)? Give reasons for your answers and illustrate them by reference to material from the chapter.

3. What is the most appropriate element of curriculum theory: the idea, the written work, an individual author's body of work, the work of all authors belonging to a particular school of thought, or the sum total of writing on a particular topic by all authors? Give reasons for your answer.

4. Some maintain that all thought must rely on *some* theory, however scant or incoherent. Therefore, any writing that urges people to offer this or that kind of curriculum must rely, explicitly or implicitly, on some form of curriculum theory. Do you think this view is correct? Give reasons for your answer. If you answer affirmatively, illustrate your conclusion by identifying the theory in a brief statement (one page or less) on curriculum clipped from a newspaper or magazine. If you answer negatively, explain where the ideas come from and what relation they bear to ideas found in curriculum theory, illustrating your conclusions with reference to a brief extract of curriculum writing.

5. Why do you think some works of theory are generally regarded as more important than others? Is it because of the intrinsic qualities of the works or does it reflect the fit between the works and our shared values, or is there some other reason?

6. Curriculum theory often makes extensive use of concepts and terms borrowed from other fields of study. For example, conceptions of the child, and of learning from psychology; concepts of knowledge, and ethical principles from philosophy; and concepts of society, and culture from the social sciences. This is so characteristic of all educational thought that educational writers and philosophies are often studied as instances of some philosophical tendency of thought. Plato's ideas are said to reflect idealism, Rousseau's to reflect romanticism, Dewey's pragmatism, and so on. Based on what you read in this chapter, do you think curriculum theory borrows a great deal from other fields of thought? Do you think this intellectual borrowing is good or bad? Do theorists have a choice about using ideas drawn from other fields? Do you think labelling an author with the name of a school of thought helps (or could help) people understand it better? If so, how? If not, why not and why are such labels used so often?

7. Consult a journal that regularly publishes works of curriculum theory. (See Recommended Reading at the back of this chapter for some journal titles.)

Read an article on a topic in curriculum that appeals to you. Is it a work of curriculum theory? Explain how you decided. If it is, into which of the streams of contemporary curriculum work does it fit best? If it is not, explain whether the author's purpose in the article could have been achieved by using one of the forms of theory, showing how or showing why not.

8. Examine the quotations presenting progressive and traditional views in Boxes 3-1 and 3-2. For each pair of statements, identify the difference in fundamental values that most separates the two positions.

9. Study closely the language used in Boxes 3-1 and 3-2. For instance, look at the use of active and passive voice, abstract and concrete terms, colloquial and formal tone, and resort to dramatic and figurative expressions. Identify those features of language that seem to separate the two orientations most clearly. Does analysis of the language provoke any insights about the two orientations and those who gravitate toward them?

RECOMMENDED READING

All of the works mentioned in the text of this chapter are highly recommended reading for those who wish to learn more about curriculum thought. Each will amply repay the time and effort needed. Readers who want the quickest, simplest introduction to all the main traditions of curriculum theory would do well to proceed chronologically, beginning with Robert Ulich's marvelous *Three Thousand Years of Educational Wisdom* (1947) and supplementing this with any good translation of Plato's *Republic,* Aristotle's *Politics,* and Rousseau's *Émile.* The Twenty-sixth Yearbook of the National Society for the Study of Education, Part II (Rugg 1927) is an excellent single volume introduction to some of the best and worst of the progressive/traditional debate in curriculum. Unfortunately, it is out of print and available only in college and university libraries with good collections of historically important material in education. Reginald Archambault's *John Dewey on Education* (1964) is a good brief introduction to Dewey's thought. Dewey's *Experience and Education* (1938), *School and Society* (1900), and *The Child and the Curriculum* (1902) are recommended. Convenient sources of contemporary curriculum theory are harder to find. From time to time edited books of readings on curriculum are published that capture some movements of thought conveniently between two covers. For example, Bellack and Kliebard's *Curriculum and Evaluation* (1977) gives a good overview of writing in the 1960s and 1970s. Generally, however, it is necessary to read the originals. I have tried in this chapter to say enough about many contemporary authors doing outstanding work in curriculum theory to enable the reader to select individuals for study.

Readers who wish to pursue curriculum theory to greater depth should choose a topic, an author or, better, a group of authors working in compatible ways, and make an intensive study of the pertinent writings. Harold Dunkel's (1965) small book, *Whitehead on Education* sets an excellent standard for studying an author's body of writing. Intensive study of a small corner of the literature is much more educative for one who wants to become a connoisseur, critic, or author of curriculum theory than wide but superficial reading. The following topics have been lively ones in curriculum theorizing in recent years. I have indicated for each topic a work that I would recommend as a starting point: the hidden or implicit curriculum (Vallance 1977), feminist perspectives on curriculum issues (Noddings 1985), the arts and aesthetic perspectives on curriculum (Eisner 1982), neo-Marxist criticism of American education (Apple 1982), the place of teachers in curriculum decision-making (Clandinin 1988), and theoretical analyses of historical trends and developments (Goodson 1987). Leafing through recent issues of *Curriculum Inquiry, Journal of Curriculum Studies, Journal of Curriculum and Supervision, Educational Theory, Teachers College Record, American Education,* and *Harvard Educational Review* (be sure to look at book reviews) is an excellent way to get a quick picture of recent work in curriculum theory.

Because the topics and works are so specialized, it is rare to find courses on them. Students should regard courses that offer an opportunity for intensive study of an author or topic in curriculum under the guidance of a good teacher to be an extraordinary opportunity.

REFERENCES

Apple, Michael W. 1979. *Ideology and Curriculum.* London: Routledge and Kegan Paul.

Apple, Michael W. 1982. *Cultural and Economic Reproduction in Education.* London: Routledge and Kegan Paul.

Archambault, Reginald D. 1964. *John Dewey on Education.* N.Y.: Modern Library.

Bantock, G. H. 1968. *Culture, Industrialization, and Education.* London: Routledge and Kegan Paul.

Bantock, G. H. 1980. *Dilemmas of the Curriculum.* N.Y.: Halsted Press.

Beard, Charles. Feb. 29, 1936. The Scholar in an Age of Conflicts. *School and Society* 43: 278–279.

Bellack, Arno, and Herbert Kliebard (eds.). 1977. *Curriculum and Evaluation.* Berkeley, CA: McCutchan Publishing Corporation.

Bloom, Benjamin S. (ed.). 1956. *Taxonomy of Educational Objectives: The Classification of Educational Goals, Handbook 1: Cognitive Domain.* N.Y.: McKay.

Bobbitt, Franklin. 1918. *The Curriculum.* Boston: Houghton Mifflin.

Bobbitt, Franklin. 1924. *How to Make a Curriculum.* Boston: Houghton Mifflin.

Bode, Boyd H. 1927. *Modern Educational Theories.* N.Y.: Macmillan.

Broudy, Harry S., B. Othanel Smith, and Joe R. Burnett. 1963. *Democracy and Excellence in American Secondary Education.* Chicago: Rand McNally.

Charters, William W. 1923. *Curriculum Construction.* N.Y. The Macmillan Co.

Clandinin, Jean. 1988. *Teachers as Curriculum Planners.* N.Y.: Teachers College Press.

Committee on the Reorganization of Secondary Education. 1918. *Cardinal Principles of Secondary Education.* Washington, D.C.: Government Printing Office.

Counts, George S. 1926. *The Senior High School Curriculum.* Chicago: University of Chicago Press.

Counts, George S. 1932. *Dare the School Build a New Social Order?* N.Y.: The John Day Co.

Dahllof, Urban. 1971. *Ability Grouping, Content Validity, and Curriculum Process Analysis.* N.Y.: Teachers College Press.

Dewey, John. 1900. *The School and Society.* Chicago: University of Chicago Press.

Dewey, John. 1902. *The Child and the Curriculum.* Chicago: University of Chicago Press.

Dewey, John. 1916. *Democracy and Education.* N.Y.: Macmillan.

Dewey, John. 1938. *Experience and Education.* N.Y.: Macmillan.

Dunkel, Harold. 1965. *Whitehead on Education.* Columbus: Ohio University Press.

Eisner, Elliot. 1982. *The Educational Imagination* (2nd ed.). N.Y.: Macmillan.

Freire, Paolo. 1970. *Pedagogy of the Oppressed.* N.Y.: Herder and Herder.

Goodman, Paul. 1964. *Compulsory Mis-Education.* N.Y.: Horizon Press.

Goodson, Ivor. 1987. *The Making of Curriculum.* N.Y.: Falmer Press.

Greene, Maxine. 1988. *The Dialectic of Freedom.* N.Y.: Teachers College Press.

Grumet, Madeline. 1988. *Bitter Milk.* Amherst: University of Massachusetts Press.

Holt, John. 1966. *How Children Fail.* London: Pitman.

Hopkins, L. Thomas. 1929. *Curriculum Principles and Practices.* N.Y.: Benjamin H. Sanborn and Company.

Hopkins, L. Thomas. 1937. *Integration: Its Meaning and Application.* N.Y.: Appleton.

Hopkins, L. Thomas. 1938. *Pupil-Teacher Learning.* Wilmington: The Delaware Citizens Association.

Huebner, Dwayne. 1975. The Tasks of the Curriculum Theorist. *Curriculum Theorizing* (William Pinar, ed.). Berkeley: McCutchan.

Kilpatrick, William H. 1918. *The Project Method.* N.Y.: Teachers College Press.

Kilpatrick, William H. 1926. *Foundations of Method.* N.Y.: Macmillan.

Kilpatrick, William H. 1936. *Remaking the Curriculum.* N.Y.: Newson and Company.

Kliebard, Herbert M. Feb., 1970. The Tyler Rationale. *School Review* 78: 259–272.

Noddings, Nel. 1985. *A Feminine Approach to Ethics.* Stanford: Center for Research on Women.

Ong, Walter. 1971. *Rhetoric, Romance, and Technology.* Ithaca, N.Y.: Cornell University Press.

Pinar, William. 1974. *Heightened Consciousness, Cultural Revolution, and Curriculum Theory.* Berkeley: McCutchan.

Plato. *The Republic.* (Available in many translations.)

Rousseau, Jean Jacques. *Émile.* (Available in many translations.)

Rugg, Harold. 1927. *Foundations and Techniques of Curriculum-Making,* Twenty-sixth Yearbook of the National Society for the Study of Education, Parts I and II. Bloomington, IL: Public School Publishing.

Rugg, Harold, and Ann Shumaker. 1928. *The Child-Centered School.* N.Y.: World Book Company.

Rugg, Harold, G. Axtelle, Harold Caswell, and George S. Counts. 1936. *American Life and the School Curriculum: Next Steps Toward Schools of Living.* N.Y.: Ginn and Company.

Tyler, Ralph W. 1950. *Basic Principles of Curriculum and Instruction.* Chicago: University of Chicago Press.

Ulrich, Robert (ed.). 1947. *Three Thousand Years of Educational Wisdom.* Cambridge: Harvard University Press.

Vallance, Elizabeth. 1977. Hiding the Hidden Curriculum: The Language of Justification in the Nineteenth-Century Educational Reform. (In Bellack and Kliebard 1977, 590–607.)

Young, Michael F. D. (ed.). 1971. *Knowledge and Control.* London: Collier: Macmillan.

PART II
Theory and Practice

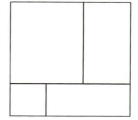

What comes over a man, is it soul or mind—
That to no limits and bounds he can stay confined?
 . . .
Why is his nature forever so hard to teach
That though there is no fixed line between wrong and right,
There are roughly zones whose laws must be obeyed?

Robert Frost
American poet, twentieth century

CURRICULUM THEORY

chapter 4

What is now proved was once only imagined.

William Blake
English poet, eighteenth century

PURPOSE OF THE CHAPTER

- to explain what curriculum theory is intended to accomplish
- to show how to make defensible judgments on the merits of curriculum theories, identifying strong and weak points
- to explore the potential and limitations of curriculum theory in improving curriculum practice
- to show how to read critically and analyze theoretical curricular discourse, identifying key arguments, assumptions, ideas, beliefs, and values

OUTLINE

The Project of Curriculum Theory: Practice Grounded in Ideas

A Definition of Curriculum Theory

Marks of Quality in a Curriculum Theory

***The Paideia Proposal:* A Curriculum Theory in Action**

Assessing the Quality of Adler's Theory

Reading Curriculum Theory

Reflections on the Value of Theory in Curriculum

THE PROJECT OF CURRICULUM THEORY: PRACTICE GROUNDED IN IDEAS

The distinct traditions of different fields of study have led to many different meanings for the term *theory*. In mathematics, a theory is a system of formal definitions and assumptions. In the natural sciences, a theory is a set of testable propositions. In the social sciences, although theories are not as precise or as complete, and therefore are not as testable, they also tend to have the form of scientific theories. In philosophy, by contrast, any systematic body of ideas on a subject may be termed a theory. In applied fields like law or business the term is used much more loosely to mean *an account of,* or *an interpretation of,* as in theory of the firm or a theory of liability. In everyday life we often speak loosely of theories as any set of competing explanations of a single event, as in newspaper discussions of different theories about the stock market crash of 1987.

The common aspect in these different definitions of theory is that a theory is a careful, systematic use of a well-defined set of ideas. In the previous chapter more than a dozen sets of ideas that qualify by this general definition of *theory* were sketched. We shall be concerned in this chapter, however, with a more specific meaning of the term. The type of curriculum theory that will concern us in this chapter is what was called in the previous chapter "the mainline tradition"—that is, theory that provides an intellectual foundation or grounding for practice. We will study one such theory intensively and comment on the general project of theory in curriculum in light of this example.

A DEFINITION OF CURRICULUM THEORY

A curriculum theory is a coherent and systematic body of ideas used to give meaning to curriculum phenomena and problems and to guide people in deciding on appropriate, justifiable actions.

We will speak of these uses for curriculum theory collectively as **grounding.** So, curriculum theory backs up curriculum practice; **theory conceptualizes practice and gives it meaning.** First, it names the problem and its elements, the factors related to and contributing to the problem, the resources available for handling the problem, and the positions and actions we might take in response to it. And these names are not just empty labels but part of an account, an image or model or story, or most generally, a conceptualization of the situation. Theory thus provides us with a way of viewing the matter, of thinking and talking about it, of relating it to the rest of our thinking. The conceptualization identifies some things as of greater significance than others and thus implicates values. Since the elements involved in curriculum theory—indeed, in education—are always infused with values, conceptualizations are inherently value laden. Theory helps to show how the various and variously valued elements are related to one another and to our value systems. We summarize all these contributions in the phrase *gives meaning to practice.*

Theory guides (or informs) practice. Secondly, theory includes substantive propositions about how the world works and should work that we can use to draw out implications about what we should do. What is our world like? How do children learn? Theory can suggest possible causes of problems and can point to constructive courses of action. In short, theory informs practice.

Theory justifies practice. Theory helps us to answer such questions as: "Why do you propose to do X?" "Why is curriculum A better than curriculum B?" and "What are the advantages and disadvantages of doing this about that curriculum problem?" Theory thus helps us to justify our decisions and actions when we are in doubt or when others challenge us.

We can find other ways to ground practice without the aid of theory. Custom and tradition can impart meaning, guide practice, and justify practice. Religion and the arts can do the same, as can feelings and emotions. Common sense and ordinary language can be used for these purposes. When we use theory, however, our practices rest on a coherent, systematic, explicit, examined, intellectually defensible set of ideas. The grand intellectual project of curriculum theory is to ground practice in ideas in the same sense that religious theory grounds morality in theology or the same sense that scientific theory grounds engineering practice.

The significance of the claim made on behalf of theory becomes clearer if we consider a counter-example, an instance where important curriculum issues are treated without the help of theory. James Conant's influential book, *The American High School Today* (1959) offers one such example. In the book Conant endorses the main outlines of the American comprehensive high school while proposing some significant modifications. The language is simple, plain, direct, and the perspective is that of the educated layman. In no passage does Conant get any closer to the use of theory than this:

> What are the arguments in favor of an academically talented student's electing a wide program of at least eighteen courses with homework? To my mind the most compelling argument is that the student in question has potentialities shared with only a relatively few contemporaries, probably not more than 15 percent of his age group. If these potentialities are not

developed as far as possible during the school years, they may never be fully developed. . . .

The loss to the individual from not electing a suitable program in high school is clear. So too is the loss to the nation. From the 15 percent of the youth who are academically talented will come the future professional men and women. These people ought to have as wide and solid an education as possible. It is in the national interest to have them develop their capacities to the full and to start this development as early as possible. . . . (Conant 1959, 59–60)

The critical terms in this argument—"potentialities," "loss to the individual," "loss to the nation," "wide," "solid," "develop their capacities to the full"—are assumed to have referents that are so clear and familiar as not to need elaboration or justification by theory.

Conant treats nearly every aspect of the curriculum of the American secondary school in just such terms. He never spells out his conception of American society, for example, and he does not claim that his proposals will help to realize some particular conception of the good life or the good society. He assumes that Americans generally know and agree about what a good education should be. He does not attempt to offer his own statement or to explain why we should prefer one conception of a good education to another. Instead, he offers narrowly practical justifications such as "it is in the national interest" and simple claims that the program he recommends will realize undefined goals we all want, such as "full development of capacities." In short, Conant's proposals are grounded in common sense, not in any coherent and systematic body of ideas. So theory is not the only way of addressing curriculum problems.

The set of ideas that make up a curriculum theory generally include ideas about the purpose, content, and structure of education, of course. These are needed to conceptualize curriculum problems and practices. But in what terms are these to be grounded? Curriculum theories have long been known to rely on four fundamental conceptual reference points, called the *commonplaces of curricular thought:* 1) the student; 2) the subject or what is to be learned; 3) the milieu in which education takes place (the environment, from the classroom to the entire society or culture); 4) the teacher or other educative agent, such as the textbook author, the school as an active institution, and so on (see Figure 4-1). Any set of ideas that gives meaning to, guides, and justifies curricular practice must make some reference, explicitly or implicitly, to some conception of each of these commonplaces. A curriculum theory, then, at least grounds practice in conceptions of these commonplaces, and possibly in an even wider range of considerations.

A completely successful curriculum theory would be able to show, for any proposed practice, whether that practice was or was not consistent with the theory. It would also explain why that practice was or was not a good idea. Any curriculum problem could be analyzed in terms of the theory, and the analysis

FIGURE 4-1

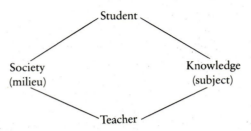

Four commonplaces of curricular discourse

would provide criteria for verifying that a proposed solution would in fact solve the problem. A successful theory would even provide hints that would help us find a solution. Of course, no curriculum theory is ever completely successful, but we are looking at the ideal.

The advantages of having a body of ideas that would serve all these functions would be immense. Every time a curriculum question arose, we would know where to turn to find the answer. Instead of puzzling or arguing over what to do about every curriculum problem that arose, we could puzzle and argue over more general issues of theory and, having settled a few theoretical issues, dispose of an infinity of potential problems of practice. Think of the confidence with which we could act if some curricular practices could be shown to be most consistent with the best available contemporary understandings, the most warranted findings of science and scholarship. We would then have a strong reason to adopt these practices. We would minimize our need for seers, pundits, or wizards, because the theory would be explicit and open to everyone's inspection. Genius might be required to apply it to difficult cases, but the results of genius could be checked by the merely competent. When all issues could be submitted to the bar of theory, we would have minimized our need to resort to arbitrary authority. If the theory was just, correct, and complete, we could be confident about all the practices grounded in it. In seeking to ground practice in theory it would seem that we aspire to maximize the role of mindfulness in decision and action. Such an ideal cannot be taken lightly.

The preceding remarks indicate criteria of form and intent that would qualify a set of ideas as curriculum theory. We have already seen in the previous chapter examples of ideas with this general form and intent, so we have candidates for the status of curriculum theory to examine. In fact, we have an embarrassment of riches in curriculum theories. There are so many varied and contrasting candidates that our greatest problem will be to determine whether any are good and, if so, which are better. So, before we study one example in detail, let us consider what the marks are of quality in a curriculum theory.

MARKS OF QUALITY IN A CURRICULUM THEORY

What characteristics should a theory have in order to perform its functions well? Correctness or validity is obviously desirable. Other generally acceptable marks of quality in a curriculum theory include the power to lead to interesting conclusions that are not obvious without the theory and that increase our ability to resolve important issues; serviceability in practice; and morality or consistency with standards of good or right conduct. Beyond these basic criteria, curriculum theories can be in good theoretical form, that is, good as theories, in a number of other ways. For instance, a more complete theory is better than a less complete one, all other things equal, and a briefer and simpler theory is preferable to a longer, more complicated one that accomplishes no more. We will consider each of these criteria in turn.

Validity

Validity or correctness in a theory has at least three components:

meaningfulness: Is it clear, unambiguous, well-defined?
logical consistency: Is it free of internal contradictions?
factual correctness: Is it consistent with everything else we know?

Meaningfulness as a Component of Validity   Meaningfulness is partly a matter of good written form, but primarily a question of adequacy of communication. A rough and ready standard is that if persons suitably qualified by training and experience agree on the meaning of the terms and propositions in a theory, then it is meaningful. To apply this standard we simply ask people what they understand the writing to mean or read what others have written about the theory to see if they agree on what it means. We may also observe what those who say they are using the theory do and why they say they do it. This standard is certainly fallible inasmuch as whole communities can be deceived—remember the story of the emperor's new clothes.

In making our own independent judgment of the meaningfulness of a theory, it is helpful to produce a glossary of key terms and a list of key propositions. If we have few doubts about the meaning of the terms, if they are clearly defined and then used consistently throughout, then the statement of the theory is at least formally adequate. We must then look at examples and instances cited to see if they fit the definition. We should invent our own examples to see if we can find borderline cases, unclear cases, cases covered under both of a supposedly mutually exclusive set of terms, and so on. Then look at the key propositions to verify that the terms are actually used consistently with their definitions.

All too often the key terms in a curriculum theory are glittering abstractions like *social adjustment* and *high-grade living* that are not defined or defined so loosely that we can fill them with whatever good things we wish. Each of us may have in mind examples that make propositions expressed in terms of glittering abstractions meaningful to us individually, but when we compare notes we may find that the theory means very different things to us. Such concepts, therefore, give us the illusion of understanding. For example, the definition of the term *needs* is generally accepted as being self-evident. Adequate nutrition, exercise, and rest are clearly physiological needs. When it comes to needs that can be satisfied through education, though, virtually anything anybody wants to teach has been claimed to meet students' needs.

Some observers want to make curricular definitions more rigorous and scientific by insisting that key terms be defined operationally. An operational definition of a concept specifies the procedures (operations) anyone would use to detect and measure any purported instance. We could, for example, define democracy in terms of observations we could make on an unknown society to determine if it was democratic, such as observing whether it had free and open elections; a one-person, one-vote system; and so on. It is now generally conceded among philosophers of science that the attempt to define all concepts operationally is self-defeating even to a purely scientific theory. Theory's power arises precisely because its central concepts can be measured in several ways and are robust enough to remain meaningful even when different measurement techniques are used. It is unclear whether all the terms one might want to include in a curriculum theory could, even in principle, be defined operationally. In particular, it is a puzzle how to define value laden terms—the good life, the good society, the worth of knowledge, the utility of knowledge, good citizenship, and the like. Meaning is at least as much a matter of values as a matter of fact in curriculum discourse. Still, we can always improve the meaningfulness of curriculum theories by showing how any particular instance qualifies under the terms of the theory.

Logical Consistency as a Component of Validity   To judge logical consistency we look at the key propositions of a theory in purely formal terms. One way to accomplish this is to give each key term in the theory a symbol. You will usually find that these terms take on three main forms, corresponding to parts of speech: 1) entities, corresponding to nouns; 2) events, corresponding to verbs; and 3) qualities, corresponding to adjectives and adverbs. It is often helpful to list key terms in three columns, one corresponding to each of these forms, and to represent each by a symbol. For example, you might write "the vocational proposal" to represent an elaborate plan the author proposes, or the word "academics" to represent an entire value system. Key propositions of the theory can then be expressed in terms of these primitive symbols. Formal representation of a theory in this way helps to clarify the logical relationships being asserted and may reveal gaps or inconsistencies in the theory.

Factual Correctness as a Component of Validity   The factual correctness of a theory can only be assessed by comparing its observable consequences with actual observations. You will remember that the essential logic of curriculum theory in use is to conclude that something should be done because some valued end would be furthered. The proposition that doing A furthers B is empirically testable, in principle, if A and B are meaningful and the relationship is logically coherent. The most powerful tests involve making observations specifically to test this proposition—in other words, an empirical study designed to test it. Sometimes it is also possible to test the factual correctness of the theory by inspecting existing records, either formal records of things like grades or enrollments or the record of history. Also, each of us can test the theory's consequences against our own experience. The following chapter includes examples of all these means of verifying the factual correctness of curriculum theories.

Theoretical Power

We speak of theories as more powerful when they make greater contributions to our understanding and to our ability to predict and control events. Powerful curriculum theories enable us to act effectively in a wide range of situations because we can deduce from them what are likely to be the consequences of acting in different ways. By contrast, weak theories yield few deductions and the few they yield do not advance us far beyond the point where common sense would have taken us anyway. As theories go, curriculum theories tend to be relatively weak. Humankind has not yet seen a curriculum theory that revolutionized practice to the extent, say, that the germ theory of disease revolutionized medicine, or Freud's theories revolutionized psychiatry, or Marx's theories revolutionized political economy. Curriculum theories offer the possibility of new perspectives and improved results, but not the prospect of scientific or philosophical breakthroughs —not yet anyway.

Serviceability

A theory both valid and powerful would still be of little use if it could not be applied under realistic conditions to help resolve the important curriculum problems people actually face. A curriculum theory of great serviceability helps us with the problems we actually face, under realistic conditions, in a timely and economical way.

Theories can fail to be serviceable for many reasons. One of the most common, surely, is that the theory requires conditions not attainable in practice. It was said of progressive education, for example, that it demanded too much knowledge, skill, and dedication from teachers. Critics wrote of the *impossible role* of the teacher in progressive education, who was expected to plan a unique classroom program tailored to that group of students, involving individual work for each student and joint work by the class as a group, who was responsive to daily shifts in mood and in events in and out of the classroom. Important aspects of serviceability include functionality, efficiency, economy, appeal, and relevance.

Morality

Those who would use a curriculum theory for its intended purpose cannot avoid, even if they want to, making judgments about the values it employs and the priorities it establishes. In fact, the influence of a valid, powerful, highly serviceable theory built on misguided values is to be feared greatly. Shallow, evanescent values will more likely be emphasized over deeper, more enduring ones. If there were a clear, prevailing set of moral standards, judging the morality of a curriculum theory would be no more difficult than judging its validity, power, and serviceability, but the evident diversity of moral standards found in contemporary society complicates any application of this criterion. Most Americans acquire their moral standards in their family and religious groups, and these are enormously diverse. Yet public education is secular and universalistic. Our public life upholds certain political and legal standards common to all, but not common social mores and religious beliefs.

Consequently, books that are classics to some are immoral in the eyes of others (*Huckleberry Finn,* Darwin's *The Origin of Species,* Salinger's *Catcher in the Rye*). Texts sacred to any religious group may not be studied lest they offend those who belong to other groups or hold other beliefs. Subjects that some regard as needing extensive public discussion, such as sex, drugs, and social problems, others consider taboo. Some parents give moral reasons for preferring highly structured, authoritative classroom environments with a serious businesslike atmosphere, while others give equally moral but quite different reasons for preferring classrooms to be open, unstructured, and playful.

Under these conditions of a society with fragmented moral doctrines, we must content ourselves with evaluating the morality of theories by reference to some appropriate moral standards. These may be a prevailing code accepted by a consensus among the relevant community, the code accepted by a dominant group or a particular minority group, or even the code of a single individual. Naturally, the same theory may be highly laudable by some of these moral standards and odious by others. It is not the province of the professional to choose among moral codes accepted by groups of clients, however, but it is the province of the professional to clarify the values used in any particular theory and to show how these fare when judged by varying moral standards. Just how active a role professionals should play in advocacy of values within the larger community and just how conflicts between professionals and their clients over values should be resolved is a matter of some controversy. It seems clear, though, that the professional in any field cannot claim by virtue of professional expertise any special ability to make moral judgments or any right to impose moral judgments on clients or the public.

When communities contain groups with different moral standards, curriculum leaders have two fundamental options: tolerate different moral judgments or search for common ground. To tolerate some different sets of moral standards does not necessarily imply abandonment of all morality, but to tolerate any and all moral standards does. Thus, toleration has its limits. In practice, American public school systems tend to abandon any practice that is objected to on moral grounds by any major religious or ethnic group in the local community.

Nearly all professional writing on curriculum questions asserts or assumes a commonly accepted set of values in the form of an agreed-upon list of goals. For example, Goodlad (1984) lists sixty-two goals for schooling under four broad headings: academic; vocational; social, civic and cultural; and personal. Goodlad's list probably reflects nearly all of the educational values important to any major segment of the American public, but any such inclusive list begs the crucial question of what priority should be given to the many goals. Finding common moral ground among established communities who place different priorities on various values is much more difficult than producing an inclusive list of general goals.

In conflicted social contexts it is not possible to set down general rules about which values are appropriate to assessing a theory's moral acceptability. The most democratic course of action for the analyst in assessing the quality of a theory is to examine it in light of all values held by all parties to the issue. This can be costly, however. In many cases the best course of action will be to use prevailing mainstream values and also one or a few of the most widely held alternative value systems. In any event, as we shall see in later chapters, the contending parties are seldom willing to leave the decision about which values to use to analysts.

THE PAIDEIA PROPOSAL: *A CURRICULUM THEORY IN ACTION*

We are ready now to study intensively one example of curriculum theory, a clear, noncontroversial case of curriculum theory being put to use. One of the most fundamental curriculum issues is **curricular differentiation,** or, looked at from the other side, the issue of a common curriculum. We can pose the issue this way:

> Should the same curriculum be provided for all students in public elementary and secondary education, or should different curricula be provided for different categories of students?

This issue has been especially pivotal for American education from the nation's beginnings. American educators, seeking forms of education that would prepare citizens for a democracy, had established by 1850 the institution of the common school, founded on the principle of a common curriculum for all students. In the 1890s the Committee of Ten outlined three programs of study for high schools —Classical, Latin-scientific, and English—but stipulated that satisfactory completion of any one of these courses should qualify students for admission to corresponding courses in colleges and scientific schools. The same philosophy of parallel independent courses of study justified the provision of separate vocational education programs in secondary schools under the federal Smith-Hughes Act of 1917. During the middle decades of this century it became common practice in high schools to offer three tracks: a general track intended for most students, an academic track intended for gifted students, and a vocational track. In elementary schools, special programs for the gifted and for students of low academic ability became widespread. In recent years, many large urban school systems have created specialized high schools—schools for the arts, for science, or for languages, for example—intended to attract students with special interests and talents from all over the urban area. Gradually, it seems, the prevailing view has come to be that students should be given programs that meet their individual needs, that society is best served by programs that meet the varied needs of a complex, highly differentiated modern society, and that these needs are best met by a diversity of programs among which students and parents may choose, with the advice and counsel of school officials.

In the 1980s the issue of curricular differentiation was raised to prominence again in public discussions of education by the publication of *The Paideia Proposal* (1982) by Mortimer Adler, a philosopher instrumental in founding the Great Books Program of adult education. What makes the book particularly interesting for us here and now is that Adler grounds his proposal for a common academically oriented curriculum for all American schools in a systematic and coherent body of ideas. Let us examine this grounding in detail.

The Proposal in Brief

In *The Paideia Proposal* Adler calls on Americans to realize "that a democratic society must provide equal educational opportunity not only by giving to all its children the same quantity of education . . . but also by making sure to give to all of them, all with no exceptions, the same quality of education" (Adler 1982, 4). He proposes a one-track system of schooling to create an educationally classless society, with the same objectives for all. He endorses Dewey's claims in *Democracy and Education* that democracy demands universal and equal educational opportunity, embracing the Deweyan principle that advocates "the best education for the best is the best education for all." Adler criticizes those who have claimed that many children are not educable, maintaining instead that, "There are no unteachable children. There are only schools and teachers and parents who fail to teach them" (Adler 1982, 8).

Adler sketches a plan for a common curriculum devoted to three purposes, corresponding to the three callings common to all: personal growth, citizenship, and preparation for earning a living. The common curriculum should be general and liberal, not narrowly specialized and not aimed at job training. He proposes that the content of this common program include language, literature, the fine arts, mathematics, natural science, history, geography, and social studies. He also proposes that instruction proceed by reading, lectures, discussion, coaching and supervised practice on exercises, and involvement in artistic activities. He advocates including physical exercise and sports for all, some training in manual skills (woodshop, crafts), and, in the later years, an introduction to the wide range of human work (typing, health). Specific job preparation and preparation for specialized study can come after basic schooling is completed in two-year community colleges, in technical institutes, or on the job itself. This common program should be adjusted administratively in subtle ways to provide for individual differences in students' abilities and interests. Remedial instruction should be provided for those youngsters who need it, to insure that no one is ever allowed to fall behind irremediably. Otherwise, the emphasis should be on the abilities and inclinations that all humans have in common, rather than on the relatively unimportant differences of degree among them. "The facts of sameness . . . justify the sameness of objectives at which our program for basic schooling aims" (Adler 1982, 43).

Adler claims that children trained for jobs instead of being educated in this general and liberal fashion are being shortchanged. They are not prepared for the duties of self-governing citizenship or for the enjoyment of the various things that make a good life. The underprivileged children who are shunted onto the lower tracks of the existing differentiated curriculum encounter an educational dead end. Adler believes that schooling should instead prepare young people for continuation of learning in adult life by giving them the skills and stimulation that will motivate them to keep their minds actively engaged.

Adoption of the Paideia Proposal by a contemporary comprehensive high school would entail major adjustments to the curriculum of elementary, middle, and high schools. Current tracking systems would have to be abolished, many nonacademic courses dropped, the vocational program eliminated or redirected to provide manual training and work orientation for all students, and the academic subjects treated more as occasions for liberal education than as specialized preparation for college. The Proposal seems to appeal to a wide audience. The issue before the public then, is "Should American schools undertake the curriculum reforms needed to realize the Proposal?"

Adler's Case for the Proposal

Adler grounds his Proposal carefully and systematically in a body of ideas of which the most central are democracy and human nature. Let us look in detail at how he does this. For purposes of discussion, we can divide the Paideia Proposal into two broad recommendations:

1. The same compulsory basic schooling should be provided at public expense for all American children.
2. The curriculum of this schooling should focus on the aims of personal growth, citizenship, and preparation for earning a living, these purposes to be achieved through reading, study, and discussion of ideas drawn from the traditional academic subjects.

The first recommendation is of most immediate concern to us. If true, Americans should avoid all forms of curricular differentiation in basic compulsory schooling.

Adler presents the following four arguments to support this recommendation.

1. Democracy requires that schooling be provided for all.

Following a line of thought prominent in the writings of Thomas Jefferson and any number of later writers, Adler argues that maintaining the American system of government—the rule of law under a constitution with government by the people—requires an educated citizenry. Universal suffrage requires universal schooling. The overwhelming body of Americans, both the general public and educational leaders, accept the truth of this relationship, so Adler asserts nothing controversial in this first step of his argument. But to say that our form of government requires that all citizens be educated is not necessarily to say that all must be given an identical curriculum. To reach this latter conclusion Adler must offer additional arguments.

2. Democracy requires the same quality of education as well as the same quantity.

To buttress the claim that democracy requires a common curriculum Adler cites Dewey's *Democracy and Education,* claiming that its revolutionary message of equal opportunity in education is fundamental. Dewey's doctrine may also be interpreted as calling for different programs equally suited to varied needs, however.

3. The gross inequities of the present differentiated system of education demonstrate that differentiation leads to unequal educational opportunity.

Adler cites the existing tracked system of education as an argument against the idea that varied programs can offer equal opportunity, claiming that it provides an inferior education for students on the lower tracks. "If . . . [students] are divided into the sheep and the goats, into those destined solely for toil and those destined for economic and political leadership and for quality of life to which all should have access, then the democratic purpose has been undermined by an inadequate system of public schooling" (Adler 1982, 5). The failure of the present system to prepare many of its students for political leadership and a high quality of life, if true, certainly shows that this one tracked system *does* undermine democratic ideals, but it does not necessarily imply that all differentiated curricula would do the same or that a common curriculum would correct the inequities.

4. All other educational programs are inferior to a broad liberal education in preparing students for democratic leadership.

Adler maintains that a broad liberal education prepares students for democratic leadership and a high quality of life better than any other educational program known. Any other program of education therefore provides an inferior education and does not provide equal educational opportunity. So, Adler concludes, distinctions among programs are sure to lead to invidious distinctions among students that will lead, in turn, to invidious distinctions among citizens, thereby undermining democracy. If true, this last argument clinches Adler's case.

Taken together, this network of four interconnected arguments, which I will refer to as the *democracy rationale,* makes a coherent rational case for Adler's proposal that American schools should offer a common curriculum for all students.

Adler also offers a second set of arguments, the *human nature rationale,* to justify a common curriculum. He argues that in important respects all human beings are the same and that this sameness, contrasted with the relatively superficial differences among human beings, call for the same education. In particular, Adler argues that students are biologically more similar than different. "They all have the same inherent tendencies, the same inherent powers, the same inherent capacities" (Adler 1982, 43). Differences are always merely differences of degree. In a democracy people are also the same in another way—they have the same rights and duties and are therefore equal under the law. "These are the facts of sameness that justify the sameness of the objectives at which our program for basic schooling aims" (Adler 1982, 43).

Adler's case rests ultimately on these two lines of argument, the democracy rationale and the human nature rationale. In articulating these rationales for the Paideia Proposal, Adler gives meaning to the decision of whether to offer a common or a differentiated curriculum by showing how some of our most important and widely held ideas and values may be implicated in this curriculum decision. At the same time, his rationale justifies the Proposal, for, if his theoretical analysis of these issues is correct, then adopting a differentiated curriculum would violate democratic ideals and run counter to human nature. Adler uses his conceptions of democracy and human nature to help him build the common curriculum he advocates. *The Paideia Proposal* is, then, a clear case of curriculum theory being put to use, and we have been able to see precisely how this theory does its work.

ASSESSING THE QUALITY OF ADLER'S THEORY

Let us look at Adler's theory in light of the marks of quality presented earlier in this chapter: validity, power, serviceability, and morality.

Validity

Meaningfulness   On the surface, at least, Adler's proposals and the case he makes for them are quite clear and should be easy for any reader to comprehend.

The book is written in plain English, is free of technical jargon, and reads easily. We have already discussed the two key propositions of *The Paideia Proposal,* the democracy rationale and the human nature rationale. The key terms are *democracy, human nature,* and *liberal education.* Unlike Dewey, Adler does not introduce any special meanings for these key terms. Although he does not define democracy or human nature, he seems to use their common dictionary meanings. A serious scholarly study of the adequacy of Adler's rationales for a common curriculum would eventually require a more complete and precise definition of human nature, but the dictionary definition is adequate for most purposes. The meanings of key terms appear to remain constant throughout the work. On the whole *The Paideia Proposal* deserves high marks for meaningfulness.

Logical Consistency   Let us examine critically the two rationales Adler offers in support of his proposal. Adler argues that democracy requires a common curriculum by sketching a heroic version of American education progressing toward equality of schooling as part of the general triumph of democracy. "We are on the verge of a new era. . . . Democracy has come into its own for the first time in this century. . . . Not until this century have we conferred the high office of enfranchised citizenship on all our people. . . ." (Adler 1982, 12) Equal quality of education is presented as the next logical step in this progress. Conclusion: if we are to maintain our progress toward ever more perfect democracy, the same curriculum for all students should be our goal.

This is obviously a simplified, idealized version of the history of American education, but leaving aside its correctness for the time being, it is certainly a coherent practical argument. If it is true that Americans have been struggling for generations to provide equal educational opportunity and if the next step in that struggle is to provide a common curriculum for all, then, in the absence of compelling reasons to the contrary—such as showing that we have gone far enough or that further steps would have undesirable effects—we should certainly want to take that next step.

Adler argues that, since each citizen must be prepared for self-government, all should have an education that prepares her or him for political leadership. All curricula that do not so prepare students, especially vocational curricula, but also all curricula other than broad liberal studies, are inferior. The logic of this argument is impeccable.

Adler endorses the ideas of John Dewey on democracy and education, quoting and paraphrasing his arguments. Such an appeal to authority is a legitimate way to show that others of distinguished reputation who have given the matter much thought agree with one's positions or arguments. This move on Adler's part also serves another subtle purpose. It tends to forestall the charge of elitism that has dogged advocates of liberal education since at least the 1890s. Dewey's ideas are revered by many educators who espouse egalitarian values. Now Adler claims their chief spokesman for his ally. If Adler is correct in this claim, then he can claim that the life work of a distinguished scholar who has studied the matter deeply and who demonstrated a deep and lasting commitment to equality supported his position. This is clearly a sound reason for others committed to the same values to support the position. So, again, the argument is logically sound.

Adler claims that American society is politically classless and therefore should also be educationally classless. The logic here is unclear. Is Adler invoking a general principle that political classlessness implies classlessness in all aspects of life or only in education? If the former, then presumably he would also argue that we should be economically and socially classless, an unlikely position. Presumably, he invokes again the principle that democratic citizenship demands a certain kind and level of education and that if all citizens are going to be politically equal, they must be educationally equal. It is not clear that such a principle can be defended. Certainly Adler does not himself defend it. Rhetorically, this argument taps American pride in being less class-ridden than European societies and appeals to Americans' desire to be seen as a classless society, thus forestalling charges of elitism often leveled at advocates of solely academic curricula.

Adler contrasts the simple justice of a common program for all with the pernicious inequities of the present system. This is an unfair rhetorical device. He compares his proposal in its ideal form with the reality of the present system. A fair comparison of course, would compare ideal against ideal and reality against reality. At least a plausible case can be made for the ideal of differentiating curricula to suit individual students or groups of students. Adler does not consider this case. And Adler offers us no real instance of a common curriculum in actual practice to compare against the present American system.

Adler anticipates the potential objection that some students could not succeed in a curriculum that is demanding enough for the most able. He implies that this is the major reason why people have not adopted a single curriculum. He counters the objection with the assertions that "there are no unteachable children," and "every child is educable up to his or her capacity" (Adler 1982, 7).

This argument does not show what Adler claims it does. To say that there are no unteachable children is not to say that all children will do as well under a common curriculum as under one differentiated to meet varying needs. An opponent might well reply, "Yes, all children are teachable, but some learn better in one way and others in another." That all children are teachable is not really relevant to the issue of whether all students can and will succeed in Adler's proposed common program. To say that every child is educable up to his or her capacity is a tautology; that is what we mean by *educable*. The statement counts neither for nor against Adler's proposal. Adler evades the critical issue: whether any single program will educate *all* children to their capacity.

Adler offers some equalitarian homilies such as "All should aspire to make as much of their powers as they can," "Every child should be able to look forward not only to growing up but also to continued growth in all human dimensions throughout life," and "Basic schooling should prepare [children] to take advantage of every opportunity for personal development that our society offers" (Adler 1982, 16).

These statements invite readers to recall and renew their commitment to democratic and egalitarian ideals and thus support the value bases for Adler's arguments. He offers no new argument to supplement the one unfair argument he offered earlier—comparing the reality of the present system with the ideal system he proposes—to show that a single common program will promote equalitarianism to a greater extent than a differentiated program.

To support the human nature rationale, Adler offers an archaic form of argument. He claims that Homo sapiens is the least specialized species. It is not clear that the concept of specialization is well enough defined to permit this claim to be tested, but perhaps so. He then argues that general, nonspecialized schooling most suits unspecialized human nature (Adler 1982, 19). The logic here presumably relies on some principle that the education should fit the organism, for it does not follow necessarily that a nonspecialized organism needs a nonspecialized education. We might equally well argue that such a species needs more specialized education to compensate for its natural lack of specialization. Adler claims that the facts of human sameness are more significant than the facts of human differences. In support of this conclusion he offers the argument that no child is more or less human than another, a biological tautology that he seems to think should somehow count in favor of sameness and against differences in educational programs.

The scholastic origins of Adler's ideas are most evident when he offers the argument that differences between individual humans are differences of degree only, not differences of kind. Distinctions between differences of kind and of degree were a favorite rhetorical tactic in the scholastic tradition, but these distinctions have serious logical defects. Whether a difference is one of kind or degree depends on how terms are defined. Lights colored red and green differ in kind when they are defined in terms of human sensations, but when defined in terms of frequencies they differ only in degree. Differences between animals in the same species may be either a matter of degree or a matter of kind, depending on one's purpose in making the distinction. To say that some conclusion follows from a certain difference being of degree rather than of kind is to say that something follows from the conceptualization, not from characteristics, of the phenomenon itself. The question of whether, in the context of basic schooling, people are similar enough to be treated identically is the real issue. To answer that they are because people by nature differ by degree rather than kind does not advance the argument.

In summary, Adler's democracy rationale appears to be meaningful, logically sound, and coherent. His human nature rationale is less secure. Serious questions can be raised about the meaning and logical coherence of its key terms and propositions.

Factual Correctness   The central empirical claim of the democracy rationale is that democracy requires a citizenry with a common basic education, specifically, a broad liberal education of the kind Adler proposes. It would not be practical to test this by experiments in which we assign people with varying educations to live under democratic forms of government and see which governments persist. We can ask about those democracies which have existed and we can ask for the judgment of those who have thought the most about and had the most experience with democratic government. On these admittedly weak grounds, the proposition is more supported than opposed, although the evidence is equivocal and depends on how one defines democracy. Was Athens in the Golden Age a democracy? Is contemporary England, with its monarchy and the House of Lords, a democracy? We can at least array both historical and contemporary societies on a rough continuum from more to less democratic and ask to what extent each society offers a common compulsory basic education of the sort Adler proposes. The construction of such a chart would depend so critically on so many complex judgments about each society that the results would probably be endlessly disputed.

Adler does not attempt this or any other form of systematic empirical support for this claim. He writes as though the actual connection between education and democracy in real societies is irrelevant. And so it is, for him. He is interested in approaching the ideal of genuine democracy. That a common education would contribute to the realization of this ideal is a consequence of the theory of democracy, not an observed fact of actual democratic societies. Adler proposes that we accept this claim because it can be justified by arguments based on the theory of democratic government.

As we have already seen, the human nature rationale rests on arguments that are not capable of an empirical test. Whether the samenesses or the differences between people are more significant is not empirically testable, nor is the question of whether the differences are of kind or of degree only.

Adler asks for faith grounded in reason; he neither asks for nor attempts to provide evidence from observations of real societies or from studies of real human similarities and differences. He does provide brief sketches of arguments that appeal to historical evidence, and factual correctness of the historiography could in principle be judged, except that Adler does not cite any historical evidence—not even a reference to an historian. Similarly, although he does mention some schools that are implementing programs like *The Paideia Proposal,* he does not cite any evaluations of these programs. This lack of interest in observations of the real world and this willingness to rely on reasoned deduction from ideals that are accepted on faith were prominent in the intellectual life of medieval and early modern times. The mainstream of modern thought has developed in a more empirical and scientific direction. The earlier tradition, which today we label *rationalist* and *scholastic,* has not proven to be as productive of new knowledge and theory as the more empirical, scientific tradition. In reverting to this earlier tradition, Adler asks us to reject the dominant forms of thought of our time, for which entreaty he earns the label of a contemporary scholastic.

Where does this leave us on the matter of the correctness of Adler's ideas? If we judge it on the criteria most important to him—meaningfulness and logical coherence—the democracy rationale stands up pretty well, but the human nature argument is weak. On the criterion of factual correctness both rationales stand completely unsupported. Factual evidence could certainly be adduced on the democracy rationale and, with suitable revisions, possibly on the human nature rationale, but Adler provides none.

Theoretical Power

Adler's proposals and the two rationales he offers in support of them are principles of enormous scope and power. Those who accept them are greatly helped in making countless decisions about what should be the purpose, content, and structure of common basic education. The conclusions Adler comes to are not the obvious ones that common sense would suggest. They challenge the prevailing view among both educators and the public that different types of students should have different programs of education. That our commitment to democracy requires instead the same curriculum for all students and that, in spite of superficial diversity, human nature requires a common curriculum, are in the present context interestingly novel conclusions. Thus, Adler's ideas are extremely powerful theoretically and this is doubtlessly a major reason for their success.

Serviceability

Adler's proposals are clear enough and simple enough to be understood by most educated persons. Superintendents, principals, and teachers should be able to work out the additional details required for implementation in their schools. The chief issue concerning serviceability is, as Adler anticipated, feasibility. Would it be possible to sustain such a program with inner-city, rural, and suburban students, with low-achieving students, with students whose interests lie elsewhere than academics? Will traditionally blue-collar communities concerned about jobs accept it? Can enough qualified teachers be found to bring it off? And so on. Adler promises a second volume devoted specifically to such issues. Here, he asserts confidently, but without argument or evidence, that it can be made to work in all communities, with all students. Again, we are asked to accept conclusions on faith and rational argument.

Morality

Adler appeals to core American values—democracy and human equality—that are widely supported and deeply held by Americans. His commitment to the intellectual traditions of Western civilization will find wide support, but also some opposition on grounds of cultural chauvinism and social elitism. In spite of his strenuous efforts to show that his proposal is democratic, some will still charge him with elitism because the content he proposes is drawn exclusively from the traditional high culture. Some will also level the charge of cultural chauvinism and parochialism, arguing that the Western tradition systematically rejects the perspectives of women, the poor, and cultural minorities. It is unlikely that many would raise moral objections to the values Adler takes as central, but some might object to his priorities. For example, some people would put a higher priority on preparing students to work in and to sustain a flexible, sophisticated, highly technological economy in a competitive global environment. Some people might place a higher priority on fostering social harmony and interpersonal caring. In general, most of those who adopt a traditionalist perspective will probably find Adler's values and priorities congenial, whereas most progressives will not.

Adler's theory considers primarily only two value bases—democracy and human nature. The clarity and simplicity he achieves thereby is one of the sources of the theory's power and appeal. But it is also a limitation. Adler does not consider what may be the educational demands of other values, say, economic efficiency or economic justice, social unity, psychological well-being, or spiritual growth, all of which have been perennially important in educational thought, and therefore he does not address the values of greatest concern to some Americans. In fact, he strongly implies that political considerations are paramount, and thus that these others are less deserving. Adler's theory is therefore built on a strong, but rather narrow, moral foundation.

Summary Assessment of Adler's Theory

We now have a solid basis for making some judgments about the strengths and weaknesses of Adler's curriculum theory. It is well and carefully argued, but lacks empirical support. It offers us a few extremely powerful principles of wide appeal, but leaves out of consideration a variety of other values regarded as important by many. It yields clear suggestions for improving many aspects of educational practice, but they may not be feasible for many real situations. We now see further tasks for analysis. We could try to reformulate Adler's human nature rationale in modern terms. We could seek more information about the actual correlation between democracy and a common curriculum in contemporary and historical societies. We could look further into the philosophical and historical roots of the beliefs and values most fundamental to Adler's argument. Especially, we could study and apply other relevant theories of democracy and human nature. We could even develop other rationales of our own for a common curriculum and compare these with Adler's. How far we continue our analysis depends on our judgment about the likelihood that further analysis will change our assessment of the strength of the case for the Proposal. In my judgment, additional analysis is unlikely to change my assessment of the strengths and limitations of Adler's case for a common curriculum. The scaffolding of arguments and the beliefs, values, and conceptualizations on which they rest seems clear to me.

In a free and pluralistic society, each person must weigh Adler's Proposal in terms of their own values and priorities in order to decide what to do about it. It might be helpful if I described the conclusions I draw from this analysis. I regard the Proposal as making an important contribution to current curricular debate because it advocates the general value of academic and intellectual studies, a perspective that I think has been neglected in American educational discussions for several decades. In my judgment Americans and their educational leaders have been too ready to dismiss fundamental academic and intellectual studies as simply vocational preparation for the college bound and to focus instead on social and economic priorities over political and intellectual ones.

Adler's democracy rationale confirms my preexisting belief that democracy requires us to presume a common curriculum until a convincing case is made to differentiate in some particular case. The burden of proof in a democracy must lie with those who advocate that public schools should teach some particular students something that others are not taught. Only then should we make an exception. But I believe there will be situations where a strong case can be made for an exception. I think, for example, a strong case can be made for individual students to specialize in some part of their school studies during the last two years of high school. For those with no intention of pursuing further academic studies, this specialization might consist of vocational education.

I am concerned about what might go wrong if the Proposal, even in a modified form, were adopted. I share the concerns Adler expressed about whether the Proposal is feasible in real schools as we have them today. But I have even more serious concerns. Many idealistic curriculum proposals have had effects quite opposite to their advocates' intentions. In this case, I worry that the combination of strictly academic curriculum and a competitive school climate could create in many schools a profoundly undemocratic academic class system based on differing achievement in the common curriculum. I would value the judgments of experienced teachers and principals and of sociologists and social psychologists on this question. Before urging widespread adoption of any form of the Proposal, I would want to see it implemented in a variety of schools and the results studied closely for signs that this type of invidious class system might be emerging.

Also, I am troubled by Adler's failure to address and to rebut arguments given by Dewey and other earlier advocates of education for democracy to the effect that students need to develop habits of initiative and independence as part of training for democratic living. They maintain, and I concur, that students cannot be merely told about democracy and expected to practice it. They need to practice it all along. This seems to me to require that we arrange somehow for students to pursue their own independent paths in learning. It is not clear to me whether Adler would endorse these arguments and, if so, how he would accommodate them in his Proposal.

My inclination, contrary to Adler's, is to assume that human nature is almost infinitely variable and pliable; the profound differences everywhere manifest among individual personalities, as well as human cultures, seem to me strong evidence for my belief. Nevertheless, I agree with Adler in that I regard this variability as calling for more, not less, curricular commonality. If we are to live together well as adults, we must begin by living and working together well in school. A common heritage offered through the school can build a foundation for a common culture.

Democracy is not the supremely important value for me that it is for Adler. I regard economic well-being, social amity, and cultural achievement, for example, as values on a par with democracy. If the proposal for a common curriculum were considered in light of this wide array of values, I am not confident that the rationale would be as strong.

My objections are not serious enough to send me to the front lines to fight against adoption of *The Paideia Proposal*. On the contrary, I am optimistic that its most serious shortcomings would be found out and compensated for in some way during the process required for its adoption in school systems. Opponents would insist on checks, balances, and compromises to protect their interests. Teachers would soften its hard edges and enrich it with other values as they put it to work in their classrooms. If I thought that adoption of the Proposal would lead to abandonment of the harmful systems of tracking all too common in large school systems today, that in itself would be enough to cause me to favor it. But I think we can do better. Indeed, I think better proposals exist already. What do you think?

We see from this analysis of *The Paideia Proposal* that we cannot demonstrate the truth or falsity of a curriculum theory the way we could a mathematical theory. Nor can we confirm or disconfirm it by experimental evidence in the way scientific theories are tested. We can check the logic of its arguments and the soundness of the evidence on which it is based, but even when we have done this, people may legitimately reach quite different judgments about the merits of the theory based on its values or practical usefulness. The best we can do is what we have just done with Adler's ideas: study them, check the logic and evidence, and make considered judgments about the theory's strengths and limitations.

READING CURRICULUM THEORY

To read curriculum theory closely and analytically is a more active process than everyday reading, but the skills involved are not obscure or difficult and with a little practice anyone can learn to do it. What you must do is identify the lines of argument that are fundamental to the theory, then the fundamental ideas and values on which these lines of argument rest, and finally, read between the lines by asking yourself what alternative arguments, ideas, and values might have been used instead. Once you have exposed the theory's scaffolding in this way, you will find it easier to draw convincing conclusions about its validity, power, serviceability, and morality. And, when you cannot reach a firm judgment, you should at least have a better idea of what further information would most help you confirm your judgment. Try the following procedure.

1. *Read the work straight through,* just as you would any expository writing, trying to recover the author's meaning, noting for future reference the passages that make a particularly strong impression. Summarize the manifest content the author treats in the work, conclusions reached about this concern, and main points made in support of this conclusion. This is the main skeleton of the argument.

2. *Make a list of key terms and their defining phrases.* When a term seems value-laden, try to identify the value in a word or brief phrase. Quote brief phrases that express each value most vividly. Look for the key ideas and central values on which the case rests, ones which, if changed, would make the greatest change in the overall message of the work. If you have trouble sorting out relationships among ideas, create a table listing each idea along both the top and the side margin of the table and place a check in each box where there is a strong relationship between ideas.

3. *Check the soundness of each step in the argument.* What grounds does the author give for the truth of the arguments' premises? Note strong and weak arguments as well as ones about which you are most uncertain. Look for unstated premises and hidden assumptions; often these are more dubious than stated ones. Note the historical and intellectual origins of key terms and ideas. Often, knowing the fields of study, philosophical doctrines, or historical periods where ideas originated suggests assumptions or values that the present ideas may share with the older ones. Give special attention to turns in the argument that seem arbitrary, to places where you find yourself wondering, "Where did this come from?" Such unexpected twists in the argument may give clues about an unstated assumption or value. Look for gaps and holes in the argument.

4. *Consider the theory in the context of alternative views.* Try to find strong, credible alternatives to the author's key ideas, values, and assumptions. Then, ask yourself why the author chose to rely on the ones actually used instead of these alternatives. In what other ways might the issue be posed? In particular, what is the common sense view of the issue, and what are the major well-known views that run counter to the author's? Why might the author have chosen to address this issue instead of others? What may be inferred from the author's decision to pose the issue in that particular way instead of one of the others? What other positions are not considered? What other reasons could be given? What other grounds? In each case, what can we infer from the choices the author made? Is there, for instance, a pattern to the author's choices that suggests a purpose other than the stated purpose or values not explicitly embraced? Speculate about the possible significance of the author's choices. For example, which interested parties

would support or oppose them? Examine the author's language for subtle cues to purpose and value. When is the tone conciliatory and when combative? How does the author use words to make something appealing or repulsive? What rhetorical or persuasive strategies does the author employ?

5. *Put together everything you have learned from studying the work into overall judgments about its strengths and limitations.* Would you embrace these ideas? What changes would make them more embraceable? Are other competing ideas still more appealing? How would you judge their validity, power, serviceability, and morality? What uncertainties make it difficult for you to reach a judgment about the overall quality of this work, and what further steps would reduce these uncertainties? Make allowances for the way the author framed the work, for no work can address all problems. For example, if the work is a brief essay sketching out a direction of thought on an issue, do not expect it to provide a completely worked out solution. If the author's purpose is to develop a view that will serve as a partisan alternative for use by those, perhaps a minority, who share certain values, do not criticize it for ignoring prevailing values. (Box 4-1 summarizes these steps.)

REFLECTIONS ON THE VALUE OF THEORY IN CURRICULUM

Has the grand intellectual project of curriculum theory been achieved in this case? Has practice been grounded in theory? Has Adler's theory settled the issue of whether to offer a common curriculum to all students? As we have seen, the theory has flaws. But suppose we could fix them. The democracy rationale and the human nature rationale would then certainly offer us a way of settling the issue of curricular differentiation, but whether we accept it or not would depend on whether we accept the theory. Has anything been gained by shifting the debate from the merits of curricular differentiation to the merits of Adler's theory? I think so. We have gained intellectual coherence, for one thing, a greater understanding of what larger matters may be at stake in this one practical decision. We now know why we should care about this decision. Those who disagree about whether to offer a common curriculum can now go beyond the stage of shouting or fighting about it to discussing exactly why they favor one side or the other.

But, in spite of these many important gains from the use of theory, the efforts of a generation of scholars to realize the grand intellectual project of placing curriculum practice on a firm theoretical foundation has not been completely successful. In the next chapter we will consider some of these limitations of theory and an alternative way to think about grounding practice in ideas.

BOX 4-1   A Plan for Intensive Reading of Works of Curriculum Theory

1. Read the work for sense noting your responses
   Summarize concerns, conclusions, main arguments
2. Study the argumentative scaffolding
   a. main lines of argument
      What issue is addressed? What position is taken? What other positions are considered? What reasons are given for taking the chosen position? What supporting grounds are given for these reasons?
   b. key ideas
   c. central values
   d. connections and relationships
3. Check the soundness of arguments
   a. logical validity
   b. strength of evidence
   c. hidden premises?
   d. gaps?
4. Consider the work in light of a context of alternatives
   a. other ideas
   b. other values
   c. other assumptions
   d. other language and rhetorical form
   e. origins may suggest other strengths or weaknesses
   f. what can be inferred from the author's choices?
5. Reach a summary judgment of the quality of the work
   a. validity
   b. power
   c. serviceability
   d. morality
   e. would I embrace it? with changes?
   f. judged in relation to the author's project

QUESTIONS FOR STUDY

1. Write a summary judgment of Adler's ideas, based on your own values and your own judgments. Compare this with other summaries and try to understand why your judgments are the same or are different.

2. Discuss the issue of curricular differentiation informally with a friend. You might broach the subject with a casual question such as "What do you think of specialized high schools?" or "Do you think all children should study the same things?" Listen carefully to the answer. Does your friend use any of Adler's arguments? If not, offer some of Adler's arguments on behalf of a common curriculum and ask for a reaction. Has your friend thought of these arguments

before? Were your friend's views changed in any way by hearing Adler's arguments? What does this suggest about the value of theory in considering curriculum questions?

3. Read Adler's *Paideia Proposal* in its entirety. Find additional arguments he offers on behalf of his proposal. How powerful do you find these new arguments? Analyze them in the manner demonstrated in this chapter. Did this process affect your assessment of Adler's views?

4. Which of the commonplaces of curricular thought do you think Adler emphasizes most? Which does he most neglect? Explain.

5. Hold a debate on the merits of Adler's *Paideia Proposal* for use in a school in your community. Keep a careful record of all the arguments presented on both sides. Discuss which arguments were most telling and why. Reflect on the relation, if any, of these arguments to Adler's theory or to other curricular theories you know.

6. Choose a curricular practice that you think should be more widely used. Defend it to friends who have not considered their position on this practice yet. List as many strong arguments for the practice as you can think of. Examine these arguments. Do they seem to reflect a single theory? If so, does this strengthen the case? Why? Why not?

7. Imagine two experienced teachers who are both highly respected by their colleagues, students, and their students' parents. One of them has read many books about curriculum, has a well thought out philosophy of education, and loves to explain why this or that practice is good or bad. The other is not well-informed about theories and seldom can explain why she prefers one practice over another, but she usually has a clear preference and her judgment in such matters usually seems to be quite good. Should this difference between them weigh in decisions about hiring, promotion, or honors? Which way, how much, and why?

8. Find a recent work of curriculum theory. (Chapter 3 summarizes several. Articles can also be found in journals in curriculum and in philosophy of education.) Follow the procedure suggested in this chapter to analyze the work and identify its strengths and limitations. Identify the key values on which it rests.

9. Apply a curriculum theory, Adler's or another in the mainstream tradition, to a particular curriculum issue. Use the principles of the theory to decide how this issue should be settled. How certain are you that your conclusions are correct applications of the theory? Do you think there are other conclusions also consistent with this theory? If possible, compare your application to that of another person or group and discuss any differences. What do you conclude about the theory and about the rigor possible in applying curriculum theories?

10. With the assistance of an experienced person, identify a contemporary curriculum issue and two different sets of theoretical ideas in curriculum bearing on that issue. (For example, should schools foster bilingualism among students whose native language is not English? Adler's theory is relevant. So are G. H. Bantock's and Michael W. Apple's.) Apply each theory in an effort to solve the problem. Note the difficulties you encounter in applying each theory. Do the theories yield similar or different recommendations? If different, how could we and *should* we cope with these conflicts?

11. Many observers claim that there is a huge gap between theory and practice in American education, that practitioners ignore theory and that theory is irrelevant to practice, with the result that the curriculum students experience is not affected by ideas, but only by tradition and passing fads. Suggest several reasons why theories such as Adler's might not be used by practitioners. What changes in either theory or practice might overcome these difficulties? Do you think these changes can or should be made?

12. Choose any recent work proposing curriculum reforms. Select a brief passage that you consider to express ideas fundamental to the proposed reform. Analyze this passage in detail. What question is addressed in that passage? How is the question expressed? Are any assumptions or presuppositions hidden in this formulation of the question? What position does the author take on the question? What reasons does the author give to justify this position? What are the most fundamental educational values and human values that are behind this justification? What other values, also important and relevant to the question, go unmentioned? How would you characterize the perspective or point of view implicit in this passage?

13. Consider a school that you know well. To what extent do the faculty and administration of this school share a common theory about its curriculum? Do you think they would react in the same way, for example, to Adler's proposal? If *yes,* to what extent and in what ways is this shared point of view on curriculum reflected in the curriculum actually offered by the school? If *no,* what do you think are the implications of these differences? Are theories such as Adler's useful in schools such as these?

RECOMMENDED READING

The best way to sharpen your skills of analysis of curriculum theory is to read additional works of theory and write your own analyses of them. This also gives you wider knowledge of curricular ideas and deepens your understanding by showing how different thinkers have approached the same issues in different ways. Dozens of references to contemporary theorists and recently published books and articles appear in Chapter 3. If you are using this book in a course, ask your instructor to recommend writers whose ideas are timely and important. For those working without such guidance, here are names of a few contemporary curriculum theorists whose work I recommend, listed in alphabetical order: Bereiter, Carl;

Bernstein, Basil; Bloom, Benjamin; Broudy, Harry S.; Bruner, Jerome; Eisner, Elliot W.; Foshay, Wells; Greene, Maxine; Lawton, Deniss; Musgrave, P. W.; Keddie, Nel; Noddings, Nel; Peters, R. S.; Phenix, Phillip; Ravitch, Diane; Thelen, Herbert; Wilson, John.

It is also helpful to read published analyses of educational theories. Boyd Bode's *Modern Educational Theories* is a classic of the genre. His analyses of the strengths and limitations of both progressive and traditional educational thought in the early decades of this century remains useful in dealing with contemporary ideas. One of the most astute analysts of contemporary educational ideas is Harold Dunkel. Reginald Archambault's edited volume, *John Dewey on Education* offers thoughtful analyses of Dewey's seminal ideas. Any good education library will have books on the ideas of various important educational writers. The journal *Educational Theory* frequently carries articles on the educational thought of particular authors.

REFERENCES

Adler, Mortimer. 1982. *The Paideia Proposal.* N.Y.: Macmillan.

Archambault, Reginald D. 1962. *John Dewey on Education.* N.Y.: Random House.

Bode, Boyd H. 1927. *Modern Educational Theories.* N.Y.: Macmillan.

Conant, James. 1959. *The American High School Today.* N.Y.: McGraw-Hill.

Dewey, John. 1916. *Democracy and Education.* N.Y.: Macmillan.

Dunkel, Harold B. 1965. *Whitehead on Education.* Columbus, OH: Ohio State University Press.

Goodlad, John. 1984. *A Place Called School.* N.Y.: McGraw-Hill.

chapter 5

CURRICULUM AS A PRACTICAL ENDEAVOR

The reasons why any particular society follows the educational curriculum which it does follow are always exceedingly complex. Because, in being a preparation for the future, it is inevitably a communication of what is available from past experience, only secondarily a matter of theory. The theories concerning the handling of this experience never quite compass the actuality and totality of the experience itself. They are generally rationalizations, afterthoughts, however valuable or venturesome they may be under certain of their aspects.

Walter J. Ong
American scholar, 1971

PURPOSE OF THE CHAPTER

- to articulate the perspective that curriculum is a practical field of work and study
- to argue the case that curriculum problems are fundamentally practical rather than theoretical
- to explain the mode of reasoning appropriate to dealing with practical problems
- to show how to analyze the structure of practical discourse

OUTLINE

THE PRACTICAL: ANOTHER WAY TO GROUND PRACTICE IN IDEAS

The intellectual project of curriculum theory is to ground curriculum practice in a single coherent, systematic body of ideas. The previous two chapters showed something of the promise of this project, and also showed that the project had not been fully realized. In 1967 at the Annual Meeting of the American Educational Research Association in Los Angeles, Professor Joseph Schwab (Figure 5-1) of the Department of Education at the University of Chicago charged curriculum specialists with over-reliance on theory and proposed an alternative. In this chapter we consider Schwab's arguments and his proposal to reorient intellectual work in the curriculum field from theory to practical reason.

In his address Schwab condemned "the inveterate and unexamined reliance on theory" in curriculum work and declared that the field would not regain its intellectual vitality until and unless it reconsidered its commitment to theory. He pointed out three radical deficiencies inherent in the project of theory in curriculum. First, Schwab maintains that many theories of quite different kinds are needed. Curriculum issues generally depend on theories of a number of fundamentally different subject matters, including conceptions of the learner, the teacher, the subject, and the milieu. No single theory can hope to unite such diverse subject matters into one all-encompassing body of ideas. Second, theory must be applied to specific, unique, real, three-dimensional cases of people grappling with curriculum problems. No theory, especially theory dealing with human conduct, ever completely captures the relevant features of the individual case that must be considered in making wise curriculum decisions. Third, theories from the humanities and the human sciences are "marked by the coexistence of competing theories. . . . There is not one theory of groups, but several. There is not one theory of learning, but half a dozen. All the social and behavioral sciences are marked by 'schools'" (Schwab 1970, 28). Basing curriculum decisions on only one theory when several may be contending for acceptance can leave us with a brittle resolution, one that falls apart easily when one theory is overturned in favor of a close competitor. Schwab maintained that these difficulties of principle were serious enough to call into question the intellectual project of theory in curriculum. He was suspicious, he said, of "the dispatch, the sweeping appearance of success, the vast simplicity which grounds [a] purported [theoretical] solution to the problem of curriculum" (Schwab 1970, 21).

Schwab proposed an alternative way of giving thought to curriculum problems, a way he claimed was better suited to the nature of curriculum problems than curriculum theorizing. He recalled Aristotle's distinction among three types of

Joseph Schwab, 1909–1987

knowledge—theoretical, practical, and productive. Aristotle maintained that different types of problems demanded different modes of thought and resulted in different types of knowledge. Theoretical knowledge was appropriate for solving problems in the realm of ideas—questions about terms, concepts, principles, and other abstractions, for example. Philosophy was the paradigmatic theoretical activity, and Aristotle developed the now-familiar Aristotelian logic to describe correct patterns of reasoning in the realm of the theoretical. Practical problems, on the other hand, were those that arose when we took action in the world. The realm of the practical included the kinds of thinking used in making decisions and in planning and carrying out actions. Politics was the paradigmatic practical activity because it was concerned with making decisions about actions to be taken in public affairs. Aristotle's realm of the productive encompassed the kind of thought used in making things. All three employed mankind's higher faculties, but in fundamentally different ways. Curriculum problems, Schwab argued, belong to Aristotle's realm of the practical, not to the theoretical.

Practical problems arise when someone identifies conditions that they want to ease or eliminate. A practical problem can only be settled by an action or a decision to undertake a course of action designed to eliminate the problematic conditions. If we believe that thoughtful, considered actions are more likely to be effective, then decision-makers should consider in light of the best available knowledge what action, if any, is best for this situation, all things considered. This consideration of possible actions is called *deliberation*. Schwab described deliberation in these terms:

> [Deliberation] treats both ends and means and must treat them as mutually determining one another. It must try to identify, with respect to both, what facts may be relevant. It must try to ascertain the relevant facts in the concrete case. It must try to identify the desiderata in the case. It must generate alternative solutions. It must take every effort to trace the branching pathways of consequences which may flow from each alternative and affect desiderata. It must then weigh alternatives and their costs and consequences against one another, and choose, not the right alternative, for there *is* no such thing, but the best one. (Schwab 1970, 36)

Theoretical problems are solved once and for all time by an idea or invention of the mind; productive problems are solved by skilled performance in manipulating material objects with one's body; but practical problems are *resolved*, not solved, and not by an idea but by a decision. When the person or group confronted with the practical problem decides what to do, that particular practical problem is resolved. The conclusion that a certain action is best for this situation is called a *practical judgment* (Gauthier 1963). Strictly speaking, a practical problem can be considered fully resolved, as distinct from resolved in principle, only after the fact, when action has been taken and the problem is gone. Whereas with genuinely theoretical problems we can sometimes find ideas that completely satisfy all the conditions of the original problem, the actions that resolve practical problems usually lead to a new set of conditions only somewhat less problematic than the original ones.

As an example, consider a school facing the curriculum problem considered at length in the previous chapter: whether to differentiate the school curriculum or to maintain a common curriculum for all students. This is a problem that calls for the school community to decide on a course of action to follow in that school. A committee would typically be appointed to consider the question and make a recommendation to the Superintendent and to the school board. The committee would probably be charged to consider fully the pros and cons of each alternative. In the process the committee might well consider the arguments Adler offers in *The Paideia Proposal*, along with various other ideas and theories, including some easily framed in common sense terms, such as the cost of the alternatives and their appeal to parents, teachers, administrators and students. Having given the matter due consideration, the committee would reach a judgment that one course of action was preferable for their school at this time.

Let us suppose they recommended a common curriculum. Their recommendation to this effect might signal the end of the deliberation, but more likely it would mark the beginning of another round of public discussion as the Superintendent and school board make an official decision. The official decision resolves the curriculum problem in principle. After the decision has been implemented, it may happen that a common curriculum has led to serious and widespread difficulties in the school. Parents of gifted or handicapped children may complain that the common curriculum is unsuitable for their children. Or teachers may be unable to agree on what should be included in the common curriculum. Such difficulties might lead the Superintendent or the Board to reconsider the issue. On the other hand, those involved may consider the matter settled and regard these new difficulties as new problems to be resolved within the framework of a common curriculum, in which case the original problem will now be fully resolved. Clearly this case can be construed as a practical problem. Equally clearly, it is not a theoretical problem.

All questions of curriculum policy or practice will qualify as practical problems. For example:

> What curriculum should we offer for these students in this educational situation?

> What actions should we take in order to maintain and improve the quality of this curriculum?

It is only when we take the basic questions of curriculum to be like those that follow that we naturally look to theory for answers.

> What should be the aims of education?

> What is the nature of the good and how can education enable humanity to achieve it?

> What knowledge is of most worth?

> What is the proper role for education in society?

Adopting a practical perspective on curriculum matters refocuses our attention on decisions and actions in concrete situations rather than abstract notions.

Both ways of treating curriculum problems use ideas, but in quite different ways. Curriculum theory begins with ideas and applies them to particular cases, whereas the practical begins with the case and asks what ideas may be helpful in dealing with it. A theoretical approach insists that curriculum problems be grounded in ideas that form a coherent and systematic body, a curriculum theory, whereas the practical permits grounding in an eclectic variety of ideas. Theory strives for the greatest possible degree of abstraction and generality, whereas the practical is content with principles at any level of abstraction that helps to resolve the problem. Theory looks for better answers to deep questions, whereas the practical looks for better decisions. Let us consider an example of a practical approach to a real curriculum problem.

A CURRICULUM PROBLEM RESOLVED

The following example of curriculum deliberation is taken from my personal collection of tape recordings of actual discussions among a team of curriculum developers. The team included scientists, teachers, and science education specialists, about a dozen people altogether. The team was collaborating on a project at the University of California at Berkeley, funded by the National Science Foundation, to develop curriculum materials for elementary science. The project was called the Science Curriculum Improvement Study (SCIS).

The meeting that will concern us here began with one member of the team demonstrating some apparatus that had been designed for use in elementary school science classes. He first demonstrated a simple pendulum made of a piece of nylon fishline with a lead sinker tied on its end, which was clamped to the back of the child's desk in a way that made it possible for the sinker to swing freely as a pendulum (Figure 5-2). He commented:

> The general object of the exercise as I saw it was to have the children investigate, in the first place, how you describe the system, and in the second place, how you describe the motion, and in the third place what properties of the pendulum are important in determining what kind of motion takes place. . . .

Those present were encouraged to examine the apparatus and its motions.

Other pieces of apparatus being considered for use in this same lesson were similarly demonstrated, including various simple arrangements of balls rolling in curved tracks, and various arrangements for comparing the motions of different swinging or oscillating objects. The presenter noted that two balls of different size (radius) can be placed side-by-side in curved tracks and, when released together, will roll back-and-forth in unison for a considerable time. He noted that the balls stay in step longer if the apparatus is larger and commented that therefore the experiment is more convincing if the class uses a larger apparatus. He noted that if you use tracks with different curvature, the balls do not stay in step at all, commenting that it's very easy for students to see that the shape of the track is important and that the motion is nearly independent of the radius of the ball. He pointed out that once these phenomena have been demonstrated, the children can be led to ask similar questions about the pendulum and the factors that determine its back-and-forth motion.

He then demonstrated how the children were supposed to use the pendulum to answer these questions.

> One way we've tried that worked well for some children, at least, was to use the clock's second hand and ask them to count the number of swings in half a minute . . . and they very quickly come to the conclusion that, yes, the length of the pendulum does indeed make a difference—the longer the pendulum, the fewer swings you have. Then we can ask another question.

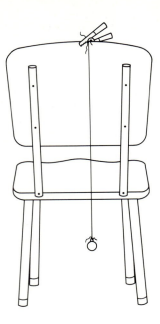

Does the size of the weight on the end make any difference? And there we have to be careful because some of us already know the answer, and that's a disadvantage. The answer is, no, it doesn't make a difference, but you ask the children to try this out and they will almost invariably come to the conclusion that, yes, it does make a difference, and then you have to go into the business of, well, how big a difference and is it an important difference or not.

He then described several approaches that they had considered for dealing with the problem, concluding with the one that his subgroup believed resolved the problem most satisfactorily.

So we thought we'd approach it rather obliquely in this way. Make two pendulums side by side. Don't say anything at all about the length of the two pendulums (which have different weights) but ask the children to take one pendulum, set it in motion . . . and then ask what length does the other pendulum's string have to be to swing exactly in step with the first pendulum. We tried this out just yesterday . . . and they did in fact discover that in order to synchronize the two pendulums the lengths must be less than one half inch different. It is interesting that they were able to adjust the pendulum precisely enough to synchronize the motion of the two pendulums quite precisely so that they'll stay in phase for several swings.

Someone then asked whether all the weights were the same size. No, they were different both in size and weight. Someone remarked and all agreed that, ideally, they would have weights that were the same size, but different weight. The presenter continued:

> That'll involve some bother, making those. Make one out of wood, one out of lead. But that will eliminate the uncertainty that I think accounts for the half-inch, because that half-inch is pretty surely the result [of the fact] that they don't know whether they should measure to the center of the weight or the point where the thing is attached to the string, and we haven't gone into this question. In fact, that's too subtle a question to settle anyway, but that whole question will be circumvented if we use two objects of the same size.

The presenter then went on to indicate that the next question for the children to take up was whether the amplitude of the swing (the range of its back and forth motion) makes a difference in the time taken for each swing. He pointed out that it does make a slight difference, especially at larger amplitudes, but that he doubted whether the children would be able to detect the difference with their method of timing. He pointed out that the effect might be detected by comparing two identical pendulums set in motion with different amplitude, but they had not yet had a chance to try this in their experimental classrooms.

He then demonstrated a different oscillating system, a flat saw blade clamped to a table at one end so that it could be bent and released to vibrate freely. He showed how the vibration could be slowed down by clamping weights and moving them back and forth along the length of the saw blade. This contrasted with the pendulum where weight made no difference.

A question then came from the floor asking how kids could understand the difference between pendulum motion and the vibrating blade.

> I'm not sure that they will understand. I'd hope they will understand it. In fact, they understand that gravity is an essential ingredient for this pendulum because we described this system [in an earlier unit]. . . . But I think we have to make it clear that for the pendulum the earth is an essential part of the system . . . [whereas] for this system [the spring] the earth is not really essential. . . .

There were then several interchanges among those present on this question, pointing up the complexity of the situation in the case of the saw blade and the difficulty of making the comparison they wanted the children to make. As he returned to his demonstration of the saw blade and how children would use it to answer the same sorts of questions as they had answered for the pendulum, he mentioned, as an aside, a difficulty they had encountered in using the materials.

> The guiding principle in all this has been to try to get the children to think about what things are really of primary importance in deciding how the system operates, what things are not very important, and along with that trying to get them interested in making some reasonably precise

measurements so that we try to encourage them . . . to actually measure the length of the pendulum and to actually tell us the number of swings in a given interval of time. We try to underline the importance of making quantitative observations, which they are very reluctant to do. This is a real stumbling block. . . .

This question of how to stimulate children to make accurate measurement, how to show them the value of precise measurement, how to give them a reason for it, dominated the rest of the two-hour meeting, although it had not been on the agenda.

In the subsequent course of the deliberations of this meeting, several possible courses of action to make students appreciate measurement were proposed and considered. Instructors could:

- simply tell the children that measurement is important, that qualitative description is not enough;
- set a problem that would lead children to feel the need for accurate measurement;
- relate measurement to overcoming problems commonly encountered in children's daily lives;
- give children data and have them infer the existence of something hidden, in order to illustrate the power of quantitative data;
- give children a table of data on pendulum lengths and times and have them construct a pendulum the data applies to;
- have children take additional measurements to extend a table of data they would be given in the curriculum materials.

As the merits of each of these alternatives were considered, a wide range of desiderata was advanced, including whether it would interest the children, whether it would be too difficult for them, whether it was good science, whether it would serve as a sound basis for later work in measurement, whether the lesson fitted well in this place in the course, whether it would encourage the proper balance between doubt and commitment in the budding scientist, as well as the cost of the activity.

The strategy that met with most favor and emerged as the resolution was the option to design the activity so that children were asked to begin with two identical pendulums, show that they took equal times to swing, then add weight (or amplitude) to one and find out, as exactly as possible, how much longer or shorter the second pendulum must be made to compensate for its heavier weight or larger amplitude. The request for a quantitative answer (How much longer?) and for explicit comparison rewarded attempts at precise measurement and revealed its value in scientific work. The children would then follow a parallel procedure in studying the vibrating saw blade. Their measurements would be accurate enough to show that the weight attached to the saw blade made a definite difference in its swing-times, in contrast to the case of the pendulum. Thus, children would see the value of taking careful measurements.

At this point, showing evident satisfaction with the work they had done, the group adjourned.

This episode is a good illustration of deliberation as it occurs in curriculum development. Episodes of deliberation about other kinds of curriculum problems such as those encountered in school or school district curriculum planning would be similar in form. Note the following general features of curriculum deliberation apparent in this example.

1. Its purpose is the attainment of agreement on the part of the deliberating body on a course of action to be taken on some curricular problem or issue.
2. It is centered on quite particular courses of action. General, abstract issues or questions may arise in the course of deliberation but these are discussed as means of deciding on a particular action.
3. In reaching agreement on a course of action the group must subjectively weigh competing considerations of very different orders drawn from different realms of discourse, including:

    ▪ theoretical principles from philosophy or the human sciences, as well as from the physical science being taught
    ▪ practical experience or judgment (for example, about what kinds of evidence children will find convincing)

4. The issue is resolved for the group when they hit on a course of action that they can accept as better than any others they have considered and that they judge will eliminate the difficulties that launched the discussion, or at least reduce them to tolerable levels.

Notice that each of these characteristics marks out a trait that theorists seek to eliminate or circumvent. The seeker of universal truth must look beyond the particularities of time and place with which deliberation deals directly.

FUNDAMENTALS OF PRACTICAL REASONING

Those who seek resolutions for practical problems face many quandaries. We will consider some of these under two main headings: posing the problem and reaching a satisfactory resolution.

Posing the Problem

Practical problems originate in feelings of unease, discomfort, dissatisfaction, and the like, or in a sense of challenge, of opportunity, of a feeling that something better is possible. We call these feelings a sense of the problem. A sense of the problem includes feelings and beliefs about what one wants or does not want to happen, as well as feelings and beliefs about the present state of affairs and why it is important enough to demand action. A person's sense of the problem is directly accessible only to that person, but we can try to communicate our sense of the problem to others explicitly in words or implicitly through such nonverbal means as behavior, body language, cries, and tones of voice or other sounds. Sometimes our sense of the problem seems quite clear, even though we might have difficulty expressing it in words. At other times our sense of the problem presents itself to us in the form of a vague uneasiness or dissatisfaction, a feeling that something is not right, a longing for something more, an intuition that something better is possible. We may even experience difficulties of which we are not consciously aware, becoming aware of them only when someone else describes them in ways that we recognize. Life is filled with discomforts that we learn to live with and never identify as problems.

To pose a problem is to transform this inarticulate sense of the problem into an explicit statement of the problem that we can communicate to others who cannot feel what we feel. The act of posing a problem is familiar to most of us only in relation to domestic or personal problems, because public issues usually arrive in the newspaper or over television and have already been posed by others. For the most part we recognize that our children or our schools have a problem of a certain kind, and therefore, the problem comes to us already posed. Our task is then to decide if a problem is adequately posed. So we have little practice at posing problems afresh, starting with our own sense of the problem.

Posing problems requires highly developed conceptual and verbal skills. Just describing difficulties we experience in a way that says nothing about their causes is an important step. If we can pose the problem in a way that also reveals its underlying causes, we are closer to a solution. The most direct way to pose a practical problem is simply to point out what is wrong with things as they are and describe how they should be instead. We can do this with a low-inference description that makes few assumptions and mostly points to things and how they appear to our senses. Or, we can resort to high-inference description that goes beyond describing symptoms and makes a diagnosis. It is a much more powerful statement of the problem, but also a riskier one since it makes many assumptions about the significance of the symptoms, their relationship to one another, their likely causes, and even the prognosis for the course of the problem, treated or untreated. For example, we can say of the problems identified in *A Nation At Risk* that American students' test scores are too low, a low-inference description, or that the curriculum they are being offered is not sufficiently challenging, a high-inference description that amounts to a diagnosis of the causes of the problem. The former statement makes few inferences but is correspondingly unrevealing. The latter gives much more guidance but at the cost of making assumptions that might not be true.

The ideal to be sought in posing problems is to describe the problematic situation so that relevant and important features and values are foregrounded. This demands a deep understanding of the problem, of the conditions that cause the pain and other conditions that maintain and support these, of the origins and causes of the problem and of its ramifications and consequences. A completely adequate posing of a problem offers a model of the problem, which explains its symptoms, origins and causes, and an interpretation of the problem's significance, which explains why this problem deserves attention and cannot be lived with any longer.

An adequate posing of a practical problem is an intellectual achievement in itself. In *Value Systems and Social Process* (1968), Sir Geoffrey Vickers calls this "an appreciation of the situation," and maintains that reaching agreement on a shared appreciation of the situation that is adequate to the demands of the problem is the heart of practical problem-solving. In most instances, posing a curriculum problem well is an important part of discovering a resolution for it, often the most difficult part. When we know what the problematic conditions are as well as the causes, supporting conditions, origins, and ramifications of these conditions, we may truly say we understand the problem. Often, then, it is but a short step to finding a satisfactory resolution. As the saying goes, a problem understood is half solved.

The deliberations of the science curriculum development team illustrate the importance of how the problem is posed. The team began by trying to create a science activity that would encourage students to describe a physical system that exhibited regular repeated motion and then to investigate the factors that affected the motion of that system. This initial formulation of their problem arose naturally from their conception of science as a study of systems and their interactions. Acting on this understanding of their practical problem, the team devised some activities. When they tried these activities, they discovered that students were too easily satisfied with their own rough estimates and saw no need for careful measurement, as a result of which many students confirmed some of their misconceptions about the pendulum's motion. The lesson therefore did not satisfactorily resolve the educational problem. These field trials gave the deliberating group a better, more refined appreciation of the situation they were dealing with and led them to redefine their problem as one of devising an activity that would make students aware of the need for careful measurement in studying this system. They were eventually able to resolve the problem when they posed it differently.

REACHING A SATISFACTORY RESOLUTION

Resolving Practical Problems Versus Solving Theoretical Ones

To resolve a practical problem is quite a different operation from solving a theoretical problem. If we are given a proposed solution to a theoretical problem, we can determine with certainty whether the given answer actually solves the problem by simply substituting the proposed answer into the problem as originally defined; if it satisfies all the terms of the problem, it is a solution and solves the problem for all time. If we also want to know whether the theoretically correct solution conforms to observed fact then we need an additional test of the empirical adequacy of the theory's predictions. For this we make observations under specified and controlled conditions, comparing theoretically predicted results with actual observations. A practical problem, by contrast, is resolved in principle when those addressing the problem find a course of action that they judge to be better than any others known to them. It is resolved in fact—in other words fully resolved—when the course of action has been completed and the results found to be satisfactory.

Solution of theoretical problems and resolution of practical problems both depend ultimately on human judgment, but the form and process of judgment differ radically in the two cases. When experts exercise judgment in determining whether a proposed solution does or does not solve a theoretical problem, they exercise a limited, circumscribed form of judgment, one they are extensively trained to make, and one that is hedged about with checks to ensure agreement among experts. If mathematicians agree that a certain proof demonstrates that the ratio of the circumference of a circle to its diameter is not a rational number, the likelihood that a lawyer, business proprietor, or psychologist can add anything useful to their collective judgment on this professional matter is essentially zero. The considerations relevant to the judgment are limited and the community of mathematicians have accumulated generations of experience in making this kind of specialized judgment. We can summarize this by saying that specialists' judgments on theoretical questions are limited judgments. By contrast, the resolution of most curriculum problems requires open-ended judgments. Open-ended judgments are ones for which the relevant considerations cannot be limited in advance. Most major life decisions are open-ended. We cannot produce a checklist of all the important things to consider in choosing a friend, having a child, or taking a job. Nor can we tell in advance what considerations will be important in establishing the major aims, content, and structure of an educational program. These judgments are open-ended. Once some open-ended judgments have been made, later judgments—for example, of particular objectives and details of content and structure—are then limited by the earlier open-ended choices, but still much more open than is typical of theoretical issues.

Open-ended judgments involve bringing many values to bear on each alternative. In resolving practical problems incommensurable criteria of merit must somehow be weighed on a common scale of value. In comparing two curricula we may find that one leads to better achievement among academically able students while the other leads to better achievement among low achievers. How do we weigh these competing merits in a common scale in order to decide on a curriculum? On what rationally defensible grounds can we choose between adding economics, music, or sex education to an already full elementary curriculum, assuming we have sound proposals and strong support for each? These are examples of **multi-valued choices.** Since the alternatives in a multi-valued choice do not claim to offer the identical benefits to the same recipients, no straightforward calculation of overall merit is possible. Instead, we must ask what trade-offs people are willing to make among competing but incommensurable values. All resolutions of curriculum problems involve such trade-offs. When those involved in the decision disagree on values or priorities, the process of reaching a common judgment is further complicated. How different this is from solving theoretical problems.

Solutions of theoretical problems are eternal and absolute, but resolutions of practical problems must be adapted to the particulars of local circumstances. When even one person has found a solution to a theoretical problem, it remains a solution for all persons and all circumstances, so long as the terms of the problem and the standards of the discipline remain the same. And any expert, given the problem and the proposed solution, can reach a conclusion about the adequacy of the proposed solution. By contrast, resolutions of practical problems are relative to all the particularities and realities of life. Actions taken too late will not resolve the practical problem, nor will actions that are too expensive, too complicated, or lack political support. Resolutions of practical problems must also be adapted to realities of limited time, resources, knowledge, and skill. Theorists may take generations to settle a dispute, but those faced with a practical problem do not have the luxury of suspending judgment. For them, not to act is to act. To judge the adequacy of a proposed resolution of a practical problem, therefore, one must be acquainted with the particularities and realities of the situation in which the problem exists.

The Process of Reaching a Resolution

The process by which either individuals or groups come to a judgment about what they will do about a practical problem is complex and mysterious. Clearly the process involves subconscious components, subjective meanings, and the operation of all sorts of psychosocial needs such as those for power and prestige. For now we will neglect these mysteries and pretend that the process is fully rational in the broad sense of the term. That is, we will assume that people have reasons for their judgments and that they can express these reasons publicly. Their reasons may hold only private, personal significance, they may be complex, inconsistent or incorrect, but we will assume that they have reasons and that they can express them if they wish. We will not assume that people's reasons will always seem good to others or even make sense, only that they have them and can express them if they wish.

Given this assumption, the essential logic of the process of reaching a shared judgment on a public course of action is straightforward. We imagine a course of action that might possibly resolve the problem and ask ourselves, "Would this eliminate the problem?" Using our knowledge and experience, or by reasoning or guesswork, we reach a judgment: yes, no, or not sure. We compare our answers with others' and, when we disagree, we ask for and give our reasons for our judgment. We continue in this way, eventually choosing the one of our imagined actions that seems best, all things considered. The process is a form of mental trial-and-error in which we substitute some form of judgment for the trial itself. "Suppose we did this," we say. "What would happen, and how would we like it?"

People can generate plausible courses of action in many ways, such as by recalling ones that seem appropriate to the present problem or using common sense, guesswork, or intuition. A more systematic and dependable method for developing promising courses of action would obviously be desirable, but no generally useful method is possible because the action must be suited to the specifics of the problem. When we have a model of the problem that describes the factors that produce and sustain the problem, we can use it to develop courses of action that should mitigate the problem if the model is correct. For example, the science education development team shared a sophisticated model of science as the study of systems in interaction, and they used this model repeatedly in designing classroom activities. When we lack a model of the problem we are thrown back on our own resources of mind to find or invent a plausible course of action, but we are free to use any of our inventive faculties without restriction.

When a course of action is proposed and its merits have been debated by a deliberating body, it often happens that an even more promising course of action can be generated by modifying this one so as to accentuate its strong points and overcome its weak points. Thus the proposal is shaped in the course of deliberation. We may then speak of the problem as having been resolved by design. Often when a curriculum problem is resolved by design the resolution is not expressed in words or symbols but in curriculum plans or materials that embody design principles. By following the ramifications of each potential action through all of the factors relevant to the problem, and adding or subtracting other actions, features, or components of our action, we could design a solution in much the same way that a composer solves a musical problem, a product designer or an architect solves a problem in material design, or a business analyst solves a problem in business strategy.

Resolutions achieved by design may be more subtle and intricate than resolutions achieved verbally. Resolution by design is therefore particularly appropriate when the success of a course of action depends crucially on many details. In such cases broad principles are insufficient guides to action, and the deliberating body must find a way to specify in detail the configuration of factors they believe to be crucial to the success of the course of action. To do so abstractly is usually impractical. Verbal elaboration can be tedious and is often ineffective in communicating such fine details. A live demonstration with opportunity for questions would be ideal. (Recall that the science curriculum deliberations presented earlier centered around just such a presentation.) Often the best way to communicate resolutions of curriculum problems to many people unknown to and distant from the deliberators is to design objects that embody the desired relationships (curriculum materials) or to design plans or procedures that others can use like recipes to realize and thus to understand the developers' intentions.

The Quality of Resolutions

Obviously, the quality of any resolution that emerges from such a process depends critically on the basis we have for our judgments about 1) what would happen if we acted in a certain way and 2) how we would like the world we would create by our action. A *basis* is a reason given to support a judgment. The basis for a judgment is the complete set of reasons given to support it. If all you can say to justify your judgment is "It seems to me that a common curriculum would be better for our school," then your intuition is the only basis for your judgment. Your judgment is then completely subjective, since no one else can know how you made it or what lies behind and supports it. This does not mean that the judgment is necessarily bad: some people have very good intuition about some things. But the best others can do to discover the likelihood that your judgment will be good is to check your record in past decisions of a similar kind.

When you provide a more objective basis, others can check or validate your judgment. For example, you might point to other schools that have adopted a common curriculum and argue that they, their students, staffs, and communities are better off than comparable schools that have offered a differentiated curriculum. Others can then study these schools and decide if they agree that schools with a common curriculum are better off. Or, following Adler, you might argue that only a common curriculum is consistent with democratic ideals. Others can then study this argument, as we did in Chapter 4, and decide if they agree with it.

We may represent the rational core of resolution as a process of considering relevant evidence and arguments. From this point of view, those judgments are soundest that are the best informed or most considered. Qualitatively, this means that the most important arguments and evidence are considered and that these are individually sound. Quantitatively, it means that the greatest number and widest range of relevant arguments and evidence are considered. If, after due consideration (another complex judgment), one course of action seems better on balance (still another judgment) than another, then the better must be compared against the next candidate until at last the best course of action is determined.

Resolutions of practical problems reached by deliberation are seldom final or definitive. The reasoning employed in deliberation is plausible inference, not formal logic, mathematical proof, statistical inference, or scientific verification. These rigorous forms of substantiation are not achievable in practical curriculum disputes, not even in principle. In particular, the final weighing of the relative force of various arguments for and against proposed alternatives can never be demonstrated to be superior to other final weightings. It is appropriate, though, to ask whether the resolutions reached are supported by the available evidence, formal and informal. And it is appropriate to ask that the resolution settled on be better supported by the available evidence and argument than any other resolution proposed and considered. But the best that can be expected from deliberation is a resolution *relative* to a limited set of considerations and *relative* to the abilities, values, priorities, and perspectives of the deliberating body. What may seem at the time a final resolution, always turns out to be a temporary one sustained by the shared limitations of a particular view that happened to prevail at the time. When circumstances or advances in knowledge change the prevailing view, the resolution stands revealed as only a partially valid resolution, and calls are heard for new reforms to bring practice in line with newly emerging views.

Although resolution by design adds additional flexibility and power to the possibility of an abstract resolution of curriculum problems, resolutions by design remain subject to the limitations inherent in all practical problems. Resolutions, whether expressed in a design or verbally, are still relative to the judgment of the deliberating body, and therefore different deliberators may reach different resolutions. Any resolution may be upset by the discovery of an alternative course of action not previously considered or a previously unknown line of argument. Any resolution requires weighing incommensurable considerations, and a different weighting may result in a different resolution.

Is Practical Reasoning Worth the Effort?

Since it does not lead to definitive resolutions, should we take practical reasoning seriously, then? Will we be squandering our limited time and energy in deliberation when no resolution can ever be shown definitively to be best? If resolutions are mere matters of opinion, why not just express the opinions in the first place and avoid the hassle of deliberation? In considering these important questions we must be careful to avoid polarizing all possibilities for the status of resolutions into two extreme opposites: truth and opinion. In such a dualism all answers to curriculum problems fall into the realm of opinion, and so all effort at rationality seems futile. Even if we cannot reach the perfect solution possible in theoretical problems, we can still aspire to make better decisions than we would had we simply acted on our first impressions.

Whether the benefits of deliberation are worth the effort depends on the situation and on how well it is done. Decisions can be over-considered as well as under-considered, as the great English essayist and wit, Samuel Johnson, pointed out so eloquently more than 200 years ago when he said:

> Life is not long, and too much of it must not pass in idle deliberation how it shall be spent; deliberation, which those who begin it by prudence, and continue it with subtility, must, after long expense of thought, conclude by chance. To prefer one future mode of life to another, upon just reasons, requires faculties which it has not pleased our Creator to give us. (Boswell 1952, 368)

Whereas theoretical problems generally have only one solution, and that one perfect, practical problems generally have many imperfect solutions. Infinitely fine gradations of resolution are possible. The quality of resolutions will in general depend on the situation: A course of action may be better than all known alternatives for urban schools, but not rural ones, for large schools but not small ones, for academically talented students but not for average ones, for communities where children have few other opportunities but not for communities with a surfeit of juvenile options, and so on indefinitely. The quality of resolutions may legitimately depend on the perspective of the person making the assessment: A course of action may be better than all known alternatives in the judgment of educational psychologists but not in the judgment of professional educators in the field, in the judgment of educators but not of the lay community, in the judgment of the better educated but not of the less educated, in the judgment of progressives but not of traditionalists, and so on indefinitely. The more the judgments differ, the more nearly a resolution seems to be a matter of mere opinion; the more they converge, the more nearly resolutions seem to be solidly grounded in something approaching truth. But the territory between these two extremes is the domain of the practical and it is there, where rationality guides but does not dictate, that most curriculum decisions fall.

From a humane perspective, the fact of being generally unable to reach universally acceptable, completely adequate resolutions to practical problems is an asset as much as a liability. It leaves us with a rich diversity of defensible actions. Who, after all, would want to live in a world where rationality dictated our every move? When, after due consideration, several courses of action seem defensible, then we have scope for freedom, self-expression, invention, assertion of will, even playfulness. Surely the world is a better place when scope for human choice can coexist with rationality.

THE STRUCTURE OF PRACTICAL ARGUMENTS

The basic argumentative strategy in practical reasoning is to generate courses of action that are candidate resolutions for the practical problem and then to rule out candidates by using arguments that appeal to evidence and values until one is reached that is on balance superior to all the others. The forms of such arguments have been extensively analyzed by Stephen Toulmin in *The Uses of Argument* (1958). Toulmin maintains that the basic form of all practical arguments is expressed in the following sentence-pattern, which I have slightly rephrased, intending to retain the original sense.

Since we are committed to P, we must rule out anything involving Q; to do otherwise would be R, and would invite S.

P stands for the principle that is being appealed to as grounds for the argument;
Q stands for the course of action under consideration;
R stands for the wrong that would be committed;
S stands for the penalties risked.

Some curricular arguments we encountered in the science curriculum development deliberations can readily be cast in this form. For example, consider the following paraphrases:

1. Since <u>students should learn to think as scientists do, which among other things requires that they decide for themselves when their data are adequate</u> (P), we must rule out <u>telling them they must measure more accurately</u> (Q); to do otherwise would <u>give them the wrong impression of scientific work</u> (R) and invite <u>formation of inappropriate authoritarian, unscientific attitudes</u> (S).
2. Since <u>students should not learn incorrect or misleading scientific principles</u> (P), we must rule out <u>allowing them to conclude erroneously that the period of a pendulum varies with its amplitude or mass</u> (Q); to do otherwise would <u>teach falsehoods</u> (R) and invite <u>criticism from scientists, parents, and educators</u> (S).

Notice that the principles are normative statements rather than descriptive ones—in other words, they state what should be the case rather than what is. Notice also that the courses of action spell out in detail what it is that is ruled out. Notice that the offense to be avoided in each case is a violation of peculiarly educational norms. While it is conceivable that a curricular argument would devolve on the avoidance of some more generic social ill, such as class bias, diminished economic prospects, or incapacity in the role of citizen, it is much more common for curricular arguments to devolve on specifically educational norms and ideals. Finally, recall that these arguments are part of an ongoing deliberation and that they appeal to a common set of agreed-upon principles so that debate about the principles themselves is therefore presumably no longer necessary.

Suppose we now adopt a skeptical attitude toward such arguments. We ask: "How do you know that this principle rules out that course of action?" In responding to such a challenge we must, according to Toulmin, refer to some data, some facts that we regard as supporting our claim, and to some warrants, some rules or principles that we believe justify the connection between the data and the conclusion and thus give the argument its force. We may also need to give some qualifiers, statements of conditions under which the general claim made by data and warrant may not hold. This type of argument we may call a justification. The general form of justifications can be diagrammed as follows:

Data — > Conclusion
　　　　ᴧ　　　　　　　　　　　　　　　　　　　　　　ᴧ
　　　　⋮　　　　　　　　　　　　　　　　　　　　　　⋮
　　　　⋮
　　Warrant　　　　　　　　　　　　　　　　　　Qualifier

(Recall that conclusions are courses of action that the justification either rules out—(less categorically, counts against)—or supports.)

In the first of the two arguments above, the conclusion is that the activity should not depend on some authority (the teacher or the curriculum materials) telling students to make more accurate measurements. The data in this case are the classroom observations that students did not see the need for careful measurement even when given various hints and also that the proper understanding of the system under study (the pendulum) demands more careful measurement than students make, even when given hints. The warrant for this conclusion would be something like this: students should generally rely on their own judgment rather than on authorities in judging what data to collect to resolve a scientific question they are studying. One might qualify this conclusion as applying only or especially to the study of science, and perhaps also qualify it to permit exceptions when the acceptance demanded is temporary and students are assured that everything will be explained soon. In the second argument, the conclusion is that students should not be allowed to leave the activity with false and misleading conclusions about the laws governing the motion of a pendulum. The data again comes from classroom observations that many students did draw erroneous and misleading conclusions from their participation in the activity. The warrant is presumably: Students should generally not be taught or allowed to learn incorrect or misleading things. We might want to qualify this in any of several ways, such as 1) whenever this can be prevented with reasonable foresight and effort or 2) except in the case of "useful fictions" that are not too far wrong and that facilitate learning of the correct thing when students are able to comprehend it.

Notice that in both examples, the warrant is not empirically testable, even in principle. One could design studies to determine whether feeding students conclusions they did not understand made them more accepting of other conclusions from authorities. But even if the studies found no such effect, the scientific community still upholds as a general value reliance on the independent judgment of each scientist and frowns upon imposition of methods or conclusions by any authority, no matter how respected. The warrant in the second example simply asserts as a value commitment that students should not be taught falsehoods. If pressed, one could no doubt find empirical consequences of teaching falsehoods, but even if solid evidence were found to show that in many cases no serious consequences follow from teaching falsehoods, the norm of teaching truth and avoiding falsehood would remain in force.

Notice also that in both examples the data are the key to the argument. The warrants are obvious truisms, though the choice of which among many possible truisms to apply is not an obvious one. The practical problem being addressed in each case arose from observations of students' reactions to the preliminary versions of the activities—reactions which no one, not even the planners who designed the activities, could have predicted. For this reason we would be justified in calling these arguments data-driven. Not all curricular arguments are data-driven. Presumably, at an earlier point in their deliberations, when the team decided to undertake an activity such as this one, an activity that involved studies of the variables influencing a system, an activity that would demonstrate the value of careful measurement, they employed mainly theory-driven arguments, arguments in which the key elements were general statements about education, science, science education, society's needs, children's needs, and the like, and the data are provided by the ordinary experiences of students and teachers.

Some such justification as this lies behind each argument given for adopting a course of action or ruling one out. The grand or ultimate conclusion that "We should do Q" rests on many arguments for and against many potential courses of action, and each of these arguments implies data, warrants, and qualifications. It is this entire web or network of practical argumentation that forms the basis for and justifies the ultimate conclusion. Curriculum theory focuses our attention on the principles and values in which such arguments are grounded, to the neglect of the data, the specifics of the courses of action, and the qualifying conditions. Theory plays an indispensable part in deliberation by supplying and clarifying terminology, principles, and lines of argument and by drawing out hidden implications, pointing out needs for additional data, and the like. But the attempt to decide what should be the purpose, content, and organizing principles of an educational program by the use of theory alone (or first, before practical considerations are taken up) sacrifices the intimate interplay of data, warrants, qualifications, and conclusions. Achieving a productive interplay of principles and data in making the many judgments and decisions that must go into any curriculum is the goal toward which we must strive.

No objection can be sustained, however, against the use of theory as a resource for identifying, discussing, and resolving practical problems. Theories of various kinds can provide the concepts needed for posing and discussing problems, the substantive principles on which to base arguments showing that one course of action is better than another, and even the criteria by which a resolution may be judged. We can now see how it is possible to resolve curriculum problems rationally without fulfilling the impossible requirement to build a comprehensive theory to answer all the questions that arise in curriculum practice.

CONCLUSION: CURRICULUM AS A PRACTICAL ENDEAVOR

This, then, is the other way of grounding curriculum practice in ideas promised at the beginning of the chapter. The grand intellectual project of the practical is to ground practice in a rich, strong, and productive interplay of principles and data, not in a curriculum theory. The result hoped for from this project is better curriculum decisions, not new ideas or authenticated knowledge, though these may arise as a byproduct. Those who embrace the intellectual project of the practical must abandon the grand project of curriculum theory as misguided, although theory still plays an honorable, if more modest, role in curriculum considered as a practical endeavor.

Good deliberation is the main strategy for realizing the project of the practical. But deliberation is not a panacea. To do it well is an art that demands much study and long practice and entails much trouble and expense. The best-considered decision can lead to poor results because of human ignorance or unforeseeable events. Yet all hopes for rationality in human affairs rest on the assumption that more well-considered choices will turn out better, on the average and over the long run, than less well-considered choices. The alternative is to assume that our minds are impotent and our actions are beyond our understanding. Even good deliberation can go awry and cause harm, especially the harm of wasted resources and delay. As for poor deliberation, even the most inveterate and unexamined reliance on theory can be no worse than deliberation done poorly.

A major purpose of this book is to show how curriculum practice can be strengthened and improved through the adoption of a practical perspective and mastery of the associated practical arts. The next chapter presents some of the arts of curriculum deliberation.

QUESTIONS FOR STUDY

1. Classify the following types of problems as theoretical or practical and explain why.

    finding the best location for a bridge
    deciding whether to build a new school
    determining the occupation a person is best suited for
    determining the winning essay in an essay contest
    deciding whether a mathematical proof is correct
    deciding whether a sentence is grammatically correct

    In general, how can a person determine whether a given type of problem is practical or theoretical?

2. Consider the curriculum questions that divided progressives and traditionalists, as explained in Chapter 3. Which of these are posed as theoretical questions and which as practical ones? Do you think these questions were correctly posed or were practical questions sometimes mistaken for theoretical ones or vice versa?

3. Refer to the limitations of theory noted in Chapter 4. Consider whether the limitation you regard as most serious is overcome by adopting a practical perspective on curriculum problems.

4. Consider the following situation. A private boarding school (secondary, 1,000 students, college preparatory) in rural Massachusetts has adopted an annual schedule in which the fall semester ends at Thanksgiving and the Spring semester begins after the holidays in January. During the month between Thanksgiving and the Christmas/New Year holiday the school offers an array

of minicourses designed by teachers to be interesting and worthwhile to students. Students must enroll in a full schedule of minicourses and must choose at least one in each major academic area and one in physical education. To relieve the academic pressure and to encourage students to explore unfamiliar subjects, no grades are given for minicourses. The physical education department has devised what the teachers think is an attractive array of minicourses, including jogging, free swimming, stretching and flexibility, handball, and various other games and sports, yet they have an attendance problem. Students cut classes during the minicourses with much greater frequency than during the regular semesters. (Students are required to be enrolled in some physical education class or sport at all times.) What should the physical education department do?

5. Choose a real curriculum issue facing a school you know.
   a. Through simulated deliberation identify at least three promising courses of action.
   b. Discuss the merits of these alternatives, tailoring and redesigning them as appropriate to respond to valid criticisms. List the main arguments used in your deliberation.
   c. Suggest how the problem might be resolved to the greatest satisfaction of all interested parties. Is yours a resolution at the level of theory? Does it contain any elements of a resolution by design? Does your resolution do justice to the highest values of all interested parties? Do you personally favor this action? If not, would you oppose it? Explain.

6. Read an article that proposes a curriculum reform. *Educational Leadership, Phi Delta Kappan, Clearinghouse,* or a similar journal intended for local school officials are good sources. Identify the words and phrases that express the author's posing of the problem. Identify the courses of action the author considers and the main arguments given in behalf of each. Examine the data (evidence) and warrant (principles) for each argument. Comment on the quality of the practical reasoning in the article.

7. Examine the claims made for some school subject by its advocates and compare these claims with what actually happens when the subject is taught. For example, physical education is often said to promote an integration of mind and body ("a sound mind in a sound body"), but to what extent do actual courses in physical education accomplish this or even seriously attempt it? Also, foreign languages are justified on grounds of intercultural understanding, yet they often consist largely of drill on vocabulary and syntactic patterns. If your finding is typical, what do you conclude about the relationship between deliberation and action, and what implications does your conclusion have for using a practical approach to curriculum problems?

8. Discuss the following statement from the standpoint of either an advocate or a critic of a practical approach to curriculum problems. Better still, stage a debate.

The trouble with curriculum thought and practice in this country since *Sputnik* is that it has been attempted without reliance on theory. Hence, curricula have been piecemeal, uncoordinated, and formless. Attempts to guide learning without a theory of learning, to transmit knowledge without a theory of knowledge, to alter attitudes without a theory of personality, and to reform society without a theory of society, are doomed to failure.

RECOMMENDED READING

The seminal work on the topic of this chapter is Joseph Schwab's *The Practical: A Language for Curriculum* (1970). It is powerfully argued, elegantly written, and makes demanding reading, but it amply rewards close study and many careful readings. Israel Scheffler's article "Justifying Curriculum Decisions" (1958) reaches many of the same conclusions from a more purely technical analysis of the logic of justifying curricular decisions. W. A. Reid's *Thinking About the Curriculum* (1978) contains useful ideas on the application of practical reason to curriculum.

On the more general topic of practical reasoning, we are fortunate to have several excellent works easily accessible to the beginner. Aristotle's *Politics* in any of its contemporary translations is still a useful beginning. Thucydides' *History of the Peloponnesian War* (Feetham 1958) includes many powerful testimonials to Greek ideals of deliberation. David Gauthier's spare volume, *Practical Reasoning* (1963), is a sparklingly clear philosophical introduction. Stephen Toulmin's *The Uses of Argument* (1958) meanders about several themes, but the parts on construing practical arguments are still the best elementary treatment of the logic of practical reasoning.

Sir Geoffrey Vickers seems to me to be the most eloquent contemporary spokesman for practical reason as the preferred method for making public decisions in a democracy. *Value Systems and Social Process* (1968) is the most relevant to the concerns of this chapter.

REFERENCES

Adler, Mortimer. 1982. *The Paideia Proposal.* N.Y.: Macmillan.

Boswell, James. 1952. *Life of Johnson.* London: Oxford University Press.

Feetham, H. B. (tr.) 1958. *Thucydides' History of the Peloponnesian War.* Chicago: Encyclopedia of Brittanica.

Gauthier, David. 1963. *Practical Reasoning.* Oxford: Clarendon Press.

National Commission on Excellence in Education. 1980. *A Nation at Risk.* Washington, D.C.: Department of Education.

Reid, William A. 1978. *Thinking About the Curriculum.* London: Routledge and Kegan Paul.

Schwab, Joseph. 1970. *The Practical: A Language for Curriculum.* Washington, D.C.: National Education Association.

Toulmin, Stephen. 1958. *The Uses of Argument.* Cambridge: Cambridge University Press.

Vickers, Geoffrey. 1968. *Value Systems and Social Process.* N.Y.: Basic Books.

chapter 6

THE ART OF CURRICULUM DELIBERATION

Life is brief, the art long, opportunity fleeting, experiment perilous, judgment difficult.

Hippocrates
Greek physician, fourth century, B.C.

PURPOSE OF THE CHAPTER

- to acquaint the reader with the difficulties encountered in real curriculum deliberation
- to describe the skills required to handle real curriculum problems competently by means of deliberation
- to assess the strengths and limitations of deliberative approaches to curriculum problems in comparison with alternative approaches.

OUTLINE

THE DELIBERATIVE IDEAL

Issues of what to do about the purpose, content, and structure of educational programs can never be resolved with the finality and certainty of some theoretical questions, but this does not mean that curriculum issues are simply matters of opinion or that all proposed resolutions are equally satisfactory. In the ideal case, good deliberation will show that some courses of action are better, given certain values and certain beliefs. Unfortunately, the ideal case is far-removed from real curriculum deliberation.

Looking at the ideal, full and fair curriculum deliberation would 1) construe the problem in the most defensible way (or ways); 2) consider all the most promising alternative courses of action; 3) consider in full the merits of each alternative, taking into account all relevant knowledge and using valid arguments to examine the bearing of this knowledge on the issue; 4) explore the points of view and values of all interested parties to the decision; and 5) reach a fair and balanced judgment. Deliberation that fails on any of these criteria would be clearly inferior to deliberation that meets them all. This is obviously a difficult ideal to attain. In fact, it is easy to see that the ideal can only be reached with complete knowledge and with perfect justice in dealing with disputed values. The ideal's usefulness, then, lies in setting an absolute standard in terms of which real deliberations may be compared. We can understand a great deal about the quality of real deliberations by comparing them against this standard.

Difficulties of Deliberation: Limitations in Principle

Deliberative bodies cannot avoid some difficulties. To be certain of attaining the ideal, a deliberative body would, among other things, have to possess complete knowledge of both principles and the particulars of the contexts in which the action would be taken, to agree on value priorities, and to possess the power and resources needed to deliberate and to act on their conclusions. In practice, deliberative bodies never meet all these conditions; they rarely even approach them. The gaps between the conditions presupposed and those actually prevailing in deliberation give rise to some inherent difficulties with which deliberating bodies must learn to cope.

Limited Knowledge of Principles

When we do not understand the problem or its causes and consequences, we cannot possibly know whether we have construed it properly, considered the most promising courses of action, or examined all the merits of each correctly. Mistaken beliefs are more common and even more dangerous than simple ignorance. Curriculum theory is supposed to provide decision-makers with the principles necessary for curriculum decisions, but the help provided by curriculum theory, as we saw in earlier chapters, is imperfect, and sometimes even downright misleading. For example, at the turn of the century, the prevailing view among educators was that having children practice a difficult learning task improved their ability to learn new material of that type. This belief is a curriculum theory based on the faculty theory of the mind. Acting on this belief educators filled the spelling curriculum with long and arcane spelling words, the mathematics curriculum with intricate calculations, and so on. This mistaken belief misguided curriculum deliberations and led to resolutions of curriculum problems that were ineffective and mis-educative.

Of course, we can never be certain that what we believe we know to be true is actually true. In general, the best we can do is to rely on the beliefs most accepted by the community of scholars that studies that subject. Proponents of this prevailing view may be challenged by others favoring alternative contending views, in which case the deliberating body may choose among the contenders or they may use what Schwab (1970) calls the arts of eclectic, using and combining parts of several theories selectively. For major efforts involving extensive deliberation, the deliberating body may adopt its own distinctive deliberative platform, a body of beliefs on which they intend to base their deliberations, a kind of tailor-made theory. Real deliberators must make some such compromise with the ideal of full and fair deliberation whenever they have limited knowledge of the principles implicated in the phenomena they are dealing with.

Lack of Knowledge of the Particulars of the Context

Deliberators must choose actions for particular situations: a particular period in the history of a particular country, state, and community, in one or more particular schools or school systems, staffed by particular individuals, and attended by particular students. The deliberators must know the particulars of this situation. However, no one can have full knowledge of the situation of even one school or classroom. Even the keenest, most well-placed observer can experience at best a small sample of the realities of these settings, and even this part is filtered through a particular perspective. Understanding human interactions in schools and classrooms requires skills on the same order as understanding the interactions of individuals in families, and this understanding often eludes even the skilled therapist.

Lack of Agreement on Value Priorities

Even when knowledge is essentially complete and deliberation is thorough, arguments about the comparative merits of different courses of action always appeal to some values. A different set of values or different priority ordering among them may lead to a different final judgment given the same beliefs. For example, members of a school community council may agree that teaching students how scientists and scholars verify knowledge claims makes students more intellectually independent and willing to challenge authority, but the members may disagree about the desirability of this aim in comparison with teaching children to respect authority. Curriculum decisions seem to be more suffused with values than many other types of public decisions, perhaps because they deal so intimately with matters of personality and culture. Whatever the reason, curriculum decisions often hinge on value questions at least as much as on questions of knowledge and belief.

Limited Resources and Power

For deliberation to be effective, the deliberating body must have the resources to carry out whatever deliberations the problem requires. In some cases, resolving a curriculum problem through full and fair deliberation may require extensive background research, advice from experts in dozens of fields, months or even years of hearings and discussions, and years of experimental programs, evaluations, and revisions. Assigning such a problem to a committee with a budget of $1,000 and four weeks time produces a travesty of deliberation, but even the most ambitious efforts we could envision—say, a $20,000,000 project with a five year life—would still be forced to leave many promising possibilities unexplored.

Few deliberative bodies have the power to make curriculum decisions by themselves, let alone to carry them out. Typically, some official or governing body asks the deliberators to *recommend* an action. The recommendation is then subject to some form of ratification—perhaps a period for public comment followed by a vote of the school board, in the case of local school systems. Even those officially empowered to decide may lack the power to act. Superintendents and school boards, for example, cannot bring an adopted program into reality in schools and classrooms without the collaboration of teachers and principals. When deliberative bodies lack power to decide and to act, their only option is to attempt to influence those who have the power. This complicates and distorts the deliberation by introducing a different criterion for a good resolution: one that the powers-that-be will accept. Persuading those with the power to act can become an end in itself rather than the means of implementing good curriculum decisions. On the other hand, ignoring the wishes of those with the power to act risks losing the practical point of the deliberation. Why waste time resolving a problem if those who can do something about it do not listen?

Deliberators in the real world must always keep in view the end of building or retaining a base of power in addition to resolving the practical problem at hand. All too often those who discuss curriculum issues lack any power to act and their first priority is to acquire some influence over those who do. As we shall see in detail in subsequent chapters, the authority to make curriculum decisions in the American system of educational governance is widely distributed and constantly shifting. Therefore most discussions of curriculum questions are designed to influence the general public, the profession at-large, key educational decision-makers, or an undefined combination of the three. Whatever genuine deliberation may occur in these discussions is done by those with a special interest or particular viewpoint to advance and consists of seeking those actions most likely to gain them power by attracting support from the public, the profession, other powerful interest groups, or key decision-makers and leaders.

Strictly speaking, then, full and fair deliberation requires conditions never fully realized and seldom closely approached. The ideal remains useful, however, if we understand that our goal need not be to attain it but rather to approach it as closely as circumstances permit.

DELIBERATIVE ART

There are no rules for carrying on the fullest and fairest deliberations possible under particular circumstances. Those who would succeed at this task must master many skills and use them artfully. In this section we will briefly survey some techniques for coping with some serious difficulties commonly encountered in curriculum deliberation, including techniques for using ideas constructively, for considering context, for managing value conflicts, and for adapting deliberation to economic and political realities.

Building a Sound Base of Knowledge

Behaving as though we know everything relevant to our decisions and as though all our beliefs are true is not a constructive response to curriculum problems. Our understanding of most curriculum issues is clearly limited and fallible. Furthermore, members of a deliberative body typically enter the deliberations with quite different beliefs. What we need are constructive ways of proceeding with deliberations in the face of such limitations.

One important response to these inherent limitations is for the deliberators to give explicit attention to the knowledge and beliefs they will use. In curriculum deliberation we often find that a working group adopts its own distinctive set of shared ideas, often including some that are not among those prevailing in the educational community. This set of ideas constitutes a kind of deliberative platform, by analogy with a political platform, on which the work of the group is built. The science curriculum planning team quoted earlier relied on a platform of ideas that included the following:

- Youngsters can and should actively manipulate scientific apparatus themselves and collect data of their own.
- Youngsters should not be asked to accept a scientific conclusion unless they are convinced of its correctness by the force of the data.
- Children's natural or inherent curiosity should be respected and nurtured.
- Children learn best by doing and experiencing the results of what they do.

The planning group used such ideas as these in making the decisions that shaped the curriculum materials they designed. The sample of deliberations presented earlier shows how such a deliberative platform is used, along with data from actual classroom trials and the judgment of experienced educators, to construe curricular problems. When this episode of deliberation began, the group had chosen to address the problem of how to teach children scientists' ways of describing and investigating physical systems. The planner's shared views about science teaching made this problem seem important enough to deserve the children's attention. The planning group believed that most elementary school children were not learning these important skills. Had anyone questioned these convictions, any member of the team could have offered such explanations as: children need to learn to think as scientists think; children need to master fundamental concepts of science; or children need to discover or rediscover scientific knowledge for themselves. As the team examined the materials they had designed for this purpose and listened to accounts of tryouts of the materials in classrooms, they discovered other problematic elements in the situation. And so the initial posing of the problem was refined and transformed as they worked with it.

The planning team was not troubled much by the question raised by one member about the activity being too far removed from the children's everyday experience. Their shared platform of ideas did not include a commitment to connecting scientific principles to everyday experience. Had such a commitment been prominent, the activity they chose might have been quite different. For example, they might have measured heart rates or breathing rates or studied children on playground swings. Had they shared the then-prevailing view among educators, they would doubtlessly have emphasized nature study to a much greater extent than they did. Then their activities might have included collecting leaves, studying the weather, making maps of the area, and the like. But then there would have been little need for a curriculum materials development project whose whole point was to develop materials to support an alternative view of science education.

Constructing deliberative platforms explicitly early in the life of a deliberative group and updating them periodically during the group's work can be a helpful tactic. It is important that the deliberative platform include explicit models of the curriculum problems or issues with which the group will be concerned. Why and how did the problem arise? Why has the problem persisted? What are its causes? Its consequences? Where, as will often be the case, the deliberative group is uncertain about answers to such questions, the members should make assumptions and explicitly label them as such. Where alternative assumptions seem about equally plausible, they should state the alternatives and strive to study the problem further until they can reconcile them or show that one is preferable.

Deliberators can guard against some of the pitfalls of theory both in building platforms and in deliberation by grounding terms in shared experience of real phenomena. They can develop a habit of discussing issues by reference to real cases, instances, and examples. When these are not available, they can construct hypothetical ones. In considering courses of action, deliberators need not stop with verbal descriptions. Right from the beginning, they can develop hypothetical models or sketches of proposed actions and schematic or physical models or prototypes. Those who commission deliberation on curriculum issues might well sponsor a sort of design competition among deliberative bodies, in which each is invited to submit preliminary platform statements and plans to the commissioning group. The commissioners can then solicit comment and criticism from the public, the profession, and various kinds of experts about concrete proposals. Precedents can be systematically studied, especially where some precedents succeeded and others failed, so that some comparative analysis of faults and causes of failure becomes possible.

Good deliberators are self-critical. They study their own deliberations to identify weak arguments, unexamined assumptions, and overlooked considerations. When they find a gap or contradiction in their platform, they welcome the discovery as an opportunity to extend and deepen their understanding and to reach a more satisfactory resolution of the problem they are considering. Good deliberators actively seek additional knowledge by consulting appropriate experts, reading, and even by commissioning briefing papers. They keep their work open to scrutiny by others and welcome comment and criticism. They seek out informed and able people to comment on and criticize their work, including platform statements, design prototypes, and draft materials. They try out promising solutions early and often and discuss the results intensively. They may even commission research or evaluation by others.

Making Artful Use of Knowledge through Argumentation

A good knowledge base by no means guarantees good deliberation. Deliberators must also be artful in applying their knowledge to particular problems. This application, as we saw in the last chapter, involves the construction of practical arguments. These arguments come thick and fast in the heat of discussion, so it can be helpful to keep minutes and condensed records of deliberations, outlines of issues considered, proposals made, and arguments accepted and rejected. Expert or representative reviewers (or both) can be asked to comment critically on the deliberations or to assist with difficulties encountered by the deliberating body. When more intensive deliberation seems needed, the deliberating body can explore more alternative proposals in more depth. Doubters and dissenters can be deputized to explore promising alternative paths. When comprehensiveness of deliberation is particularly important, checklists can be employed to guide deliberation and maps made and displayed showing issues and arguments explored so far.

It is convenient to think of two modes of deployment of practical arguments. One uses arguments to generate courses of action that are likely to be worthy of later consideration; the other uses arguments to examine the merits of a course of

action. The prevailing view regards generative processes as mysterious manifestations of nonrational sides of our personalities, but the most careful studies of
creative work in various fields imply that creative work is a form of rationality
similar to ordinary reasoning. David Perkins, a psychologist at Harvard University,
has studied the creative process in persons of outstanding achievement in various
fields by asking them to think aloud or report their thoughts immediately after
episodes of invention. His subjects reported many experiences that felt like mental
leaps or flashes of insight, but he concluded after careful study that these were only
rapid, effortless reasoning. In Perkins' words,

> Many mental leaps are explained by the ordinary mental
> processes . . . that . . . accomplish quickly what one might attempt more
> consciously and deliberately over a somewhat longer period. (Perkins 1981,
> 65)

Perkins' studies led him to conclude that "creating occurs when ordinary mental
processes in an able person are marshaled by creative or appropriately 'unreasonable' intentions" (Perkins 1981, 101). The roles played by feelings and emotions in
creativity were not inconsistent with rationality, either. On the contrary,

> Cognition and affect are not distinct aspects of creative experience.
> Emotions provide knowledge, point to knowledge, and constitute
> knowledge crucial to the maker. Emotions are a way of knowing. (Perkins
> 1981, 121)

The generative thought processes in deliberation are a form of reasoning, a form
that seems mysterious when we are somehow able to propose a creative course of
action even though we cannot readily recount the arguments that led to our
discovery. When we have an explicit model of the problem we can use it to
generate actions that would have desired effects. Without a model of the problem,
we can only guess, and then the sources of our guesses seem mysterious. We cast
about for anything at all in our accumulated experience that might help us
understand this situation. An insight here, a plausible guess there, and a dimly
remembered similarity, and, without our being aware of what has happened, we
find that a proposed course of action has sprung to mind. Once it has been stated,
we can consider its merits. We can shore up its weak points. We can compare it with
still other proposals that are like it in most respects but without objectionable
features. If we look carefully, we will find that when a proposal comes to us in a
flash, we were using an implicit, intuitive, perhaps crude and incomplete model of
the problem. Good deliberators will cultivate this implicit model and work to make
it explicit and thus accessible both to others and to ordinary processes of thought.

SOME COMMON ARGUMENTATIVE PITFALLS

Sound fundamentals are vital in any art, yet my impression is that mistakes in fundamentals are surprisingly common in curriculum deliberation. In 1977 James Hessler, then a graduate student in the School of Education at Stanford, studied the quality of argumentation in professional journals in education. Such writing is not itself deliberation, but Hessler made the assumption that, since consideration of the merits of possible educational reforms is a primary purpose of the writing, journal articles should, taken as a whole over a period of time, reflect good deliberation. He used content analysis to study assertions made about individualization of instruction and the evidence cited for these assertions in a random sample of one-fifth of the articles published in professional journals between 1929 and 1974. He expected to find that the claims made for or against individualized instruction in this large body of professional literature would be balanced, complete, and appropriately qualified. For each assertion he found he recorded the following information:

1. Did the assertion identify a strength, a weakness, or was it simply a neutral claim?
2. Was it a global, undifferentiated claim or a qualified, differentiated claim? (For example, an undifferentiated claim would be something like: "Individualization increases students' motivation"; a more differentiated claim would be something like: "Individualization increases motivation for those students who do not set their goals with reference to their peers.")
3. Was evidence stated or implied to back up the assertion? (If so, was it supportive, opposing, or neutral to individualization? Was the evidence empirical, based on personal experience, authorities, popularity, *a priori*, or other argument?)

Hessler analyzed a total of 252 articles on individualization. For comparison, he studied 29 medical articles on heart bypass surgery. Box 6-1 summarizes his results.

Hessler found that in the individualization literature a few articles cited most of the evidence while the bulk of the articles seldom cited evidence. Of those articles that cited evidence of any kind, the greatest number cited the authors' personal experience—nearly 40%. Only about 25% of the citations were of empirical evidence.

In short, this educational literature consisted largely of simple claims for or against a named practice that was seldom carefully defined, with little evidence provided and that drawn mostly from the authors' personal experience. Hessler concluded that

> The literature of education is dominated by the repetition of assertions which are often unsupported by any sort of evidence. . . . The literature

BOX 6-1   Comparison of Evidence Cited in Arguments from Articles in Professional Journals in Education and Medicine

	Education (individualization)	Medicine (heart bypass)
median assertions per article	6	9
ratio of supporting arguments to total arguments	2/3	2/3
% of claims above level 2 on 1–4 scale of differentiation	10%	40%
median citations of evidence per article	3	10
% of articles citing empirical evidence for more than 2/3 of assertions made	18%	50%

SOURCE: (Adapted from Hessler 1977)

provides insufficient information to the reader to permit judgment about the worth of particular findings or suggestions, or to relate the findings and suggestions of one author to another. . . . [In comparison,] the articles in medicine contain a consistency of expression beyond jargon, syntax or semantics . . . which is not evident in the literature of education. (Hessler 1977, 85).

In addition to the problems Hessler found, the following fundamental mistakes in deliberation are surprisingly common.

1. **Failure to consider alternatives.** Sometimes deliberating bodies become convinced at an early stage in their deliberations that one alternative is clearly superior to all others and then confine their deliberations to questions of how to achieve it. Sometimes people are impatient or anxious to avoid divisiveness and delay. Sometimes people simply do not perceive what they are doing as deliberation. Rather, they think of themselves as making decisions and perceive true deliberation on genuine alternatives as indecisive. Whatever the reasons for it, failure to consider the relative merits of several promising alternatives reduces deliberation to strategizing about implementation.

2. **Failure to consider arguments against courses of action.** Many people are reluctant to argue against a promising proposal. They fear alienating its proponents, gaining a reputation as a negative person, as disloyal, or as being "not a team

player," or interfering with the formation of the consensus needed for action. Some argue that no one ever made a reputation as a dynamic leader by raising objections. Objecting to a proposal backed by a dynamic leader is hardly an heroic role and may endanger one's career prospects. Yet, to enter into a process of educational reform without having considered what can be said against the reform would be naive to the point of irresponsibility. More likely, what happens in such cases is that the negatives are considered privately, while an entirely positive image is displayed to the public. What the public hears, then, is not genuine deliberation but advocacy in disguise. Alert, experienced, self-respecting audiences will not be fooled, but they may not always have the power to insist on genuine deliberation.

3. **A restricted range of arguments.** Deliberation is easier and less threatening when arguments considered pro and con for the various alternatives are restricted to a few topics or are not pursued to sufficient depth. Any proposal can be made to look good if only its best features are considered, or made to look bad if only its worst are considered. It is easy to produce arguments based on personal impressions and common sense, but difficult to support them when they are seriously challenged. Deliberations in which superficial arguments and merely plausible claims go unchallenged can proceed smoothly to a neat conclusion based on the flimsiest of evidence and argument.

4. **Oversimplification.** The maladies of deliberation mentioned so far have been detectible from the form of the deliberations. But even if the form is perfect, argumentation can go wrong. One of the most common substantive shortcomings of curricular arguments is implicit reliance on oversimple models of causation. "A few more minutes of instruction per day in mathematics will lead to substantial improvements in mathematics achievement." "Expose students to examples of excellence in literature and they will develop good literary tastes." "Individualization develops children's initiative." Any experienced educator who gives the matter more than a moment's thought can easily think of other factors that must also be present if the promised results are to be realized. It is the rule in curriculum matters that several factors must be present and operating in conjunction for results to be achieved: students must be motivated, they must possess prerequisite knowledge and skill, they must have an effective source of information or instruction, they must have time to learn, opportunities for practice with immediate knowledge of their results, and so on. These other factors need not always be mentioned, but they must always be kept in mind in deliberations and will likely arise with some regularity in considering the merits of realistic proposals.

5. **Reductionism.** An argumentative problem common in curriculum work with a strongly technical orientation is reductionism. The difficulty here is that those aims or arguments that cannot be reduced to some prespecified form are eliminated from consideration. A common example is the insistence on rigid behavioral specification of objectives. In deliberation, it then becomes impossible to raise such issues as developing a mathematical intuition or developing positive attitudes toward mathematics. One must instead speak of explicit performances, such as "can estimate answers to problems within an order of magnitude" or

"freely chooses to engage in mathematical recreations" that are, at best, only possible manifestations of the underlying dispositions to which one would like to refer simply.

Curriculum argumentation is subject to all the ordinary pitfalls of argument, such as guilt (or virtue) by association, confusion of co-occurrence with true causation, teleological arguments, and outright errors of logic. Appeals to authority often substitute for substantive arguments. People seek to persuade through rhetorical tricks when sound arguments fail them. In addition, there are unavoidable difficulties associated with defining proposals in such a way that it makes sense to argue for or against them. For example, some authorities claim not to be able to make sense of arguments that say something should be taught unless they also know how it is to be taught.

Learning to avoid such pitfalls as these is an important part of developing fluency in deliberation, which is, in turn, an important ingredient in curricular expertise. Doing good curriculum work of any kind—policy-making, management, development, implementation, evaluation—requires fluency, power, and precision in handling a vast field of curricular arguments. Specialized knowledge and skill with specifically curricular arguments demands both wide reading in the history and theory of curriculum and deep, careful analysis of cases of curriculum deliberation. You may find Figure 5-2 (p. 166) helpful as a framework for classifying curricular arguments. Such a framework is, of course, no substitute for a detailed study of particular arguments. It is simply an aid in locating the particular argument among others you encounter. Box 6-2 presents a way to keep track of what can otherwise be a bewildering variety of lines of thought about curricular matters. There is no general agreement on such a framework among curriculum scholars or practitioners, as there is in biology or law, so you should not hesitate to develop one of your own. Before you do, though, I suggest you spend an hour or so fitting curricular ideas into this one.

Posing Problems

Once we are aware of having a problem, some questions about it are always in order. How did this problem come to be? Has it always been a problem? Then why has it not been recognized as such or, if it has, why has it not been solved? If it has become problematic only recently, then what accounts for its becoming problematic now? Also, what sustains this problematic situation? In most cases people act, individually or collectively, to overcome situations they consider problematic. Have they done so in this case? If so, why does the problem persist in spite of these efforts? If they have not acted, why? Also, are there other plausible ways of posing this problem? What can be said for them? Is one way of posing it unquestionably

■
BOX 6-2   An Outline of Common Curricular Arguments

Some important lines of argument
  arguments claiming simple desirability: Doing X will:
    realize an ideal, attain a goal (or avoid ills)
    realize inherent potential (of students, society, humanity)
    conform to tradition (classics)
    achieve freshness, novelty
    allow students to have experiences judged to be inherently good
    satisfy wants, desires, preferences, interests
    be natural, conform to natural law

  arguments claiming utility: Doing X will:
    lead to results that will be directly useful in life outside school
    meet needs (students', society's)
    be consistent with social trends
      society will embrace it
    be instrumental to ideal realization
    be instrumental to further important learning

  arguments claiming obligation: Doing X will:
    meet (fail to meet) a moral obligation, such as:
    minister to basic human needs
    be just, fair
    promote equality
    promote freedom, liberty
    promote human dignity
    be consistent with a moral code
    meet (fail to meet) a legal obligation, such as:
    a constitutional right
    provisions of a duly enacted law

  arguments claiming feasibility: Doing X will:
    achieve (fail to achieve) the results we seek
    require resources we can (cannot) afford
    impose time requirements we can (cannot) meet
    produce desirable (undesirable) side effects
    incur acceptable (unacceptable) transition costs
    require human abilities we can (cannot) expect to find
    require human willingness we can (cannot) expect to find
    require social/political/institutional acceptance, support we can (cannot) expect to
      receive
    expose us to risks we can (cannot) bear
    achieve a satisfactory (unsatisfactory) overall benefit/cost ratio

  Selected argumentative strategies
    Show inconsistency:
      between two aims or ideals
      between actions and ideals
      between two actions   *(continued)*

(Box 6-2 continued)

Show failure to resolve the problem as construed
Show faulty assumptions
Produce counter-evidence
Produce a superior problem construal
Challenge a value expressed or implied
Identify a value that is neglected or violated
Show superior comparative advantage (If X is good, Y is better)
Show undesirable holistic or emergent properties of the curriculum, such as:
 balance
 comprehensiveness
 integration, coordination, unity, coherence
Show lack of relevance to contemporary life

---

better or is it possible that *the* problem is really a problem complex made up of many overlapping problems of separate origin?

In deliberation about problems of public education, getting agreement on how the problem should be posed—in other words, on what the problem really is, becomes the first order of business. The varied and contradictory points of view people hold about curriculum matters result in different ways of interpreting the 'same' situation. As Anatol Rappoport expressed it in *Fights, Games, and Debates,* "Without falsifying a single fact, entirely contradictory descriptions can be and are given of . . . situations . . . by selecting (often unconsciously) only the features which support preconceived notions."

Problem identification always involves a reference group. We should routinely read into all curriculum problem statements the preamble "This is the problem as viewed by . . . ." In most cases those who construe a curriculum problem in a certain way have in mind that their formulation applies to some extensive population. The members of the science curriculum project thought of themselves as dealing with problems faced by essentially all American elementary school students and probably by those in many other nations as well. Members of a district curriculum committee generally think of themselves as planning for all the schools, students, and teachers in the district. Individual teachers, however, generally define their curriculum problems in terms of their class and even of individual students in the class. Sometimes disagreements over curriculum problems can be resolved when the parties realize that they have different reference groups in mind.

In my experience, persistent, widespread curriculum problems are always complex and therefore can never be posed adequately in any simple statement. For example, the marginal place given the arts in American public school programs can be posed as a cultural problem—how do we persuade Americans to value the arts as much as they do "serious" academic subjects? Alternatively, it can be posed as a political and economic problem—how do we empower supporters of the arts? It can be posed as an organizational problem—how do we develop professional organizations that represent all the arts, political lobbies at local, state, and national levels, and so on? Or, we could pose the problem in terms of pedagogical deficiencies—how do we encourage better goals and methods of arts education, and prepare enough sufficiently well-educated teachers and teacher educators? All these are likely to be sources of the difficulties comprehended in the perennial problem of lack of attention to the arts in the curricula of American schools, but none is an adequate way to pose the problem.

Several argumentative tactics are common in debates about the merits of two or more ways of posing a problem. One is to explain the problem away by revealing its historical or sociological origins. For example, we could point out that Dewey's concern that public school curricula promote freedom and democracy only became widely shared when Western democracies were threatened from both fascism on the right and communism on the left. Another common rhetorical tactic is to take away the threatening aspects of the negative values implied in the problem. We might, for example, point out that the United States is not a pure democracy, but rather a republic, and that sustaining republican government presupposes that individual freedoms are balanced by civic obligations. Mastery of such rhetorical forms is essential to fluency and power in dealing intellectually with conflicts over how problems are posed.

Willingness to reconsider how the problem under deliberation is posed is the fundamental test of open-endedness in the deliberation and therefore of the status of the issue as truly a practical problem. If the problem itself is not subject to deliberation, if people are prevented from asking whether this is really the problem and, indeed, the most important problem, then the deliberations are limited and the problem is to that extent being treated in a technical rather than a practical way.

Points of View

Ideas are the mainstay of deliberation. These ideas take various forms, including images (exemplars, stereotypes, archetypes), words (names of objects, actions, or events, classification systems), and procedures, together with their associations, interconnections, and relationships. Even the most modest proposal and the most commonsensical reason given in its support presupposes a way of interpreting experience that gives the words their meaning and enables us to make judgments about the proposal and its justification. An individual's ideas about a particular subject are an integral part of a larger fabric or framework of more or less consistent ideas that form that person's educational point of view. In practice, deliberators cannot approach the ideal of a fully informed decision using isolated bits of knowledge only, but rather they must use knowledge embedded in an educational point of view that encompasses and integrates them. Attempting to add or change one idea may create tensions or conflict within a person's point of view, with unpredictable results, and so people will usually resist adopting any such idea until they can reconcile it with their point of view. It is their entire point of view that people bring to deliberation.

When a particular worldview is shared by most people or by a dominant group, we speak of the dominant view or the prevailing view. Most curriculum problems encountered in the daily work of educators are posed in terms of the worldview the educator brings to the situation, which would most commonly be the prevailing view among educators. The sample of elementary science curriculum materials deliberations quoted at length in the previous chapter includes many examples of reliance on the prevailing view among educators, such as that youngsters can and should be taught science, correct science, in classrooms, that children can and should be constructively motivated to participate in science learning, and that classroom activities can and should be carefully designed so that youngsters are likely to learn important things and unlikely to be misled or to fail in their efforts.

In addition to the prevailing view, many other views exist and contend for dominance. Those at odds with the prevailing view generally try to call attention to their views in hopes of attracting adherents. Those who adhere to the prevailing view seldom talk about it, taking it for granted more often than not. For this reason, full statements of the prevailing view and the rationale for it are hard to find. Historical documents from times when the currently prevailing view was challenging an earlier one usually present the case more fully and vigorously than contemporary documents. Current literature defending widely accepted views, where it can be found at all, concentrates on those aspects that are most challenged. The great bulk of prevailing ideas, including some of the most fundamental ones, exist in a state of tacit, unquestioned acceptance. Before people can entertain an alternative view they must come to realize that they have tacitly accepted a prevailing view, that acceptance of this view has consequences, and that there are alternative views with different consequences. Finding ways to bring people to reconsider their commitments is one of the arts of fostering change, and a very high and difficult art.

THE ROLE OF CURRICULUM THEORY IN DELIBERATION

A theory is a more formal, explicit, and coherent set of ideas than a point of view. It should be obvious that theory can play a vital role in forming platforms and posing problems. One of the greatest benefits of theory in any field of knowledge is that it provides a framework of concepts that can be used to pose a certain class of problems such that any problem of the class, when correctly posed using this framework, is meaningful and can be solved in principle. Thus, Adler's theory provides a way of posing problems involving the relationship of the curriculum to the society in a democracy. Adopting a theory simplifies the deliberator's task. The deliberator committed to a behavioristic theory of learning, for example, can use this theory to deduce the most effective way to facilitate learning in any curriculum activity. When theories are correct and essentially complete, resolutions correctly derived from them will behave as predicted. But as we saw in earlier chapters, curriculum theories that are sufficiently correct and complete to serve as sole and unquestioned bases for practical decisions do not exist. Deliberators who behave as though the theories to which they are committed are fully satisfactory may be said to be making an ideological use of theory. Embracing a theory as an ideology simplifies deliberation and makes the deliberators' commitments explicit, but it hinders pursuit of the ideal of full and fair deliberation by closing deliberators' minds to other aspects of reality and other values. We will consider this matter further under the heading of value conflicts later in this chapter.

Considering Context

The conditions under which deliberation occurs are set by the social and institutional context, so the context is a real force affecting deliberation, not just something to be considered or ignored as the deliberators wish. The social and institutional context typically determines membership on the deliberative body, its charge, its authority, and the resources at its command, for example. We are concerned here, however, with the efforts of the deliberating body to take context into account explicitly in its deliberations. Members of the deliberating body who have lived and worked within the immediate context will know it from personal experience. Their minds will be stocked with specific memories of people and events, generally accepted accounts of what typically happens under various circumstances, stereotypes, and genuine theoretical models of how something works. These images generate gut feelings about issues, and surround and suffuse articulate, formal thought and discourse. Each person will have a unique set of images, but they will overlap to some degree with the images of others. They will rely on these images in many ways during deliberation. For example, they may perform thought experiments in which they try to predict how the people in their school might respond to a proposed course of action. Or, they may use their knowledge of classrooms to generate a new course of action for consideration.

The problem for those who would achieve fuller and fairer deliberation is to extend, deepen, and correct these individual images and to reconcile conflicts among them to achieve a sufficiently common basis for judgment and action. Arrange for deliberators to experience the context at first hand whenever possible. Images derived from first-hand experience with the context carry a conviction that is not possible in any other way. Some obvious, staple approaches include:

- observing classrooms and schools,
- holding public hearings, inviting comments,
- interviewing individual students and teachers,

- examining student work,
- touring communities, visiting homes and businesses.

In some cases people are reluctant to show critical features of the context to outside observers, and so other approaches may be needed that catch them off guard, such as shadowing—following an individual (student, teacher, school official) through all the events of one or more days—or going incognito by pretending to be a student, teacher, or school official for a time.

The chief shortcomings of first-hand experience are its cost and the difficulty of ensuring that any one person's inevitably limited sample is typical. Selecting deliberators with extensive prior experience in a variety of roles within the setting can guard against the latter shortcoming, but may introduce other biases common among those who have chosen to remain in a setting for a long time. Consulting individuals with varied experience can be an economical way of extending the experiences of the deliberators, at the cost of introducing still other possibilities of bias. Studies, such as opinion polls and demographic projections, can often provide more valid and extensive knowledge of the context than is accessible to personal experience.

Taking context into consideration in deliberation involves difficult and delicate judgments. For one thing, the rights of individuals and role groups may be affected. Where the problem concerns a specific site—a classroom or a school, for instance—the characteristics of the people involved assume a great importance. The teacher is the main feature of the classroom setting. To discuss a curriculum problem in Mr. Varnett's third grade classroom without knowing Mr. Varnett and considering his habits, abilities, and inclinations is ludicrous. Similarly, the principal is the main feature of the school setting and must be taken into consideration in any deliberations concerning that school. Unless a teacher or principal requested it, establishing a group to decide on a course of action for a teacher or a principal would be an awkward and threatening action. It would intrude on their privacy, perhaps on their professional autonomy, and inevitably would put them in the position of having the quality of their prior work evaluated. When the curriculum problem involves a number of sites, the threat to individuals is less immediate, but the threat to role groups remains strong. When a deliberative body considers curriculum decisions that affect a large group of teachers or principals and attempts to take into consideration their characteristics as a group, members of these role groups have a right to be concerned that they are fairly and accurately represented as a group. Situations so crucial to the welfare of those concerned must be handled in ways that respect the legal and moral rights of those affected.

Those who would master the arts of deliberation must develop sensitivity to the moral and legal rights and obligations of all affected by a decision and learn to arrange deliberation in ways that consider the particular human and institutional context without undue threat to those involved. This means, among other things, deciding which matters to consider publicly and which to handle privately, determining which authorities have jurisdiction over various matters and giving them appropriate roles in the process, negotiating roles for the parties involved and procedures for assigning individuals to those roles, and arranging for appropriate places, times, and auspices for meetings. The role of context is so important in curriculum deliberation that to go much further with the topic than we have so far requires us to begin to consider deliberation in specific kinds of contexts. The chapters that follow will treat three primary contexts for curriculum work: classrooms, schools and their communities, and the society at large.

Managing Value Conflicts

Matters of fact and matters of value can only be separated for purposes of analysis. In practice, all curricular arguments involve both a factual claim and commitment to a value, and typically the two cannot be separated without doing violence to the meaning intended by those expressing the argument. Consider the statement by Michael Cole, quoted earlier, that

> People will be good at doing the things that are important to them and that they have occasion to do often. (Cole 1971, xi)

This may seem to be a purely factual claim, but it implies that everyone will be good at some things, suggesting an egalitarian value. Furthermore, the statement implicitly embraces a value of cultural relativism, since the author considered the fact of these things being important to them as worthy of mention, in contrast with the question of their importance to others. Statements or propositions may explicitly state only a factual claim, but the meaning of even the most neutral-seeming statement to an individual or a cultural group is inherently suffused with values.

Value assertions in their simplest form just claim that something is good or bad. The something may be a state of affairs to be sought or avoided, a course of action to be undertaken or prevented, a belief to be embraced or shunned, or a process to be fostered or hindered. The description or specification of that which is claimed to be good or bad inevitably involves a factual claim: at minimum, the claim that such an entity as the one deemed to be good exists or could exist in principle. Most value claims in curricular contexts are not stated outright but rather are implied by such phrases as *should, ought, must,* and the like, or by statements of goals, preferences, or intentions. Certain values are so taken for granted that they are rarely stated explicitly, yet often figure prominently in curricular argumentation. It goes without saying, for example, that resources should not be wasted, so if one course of action requires fewer resources than another to achieve the same ends, it is preferable, all else equal. It goes without saying that effort should not be wasted unnecessarily undoing what was formerly done. This is ultimately the argument, by the way, against teaching falsehoods, even the little white ones. If they are indeed falsehoods, then we will have to correct them later. Similarly, it goes without saying that a course of action should be feasible. Is it feasible, for example, to teach children of elementary school age to make their own judgments on scientific matters? Whether we think so or not, the argument that it is not feasible appeals to a value universally acknowledged to have force in curricular deliberation.

The most elementary curricular arguments involving values simply assert that a course of action is good or, in comparative form, better than another. The question "Why do you think so?" typically provokes a reason that invokes other than educational values. For example, Adler argued that a common curriculum for all students was good, and one of the reasons he gave invoked the value of democracy. A persistent inquirer might continue to ask why Adler thought democracy so valuable, but in contemporary American educational contexts, the value of democracy can normally be taken for granted. It is possible in principle for someone to assert and defend a distinctively curricular or educational value as inherently worthy of our allegiance, but few curricular or educational values can be safely taken for granted in contemporary American discourse. In contemporary America there are many educational values that are widely supported—literacy, the liberally educated person, or the person capable of continued learning, for example—but none that may be safely taken for granted to the same extent as such general social values as democracy, equal rights under law, or economic well-being. So, in contemporary curricular discourse curricular arguments rest upon values that invoke other, more encompassing human and social values.

The possibility of relying on different sets of values makes creativity and variety possible in curriculum decisions. People who believe that each great age in history embodies a certain spirit and who value these spirits and want their children to experience them in school can build a curriculum on these beliefs and values. This source of curricular diversity is opposed by the need for widespread, long sustained collaboration to sustain a curriculum. Curricula based on widely shared, deeply held, enduring values are more likely to survive and spread than those with a shallower, narrower, more fleeting base of support. The unlimited diversity of curricula that can be generated by relying on different sets of values are thus subject to a kind of selective pressure in favor of those grounded in widespread, deeply shared, enduring values.

Advocates of particular curricula, sensing the advantage of such a grounding, offer arguments to the effect that adopting their curricula will foster the most widely held, deeply-felt values of the community. Such justifications are helpful, of course, if they are sound. But there is a temptation to make too ready and superficial a resort to ultimate values in justifying curriculum proposals. We hear it said, for example, that children should study languages so they will acquire a global consciousness and that school sports make responsible citizens. These assertions may be true, but the prudent listener will want some plausible explanation of how these programs bring about these effects. Even serious writers on curriculum often take too little care to show the connection they claim between their proposals and ultimate values. For instance, Adler claims that we should teach academic subjects to all pupils if we want to uphold democratic ideals, but others claim with some plausibility that the so-called academic subjects are largely a badge of elitist standing and that democratic ideals demand that we teach more practical knowledge more directly relevant to contemporary society. To evaluate the merits of these conflicting claims we need more elaborated and detailed arguments. How exactly does learning academic subjects foster democracy? What conception of democracy is being invoked? In what sense are these subjects elitist and how is elitism in this sense inimical to democracy? And so on.

But even when we make allowances for temptations to make simplistic claims about ultimate values, we must admit that holding different social values nearly always leads one to prefer different curricula, and also then to justify these preferences in terms of those values. We might say that curriculum decisions are value-driven, meaning that differences in values make a greater contribution to shaping curricular practice than do differences in facts or beliefs about how the world is or works. In medicine, by contrast, decisions are more fact-driven. It is a safe assumption that value conflicts underlie all substantial, continuing disagreements in curriculum deliberation. Disagreements about purely factual matters can generally be accommodated in some way relatively easily. It may happen that one or more of the parties to a dispute hold a mistaken point of view that arises from a purely factual error, but in this case the remodelling of the whole point of view will almost certainly implicate values as well as facts, and hence this case should be considered a case of value conflict.

CURRICULAR DECISIONS ARE MULTI-VALUED, COLLECTIVE CHOICES

We saw in the previous chapter that curriculum decisions involve trade-offs among multiple values. Economists have studied these trade-offs extensively. Typically, they construct plots of one value against another and represent a particular value system as a series of curves, called *indifference curves,* such that a person is equally satisfied with any proportion of the values that falls on the curve. Economists also recognize that the value people set on a thing is not constant but depends on how much of that thing we already have. They express this in the concept of *marginal utility.* It seems quite feasible to study the preferences of those involved in a curriculum decision by confronting them with choices among dissimilar content or goals and observing how they make their trade-offs. Negotiations could be held in which people bargained with one another to achieve a mutually satisfactory result. People's preferences for various designs can be studied using the same techniques used for studying consumer preferences. People can be asked to rate curriculum plans or materials on various dimensions so as to create profiles of relative perceived strengths and weaknesses. The utility of such approaches to multi-valued choices for curriculum remains to be demonstrated, but the fundamental concept of trade-offs among competing goods is certainly fundamental to judgments of value about curricula.

Curriculum problems generally require collective choices, and this fact complicates problem resolution further. Rarely does a curricular proposal benefit everyone equally. In some cases there are winners and losers. Even when everyone wins, some will win more than others. How does one define an optimum result for a collective body when not everyone wins or loses equally? This is a very deep problem in the theory of value, one that challenges the very notion of rational collective decisions. One criterion frequently employed is Pareto optimality. A resolution is Pareto optimal if no one is worse-off and at least one person is better off than they would otherwise be. Economist Kenneth Arrow (1951) has demonstrated that Pareto-optimal decisions are impossible under most real conditions of collective social choice. In curricular decisions, the time—of students and teacher—is one primary resource that must be allocated to various purposes and content. Decisions to increase time spent on one thing reduce time available for others. If we assume that individuals set different values on different types of content and different purposes, then a Pareto-optimal decision about curricular time might still be possible. However, we know very little about how people actually value different curricular elements or about who believes themselves helped or harmed by different curricular decisions, and we know next to nothing about how curricular decisions allocate benefits and costs among individual students or large demographic groups. It seems likely that our understanding of how values enter into curriculum decisions would be advanced by applying techniques developed in economics and the other social sciences for studying values.

The resources represented by the arts and humanities seem also promising for dealing with value concerns in curriculum deliberation. The arts, in particular, provide a most flexible, accurate, and powerful means of communicating values. A play or story can show what it feels like to be put in a situation, bringing into the picture complexities of interpersonal relationships, differences of character and values among individuals, and the subtleties of the situation more powerfully and accurately than mere talk about value questions can ever do. Since practical problems originate in real human difficulties and since the resolutions of practical problems have real human consequences, human qualities of character such as courage or compassion are inevitably implicated. All human action is subject to moral judgment; curriculum actions are certainly no exception. The deliberating body can choose to put moral considerations ahead of practical ones or to ignore them altogether, but the resolution they reach will be subject to moral judgments by others in any event. Changing ourselves—our wants, values, perceptions—is an option always open in deliberation. Such decisions shape us as individual human beings and as a society. They are the special province of the arts and humanities.

> We believe that according to our desire we are able to change the things round about us, we believe this because otherwise we can see no favourable solution. We forget the solution that generally comes to pass and is also favorable: we do not succeed in changing things according to our desire, but gradually our desire changes. The situation that we hoped to change because it was intolerable becomes unimportant. We have not managed to surmount the obstacle, as we were absolutely determined to do, but life has

taken us round it, led us past it, and then if we turn round to gaze at the remote past, we can barely catch sight of it, so imperceptible has it become. (Proust 1930, 123)

Curriculum criticism, drawing on traditions of artistic and literary criticism, can illuminate the value implications in curricular proposals and arguments. The techniques of analytic philosophers can reveal subtle ambiguities of meaning that may lead us to mistaken support of positions that really do not advance our interests. The value-driven character of curriculum decisions accounts for the greater prevalence of writing drawn from the traditions of the arts and humanities in curriculum discourse than in most educational discourse, and does much to give work in the field its distinctive character. Curriculum studies are more nearly applied arts and humanities than applied human or behavioral sciences.

When Deliberators Differ on Fundamental Commitments

Agreement on fundamental factual and value commitments among members of a deliberative body is extremely desirable. A curriculum planning group that disagrees about fundamental commitments will experience difficulty in reaching agreement on a formulation of their problem, let alone on its resolution. The deliberations of a deeply divided group are inevitably contentious, and progress is slow and painful. Nevertheless, in public education people who disagree about fundamental beliefs and values must often decide together on a common course of action.

When a deliberative group includes individuals with divergent points of view, they can have no hope of reconciling their differences until they understand each others' points of view. Mutual comprehension of the contending points of view is an essential preliminary. In principle this involves learning the images, ideas, and judgments that constitute the others' point of view, learning what it emphasizes, what it leaves out, and what it depends on, and appreciating the value commitments that support it. In practice, it means not only a great deal of talking and listening but also attentive monitoring of one another's decisions and actions with reference to cases, real and hypothetical. Comprehending others' different points of view is difficult work intellectually and emotionally, and it can take a long time. People need strong reasons to undertake it. Those who enter curriculum deliberation with the commonest of motives—to make important decisions, to influence the course of events in a particular direction—will perceive the laborious process of understanding an alien point of view as a distraction, at best. Many will feel threatened when it becomes apparent, as it usually does, that the other view has much to be said for it. Deliberators will exhibit various forms of avoidance and withdrawal, as mild perhaps as attempting to steer the discussion away from sensitive issues or as pronounced as resignation from the group. Those responsible for the deliberations must make a delicate judgment as to whether the potential benefits of successful deliberation outweigh the costs of attempts to reconcile conflicting points of view.

Assuming further effort is warranted, a constructive next step in seeking to reconcile conflicting points of view is to search for regions of validity for each position—those cases or situations which each view seems to handle best. Anatol Rappoport argues convincingly in *Fights, Games, and Debates* that until the parties acknowledge the validity of one another's views in their most favorable cases, they have no basis for further dialogue. When the parties are able to acknowledge at least some region of validity for the others' views, remaining disputes can be approached more constructively. It often happens in curriculum issues that all views rest on a limited base of experience. The clash of opposing views offers an opportunity to devise practices that will be deemed satisfactory from many points of view and perhaps also an opportunity to enlarge our ideas. Even when we remain unalterably opposed to a view, we can gain from understanding it.

Given a relatively non-threatening situation, a strong desire to undertake common action, and enough time, some sort of temporary accommodation, at least, can generally be reached on curriculum issues, even when differences are deep. When these conditions are not present, deliberation may be inadvisable. For instance, when one or more parties want to fight over curriculum issues and perceive the costs to them of continued fighting as low, little anyone can do will make deliberation constructive. Attempting deliberation will only create occasions for conflict. Deliberation is easily disrupted. A participant with no desire to reach an accommodation can delay action by raising irrelevant issues, dwelling on disputed questions, quibbling over terms, and generally filibustering. When confronted with such a situation, those responsible for deliberations should try to increase the incentives for filibusterers to reach a commonly acceptable decision. For example, funds might be made available for implementing proposals on the condition that all parties endorse them. If those responsible cannot increase the incentives enough to secure willing participation, deliberation is probably inadvisable. Similarly, when some deliberators refuse to consider the possibility that opposing views could have any merit and dogmatically insist on their own viewpoint, those responsible for the deliberations should try to increase the incentives for toleration and openness to other points of view. For example, deliberation could be conducted in public, where intolerance would create an unfavorable impression on the uncommitted and thus penalize partisan dogmatism.

Those responsible for the deliberation must take care to see that weaker parties are not unduly coerced into participating in deliberations on unfavorable terms. Dominant groups can arrange deliberation so that weaker groups are forced to agree to conditions they would not freely accept. Views of minorities or less powerful subgroups within the deliberative body that are unacceptable to the majority or dominant subgroups may simply be ignored and the views of the dominant ones adopted as the group's joint view. All deliberation is somewhat coercive, but there are moral and legal limits.

The path of least resistance when faced with fundamental differences of belief and value among deliberators is to let the contending parties go their own way without attempting to resolve conflicts. Those unhappy with a look-say reading program are invited to attend another classroom or school using a phonics approach. Those unhappy with one school simply move to another community and attend another school more to their liking. Why argue? Let everyone have what they want! This tactic can be constructive, but its usefulness is limited. When it frees representatives of different points of view to develop their own resolutions based on their separate values, it enriches everyone's options. But it costs more to maintain several alternatives and, since no society can ever afford to provide every curricular option anyone might want, the necessity for making hard choices still remains for some. Administration of curricula with multiple alternatives is more complicated. Families must invest more time and effort in studying the merits of the alternatives and making a choice. Curricular differentiation promotes social fragmentation and undermines social unity, as different economic, social, ethnic, or economic groups enroll in different curricula. Later in this chapter we will discuss conditions under which this tactic seems advisable. For now, we note that it is an alternative to deliberation as a method of resolving certain kinds of curriculum problems.

Expressing Values Aptly in Deliberation

There is an inevitable tension between formulating values so that they will command the widest support and formulating them so that they will be most useful in deciding on a course of action. All else equal, values that are more general will be supported by more people than more specific values. For example, a just society is endorsed as a value more widely than equality of educational opportunity that in turn commands wider support than an common academically-oriented education for all. All else equal, values that are stated in absolute, unqualified terms will be more widely endorsed than ones expressed more cautiously. For example, slogans like "Every child can learn," and "The school must take the lead in building a new, more just society" command wider support than properly qualified statements such as "Every child can learn most of what is taught in school, given enough time and help." But glittering generalities are subject to widely different interpretations when attempts are made to apply them to concrete decisions.

General aims of education expressed in such high-sounding phrases as:

- understanding: to comprehend the world, oneself, existence,
- social adequacy: relationships with others, economics, politics,
- personal development: fulfillment of basic human needs, realization of individual potential,
- cultural advancement: enriching and upholding traditions, growth of human knowledge,

somehow never do justice to what it is people actually value. They are helpful in pointing to the general direction of what it is that people value, but they are not helpful in predicting or explaining people's real choices. The reality of human values is more complex and subtle. Rousseau's *Èmile* expresses a system of educational values, among other things. To reduce this work to some label such as *naturalism* or *romanticism,* or to some phrase such as "break the chains of social conformity," or "nurture individual growth through informal experiences" or even to some one-page abstract, unless this is done to remind the reader of the subtler and more complex texture of the work, caricatures it and the values it expresses. On the other hand, human memory is far too limited to permit us to recall at will the details of even this one work for more than a few weeks after studying it.

What happens, presumably, is that our personal values are changed by our dialogue with works that express other values. Sometimes we embrace these other values; sometimes we reject them. Sometimes they stimulate us to our own inquiries that result in subtle or profound changes in our value systems. Our personal value systems bear the marks, so to speak, of our encounters with expressions of other values, even though we have forgotten the details. As a result, our personal value systems are generally much more textured and richly detailed, and much more disorderly, than anything that would appear in a list of ultimate curricular values such as the one above. Reading such a list, each person tries to match the subtleties and disorder of the inner value system with the crude orderliness of the list and to make some kind of judgement about how adequately the one reflects the other.

Tension between inward, personal representations of values that are only accessible to us privately, and the outward expressions of value that we must use for communication is inherent and inevitable. What we must learn to do is to run back and forth along a scale of detail. When circumstances demand a quick shorthand, we must be able to produce and decode it. When circumstances call for a delicate, intricate attention to the details of values, we must be able to do that. Most importantly, we must be able to negotiate and to reconcile expressions at different scales, to begin with a list and flesh it out into a platform of ideas and beliefs and then use these as ingredients in arguments that direct decision and action.

STRENGTHS AND LIMITATIONS OF DELIBERATION IN CURRICULUM

Recognizing that curriculum problems are fundamentally practical and that deliberation is the essential method for resolving them in a principled way merely starts us off on the right foot. Much artfulness is required if we are to reach a sound resolution. Appointing a committee to conduct deliberations is not necessarily the appropriate response to every curriculum problem. Some problems are so easy and straightforward that an experienced person, working alone, can formulate the problem, devise the most promising alternatives, anticipate the main arguments pro and con, and reach a satisfactory resolution without the need for public deliberation. In other cases the differences in point of view and values among parties may be so great, so longstanding, and so bitter as to leave little hope of agreement through deliberation and to risk open and acrimonious conflict. In fact, full face-to-face deliberation by representatives of the major interested parties to a decision is a relatively specialized technique that requires some rather unusual conditions. (Box 6-3 lists some of these conditions.) Situations in which all these conditions are met seldom arise spontaneously in curriculum planning. Those responsible for curriculum decisions must consider carefully whether each curriculum decision is amenable to satisfactory resolution through full and fair public deliberation, and they must work hard to maintain conditions conductive to good deliberation in those cases.

BOX 6-3   Conditions Necessary for Effective Deliberation

Deliberation is primarily helpful when:

- the community that sponsors and supports the deliberations agrees to resolve the problem by rational search for a common, defensible course of action, in preference to such other methods of resolving the problem as power politics, voting, leaving decisions to be made in a market, or violence,

- the parties to the deliberations are in genuine doubt about which course of action is best, as contrasted with a situation in which some or all of the parties are convinced in advance that one course of action is best and enter deliberations to convince the others,

- deliberators agree on fundamental commitments, or, failing that, when all contending parties have a strong desire to reach a common resolution, and when institutional arrangements have been established for resolving conflicts definitively on the basis of rational arguments,

- deliberators are empowered to make the final decision, or, failing that, when the resolution recommended as a result of the deliberations will carry more weight with the actual decision-makers than other recommendations,

- the problem is important enough to justify the trouble and expense of deliberation,

- enough knowledge exists to give a sound rational basis to the discussions, insuring that it is not just a clash of insupportable opinions,

- deliberators have or can get the knowledge, expertise, resources and time needed to resolve the problem,

- the social and institutional context leaves the deliberators free to consider all points of view.

Those responsible for curriculum decisions must find a golden mean between wasting time on overly elaborate deliberations and fostering superficiality by faint-hearted efforts. Probably the most common shortcoming of curriculum deliberation is superficiality. Most curriculum decisions at all levels and of all types are made under tremendous pressures of time and resources, with the result that most are made after only a cursory examination of the merits of a few prominent alternatives. All too often, for example, decisions about curriculum materials are made entirely on the basis of cost. Deliberation is clearly superfluous in such cases and yet all districts go through the motions of establishing selection committees. On the other hand, large investments in full deliberation can easily come to nothing. Compared to other methods of making curriculum decisions, such as by vote or tradition or delegation to an expert, conducting good deliberation requires large amounts of resources and time. Unless one expects the results of deliberation to be substantially preferable to these simpler techniques, deliberation is a poor investment. One of the most important arts of deliberation is to know when full deliberation is justifiable and when something less than or other than deliberation will suffice.

Forms of Curriculum Deliberation

We have mainly been concerned in this chapter with deliberations that make a serious attempt to attain the ideal of full and fair deliberation. Those responsible for curriculum decisions may choose from a wide variety of other forms of deliberation as well. One of the most common forms is partisan deliberation, in which like-minded participants decide what course of action they will advocate later when they are in a group of people who do *not* agree with them. A group of parents and teachers who favor the teaching of character and traditional values, for example, may deliberate about the kind of program they should propose to a school board, before they are faced with people who do not agree.

Deliberations may also be limited to one or a few issues, points of view, or proposals. For example, a board of education may charge a committee considering a curriculum change to consider only its impact on achievement and equity. Box 6-4 lists some other common types of curriculum deliberation.

Decision-makers can compensate for shortcomings of full deliberation by crafty use of various subtypes of deliberation. For example, if some national body has explored the general pros and cons of adopting an activity-based science program for the elementary school, a deliberative body appointed by a local school superintendent might begin by reading that national report and singling out those factors that seem most problematic in their particular schools. Several school systems might band together to establish a joint deliberative body to explore an issue of common concern, thus spreading the expense of full deliberation more widely, though at some risk to the quality of the deliberations, since the joint body will presumably not be empowered to make decisions for the separate jurisdictions.

BOX 6-4   Some Common Subtypes of Curriculum Deliberation

Partisan deliberation: deliberation that adopts the point of view of one group in a conflicted context and does not pretend to include all points of view

Limited deliberation: deliberation in which only certain factors are to be considered, or in which certain factors are forbidden to be considered.

Defined deliberation: deliberation in which the problem has been defined for the deliberators who are not authorized to redefine it.

Quasi deliberation: deliberation about aims, ideals, basic principles, long range goals, philosophy, and so on, rather than about actions to be taken.

Hearings: discussions to inform decision-makers prior to deliberation and decision.

Sometimes decisions can be structured so as to recruit the services of partisans and thus augment the resources available for deliberation. For example, advocates of particular points of view might be asked to present arguments on behalf of various proposals under consideration or even to develop plans for consideration by the deliberative body.

Alternatives to Deliberation for Resolving Curriculum Problems

A practical perspective demands that we consider the pros and cons of the most promising alternatives before we decide to use one or another form of deliberation to resolve curriculum problems. Any such list will be incomplete and perhaps overlapping as well, but Box 6-5 is one attempt. As we have seen from our brief study of the history of the American school curriculum, Americans have at one time or another used each of these alternatives to resolve curriculum problems.

Presumably we can regard the exercise of raw power as a last resort on both moral and practical grounds, though it is an important last resort for those whose other actions go unheeded. Tradition in its various forms is most convenient, effective, and economical until circumstances change or new alternatives become available. Delegation to an expert merely displaces the responsibility for deliberation from the authorized body to the expert, a desirable displacement in fact-driven decisions where specialized knowledge or intricate calculations are appropriate. Reliance on unconstrained choices by individual teachers, students, or parents limits the need for official decisions, but does not eliminate it since someone must still decide which options to offer. In a market even this decision is left to sellers.

■
BOX 6-5   Alternatives to Deliberation for Resolving Curriculum Problems

- precedent, custom, routine, tradition,

- unconstrained choice by individuals,

- power politics (organizing, demonstrations, voting, and so on),

- choices of buyers and sellers in a market,

- raw power (threats, violence, domination),

- formal negotiation (bargaining),

- delegation to an expert.

Formal negotiation seems appropriate only when attempts to secure agreement through deliberation have failed.

On balance, the most promising alternatives to some form of deliberation for the general case of making major curriculum decisions seem to be individual choice from either officially provided options or from those options provided by a market and some sort of direct expression of political power, such as a vote. The other techniques would seem to have specialized roles in particular situations. The adoption of the elective system in colleges and high schools has been a major shift of curricular decision-making authority from official bodies to individuals. In colleges and universities today, the decision of what courses and programs to offer is the only remaining official institutional curriculum decision. High schools are more constrained by statewide graduation requirements and university admission requirements, but there, too, decisions about course offerings are the main institutional action taken about curriculum. The much-discussed voucher system would create a market in schools from which students and parents could freely choose and schools would probably respond by adjusting their offerings to suit customer preferences, thus creating a market for courses and programs as well.

The chief contrasts between market mechanisms and deliberation is that deliberation is inherently and fundamentally public and verbal, whereas markets operate privately by direct actions of buyers and sellers. The highly verbal, public processes of formal deliberation may not always be the most suitable way of making curriculum decisions. Nathan Rosenberg and L. E. Birdzell, Jr. express this point well when they contrast political decision making with economic decision-making via the market.

> The verbal method of decision making allows extended debate, further experiment, a weighing of costs and benefits, conflicts of expert opinion, successive resort to different political jurisdictions each with the authority to

> obstruct change, pleas for reconsideration, and other familiar exercises in
> decision making and law. . . . The use of verbal decision
> making . . . implies . . . that the benefits of the innovation are sufficiently
> understood and predictable that they can be persuasively verbalized in
> advance of its adoption. (Rosenberg and Birdzell 1986, 310)

Because of its verbal nature, deliberative decision-making tends to favor those who are articulate in public debate, which means well-educated, economically advantaged groups are favored, along with professionals trained in the use of specialized language.

Because deliberation is a public performance, conventional ideas have a better chance of favorable reception. Less familiar ones are more likely to seem strange and thus threatening or laughable, and so may not be taken seriously. Extremely unpopular ideas also stand little chance of gaining a fair hearing in such a setting. And there is a whole universe of considerations that are of great personal importance but that are not considered appropriate bases for serious public decisions in our culture—sentimental or emotional attachments, family values and traditions, and so on. Individuals making their own decisions about what to study, by contrast, are free to consider whatever they please in complete privacy. Reliance on individual decisions made in private, on the other hand, sacrifices the possibility that truth may emerge from a dialogue, although an attenuated form of dialogue is still possible as people comment on one another's choices in public. These contrasting characteristics of deliberation and market choices suggest that they may complement one another and that it might be desirable to allow both to come into play in some way in curriculum decision-making.

Deliberation appeals mainly to those who place a high value on rationality, a value priority usually traced to the Enlightenment in Western cultural history. By contrast, those who value the ineffable, the inscrutable, the mysterious, and the deeply personal will object to placing so much emphasis on what people say. What we say, some believe, bears little relation to what we believe or do. And in any event, we can perceive, experience, and understand much more than we can say or explain. Those who believe that people are more than rational beings and that this other-than-rational part of us is not just a dark side full of disreputable impulses, but is a form of higher consciousness that manifests itself in feelings, intuition, creativity, playfulness, humor, and art, will find purely verbal deliberation far too limiting. It is certainly true that purely verbal deliberation conducted in the formal manner of most public business neglects such nonrational modes of expression. Even though no rule says that deliberation must be confined to formal prose, as a matter of fact it usually is, and our leading institutions—government, business, and science, for example—enforce norms of decorum and formality that actively discourage playful uses of language. Ironically, such limitations, adopted in the name of fostering rationality, may actually serve the irrational side of our culture and personality by excluding important facets of human nature and intellect from the decision-making process.

The inhibiting effect of context on deliberation can be controlled to some extent by modifying the context. For example, people may be more likely to express their true feelings when deliberations are held in settings where they feel comfortable, when the mood is kept informal and the atmosphere light, and when those in charge seem genuinely interested in hearing their views. Still, major public decisions arouse tensions that inhibit some people from expressing some views and that encourage others to express other views. Markets and individual choices are less inhibited by these public norms. In general, then, individual choice and market mechanisms seem to provide useful alternatives to deliberation as methods for resolving curriculum problems. Which is better will depend on the situation.

Direct exercise of political power, on the other hand, seems more like an evil that cannot be entirely eliminated. American institutions of government emphasize the use of reason in decision-making by prescribing deliberation of particular types at various points—passage of legislation, adoption of regulations, trials, and so on. These are intended as safeguards against the arbitrary exercise of power. The line between arbitrary power and legitimate authority is usually hazy, however, especially so in the relatively undeveloped legal territory of curricular governance. A tried and true recipe for an interest group to change the curriculum of local schools is to organize themselves, elect a sympathetic board, intimidate or replace an unsympathetic Superintendent, and proceed to implement the change. In such a context, deliberation, except for partisan purposes, is wasted breath. Such purely political struggles are sometimes required in order to establish the right of excluded groups even to participate in deliberations, and further displays of political power may be needed to get others to listen. It should not be surprising that the winners in these political struggles often simply claim the right to make the decision, without deliberation, by the direct exercise of political power. This is a reality those responsible for curriculum decisions must face, but it does not detract from the ideal of full and fair deliberation. It complicates the work of those responsible for the decision by requiring them also to decide when and how and to what extent the deliberative ideal can be pursued.

Individuals or small groups charged with responsibility for curriculum decisions can do a great deal to check the arbitrary exercise of political power and to foster conditions required for true deliberation. For one thing, they can learn to recognize partisan manipulation of deliberation and expose it. Deliberation can be subverted all too easily with such tactics as hand-picked committees stacked in favor of one alternative, obfuscation and mystification through the use of jargon, unrealistic limits of time and resources, grandstanding, bandwagoning, sloganeering, even intimidation and coercion. By establishing conditions that make it necessary for the politically powerful to employ such tactics openly, political opposition can often be aroused to check their power. Administratively, deliberation is subject to subversion by bureaucracy, red tape, and unreasonable formalism, ills that alert and vigorous leadership can forestall. On the positive side, tendencies in the community and the institution that foster full and fair deliberation can be cultivated, tendencies such as the propensity to resolve conflict in principled ways, the propensity to maintain an open mind and to consider other points of view, and a willingness to trust the others involved in making and implementing decisions—at least until they prove unworthy of trust. The best ways to cultivate such tendencies are by example and by heaping public honors on those responsible for conspicuous instances. Those responsible for institutional decision-making procedures can arrange for conditions that foster good deliberation, such as by providing sufficient resources to cover its costs, and by maintaining open, representative institutional procedures.

In addition to the pros and cons of deliberation mentioned previously, deliberation has one advantage that is of special interest to any profession. Professions are grounded on specialized knowledge that their practitioners have that the general public does not have. Done properly, deliberation helps to build a body of professional knowledge by facilitating our efforts to learn from our actions. We can gain useful information when we observe the consequences of our action. If what we planned for happens, we have greater confidence in the point of view, assumptions, and reasoning that support our actions. If we are surprised at the outcome, we can make informed judgments about how our thinking went wrong and make adjustments the next time. Neither markets nor direct political action supply us with explicit rationales for actions, so we are less able to interpret the significance of either success or failure.

Taking all these factors into account, it seems prudent for professionals to regard deliberation as the first preference for resolving important curriculum problems. When conditions make deliberation impractical, unnecessary, or unlikely to succeed, other methods can be employed. When those who govern the educational system determine that a market or direct exercise of political power will be employed in preference to deliberation, professional educators have neither the right nor the power to say no, but they can still carry on full and fair deliberation in their own professional groups and work politically and professionally to expand and enhance deliberation in the public context. Above all, professionals have a public responsibility to use deliberation wisely, appropriately, and when conditions are right.

In the long view, the most fundamental limitations of deliberation are those so embedded in our worldview that we are unaware of them. We could say of curriculum decision-makers what David Perkins says of mathematicians and poets about the dependence of their work on a larger culture.

> Behind the building up the mathematician and poet do on a particular occasion lies a whole saga of preselection—years of training and striving for the individual maker, centuries of history in the discipline, millennia of general cultural evolution, billions of years of biological evolution, and, behind all that, the physical evolution of the universe. Taking this long perspective, we discover that the maker's work on the occasion is the least part of the work. The language, the symbols, the concepts, the cultural and personal style, even the particular task, already have been chosen. The

maker of the moment merely puts the last block on the top of a pyramid of
selection, a tower of ever higher and narrower ranges of possibility which
finally finds its summit in a particular creative product. (Perkins 1981, 278)

Deliberation, along with all other methods of curriculum decision-making, is
subject to the limitations of the culture it operates within and of the human
situation. Curriculum planners cannot step outside their culture, no matter how
hard they try. As a species, our knowledge is limited, and learning more can be a
long and costly process. Decision-makers never have complete power to put into
effect whatever measures they think the situation calls for, and exerting what
powers they have usually brings costs and risks and often unforeseen consequences. The success of our curriculum improvement efforts, as in all human endeavors,
depends heavily on timing and on events beyond anyone's control. Through
deliberation, it is possible, though, to use whatever limited knowledge and power
decision-makers may be able to get to determine—not with certainty but with
some plausibility—which actions best accord with our purposes and ideals. This
result is less satisfying than mathematical proof, scientific confirmation, or
scholarly substantiation, but it is the most that we can aspire to in human affairs,
and achieving even this is difficult enough.

QUESTIONS FOR STUDY

1. Conduct deliberation on the question of whether to differentiate the curriculum of one particular school. Let all members of the deliberating body raise
   whatever issues they feel are important and take whatever side they wish.
   Appoint a recorder to list issues raised and main arguments offered. After at
   least half an hour of deliberation, conduct a debriefing session during which
   you consider the principles (warrants) appealed to in the course of the
   deliberations. Compare results with Adler's theoretical approach to the same
   problem as described in Chapter 4. Were any of Adler's principles used? What
   other principles were used? To what extent would Adler's theory offer an
   adequate basis for this decision?

2. The members of a national science curriculum development group are divided
   over the question of whether to include a unit on health and safety in their
   elementary science textbook for grades 4–6. Examine the following arguments
   offered in the course of deliberation on this issue and choose those that you
   think offer the strongest support for each position. If these were the only
   arguments considered, would you judge the deliberation to be full and
   complete? If not, what types of considerations have been neglected? Find a
   course of action that meets the concerns expressed in as many of these
   arguments as possible. What course of action would you recommend, all
   things considered? Why?

a.   Health and safety (h & s) are important topics. They save lives.

b.   As a curriculum topic h & s consists of nothing more than a collection of dos and don'ts. This is inconsistent with science, which consists of fundamental principles and methods of inquiry.

c.   Several states have laws requiring schools to teach h & s to every student every year. Most schools satisfy this requirement in science classes.

d.   H & s content goes out of date very quickly as new hazards appear (AIDS, crack cocaine, and so on) and new safeguards are developed.

e.   Children are interested in h & s.

f.   H & s are excellent topics for teaching how science can be applied to improve human life.

g.   Problems of h & s need to be handled near the time and place where precautions should be taken. Teaching them in the abstract, in a classroom, in advance of any real felt need to know will be futile.

h.   H & s are problems for the medical, police, and emergency services to handle, not for schools.

3.   A group of teachers from one elementary school have proposed to individualize their mathematics program. Discussions of the proposal in the district mathematics curriculum committee have led to the identification of the following list of claims and criticisms of individualized programs in mathematics, each of which is believed to be true and important by at least two members of the seven member committee. Outline a plan for individualization that incorporates as many of the claimed advantages as possible while it avoids or minimizes the dangers envisioned in the criticisms.

Claimed advantages of individualization

- allows all students to learn at their own pace
- everyone doesn't have to study the same thing
- children make more progress when instruction is tailored to their specific needs and abilities
- no child will experience chronic failure because their goals will fit their abilities
- children can use their own preferred learning styles; they can learn in whatever way they learn best
- American society is diverse and needs diverse talents and know-how; it makes no sense to teach all students the same things

Criticisms of individualization

- children get lost because it is so hard to keep track of their progress
- it hinders social development; they need to learn to work together, to subordinate their own needs in favor of the group; it encourages disregard of others, doing your own thing
- it fosters inequality; good learners go further, poor learners fall further behind

- it sacrifices the strong social pressures to keep up and conform; some children need these to motivate them to learn
- children do not know how much they can achieve; having adults set challenging standards extends them more
- it encourages one-sided development; children have no incentive to do the kinds of learning they are not good at doing

4.   Identify a contemporary curricular disorder, muddle, or perplexity and pose at least two different problems that might plausibly correspond to the experienced difficulties. Possible perplexities: drop-outs, low test scores, accommodating the range of ability from gifted students to learning disabled, narrowly academic focus of the school program, bilingualism, or inequities of educational outcomes among blacks and hispanics as compared to mainstream white students. Find any differences in assumptions and values, explicit or implicit, between these two ways of posing this perplexity as a problem. If these two formulations were competing for use in a real decision-making situation, how would people decide which to use?

5.   Divide your class into two groups. Let each accept a different formulation of the same problematic situation and proceed to discuss the merits of alternative courses of action. Compare results and discuss the extent to which the way a problem is posed affects the solutions considered and accepted.

6.   Present a package of commercial curriculum materials (textbook and teachers guide, at least) to a group of teachers. Ask them to identify what they consider to be the program's strong and weak points. What principles and values seem to underlie the strengths teachers identify? Are these the ones intended by the developers? Determine the extent to which the objections they raise can be overcome through redesign of specific features of the curriculum materials. What could or should be done about the remaining objections?

7.   Write an editorial for school curriculum officials on a contemporary curriculum reform movement. Assume your audience is knowledgeable about deliberation. They need for you to warn them of subtle but important difficulties they might encounter. Suggest the main considerations you think they should take into account in deciding what to do about this reform. Suggest pitfalls they should watch for.

8.   Prepare a briefing paper for local school decision-makers on some curriculum issue they face. Through interviews, by attending meetings, or by reading minutes of previous meetings, discover how they conceptualize the issue. Provide them with whatever you think they need in the way of background knowledge, perspective, and evidence to reach a better resolution of their problem. If possible, listen to their subsequent deliberations and interview them to discover what difference your briefing paper may have made.

9. Comment on the following statement.

> What should be taught is a value question, pure and simple. This means it
> will never be resolved by arguing. Deliberation just masks people's
> preferences in high-sounding phrases. We should simply take a vote or do a
> poll or let people choose the curriculum that suits them and dispense with
> all this rationalization.

RECOMMENDED READING

There is a dearth of writing about the art of curriculum deliberation. Schwab's Practical papers (Schwab 1969; 1971; 1973) are indispensible and will reward repeated reading and careful study. My own investigations of the deliberations of several curriculum projects (Walker 1969; 1970; 1971 a, b, c; Walker and Reid 1975) provide analyzed examples of real curriculum deliberations. Graham Orpwood's (1981) dissertation, "The Logic of Curriculum Policy Deliberation: An Analytic Study from Science Education," offers records, transcripts, and insightful analyses of deliberations of science education policy-makers in Ontario.

We are in better shape with respect to the arts of deliberation generally. David Perkins' *The Mind's Best Work* (1981) shows how creative work can be considered under the framework of practical reason. The world of business and economics has much to offer the student of decision-making in curriculum. Raiffa's *Decision-Analysis* (1968) is a readable introduction to the basics of that formal discipline. Thomas Y. Sowell's *Knowledge and Decisions* (1980) is a brilliant exposition of the difficulties of basing public decisions on knowledge. Kenneth Arrow's works provide powerful insight into the possibilities and especially limitations of formal decision-making processes in social situations. *Social Choice and Multicriterion Decision-Making* (1986) is his most recent relevant work. *Social Choice and Individual Values* (1951) and *Social Choice and Justice* (1983) are also classics. Amos Tversky's studies of individual decision-making, (1982) offer provocative insights into possible deviations from rationality in curriculum decisions.

REFERENCES

Arrow, Kenneth. 1951. *Social Choice and Individual Values*. N.Y.: Wiley.

Arrow, Kenneth. 1983. *Social Choice and Justice*. Cambridge, MA: Belknap Press.

Arrow, Kenneth. 1986. *Social Choice and Multicriterion Decision-Making*. Cambridge, MA: Belknap Press.

Boswell, James. 1952 (1766, original). *Life of Johnson*. London: Oxford University Press.

Cole, Michael. 1971. *The Cultural Context of Learning and Thinking*. N.Y.: Basic Books.

Hessler, James. 1977. A Comparison of Professional Writing in Education and Medicine. Unpublished Ph.D. Dissertation. Stanford University.

Orpwood, Graham. 1981. "The Logic of Curriculum Policy Deliberation: An Analytic Study from Science Education." Unpublished Ph.D. Dissertation. University of Toronto.

Perkins, David N. 1981. *The Mind's Best Work*. Cambridge, MA: Harvard University Press.

Proust, Marcel. 1930. *The Sweet Cheat Gone*. (Scott Moncrief, tr.). N.Y.: Modern Library.

Raiffa, Howard. 1968. *Decision-Analysis*. Reading, MA: Addison-Wesley.

Rapoport, Anatol. 1960. *Fights, Games, and Debates.* Ann Arbor: University of Michigan Press.

Rosenberg, Nathan and Luther E. Birdzell. 1986. *How the West Grew Rich.* N.Y.: Basic Books.

Schwab, Joseph. 1969. "The Practical: A Language for Curriculum." *School Review* 78: 1–23.

Schwab, Joseph. 1971. "The Practical: Arts of Eclectic." *School Review* 79: 493–542.

Schwab, Joseph. 1973. "The Practical 3: Translation into Curriculum." *School Review* 81: 501–522.

Sowell, Thomas Y. 1980. *Knowledge and Decisions.* N.Y.: Basic Books.

Tversky, Amos. 1982. *Judgment Under Uncertainty.* N.Y.: Cambridge University Press.

Walker, Decker. 1969. "A Case Study of the Process of Curriculum Development." Research Report. School of Education: Stanford University.

Walker, Decker. 1970. "Toward More Effective Curriculum Projects in Art." *Studies in Art Education* 11: 3–13.

Walker, Decker. 1971 a. "A Study of Deliberation in Three Curriculum Projects." *Curriculum Theory Network* 7: 118–134.

Walker, Decker. 1971 b. "The Process of Curriculum Development, A Naturalistic Model." *School Review* 80: 51–65.

Walker, Decker. 1971 c. "Strategies of Deliberation in Three Curriculum Development Projects." Unpublished Ph.D. Dissertation. Stanford University.

Walker, Decker and William A. Reid. 1975. *Case Studies in Curriculum Change, Great Britain and the U.S.* London: Routledge and Kegan Paul.

PART III

Curriculum in Context

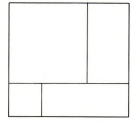

The central problem of the curriculum reaches down too far into the structure of our civilization to be changed overnight.

Boyd Bode. *Modern Educational Theories.*
American Philosopher of Education, 1927

THE CURRICULUM IN CLASSROOMS

One who studies such reports can scarcely escape the conclusion that the work of the typical American classroom . . . has been and still is characterized by a lifeless and perfunctory study and recitation of assigned textbook materials.

William Bagley, American educator, 1931

PURPOSE OF THE CHAPTER

- to describe conventional classrooms as settings for a curriculum
- to explain why the central features of classrooms resist change and maintain their conventional form
- to analyze common approaches to changing classroom curricula and to assess the strengths and limitations of these approaches in light of the realities of life in classrooms

OUTLINE

The Conventional Classroom

The Curriculum at Work in Conventional Classrooms

Teachers' Ambivalent Attitudes toward the Curriculum

Curriculum, Control, and Mutual Adaptation

Teachers and the Implicit Curriculum

THE CONVENTIONAL CLASSROOM

Classrooms are the primary setting for formal education, as they have been for over a century, in schools around the world. Until the curriculum comes to life in the classroom, it remains only a plan, and unless it reaches the students there, it makes no difference in what they learn. Schools do sometimes sponsor educative activities outside the classroom: extracurricular activities, assemblies, arts performances, and contests of various types, for example. And students carry on activities of their own in school—that may be educative or miseducative—before, after, and between classes. Although these extracurricular activities may sometimes be more important to some students than what happens in classrooms, the main work of the school is nevertheless still done in regularly scheduled classes, and the curriculum is realized, if at all, in classes. So, to understand curricula we must understand how they work in classrooms. Whatever else may influence what students study and learn in school, the final, determinative steps are taken when teacher, student, and curriculum materials come together.

Curriculum reformers often assume that classrooms are a kind of neutral stage on which teachers can enact any curriculum assigned to them. But classrooms are highly structured social settings. Research over the past two decades has shown that teachers and students behave in highly patterned, almost stylized ways in classrooms. Curriculum plans that call for teachers and students to act in ways that are inconsistent with these patterns probably will not be widely implemented. If we understand the classroom as a social setting and how the curriculum operates in the classroom, we may be able to improve the odds on implementing effective curriculum improvement.

All of us know from our time in school that in many respects classrooms are alike. They contain one adult, the teacher, and thirty or so children, the students. The students are all about the same age. These same people occupy the classroom during the same times every school day. They enter the classroom together at the beginning of the class period and leave it together at the end. They sit at identical desks. They are under constant supervision and their behavior is controlled by rules governing when they can move or speak and limiting the noise and disturbance they may cause. They raise their hands to be recognized to speak. They respond to questions, follow instructions, and obey the rules. Teachers are in charge. Teachers do most of the talking. They stand in the front of the room near the chalkboard. They ask questions, make assignments, plan and supervise work, explain things to students, and move about the room monitoring and controlling what takes place.

Lessons are closely related to the content of a book of which everyone has a copy. Classroom work is almost exclusively verbal, consisting mostly of speaking and listening, with a modicum of reading and writing. The group is instructed as a whole. Everything is public.

Some kinds of events that are common elsewhere are rare in classrooms. We seldom see more than one adult in classrooms. When we do, the other person is either a passive observer or under the teacher's direction (an aide, volunteer, or student teacher). Once a class is established, they stay together as a group for months; we seldom see new faces added to the cast or familiar ones leaving. We seldom see much moving about or independent conversations among students. Small group work and individual consultations of more than a few minutes duration between students and teacher are also relatively rare, as is quiet reflection. Play, the nearly universal occupation of children in other settings, is seldom seen. Students seldom use apparatus or equipment of any kind other than books, papers, and pencils.

Those who have studied classrooms have also noted that behavior is highly predictable; classrooms are places where certain standard types of behavior typically take place and where there are standard ways of doing recurring activities at particular times or on particular occasions. Elementary classrooms are often arranged to include a reading circle to which students come for reading lessons, a math corner where various activities and materials for math learning are located, and a daily and weekly routine that cycles through opening exercises, reading, writing, spelling, arithmetic, science, music, art, recess, lunch, and clean-up in a regular procession. The teacher, guided to varying degrees by a school or district course of study, schedules specific activities and their times and places. In secondary school classrooms, times and places for major activities are incorporated in the student's schedule of classes. Within each class, teachers schedule activities in a fashion quite similar to that of elementary teachers, though with appropriate variations depending on the subject, the pupils' maturity, and the teacher's style. Tests are special occasions that occur only once every few weeks. During tests students read and write individually at their desks and are forbidden from working with each other. Teachers scrutinize students' performance on tests closely and make fine judgments about the quality of their responses.

It doesn't always go smoothly, but, to a remarkable extent, a single broad pattern of behavior prevails in classrooms throughout the world. It is teacher-centered, teacher-directed, largely oral, and almost exclusively verbal, whole group instruction based on a textbook and punctuated by frequent tests. It is called, variously, traditional teaching, the teacher-centered classroom, the recitation, or, the term to be used in this chapter, the *conventional classroom*. In this chapter we consider how the curriculum works in conventional classrooms. In reality every classroom is unique, but as we've seen, most share certain basic features. Treating these commonalities as if they defined a universal classroom pattern will enable us to discover some general principles useful in understanding how curriculum works in real classrooms.

THE CURRICULUM AT WORK IN CONVENTIONAL CLASSROOMS

The Curriculum and the Teacher's Actions

Insofar as the curriculum plays a role in the classroom, it does so under the direction of the teacher. Among all those concerned with education, only the teacher knows the specifics of a particular learning situation and has the power to act in that situation. As the single agent empowered to marshal and orchestrate all of the ingredients in the educational situation of that classroom, the teacher clearly directs the classroom curriculum. The teacher's power in curriculum matters is not absolute, as we will see, but other influences must be exercised with, through, or around the teacher. Therefore the teacher's influence on the classroom curriculum is far more direct and usually far greater than that of any other single agent. The generalization that teachers control the classroom curriculum is closer to being true than any other equally simple statement.

We therefore begin our study of the classroom curriculum by looking at what teachers do. Teaching is a notoriously complex, many-faceted, and mysterious art. We shall be concerned here not with the subtleties of interpersonal interaction and the details of pedagogical craft, but with certain broad and basic aspects of teachers' work that are especially important in realizing curriculum plans in the classroom. For this purpose, it helps to think of teaching as essentially inducing students to participate in educationally valuable activities, whether these be as private as reflecting silently on what they read or as public as singing a song. We will treat classrooms as *settings* where students engage in educationally valuable activities under the teacher's direction.

From this perspective the following classroom responsibilities of teachers are crucial to realizing any curriculum in the classroom:

- selecting classroom activities,
- scheduling and pacing activities,
- presenting activities to students,
- adapting and adjusting activities, pacing, and presentation to the particular circumstances of the classroom,
- motivating students to engage in the activities,
- finding out what students have learned from participating in the activities.

These actions define the purpose, content, and structure of the classroom—the classroom curriculum. Students who experience this classroom curriculum receive a substantial opportunity to learn what these activities teach. (See Figure 7-1.)

Clearly, then, the curriculum is not something teachers do as a distinct and separate part of their work, but rather it is thoroughly mingled with nearly every aspect of teaching. Distinctions between curriculum and instruction, curriculum and teaching, curriculum and pedagogy, or the like may be useful for purposes of discussion, but these distinctions do not correspond to real differences in teachers'

■ FIGURE 7-1   Components of the Classroom Curriculum

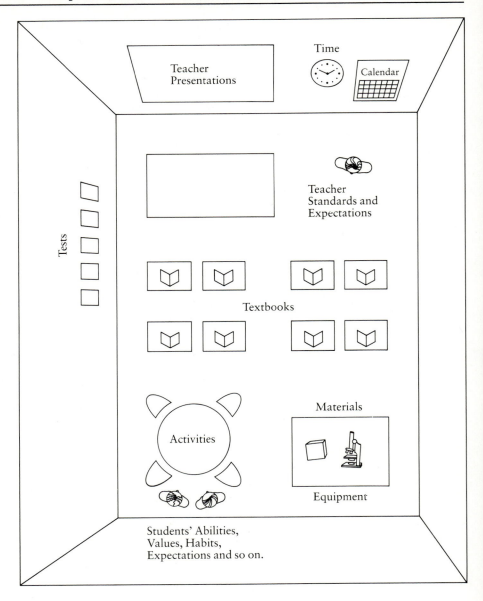

actions. For teachers, these decisions are all tied up together. Davis and McKnight (1976) give a hypothetical example that illustrates the intricate connections to be found among apparently distinct decisions in classrooms.

One can attempt to restrict a mathematics curriculum to a sequence of undemanding tasks, done individually in workbooks. This leads to a quiet and orderly classroom, but, we suspect, implies limitations on the mathematical content that will be learned. . . . As the problems in a workbook are made more challenging, students will need more help from the teacher. This, at the least, will lead to many students wanting to see the teacher for help, which, in turn, means a need to wait, with attendant impatience and temptations to disorder. If the subject is genuinely profound, most students may be unable to learn it from independent reading, and class discussion may be necessary—but this means, in many cases, large group instruction. . . ." (Davis and McKnight 1976, 216–217)

As we discuss some of the particulars of how the curriculum is realized in the classroom, keep in mind that the curriculum plays a part in nearly everything that happens in the conventional classroom.

Although it is difficult to single out any one of these things teachers do as more important than the others in realizing the classroom curriculum, the teacher's contribution is probably most irreplaceable in motivating students. Perhaps this explains why in judging others' teaching, teachers rate the ability to motivate students as very important. Sociologist Dan Lortie conducted intensive interviews with several hundred elementary teachers asking about every aspect of their work.

It is evident that [teachers] are impressed by teachers who establish and sustain cordial, disciplined, and work-eliciting relationships with students. (Lortie 1975, 133)

Teachers' efforts to maintain appropriate depth and quality of attentiveness and mindfulness on the part of students despite distractions and turbulence give the classroom environment its purposefulness and thus make it possible for the curriculum to be realized. By helping students to make sense of activities, to see them as contributing to larger long term goals, and to understand why they are doing these activities, teachers help students to internalize the purpose of the activity and thus to connect the planned purposes of the curriculum to the students' *own* purposes. Any sound curriculum can be realized in a classroom in which study and learning are central, spontaneous, intrinsically rewarding, and therefore self-sustaining. No curriculum can create such an environment without the efforts of a teacher.

TEACHERS' AMBIVALENT ATTITUDES TOWARD THE CURRICULUM

Both the central place of the curriculum in teachers' work and the dominant role teachers play in realizing the curriculum in their classroom argue that teachers should put curricular concerns at the center of their professional lives. In fact, though, curriculum is seldom at the center of teachers' concerns. Most teachers simply want a good set of written curriculum guidelines to use so that they can devote their attention to working with students. Yet most teachers want this curriculum to be consistent with their own philosophy and values and many want the professional autonomy that allows them to make their own curriculum decisions. Therefore, many teachers have deeply ambivalent feelings about curriculum. They both love and hate it; they both want its help and want to be independent of its control.

Although the curriculum is an integral part of their work, teachers must often give it separate attention, and, when they do, their work assumes a different character, one not to many teachers' liking. Most teachers derive their greatest job satisfactions from working with students. Lortie (1975) found that the main attractions of teaching for the experienced teachers he interviewed were interpersonal—namely, the opportunity for extended contact with young people—and service-oriented. Lortie writes of teachers' concern for reaching students, for maintaining good relationships with students, and how important it is to them to have a good day in the classroom with their students. Lortie suggests that these attitudes are a necessary adaptation to the ambiguity and unpredictability of teaching. The immediate interpersonal satisfactions of the classroom—reaching students, seeing eyes light up, bringing smiles to faces—give teachers a reliable source of tangible daily satisfaction, whereas a focus on the production of lasting learning outcomes would yield meager, deferred, and uncertain satisfaction, at best. Working on their classroom curriculum takes them away from working directly with students and this, for many, brings less satisfaction.

Curriculum work typically calls for quiet reflection, systematic analysis, cool-headed advance planning, and attention to things and ideas rather than people. These activities and attitudes are quite different from those found in the richly peopled, hurried, live classroom environment. Those who choose teaching as a job do so because they find classroom life rewarding. From an extensive review of research on teachers, Philip Jackson (1968) concluded that they tend to be personalistic, people-oriented, and service-oriented.

> The personal qualities enabling teachers to withstand the demands of classroom life have never been adequately described. But among those qualities is surely the ability to tolerate the enormous amount of ambiguity, unpredictability, and occasional chaos created each hour by 25 or 30 not-so-willing learners. (Jackson 1968, 149)

Jackson refers to teachers as valuing immediacy, informality, and individuality. Yet curriculum planning calls for a certain emotional distance, for systematic analysis, and for moving students' individualities to the background of attention. Jackson characterizes teachers' thought processes in terms of *conceptual simplicity, simple causality, intuitive* rather than analytical modes of thought; *opinionated* rather than open-minded attitudes toward teaching decisions, and *narrow interpretation of abstractions* (Jackson 1968, 151). These are not habits of mind that would cause one to gravitate toward curriculum planning.

CURRICULUM, CONTROL, AND MUTUAL ADAPTATION

These fundamental conflicts between working with the curriculum and what teachers consider to be the most essential and rewarding part of their work would be enough to give most teachers conflicting attitudes toward curriculum matters. But the most serious curriculum issue for teachers is the issue of control over their work. The officially prescribed school curriculum is one of the main avenues through which the teacher's organizational superiors seek to control what happens in the classroom. Textbooks, tests, and other curriculum materials bring content, purpose, and structure from outside into the classroom and teachers are forced to deal with these outside influences. As we have seen, the curriculum enters into virtually every nook and cranny of the teacher's work. To relinquish control over the curriculum seems very nearly tantamount to relinquishing control over teaching. Instead of autonomous professionals, teachers without control over curriculum become more like actors following a script or musicians following a score.

A teacher may be placed in an ethically untenable position if the official curriculum contravenes a deeply held personal belief. For instance, teachers who believe that education involves a genuine human interaction about matters of importance to the student at the moment the situation occurs will be unable to maintain their personal integrity if they follow a curriculum that calls for prescribed units planned to achieve specific behavioral objectives. Likewise, an English teacher who is personally committed to maintaining traditional standards of good English usage will have trouble accepting Black English or Spanglish as equally worthy of respect, even if the official curriculum guide says they should. For teachers to follow a curriculum that conflicts with their beliefs and values means that they must work constantly with divided minds and divided loyalties. It should be no cause for wonder, then, that teachers crave the power to control their curriculum, to teach what they see fit, as they see fit, using or not using at their discretion any curricular assistance offered.

The curriculum, in one form or another, is often the occasion of conflict between teachers and school administrators, because administrators see it as one of the few means they have for influencing what happens behind the classroom door, while teachers see it as rightfully their professional prerogative. Teachers' intense desire for independence and autonomy in their classroom inevitably collides with efforts of local policy-makers and administrators to implement school-wide or system-wide programs. Yet teachers do not merely want to replace local governance processes with collegial professional norms. They want freedom from all organizational authority in matters that concern their conduct in the classroom. Lortie summarized the results of a survey of teachers in Dade County, Florida, asking about their preferences for different types of organizational control: "These teachers want to loosen organizational claims in favor of teacher decision-making in the classroom" (Lortie 1975, 164). The obstacles these attitudes place in the way of implementing school-wide curriculum changes are formidable.

The idea implicit in the term *curriculum implementation,* that teachers should faithfully follow the formal written curriculum, is the school administrator's or policy-maker's counterpart of the teacher's dream of autonomy in the classroom. Neither is a realistic account of what happens. For the most part, teachers use the curriculum materials provided by the school, but with their own little twist. "Many teachers want to add something personal [by way of emphasis] to their curricular responsibilities" (Lortie 1975, 111).

What teachers try to do when confronted with an official curriculum they disagree with is to find ways to satisfy both the external demands and their own professional taste, standards, and conscience. Usually they have enough leeway to enable them to do so. For example, district policy changes may dictate that children be taught to balance checkbooks in math class, and that policy may conflict with some teachers' deeply held beliefs. Teachers can ease the tension of this conflict in several ways:

- by completing the checkbook-balancing lessons ahead of schedule, leaving time for problem-solving,
- by devising problems with significant mathematical content within the format of checkbook balancing,
- by creating materials to teach checkbook balancing as homework and seatwork so that no additional class time will have to be diverted to this topic.

None of these expedients is as good from a teacher's point of view as having a free hand to follow one's own mathematics curriculum. But all meet the letter of the law while preserving the teacher's integrity. This is mutual adaptation (Greenwood, Mann, and McLaughlin, 1975). It is the same process school officials use when pressured by an outside agency to implement school-wide or system-wide reforms not entirely to their liking. In mutual adaptation individual teachers negotiate the best compromise they can between their own preferences and those being pressed on them from beyond the classroom.

TEACHERS AND THE IMPLICIT CURRICULUM

Some of the most important things schools teach are never mentioned in the official curriculum or the textbook. Their educational significance is not discussed explicitly, and yet they constitute a definite program of social training, one that probably receives as much attention from teachers, students, parents, and administrators as the formal curriculum. We speak of these as constituting an *implicit* (or hidden) *curriculum.* The implicit curriculum includes tacit understandings teachers establish, such as those about expressing strong emotions in the classroom, about doing your best, respecting others' rights, and being fair. It includes rules such as those defining cheating, those regulating movement about the classroom, noise, and speech. It includes unwritten structural characteristics of classrooms, such as that teachers may evaluate students at any time on any aspect of their learning.

In *On What is Learned in School* (1968), sociologist Robert Dreeben argues that the implicit curriculum helps children make the transition from family life to public life by teaching them "the principles of conduct and patterns of behavior appropriate to adulthood" (Dreeben 1968, 4). These principles and patterns—*norms* is the sociological term—are not taught didactically as part of the formal curriculum, but experientially through the implicit structure of the school experience. Specifically, Dreeben argues that schools teach these norms by such structural features as:

> *annual promotion*—important relationships with adults and classmates are established, then severed periodically
> *low ratios of adults to children*—it is virtually impossible for teacher-student relationships to develop the emotional intensity and personal significance of family relationships
> *publicness*—everything the student does is visible to everyone all the time

Such features of school as these begin to accustom children to functioning in a public world peopled neither by strangers nor by intimates but by fellow citizens, members of a common society.

Dreeben singles out four norms he regards as particularly important to learn if one is to function as an adult in this society: independence, achievement, universalism, and specificity. Teachers teach independence in the classroom by rules that limit students' access to teacher help, requirements to "do your own work," and by individual testing and grading. Classroom emphasis on achievement is obvious in nearly every feature of classroom practice. Even so, some children persist for years in trying to be graded for charm or need or some other personal quality instead of their achievement. Universalism is taught by treating all pupils alike, making it clear that no one is entitled to special treatment. Specificity is the recognition that sometimes people do have particular qualities that make them exceptions to a general rule, that special treatment is sometimes appropriate for special people. For example, specificity is taught by grading students according to age and giving different privileges to students in different grades. Dreeben argues persuasively that schools and classrooms are designed to teach such norms as these. These are parts of a curriculum as real for students and teachers as the mathematics curriculum.

Teachers would be in a less ambiguous and vulnerable position if this implicit curriculum were explicit. Teachers are subject to sanctions if they fail to teach the implicit curriculum, just as they are with the formal curriculum, perhaps more serious sanctions. Yet the teaching of these norms remains largely tacit, so teachers have nothing official in writing to guide them. This was not always the case. As Elizabeth Vallance (1973) shows in an article entitled "Hiding the Hidden Curriculum," the implicit curriculum was quite explicit until we became uncomfortable with it. When Americans shared a consensus on firm discipline, the rules were spelled out clearly. Schools were, first and foremost, places where children acquired discipline and moral training. Under the influence of Rousseau, certain readings of Freud, and Progressive education, American attitudes toward discipline, especially educators' attitudes, changed. Strict discipline fell out of fashion. A whole range of more positive, warmer, and kinder approaches to socialization came into vogue. But practice has not always followed preachment. Schools and classrooms still have rules—fewer, broader ones, and not so harshly enforced—but we are not agreed on the rules or on why we have them, and so they are not a subject anybody much likes to talk about. Teachers inherit vague and conflicting public expectations that they must somehow take into account in establishing their own classroom routines and climate.

The Curriculum and Students' Actions

What students do determines what they learn. Regardless of how much direction, help, and influence a teacher may give, students must look, listen, selectively note and recall, and marshal their personal abilities in active efforts to learn. The most fundamental thing students do that affects what they learn in school is simply to expose themselves to the classroom environment, to attend, to participate in class activities, and to follow instructions. Students can sometimes choose among alternative activities offered within the classroom, but they can also choose between tending to the current classroom activity or to their own private thoughts. To attend and participate as directed presumes voluntary control of attention and willingness to exercise that control under the direction of the teacher, the curriculum materials, and the ongoing activity. The emphasis given in school rules to listening well, following instructions, and doing one's best testifies both to the importance of these matters and to the tendency of students to make their own independent decisions about them.

To learn what is included in the classroom curriculum students must manage the mental, physical, and emotional processes involved in performing classroom activities and in learning from them. We do not know very much about what specifically goes on in their minds and bodies when people are engaged in school learning. Psychologists call these processes mathemagenic, a coined term meaning *giving birth to learning* in Greek (Rothkopf 1970). It is clear that mathemagenic processes include volitional control of attention, physiological and cognitive processing of sensory data, strategies for remembering and for relating one item of information to another, monitoring one's own state of knowledge or ignorance, and other mental actions that control the use of one's abilities for learning. But it is seldom clear exactly which processes are used in which ways on any specific classroom task. These processes play a crucial role in making the classroom curriculum accessible to students, but they are not directly accessible to anyone other than the learner and so fleeting and inchoate that even the learner finds it difficult to speak accurately about them. For the most part, we speculate.

Hope Jensen Leichter, for example, speculates that every person has an educative style. She identifies a number of components of educative style, including: modes of integrating experiences over time, the manner in which an individual responds to cues from others, the way an individual appraises the values, attitudes, and knowledge encountered, the process by which an individual scans and searches the environment for educational opportunities, and the individual's strategy for contending with embarrassment (Leichter 1973). Surely as important are the moment-to-moment evaluations students make of the success and promise of their own covert mental actions: Is this the right thing to do now? Have I done things properly so far? Should I stop here and check to see that everything is in order before I proceed? How well am I doing in my efforts to learn this? We need to know much more about how these mathemagenic processes enter into students' learning in school. Even when we know all we care to know about them, however, our capacity to intervene and to influence students' mathemagenic activities in classroom interactions will remain limited, and students will therefore remain in control of the details of their own learning processes.

How, then, *does* a curriculum influence students? It does so mostly through very rough, crude, but powerful social mechanisms that do not make strong assumptions about the nature and details of the mathemagenic processes required of students. For example, content is presented to students in classrooms by the teacher, by curriculum materials, and perhaps by other students. A task analysis of the cognitive, psycho-physical, and emotional demands of any one of these presentations would be beyond the state of the art of modern psychology, but curriculum planning proceeds on the simple and crude assumption that things can be said, written, or done that will be sufficient for students, on the average, to learn what was intended. Teachers and curriculum developers may rack their brains to find activities that will, in fact, give students a reasonable chance of learning that content. They will try anything reasonable and combine different strategies to achieve a mix with broader effectiveness. They may even conduct controlled studies to evaluate the effects of different ways of presenting an idea, but even these will fall far short of illuminating the details of students' psychological processes.

In spite of the crudeness of the psychological basis for most classroom activities, students usually respond to them in roughly the intended way and learn more or less what they are expected to learn. As Philip Jackson concluded from his review of a half-century of research on children's attention to classroom activities,

> Although the amount of attention may vary considerably from class to class and even from minute to minute within a class, it would seem that most of the time most students are attending to the content of the lesson. (Jackson, 1968, p. 101)

As a result, students' learning usually reflects the pattern of inclusion and emphasis of the curriculum (Walker and Schaffarzick 1975). In spite of differences in students' ability, learning style, and interest, teachers' style and the quality of their preparation, classroom climate, and so on, for the most part students learn what they are taught. Where this is not true, the curriculum ceases to be an important educative influence.

SOURCES OF STUDENTS' DIFFICULTIES WITH CURRICULA

Obviously, real curricula do not always function as smoothly and powerfully as this. If they did, we would not hear so many calls for reform and read so many indictments of the scandalously poor quality of schools today. For a variety of reasons, students often fail to learn all that our curriculum plans propose. Whatever the ultimate explanation of such failures, their immediate causes must be attributed to the students' interactions with the classroom curriculum. One common failure observed in these interactions is lack of engagement of students with the classroom activities: students do not attend at all or put forth half-hearted efforts. When asked about this, students may say that they believe they are doing their best, or they may say that they find the activities boring (which is more symptom than cause: why are they boring?), or they may cite some factor in the classroom itself, such as that the activities are too difficult or the teacher too disorganized. Many factors contribute to lack of attention by a student and therefore many different changes in the classroom curriculum might improve engagement. For example, changing the difficulty of the activities may improve engagement, but increasing incentives for better performance on the unchanged activities may work as well or better.

Sometimes the curriculum plans and materials are clearly faulty and should be changed. The classroom activities they suggest may not offer students a sufficient opportunity to learn what students are expected to learn, for example. Or, the suggested activities may be poorly matched to students' abilities or interests. Or, they may be unnecessarily dull, failing to show the intrinsic value and interest of what is being taught. Or, the content and purposes they embody may not be the highest and best possible under the circumstances. Sometimes teaching is clearly at fault. When a teacher fails to maintain sufficient order in the classroom, even students who want to attend may be unable to. A teacher who knows too little of the subject may be unable to answer students' questions or help them when they make mistakes or lose their way in the curriculum.

The explanation of poor engagement with classroom activities may even lie outside classrooms. Students may be so distracted by outside activities—television, sports, dating, part-time jobs—or stressful events in their lives or their families—divorce, remarriage, illness or death in the family, violence at home or in the neighborhood—that they cannot concentrate on school work. They may become so accustomed to slick, dramatic, entertainment on film and television that school work of any kind seems dull by comparison. Students, their parents, and peers may set little value on school learning.

So, in most cases where curricula clearly fail to work as intended and fail to produce the intended learning, a combination of causes is probably at work. For example, anthropologist John Ogbu (1980) studied low achieving students in a California high school and found that many were happy with grades of C or even D. After all, they passed, didn't they? Students believed they knew something simply because they had been exposed to it, whether they had mastered it or not. Their attitude was, "I've had that already." Teachers failed to make it clear to these students and their parents that their performance would not qualify them for the further schooling and the employment to which they aspired. The curriculum materials provided enough easy content and activities to give all students the impression they were succeeding, no matter how little effort they expended or with how meager results. Somehow nothing they encountered in school conveyed a realistic appraisal of their performance. It is not easy to convince young people to raise their sights when their progress is satisfactory in their own eyes.

Faced with low levels of engagement with the classroom curriculum or with low levels of achievement, the path of least effort for teachers and students is to reduce the standards of performance expected from students and to make the materials simpler and more inviting. The possible negative life consequences of doing less than one's best in school are seldom apparent to either teachers or students, whereas the short term costs of working harder or better are obvious. It is important that ways be found to guard against this tendency toward *dumbing down*. One way to guard against gradual lowering of expectations is through achievement tests designed to reflect standards of performance expected in life outside the school. In addition to maintaining performance standards, such tests also help to make the eventual costs of easy adjustments more apparent to teachers and students at the time. The threat of low test scores at year end is more immediate, definite, and tangible than the threat of failing to qualify for entrance into a college or a profession many years later.

When students have difficulty with a curriculum, officials must determine if it is due to inadequate engagement and effort. If it is , and if the curricular content and purposes are clearly important, then every effort should be made to maintain curricular standards and find ways to secure students' engagement. When individual students have difficulty learning what is included in a curriculum even though they are engaged and try hard enough, the temptation is to conclude that they lack the basic ability to learn the material, and then to either to drop the material as too difficult or to dismiss the students as being unable to learn it. More commonly, though, such failures will arise from deficits in prerequisite learning or from misjudgment by students of the kinds of effort required.

For instance, many high school students who never previously had trouble learning in school experience problems in high school chemistry and physics courses. Some of these difficulties arise from weaknesses in arithmetic, algebra, or trigonometry. Some arise from lack of personal experience with chemical and physical phenomena and consequent absence of intuition about the material covered in the course. Others arise from the need to adjust to changes in unwritten rules of the high school science classroom, such as the requirement to learn how to solve new and unfamiliar problems. Still others arise simply from the pacing of the courses; the students are not accustomed to the high rate at which unfamilar ideas are introduced. As a rule of thumb, students who have dealt adequately with the tasks of school for ten years can be assumed to have the basic psychological ability to do any tasks presented in school curricula. Failures in particular courses by such students that are not explainable by lack of engagement can be presumed to indicate a curriculum problem, though the solution might require a strengthening of earlier courses rather than easing standards in this one.

HOW STUDENTS INFLUENCE THE CLASSROOM CURRICULUM

Although students are overmatched in social power in the classroom, they can counteract unwelcome influences by controlling their own covert thoughts and evaluations. In *The Ogre,* the French writer Michel Tournier presents a dramatic fictional account of a student putting the material of the school curriculum to personal use in ways completely contrary to those intended by the school. The hero narrates:

> I had crossed out the teachers, and the world of the mind into which they were supposed to initiate us. I had got to the point—but have I ever been at any other?—of considering every author, historical personage or book, any educational subject whatever, as automatically null and void as soon as it was annexed by adults and dished out to us as spiritual nourishment. But here and there, leafing through dictionaries, picking up what I could in textbooks, watching out for fleeting allusions to what really interested me in French or history lessons, I started to build up a culture of my own, a personal Pantheon that included Alcibiades and Pontius Pilate, Caligula and Hadrian, Frederick William I and Barrabas, Talleyrand and Rasputin. There was a certain way of referring to a politician or writer—condemning him of course, but that was not enough, there had to be something else as well—which made me prick up my ears and suspect that this might be one of mine. I would then start an inquiry, a sort of preliminary to beatification, carried out with all the means at my disposal, at the conclusion of which the gates of my Pantheon would either open or stay shut. (Tournier 1972, 10–11)

Covert subversion by students of the official curriculum, in milder forms, is commonplace in classroom life.

Students also play active, overt roles in shaping their classroom curricula, though this is not widely acknowledged. Students influence the pacing, the standards of mastery, the emphasis, and even the coverage of all their courses. By giving or withholding their cooperation, students can, in effect, bargain with teachers over the terms of their work in the classroom. Studying medical schools, Becker et al.

(1961) coined the term *grade-performance exchange* for this negotiated agreement between teachers and students on the terms of their trade. The deal is that teachers award grades in exchange for specified levels of performance from students. When teachers make it more difficult for students to achieve high grades, students counter by making classroom life more difficult for teachers, perhaps by complaining or misbehaving or by withholding responses they know the teacher wants, such as friendliness, enthusiasm, timely delivery of assigned work, or even class attendance and attentiveness, in an effort to induce the teacher to adopt more favorable terms of exchange.

A class in which students hold the teacher's performance demands to a minimum may cover less content and realize less lofty goals than another in which students and teacher negotiate a grade-performance exchange that calls for higher performance standards. Speaking informally with students in a high-income, academically oriented Bay Area high school, I found that many of them made quite intricate calculations of the time and effort they needed to allocate to different curricular and extra-curricular activities in order to achieve the grades and honors they believed they needed in order to be admitted to the colleges of their choice. When a teacher's excess demands upset their plans, they were quite forward in discussing the matter with the teacher. Teachers reported feeling pressures from students and from parents anxious about their children's academic success. Some teachers reported that such pressures led them to organize their courses more fully in advance, to make the terms of their grade-performance exchange explicit, and to limit or eliminate open-ended assignments, surprise quizzes, and anything else that added to the uncertainty of the grade-performance exchange. The phenomenon noted by Doyle (1977) that students work to reduce the ambiguity and risk they bear in the grade-performance exchange seems widespread, perhaps universal. And it can play a major role in shaping the classroom curriculum.

So, students are by no means powerless in their interactions with the curriculum. On the contrary, their active efforts are essential to the success of any curriculum, and by helping to set the terms under which they cooperate, students do a great deal to determine the curriculum they actually receive. If students' efforts in this regard are so often negative, it is surely at least in part because they are unaware of the eventual costs they bear when they use strategies that reduce the expectations placed on them. Our aim should surely be to encourage students to think of the curriculum as an opportunity and of meeting curricular standards as a matter of personal pride.

FRAMES, MATERIALS, PLANS, AND THE CLASSROOM CURRICULUM

Because the curriculum is an abstract pattern of content, purpose, and form found in classroom activities, it can only be isolated from the activities themselves by an act of abstraction. We have seen how the curriculum is embodied in the actions of teachers and students in the classroom. The classroom curriculum manifests itself in classroom events in at least three additional ways. First, the curriculum is an integral part of the frames that define and limit the goals and resources of any given classroom. Second, the curriculum is embodied in the curriculum materials used by teacher and students. Third, the curriculum enters into teacher planning.

The curriculum is realized in part by the institutional decisions and actions that lead to this classroom existing in the first place and to the scope and direction assigned to the work. Contemporary secondary schools offer courses in English rather than separate courses in grammar, rhetoric, and composition, for example, and this fact influences what students and teachers do in their classes. A high school's decision to offer or not to offer a high school course in Parenting determines whether students and teachers will be brought together in classrooms with this content and purpose at all. The most important classroom frames, from a curricular point of view, are:

- time—the amount and distribution of time in the school schedule allocated to a class
- teacher—characteristics of the teacher assigned to the class, such as subject-matter competence
- students—characteristics of the students assigned to the class, such as ability and prior achievement
- materials—type of teaching/learning materials and facilities supplied for use in the class
- expectations—what teacher and students are expected to accomplish, the standards by which their performance is judged

The decisions that establish these frames limit and direct what teacher and students do within the classroom. Generally speaking, these frames are set by curriculum policy decisions made by the school and school system that are, in their turn, constrained by frames established at state and national levels.

The curriculum materials available in a classroom exert a powerful influence on the content covered. Students can learn from the materials directly, and what they learn may complement, supplement, or contradict what the teacher teaches. But materials affect classrooms most powerfully by influencing teachers. Komoski (1978) claimed that 90–95% of all classroom instruction involves published instructional materials. A national survey by the Educational Products Information Exchange (EPIE), admittedly not a disinterested body, maintained that more than 90% of the time that students are engaged in learning activities in the classroom is spent with instructional materials in one form or another. Smith (1977) tried to measure the extent of teachers' independence from the textbook by recording the amount of time teachers spent using teacher-made materials and published materials. He found that primary school teachers spent more classroom time working with teacher-made materials (42%) than upper elementary teachers (37%), and that more experienced teachers made more use of teacher-made materials than less experienced teachers (38% versus 30%). McCutcheon (1980) studied 12 elementary teachers and reported that they all relied on the textbook as the major source of their classroom activities.

> From 85–95% of reading and mathematics activities in these twelve classrooms was based on suggestions in the teacher's guide. (McCutcheon 1980, 8)

While the range of these estimates is large, from 60% to more than 90%, clearly curriculum materials play an important role in determining what happens in classrooms. To cover content not in the standard curriculum materials provided to each student requires teachers to do the additional work of presenting material themselves and of creating, selecting, acquiring, and distributing materials of their own. Also, teachers must assume full responsibility for material they introduce into their classroom, whereas they are protected by the authority of the institution when they use materials provided. So, while teachers in many cases have the ability to control the content of classroom instruction, they do not have clear authority to do so, and doing so costs them time, energy, and effort. For these reasons, the officially selected and supplied curriculum materials exert a powerful influence on the content covered in most classrooms.

Tests provided for use in the classroom may be considered a special case of curriculum materials, one with a particularly important influence over the criteria teachers use to judge students' progress and mastery. Again, it is possible but difficult and time consuming for teachers to write their own test items or to develop an alternative to tests. Standardized tests administered to students by the school are best considered as one of the classroom's frames. Tests of all kinds are the most direct reflection of purpose in the classroom curriculum.

The classroom curriculum manifests itself quite directly in teachers' planning. Teachers typically plan a rough outline of the year's work at the beginning of the school year and then make plans for each week or for units of a few weeks' duration throughout the year. All studies of teacher planning show that teachers generally begin their planning by considering one of the classroom frames: the content to be covered (Zahorik 1975; Taylor 1970; Peterson, Marx, and Clark 1978; Clark and Yinger 1978; Yinger 1978). Teachers' first consideration in planning is content, even before consideration of students' interests and course objectives. A close second is consideration of curriculum materials, another critical classroom frame. After content inclusion and emphasis, class activities are the most frequent focus of teacher planning. Again, the teachers' guides that come with textbooks commonly suggest class activities, as do the courses of study and curriculum guides provided by the school district. These are only suggestions, and teachers feel quite free to use other activities instead. Teachers can find other activities described in teaching methods texts, professional journals, teachers' guides accompanying other textbooks and curriculum guides from other districts. Figure 7-2 illustrates some of these frames graphically.

FIGURE 7-2   Curriculum and Its Frames

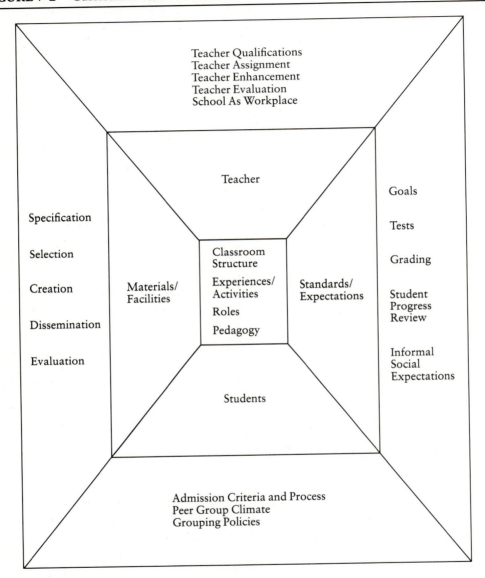

Teacher Qualifications
Teacher Assignment
Teacher Enhancement
Teacher Evaluation
School As Workplace

Teacher

Goals

Specification

Tests

Selection

Grading

Creation

Materials/
Facilities

Classroom
Structure
Experiences/
Activities
Roles
Pedagogy

Standards/
Expectations

Student
Progress
Review

Dissemination

Evaluation

Informal
Social
Expectations

Students

Admission Criteria and Process
Peer Group Climate
Grouping Policies

Why the Conventional Classroom Persists

Classrooms did not always take the form that we now regard as conventional. Instruction in schools was predominantly individual until the latter half of the nineteenth century. Schoolrooms held a schoolmaster and a collection of pupils of various ages and levels of achievement and ability. Pupils would be called individually to the master's desk to recite orally. Then, as we learned in Chapter 2, reformers following the lead of William T. Harris brought group instruction, grade levels, textbooks, and common examinations into common use in American schools. By 1890, the classroom in essentially its modern form prevailed in American elementary and secondary schools. By then it was already under attack from Progressives, who believed that the recitation had served its purpose and should now pass from the scene in favor of more modern methods, by which they meant student-centered, activity-oriented modes of instruction. After the turn of the century the recitation found few defenders among educational authorities. Even the arch-traditionalist William Bagley would not defend the recitation as typically practiced.

> One . . . can scarcely escape the conclusion that the work of the typical American classroom . . . has been and still is characterized by a lifeless and perfunctory study and recitation of assigned textbook materials. (Bagley 1931, 8)

Yet the conventional classroom persisted. Subsequent studies, extending right into the present decade (see reviews by Hoetker and Ahlbrand 1969, and Cuban 1985) continue to find the pattern of teacher-centered group instruction prevalent in American classrooms at all levels.

The most satisfactory answer to the question of why these traditional patterns are so pervasive and persistent, despite so much opposition, is that they permit teachers and students to cope with some rather difficult situations in the classroom. Conditions prevailing in classrooms make many demands on both teachers and students and place strict limits on the resources available for meeting these demands. Meeting all the demands within all the imposed limits is not an easy job. The recitation makes the job easier.

One formulation of the expectations placed on teachers and students lists these four items:

- coverage—of topics, content, material to be learned
- mastery—of knowledge, skill, and the like included under each item of content
- affect—maintenance of good feelings and attitudes
- order—quiet, good conduct, discipline

(Westbury 1973)

Teachers and students are expected to maintain acceptable overall levels of performance in all four of these areas.

These expectations must be met in an environment that is in some respects quite limited. It is limited in space to one room, which must accommodate 20 to 40 students. It is limited to one teacher with just so much talent and preparation, to those students who happen to be assigned to that classroom and who elect to attend, to such facilities and equipment as can be afforded and accommodated, to a few textbooks per pupil and a few other books for the use of the class as a whole, and to a fixed number of hours per day and days per year. These limitations do a great deal to determine what sort of social interactions will be successful in classrooms. Because mastery is expected of students, evaluation of students is necessarily a prominent feature of classrooms. Since classrooms are crowded, evaluation, along with everything else that happens, is necessarily public. Under these circumstances, competition is almost unavoidable. Because the ratio of children to adults is so large, and because space is so limited, interactions between children are likely to be frequent and, unless the children are exceptionally well socialized, many of these interactions will be noisy, violent, or otherwise disruptive. Maintaining enough order so that demands for coverage, mastery, and affect can be met requires a great deal of attention and effort from the teacher. Under these conditions, a focus on strict discipline is almost unavoidable.

The conventional classroom interaction pattern, competently implemented, enables teachers to cope with these rather restrictive demands and limitations. A good teacher running a conventional classroom establishes rules and routines early in the year that limit students' movement, actions, and noise, and thus fulfill the demand for order while simplifying what would otherwise be an excessively distracting environment. By dealing with the class as a whole in a single set of classroom activities, the situation is further simplified. The teacher plans activities to suit as many students as possible, and paces activities to ensure adequate coverage of the content assigned to the course. The textbook presents content to be learned, offers exercises for practice, and problems to test mastery. By questioning pupils, the teacher discovers what they have and have not learned, and, if necessary, provides remediation, perhaps by presenting material a second time in a different way. Intermittent questions and continual supervision help the teacher keep students' attention.

The secret of the success of this formula is that it does so many things reasonably well in such a variety of circumstances, while economizing on limited resources, especially the teacher's time, energy, and expertise. Conventional classrooms carry out simultaneously the functions of custodial care, socialization, and academic training. They require only one adult with relatively unspecialized training to supervise 30 or more children. They require almost no capital or technology. They can be set in operation in an almost identical form in any location. They can be adapted to virtually any language or culture. They can coexist comfortably with both family and government. They can be adjusted easily for age ranges from kindergarten to graduate school and for virtually any subject, academic or otherwise. (Cuban 1985 presents a careful analysis of historical data in support of this and competing interpretations of the persistence of recitation.)

Compared to individual instruction, for example, the conventional classroom achieves test results that are at least comparable and often superior (Hedges and Olkin 1985; Begle 1979) while placing less severe demands on the teacher's resources of time, skill, knowledge, attentiveness, imagination, and energy. Individual instruction requires a greater variety of more carefully designed and expensive self-instructional curriculum materials. It requires specialized teacher training in managing a more complex classroom organization and record system. If we could afford a very much smaller pupil-teacher ratio, we might see more individual instruction and tutoring, but schools would then be more expensive. If we would invest more capital in self-instructional materials and educational technology, we might substantially improve achievement in an individualized system. No doubt teachers could be trained to operate classrooms with more varied and complex social interactions—including, say, students helping one another and flexible use of a variety of media by small groups of students—but such classrooms could only be operated by teachers with specific training, whereas conventional classrooms are less demanding of teacher skill. The more specialized alternative would have to offer definite benefits to offset this greater cost and fragility. The recitation persists, then, not because it does any one thing optimally, but because *it can be made to do a number of important things reasonably well under almost any conditions.*

There can be no question that the conventional classroom is a limited and limiting form. It makes very inefficient use of students' time, energy, and talents, much of which is wasted in waiting or in frantic efforts to keep up and in studying things they already know or are not yet ready to learn, or simply in sitting and listening when they could be using and testing what they are learning. It is not effective for teaching manual skills, eye-hand coordination, or other forms of non-verbal learning. Social interactions among peers and between adults and children are so restricted by classroom interaction patterns that social learning is, if anything, hampered. But until a more serviceable alternative is available, conventional classrooms will continue to prevail. Although the conventional classroom will doubtlessly continue to be challenged by an ever greater variety of classroom innovations, it will continue to be widely used until a clearly better alternative emerges that is as robust and widely useful. When such alternatives become available, the conventional classroom, with few fervent advocates, could fall precipitously from its dominant position, perhaps in less than a decade.

Summary

Classrooms are not neutral stages on which any sort of curriculum can be enacted, but social settings so constrained by expectations and limitations that only a few specialized activity patterns diffuse widely and endure. The classroom curriculum is so thoroughly fused with these patterns that it, too, is highly constrained. To determine whether a proposed curriculum can take root in classrooms and maintain itself without special attention requires a close analysis of its demands on teachers and students and its compatibility with curriculum materials and frames.

CHANGING THE CLASSROOM CURRICULUM

Teacher-Initiated Efforts to Change

When teachers try to change the curriculum in their own classroom, they do not have to leap the highest hurdle: how to secure the willing cooperation of the single most powerful figure in the classroom—that is, the teacher. Still, teachers embarking on curriculum change efforts in their own classroom must overcome a number of obstacles, the most serious of which fall under three broad headings: resources, expertise and authority.

Essential resources include time to plan and access to curriculum materials. Teachers are usually allotted one class period per day for preparation, which includes planning curriculum changes as well as planning ordinary lessons, grading homework and tests, consulting with students and colleagues, and all the other planning and housekeeping duties associated with teaching. A new unit of, say three weeks' duration, will take several dozen hours to plan, so it will probably absorb all of the teacher's discretionary time in school for at least a month and most likely additional time at home as well. Unless teachers devote evenings and weekends to the project, this time all comes in brief snippets of an hour or less. Curriculum materials may include printed material, audio or video recordings, or apparatus of any kind needed for the activities the teacher plans. Unless the teacher proposes to provide all the information by lecture, or unless it is readily available in the textbook, some additional material will be needed. Teachers often make these materials or scrounge for them, both of which add to the demands on their time. Teachers often buy materials with their own funds to avoid the delay and red tape required to arrange for the school to buy them.

All teachers presumably acquire the expertise for lesson planning during their professional training, and this is presumably sufficient for them to make incremental changes in content, purpose, or organization of the educational program in their classroom. Planning a substantial change in the classroom curriculum, on the other hand, typically requires expertise of several kinds not routinely provided during teacher training. If teachers must introduce substantially new content, such as mathematical proof, inequalities, or number systems in bases other than base ten, then teachers will need to acquire expertise in the new content. If teachers must prepare new curriculum materials for students to use, they will need at least amateur competence as a writer, as an applied psychologist, as a graphic designer, and as an evaluator. When a curriculum change calls for new patterns of classroom interaction, teachers may need to learn new skills in order to enlarge their repertoire of teaching styles. For example, a teacher would be foolhardy to use peer teaching or small group learning without at least reading about these techniques and rehearsing them. Formal training under the supervision of someone who has mastered these teaching styles would be advisable.

I am not aware of any data on the frequency with which teachers initiate curriculum changes of varying magnitude, but my experience and reading suggest to me that teachers seldom attempt changes that require expertise they do not already have. Teachers who have developed a talent for writing word exercises for language instruction may spend considerable time preparing such materials, but other teachers will not. Teachers whose repertoire of teaching techniques already includes cooperative work groups will develop lessons that call for cooperative work groups, but other teachers will not. When teachers can rely only on their own expertise, they are unlikely to attempt really ambitious changes except in those areas in which they already feel expert. Too often curriculum changes teachers make on their own are merely incremental, timid adjustments made in the interest of a narrow practicality, or one-sided, reflecting the teacher's hobby-horse. Greater access to a wider range of deeper expertise would strengthen most teacher-initiated curriculum change efforts. On the other hand, one can be confident that teacher-initiated curriculum changes can be made to work under realistic classroom conditions, which cannot always be said about externally-initiated curriculum changes.

Making major changes in the classroom curriculum on their own initiative is not a normal job requirement for teachers. A teacher who initiates a major curriculum change makes a public statement that may be seen as implying dissatisfaction with the officially adopted curriculum and thus as criticism of superiors and colleagues. Even if teachers had full authority to shape their own classroom curriculum, they would still need to worry about possible opposition to the change from colleagues and superiors, as well as students and parents, all of whom can make life difficult for teachers if they try. But, as things are, school administrators, school boards, and the public do not acknowledge an unlimited right of teachers to plan their own classroom curriculum. They do acknowledge teachers' right and duty to adapt official plans and materials to the specifics of their individual classroom. The line between planning and adaptation is vague, and different schools draw it differently, but the one universal unwritten rule is: *Don't make waves.* If a curriculum change comes to public attention, the school system will be forced to assert its authority and either pronounce the teacher's initiative to be official school policy or reject it. Either way, committees will need to consider the change using officially prescribed procedures for curriculum planning in the schools of that community, usually a time-consuming, bureaucratic process.

In schools in which controversy arises frequently over curriculum matters, teachers are well-advised to seek approval for their initiative from the department chair, principal and perhaps also central office personnel in advance. In less conflicted contexts, teachers may be encouraged to try even substantial changes with only a requirement to report after the fact what they did and how it worked. In some cases, controversy is so rare that teachers are given broad discretionary authority over their classroom curriculum. Such freedom in curricular matters is reported to be one of the attractions of private school teaching.

But teachers' autonomy in regard to their classroom curriculum is also limited by the need for coordination among teachers and among curricular components such as tests, textbooks, and curriculum guides. Because students stay with teachers for only a year and, after the first few grades, for only a small part of each day, the work of one classroom must be coordinated with that of others if students' school programs are to retain any coherence. Substantial changes in any one curriculum will require adjustments in all those subsequent or concurrent curricula that depend on it. This dependency is greatest in the skill subjects of mathematics, reading, writing, and foreign languages, but it is evident to some degree in all subjects. Also, curriculum changes have implications for tests, textbooks, and curriculum materials that may impact other parts of the school.

In short, the curriculum, even the classroom curriculum, is a public matter given in trust to schools and delegated by them to varying degrees to teachers. Legally, teachers and school officials are public servants in regard to curriculum matters, not professional experts. And the classroom curriculum is not, therefore, the teacher's private preserve or professional prerogative.

In general, making minor changes in the classroom curriculum presents teachers mainly with the problem of finding the time and resources and enduring the small risk of controversy. For teachers who enjoy curriculum work, these problems are minor annoyances that the satisfactions of planning far outweigh. For many others, curriculum work of this sort is an unpleasant chore. But making substantial changes in the classroom curriculum is a different matter altogether. The more a proposed curriculum change disrupts established classroom routines, the more time-consuming will be the planning, the greater the expertise required in planning, the more difficult it will be for the teacher to implement that change, the more visible the change will become within the school and community, and the greater will be the risk of controversy. Teachers who initiate major curriculum changes in their classroom on their own, who succeed by local standards, and who gain the respect of colleagues and superiors for their work, become local experts on curriculum matters and often assume leadership positions in official curriculum change efforts of the school or school system. They may also develop curriculum materials for publication. In effect, they carve out an uncertified professional specialty in curriculum planning.

Externally Initiated Change Efforts

When others try to initiate changes in the classroom curriculum, they must rely on teachers to realize their plans. The obvious and natural strategy for an outsider intent on initiating change in the classroom curriculum is therefore to try to get teachers to treat the initiative as if it were their own. Experienced hands speak of *ownership* of the change by teachers, by which they mean getting teachers to regard it as their own initiative. When this happens, implementing externally initiated changes in classrooms reduces to the problem of helping teachers to bring about their own changes in the classroom curriculum. If external agents can also provide additional time for teachers to plan, curriculum materials or funds to acquire them, appropriate expertise, and the backing of school authorities, then the obstacles to classroom curriculum change are minimized.

There are no formulas for winning over the hearts and minds of teachers to a proposed curriculum change. Approaches range from advertising and public relations to inspiration, co-optation, intimidation, and education. Traditionally curriculum reformers play to teachers' idealism and try to persuade teachers that implementing their reform will help their students or contribute to a better society or both. They also try to get a bandwagon rolling, to create the impression that teachers who implement their reform will be in the vanguard setting the direction other schools will later follow. Local school officials often attempt to co-opt teachers by involving them in planning the details of reforms to be adopted. School systems also sponsor speakers, training sessions, buy books for the teacher's lounge, and even reimburse teachers for college courses, in an effort to win them over by education.

Sometimes authorities avoid the problem of winning over teachers by simply mandating reforms. Simple mandates have a miserable record of effectiveness. Every state has laws on its books requiring that something be done in classrooms— teach the evils of alcohol, drugs, and tobacco in every class every year or offer 15 minutes of vigorous physical activity every day. Unless school officials enforce these in some way, they are largely ignored. Enforcement by direct observation of classrooms is impractical, although tests seem to be an effective enforcement tool. In general, though, teachers have such broad discretion in managing their classrooms that willing initiative is much more likely to be effective than grudging compliance. Still, grudging compliance may be preferable to noncompliance from the point of view of legislators or educational authorities.

Outsiders may also hope to influence the classroom curriculum indirectly by changing curriculum materials, classroom frames, or even by influencing what students do. Change agents may hope that such changes will bring pressures to bear on teachers and cause them to change or that such changes will bring about curriculum change directly, even when the teacher does not change. The situation in which teachers are presented with an externally developed program in the form of written plans and materials has been extensively studied. It is clear that teachers are usually influenced by the plans and materials to change what they do in their classrooms, but it is also clear that teachers transform the prepared program. What happens in the classroom is neither what was happening before the external program was adopted nor exactly what was proposed by the program's developers, but some sort of compromise. This is mutual adaptation again.

The net effect of mutual adaptation is to ward off, redirect, or blunt attempts to control the curriculum from outside the classroom. Experienced teachers whose schools have adopted many of the national educational reforms produced during the last quarter century have become adept at meeting official guidelines while retaining their professional integrity and continuing to exercise their professional judgment. Those who thought they had revamped the school's mathematics curriculum by winning the school board's endorsement of checkbook balancing in the mathematics curriculum will be disappointed to discover that they have only made a marginal change. But they will have made some change, which is more than the teachers who opposed it would have liked. The art of negotiating changes in classrooms with teachers lies at the heart of facilitating curriculum change. We will consider it in detail in a later chapter.

In the case of a distant reform adopted by state or district officials but not supported by local school administrators, no one is present in the local school to bargain with teachers, and so those who do not prefer the reform do not implement it in their classroom. If all the curriculum reformer has to bring to the negotiating table—which also happens to be the teacher's desk—are written documents exhorting teachers to change, the result is a foregone conclusion. On the other hand, if proponents of the curriculum change have even one person who is an experienced, respected member of the local school staff and who will act as a champion of the reform, will defend its more costly and risky features, talk up its benefits, and in general advocate it, chances for implementation of the reform are much better. And if, in addition, a strong administrator is willing to bargain hard, using up political capital in the process, then it may be possible to persuade teachers to go along with an unpopular change.

Changing classroom frames is in some respects easier and in others much more difficult than other ways of influencing the classroom curriculum. It is much easier for a local school official to create a new course or special program in the school, recruit teachers committed to the change to staff it, buy new curriculum materials, and so on, than it is to try to change the hearts, minds, and classroom actions of dozens of established teachers in their conventional classrooms. The administrator controls most of the frames directly, few teachers' routines are disrupted, and no teacher need be coerced into adopting a curriculum change. On the other hand, changes in frames often have budget implications and require personnel changes and changes in teacher and student assignments that must be approved by others.

In principle, it is possible for external agents to try to influence classrooms by working with students, though only a few gestures are ever made in this direction. Measures that increased students' active efforts to learn, for example, or redirected them in more productive channels could certainly result in greater coverage and mastery and improve classroom order and affect. Students' efforts could be co-opted as teachers' are by involving them in planning changes in the classroom curriculum. Students could even be trained to help maintain a different classroom pattern. For example, students could be trained in peer tutoring and cooperative group learning in order to make it easier for teachers to implement such reforms in classrooms. Even just explaining the rationale for the change and asking for students' help in bringing it about would be likely to facilitate change in the classroom curriculum.

The most prominent curriculum reforms of this century have demanded extensive changes in classroom routines. Progressive education called for nothing less than a complete transformation of the classroom. The new math demanded not only the teaching of new content unfamiliar to most teachers, but also teaching young children to prove mathematical relationships, to solve unfamiliar and difficult problems, and to explore and discover mathematics on their own. It called for the use of blocks, balances, beads, geoboards, and a host of other apparatus. The teaching of writing across the curriculum demands major adjustments from secondary school teachers who had never before considered this part of their responsibility. The use of computers in science, math, or English classrooms is requiring major adjustments. Such changes as these require enormous amounts of time and effort from teachers sustained over years. They are almost equivalent to learning to teach again in a new way. This can be done with several hours of work per week sustained over several years and appropriate opportunities for practice, feedback, discussion, and psychological support. But in most cases teachers were expected to make these changes after at most a single college course in the evening or over a summer.

Even changes that preserve conventional classroom patterns and call for only incremental changes usually require extensive adjustments in several aspects of classroom routines. Just substituting one unit of content for another within an existing course requires changes in the curriculum materials, tests, and teacher's plans, and may possibly also require that teachers learn new content, revise their understanding of the subject, or learn new teaching skills or strategies. Teaching is seldom divided into units so independent that one can be changed without affecting others. Even the incremental curriculum changes typically attempted in schools, such as adopting a new method of reading instruction, increasing emphasis on writing in the upper elementary grades, making mathematics more or less practical, or updating science content, require far reaching adjustments throughout the curriculum.

Every curriculum change demands a change from teachers. At a minimum, teachers must revise their plans to include the changes in content, purpose, or form, and revise their class activities to realize these changes in plans. They may also need to learn new content. They may need to reconsider their conception of the subject, the student, teaching, education, or society and to reconcile new ideas and values with familiar ones. They may need to learn new teaching skills and strategies. The more difficult and extensive the changes demanded of teachers, the more difficult it will be to implement that curriculum change in the classroom.

Teachers need incentives to make the changes required to modify the classroom curriculum. They must envision possible benefits from making the change that might exceed their costs and risks. These may be material incentives such as extra pay. They may be intangible incentives such as professional pride and recognition. As we have seen, teachers feel rewarded by their contacts with students and by being able to help them. Making a curriculum change that they believe truly benefits students substantially may therefore be so inherently rewarding that it requires no extrinsic rewards of any kind. Teachers can readily see, though, that few teachers achieved rewards other than intrinsic ones for their efforts in implementing earlier curriculum reforms. Champions of one reform movement may have become heroes for a time, but they eventually endured criticism when reactions came or obscurity when the next wave of reform crested. Teachers found themselves criticized as causes of the current problems by each successive band of reformers. Newspaper headlines never trumpeted their success. By contrast, in the Progressive era teachers who labored to realize the new student-centered, activity-oriented reforms were hailed as heroes helping to usher in an enlightened modern era, to create a fuller democracy, and to realize the potential inherent in each child.

Summary

For all these reasons, achieving substantial, lasting changes in the curricula of large numbers of classrooms is the greatest challenge facing those who work on curriculum problems. It is probably not impossible, though it has not been done in this century. The most serious challenge to the conventional classroom has been Progressive Education—the broadened content of elementary school programs, the modern school subjects, the appealing textbook. While certain aspects of Progressive practice have diffused into typical contemporary classrooms, no one would argue that many American classrooms today realize Progressive ideals to any substantial degree. Nor has the teaching of science and mathematics been transformed by the post-Sputnik reforms. The Great Society reforms have not realized equal educational opportunity in today's classrooms. It is too soon to tell what changes the major state educational reforms following *A Nation At Risk* may have made in classrooms. If we are to transform the classroom or even to realize the greatest effectiveness from the conventional classroom pattern, we will have to develop much more intensive and considered strategies for changing the classroom curriculum.

QUESTIONS FOR STUDY

1. Describe how Progressive classroom practices satisfy or fail to satisfy the demands of order, affect, coverage and mastery. What does your analysis suggest about the challenges that face a school intending to adopt Progressive classroom practices?

2. The conventional classroom takes on significantly different forms in different grades and subjects. Choose a subject and grade you know well and describe as exactly as you can the conventional pattern of teaching in those classes. Compare your description with others' descriptions. Speculate on reasons why these differences might arise. (You might want to consult Barr and Dreeben (1983) and Stodolsky (1988) to discover findings of research on these questions.)

3. Seatwork is a common pattern found in classrooms. In seatwork students complete paperwork independently at their seats. Compare and contrast

seatwork with the conventional classroom interaction pattern as described in this chapter. Does seatwork help teachers to cope with the demands and limitations of the classroom setting? Under what conditions would you expect that seatwork might be better suited to the demands and limitations of classrooms than the conventional pattern? What difficulties would you predict an accomplished conventional classroom teacher might face in attempting to use seatwork?

4. Compare and contrast individualized instruction with the conventional classroom interaction pattern. What are the advantages of individualization for teachers? For students? What are the costs and risks for teachers of switching from a conventional pattern to an individualized one? On balance, how strong do you think the incentives (or disincentives) to switch would be for an experienced classroom teacher? What actions on the part of a principal might contribute most to improving the incentives for such a teacher?

5. Expand or enlarge one of the frames to which classrooms are now subject and see whether teachers would have more options for ways to satisfy the demands of coverage, mastery, affect, and order in their classrooms. Which frame do you think puts the most severe limitations on teachers' options? Why? Why do you think this frame remains as confining as it is?

6. If students generally go along with the curriculum provided in the classroom and if they usually learn what they are taught, then why wouldn't issuing more demanding curriculum plans and textbooks improve students' achievement?

7. Examine your own mathemagenic activities during a classroom lesson. Reserve at least two hours immediately after one of your classes. Tape record the class. Immediately afterward, play back the tape and record the thoughts you had at the time as well as you can recall them. Note times when your attention wandered, times when you were puzzled and how you coped with your puzzlement, times when you questioned the ideas presented, and so on. Would you describe your role in this lesson as especially active? If you can, play the first few minutes of the tape for a friend who has never studied the material, and compare your thoughts with your friend's. Chances are, you did some things while listening that made you a more effective learner in this lesson than your friend. Describe them.

8. Try to write out the implicit curriculum in a classroom you know well. Do this by listing the norms and expectations that are generally followed there. What do you think would happen if these were written out and presented to students at the beginning of the school year in every class? If you think doing so would be a good idea, explain why the practice has not caught on. If you think it would be a bad idea, explain its bad effects.

RECOMMENDED READING

Philip Jackson's *Life in Classrooms* (1968) and Dan Lortie's *Schoolteacher* (1970) are so compelling and literate on the subjects of teachers and teaching that anyone interested in the relation of these to curriculum must read them, even though more recent works on their subjects are now in print. Dreeben's *On What Is Learned in School* (1968) remains the seminal work on the implicit curriculum. Barr and Dreeben (1983) and Stodolsky (1988) offer provocative extensions of the work on conventional classrooms.

The *Handbook of Research on Teaching* 3rd ed. (Wittrock 1986) is a treasure trove of recent research and scholarship on all aspects of teaching. Walter Doyle's chapter in the Handbook on "Classroom Organization and Management" (Wittrock 1986, 392–431) is a wonderful summary of research on conventional classrooms and other patterns of classroom organization. Courtney Cazden's chapter, "Classroom Discourse" (Wittrock 1986, 432–463), gives a lively overview of the role of language in classroom interactions. Penelope Peterson and Christopher Clark's jointly written chapter, "Teacher's Thought Processes" (Wittrock 1986, 255–296), summarizes the teacher planning literature and other aspects of teacher thinking as well. Wittrock's twin chapter, "Students' Thought Processes" (Wittrock 1986, 297–314) is the most comprehensive summary I have seen of the relatively scant literature on the role of students' thinking in classroom learning.

REFERENCES

Bagley, William. 1931. The Textbook and Methods of Teaching. *The Textbook in Education*. (Guy M. Whipple, ed.) Thirtieth Yearbook of the National Society for the Study of Education, Part II. Bloomington, IL: Public School Publishing Company.

Barr, Rebecca and Robert M. Dreeben. 1983. *How Schools Work*. Chicago: University of Chicago Press.

Becker, Howard, B. Geer, E. Hughes, and A. Strauss. 1961. *Boys in White: Student Culture in Medical School*. Chicago: University of Chicago Press.

Begle, Edward G. 1979. *Critical Variables in Mathematics Education*. Washington, D.C.: Mathematical Association of America.

Bode, Boyd. 1927. *Modern Educational Theories*. N.Y.: Macmillan.

Clark, Christopher and Robert J. Yinger. 1987. Teacher Planning. *Talks to Teachers*. (Berliner, David and Barak Rosenshine, eds.) N.Y.: Random House.

Cuban, Larry. 1985. *How Teachers Taught*. N.Y.: Teachers College Press.

Davis, Robert B. and Carolyn McKnight. 1976. Conceptual, Heuristic, and Algorithmic Approaches in Mathematics Teaching. *Journal of Children's Mathematical Behavior* 1:271–286.

Doyle, Walter. 1977. Learning the Classroom Environment: An Ecological Analysis. *Journal of Teacher Education* 28:22–34.

Dreeben, Robert. 1968. *On What Is Learned in School*. Reading, MA: Addison-Wesley.

Greenwood, Peter W., Dale Mann, and Milbrey W. McLaughlin. 1975. *Federal Programs Supporting Educational Change, Vol. III: The Process of Change*. Santa Monica, CA: Rand.

Hedges, Larry and Ingram Olkin. 1985. *Statistical Methods for Meta-Analysis*. N.Y.: Academic Press.

Hoetker, James and David Ahlbrand. 1969. The Persistence of the Recitation. *American Educational Research Journal* 6:145–167.

Jackson, Philip W. 1968. *Life in Classrooms.* NY: Holt, Rinehart, and Winston.

Komoski, Kenneth. 1976. Educational Products Information Exchange. *EPIEgram* 5:1.

Leichter, Hope Jensen. 1973. The Concept of Educative Style. *Teachers College Record* 75: 239–250.

Lortie, Dan C. 1975. *Schoolteacher.* Chicago: University of Chicago Press.

McCutcheon, Gail. 1980. How Do Elementary Teachers Plan? The Nature of Planning and Influences on It. *Elementary School Journal* 81:4–23.

Ogbu, John. 1980. *The Next Generation.* N.Y.: Academic Press.

Peterson, Penelope, R. W. Marx, and C. M. Clark. 1978. Teacher Planning, Teacher Behavior, and Student Achievement. *American Educational Research Journal* 15: 417–432.

Rothkopf, Ernst Z. 1970. The Concept of Mathemagenic Activities. *Review of Educational Research* 40: 325–336.

Schaffarzick, Jon. 1975. The Consideration of Curriculum Change at the Local Level. Unpublished Ph.D. Dissertation. School of Education, Stanford University.

Smith, J. K. 1977. *Teacher Planning for Instruction.* (Report No. 12) Chicago: CEMREL Studies of Educative Processes.

Stodolsky, Susan. 1988. *The Subject Matters.* Chicago: University of Chicago Press.

Taylor, Philip. 1970. *How Teachers Plan Their Courses.* Slough, Berkshire, England: National Foundation for Educational Research.

Tournier, Michel. 1972. *The Ogre.* (Barbara Bray, trans.) Garden City, NY: Doubleday.

Vallance, Elizabeth. 1973. Hiding the Hidden Curriculum. *Curriculum Theory Network* 4: 1–13.

Westbury, Ian. 1973. Open Classrooms, "Open" Classrooms and the Technology of Teaching. *Journal of Curriculum Studies* 5: 99–121.

Westbury, Ian. 1978. Research into Classroom Processes: A Review of Ten Years' Work. *Journal of Curriculum Studies* 10: 283–308

Yinger, Robert. 1979. Routines in Teacher Planning. *Theory Into Practice* 18: 163–169.

Zahorik, J. A. 1975. Teachers' Planning Models. *Educational Leadership* 33: 134–139.

THE CURRICULUM IN THE SCHOOL AND THE COMMUNITY

I am not suggesting that there have not been and are not now revolutionary innovations in methods of teaching and learning being tried in some schools. But I do suggest that these tend to be rare, that they probably require a particularly fortunate combination of either enlightened or indifferent (but willing to pay) citizens, an imaginative, brave, and somewhat iconoclastic administration, and a teaching staff dominated at least to some degree by a group willing to try new things, to break out of the old patterns. There are no easy answers here.

Gertrude McPherson
American ethnographer, 1972

PURPOSE OF THE CHAPTER

- to describe schools as settings for the operation of a curriculum and to show their relations to the community that supports them
- to show how the school curriculum works
- to explain what is involved in changing the school curriculum and how schools typically approach this task

OUTLINE

Communities and their Schools

Schools and School Systems

The School Curriculum

Maintaining the Quality of the School Curriculum

Changing the School Curriculum

COMMUNITIES AND THEIR SCHOOLS

School-Community Ties Are Close and Strong in the United States

Public schools in the United States have traditionally maintained very close relationships with their local communities. Parents with school-age children are directly and daily affected by the school system. Especially in smaller communities, school activities—athletics, arts performances, and school-affiliated clubs—are often a vital part of community life. Most local employers fill their entry-level positions with graduates from the local school system. In small communities the school may be a major employer and a strong economic factor in the community. Many teachers are also members of the community; in some communities local residence is virtually a condition of employment. Community conflict often spills over into the schools, even when the issue is not fundamentally educational, simply because of the strength, closeness, and multiplicity of the ties between school and community. As one student of the subject puts it, "Almost nothing happens in a school that is not or cannot become the community's business" (Saxe 1975, 9). These many ties of sentiment and personal relationship, as well as of economics and politics, ensure that schools will not stray far from a course approved by the local community.

Such strong, close ties between local communities and their schools may seem natural to those who have grown up with them, but they are found in few other places in the world. In most of the world, schools are an arm of the national or state government, financed, staffed, and governed by the central authority. Teachers are not even employed by the local school, and local school officials are not answerable to the local community politically, legally, or financially.

Because of close ties between school and community, any community problem that concerns school-age children will certainly be confronted by and in the school. It seems odd to most Americans *not* to have the local school confront such problems as dangerous driving, delinquency, drug abuse, or teenage pregnancy. It is, after all, *our* school, serving *our* children, run with *our* taxes, and it is the one place in which most of our youth can be reached at once. Even problems that have no necessary connection with young people are often addressed through the schools—problems such as interracial or intergroup conflict, poverty, or decline in local industries, for example. After all, Americans seem to reason, our children face these community problems along with us, and if we can help them to cope, the entire community will eventually benefit. And besides, it is easier to deal with many problems when people are young and habits are less ingrained. So, communities concerned about racial discrimination are more likely to institute a school program on interracial relations than to step up enforcement of equal opportunity in housing and jobs. In this way, the American public school has in many communities become a generalized community service agency.

On the other hand, many Americans want public schools to concentrate on academic goals. Tension between advocates of academic programs and advocates of broader social purposes for schools is a continuing source of conflict in American public policy. The ability to resolve this tension in different ways in different communities is one important advantage of a decentralized local system of school governance.

Governing Public Schools

Public schools in the United States are governed by the local school district or school corporation, which is legally separate, in most states, from other local government. The school district is empowered to levy taxes and to incur indebtedness on behalf of local taxpayers, subject to their approval in local referenda. Local school districts are governed by a school board (sometimes called a board of trustees or directors of the school corporation) elected in special local elections in most states, though appointed by mayor, city council, or even state courts in some states. The board is legally responsible for the operation of the school system and approves all major actions. Members of the board serve without pay or with modest honoraria and expenses. Typically they devote two to four evenings a month to their duties.

The school board selects a superintendent of schools who administers the system according to its policies. The superintendent serves under a contract that may run from one to five or more years and may be renewed indefinitely. The superintendent chooses personnel to operate the school system, subject to board approval. Most superintendents have one or a few deputy or assistant superintendents and delegate responsibility for finance, personnel, curriculum and instruction, and similar categories of administrative work to them. Sometimes superintendents delegate responsibility for curriculum matters one layer further down in the hierarchy to someone with a title such as director of curriculum or curriculum coordinator.

The line of authority for operating individual schools usually runs directly from the superintendent to the principal of an individual school. Officers in intervening positions, referred to here as central office staff (COS), may be given certain of the superintendent's powers in relation to principals, but principals do not normally report to COS. The principal is usually responsible for all aspects of the operation of the local school, although in some districts the principal's authority is closely circumscribed by central office directives. The principal may have one or more vice principals and may also delegate some authority to a committee or to a department or department chair. The board of education must approve all appointments and promotions after they have run the gauntlet of board-approved screening processes by professional staff.

Local school systems are thus staffed, managed, and operated by professionals answerable to a public governing board representing the local community. While in theory this board has complete legal authority over the affairs of the district, in practice they must depend on the superintendent and the professional staff to make most decisions and confine themselves to setting goals, making policy, and resolving serious issues. As we will see later, this makes school administrators the crucial link between school and community.

Control of their schools by local school districts is not complete and seems to be gradually eroding. School districts are subject to a wide variety of pressures and influences from many organizations, official and unofficial, national, state, and local, including state and national constitutions and laws, which may, for example, require schools to offer certain courses, set high school graduation requirements, specify in detail the health and safety requirements of all school buildings, establish procedures for hiring, awarding tenure, and dismissing teachers, and even set limits to the amount of money local districts may collect in taxes, despite the wishes of taxpayers. In some districts a substantial proportion of the time of board and top administration is filled with meetings and paperwork pursuant to the requirements of external authorities. Control of local schools by school boards is also limited by collective bargaining agreements with teachers' organizations. State, national, and even international influences on local public schools are increasing. Some board members, superintendents, and observers consider that such encroachments on local control have become so extensive as to threaten the principle itself. Nevertheless, local school boards retain considerable authority and can, with determination and when supported by the local community, be decisive on any issue not directly governed by state or federal law.

Local School Politics Are Distinctive

Political scientists assure us that "a governmental unit with an elected governing board making policies cannot exist in a democracy without politics" (Iannaccone and Lutz 1970, 16). Yet getting the schools out of politics has been a major goal of American educational reformers for more than half a century. The result of these efforts has been to create a unique form of low-profile, unrepresentative local politics of education that can often be surprisingly unresponsive to the wishes of the local populace.

In most communities, a relatively small in-group of laypeople involve themselves in local school affairs. Like school board members, they tend to be economically and politically more conservative than their communities, better educated, older, and more prosperous. These are the supporters of the public schools. Iannaccone and Lutz (1970) speak of a politics of insiders, invisible politics, and a closed system. Membership in this active group generally comes mainly from the social and economic elite of the community, the same segment that supplies most school board members. As Iannaccone and Lutz describe it:

> School systems . . . increasingly tend to be encased in a network of extra-governmental friends and allies. A civic cocoon of advisory groups, lay committees, parent-teacher organizations, grade mothers, Girl Scout Brownies, and athletic boosters surround, politically protect, and nurture the local educational leaders in school district matters. . . . Here the discussions and debate of proposed solutions for school district problems takes place before these solutions are put before the school board. (Iannaccone and Lutz 1970, 18–19)

In general, open public conflict on school issues is discouraged. Elections of school board members are notoriously tame and draw extremely low voter turnout. According to Clifford (1975, 23) only about 12% of registered voters participate in school elections. Even a rare hotly contested election seldom draws more than 50% of the voters. In communities with a history of hotly contested elections, and therefore high voter turnout, many of the community elite refuse to run for election. Some boards place a high value on professionalism and on technical quality of decisions and less value on norms of participation and representation. They experience less conflict than other communities that emphasize the political values of participation and representation more than technical and professional expertise. Salisbury notes that citizens who participate in local school affairs tend to avoid community conflict.

> School activists dislike conflict. They are uneasy about political parties because, in part at least, partisan involvement implies directly competitive struggle. (Salisbury 1980, 198)

Tucker and Zeigler studied eleven school districts in the Northwest. They reported that:

> Of greatest importance (to boards) is unanimity in decision-making, especially voting decisions. Dissent should be minimized and should not be articulated once a majority position has been established. (Tucker and Zeigler 1980, 133)

They quote a manual for school board members as stating:

> Nothing is more damaging to a board—to its internal relations or its prestige with the public—than for a board member to quarrel publicly with a decision a board has made. (Tucker and Zeigler 1980, 133)

They found that the eleven boards they studied voted unanimously 85% of the time.

The effect of conflict avoidance is to dampen debate and forestall direct confrontation of contending parties. The politics that results is the "low-pressure, invisible politics of the initiated rather than the high pressure, colorful politics of the marketplace," a politics that seeks consensus by polite, informal means rather than by facing conflict directly and seeking to negotiate a resolution (Iannacone and

Lutz 1970). Since a certain amount of difference of opinion is inevitable in any community, even among the elite, differences must be worked out quietly behind the scenes before the matter is raised officially in public. This behind-the-scenes preliminary discussion takes place in a variety of school-community forums populated largely by influential laypeople and professional leaders.

Once an issue emerges from the murky world of informal school politics and becomes a formal proposal put before the Board by the Superintendent, the Board's options are limited.

> The board is faced with the extreme alternatives of accepting staff recommendations *in toto* or rejecting its professional staff. (Iannacone and Lutz 1970, 21)

The voters' choices are even more limited:

> The public is most often confronted at the polls with a choice between electing candidates supporting the local educational establishment, or individuals representing extreme factions of the community hostile to the basic goals of American education. (Iannacone and Lutz 1970, 21)

Thus, while the formal governance mechanism of public schools appears to be democratic, even populist, the effect of keeping schools out of politics has been to create a behind-the-scenes informal local school politics dominated by community elites and professional leaders, a politics that insulates schools from the voting public most of the time and deprives most voters and taxpayers of any direct say in the running of local schools.

Administrators Link Communities and Schools

The formal social, economic, and political ties between school and community are all mediated by school administrators, and in many cases so are the informal ties. Except for personal communications from students, teachers, or non-teaching school staff, all of the community's contacts with the school are mediated by administrators. This linking role puts administrators in a pivotal position that is both powerful and risky, powerful because only the link knows about and deals with the total situation, risky because the parties to be linked have different interests and tend to have different views on educational questions. Community members tend to favor more traditional pedagogical practices and procedures for grading, promotion, and the like than the professionals who run their schools (Gross 1958). If we were to define a spectrum of educational values on a liberal-conservative continuum, students would lie at the liberal end and parents at the other. Teachers would rest near students, the community elite near parents. School administrators would occupy the middle (Elam 1978). Such an ordering makes sense in view of the roles individuals from each group must play in the educative process. Yet, it implies that the core educational values of those who spend their days in schools—students and teachers—differ markedly from those of the community that supports and, in theory, governs the school system. School administrators must reconcile these conflicts.

Contact of both sides with administrators insulates them from potential occasions for conflict and, as if in return, administrators gain greater influence over school operations. Where the community elite and top school administrators share stable educational priorities, the schools will reflect them, even when teachers or the majority of the community do not share them. In theory an alliance between teachers and a grass-roots community majority could overcome the combined power of top administrators and the community elite, but such an alliance is improbable because of the extreme differences in educational views and values that typically separate these two groups.

School-community interaction centers around relations between the school board and the school administration. Tucker and Zeigler studied the operations of local school boards in eleven school systems in the Northwest "to explore the extent to which school district officials are responsive to their lay publics" (Tucker and Zeigler 1980, 6). The title of their report, *Professionals Versus the Public: Attitudes, Communication, and Response in School Districts* reveals their conclusion. They found that school administrators dominated school board meetings. Administrators set the agenda and put forward nearly all the proposals the board considers. They provide the board's only source of professional advice and expertise. Administrators regularly make their policy preferences known, and boards accept nearly all administrative recommendations.

One of the first generation of strong superintendents, Carleton Washburne describes his relationship with the Winnetka, Illinois, Board of Education this way:

> Legally, the Board of Education has all power, the superintendent none. But the Board, if it is wise, delegates most of its power on all professional matters to the superintendent. . . . It was . . . my responsibility and that of my successors to see that the board did not step out of its role and interfere with the detailed administration of the schools, or try to substitute lay judgment for the professional decisions of the teaching and supervisory staff of the schools. (Washburne and Marland 1963, 149)

Administrative dominance is particularly great on issues of curriculum and instruction. Tucker and Zeigler assert that "virtually all studies which classify issues coming to the attention of the board find that the educational program receives scant school board attention" (Tucker and Zeigler 1980, 11). They note that "district operation (maintenance, facilities, materials, and so forth) was the most frequently discussed topic in the board meetings of these eleven districts. . . . In most districts, the school board agenda is devoted largely to housekeeping matters. Conspicuously absent from these agendas are topics of educational governance. . . . Also curious is the small proportion of discussion devoted to curriculum matters" (Tucker and Zeigler 1980, 113–114).

In relations with other community groups, the superintendent attracts attempts to influence the schools like a lightning rod. When influence attempts conflict with one another or with district plans or procedures, the superintendent becomes the focus of conflict. Many superintendents find that they must assume an overtly political role if they are to manage this conflict. Blumberg quotes a superintendent he interviewed as saying:

> Being political means having a real sense of the workings of groups—power groups, pressure groups, decision-making processes. You're dealing with different constituencies, with people interacting with each other with their own special interests. And you really have to have that all sorted out so that you can anticipate their reactions. You have to be political! (Blumberg 1985, 54)

Principals must manage conflict between teachers and parents. Teachers feel vulnerable when they confront parents or community members who challenge their professional authority. In *Small Town Teacher,* McPherson entitles her remarks on this subject "Natural Enemies: Teachers and Parents." She quotes one experienced teacher in her school:

> Whatever you do is wrong with the parents. You have to be so careful what you say. I won't give any more F's. It's not worth the struggle with them. (McPherson 1972, 124)

Parents feel equally helpless. McPherson quotes one parent as saying:

> What can a parent do? You bring up your child as well as you can and then you send him off to school. He has all kinds of teachers—cruel ones and ones without any experience—and when you try to object to something, they give you the runaround. It is frightening. (McPherson 1972, 125)

Parents expect principals, as public officials, to defend their interests. After all, they are taxpayers, clients, and members of the community that governs the school. Teachers, on the other hand, expect principals, as professionals, to defend their interests. Saxe puts the matter in these terms:

> Teachers . . . look to administrators to protect them from parents. And, because teaching is so far from being a science, the teacher expects precisely that the administrator will back him in all situations, whether he has acted wisely or unwisely, rightly or wrongly. The belief among teachers is that a united front must be presented to outsiders and that any criticism of the teacher that the administrator might have must be delayed until the confrontation is over and then given in strictest confidence. (Saxe 1975, 27)

Their monopoly of the school-community linkage gives local school administrators a great deal of power in dealing with those curriculum issues in which the community takes an active interest. It should come as no surprise that the fate of any proposal to change the local school curriculum depends most on the attitudes, talents, and actions of the principal and the superintendent. But even they cannot override determined opposition from community leadership.

SCHOOLS AND SCHOOL SYSTEMS

Schools Perform Many Functions for the Public

Schools are much more than simply places for formal education. They are also workplaces for teachers, principals, secretaries, and janitors, and formal organizations in which employees carry out their assigned responsibilities. They are places in which several hundred or a few thousand people live a significant portion of their lives, the scene of struggles for power and esteem. They are places in which children grow up, develop identities independent of their families, and practice living in a larger, more impersonal public world. They are places with which people identify—we give them names and we care about them. Schools often define the identity of whole communities.

In fact, schools resemble miniature communities more than they resemble any other familiar institution. Schools are not single-purpose organizations with a bottom line of profit or loss, like corporations, though they could probably be made to run this way if we wanted them to badly enough. Schools are not primarily about intimate personal relationships among their denizens, as families are, although many such relationships typically exist and some schools have made them more important than everything else that goes on there. Schools, like communities, must include many people with diverse purposes, and allow many of the things that make up a full life to happen there. In the larger community, we use the power of the law to guarantee individuals the freedom to pursue their varied legitimate purposes. In the almost-community of the school, everyone is considerably more constrained, students by compulsory attendance and public grading of performance, for example. But school nevertheless remains a public place governed by the public to serve public purposes, not a private contractual arrangement to serve the private purposes of the contracting parties, and so those included in the school are entitled to participate in determining what purposes will be legitimate in schools. In American schools, as we have seen, there has traditionally been strong support for the pursuit of a broad array of purposes within the framework of the school.

Schools As Formal Institutions

Individual citizens of the United States are free to learn and to teach anything they wish, any way they wish, any time or place they wish, with very few limitations. (They may not abet criminal action, advocate the overthrow of the government, infringe on the rights of others, and the like.) But the right to *establish* a school is another matter. Throughout the world, the state claims a primary interest in the provision of schooling for minors. In the United States, this right is vested in the fifty individual states, which compel citizens below 16 years of age (in most states) to attend a state-approved school; which set standards schools must meet; which tax citizens to support public schools, and to establish and enforce laws to govern their operation; and which exempt private schools from the property and business taxes levied on other businesses. Therefore, schools are formal institutions established by the authority of the state and run by government, in the case of public schools, or regulated by government, in the case of private schools.

A public school system serves a defined geopolitical district. In large cities the student population living within district boundaries numbers in the millions; in some rural areas school districts nearly as large as Rhode Island contain only a few hundred students. Despite this diversity, schools and school systems show many similarities as organizations. Because schools are public institutions, they become bureaucratic very easily. Roles and responsibilities must be contractually defined in writing. Procedures must be established for exercising the authority granted by the state to the school. Parents and teachers demand fair and equal treatment, and schools must institute procedures to see that they get it, or else face lawsuits. Records must be kept to satisfy legal requirements—employment records, attendance records, records of expenditures, and so on.

In general, the larger the school system, the more hierarchical its pattern of organization, the more rule-bound its operation, the more reliance on paperwork, the less reliance on face-to-face conversation, and the more time taken up with meetings. Similar relationships hold for large schools as compared to small schools. Whereas the principal of a small school could simply confer with teachers to select a reading series, in large school systems the process involves months of work by large committees. In large school systems several levels of authority separate the superintendent from the teacher. There may be Deputy, Associate, and Assistant Superintendents; Directors or Coordinators of Curriculum, Instruction, Evaluation, or the like; Supervisors of this-and-that subject; Principals; Associate, Assistant, and Vice-Principals; Department Chairs; Counselors; Lead teachers. Each of these positions in the hierarchy carries with it a sphere of authority over those below and responsibility to those above. To mitigate some of the problems of size, large districts sometimes decentralize, giving each individual school more autonomy, sometimes to the point of establishing regional subdistricts.

Individual schools also have a formal administrative and governance structure. The principal is responsible for assignment and evaluation of all personnel, for preparing and administering the school budget, for establishing and enforcing school-wide policies, and so on. In secondary schools teachers are assigned to departments, in elementary schools to grade-level teams. Much of the school's curriculum planning may take place in these units. The department chair or team leader may be delegated by the principal some power to budget, to select curriculum materials, to determine grade-level or subject guidelines, to monitor teachers' compliance with these guidelines, and the like. Individual teachers retain authority over grading of students and over activities in their classroom. Committees are established to deal with certain kinds of issues; sometimes they report to the whole faculty, sometimes to an official steering committee or executive committee, and sometimes directly to the principal. Channels of authority are mapped out leading from teacher, student, or parent through different levels of authority in the school up to the principal and then to the superintendent and board of education. Box 8-1 lists some additional organizational characteristics that most schools share.

The school principal generally has a more important voice in decisions about an individual school than any other person in the school. Principals are generally responsible for evaluating teachers' work performance, with such consequences as pay increases (in school districts with merit pay), desirable classes, assignment to special committees and projects, promotions to department chair, team leader,

---

BOX 8-1   Some Organizational Characteristics of Schools

1. **Schools are traditional organizations.**
   People judge them by how well they sustain certain valued activities more than by their results.
2. **Schools are custodial institutions.**
   One group maintains them, adult citizens, to serve another, students, who are compelled to attend and not allowed to determine how the institution is to be run. Custodial institutions have trouble enlisting enthusiastic participation from their charges. Schools are caught in the middle when these two groups conflict.
3. **Schools are organizations of professionals.**
   Professionals claim expertise and corresponding discretion in their practice. Professionals demand a greater voice in the operation of their organizations, and nonprofessionals are excluded from judging the quality of work done by professionals. Work is lightly supervised.
4. **Schools and school systems are aggregates rather than true hierarchies.**
   Schools are collections of classrooms; districts are collections of schools; state systems are collections of districts; the organization grows by adding new units that are treated organizationally like the existing ones.
5. **The various units aggregated in a school organization are only loosely coupled with one another.**
   They are loosely tied by authority, exchange few resources, and seldom communicate about vital matters and are therefore poorly equipped for coordinated action. State departments of education are loosely coupled to school districts, districts to schools, and schools to classrooms.
6. **Work in schools is not very interdependent.**
   Division of labor is infrequent and unimportant; the work of one teacher depends little on that of another.
7. **Schools have only weak organizational incentives.**
   Securing conformity to the school's purposes is therefore more difficult.
8. **Schools are labor intensive.**
   They make very little use of capital goods to increase productivity.

counselor, vice-principal, and so on. The school has its school-wide rules and regulations, some of which are rigorously enforced. Schoolwide policies on student behavior are common—when students may leave the room or the school building or the school grounds, policies on tardiness or absence, and the like. Most schools have school-wide policies on record-keeping by teachers, on assignments of homework, on grading, on field trips, and similar matters that affect what an individual teacher can and cannot do in the classroom. Also, principals have closer contact with parents than district administrators.

Curriculum policies and guidelines are often established district-wide, in which case decisions of those in the individual school are constrained to some degree by district policy. In many districts supervisors are assigned to coordinate the programs of, say, English and language arts throughout the schools in the district. Districts may also administer standardized tests to the students in every school and use the results as an indicator of the quality of the school and of the work of its staff. Textbooks and curriculum materials are usually selected on a district-wide basis, both because unit costs are lowered in larger orders and because it helps to coordinate the curricula of the various schools within the district. Each school will normally also have its own budget drawn up by the principal and approved by the superintendent's chief financial officer.

Probably the most frequent criticism made of schools is the prevalence of rigid and deadly routine. Much of the rule-bound quality of school can be explained as an adaptation to a few basic characteristics all schools share. First, they are crowded. Compared to homes, offices, stores, and factories, schools have more people per square foot of floor space than virtually any other setting. When we consider that the people involved are immature and therefore not fully socialized, we can appreciate that rules are needed simply to avoid bedlam. Second, schools are compulsory. This places a heavy custodial burden on them. Schools are legally obligated to know where students are all the time and to provide adult supervision for them wherever they may be. Third, schools are heavily regulated. This means that records are required to substantiate everything. Fourth, the expectations various publics hold for what should be accomplished by the school are, taken together, many times greater than the schools could possibly meet. Schools adapt to these conditions by instituting routines, standard operating procedures. Establishing and enforcing such routines as fixed class periods, daily schedules, hall passes, and written excuses for tardiness and absences inconveniences everybody, but the chaos that would result without them would be even more inconvenient, and unmanageable besides.

Even though schools are service organizations doing people work, they must establish routines, and this creates a tension that can be troublesome. Idealistic beginning teachers, attracted to teaching as an opportunity to help young people, may be upset to find that they must play the role of rule-enforcer. Others are temperamentally attracted to the enforcer role to such an extent that the rules become an end in themselves rather than a necessary evil. Different schools resolve this tension differently. A curriculum that works fine under one set of routines may sputter under another. For example, a biology program that calls for frequent field work on school grounds or in nearby parks may work fine in a school that tolerates hall traffic, but be unworkable in a school in which doors must be locked and halls patrolled by guards. Making a curriculum work within a particular school's routines is one of the important skills of local curriculum work.

Teachers' Autonomy in the Classroom

In spite of the foregoing indications of hierarchical unity, schools are in many ways loosely related collections of largely independent social units. Schools are rarely organized so that teachers work in truly interdependent teams like the cast of a play or a team of surgeons. The typical school more nearly resembles a building full of dentists' offices in which similar professional services are offered independently. Each teacher operates as a nearly independent professional within his or her own classroom. Schools do have some guidelines teachers are expected to follow, but monitoring is usually light. Teachers question the right of other persons to pass judgment on their work. This applies to principals, supervisors, and peers who, though professionally qualified, lack specific information about this particular class and its history. In *Small Town Teacher*, McPherson notes this tendency:

> Although [every teacher] recognized [the elementary supervisor's] right to visit and advise, she objected to her advice because of the inevitable difference between her perspective as teacher and the perspective of [the] supervisor. She was convinced that no administrator, even one specially trained, could understand her problems or her needs. She succinctly summed it up by saying that [the supervisor] had 'forgotten what it is to be in a classroom'. (McPherson 1972, 161)

The tradition of academic freedom supports teachers in this kind of assertion of their autonomy. Teacher organizations also support this principle and oppose measures such as merit pay that would strengthen the hand of school administrators in evaluation of the work of teachers. The result is that teachers are monitored lightly in most school systems once their initial probationary period has passed, and the sanctions available to those who evaluate teachers are few and weak.

Except in extreme cases, the character and quality of students' school experience are likely to depend more on which classrooms and which teachers they are assigned to than on which school they attend. Studies have shown that, indeed, the range of achievement within a single school is greater, on the average, than the achievement differences between schools (Cohen, 1983). A classroom may be viewed as a social niche within the school in which certain patterns of behavior are expected, others welcomed, and still others forbidden or frowned on. Thus, students who like to clown around, to act out their feelings, to improvise, to put on a show for their peers, may gravitate toward an English teacher who encourages this behavior and incorporates it into theatrical productions and informal class dramas. A science teacher who runs a laboratory-based class and who demands quiet, businesslike demeanor, and judges students only on their test and laboratory results establishes a quite different social setting. Some students may feel comfortable in both settings, but many will show a strong preference and choose elective courses accordingly and, if assigned to an uncongenial class, will spend as little time there as possible and remain as aloof as possible.

Schools Support a Rich, Informal Social Life

Intangible social qualities of individual schools may be even more important than the formal characteristics of the school as an institution. School spirit, school climate, the quality of the school environment—these are some of the expressions we use for these real and important, yet elusive qualities. In some schools everyone, students, teachers, administrators alike, seems to concentrate on schoolwork, producing a busy, no-nonsense atmosphere. In other schools work takes place in a varied, lighter, more social atmosphere. For example in some schools athletics form the center of school life, whereas in others various school activities may play a central role. In some schools, students enrolled in various programs and grades and students of different family backgrounds mix quite freely, while in others students tend to cluster in groups of the like-minded or even of the same racial, religious, or ethnic origin. A principal's strong personality can influence the school climate, as can an established teaching staff's shared traditions. As the most numerous category of school inhabitants, students contribute most directly to the look, sound, and feel of the school. Parents, teachers, and school administrators influence the climate mainly through their influence on students' behavior.

The curriculum both reflects and affects the climate of a school. A serious, businesslike climate can coexist nicely with a solid academic curriculum, but a school with a diverse, student-centered, innovative curriculum is more likely to come with an enthusiastic, boisterous climate. The attractiveness of various curriculum innovations to a school will depend on their compatibility with the school's existing climate. Curriculum changes are one way for a new principal to influence a school's climate.

Schools house many other activities in addition to classroom teaching, including informal exchanges before and after school and between classes; organized extra-curricular activities, such as sports, school-sponsored plays, dances, and other events; and school-sponsored organizations such as the 4–H club, the Future Farmers of America, or their urban/suburban counterparts. These other activities serve as the nucleus for voluntary, self-selected social groups, whereas classrooms are public settings whose norms enjoin universal participation on an equal footing. Often these extracurricular activities have strong connections with relevant organizations in the community. In many schools there are junior versions of such community service organizations as the Lions, the Rotary Club, the Chamber of Commerce, the League of Women Voters, or the like. Most high schools have organizations of sports boosters in the community. The band may have a community group that helps it raise money for uniforms, instruments, or trips.

Elementary schools have their carnivals, fairs, and performances and their groups of parents with special interests in sports, scouting, music, drama, and the like. Schools are thus attached socially to their communities through a host of special relationships between subgroups occupying special niches within the school and particular organizations in the community at large.

James S. Coleman in *The Adolescent Society* (1961) argued on the basis of his studies of ten high schools of various types that adolescents form their own societies within schools, with their own values distinct from and often in opposition to those of the adult society around them. He noted that adolescents were particularly sensitive to the opinions their peers held of them, and that the status awarded to individuals by the adolescent society was often a more powerful incentive to behave in accordance with its values than were the grades, awards, and approval the school could bestow. The leading crowd in the schools Coleman studied was not intellectual in its orientation. Athletes were generally accorded highest status by their peers. Students with *personality*—socially active, well-liked, students—were also held in high esteem by their peers. Good students were not generally accorded high status unless they were also athletes or personalities.

Teachers, too, have an informal social system that determines to some degree what happens in that school. In some schools dominant teacher cliques are so powerful that not even the principal and superintendent united can prevail against them. McPherson reports such a clique, which she named "The Old Guard" in the small New England elementary school in which she taught and observed. She describes the systematic efforts of the Old Guard to undermine a music program that they opposed:

> [The teachers] were much less willing to accept [the music teacher's] program of instrumental instruction, which was approved but not formally scheduled by the administration. . . . His struggle for acceptance took five hard years, subjected as he was throughout to indirect harassment that included teachers scheduling tests during his music lessons, refusing to send the pupils, asking them to return to classes during band practice, refusing to allow a pupil to play an instrument because his grades were too low, and even on various farcical occasions hiding the instruments. (McPherson 1972, 79)

Schools are, then, an aggregate of social niches, each of which may have its own distinctive goals and may compete with the others for resources to achieve these goals. When elements of the curriculum become the customary preserve of one group of teachers, students, parents or others, the principal or district administration may find they have to persuade these influentials in order to bring about change in their part of the curriculum. Whatever the job description and the organization chart may say about responsibilities for curriculum decisions in the local schools, effective exercise of authority over the local curriculum depends on the cultivation by formal leaders of avenues of influence over those who control the various social niches. Principals and district administrators do not have very strong incentives to offer—no bonuses, pay increases, or promotions, as in private business. They must exercise their leadership in more personal ways. Strangely, then, local school leaders must depend on personal qualities of leadership and on their skill in interpersonal influence in order to realize the power over curriculum matters formally delegated to them.

THE SCHOOL CURRICULUM

The main features of the school curriculum are deeply ingrained in the operations of school and school system. One can no more separate a real curriculum from its school than a skeleton from the body it supports. Teachers are certified to teach some subjects but not others. Some teachers' loyalties and even their professional identities are strongly attached to the subjects they teach. In some schools teachers are organized in departments by curricular categories. Textbooks and other materials are selected by curricular area. Tests are given and grades assigned by curricular area. The school's schedule allocates teacher and student time to the study of various curricular elements. Students consider themselves good at mathematics but not so good at English on the basis of how they perform in these classes, as do parents, potential employers, and college admissions officers. To understand the school curriculum we must recall that the curriculum is a pattern in the operations of a school, not a specific set of activities. In order to track the school curriculum through the jungle of school operations, we need a concept that focuses our attention on the abstract pattern. Opportunity to learn is the concept we need.

Learning Opportunities

A school provides opportunities to learn, but a student can only be said to have an opportunity to learn when at least the following essential items are provided:

1. A source that presents what is to be learned in a form comprehensible to the student,
2. Time and space, free of distractions, for students to comprehend the message and incorporate it into their bodies of knowledge and skill.

In addition, the following items are also important in most cases:

3. Signals pointing out this particular information as more important to learn than other information present in the environment,
4. A procedure for determining whether the item has been learned well enough,
5. A person who has mastered the information and can guide students in their efforts to comprehend it and help them overcome difficulties,
6. Incentives for students to apply themselves to this learning task until success is attained,

7. Equipment or facilities that may be needed to take advantage of the learning opportunity.

We may think of these as facets of a learning opportunity. In contemporary classrooms these are provided by:

qualified teachers: (numbers 1, 3, 4, 5, and 6)
suitably equipped classrooms: (2 and 7)
textbooks: (1 and 4)
tests: (4 and 6)
curriculum materials and apparatus: (7)

If students' learning is to be cumulative then the learning opportunities they encounter must be coordinated with one another over an entire school career. Schools accomplish this coordination by such means as:

designations of requirements and electives
time allotments
school schedules
entrance requirements and standards
graduation requirements and standards

We can speak of the school curriculum, then, as the learning opportunities provided in and by the school, together with the conditions and constraints schools attach to them. Figure 8-1 represents these components of the school curriculum.

Generally speaking, the school curriculum is organized in the form of a series of courses at the secondary level, and a series of programs (reading, writing, mathematics, and so on) at the elementary level. Every student completes all of the elementary school curriculum, but no student can complete more than a small fraction of the courses offered in a reasonably large high school. A differentiated curriculum, such as that offered in high schools, is a network of possibilities through that each student follows an individual path by choosing or being assigned to electives, while a common curriculum guides everyone down parallel paths.

The school curriculum is shaped by many school level decisions, among which three stand out as fundamental.

1. Decisions about what learning opportunities to offer,
2. Decisions about coordination among those opportunities over the years of a student's school career,
3. Decisions about conditions of access and equity of access to the school's learning opportunities.

Considered together, these three decisions about the school have a greater impact on what teachers teach and students learn than any others. Compared to them, such decisions as textbook selection, course of study development, and selection of tests are mere details.

FIGURE 8-1   **Components of the School Curriculum**

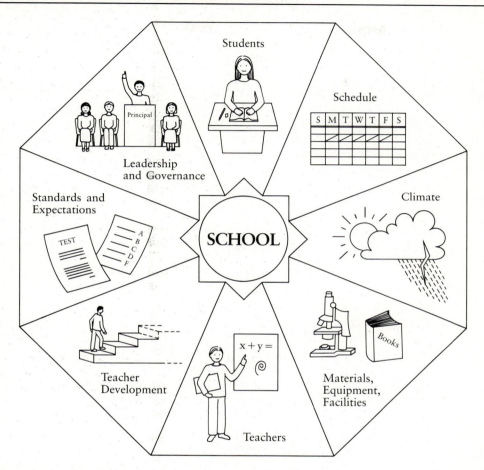

Stability and Change in School Curricula

The school curriculum is built to last. Course offerings are assumed to continue from year to year unless something happens to cause a change. The school schedule-maker begins with last year's schedule and makes only necessary changes. Adding a new offering usually requires approval from the principal, central office staff, and board of education; dropping one is only slightly easier. Textbooks have a useful life of 5–10 years. Tests do not change greatly from year to year. Teachers have tenure and in most communities the turnover rate among teachers is low. Only enough funds are budgeted for curriculum revision to permit a small fraction of the total offerings to be officially reconsidered each year.

Yet change does happen. This year's students choose different electives than last year's. Some teachers do leave and some new ones are hired. The qualifications of the incoming teacher never exactly match those of the departing one, so adjustments in teaching assignments or even course offerings may be needed. When new principals, superintendents, or central office staff members assume their posts, they often sponsor curriculum changes. Textbooks wear out and become obsolete. Tests and test norms do change from year to year and in a few years can drift noticeably. Most important, the preferences and expectations of teachers, parents, and school leaders can change, leading to calls for curriculum reform. Curriculum reform movements often inspire changes in local course offerings—the addition of Advanced Placement courses or, in earlier years, courses on black literature. And offerings change simply because teachers get bored teaching the same course, lose enthusiasm, and need refreshment.

These forces for change chip away at the neatly planned school curriculum and, unless someone pays careful attention, a strong, coherent, eminently serviceable curriculum can become a shambles in a year or two. In some schools, the disruptions are so great that even the best efforts of everyone involved are not enough simply to maintain the quality of the school curriculum. It does not take much to disrupt a school curriculum. Two or three of the following happening in one year could be enough: resignation of a few key teachers, appointment of a new principal or superintendent, curricular controversy in the community, a teacher strike, a hotly contested school issue on the ballot, enrollment increases or declines, or changes in the demographic composition of the community. Under such circumstances school leaders must give up all hope of achieving improvements and do their best to hold the line. In fact, during good times and bad, most of the energy and resources devoted to curriculum work in schools goes simply to maintain a desired level of service and quality. Figure 8-2 shows some of the frames that shape the school curriculum.

MAINTAINING THE QUALITY OF THE SCHOOL CURRICULUM

Maintaining the quality of a school's curriculum—even when nobody is complaining and no improvement projects are under way—can be a struggle. The work needed to keep the curriculum going is seldom conspicuous; for the most part, it is folded into the routines of running a school. For example, ordering textbooks is an essential part of maintaining a school's curriculum, but it is often treated as a routine part of the requisitioning of supplies. Securing teachers qualified to teach what is offered in the curriculum is clearly an essential part of maintaining a good curriculum, yet this function is typically assigned to a personnel department that operates independently of the curriculum planning process. Assigning teachers and pupils to classes is an essential part of maintaining a curriculum, yet scheduling

FIGURE 8-2   The School Curriculum and Its Frames

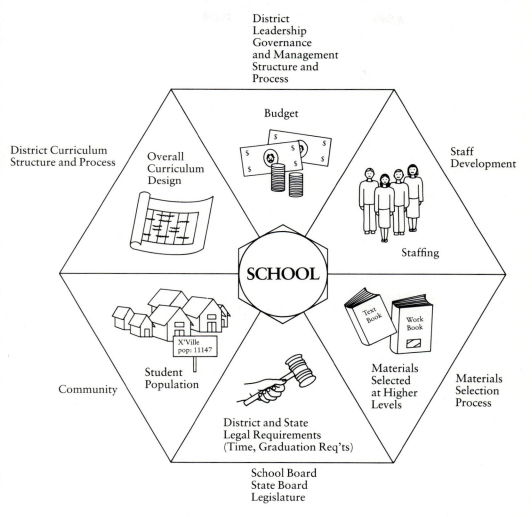

is generally treated as a routine administrative chore. Thus, the small fraction of the effort of running a school that is devoted specifically to curriculum work is mostly accomplished as part of general administrative tasks, and distributed widely among different branches of the school and district organization. Let us call this work, these low-profile but important tasks, curriculum management.

Nearly all of the resources and time devoted to curriculum goes to curriculum management. One of the foremost students of educational innovation, Matthew B. Miles, laments this fact:

> The major portion of available energy goes to carrying out routine operations and maintenance of existing relationships within the system. Thus the fraction of energy left over for matters of diagnosis, planning, innovation, deliberate change and growth is ordinarily very small. (Miles 1964, 437)

When we consider the small amount of energy available, it is no cause for wonder that most of it is consumed in curriculum management. The paramount concern in day-to-day management of a school curriculum must therefore be conserving resources, time, and energy. The work of maintaining the quality of the school curriculum must be routinized to minimize their demands on these limited resources.

School Routines

Smooth school routines are the most common indicator people use to define good school administration, for the same reason that smooth classroom routines are the most common criterion of success for teachers: to make such complex social systems function at all requires an exacting discipline. The school routines that do the most to structure curriculum management activities in contemporary schools are:

scheduling
the organization of professional staff
ordering curriculum materials
provisions for in-service education
teacher-performance assessment procedures
arrangements for monitoring and advising students

The School Schedule The school schedule is the master school routine. It brings together teachers, students, curriculum materials, and facilities and provides a framework for assigning purposes to occasions. It defines the curriculum offerings of the school on a yearly time scale. Teachers adjust their activities to fit the length of school periods, the rhythm of the school week, and the scope of the school year. All other school officials match their schedules to the school schedule. For example, textbook adoption must be completed so that books arrive on time for the start of classes, and new teachers must be hired so that they arrive by then. Because so much else depends on it, the construction of the school schedule is perhaps the single most powerful tool school leadership has for shaping the school curriculum.

The dictates of the schedule are most consequential for the more peripheral elements of the curriculum. The academic core of elementary education—reading, writing, and arithmetic—and secondary education—English, math, required science, social studies, and physical education courses—can be expected to appear on every master schedule as a matter of routine. But more peripheral subjects must struggle for a place in the schedule every year in life-or-death competition with other subjects for students' elective choices. The school schedule may substantially affect the nature and quality, if not the existence, of offerings even in core academic subjects. The number of semesters or sections of an established subject may be increased or reduced. Optional elective course offerings in a required subject may be expanded or reduced. Students of varying abilities may be distributed in various ways across the courses in a core academic subject.

School Staff Organization How the teachers and school administrators employed by the school are utilized, how responsibilities are allocated, and how individuals in various roles interact with one another determines how curriculum work will get done. In some schools, individual teachers are given virtually complete autonomy over the curriculum in their classrooms, subject only to the implicit requirement to follow official school or district curriculum guidelines, and in many cases compliance with even this requirement is not monitored. In other schools, the principal exercises close control over the curriculum, sometimes to the point of insisting that teachers make and submit weekly lesson plans. Some schools have more differentiated staffing arrangements in which teachers and school staff are organized into teams or departments with some autonomy and authority, often including a budget, for completing their assignment.

Depending on how the school staff is organized, curriculum work may be collaborative or individualistic, integrated or compartmentalized, centralized or widely distributed. Patterns of staff organization also influence the priority put on curriculum work within the larger set of tasks required to run the school, as well as the expertise of the persons who make curricular decisions. A differentiated staff organization based on curricular categories—team leaders and specialists in reading, mathematics, music, and so on—will generally give curriculum work a higher priority and bring more expertise to bear on it than will a grade level staffing pattern or an undifferentiated pattern in which all teachers share equal responsibility and report to the principal. Still, differentiating by curriculum area brings its own set of problems, such as how to coordinate the work within the separate subjects. Specialization erects barriers to reallocation of staff. More differentiated organizations foster wider participation, but they also take more time and make interpersonal conflict more likely. So, though the specific work required to maintain a good curriculum will differ substantially depending on the staffing arrangements, it is not clear that one type of organization is always superior from a curricular standpoint.

Provision of Curriculum Materials The availability of curriculum materials limits what teachers can realistically hope to cover in their classrooms, and hence is an important frame for the classroom curriculum. Textbook series coordinate the content presented over years of study in a subject, often from kindergarten through grade 6 and sometimes even through grade 12. Decisions about adoption of a textbook series come only every 5–10 years, the useful life of the books. But selection of workbooks, supplementary books, films, laboratory apparatus, computer software, art supplies, posters, and other equipment and supplies happens annually. The timely delivery of curriculum materials is critical to supporting teaching and learning in the classroom. The cost of these materials, together with the implicit cost of the time involved in selecting, ordering, budgeting, and processing them, is the major part of a school's budget for curriculum. Changes in the budget for materials can trigger substantive changes in the curriculum. In one school, an English program built around the reading of novels in paperback was eliminated when school budgets were reduced, and the department reverted to a program based on a cheaper anthology. Costs of apparatus have been a significant factor hindering widespread adoption of hands-on science programs in many elementary schools.

In-Service Education In most schools the only way for teachers to do curriculum work on school time is to call it in-service education. Except for an hour or two a month set aside for faculty meetings run by the principal, in-service education for teachers is the only time most schools provide for teachers to interact with one another over professional matters. Teacher meetings are barely adequate for disseminating essential information about curriculum policy such as changes in entrance or graduation requirements, testing, or the logistics of providing curriculum materials. If, say, a consultant is needed to help a school consider how to improve students' writing, the work must be called in-service education. As a result, curriculum work competes with improvement of teaching skills, dealing with students' problems, and handling school organizational and interpersonal issues, among many other matters, for a few days out of a teacher's year. If teachers did not spend a good deal of unpaid time and time allocated to other matters—such as computing grades and ordering supplies—on curriculum work, much curriculum management simply would not get done. In fact, a main obstacle to teachers' playing a more substantial and responsible role in curriculum work is simply the lack of time for this work in their schedules.

A school with a generous in-service education budget can afford to provide substitutes for teachers in order to release them for curriculum work. Such a school can attend to weaknesses in its program better than a school with a more constrained budget for in-service education. It can also respond better to unanticipated disruptions and can contemplate more considered, more ambitious, and more thoroughly implemented innovations. The number and scope of innovations that a school can support at any one time sets a firm limit on the rate at which curricular improvements can be made. If, as Fullan (1982) and other experts on implementation of educational innovations argue, social interaction among teachers is crucial in bringing about changes in their classroom behavior, then lack of time for such interaction may well be a major cause of implementation failures of curriculum reforms from the 1950s to the present. Schools that must rely exclusively on textbooks, teachers guides, and other printed materials to support teachers in improving their classroom curriculum may well be attempting the impossible. Accomplishing even minor adjustments needed to preserve curricular quality becomes difficult when only a few hours per year are available for teachers to work on school curriculum matters. The prominence given to curriculum issues in in-service education is an important determinant of the quality of curricular management in a school.

Teacher Performance Assessment Principals and central office staff are supposed to monitor and evaluate the performance of every teacher every year. What we know about teacher assessment (see Bridges 1986, for example) indicates that most of this effort is devoted to evaluating probationary teachers and that the major concerns of evaluation are classroom management and relationships with students. School leaders also bear a responsibility to monitor the quality of the classroom curriculum both for conformity to law and policy and to foster quality by the standards of the school and the profession. This may involve reviewing course outlines and lesson plans, observing classrooms, analyzing test results of a teacher's students, and conferring with teachers about curriculum matters. It may involve requesting advice from others—subject matter specialists, other experienced teachers—if the principal is not competent in the teacher's subject. Whatever the procedures, if principals convey a clear message that the quality of the curriculum a teacher maintains in the classroom is a major sign of good teacher performance, then teacher assessment can be a powerful process for maintaining curricular quality.

Monitoring and Advising Students The quality of a school's curriculum depends on how well its offerings are assimilated by the students who want and need them, as well as on the quality of the list of offerings. The first step in getting the offerings to students is placement in appropriate classes. Decisions about placement of students in the school program are made on the basis of records, formal and informal assessment of students by teachers, and (occasionally) other professionals, and the preferences of students and parents. Sooner or later these data find their way into the student's cumulative record file, the master file of records the school keeps on each pupil. Every student's cumulative file contains lists of every school and course enrolled in, Carnegie units completed, grades received, daily attendance records, teachers' comments, and test scores, among other items. Teachers, counselors, and, ultimately, the principal decide on placement of students, based on data included in that file and their own professional judgment.

Ideally, placement decisions should maximize the rate and extent of the student's educational progress. Officially, students' progress through school is defined in curricular terms—courses completed, grades earned, promotions achieved. A key issue the school faces for every student in every course or program every year is the readiness of the student to undertake the work in the curricular units that follow the present one. Decisions about readiness are complex, important, and difficult to justify to the complete satisfaction of professionals, let alone parents and students. When the school offers several alternative tracks or levels of study, the decision about placement of students in various tracks becomes even more difficult and complex. Evidence strongly suggests that in tracked programs early placement decisions tend to become self-fulfilling as students in more advanced tracks receive more and better instruction and are held to higher standards and so pull further away year after year.

How well the school makes its thousands of placement decisions each year is a crucial determinant of the quality of the school program. Stories of honor students who graduated from high school without learning to read signal blatant failures of monitoring and advisement, but less dramatic instances can be equally damaging: primary school students whose limited English speaking ability is misconstrued as low academic ability, high school students who are not informed that high school algebra is a prerequisite to nearly all college science and engineering majors, or students who fail because of simple oversight to take a course required for entrance to the state college system.

Given the universally acknowledged difficulty of these decisions, it seems prudent to build in as many safeguards and monitoring points as feasible. Some possibilities include:

- special reviews by qualified outside experts of the files of students in the top and bottom quartiles of assignments to tracked classes,
- conferences with students and parents beginning years in advance of crucial placement decisions, to ensure that they know the criteria that will be applied,
- special summer and after school classes to boost top students from one level or track to another or to solidify a student's readiness to remain in the present track the coming year,
- checking criteria used in making placement decisions periodically against actual student performance to make certain that the criteria and decision-rules are working out as hoped.

In general, nothing beats giving students a chance to perform at a higher level and seeing if they are able to capitalize on it. This can be done in brief units within the regular curriculum in such an unobtrusive way that students will not be under any special evaluation stress.

Maintaining Priorities in the Face of the Unexpected When everything that can be routinized has been, the events that fill the days of school people remain. Every study of what school administrators do on the job shows that they are in virtually constant communication with other people—secretaries, teachers, students, parents—that they control the time, place, and subject of only a tiny fraction of these encounters, and that most of the problems they deal with are unscheduled and unanticipated (Martin and Willower 1981). In short, school leaders spend most of their time coping with the unexpected. From a curricular point of view, the chief challenge of this fact of school life is to maintain goals and priorities in the face of this random activity. The cumulative effect of hundreds of small daily compromises can be a school program that is far different, and more probably than not, far worse, than the one planned. In extreme cases, perfectly sound plans and adequate resources to implement them can result in programs that are truncated, worn away, and trivialized by such compromises as scheduling many special school events that preempt classes, accepting unqualified substitutes for absent teachers, cutting corners on curriculum materials purchases, using in-service time for doing routine administrative business, or reallocating time intended for monitoring and advising students.

Disruptions of the daily operation of the school program should be minimized, of course, but unplanned events will probably always be frequent in schools. Children are not fully socialized and cannot be expected to conform as readily to routines; schools are crowded places in which people pursue many different institutional goals in close proximity; the school population is diverse; and children's participation is not always voluntary. Draconian measures designed to eliminate disruptions will establish an authoritarian school climate. The challenge for curricular management is to maintain consistency of purpose and priorities in the midst of all this randomness. To do so requires that all those involved be continually reminded of the importance of the school's major goals and priorities and urged to be diligent in pursuing them. School leaders must reflect this attitude in their behavior as well as in their statements. By enunciating and projecting a vision and repeatedly making split-second decisions on the basis of this vision, school leaders can guard against the erosion of program quality by the inevitable randomness of their daily work.

Maintaining a Healthy School Climate School routines exist within the total school environment, the quality of which must also be maintained. The same set of rules will function differently and have different effects in a school in which people feel they belong, believe they can succeed, hold high expectations for themselves and others, and experience an elevating school spirit, than in a school in which people feel alienated, powerless, or indifferent.

School climate is a fuzzy and complicated construct, but it seems to point to something that is vitally important both as an outcome and as a means to the more conventional ends of school achievement. Carolyn Anderson (1982, 411), in a comprehensive and thoughtful review of research on the concept, summarized the results of 38 major studies of school climate with the words "Certain characteristics of life within schools are recurring in the research in association with both climate and outcomes." Among these characteristics she includes:

- morale of teachers and students,
- administrator–teacher rapport,
- good teacher–student relationships,
- good teacher–teacher relationships,
- good community–school relationships,
- cooperativeness,
- shared decision-making,

- good communication,
- frequency of rewards,
- consistency of rewards and punishments,
- opportunity for student participation,
- principal and parent involvement with instruction,

- -

- teacher commitment to improved student performance,
- peer norms supporting academic achievement,
- high expectations for student and teacher performance,
- emphasis on academics,
- perceived quality of educational program,
- consensus on curriculum and discipline,
- clear goals.

The characteristics that appear in the top of this list above the dashed line seem to help create a positive climate by making the school's social system work smoothly and pleasantly, resulting in a social environment in which people feel comfortable and experience as rewarding. The characteristics toward the bottom of the list seem to work by focusing energy and attention on the school's institutional purposes. Clearly, a good school climate also fosters a good school curriculum. *Good curricular routines operating in a good school climate* is a plausible definition of a good school. Detailed consideration of how to maintain a good school climate is beyond the scope of this chapter, but it is important to recognize that maintaining a good curriculum means more than establishing smooth-running routines.

CHANGING THE SCHOOL CURRICULUM

Many individuals and organizations seek to change the school curriculum, and they approach the task in many different ways. The key players in school curriculum change are the teachers in the school, the principal, the school system administrators, and community leaders most concerned with education. Students and parents can play key roles when they are aroused, unified, and organized. Exactly who controls a particular decision will depend on the school subjects affected by the proposal, the age of the students affected by it (elementary, middle, secondary), and the nature of the proposal. Generally speaking, administrators are the gatekeepers who admit *some* externally initiated change efforts and exclude others. The authority for the decision often rests directly with an administrator, but even when a community group, teacher group, and the board of education are authorized to make the decision, administrators must implement it and can still do a great deal to shape it during the process of implementation. Combined with the training administrators have received to make such decisions, the access to information they have by virtue of their professional contacts, and the opportunity afforded them by their job responsibilities to spend time on the issues that concern them, school administrators have the upper hand in determining the fate of change efforts directed at the school curriculum.

Local Curriculum Planning, American Style

In the American tradition, each local school system is responsible for planning its own curriculum. Local school staffs, working under the leadership of school administrators, build a curriculum that meets the needs of their community. Contemporary practice of local curriculum planning follows a pattern laid down soon after the turn of the twentieth century, early in the Progressive era, when educators strived for a continuous, comprehensive, systematic, fully professional procedure. We can see these Progressive values in steps Harold Rugg and George S. Counts proposed in 1927 to improve curriculum development procedures in American schools (see Box 8-2).

At the time, the proposals of Rugg and Counts must have seemed revolutionary. The ordinary practice of curriculum-making in local school systems consisted of the superintendent, with secretarial help and such voluntary assistance from teachers as he or she could command, preparing courses of study for all subjects and grades and distributing them to teachers. Most districts were too small and poor to afford to do much else. Serious discussion of curriculum issues took place

---

BOX 8-2

The first step in any sound program of curriculum-revision, is the development of a research attitude toward the problem on the part of those in responsible charge. The superintendent, the supervisory staff, the board of education, the teachers, must come to recognize that the task of curriculum-making is technical, professional, complicated, and difficult in the extreme. . . . (Rugg and Counts 1927, 439)

The second step is the provision of adequate funds for the *continuous and comprehensive* prosecution of curriculum-construction. (Rugg and Counts 1927, 440)

The third step to be taken is the employment of trained and experienced specialists in curriculum-making and the organization of these workers under the direction of an executive officer. The latter should report directly to the superintendent and have control over the general function of instruction. (Rugg and Counts 1927, 440)

The curriculum bureau should develop a systematic program of appraisal, of measurement of results, of comparison of outcomes obtained from alternative procedures . . . . In accordance with the findings of the bureau and the broader contributions of educational science, the course of study should be modified continuously. (Rugg and Counts 1927, 447)

in national committees established by the Department of Superintendency (a department of the NEA), in which speakers hoped to persuade local school superintendents to revise their courses of study in some particular way. But by the late 1920s the pattern recommended by Rugg and Counts had already been tried in pioneering districts and soon became established in all the most advanced and influential districts. Box 8-3 describes an early example.

Good Current Practice of Local Curriculum Planning

A contemporary school district that can afford essentially whatever curriculum planning it wants, can do something like this. It can maintain an executive committee that meets regularly to consider curriculum matters in the district. This might be the Superintendent's Executive Committee (consisting of the Superintendent and a few most trusted aides); it might be the Superintendent's Roundtable (consisting of top administrators plus school principals); or it might be a designed Curriculum Council headed by the Associate or Assistant Superintendent for Curriculum and Instruction and consisting of COS plus representatives from each school. The executive committee can be comprised in many ways and given any of a variety of specific charges.

This executive committee monitors the curriculum, reactions to the curriculum, and data bearing on the curriculum of local schools. It routinely receives reports from the local office of research and evaluation about test scores. It receives progress reports and evaluations of curriculum improvement efforts under way in the district. It discusses curriculum issues brought before it, usually by the Superintendent or COS, sometimes by principals, and occasionally by laypeople or teachers. This activity is called needs assessment. Needs assessment can be as informal as the description above or it can be more systematic and elaborate, sometimes *much* more systematic and elaborate. Among the techniques available for needs assessment, should the occasion demand or the Superintendent prefer:

- historical studies using existing data (for example, studies of enrollment trends, achievement test score trends, and so on),
- interviews (for example, of principals and teachers by supervisors, of parents and teachers by COS assistants, of employers, and so on),
- questionnaires (for example, to teachers seeking their opinions about some curriculum issue, to parents, students, graduates, employers, and so on),
- discussion groups (for example, of parents in the homes of volunteers, of teachers and parents at PTA meetings, of students, of business and community leaders at meetings of civic organizations, and so on),
- institutional self-studies (for example, in connection with the visit of an accrediting agency, on the appointment of a new superintendent, and so on),
- community self-study (for example, in connection with a major local government planning effort or grant application),

BOX 8-3   An Early Example of Systematic Local Curriculum Planning

Beginning in 1919, the Winnetka, Illinois, public schools under Carleton Washburne pioneered an approach to curriculum planning that would later be developed into what was then called scientific curriculum making. It began with specific educational objectives and called for planners to apply scientific principles in designing activities and scientific methods in determining whether they were successful in teaching students to meet the objectives. The work in Winnetka had a nationwide and even a worldwide influence.

Washburne was a new superintendent, younger and with less experience in education than most of the 40 or so teachers in the Winnetka school system. He met with them in small groups one afternoon every two weeks, encouraging them to discuss their problems in teaching, and working with them to overcome them. Through their deliberations they devised diagnostic tests and developed a common philosophy of education. The Winnetka teachers developed a high morale, a solidarity, a unity of purpose and of feelings of mutual respect as a result of their activities in these after-school meetings. They adapted ideas from other sources—from other schools, including some in Europe, and from research reports— and they tested their ideas on children in their classrooms, striving to find scientific answers to educational problems.

Washburne describes his own role in these meetings in this way:

At the beginning I asked the teachers in each group what their objectives were—what they hoped to teach their children during the year and what problems they were finding. Very soon arithmetic became a major subject of inquiry; above the first grade, arithmetic caused more failures among the children than did any other subject, in spite of more time being given to it than to any other study.

What knowledge of arithmetic and what skill did each successive grade seek to give to the children? The answers at first were general—addition, multiplication, fractions, and so on. "But specifically what do you expect every child to know at the end of the year?" I would ask. The teachers tried to specify—and they always specified more than every child could possibly master.

"But can *every* child know all that, well, by the end of the year?"

"No, but this is what we should try to teach them. We must keep our standards high."

"But is a standard which a child cannot reach, even with every effort, a useful standard? Have we a right to tell a child he must do what he cannot do and that failure to do it will be punished by low marks or by repeating the grade the next year? Have we a right to deceive parents into thinking we will teach their children things we know many of the children cannot learn at this stage of their development?" (Washburne and Marland 1963, 21–25)

Washburne suggested that self-instructional materials might solve the arithmetic problem, and soon he had teachers volunteering to spend time after school developing their own self-instructional materials. These eventually became the first commercially published workbooks.

- citizen task force or advisory group (for example, to deal with desegregation or a similar major problem that affects schools and also requires community support),
- outside consultants (for example, to draw up demographic and economic projections to be used in planning).

These more formal efforts at needs assessment would normally be carried out under the direction of the executive committee or its chair, but sometimes under the direct supervision of the Superintendent.

Institutional initiatives that make a call on significant institutional resources must gain the approval of Superintendent and executive committee. This typically means that some member of the committee or the Superintendent must sponsor the effort and be its champion in discussions within the Committee. When the Superintendent wishes to initiate a district-wide curriculum reform, he or she will normally begin by making a presentation to this committee and directing it either to take actions or to look into the matter and recommend a course of action. Such an initiative would take precedence over other matters on the committee's agenda. When the Superintendent is ready to initiate a program of district-wide curriculum improvement in a given area, he or she submits a proposal to the board of education along with a report prepared by staff or by the executive committee. Sometimes the recommendation is to apply for state or federal assistance to carry out the work; more often, funds are requested from the annual budget. Depending on the situation, the program proposed may have some or all of the following ingredients:

- curriculum materials adoption (committees draft criteria and guidelines, review published materials, and recommend materials for adoption by superintendent and school board),
- course of study revision (COS and teachers work in the summer to revise the district's official course of study, usually taking the form of a teachers' guide),
- in-service education/staff development (workshops, lectures or demonstrations put on for teachers on days set aside for this purpose at the beginning and end of the school year and periodically throughout),
- curriculum study councils (groups of teachers, supervisors, and possibly consultants, students, parents, or others who meet in each local school, perhaps in various subjects or grades within each school, to plan a curriculum change).

Choice among these normally will depend on the situation: if teachers know how to make the change but must be persuaded to do so, study councils would be in order; otherwise, in-service education is essential; major changes in content and emphasis of a course normally require course of study revisions, and so on.

The reform, if approved, is put in the hands of the top level curriculum official in the COS, if it is substantial enough; otherwise it is turned over to a lower-ranking administrator. Progress reports are made at intervals to superiors and the executive committee. Principals must be consulted and their support and cooperation secured. A plan must be developed for carrying out the reform. Any of several standard types of plans may be adapted for this purpose or a new one devised. Among the options:

- pilot study (one or a few schools or classrooms are chosen to develop and shake down early versions of the new program),
- phased implementation (beginning in earlier grades and proceeding toward later ones in successive years, or beginning in those sites most ready and proceeding later to the others),
- demonstration site (full implementation in one site with others invited to follow its example),
- multiple local versions (let a thousand flowers bloom, then prune),
- blitz (all schools change at once, immediately).

Whatever method is followed, a staff must be assembled, usually from among district employees already holding responsible positions whose supervisors are reluctant to part with their services. The logistics of the whole affair must be arranged—people, time, buildings, materials, and so on. Cooperation of other departments—evaluation, staff development, community relations, and so on— must be secured. Lines of communication must be established with all groups potentially concerned.

The initiative is typically announced to teachers through the principals, although in some cases the Superintendent may communicate directly with the teacher in a series of appearances at regularly scheduled or special faculty meetings. The reasons for the project are explained, the plans presented. Support is requested. If volunteers are being sought for early or heavy participation, they will be called. If the reform is to be phased in gradually, individuals and schools may be invited to indicate whether they would like to be among the first to implement the reform.

If all goes well, the reform will be implemented in one or more sites, monitored carefully, results evaluated with the help of the evaluation staff, and reports made to Superintendent, executive committee and other district staff. Evaluation may be quite formal and systematic, with control groups, standardized tests, statistical analysis of data, and the like. Or, it may be informal, featuring testimonials from teachers and students who participated, reactions of observers, samples of students' work, and so on. The evidence will be presented to the executive committee, the Superintendent, and the board. It is their evaluation that determines the fate of the reform. If the reform is judged a success it will be incorporated into district policy.

Behind the scenes of this official bureaucratic process, other kinds of initiatives arise and grow. Crises arouse concern about the school curriculum among parents and the public who ask what the schools should do. Shortly thereafter, a reform initiative surfaces and shoulders aside others on the executive committee's agenda. A teacher quietly explores a new way of teaching history, with or without the principal's permission. Soon other teachers become interested and a local movement grows. When they seek official recognition and district funds, their proposals are funneled into the bureaucratic channels. A new principal or superintendent is appointed and brings new initiatives to the table.

Sometimes initiatives come to the table from outside the circle of school and community. A court may order instruction to be offered in Cantonese to children who are native speakers of that language. State law may mandate drug education programs. The state university may raise its admission requirements. The county health department may propose a program to combat rising rates of smoking by adolescents. Accreditation teams may suggest an expanded program for the physically handicapped. Some of these external initiatives will be eagerly embraced by the school leadership, but usually not. Had they perceived an urgent need for some initiative, the school leaders would have sponsored it themselves. In presenting it to them, an external agency challenges their previous priorities. Typically, local leadership responds by trying to shape the initiative so that it fits within their preexisting priorities. So, a school initiative to make greater use of parent volunteers can be used to provide Cantonese aides for monolingual teachers of Chinese students. Drug education can be incorporated into the new revision of the health and physical education course of study that was scheduled for next year anyway. Perhaps courses can be relabeled to meet the university's new requirements. And so on. This process is called mutual adaptation and we will consider it again in more detail in a later chapter. If an externally generated initiative is to remain reasonably intact as its developers intended, it will need to gain strong local champions who, in effect, sponsor the initiative locally by treating it as if it were their own, putting themselves and their reputation behind it.

Actual Practice of Local Curriculum Planning

In actual practice local curriculum planning seldom lives up to this ideal image. Sometimes it seems highly technical: everyone seems to be measuring something and the language is that of science or engineering; you would think they were building a bridge. On other occasions, it is highly communal and consensual: meetings abound; the challenge seems to be how to satisfy everybody. And sometimes it is extremely formal and bureaucratic: officially approved steps are followed; everything is by the book. Usually, it is not extremely *anything*, but a sensible, earnest effort using a variety of common sense procedures eclectically, even loosely, in the interests of reaching a satisfactory, timely conclusion.

While results of local school curriculum planning are occasionally outstanding, typical results are unimpressive from any perspective, for good reasons. Such planning procedures as those just described require substantial time from relatively expensive professionals. Few districts can afford the heavy burden of salaries this entails. Many small districts confine local curriculum planning to curriculum materials selection and adaptation of courses of study from other sources: other districts, the textbook publisher, or the state. Even wealthy districts committed to local curriculum planning spend only a fraction of the amounts commercial publishers or nationally funded projects spend, and the results of cutting corners are usually reflected in pedestrian, unimaginative, unimpressive materials.

Many local schools and communities forego curriculum planning altogether. In *Behind the Classroom Door* Goodlad and Klein observed 158 classrooms in and around 13 American cities and reported:

> We endeavored to secure evidence of curriculum plans being developed by the school faculty as a whole or by committees of that faculty. We encountered only one example but admittedly evidence here was very difficult to obtain. Nevertheless, neither observations nor interviews with teachers and principals revealed faculties at work on curriculum problems and plans. (Goodlad and Klein 1970, 64)

The local curriculum planning that does go on is seldom very effective. Notice that the curricula resulting from presumably independent local change efforts are uniform across the country. If the curriculum were in fact closely attuned to the needs of local communities, we would see life-science and biology programs tailored to the local ecology, literature that reflected local and regional traditions, and social studies units that emphasized local government and local politics. We find instead that the curricula of American schools are very much alike, much more alike than the communities themselves are alike socially, politically, or culturally. Even the extracurriculum and the peripheral elective courses are largely local selections from national options. Most local school curricula are no more local than the food in the local supermarket. Both represent at best local preferences among nationally marketed products. The curricula resulting from local planning have been the target of nearly constant public criticism and urgent nationwide reform efforts for more than a quarter-century. Local plans consistently fail to satisfy academic critics who charge that the subject matter is watered down, distorted, and neglected. They consistently fail to satisfy those who speak for the interests of the disadvantaged. Instead of revising the process to respond to such criticisms, local schools have labelled them the work of special interests, made minor adjustments, and gone their merry way. The most substantial changes in the school curriculum in the last quarter-century have come in response to outside reform movements; local planning has consisted of adapting externally generated innovations to fit local conditions, an important role, but hardly the one envisioned by Rugg, Counts, and two generations of curriculum leaders.

It is not difficult to see why local curriculum planning rarely produces excellent results. Local resources and expertise are inadequate for the job of developing excellent curriculum materials. Local school systems have little incentive to invest more resources in developing materials. This is not their business, anyway. Commercial publishers can reap profits from selling materials to a national market. Therefore, local resources go increasingly to adapting commercial plans and materials and implementing them in local schools. The process of local curriculum development, however, is focused mainly on creating documents that spell out the official curriculum and simultaneously guide teachers in realizing it in their classrooms. But documents are inadequate for the job of bringing about curriculum change in classrooms. Local resources devoted to this task are far too slight to accomplish substantial results. The costs, for example, of providing the equivalent of even 10 working days per teacher per year for bringing about improvements in the classroom curriculum, a minimum estimate of what would be needed, are far beyond what districts typically spend on change efforts of all kinds. Meanwhile, the important school-level and system-level decisions that determine what learning opportunities will be offered to students and that influence the classroom curriculum by establishing frames, decisions that are under the control of the school system, are not included in the local curriculum change process but are buried in the day-to-day operations of the organization. In adopting a comprehensive approach, local curriculum planners neglect the important decisions actually under their control, spread inadequate resources too thin, and wind up doing nothing well.

Prospects for Local Curriculum Planning

The widespread participation, initiative, independence, and concern for local conditions fostered by such local curriculum planning are an honored part of the American educational tradition, one admired but little imitated elsewhere in the world. Even at its best, it has inherent shortcomings. It consumes a good deal of time, and most of this time is spent gaining the approval and cooperation of those whose efforts will be needed to realize the change, especially classroom teachers. Top school administrators control the agenda and determine the fate of change proposals. The process does not incorporate community leaders, parents, students or outside experts, only local professionals. Critical framing decisions such as course offerings, teacher qualifications, and course sequences are generally not brought into this process but are instead left to the various other branches of the bureaucracy. The process generally concludes well before any changes have been attempted in schools and classrooms; there are no provisions for following through and adjusting the change effort in light of events in attempting to implement it or for evaluation of the changes achieved or their effects. Radical proposals that would trample somebody's turf stand a slim chance in such a process. It sacrifices national uniformity and standardization, and leaves the door open for inequities to develop and grow among regions, classes, and races. The quality of the results is certain to be uneven. Much labor will be duplicated, many wheels reinvented.

Americans, unlike citizens of other nations, have been content to suffer these shortcomings in exchange for the benefits of local independence and initiative. But Americans' views on this question may be changing. The governors who are advocating statewide curricular standards enforced by statewide examinations are finding widespread public support and strong backing from the business and academic communities. A national system of examinations, National Assessment of Educational Progress, is in place and, if continued, will hold all fifty states up to a common national standard. Since the 1970s, schools' costs have grown faster than their tax revenues, and this squeeze, combined with enrollment declines, caused many districts to curtail or eliminate local curriculum development. So, there is not much local infrastructure left to defend, even if strong voices were raised to defend it. Most local effort is now devoted to adapting externally produced curriculum materials.

If the future is as unkind to local curriculum planning as these signs suggest it might be, then we can expect the essential work of curriculum maintenance and change in schools to be shouldered by teachers, principals, and perhaps even students or community members. The result will be a retreat from the ideal of autonomous, comprehensive, systematic local curriculum planning that has guided American curriculum making for most of this century. In Chapter 11 we will consider in detail some of the new directions work on the school curriculum might take.

QUESTIONS FOR STUDY

1. Compare the description of schools given in this chapter with a school you know well. For each important difference ask yourself how you think the school you chose exemplifies American schools in general. Compare your notes with others'. If you find the school you examined differs greatly, write a couple of paragraphs modifying the generalized description given in this chapter so that it more closely reflects schools where you live.

2. Do you think schools should be generalized community service agencies or primarily academic? Why? What are the benefits as well as the costs and risks associated with each policy? How is this issue related to the issue of local control of curriculum?

3. Assess the strengths and weaknesses of the American system of school governance as a means of achieving a strong curriculum in local schools. Suggest a reform of the present governance system that you think would most improve the curricular consequences of school governance. Discuss your choice with others.

4. Stage hypothetical conflicts between teachers and parents. Have some members of your group take the role of teachers, others parents, and others school administrators (principal and superintendent). Have parents initiate varied complaints in various ways, while teachers respond. Permit teachers or parents to report to a principal, superintendent, or board member. Have administrators decide how to deal with the situation and roleplay their subsequent meetings with those involved. Discuss the long-term, large-scale effects of these types of interactions on the curriculum.

5. Do you think it is ethical for school administrators to take an active role in

local politics? Is it prudent? Is it professional? Whose interest does the politically active superintendent represent? Explain.

6. Do you think educators should try to show a united front to the public in curriculum matters? What are the pros and cons of this? What other options are open to educators in dealing with the public on curriculum matters? Which option do you believe is best? Why?

7. Interview a school board member, a school administrator, or a teacher about his or her role in curriculum matters. How does he or she perceive his or her role? Are his or her perceptions consistent with their colleagues'? What changes would he or she like to see? Why? Why does each group see curriculum matters from the perspective that they do?

8. Although many school districts have research and development departments, they seldom search systematically for new, more effective practices as many businesses do. Why do you think this is? Do you think schools would be well advised to imitate businesses in this respect?

9. Discuss the costs and risks of local curriculum planning as done in the United States. Are there any other alternatives than a centralized bureaucratic system?

10. Very large and very small schools encounter some distinctive kinds of curricular problems. Discuss these. Interview persons with experience in very large or very small schools. Adapt the descriptions of curriculum management and change presented in this chapter in accordance with your conclusions.

11. Some critics of contemporary schools argue that schools function mainly to fit young people into the slots created for them in the economy and society. Discuss ways in which decisions that shape the school curriculum can channel students into certain roles after school. What changes in the curriculum or the procedures that maintain it would alter these results? Imagine what would happen if a superintendent and like-minded community leaders tried to make these changes. Consult with an experienced educational leader if you can. What do you conclude about the school curriculum's role in relation to the society?

12. What types of changes in school organization would you expect to occur if a state adopted a voucher system in which money appropriated for public education was given to students and parents to use at any school they wish? Which of these changes do you think are virtually unavoidable and which are merely likely or even just possible?

RECOMMENDED READING

The relationships between specific communities and their schools have long been recognized as critical to understanding curriculum stability and change in local schools. The sociological studies of Middletown by the Lynds (1929), for example, have greatly influenced scholarly perspectives on this relationship. Anthropologists have recently made an enormous contribution to our understanding of this relationship. Alan Peshkin's ethnographic studies are particularly enlightening (1978, 1982, 1986). John Ogbu's *The Next Generation* (1974) provides an especially insightful perspective on black and hispanic communities and their relationships with schools. Saxe's *School-Community Interaction* (1975) provides the best overview I have found of the various aspects of the relationship. Salisbury's *Citizen Participation in the Public Schools* (1980) provides a useful summary of ways citizens participate formally in public schools. Tucker and Zeigler's *Professionals Versus the Public: Attitudes, Communication, and Response in School Districts* (1980) views the relationship as predominantly antagonistic and supplies considerable evidence to support his conclusion. On political aspects I have relied mainly on the work of Wirt and Kirst *The Political Web of American Schools* (1972) and *Schools in Conflict* (1982).

Among the critical works I find most informative are Diane Ravitch's *The Schools We Deserve* (1985), Phillip Cusick's *The Egalitarian Ideal and the American High School* (1983) and *Inside High School* (1973), and Oakes and Sorotnik's *Critical Perspectives on the Organization and Improvement of Schooling* (1986). In a more analytic vein, Barker and Gump's *Big School, Small School* (1964) is an enlightening and powerful application of the concept of behavior settings to schools with enduring value. Seymour Sarason's *The Culture of the School and the Problem of Change* (1982) is full of brilliant insights about the realities of schools. Good and Brophy (1986) have reviewed the research done over the past decade to identify characteristics of effective schools—in other words, schools whose students score better than expected on standardized tests. Other recent works on schools worthy of attention include Goodlad's *A Place Called School* (1984), Sara Lawrence Lightfoot's *The Good High School* (1983), Ernest Boyer's *High School: A Report on Secondary Education in America* (1983), and Theodore Sizer's *Horace's Compromise* (1983).

Watch for reports of a major study under way by Michael Garrett of the School of Education at Northwestern University. Jeannie Oakes' *Keeping Track: How Schools Structure Inequality* (1985) just begins to reveal some of the subtleties hidden behind routinely reported national statistics on course offerings and enrollments. Project Talent (Flanagan and Cooley 1966) has given us some valuable information that has been barely noticed and poorly integrated with curriculum thought. Michael Cohen's essay (1983) gives an inkling of the kind of thinking needed on these issues.

Michael Fullan's *The Meaning of Educational Change* (1982) is an indispensable reference on changing the school curriculum.

REFERENCES

Anderson, Carolyn S. 1982. The Search for School Climate: A Review of Research. *Review of Educational Research* 52:368–420.

Blumberg, Arthur. 1985. *The School Superintendent.* N.Y.: Teachers College Press.

Boyer, Ernest L. 1983. *High School: A Report on Secondary Education in America.* N.Y.: Harper and Row.

Bridges, Edwin M. 1986. *The Incompetent Teacher.* Philadelphia: Falmer Press.

Clifford, Geraldine Joncich. 1975. *The Shape of American Education.* Englewood Cliffs, NJ: Prentice-Hall.

Coleman, James S. 1961. *The Adolescent Society.* N.Y.: Free Press of Glencoe.

Cohen, Michael. 1983. Instructional Management, and Social Conditions in Effective Schools. *School Finance and School Improvement: Linkages in the 1980s.* (Allen Odden and L. Dean Webb, eds.) Cambridge, MA: Ballinger.

Cusick, Phillip A. 1973. *Inside High School.* N.Y.: Holt, Rinehart, and Winston.

Cusick, Phillip A. 1983. *The Egalitarian Ideal and the American High School.* N.Y.: Longmans.

Elam, Stanley M. 1978. *A Decade of Gallup Polls of Attitudes Toward Education.* Bloomington, IN: Phi Delta Kappan.

Flanagan, John C. and William W. Cooley. 1966. *One-Year Follow Up Studies.* Pittsburgh: Project Talent, School of Education, University of Pittsburgh.

Fullan, Michael. 1982. *The Meaning of Educational Change.* N.Y.: Teachers College Press.

Good, Thomas L. and Jere Brophy. 1986. School Effects. (Merle Wittrock, ed.) *Handbook of Research on Teaching,* 3rd ed. N.Y.: Macmillan.

Goodlad, John and Frances Klein. 1970. *Behind the Classroom Door.* Worthington, Ohio: Jones.

Goodlad, John I. 1984. *A Place Called School.* N.Y.: McGraw-Hill.

Gross, Neal. 1958. *Who Runs our Schools?* N.Y.: John Wiley.

Iannaccone, Laurence and Frank W. Lutz. 1970. *Politics, Power, and Policy: The Governing of Local School Districts.* N.Y.: Teachers College Press.

Lightfoot, Sara Lawrence. 1983. *The Good High School.* N.Y.: Basic Books.

Lynd, Robert and Helen Merrell Lynd. 1929. *Middletown: A Study in American Culture.* N.Y.: Harcourt and Brace.

Martin, William J. and Donald J. Willower. 1981. The Managerial Behavior of High School Principals. *Educational Administration Quarterly* 17: 69–90.

McPherson, Gertrude. 1972. *Small Town Teacher.* Cambridge, MA: Harvard University Press.

Miles, Matthew B. (ed.) 1964. *Innovation in Education.* N.Y.: Teachers College Press.

Oakes, Jeannie. 1985. *Keeping Track: How Schools Structure Inequality.* New Haven: Yale University Press.

Oakes, Jeannie and Kenneth A. Sorotnik. 1986. *Critical Perspectives on the Organization and Improvement of Schooling.* Boston: Kluwer-Nijhoff.

Ogbu, John. 1974. *The Next Generation: An Ethnography of Education in an Urban Neighborhood.* N.Y.: Academic Press.

Peshkin, Alan. 1978. *Growing Up American: Schooling and the Survival of Community.* Chicago: University of Chicago Press.

Peshkin, Alan. 1982. *The Imperfect Union.* Chicago: University of Chicago Press.

Peshkin, Alan. 1986. *God's Choice: The Total World of a Fundamentalist Christian School.* Chicago: University of Chicago Press.

Ravitch, Diane. 1985. *The Schools We Deserve.* N.Y.: Basic Books.

Rugg, Harold and George S. Counts. 1927. A Critical Appraisal of Current Methods of Curriculum-Making. *Foundations and Technique of Curriculum-Making.* (Harold Rugg, ed.) Twenty-Sixth Yearbook, Chicago: National Society for the Study of Education.

Salisbury, Robert H. 1980. *Citizen Participation in the Public Schools.* Lexington, MA: Lexington Books.

Saxe, Richard. 1975. *School-Community Interaction.* Berkeley: McCutchan.

Sizer, Theodore R. 1983. *Horace's Compromise.* Boston: Houghton Mifflin.

Stearns, Myron M. and Washburne, Carleton. 1928. *Better Schools, A Survey of Progressive Education in American Public Schools.* N.Y.: The John Day Co.

Tucker, Harvey J. and Zeigler, Harmon. 1980. *Professionals Versus the Public: Attitudes, Communication, and Response in School Districts.* N.Y.: Longman.

Washburne, Carleton W. and Sidney P. Marland. 1963. *Winnetka, The History and Significance of an Educational Experiment.* Englewood Cliffs, NJ: Prentice Hall.

Wirt, Frederick, and Michael W. Kirst. 1972. *The Political Web of American Schools.* Boston: Little, Brown.

Wirt, Frederick, and Michael W. Kirst. 1982. *Schools in Conflict.* Boston: Little, Brown.

chapter 9

THE NATIONAL CURRICULUM

General planlessness, a love of freedom, of individual enterprise, and of open goals have been characteristic of American life.

Merle Curti. *The Social Ideas of American Educators,*
1935

Cleavages in economic class . . . do not coincide with allegiances of religion, ethnicity, or political party. . . . Opportunity in American society remains profoundly structured by race, sex, and class. . . . As in every society, public schools in the United States reinforce the interests of those in power, although they also mitigate injustice in a number of ways.

David Tyack and Elizabeth Hansot
American historian and sociologist, 1981

PURPOSE OF THE CHAPTER

- to explain how the curriculum functions in national education systems
- to describe the American curriculum influence system
- to assess the strengths and limitations of the American curriculum influence system as a way of making curriculum policy

OUTLINE

NATIONAL EDUCATION SYSTEMS

The Importance of Education in the Contemporary World

People all over the world believe in the value of education and want its benefits for their children. Indeed, the available data do show substantial correlations between education and public health, economic well-being, and cultural richness, though without experiments we can never know which is cause and which is effect. Those who are rich and powerful enough to get anything they want for their children generally choose to give them the best education available. People also believe that universal schooling of children is good for the society. For one thing, education is widely believed to foster national identity and thus to provide a foundation of perceived common interest that makes orderly government possible. In the words of the political theorist Carl Joachim Friedrich (1963),

> By supporting the values and beliefs prevalent in a community, education provides the underpinning for an authority and legitimacy which . . . depend upon these values and beliefs. For it is in their terms that . . . the title to rule has to be argued. (Friedrich 1963, 620)

Culture itself must be reconstituted in each generation, and the whole corpus of human knowledge relearned. Otherwise, whole cultures could disappear, along with their languages, arts, and customs, with the finality of biological extinction. Many factors are responsible for a culture's success or failure, including skill or good fortune in war, in trade, and in technological innovation, but people generally believe that what is taught and learned in school makes a difference. Study of the native language reinforces cultural patterns of perception, increases the value of the language as a medium of communication, and widens access to literature in the language. History, civics, literature, religion, and the arts contribute to cultural and national identity. On a global scale and over a span of generations, curriculum issues could be quite literally matters of cultural life and death.

Modern Nations with National School Systems

Around the world, nations provide schools and compel children to attend them. These schools are alike in many ways. They concentrate children in relatively large groups away from the daily activities of most adults. They occupy a major part of a child's life, lasting five or more hours a day, five or six days a week, over much of the year. A lot of the content in mathematics, science, and languages—often grouped together and called the *skill subjects*—is comparable in all systems. On the other hand, literature, history, religion, and literacy in the native language—the *cultural subjects*—take on quite distinct forms in each system. The other major group of subjects taught in most schools—the *practical subjects*—vary considerably, depending on the economies of the countries involved. School systems specify grades and levels of accomplishment and then hold children responsible for meeting these expectations at a specified rate and in a particular sequence. Most systems administer comprehensive examinations to all students at particular points in their educational careers. They award officially recognized and institutionally negotiable credentials.

Socio-Economic Functions of Education Systems

In *Predicting the Behavior of the Educational System* (1980), Thomas F. Green explains why national school systems share so many common features. Green's analysis directs our attention to how the tokens of attainment within education systems (credentials, diplomas, transcripts, and the like) function as a medium of exchange. Students who acquire these tokens gain advantages in competing for scarce benefits that are allocated on the basis of educational attainment, a basis generally considered more just than others in a meritocratic society. "A basic social function of such an education system is to allocate human beings to subsequent social and economic chances" (Green 1980, 87). Those with more education receive greater social benefits—eligibility for better jobs, for instance, or greater pay or higher social status. Obviously, the national government has a compelling interest in how these social benefits are distributed, as do individual parents and students, teachers, and citizens generally.

Any education system will distribute its benefits unequally; some students will always do better than others. Some inequalities in the distribution of benefits seem just and appropriate and others do not. For example, it seems equitable that those students who have freely chosen to spend more time studying learn more. Also, greater achievement in school does not seem unjust or inappropriate if one student is more able, energetic, or determined. However, when students learn more because benefits are distributed according to such educationally irrelevant characteristics as wealth, race, sex, religion, or the like, inequalities are not justifiable.

Education systems are supposed to provide equal opportunity for all students to achieve the benefits conferred by educational attainment. Yet, as more students succeed in entering and then completing a given level of education, that level of educational attainment confers less distinction than when fewer individuals succeed in attaining it. Furthermore, a nearly saturated system does not function well as an allocator of scarce social benefits. In the extreme case in which everybody has completed a given level of the system, this attainment provides no basis whatever for allocating any scarce social benefit. So, individuals are motivated to secure still further qualifications by completing additional levels in the system, and the system expands.

This dynamic has other consequences, as well. When nearly everybody has attained a given level, the few who are left behind incur social costs. They are barred from consideration for many jobs that require completion of the given level. They experience various types of social embarrassment and discrimination as a result of not having completed the level attained by nearly everyone else. So, while the first cadre of students to enroll in and complete a new level of the education system does so in anticipation of social benefits, the last group to enter a given level *must* complete it in order to avoid incurring serious social liabilities. Motivation that was positive for the pioneering group becomes defensive for the trailing group. Couple this with the fact that low status groups within the society are invariably over-represented in the residual trailing group at any level, and the inherent unfairness of the system for low-achieving, low-status students becomes apparent. Furthermore, as the majority of individuals within a low-status group attain the hitherto unattained level, they find that leading groups have attained still further levels of education. Green calls this the *principle of the moving target*. This characteristic of education systems is not the result of any particular social system—capitalism, say, or the Protestant ethic, or Western values. It happens in all education systems in all nations. Which groups lead and which trail and how great the disparities may vary, but the dynamic is always present in any education system.

Systems may respond to the conflicting demands that they allocate scarce benefits and facilitate equal opportunity in other ways besides adding new levels. Systems may differentiate, forming distinct, parallel programs at the same level, and allocating benefits according to the type of program a student completes. Or, less reliance may be placed on educational attainment in the allocation of noneducational benefits. When fewer benefits are allocated on the basis of educational attainment, the importance of the education system declines in relation to other social institutions. Alternatively, a qualitative distinction may be made among those whose attainments within the system are formally equal. In American higher education, for example, degrees from some institutions are much more valuable in securing noneducational benefits than formally equivalent degrees from other institutions. This devalues the educational credential. No matter how the system responds, so long as education is used as a basis for allocating noneducational goods, and so long as some objective, public mark of educational attainment is taken as the basis for the exchange of educational for noneducational goods, the system will exhibit such dilemmas.

An education system thus has a life of its own. Driven by our desire for more education, our belief that other social benefits should accompany educational attainment, our desire that equal educational opportunity be extended to all, and the hard fact of scarcity, the system expands and differentiates and intensifies. It provides the eager and able with an avenue for social advancement, while it imposes social liabilities on the slow and reluctant. If these are seen as defects, they are inherent defects of all education systems, not mistakes to be corrected by this or that reform.

Education Systems As Creatures of Government

Public schools are financed by taxes and operated by the government. In many countries private schools are subsidized. Even in the United States private schools receive subsidies in the form of exemption from property and sales taxes that apply to other private businesses. Laws specify standards that apply to all schools in such matters as health and safety, qualifications of teachers, and basic curriculum to be provided. Schools for children are thus public institutions, whether they are established and run by government or not.

The public's and the government's concern for education extends beyond formal schools and is more fundamental than simple concern over public management of the institutions of schooling. Establishing a school system, assessing its performance, and revising it from time to time to strengthen it and make it better able to further the public interest are public enterprises to be carried out within the political framework. Major political changes are nearly always accompanied by reforms in the education system, and major educational reforms are nearly always achieved through political institutions.

Patterns of Educational Governing

Considering the entire globe, centralized, governmentally-directed education policy is the prevailing pattern. In parliamentary governments, a ministry of education carries out the policies of the government. In France, Austria, Spain, and eastern European countries, the ministry itself typically originates and supervises educational reforms, while the parliament itself or the Prime Minister rarely become involved. In Scandinavian countries the parliament has been more active in initiating educational reforms that were then implemented by the ministry of education. In Israel and some less developed countries, special curriculum development centers have been established under supervision and funded by either general government or the education ministry. These represent a range of involvement in curriculum policy of the lay community through political institutions, from the highly intense leadership role of Scandinavian countries to the limited, distant role of influencing a professional organization.

In a few countries, educational policy-making is decentralized. West Germany, Great Britain, the Netherlands, and the United States are prominent examples of countries with decentralized educational policy-making. In these countries the primary responsibility for educational policy lies with local agencies, units called

Lander in Germany, Local Education Authorities (LEAs) in Great Britain, and either states or local school districts in the United States. These local agencies, in turn, may adopt a centralized or decentralized pattern in their relations with individual schools. In the United States, for example, the state of Hawaii has one school district that covers the entire state and the state Department of Education specifies the curriculum for all Hawaiian schools. In Massachusetts, by contrast, most curriculum decisions are traditionally left to the local schools. In decentralized systems the central authority plays a facilitative role, in theory, although often in practice a competing role, in educational policy-making.

In Scandinavia and other countries where the general institutions of government make education policy, education reform reflects and contributes to overall programs of social reform. *Comprehensivization* of Swedish secondary schools in the 1960s, for example, grew out of a larger concern for social equity. The governing party believed that dividing Swedish youngsters between specialized academic secondary schools (traditional *gymnasia*) and more practically-oriented schools that did not prepare students for college helped to perpetuate irrelevant and unjust social distinctions. So a massive program of educational reform was planned by the legislature in consultation with unions, churches, and other institutions. Working with social scientists over a period of years, the Swedish parliament gradually shaped the educational reform and eventually institutionalized it in a series of laws. Opposition was vocal and organized. Criticism from opponents in some cases led to adjustments to the legislative program. Some features proposed were defeated. The program as finally enacted had the full authority of the government behind it. The national unity created in this process, together with the fact of widespread participation by educational leaders in shaping the program, minimized resistance of schools and teachers at the time of implementation.

In countries where the ministry of education takes the leading role in policy-making, curriculum reform typically begins with discussions in ministerial committees. Testimony may be offered or sought from any quarter, professional or lay. Politically more powerful groups usually have an easier time getting their message through than less powerful groups. Generally speaking, pressures for reform are transmitted up the various social hierarchies in an orderly manner, with presentations to the ministry being made by high officials of the relevant organizations. Other officials within the ministry and elsewhere in government will be consulted. Special commissions may be established. Studies may be conducted. Or, the matter may be referred as a matter of course to a relevant official or committee. Decisions to proceed with a reform emerge as proclamations from the minister, regardless of their origins. These are binding on all schools and all intermediate levels of the organization. Problems of compliance, when they arise, are handled by the normal processes of administrative command and control at each level in the hierarchy, processes that always appear quite rigid on paper, but which may be fairly flexible in practice.

In decentralized systems reforms may originate within a particular local or regional sub-center in much the same way as in larger national centers, or they may originate in central government agencies, or even in centers completely outside the formal education system. Often reforms originate with a national education agency (ministry, office of education, . . .), but these reforms are not binding on all local agencies. Rather, to be eligible for funds appropriated by the central government, local agencies must follow guidelines set down centrally. Sometimes, too, the central agency establishes a temporary project to produce curriculum materials or carry out research related to the reform. The products of this temporary agency are made available to local authorities in ways that encourage them to undertake a reform of the desired type. Sometimes a quasi-public or private agency will secure funding from government or private philanthropic agencies to carry on what amounts to curriculum policy formulation, again in hopes of persuading local authorities to adopt the policies they formulate.

Curriculum Matters and Education Systems

Curriculum matters are more than just activities taking place under the aegis of the education system. They are part of the system itself. The standards for awarding credentials or degrees are expressed in curricular terms—so many hours or courses in this or that subject, satisfactory examination results in certain fields, and so on. The program of course offerings defines the school. Teachers are selected on the basis of their qualifications to teach this or that subject. Their training includes study of the content and methods of that subject. Books and supplies are chosen according to course and subject categories. Even the school building and facilities are designed to accommodate certain curricular imperatives—science laboratories, machine shops, home economics equipment, music rooms, and so on.

Consider the following list of major national education policy questions. Each has significant implications for the curriculum of schools within the system.

1. Will schools be selective or comprehensive?
2. What different types of schools will be offered or allowed?
3. Will students be grouped by ability or heterogeneously?
4. What amount of funding will be provided for education by the government?
5. How will funding and other resources be allocated among schools?
6. Will schools be coeducational?
7. What are the criteria and standards for advancement from one stage to the next of the education system and for the award of degrees or credentials?

The concept of *frames* that we encountered earlier is helpful in understanding how such national policy decisions affect schools and classrooms. Resource frames determine how much of various educational resources will be available for use in curriculum policy and practice. They include such factors as the students who are assigned or permitted to attend, the teachers available, space, materials, and facilities, and the time during which all of these will be available for school use. System policies constrain local schools to operate within limits set by these resource frames. Direction frames establish goals, priorities, and rationales intended to govern all the system's operations. Frames affect school governance, finance, and administration, as well as specifically curricular matters, but they shape curricular policies in such a direct and powerful way that they need to be considered in any curriculum decision. They are, one might say, projections of the larger system into the curricular domain.

Curricula are not simply the messages of the education system. They are not like records or cassette tapes that can be changed at will to play different tunes on the same machine. Certain features of curricula are integral to the structure and operation of the education system; to change them you must change the entire system.

Curriculum Policy

The dictionary definition of policy is "a settled, coherent plan or course of action." Curriculum policy is simply a settled, coherent plan or course of action with respect to curriculum matters. While nothing prevents us from speaking of the curriculum policies of a single teacher in a single classroom, we customarily speak of policy only when the jurisdiction is much larger. This usage distinguishes between situations in which those involved can meet face-to-face and situations in which such intimacy is logistically impossible and decisions must be delegated to representatives. In this book the word *policy* is used to cover the latter situation, only. The real and important curriculum planning and action that take place in schools and classrooms will be described in other terms.

A school district's officially adopted K–6 program for teaching reading is a clear example of curriculum policy. A district's high school graduation requirements are another familiar example, as are state laws that require all schools in the state to teach physical education, the evils of alcohol and drugs, the history of the United States, or the virtues of our system of government, and federal guidelines that all federally funded vocational education programs must follow. These examples are all actions of official agencies of government and therefore have the force of law, but curriculum policy may also be shaped by unofficial agencies such as accrediting associations or professional organizations, and even by individual citizens and private for-profit firms, as we shall see.

Curriculum Policy-Making

Policy-making is a generic term for actions that shape or determine policies. It includes **formulation** (articulation, expression, statement) of the policy, as well as **consideration** of the appropriateness of a policy to a particular situation. It also includes making a **decision to adopt, adapt, or reject** this policy for this situation. Normally, **implementation** of curriculum policy—in other words, putting the policy into practice in a particular situation, and **evaluation** of policy are spoken of as separate parts of the all-inclusive **policy process.**

Curriculum policy-making is sometimes a separate activity in its own right. For example, a deputy superintendent for curriculum in a state may undertake a review of the state's recommended English curriculum. In the course of this review she may chair a committee appointed by the superintendent, hold hearings, produce documents, and recommend to the superintendent that actions be taken. Usually, though, curriculum policy-making is an integral part of general educational planning and governance. For example, educational reform legislation enacted by a state may address such matters as teacher salaries, teacher recruitment and promotion, and administrative structure, as well as curriculum matters. A local school board that increases per pupil expenditures makes it possible to offer a greater variety of elective courses in high school. Adopting a school schedule divided into more periods gives students a wider choice among electives. The decisive act in creating or terminating a special curriculum program is often a budget authorization. Curriculum policy-making is usually part and parcel of

---

BOX 9-1   Major Curriculum Policy Decisions

- Types of educational programs to be offered, and the relative or absolute size permitted to each ("Programs" means courses of study extending over several years):

  Academic
  Vocational
  General
  Classical
  so on

- The overall curriculum design of each program: criteria for admission, promotion, and graduation, required components, elective components, rules for maintaining balance among components, schedule, time allocations, and so on,

- The aims, contents, and essential features of the component elements of each program:

  syllabi, courses of study
  textbooks, teaching/learning materials
  course examinations
  topics and time allocations
  objectives
  required facilities, equipment, supplies

- Criteria and procedures for evaluating the performance of each program:

  numbers of pupils scoring above or below certain levels on external
     comprehensive examinations
  rate of admission of students to the next stage in the education system
  student or parent satisfaction
  judgment of experts

overall school governance, administration, and leadership. The activities of designated curriculum specialists are an important part of this process, but only a part.

Curriculum policy deals with those aspects of curriculum that are large in scale, pervasive and important in effect, and that may be influenced by actions of policy-makers. These would certainly include the factors mentioned in Box 9-1.

The Functions of Policy in Curriculum Matters

The most basic function of policy is to coordinate the curricula of schools and classrooms throughout some jurisdiction. This standardization facilitates transfer of students from one school or classroom to another, simplifies school management (for instance, entrance and graduation requirements, scheduling, and testing), makes possible a greater uniformity in the training and certification of educational personnel, and lends a degree of common meaning to the credentials students earn upon completion of each stage of schooling. Without standard curricular categories each local school district would have to carry out these tasks in its own way at its own expense: examine all candidates who applied for positions thoroughly enough to be certain they are qualified; invent local course titles; develop tests; and specify entrance and graduation requirements. Standardization makes possible economies of scale. Many millions of dollars can be invested in the production of curriculum materials for a mass market, for example.

Curriculum policy also serves a cultural function. It offers people the opportunity to express shared values. A decision to teach all the children of a state about the Pilgrims and Plymouth Rock says something about what the people of the state think is important to know. A decision to leave to local schools the decision whether to teach about Spanish exploration of the Southwest in colonial times says something, too. That the language of instruction in all schools is to be English, regardless of the language spoken in the students' homes affirms the society's commitment to monolingualism and to the English language. A decision that all children will be taught the theory and virtues of democracy and free enterprise affirms principles on which American society is based. Affirming such values through official policy and forbidding individual schools or teachers from omitting them or undermining them makes a strong statement about the importance placed on them by the official agencies of government, and, so long as the government is representative, about the importance placed on them by the people. Thus policy serves to symbolize and express cultural values.

Politically, policy functions as a means of achieving concerted action on a large scale in the face of divergent interests and opinions. Political scientists speak of this process as the conversion of demands and supports into decisions and actions (Easton 1965). In times when national well-being seems threatened and people call for action from the schools, policy provides a means of converting political demands into actions that can be debated and, if supported, implemented. Such crises have arisen repeatedly in this century. Schools developed programs to Americanize immigrants in response to the perceived threat of large numbers of immigrants from southern and eastern Europe early in this century. Schools instituted improved physical education and quasi-military training for boys to increase the supply of manpower for World War I. The Great Depression, World War II, *Sputnik,* the civil rights crusade, and the threat of economic competition have all produced national debate about curriculum issues, proposals for action from schools, and a variety of official, quasi-official, and unofficial policies in response. Whenever the public perceives national educational needs and insists that schools help to meet these needs, a political mechanism—policy—is needed.

Policy performs the important economic function of allocating scarce educational resources among competing curricular priorities in accordance with a plan. A policy requiring every student in a state to study English for four years of high school, social studies for three, and mathematics and science for two, making all other subjects electives, effectively allocates an array of educational resources among these subjects, including teacher time and qualifications, student time, and curriculum materials.

Policy is not the only way these political, economic, cultural, and technical benefits can be realized. Traditions that are widely accepted and followed can perform the same functions. Voluntary organizations and networks of various kinds can also achieve these results. An elective or free market system in which students and their parents choose among classes or schools solves the economic allocation problem, sidesteps the political problem by not seeking concerted action, and lets the market set whatever standards it can.

THE AMERICAN EDUCATION SYSTEM

Americans have repeatedly rejected the prospect of an official national education policy-making agency, beginning in the first decades of independence by rejecting proposals to establish a national university. From the beginning, Americans have distinguished with pride their system of governmental checks and balances from the authoritarian central governments of Europe. Formal, centralized, hierarchical, bureaucratic policy-making clashes with America's democratic, populist, republican traditions and is associated with strong negative cultural images: despotic government actions, high-handed officials, a petty bureaucracy replete with forms and documents and, probably, corruption. The legendary claims of the French Minister of Education to know at any given moment what any youngster in France is studying do not impress many Americans. The controversies that arise in Japan when a government agency decides exactly what every Japanese textbook will say about that country's actions in World War II seem to Americans to be a needless result of intrusion of government where it does not belong. Confronted with such examples, Americans celebrate their sturdy individualism, invoke their tradition of local control over education, and heave a sigh of relief that their federal government has not been given this sort of power over American public schools. If this is curriculum policy, Americans don't have it and most don't want it.

Americans have left decisions about education to each of the fifty states, and for the most part those states have by tradition further delegated these decisions to local school districts. But the American education system has the same need for the political, economic, cultural, and technical benefits conferred by policy as any other national system. And, in fact, the American education system has nearly as much standardization in curriculum matters as most centralized systems. Americans have developed ways to establish a common national education system without a national education authority.

The American Curriculum Influence System

The American approach to establishing a common national curriculum may be briefly described as a distributed system of curriculum decision-making loosely organized into overlapping and contending networks of authority and influence operating in a strong national context of ideas and institutions.

The curriculum of the American education system results from the actions of three very different types of actors:

1. Official local, state and federal government agencies
2. Quasi-official organizations such as accrediting associations and the College Entrance Examination Board, which are usually staffed and controlled by professionals or experts, and which derive their authority by delegation from legally authorized agencies
3. Unofficial agencies such as textbook publishers, the education media, special interest groups, and professional associations that control or heavily influence particular aspects of the curriculum-making process, and whose actions have real, substantial consequences that local agencies cannot afford to ignore

Each of these sets of actors controls or heavily influences certain decisions that can have a powerful effect on the curriculum of local schools.

Since federal agencies have no official authority for curriculum policy, issues that come to prominence nationally cannot be resolved by official action of the federal government. The United States Department of Education cannot compel action from state departments of education or local school districts; it can attempt to lead them and it may threaten to withhold federal funds unless they comply. State departments' control over local school districts is also weak. The official governance system of the American education system is therefore only weakly hierarchical. In the United States, national curriculum issues can be officially resolved only by decisions taken at lower levels.

This does not mean that national forces are entirely absent, however. Various unofficial actors on the national stage have positioned themselves to take actions that may strongly influence or constrain state or local decisions. For instance, professional associations are organized on a national scale, and can use their accrediting power to influence local schools. Many citizen groups, such as the Council for Basic Education and the John Birch Society, conduct national campaigns on behalf of their curricular issues. The power to make decisions and take actions affecting the curriculum on a national scale is distributed among many agencies, each controlled by different interests. In particular, the division of authority between public and profession is unclear and contested, and the roles of official and unofficial agencies are mingled. These interests contend on many occasions, in many arenas, each trying to influence many decision-makers. The actions of a network of varied national groups, overlapping, sometimes competing, sometimes cooperating, together controlling dozens, perhaps hundreds of nationally significant leverage points, can create the effect of a national policy when the net result of their struggles is a stable common course of action by many thousands of presumably independent educational decision-makers.

Box 9-2 represents the major features of the American curricular influence system schematically. Box 9-3 shows some of the main decisions that might be controlled at each of five levels of authority in a hypothetical, representative state. (Note the prevalence of overlapping authority.) Box 9-4 shows some of the actions official agencies take in order to influence the curriculum of schools throughout the nation.

There are two distinct ways these many actors may influence the curriculum of schools throughout the nation. Under normal conditions, incremental policy-making is the rule, while in national emergencies, which seem to recur every few years, a new set of rules apply: crisis policy-making. In incremental policy-making, state and local officials and top-level educational administrators play the crucial deciding roles, as they are authorized to do, while various interests try to influence their decisions. In crisis policy-making, ordinary procedures are swept aside by organized national curriculum reform movements initiated by advocates of a particular curriculum reform and given influence by a tide of public support for extraordinary actions to relieve the crisis. The actors and arenas in crisis policy-making shift unpredictably, depending on the nature of the perceived crisis and the coalition that forms in support of the reform, but to be successful a reform movement must get its message into the major national channels of communication. This involves attracting the attention of the mass media—major newspapers, magazines, radio, and network television—and of major education journals. Successful reform movements eventually solicit support from one of the agencies of general government by petitioning the President for action, requesting legislation, or bringing suit in court.

Federal Government Interventions in School Curriculum Policy

The federal government does strive to influence the curriculum of American schools, even though education is, in strict constitutional theory, a responsibility of individual states. Box 9-5 shows major actions taken by the federal government since 1950 that have affected the curriculum of the nation's schools. It is hardly a

BOX 9-2 Major Influences on Curriculum Policy

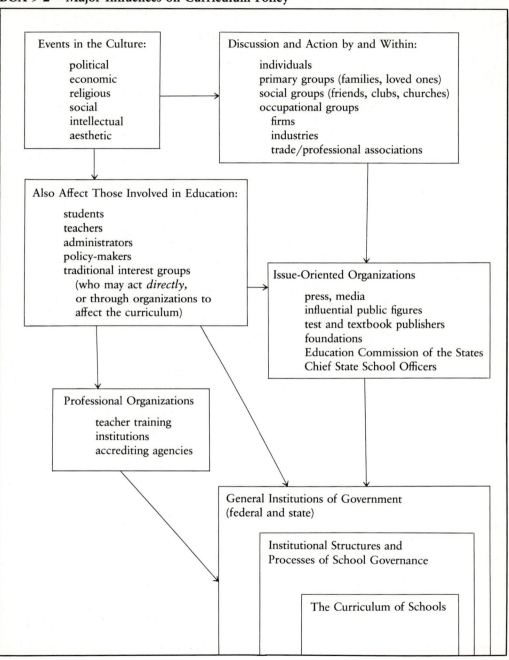

Events in the Culture:

    political
    economic
    religious
    social
    intellectual
    aesthetic

Discussion and Action by and Within:

    individuals
    primary groups (families, loved ones)
    social groups (friends, clubs, churches)
    occupational groups
      firms
      industries
      trade/professional associations

Also Affect Those Involved in Education:

    students
    teachers
    administrators
    policy-makers
    traditional interest groups
      (who may act *directly,*
      or through organizations to
      affect the curriculum)

Issue-Oriented Organizations

    press, media
    influential public figures
    test and textbook publishers
    foundations
    Education Commission of the States
    Chief State School Officers

Professional Organizations

    teacher training
    institutions
    accrediting agencies

General Institutions of Government
(federal and state)

Institutional Structures and
Processes of School Governance

The Curriculum of Schools

BOX 9-3   Major Areas of Authority for Curriculum Policy for a Hypothetical State Public School System

LEVEL	Curriculum Policy Controlled
National	<ul><li>national agenda for educational debate and action</li><li>innovative demonstration projects</li><li>monitoring of quality of the nation's schools</li><li>research and evaluation</li></ul>
State	<ul><li>minimum standards for high school graduation</li><li>required curricular offerings</li><li>mandated local minimum competency testing</li><li>innovative state-sponsored programs</li><li>annual statewide achievement testing</li><li>selection of approved textbooks</li></ul>
District	<ul><li>selection of specific textbooks from approved list</li><li>high school graduation requirements</li><li>elementary school time allotments</li><li>district philosophy and aims</li><li>course and program approval</li><li>course syllabi and curriculum guides</li><li>curriculum consultants and support services</li><li>minimum competencies at various grades</li><li>district achievement testing</li><li>in-service education of teachers</li></ul>
School	<ul><li>assignment of students/teachers to classes</li><li>selection of supplementary curriculum materials</li><li>elective course offerings</li><li>selection of textbooks for elective courses</li><li>school schedule</li><li>school-wide innovations</li><li>school philosophy and aims</li><li>school climate</li><li>in-service education of teachers</li></ul>
Classroom	<ul><li>instructional strategies and tactics</li><li>content actually covered</li><li>priorities among multiple objectives</li><li>testing and grading of student performance</li><li>use and allocation of resources: student time, teacher time, materials</li><li>classroom climate</li><li>classroom activities</li></ul>

BOX 9-4   Actions Taken to Influence School Curricula Nationwide

Incremental Policy Planning

National Level:

- textbook planning (by publishers, normally)
- design of tests for nationwide use
- setting of accreditation standards
- writing regulations administering federal law
- developing curriculum plans by professional organizations
- developing curriculum plans by public interest groups
- developing curriculum plans by special interest groups

State Level:

- laws governing curriculum (course requirements, graduation requirements, minimal standards for school programs, and so on
- administrative rules and regulations governing curriculum
- textbook adoption (in some states)
- standards governing teacher education
- developing statewide curriculum plans (frameworks, syllabi, and courses of study)

Crisis Policy Planning

National Level:

- presidential commissions
- congressional study groups
- laws (National Defense Education Act, Elementary and Secondary Education Act, and so on)
- curriculum materials development by national projects

State Level:

- governor's special commissions
- legislative study groups
- state laws
- statewide curriculum reform projects

Local Level:

- special meetings of the Board of Education
- establishment of ad hoc citizen's committees

BOX 9-5   Major Federal Curriculum Policy Initiatives Since 1950

1954   **Brown vs. Board of Education:**
Supreme court rules school segregation unconstitutional.

1958   **National Defence Education Act (NDEA):**
Authorizes funds for curriculum development, teacher training, and purchase of materials and equipment to strengthen the teaching of science, mathematics, foreign languages, and other academic subjects.

1964   Publication of Coleman Report, **Equality of Educational Opportunity:**
Huge survey research project, federally funded.

1965   **Elementary and Secondary Education Act (ESEA):**
Aid to local schools to improve the education of the educationally disadvantaged; includes Project Head Start and Sesame Street. Title I of this act is the largest program of federal aid to education in American history.

1967   **Project Follow Through:**
Additional aid for the educationally disadvantaged.

1968   **Vocational Education Act:**
An extension and updating of earlier statutes continuing and expanding this program.

1969   **Right to Read:**
Emphasis on literacy for adults and children. Done largely through libraries and public agencies other than schools.

1972   **Career Education:**
Major initiative of Sidney P. Marland, Commissioner of Education in the Nixon administration.

1972   **National Institute of Education (NIE) formed:**
Emphasis on educational research and development in areas of defined national need.

1975   **Education for All Handicapped Children Act:**
Mandates mainstreaming handicapped children into the same classrooms as other children, a major change in policy for education of the handicapped.

1978   **Basic Skills Replace Right to Read**

record of passivity and helplessness. Federal actions are justified as furthering vital national interests or protecting individual rights guaranteed by the Constitution. When the national security or welfare seems threatened, and when it seems that changes in the nation's schools would lessen the threat, pressures build on the federal government to act however it can within constitutional limits. Increasingly in recent decades the quality of public education has come to be seen as important to the national welfare, and the federal government has become increasingly active in education policy. Also, under the Constitution, the federal government has a responsibility to safeguard the rights guaranteed to all citizens. Many of these rights—the right to equal protection under the law, for example, and the right of freedom of religion—have been asserted in connection with curriculum issues, and the federal government has in some cases responded.

Federal activity in curriculum matters grew markedly in the period from 1958 to 1980. The budget of the United States Office of Education rose from $377 million in 1960 to over $8 billion in 1981. States and local districts came to depend on the federal government for the funds needed for new curriculum initiatives. The power of the purse and the strings attached to it gave federal agencies leverage to influence local curricula. The pretext, at least, and probably the main causes of this growth, were a series of national crises that were widely perceived as connected to the nation's education system. The National Defense Education Act of 1958 was a response to a perceived crisis in American scientific and technical know-how engendered by the Russians' surprise launching of the first Earth-orbiting satellite in 1957. The Elementary and Secondary Education Act of 1965 was a response to the civil rights struggles and riots in black areas of Northern cities.

The authority over curriculum assumed by the federal government during the period of these national crises still fell far short of establishing a national curriculum. The actions taken were, in fact, quite subtle and indirect by comparison with the official policy-making of most other nations. Federal courts, it is true, handed down rulings that were sometimes quite detailed and that bore the full force of law. But for the most part the federal government sought to influence state and local curriculum decisions indirectly, mainly by offering money in exchange for implementing federally sponsored reforms and by using the prestige of the government on their behalf. Nevertheless, as a result of these interventions, the federal government developed a repertoire of policy tools it can use to influence the curricula of schools throughout the nation.

Four prominent curriculum policy tools available to the Federal government are law enforcement, categorical aid programs, curriculum development projects, and prestige of office. Law enforcement is the most potent mechanism of federal influence but also the most limited one. It can be used to enforce Constitutional rights and federal laws applicable to schools. Recent examples are requiring schools to provide instruction in their native language for students whose native language is not English; to provide secular but not anti-religious instruction; to permit students to be exposed to a market-place of ideas on political issues; to provide minimally adequate programs for students with special needs; and not to treat such social and cultural differences as age, sex, race, or handicaps in a prejudicial or stereotypical way.

Categorical aid programs provide funds for certain specified purposes. They can be used to stimulate local schools to undertake certain curriculum reforms. When strings are attached, categorical aid can be used to coerce curriculum change in other areas. Recent examples are the Elementary and Secondary Education Act of 1965 that appropriated funds for creation of bilingual education programs, for programs for dropouts, and for early education programs for poor and minority children; the Education for All Handicapped Children Act of 1974 that offered local districts funds and technical assistance for programs to educate children with physical, mental, and emotional handicaps. Strings attached to the latter act encouraged an individualized curriculum structure across the school program because all teachers were required to prepare a specific written Individual Education Plan (IEP) for each student and to review this and the student's progress with parents periodically.

Curriculum development projects make new curricular options available to local schools. Federal support for curriculum development also stimulates the effort of educational entrepreneurs who hope for federal funds to support their innovative projects. Commercial providers of curriculum materials may be persuaded to offer innovative materials once they see that there is a market for them. The National Science Foundation (NSF) pioneered this approach to federal curriculum policy-making in 1958 when they funded the Physical Science Study Committee to produce a textbook, laboratory apparatus, and films to improve the teaching of physics in high schools. Subsequently both the NSF and the United States Office of Education funded other projects in nearly every school subject at both elementary and secondary levels.

Prestige of office enables Federal officials to set the terms of public discussion. Presidential commissions, congressional hearings or investigations, speeches by government officials, and sponsored research, evaluation, data gathering, or surveys all can be used to call national attention to a particular curriculum issue, idea, or proposal and lend prestige to it. Any proposal discussed approvingly in the official councils of government gains currency with the public and the profession. Pronouncements of government officials can do much to frame public and professional debate and to bring ideas into or out of currency. Since much of the funding for research and development comes from federal agencies, by selecting studies to fund, Federal agencies can influence educational debate in academic and professional circles. The Federally funded Coleman Report, **Equality of Educational Opportunity,** for example, posed issues that dominated discussion of education for a decade after its publication.

Official Curriculum Policy-Making by State Governments

In principle, state governments have complete legal authority to arrange the curriculum of public schools and to regulate the curriculum of private schools within their borders. States have as much authority to control education within their borders as any autonomous national government, except for limitations imposed by the Constitution and the few federal laws that affect education. In fact, however, few states exercise a degree of control approaching that of most other countries. Most states delegate authority for most educational matters to local school districts. The authority that remains in the capital is divided among the three branches of government and usually among several executive agencies and legislative committees.

Most states have enacted statewide policies regulating the actions of local schools in the following areas:

pupil records
high school graduation requirements
school organization
attendance
program accreditation
personnel certification

Almost half the states, however, have moved in the past decade to exercise more extensive central authority over education, including such additional curriculum matters as:

minimum competencies
state-approved textbooks
state syllabi and courses of study
statewide examinations.

In states with more centralized traditions, education policy-makers are active agents for school improvement whatever the issue, and initiatives for school improvement frequently originate at the state level or, if they originate at local or national levels, rapidly find expression as state policies.

Other states hold more strictly to the tradition of local control. They give local districts almost complete autonomy in curriculum matters that extend beyond the basic areas of regulation mentioned above. State agencies in these states generally adopt a service orientation, seeing their roles as coordinating, facilitating, and assisting local districts with local initiatives. They act as conduits for transmitting federal funds to local districts, but seldom intrude their own policy agenda.

Since 1980 the Reagan administration has attempted to reduce the federal role in education matters and to emphasize that education is a responsibility of the states. This reduction of the federal role in educational reform may have left a policy vacuum for states to fill. The public seems more impatient with public schools and more insistent on reform and in many states, governors and state legislatures are responding. In the 1980s we have seen increased state activity to deal with the issue of test score declines and, more recently, economic competitiveness. In addition to these political trends, the move toward increased state funding of local schools to remedy inequities and remove burdens from local property taxpayers has increased state control over local schools. Finally, SEAs and state legislatures are more experienced and better able to take on the challenges of vigorous central policy-making after their experience in administering the federal programs of the last two decades. It seems likely that more states will adopt forceful, central policies on education in the next few years.

Structure and Functions of State Policy-Making for Curriculum

The chief actors in official state policy-making are the state legislature, the chief state school officer (CSSO), the State Education Agency (SEA), the governor, state courts, and organized lobbies. These groups go by different names in different states and their conditions and terms of appointment or election differ. The following thumbnail sketches represent overall patterns to which no state conforms exactly.

SEAs A typical SEA has just under a thousand employees, although the largest employ several thousand. SEAs have, on the average, tripled in size in the last 15 years, largely due to the increased flow of federal funds for education through SEAs. SEAs are staffed by hundreds of specialists in little niches of expertise: finance, law, administration, certification, curriculum and instruction, buildings and grounds, and so on, serving under an appointed or elected state superintendent. Most of these specialists are busied with the paperwork required to implement state laws. Only a small fraction of SEA energy goes to development of proactive policies. SEAs do not have staff for frequent visitation or inspection of local districts or schools. Programs of technical assistance are also limited in most states. Also, SEAs do not control all aspects of education or even of public education within most states. For instance, colleges and universities are generally governed by a separate state agency, which means that the SEA does not control college entrance requirements or teacher preparation programs.

Legislatures Education is the largest single budget item in most states, and for that reason alone it is a major concern of state legislatures. Legislatures' power to control expenditures, to conduct hearings and investigations, and to authorize new programs makes them the most powerful actors on the state level when they are mobilized to legislate on education issues. Legislators, their staffs, and their committees are the primary actors in this process, but they are influenced heavily by their constituents, by organized interest groups and lobbies, by party leaders and members, and by the officials in the SEA and governor's office most concerned with education legislation.

Governors Governors do not have any direct responsibility for the routine operation of the public school system except establishing the state budget and, in some states, appointing the state superintendent. They can, if they choose, exercise initiative in education matters by proposing legislation, by executive order, or by working with the SEA and state board. Traditionally, though, governors have taken a stand on broad issues such as greater or lesser appropriations for education, rather than proposing specific programs. Since political reformers succeeded in removing education from party politics in the late 1800s, education issues have not played a very important part in general electoral politics. Very recently, since about 1980, more governors seem to be taking an active stance for such specific educational reforms as testing of teachers, lengthening of the school day, and more emphasis on academic skills.

Lobbies In most states a few organized groups that represent many thousands of voters vitally concerned with education have a strong influence on education legislation. These organized lobbies generally include teachers' organizations, school administrators' organizations, associations of school board members, PTA and other parent groups, good government groups, and single issue interest groups around such issues as education of the handicapped, vocational education, or agriculture education. In most states on most issues the profession has been, until recently, united in a single lobby that is the largest in numbers and influence. In recent years labor-management conflicts have split teacher organizations from the other professional lobbies. Sometimes more general organizations take a special interest in an educational issue and lobby on its behalf, usually effectively. For example, during the decade before and after World War I, organized groups, responding to widespread anxieties about communism, anarchism, and the perceived danger to American traditions from modern ideas and from European immigrants, successfully lobbied many state legislatures for passage of laws mandating patriotic ceremonies, Bible reading, temperance instruction, and for forbidding the teaching of Darwinism. In most states most of the time, though, the chief opposition to most education measures come from taxpayer groups whose goal is to keep taxes as low as possible.

State Courts State courts have tended to be overshadowed by federal courts on education issues. Curriculum issues, particularly, tend to be joined on Constitutional grounds and thus be decided in federal courts. State courts have tended to uphold most state law in curriculum matters, confining themselves to determining whether given state and local actions or policies are consistent with the law and the state constitution. Some recent exceptions are worthy of note, though. In New Jersey, the state court determined that the state was obligated to provide a *thorough and efficient* education to every child in the state. This would seem to establish a constitutionally guaranteed right not just to education or even to equal access to education, but to education of a certain quality. If more state courts follow this line of interpretation, state court decisions could become more important determinants of state curriculum policy.

Forms of State Curriculum Policy

States are legally authorized to use the full range of policy tools in curriculum matters, including all four available to the federal government and several more. For convenience we will distinguish here among six additional policy tools available to states: mandates, regulation, program support, assistance, examinations, and curricular alignment. Mandates are orders that schools are legally bound to follow. Regulation is a process of specifying limits within which schools must operate. States may regulate any of several aspects of the curriculum, including content coverage, course offerings, time allotments, choice of curriculum materials, entrance requirements, graduation requirements, organization or structure of the curriculum, and resource allocation among programs.

Program support offers schools resources to be used to establish, maintain, or improve a particular type of educational program. The offering of curricular assistance—expert advice, service, or consultation—may extend to any kind of curriculum problem a school encounters. Local schools often need assistance with implementation of new programs, teacher in-service education, program evaluation, and techniques demanded by new federal policies, such as the preparation of individual education plans for handicapped students. The variety of expertise needed helps to give SEAs their highly differentiated organizational structures.

Examinations of student learning are treated here as a policy mechanism in their own right rather than simply a way of monitoring students' performance. Most states now have statewide minimum competency examinations. Many of the most populous and influential states have extensive statewide testing programs for all students at several points in their school careers, for all required subjects every year and for elective subjects on a rotating basis. Examination results are front page news in many local newspapers and a major focus of discussion about education in many local communities as well as in state legislatures. Examinations cannot test everything schools attempt to teach, so any statewide examination will magnify the importance of what it measures in comparison with other goals. This magnification will be greater the more people care about the examination results. An examination that is taken seriously by the public or the profession can be a powerful mechanism for setting curriculum policy.

Curricular alignment is a process states may require local districts to carry out. It involves comparing the various curriculum instrumentalities at work in the schools of a local district—goals, curriculum guides, textbooks, tests, and so on—to ensure that they are consistent. States typically require school boards to certify the alignment process.

States do not require local schools to submit courses for approval and they do not police compliance with syllabi in any formal way. States do not accredit individual schools, but may require that public schools be accredited by a recognized professional accrediting association. Sometimes states do accredit individual programs, such as vocational education programs or early childhood programs. Guidelines for accreditation, like course syllabi, include detailed specifications of required and recommended features of the program.

Curriculum policy-making at the state level thus resembles in its basic outlines policy-making at national levels elsewhere in the world. It is carried on within a framework of official political institutions. The responsibilities of various state agencies for curriculum policy-making are established by law or tradition or both and change little from year to year. Policies adopted are put in writing in the legislation itself or in administrative rules. States have access to a full range of policy tools in curriculum matters.

Official Curriculum Policy-Making by Local School Districts

The local school district or local education agency (LEA) is the primary agency of government for American public schools. Federal and state policies, along with unofficial influences, converge on the local school board, local superintendent of schools, and the district office seeking acceptance as the official policy of the schools of the community.

We saw in the previous chapter how the 15,000 American LEAs are typically run. The highest LEA official with designated responsibility for curriculum matters is normally an Assistant or Associate Superintendent who reports directly to the Superintendent of Schools. Sometimes the responsibility is lodged one level lower in a Director or Coordinator of Curriculum who reports to an Assistant or Associate Superintendent for academic affairs. The size of the staff, often referred to as *central office staff* or COS, reporting to this official depends on the size of the district. This central office curriculum staff is divided among nearly as many areas of expertise as there are staff members: elementary, middle school, and secondary; every subject taught; every category of student including gifted, handicapped, delinquent, poor, college-bound; and various special programs—funded federally, by the state or locally—operating in the district. These staff members may be called supervisors, directors, coordinators, leaders, or by other titles, and several levels of assistants and associates may be recognized.

Central office curriculum staff tend to have a broad spectrum of duties within their assigned area of responsibility. The duties of a supervisor of secondary English, for example, might include all of the following: observe and rate teachers for purposes of certification and promotion; offer in-service education for teachers; prepare a grant proposal seeking state or federal funding for a special district project in English; serve on committees appointed by the Superintendent to investigate a possible problem with English teaching in the district; order books and supplies for English classes throughout the city; advise teacher committees doing curriculum revision and textbook selection; draft a policy statement on remedial reading programs in the district for consideration by superiors and the board; implement district plans for revising the writing curriculum; review test scores of students from the various high schools in the district and confer with principals and department chairs about them; and carry out informal surveys and studies of conditions in English classes.

Some LEAs delegate most of the authority for curriculum decisions to individual schools. Others retain central office control of curriculum matters. Decentralized districts oversee and coordinate the programs of local schools and save money by buying textbooks, curriculum materials, and supplies in larger quantities. When LEAs retain control of curriculum matters, the central office becomes the focus of efforts from within and outside the community to influence the curriculum of local schools. When textbooks are selected centrally for the whole district, salespeople from textbook publishers visit the central office and make their presentations to central office staff, rather than visiting each school and speaking with the principal, department chairs, and teachers. Notices of new state policies trigger district planning, rather than being copied and forwarded to principals. Citizen complaints about the curriculum are directed to the central office rather than to individual schools. And so on.

Except in the very largest districts, face-to-face communication is the rule within LEAs, and between LEAs and principals or teachers. Between LEAs and state and federal agencies, memos and reports are inevitable and ubiquitous, but even they often function either as a formal statement of something already discussed informally or else as a stimulus for later discussion. Those who work for local school districts usually know one another and maintain a social relationship in addition to their formal organizational relationship. Similarly, officials in LEAs usually know their communities well and in detail. They are likely to know personally those citizens who concern themselves with school affairs. LEA officials are likely to be very familiar with such important aspects of a community as educational aspirations, expectations, and achievements of parents and students, and community traditions of support for various types and levels of education.

Greater intimacy between LEA and community makes local policy different in important ways from policy at higher levels. Local districts are capable of much more finely differentiated policies than are state and federal agencies, and they are also subject to closer and more direct responses from their clientele. It is one thing to impose a strict curricular requirement for high school graduation on the faceless multitudes in a large state. It is quite another to impose that requirement while sitting across the desk from the parents of a student in danger of failing to meet it. It is one thing to design a generic curriculum in English for the schools of a state and quite another to design a curriculum well-suited to the teachers and students in one local school district.

Schools and classrooms are the primary arenas in which policy is implemented—when it *is* implemented. For this reason LEAs, in contrast to Federal and state agencies, need to be considered as both policy-makers and policy implementors. LEAs, unless they choose to delegate the role to local schools, form the crucial link between policy-making and policy implementation, playing key roles in both endeavors.

Areas Commonly Subject to District Policy

The division of responsibility between LEAs and individual schools is highly variable. Adjacent districts in the same state may function in completely different ways, depending on local tradition and the views of boards and superintendents. Staple forms of district curriculum policy are:

1. Statements of philosophy and aims
2. Structural specifications of such matters as overall curriculum organization; entrance, promotion, and graduation criteria; the school calendar, and so on
3. Courses of study
4. Curriculum materials selection
5. Special projects and programs
6. Policies required to implement state and federal mandates

Policies in these areas nearly always require approval by the local board of education.

In addition, active LEAs are likely to have policies governing:

district-wide examinations
textbook adoptions, K–12, all subjects
student placement and grouping
preferred methods of instruction
grading
homework

LEAs also take a variety of other actions that indirectly do a great deal to shape the curriculum of their schools, such as:

hiring of new teachers
assignment of teachers to schools
appointment of administrative staff of both local schools and the central office
setting pupil-teacher ratios to be maintained
construction of school facilities
in-service education of teachers
study leave, sabbatical
supervision, personnel monitoring, and evaluation

In recent years, LEAs find themselves increasingly subject to regulations from state and federal agencies and from unofficial outside agencies such as accrediting associations, test makers, and colleges and universities. The curriculum structures they adopt must not segregate students on racial, religious, or ethnic grounds, even unintentionally. Curriculum materials and courses of study must reflect the contributions of all such groups fairly and nonstereotypically. The public expects increasingly more sophisticated programs for dealing with special educational problems—handicapped students, poor students, students whose native language is not English, potential dropouts, potential illiterates, gifted and talented students, vocationally oriented students, and so on almost endlessly. Specialized programs for students who have trouble profiting from the standard school program are more costly than a single common program would be. LEAs are forced to seek additional funds to create and maintain them. Since funds are frequently available from state and local governments to support programs for special populations, LEAs apply for grants. More and more, special local projects consist of implementing generic programs some agency is subsidizing in hopes of widespread local adoption. Yet every application for funds for a special program seems to include stipulations that reduce local options. Central office staff spend more time and energy seeking grants and finding ways to achieve local goals while complying with the rules of the granting agency. Sometimes it seems as though it is more important for LEAs to please these outside agencies than their own clientele. When the local community is aroused and active on an educational issue, however, no LEA can resist, regardless of the strength of more distant pressures.

Unofficial Curriculum Policy-Making in the American System

Much of the real action in curriculum change occurs outside the official framework of federal, state, and local policy-making. In particular, the initiative for curriculum change ordinarily originates outside the formal institutions responsible for official curriculum policy. It normally comes from advocates organized to develop, propound, and secure acceptance of the change. For officials who must represent all the citizens of their jurisdiction to act as rabid partisan advocates for a course of action opposed by some constituents exposes them to danger of political reprisal. But it is accepted that private citizens who support an idea will organize and campaign for its acceptance. Advocacy groups can maintain effort on behalf of the idea for years when it is ignored or out of favor officially, awaiting a more propitious turn of events—a *Sputnik,* civil unrest, or a changing of the political guard. Then they are ready with ideas and plans and reasons why their proposals are needed.

National curriculum reform movements are probably the single most important mechanism for curriculum change, and clearly the most prominent. Their ultimate origins are impossible to trace but they first surface publicly in books or articles by advocates of reform, or major news stories about them. In the case of Progressive Education, the series of muckraking articles by Joseph Mayer Rice, the Boston physician turned educational reformer, usually referred to by the title of one of them, "The Spelling Grind," brought Progressive ideas and reforms to the public eye. In the case of the post-*Sputnik* reforms, published criticisms of schools by Arthur Bestor and Admiral Hyman Rickover were influential. Open education sprang on the public scene in the form of a series of books by John Holt, Edgar Z. Friedenberg, Neil Postman, and others critical of the authoritarianism and ritualistic ineffectiveness of public school practices. The compensatory education reforms that culminated in the Elementary and Secondary Education Act of 1967 were a direct outgrowth of the civil rights struggles of the period that dominated headlines for years and that affected schools more and sooner than any other institution of the society. In each case the initiative for the change came from organized advocacy groups. They achieved success as reform movements when their ideas gained public acceptance and their proposals were translated into legislative programs that received support from professional and government leaders.

The Institutionalization of Reform

In recent years initiation of reform movements by unofficial partisan advocates has come to be an institutionalized feature of the American curriculum influence system. Individual advocates and organized advocacy groups have developed close personal and professional ties with the officials and agencies responsible for policy in their area of interest. The official agency comes to regard these persons and organizations as allies in their common task of serving this particular educational need. They share information and opinions. The advocates carry out tasks indistinguishable from agency staff work—surveys, investigations of particular cases, drafting statements for inclusion in official speeches, and so on. The agency comes to depend on their services. The agency also comes to regard them as representing the interests of those they most directly serve. Thus, advocates of education for the handicapped come to represent the interests of the handicapped, and advocates of compensatory education are accepted as representing the interests of poor and minority families. In this capacity the advocates recommend people to serve on committees, react informally to early drafts of policy statements, and are generally treated as a convenient indicator of how the clients feel on any given issue. Such developments have been noticed in all areas of government social service and have been aptly characterized as the *institutionalization of reform.*

Thus, national curriculum reform movements are a blend of official and unofficial action, with the initiative coming primarily from unofficial sources. This melding is probably inevitable in view of the common interests of officials and advocates and the way they complement one another's strengths. The advocates have usually been around longer than the government appointees, have considerable political clout by virtue of the numbers of votes they represent and the influential voices allied with them, often have an inside track on foundation support for demonstration projects, and may include among their number the nation's most recognized authorities on the subject. The agencies have official authority but can only exercise it with widespread political support and they cannot campaign for this support themselves. When officials and advocates hold similar views about the shortcomings of the present curriculum and the changes needed, close informal collaboration is virtually inevitable.

To be successful in drawing official agencies into a reform effort, advocacy groups must maintain a strong impression of consensus among as many interested parties as possible and maintain the support of public opinion, as well. If a public official who is being pressed to adopt a policy on early education discovers that the member of Congress who chairs the relevant subcommittee opposes it or that the NEA and AFT are lukewarm to it or that organized parent groups were not consulted about it, that official would be foolhardy to take immediate action. Organization is essential to success in efforts to influence official agencies. Coalitions must be formed and maintained if official action is to be forthcoming. Serious organized opposition or open public controversy are, in themselves, usually enough to prevent official action.

Sometimes reformers ignore the entire policy apparatus and try instead to persuade teachers, students, and parents directly through books, articles, and publicity in public and professional media. The de-schooling movement and open education followed essentially this strategy. When it succeeds, this strategy leaves the reform vulnerable to decay or reversal once it becomes old news. We do not know how many participants may continue to practice it, but new converts drop off dramatically.

Nor are full-scale reform movements the only recourse of unofficial advocacy groups. They are the heavy weapons to be called up when the time is right. Many skirmishes must first be fought with lighter weapons. A foundation can be persuaded to fund a study of the schools, perhaps by a prominent and respected educator, such as James Conant, former president of Harvard University, or John Goodlad, Dean of the School of Education at UCLA, or by a talented senior reporter such as Martin Mayer or Charles Silberman. A new coalition may be formed, such as the Joint Council on Economic Education, which unites business, labor, and professional organizations advocating the teaching of economics in the schools, or the National Task Force on Education for Economic Growth, which consists of governors of 11 states and 17 other members representing business, academia, and labor, and which strives to develop a consensus on the changes demanded in our public schools. Such a group can keep up a constant stream of publicity, initiate curriculum development efforts, and coordinate efforts in the political arena. Perhaps demonstration projects can be mounted in a prominent school. The possibilities for change and reform are limited only by the imagination of the organizers.

Quasi-Official Curriculum Regulators

Other forms of unofficial policy-making take place quietly and routinely, but not less effectively, behind the scenes. Four prominent instances include: publishers of curriculum materials, including the test makers; colleges and universities, through their entrance requirements; private, voluntary accrediting agencies; and professional organizations. These groups are at work year in and year out, usually without much publicity. Their actions influence the curricula of nearly every school in important ways. They are normally forces for stability and for the preservation of traditional standards, but from time to time, in response to urgent, widespread dissatisfaction, they make changes—subtle changes of emphasis or a small addition or deletion—that then produce adjustments in schools and classrooms around the nation. Consider the following examples.

- In the late 1960s textbook publishers, under pressure from advocacy groups, developed a voluntary industry code governing the fair and nonstereotyped depiction of females and all racial, ethnic, and religious groups in textbooks. Whatever message was subliminally conveyed by the former policy was suddenly and dramatically reversed, with who knows what effects, but undeniably reversed, virtually overnight.
- When colleges dropped their foreign language requirements in the 1960s, fewer high school students elected these subjects. Later, when schools faced the necessity for funding cutbacks in the 1970s, many small classes in foreign languages were dropped.
- Accrediting agencies have consistently advocated a comprehensive secondary school curriculum that includes programs and courses catering to all segments of the student population. This position doubtlessly contributed to the proliferation of elective programs and courses in high schools that in turn shunted more and more students from the traditional academic core subjects.
- When a public demand for a return to basic skills instruction was being heard everywhere in the mid-1970s, the National Council of Teachers of Mathematics urged its members, who include most of the mathematics teachers in the country, not to relax their pursuit of problem-solving and other higher-order skills in a rush to cater to the public's demands for the mathematics of checkbook-balancing and change-making.

None of these agencies is legally authorized to make official curriculum policy, yet each of them wields power over a vital leverage point in the curriculum determination process.

So, even though nobody elected these people to control the curriculum, and even though they are not mentioned in laws or constitutions, they do exercise effective control over their own decisions, and these do influence local curricula. They constitute a kind of quasi-official policy-making and another type of blending of unofficial and official agencies.

WHY THE AMERICAN SYSTEM WORKS: NEGOTIATED DESIGN

That the American curriculum influence system can work at all seems improbable, it is so complicated, irrational, disjointed, open, and unpredictable. Yet there is a perspective from which the American system makes sense. The argument of this section is that the entire process can be thought of as a way for the contending parties who share authority for curriculum decisions to negotiate their differences. The parties to the negotiations are the many interested individuals and agencies mentioned previously as playing official, quasi-official, or unofficial roles in the curriculum influence system. The negotiations take place in many arenas, including the meetings of various official agencies at federal, state, and local levels and where quasi-official and unofficial decisions are made that affect the curriculum. Each party to the negotiations may choose which decisions to try to influence. Frequent participants tend to choose certain arenas regularly, those that make decisions of most direct concern to them. The ultimate arenas are the classrooms of the nation.

The parties have their separate goals, of course, which may be generically described as controlling some aspect of the curriculum of local schools and classrooms throughout the country (or state or district). They succeed in this goal when their views prevail in what actually happens in classrooms. All parties share the common goal of achieving a workable curriculum. The negotiations themselves succeed when the parties agree on a policy sufficiently to provide schools and classrooms with what they need (coordination, resources, legitimation) to sustain a curriculum. Not all contending parties need to cooperate actively, but their efforts to oppose the policy must not be strong enough to prevent its being carried out. The negotiations fail when there is not enough agreement to permit the state or district to take common action. Individual schools and classrooms may then offer whatever program they can, but they must operate without whatever they had hoped to obtain in the negotiations—usually resources, legitimacy, or coordination. In the worst case, schools will be unable to offer any curriculum that satisfies enough of its major interest groups, and controversy will continue. Usually, schools faced with a negotiating stalemate will resort to some temporary expedient, such as offering options that permit each interested party to choose what they prefer while a lasting resolution of the dispute is sought. All negotiated settlements are temporary, though, pending another round of negotiations in the same or another arena. Box 9-6 offers an example.

Box 9-7 shows some of the major parties to curriculum negotiations, the issues with which they are usually most concerned, what they want and what they have to offer.

The results of negotiations may be embodied in official actions, such as laws or regulations. That they *could* be enacted demonstrates a sufficiency of agreement, for the time being, at least, and among the parties active in this particular round of negotiations in these particular arenas. If enough other interested groups object to

■
BOX 9-6   An Example of Negotiated Design

Bidwell and Friedkin studied what happened in local school systems in Michigan when the governor demanded a ten percent budget cut (Tyack, Lowe, and Hansot 1984). When they analyzed how schools allocate staff, the investigators found that about 40 percent of districts had simply reassigned teachers to schools in proportion to student enrollment (an even-handed strategy), while 30 percent left proportionately more teachers in schools where students were not performing well (a compensatory strategy), and another 30 percent allocated teachers disproportionately to schools in which students were already performing above average (a rich-get-richer strategy). Exploratory case studies of individual districts revealed why local districts responded to the same external policy event in such distinct ways. The investigators discovered that this decision followed from the distinct political cultures in the three local communities.

> The city that provided additional teachers for the neediest students had a long tradition of leaders who shared a redistributive conception of public education. The district that assigned more teachers to the high-achieving schools was marked by conflict between groups in which the richest and most powerful faction won. The third case was a large suburb that lacked the "good works" ideology found in the first and the spoils system of the second. (Tyack, Lowe, and Hansot 1984, 224)

In this instance, the state made the decision that fell within the scope of its authority and that protected its primary interest—a ten percent budget cut—while the districts made other decisions within their authority—distribution of the cuts in services among schools. No doubt each school within the three districts also adapted to the district decisions differently.

The changes in educational programs that eventually result from this state policy change will not have been determined by any one policy decision, but rather by an interaction of different decisions made by different agencies at different levels.

the policy, other negotiations would ensue that could overturn the policy or render it ineffective. Results of negotiations can also be embodied in the actions of quasi-official and unofficial agencies. Once again, their enactment testifies to the attainment of sufficient agreement among the parties contending in that arena, and, once again, this result can be reversed or rendered effective by later negotiations in other arenas. Generally speaking, the door is opened for unofficial policy by the deliberate insufficiency of official policy. Schools and teachers are forced to look elsewhere for the resources, legitimacy, and coordination they need. Unofficial agencies are only too happy to help in exchange for the opportunity to influence local curricula.

If they are to affect the curriculum, the results of negotiations must eventually find their way to classrooms. Official actions arrive at the school and classroom door most commonly in the form of frames, as we have seen in previous chapters. Provided they stay within the frames they inherit from higher authorities, principals and teachers are free to exercise their judgment and discretion, subject to whatever

BOX 9-7   Some Parties to Curricular Negotiations in Various Arenas: What They Control and What They Need

In classrooms

Party	*Controls*	*Needs*
teachers	instructional planning, classroom activities, grading standards for students' work	time, energy, knowledge, recognition, curriculum materials, cooperation from students
students	cooperation, voluntary time, energy, attention	satisfactory grades, diplomas, good recommendations, preparation for success in job or further school

In schools

principal	course offerings, school schedule, teacher in-service, funds for innovation, authorization for innovations, funds for curriculum materials, access to community	teacher compliance, funds for innovation, ideas, knowledge

District

superintendent	graduation requirements, textbook selection, official curriculum guides, authority for district curriculum innovations, course offerings, overall curriculum structure	compliance from lower levels, funds for innovation, political support, expertise

State

legislature	legislative authority funds	political support, a program to sponsor, expertise
state superintendent	rules and regulations, graduation requirements, state curriculum guides, expertise, authority	compliance from lower levels, support from public

(continued)

BOX 9-7   Some Parties to Curricular Negotiations in Various Arenas; What They Control and What They Need (Continued)

National		
secretary of education	proposes federal budget, authority of position	political support, compliance from states, districts, expertise
Congress	Legislative authority, funds for innovation	support from constituents, expertise
Federal courts	a suit to decide	compliance from executive branch

---

local forms of oversight may apply. Of course, a higher authority may enact mandates that leave no discretion to principals or teachers. Between levels, the main issues are securing compliance from levels below and gaining as much discretionary authority as possible from levels above.

Policy may make its way to schools and classrooms through other quasi-official and unofficial channels. For the most part these channels exist because of curricular needs that are not being met in school and in the classroom. By satisfying these needs, any individual or agency can attain a degree of influence over the curriculum there. Sometimes what is supplied secures the desired control directly, as when a group supplies free curriculum materials that reflect their views. Sometimes promises must be extracted from the beneficiaries, as when a foundation agrees to provide funding for an experimental curriculum only on the condition that it be evaluated using standardized achievement tests. Some common quasi-official and unofficial channels for influencing the curricula of schools and classrooms include accreditation, testing, conditions attached to funds or other forms of support, design or selection of plans and materials, provision of human resources, especially teacher preparation, pre-service and in-service, endorsement by prestigious individuals and organizations, and publication of educational and pedagogical ideas that set the agenda and terms of discussion. The focus of official policy-making tends to be the local school district. Unofficial matters are under more or less continuous negotiation at unpredictable locations. The focus of unofficial negotiations tends to be the teacher/classroom and school/principal.

Achieving success in policy negotiations generally requires building a coalition that will support the proposal at various important niches and levels. Forging a coalition that can secure favorable action on enough of these sorts of fronts to realize one's policy proposal requires great organizational skill on the part of persons in leadership positions. Such organizing efforts must be sustained for years and they can be quite time-consuming. Qualified leadership, therefore, is a scarce and precious commodity in curriculum policy-making.

Schools stand the best chance of garnering resources and attention from outside agencies during times of great public concern about education, hence the predisposition toward crisis policy-making. However, such crises cannot be sustained for more than a few years, at most, and so educational reform takes place in cycles or waves, each lasting a few years and then seemingly disappearing. Reform without an injection of new outside resources requires a reallocation of resources internally. These resources are generally in high demand and are allocated in accordance with intricate, face-to-face bargaining in which teachers, administrators, powerful local lay leaders, organized groups of parents and students participate in various ways at the various levels. Although outside agencies may influence these internal negotiations indirectly, for example by establishing a climate of opinion or prevailing view through publicity or sponsorship of innovative demonstration projects, they hold a much weaker bargaining position here than in public policy arenas.

The interactions among the many actors, arenas, and decisions can become quite complex and produce unexpectedly powerful results. For example, when a committee of teachers and parents in Detroit in the 1960s documented racial and gender bias in textbook illustrations and persuaded the district to threaten to boycott textbooks with biased illustrations, other districts joined in the chorus of demands for better illustrations and together they influenced textbook publishers to make changes that affected classrooms throughout the nation. Complex interactions can also produce surprisingly weak results. For example, for at least five decades we have seen vigorous efforts from many quarters to encourage teachers to individualize their classroom instruction, with very little result beyond the primary grades. In spite of widespread support for the idea from teachers, public, and prestigious lay and professional leaders, it founders at several critical decision-points: it makes more demands on teachers' time and energy, it defeats efforts at standardization of programs and outcomes, more and more costly curriculum materials are required, and the skills teachers must acquire to make it work are more difficult to teach and are therefore not widely adopted in teacher education programs. Box 9-8 shows some of the factors that make for success in curriculum negotiations.

In short, national curriculum policy for the American education system emerges from a process of negotiated design. Instead of choosing national authorities who then design the curriculum of the education system, Americans let representatives of major interest groups negotiate the design of the curriculum directly. In this way, Americans escape the threat of a curriculum czar, but they do not achieve the cherished vision of local autonomy in curriculum matters. As we have seen, the powerful interests constantly seeking to influence school curricula do not respect local district boundaries. They resort to direct action. They turn to the organizations to which they belong, almost all of which are national in scope. A common national curriculum emerges from the struggle among these interests. Local schools, then, are subject to an impersonal, intangible, unaccountable authority. And in trying to insulate curriculum matters from partisan politics, Americans have

■
BOX 9-8   Factors Determining What Competing Proposals Achieve the Status of
          Curriculum Policy By Level

Level	Success Factor
National	extensive favorable media coverage
	complete curriculum and plan for reform available
	convincing rationale, no strong counter arguments
	seriousness, urgency of the educational problem
	seriousness, urgency of the national problem
	support of an organized political constituency
	support of leaders in power (President, Secretary of Education, Congressional committee chairs, and so on)
	broad support across a wide political spectrum
	weak, unorganized political opposition
	broad spectrum of nation seen as benefiting
	prestigious, able, active, organized professional leadership
	widespread professional support
	weak, unorganized professional opposition
State	same factors as for nation also relevant for states
	political and professional leadership critical
	funding more likely to be the key issue
	political activity more overt, standard political techniques used, established interest groups
	ability to move state department of education
	bureaucracy critical
District	support of Superintendent, key staff
	broad, deep support among principals, teachers
	weak public, professional opposition
	availability of external funding
	urgency, importance of local problem to be solved
School	support of principal
	presence of able professional leadership
	support of teaching staff involved
	weak public, professional opposition
	availability of external funding
	professional status accruing to pioneers
Classroom	understanding and support of classroom teacher
	ability of teacher to put curriculum into practice
	impact on teacher time, energy, effort, rewards
	positive student response
	availability of curriculum plans and materials
	consistency with preexisting routines
	professional status accruing to pioneers

driven those who wanted to influence their schools' curricula to seek other avenues of influence. The results have been the emergence of the system of negotiated design, which is a highly political struggle—more politics in curriculum matters rather than less.

JUST HOW WELL DOES THE AMERICAN SYSTEM WORK?

Despite appearances, then, the American system of negotiated curriculum design can, in principle, bring the benefits some people seek from policy to a decentralized national education system. How well does it work, though? Let us briefly examine the apparent strengths and limitations of negotiated design to the extent that they can be inferred from recent history.

First, the compliments. The American system of curriculum determination deserves good marks for producing workable policies and for embodying American ideals of governance. Local schools start on time and run smoothly. When curriculum policies fail, the school as an institution does not suffer. Credit for this achievement seems to belong to local school officials who place the highest priority on preserving stability and avoiding disruptions. Local schools freely adapt externally imposed changes in policy and achieve a result that, whatever its merits in other respects, fits the change smoothly into existing school routines.

Also, local governance of schools suits the American tradition of grassroots participative democracy very well. Interest group politics is a more recent tradition, less honored but much practiced, and thoroughly American. Despite recent encroachments from state and federal agencies and unofficial influences, local school systems retain a great deal of effective control over what happens in schools and classrooms, and so we must credit these arrangements with maintaining a considerable degree of local autonomy.

We should credit the American system, too, for the remarkable extent to which the curriculum of the American public school reflects the interests of an extremely diverse population. Rural schools can have a different curriculum than urban or suburban ones. While they may not reflect rural interests perfectly, they usually do so to a greater extent than is common around the world. We find agricultural education courses and programs, Future Farmer clubs, and other curricular and extracurricular activities adapted to the local social, economic, and political situation. Similarly, we find sex education programs in only those schools whose communities support them. The American curriculum influence system deserves high marks for promoting local diversity and choice of curricula within the framework of a single nationwide institution.

It also deserves credit for fostering a high rate of curricular innovation. No other country in the world can boast even a fraction of the curricular experiments that have poured out of the American system with remarkable regularity for virtually this entire century. Since the 1920s, at least, the United States has been the world's foremost source of curriculum innovation. This does not mean that other countries have contributed little—every country in Europe can boast of important curriculum innovations—but none of these countries has produced even a small fraction of the new programs in every field, at every age, reflecting every bias and orientation, that have been developed in this country almost continuously now for more than half a century. No doubt the vigorous open competition for curricular adoptions in local school districts is responsible in part for this cornucopia.

However, some serious criticisms can be leveled at negotiated design as an approach to curriculum policy-making. Few would claim that American curriculum policies rest on fully informed consideration of their merits. The system is geared to operate politically; the substance of the matter is important mainly as a means of persuading the uncommitted, even in the professional press, where one would normally expect to find objective, rigorous analysis, rhetoric dominates. Hessler (1977) found that articles published in educational journals on the subject of individualization of instruction were mainly persuasive appeals for this innovation. Advantages claimed for it far outnumbered mentions of possible disadvantages. Out of more than one hundred published articles, only one gave as thorough a treatment of the possible negatives as of the positives. By comparison, a sample of medical literature on heart bypass surgery was much more balanced. Virtually every medical article at least mentioned the major possible drawbacks of this operation, even when the article as a whole advocated bypass surgery.

The system rewards believers who shape curriculum policies that embody widely held values and who then campaign politically to have them adopted by local schools. Debate between supporters and opponents is simply irrelevant. The point is not to convince some judge, jury, or attentive audience that your policy is better than theirs, but to mobilize support for your course of action. Get enough people interested, build a credible national movement, and you win the support you need.

The professional press in education seldom functions as a forum for discussion of the merits of potential curriculum policies. One can find thorough airings of pros and cons in research reports in obscure journals, in testimony before Congressional committees, or in position papers commissioned from scholars or experts. And there is some reason to believe that this debate influences legislation, although the political clout of an interest group undoubtedly weighs more heavily with a legislature than any arguments or evidence could. So, the system of negotiated design earns low marks for producing informed, considered policies.

How much of the blame for the relative decline in academic achievement of American students over the past decade, as compared with students in the rest of the world, should be laid at the feet of the curriculum influence system? It is plausible to suppose that the easing of standards in basic academic subjects and the proliferation of nonacademic or quasi-academic courses have had some part in creating the problem. There has not been a large local constituency for upholding high academic standards in most communities, and ambitious superintendents have not been able to make a national reputation by maintaining and upgrading a solid core of academic subjects while rejecting innovative course proposals. (Both situations may be changing.)

We must also weigh both the necessity for the massive curriculum reform movements of the last twenty years and their failures against the American system of influencing curriculum. It is a sign of institutional pathology when a society repeatedly circumvents the institutions it has established for a given purpose and resorts to intervention by the general government. Things are out of hand when every other session of Congress is faced with a crisis in education requiring new legislation and new programs. And if these programs, created at great political and financial cost, then fail to alleviate the crises, something is dreadfully amiss. That is exactly what has happened in the United States since 1960. This suggests that the institutions of general government are the only mechanism people believe can move American schools to respond to urgent national priorities. Whether true or not, the perception on the part of large and influential segments of the population damns the current system.

Probably the most powerful single piece of evidence that can be brought forward to support an indictment of the American system of curriculum formation is the appalling series of defeats that have befallen every major national curriculum improvement initiative undertaken since World War II. These enormous national efforts to improve the curriculum of American schools failed to bring about substantial improvements in any aspect of the schools' performance. One of the closest students of the phenomenon wrote of:

> . . . the generally melancholy picture of how little of the reform agenda of the recent past has been achieved. . . . Programs were planned, curriculum was developed, teaching/learning units were packaged, teachers were trained, and the results were frustrating, uneven, unexpected, and temporary. . . . Most educators realize that the amount and pace of change has fallen far short of initial expectations. (Mann 1978, xi)

Looking back at the impact of the federally sponsored science curriculum improvement efforts, Wayne W. Welch, a sympathetic participant in these reforms, concluded that

> The educational system is extremely stable and efforts to change it have little effect. . . . In spite of the expenditures of millions of dollars and the involvement of some of the most brilliant scientific minds, the science classroom of today is little different from one of 20 years ago. . . . While there may be new books on the shelves and clever gadgets in the storage cabinets, the day-to-day operation of the class remains largely unchanged. (Welch 1979, 303)

Achievement test scores continued to decline over the two decades when the reforms were running at their peak. American students' tested academic achievement continued to lag behind those of students from Russia, Japan, and several European countries. Huge gaps remained between rich and poor and between children of the mainstream and minority children. The picture with respect to the massive compensatory education reforms of the late 1960s and early 1970s is similarly bleak. In both cases, there were elements of the policy that could be shown to work when properly implemented, but the policies as a whole did not bring about substantial improvements in the nation's schools.

As for managing change well, the record of the past two decades is depressing. The prevailing pattern has been a partisan political struggle for power and influence in which the winners dismantle the programs of their predecessors and replace them with their own. Genuine achievements are thrown out along with excesses and failures and new mistakes replace old ones. For example, some of the approaches to mathematics teaching developed in the post-*Sputnik* projects were valuable additions to the curriculum—emphasis on problem-solving, for example, and teaching about proof—while others—set theory, number bases other than ten, terminological fastidiousness—were less fundamental. Yet all were jettisoned when the new math fell out of favor. Math programs were developed that emphasized drill and practice on number facts, balancing checkbooks, and other everyday arithmetic skills. Well-managed curriculum change would have retained the strengths of the previous program, jettisoned its weaker parts and built the new practical math programs on that foundation. It would be difficult to make the case that curriculum change has been well-managed in the United States.

Conflict in this system is confined largely to a struggle for power. Each group strives to put its own supporters in positions of power and influence and then use supporters' time in office to dismantle the opposition's programs and install its own. Every curriculum reform of the past two decades has seen its period in the limelight succeeded by a period of backlash in which most of its programs are rescinded and others built on contrary assumptions put in their place. This is not constructive conflict management. Tactics of avoiding substantive engagement with the opposition work temporarily, but the original issue remains and, if it is serious, will emerge again. Conflict avoidance works badly when conflicts are basic, enduring, and pervasive.

Summary

The American arrangements for curriculum policy formation are flexible, responsive to local concerns, and generally effective in producing workable local policies. They are free of domination by distant central authorities, yet they permit participation by official and unofficial agencies on a voluntary basis. They accommodate a wide variety of local circumstances and local customs and yet the curricula they produce are quite uniform nationwide, certainly uniform enough so that high mobility seldom creates serious problems of adjustment. Wide participation tends to result in a continually shifting balance of powers among contending interest groups, and thus avoids domination by any one. Open, divisive conflict is generally avoided, in spite of serious differences in values and priorities among the population.

On the other hand, the American arrangements are of questionable effectiveness in bringing about sustained curriculum improvements on a large-scale. Fads seem to come and go, but little lasting change is achieved. The baroque intricacies of the policy formation arrangements limit effective participation to those who know the ropes or who have the resources to hire others who do. Issues are seldom debated openly with a view toward finding a mutually satisfactory course of action. Rather, each side plays to its constituents and struggles for a political victory that will implement its values and priorities. Both processes and results are highly variable from state-to-state and locality-to-locality. On balance, the centralized systems of other countries appear to have achieved a better record over the past quarter-century in bringing about planned, permanent, well-considered curriculum change. American schools might improve if a way could be found to achieve more considered policies about curriculum, better managed curriculum change processes, and more constructive resolutions of conflicts.

QUESTIONS FOR STUDY

1. Select features of today's school curriculum and speculate on features of contemporary culture that created and still sustain each.

2. Can curriculum changes play an important role in bringing about fundamental cultural changes? Think of as many examples as you can of curriculum changes that have helped to transform the surrounding culture.

3. Visit a school with a population largely drawn from a culture different from the mainstream culture in your area. Do you notice differences in the curriculum in this school as compared to the others you know? How are the continuities and differences you see related to the culture and its relation to the mainstream culture?

4. In what way is the curriculum "a matter of cultural life and death"? Can you give examples of curriculum changes that some in your community would regard as a threat to their culture?

5. Describe the curriculum influence system of your state. Include quasi-official and unofficial influences as well as the official policy-making apparatus. Make a diagram like Box 9-2 to describe the interactions of various influences on the curriculum of schools in your state. Compare and contrast it with the national system.

6. What national curriculum policies exist today in the United States? Should there be additional curriculum policies?

7. Choose one of the following areas of curriculum reform and identify the special interest groups most directly involved. Describe the struggles likely to ensue as efforts are made to implement reforms in this area.

   global education
   mandatory science and math for all students, K–12
   high academic standards
   environmental education
   drug abuse prevention
   educational technology
   suicide prevention
   peace education
   values education

8. Critically assess the American curriculum influence system as described in this chapter from the standpoint of one committed to local control of curriculum.

9. How do you think the American curriculum influence system could be improved? Prepare a plausible scenario describing how these improvements could be initiated and brought to fruition.

10. Suppose a state adopted the policy of replacing traditional high school subjects with larger functional categories such as home and family living, the world of work, and citizenship. Describe how implementation of this policy would affect the schools of that state. What do you conclude about states' independence in major areas of curriculum policy?

RECOMMENDED READING

Many distinguished scholars have studied the history and politics of educational reform, but the self-conscious study of these phenomena as policies and policy-making is relatively recent. Concerted professional interest in curriculum as a field for policy arose, understandably, during the 1960s when the federal government mounted dozens of large-scale national curriculum reform projects. A decade later, when Michael Kirst and I wrote a review of the research literature on the topic (Kirst and Walker 1971), we could not find a single use of the term *policy* in the curriculum literature, although clearly most states and school districts had policies about curriculum matters. Most of the studies we found were either case studies of particular episodes of curriculum policy-making or studies of schools or school systems that included curriculum issues as a subtopic. The study of curriculum policy-making as a subject in its own right is therefore barely two decades old.

Those who want to pick up the subject at the beginning should read Kirst and Walker's "An Analysis of Curriculum Policy-Making" (1971), William L. Boyd's "The Changing Politics of Curriculum Policy-Making for American Schools" (1978), and Tyll Van Geel's paper, "The New Law of the Curriculum" (1979). The book, **Schools in Conflict** (1982) by Frederick Wirt and Michael Kirst, especially pages 277–312, "Growth of Federal Influence on Education," summarizes the early work on the subject.

Dale Mann's collection of readings, **Making Change Happen?** (1978) contains many seminal pieces reflecting on two decades of energetic efforts by governments and officials to make schools change. Michael Fullan's **The Meaning of Educational Change** (1982) reviews the literature quite comprehensively and in a way that makes his synthesis useful even to those who do not share his pessimism about the value of government intervention in schools. Arthur Wise (1979) criticizes attempts to improve the performance of the education system through legislation. Diane Ravitch (1983) and Tyack, Lowe and Hansot (1984) offer useful historical interpretations of recent efforts to reform the public schools; the articles are quite different, but both suggest caution and moderation of our aspirations.

Studies of the fate of individual curriculum reform efforts in the field are a rich source for learning about the strengths and limitations of policy in curriculum. Wayne W. Welch's retrospective article, "Twenty Years of Science Curriculum Development: A Look Back" (1979), is the most thorough treatment I have found of federally-sponsored curriculum projects. The National Science Foundation's **Panel Evaluation of 19 Pre-College Curriculum Development Projects** (1975) is a rich source of qualitative judgments by a wide range of interested persons. Suzanne Quick's unpublished dissertation (1977) is a gold mine of data on one project, the Biological Sciences Curriculum Study. The case studies of the impact of science curriculum improvement efforts on classrooms by Stake and Easley (1978) are helpful in understanding the impact of these federal curriculum policies on schools.

By far the most influential evaluation study of federal curriculum efforts has been the RAND study, reported in several volumes, the most relevant of which is Greenwood, Mann, and McLaughlin (1975). Their focus on the implementation problems of federal curriculum policies and their concept of **mutual adaptation** have proven to be fundamental to subsequent research and scholarship. McLaughlin's article, "Implementation as Mutual Adaptation: Change in Classroom Organization" in Mann (1978) is more easily accessible.

Another theme not prominent in earlier treatments of curriculum change and innovation is conflict. Ernest House deserves credit for calling attention to this theme in a powerful way in **The Politics of Innovation** (1974). The idea that the policy process is a form of extended negotiation is consistent with the concept of negotiated order identified with the sociologist Anselm Strauss (1978). See also Day and Day's review of negotiated order theory (1977). Richard Elmore (1978) makes bargaining the central concept in his analysis of the implementation of social programs. To my delight I discovered Bardach's **The Implementation Game: What Happens After a Bill Becomes a Law** (1977) after committing myself to the concept of negotiation. It takes seriously the idea that policy implementation is a game with rules, stakes, and the like for its various players.

REFERENCES

Bardach, Eugene. 1977. *The Implementation Game: What Happens After a Bill Becomes a Law.* Cambridge, MA: MIT Press.

Boyd, William L. 1978. The Changing Politics of Curriculum Policy-Making for American Schools. *Review of Educational Research* 48:577–628.

Day, M. L. and E. R. Day. 1977. A Review of Negotiated Order Theory: An Appreciation and a Critique. *The Sociological Quarterly* 18:126–142.

Doyle, Wayne J. 1978. A Solution in Search of a Problem: Comprehensive Change and the Jefferson Experimental Schools. (See Mann, 1978.)

Elmore, Richard F. 1978. Organizational Models of Social Program Implementation. (See Mann, 1978.)

Friedrich, Carl Joachim. 1963. *Man and His Government.* McGraw-Hill.

Fullan, Michael. 1982. *The Meaning of Educational Change.* N.Y.: Teachers College Press.

Green, Thomas F. 1980. *Predicting the Behavior of the Educational System.* Syracuse: Syracuse University Press.

Greenwood, Peter W., Dale Mann, and Milbrey W. McLaughlin. 1975. *Federal Programs Supporting Educational Change, Vol. III: The Process of Change.* Santa Monica: Rand.

Hessler, James. 1977. The Content of Arguments about the Individualization of Instruction. Stanford University: Unpublished Ph.D. Dissertation.

Holt, John. 1964. *How Children Fail.* N.Y.: Pitman.

Holt, John. 1968. *How Children Learn.* N.Y.: Delacorte.

House, Ernest R. 1974. *The Politics of Innovation.* Berkeley: McCutchan.

Kirst, Michael and Decker F. Walker. December 1971. An Analysis of Curriculum Policy-Making. *Review of Educational Research* 41:538–568.

Mann, Dale (ed.). 1978. *Making Change Happen?* N.Y.: Teachers College Press.

McLaughlin, Milbrey W. 1978. Implementation of ESEA Title I: A Problem of Compliance. (See Mann, 1978.)

McLaughlin, Milbrey W. 1978. Implementation as Mutual Adaptation: Change in Classroom Organization. (See Mann, 1978.)

National Science Foundation. 1975. *Panel Evaluation of 19 Pre-College Curriculum Development Projects.* Washington, D.C.: NSF, Directorate for Science Education.

Porter, David O., et al. 1973. *The Politics of Budgeting Federal Aid: Resource Mobilization by Local School Districts.* Beverley Hills: Sage Professional Paper in Administration and Policy Studies, 03–003.

Postman, Neil and Charles Weingartner. 1969. *Teaching as a Subversive Activity.* N.Y.: Delacorte.

Postman, Neil. 1979. *Teaching as a Conserving Activity.* N.Y.: Delacorte.

Quick, Suzanne K. 1977. Secondary Impacts of the Curriculum Reform Movement. Unpublished Ph.D. Dissertation, Stanford University.

Ravitch, Diane. 1983. *The Troubled Crusade: American Education, 1945–1980.* N.Y.: Basic Books.

Rice, Joseph Mayer. 1987. The Futility of the Spelling Grind. *The Forum* 23: 163–172.

Rickover, Hyman. 1959. *Education and Freedom.* N.Y.: Dutton.

Schaffarzick, Jon and Gary Sykes (eds.). 1979. *Value Conflicts and Curriculum Issues.* Berkeley: McCutchan.

Stake, Robert E. and Jack A. Easley. 1978. *Case Studies in Science Education (Vol. 2).* Washington, D.C.: United States Government Printing Office.

Strauss, Anselm. 1978. *Negotiations: Varieties, Contexts, Processes and Social Order.* San Francisco: Jossey-Bass.

Tyack, David, Robert Lowe, and Elizabeth Hansot. 1984. *Public Schools in Hard Times.* Cambridge, MA: Harvard University Press.

Van Geel, Tyll. 1979. The New Law of the Curriculum. (See Schaffarzick and Sykes, 1979.)

Welch, Wayne W. 1979. Twenty Years of Science Curriculum Development: A Look Back. *Review of Research in Education 7*. (David C. Berliner, ed.) Washington, D.C.: American Educational Research Association.

Wirt, Frederick and Michael Kirst. 1982. Growth of Federal Influence in Education. *Schools in Conflict*. Berkeley: McCutchan.

Wise, Arthur E. 1979. *Legislated Learning*. Berkeley: University of California Press.

PART IV
Curriculum Practice

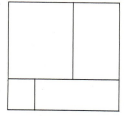

The qualities [mountaineering] requires are just those which I feel we all need today: perseverance and patience, a firm grip on realities, careful but imaginative planning, a clear awareness of the dangers but also of the fact that fate is what we make it and that the safest climber is he who never questions his ability to overcome all difficulties.

Dag Hammarskjold
Swedish diplomat, 1965

chapter 10

IMPROVING THE CLASSROOM CURRICULUM

One conclusion stands out clearly [from visits to more than 200 classrooms]: many of the changes we have believed to be taking place in schooling have not been getting into classrooms.

John Goodlad, M. Frances Klein, and associates 1970

PURPOSE OF THE CHAPTER

- to explore approaches to improving the classroom curriculum that reflect a deliberative orientation and that are consistent with the realities of classrooms, schools, and the American education system
- to show how the most important problems people encounter when they attempt to improve curricula in classrooms arise and how they can be addressed most effectively in light of the realities of classrooms

OUTLINE

Realizing a Curriculum in the Classroom

Changing a Classroom's Curriculum

Planning Classroom Activities

This chapter considers some of the problems encountered when people try to maintain and improve the quality of the curriculum actually offered in classrooms. People in many positions seek to influence what happens in classrooms, but teachers are the ones who are primarily responsible for the classroom curriculum; inevitably, then, this chapter will mainly be concerned with the curriculum work of teachers. Among the many types of curriculum problems teachers face three broad categories of problems stand out: 1) those encountered when teachers attempt to realize a standard curriculum plan in a particular classroom; 2) those encountered when teachers are presented with mandates, commands, or directives to change their classroom curriculum; and 3) those that arise when teachers make curriculum plans for other teachers. We will consider how teachers cope and might cope with these types of problems.

REALIZING A CURRICULUM IN THE CLASSROOM

Until a curriculum comes to life in the classroom, it remains only a plan and cannot affect what students learn. Whatever else may influence what students study and learn in school, the final, determinative steps are taken when teacher, student, and curriculum materials come together in the classroom.

As we saw in Chapter 7, a classroom is not merely an empty stage on which a teacher may realize any curriculum at all. Conditions in the classroom limit and direct what teachers and students can do. As we have seen, classroom interactions are teacher-centered, and almost exclusively verbal. Instruction is directed at the whole class, based on a textbook, and punctuated by frequent tests. This is the pattern called, variously, traditional teaching, the teacher-centered classroom, the recitation, or the conventional classroom. Curriculum plans that call for teachers and students to act in ways that are inconsistent with this pattern are unlikely to be carried out as intended unless accompanied by extraordinary efforts at retraining and reorienting teachers.

Realizing the curriculum is not something teachers do as a distinct and separate part of their work. Rather, virtually everything teachers do helps to realize their classroom's curriculum. Davis and McKnight give a hypothetical example that illustrates the intricate connections to be found among apparently distinct decisions in classrooms.

> One can attempt to restrict a mathematics curriculum to a sequence of undemanding tasks, done individually in workbooks. This leads to a quiet and orderly classroom, but, we suspect, implies limitations on the mathematical content that will be learned. . . . As the problems in a workbook are made more challenging, students will need more help from the teacher. This, at the least, will lead to many students wanting to see the teacher for help, which, in turn, means a need to wait, with attendant impatience and temptations to disorder. If the subject is genuinely profound, most students may be unable to learn it from independent reading, and class discussion may be necessary—but this means, in many cases, large group instruction. . . . (Davis and McKnight 1976, 216–217)

As we discuss some of the particulars of how the curriculum is realized in the classroom, keep in mind that the curriculum is an organic part of the pattern of the conventional classroom, not something influencing it from outside.

In considering how teachers realize curriculum plans, we shall be concerned not with the subtleties and the exquisite details of the art of teaching. These arts are vitally important to the success of teaching and of curriculum realization, but they depend so much on the particulars of the situation—the subject, the age and background of the students, the teacher's personality—that it would be difficult to say anything helpful about them in general. Rather, we will focus here on certain broad and basic aspects of teachers' work that are especially important in realizing curriculum plans in the classroom.

For this purpose, it helps to think of teaching as inducing students to participate in educationally valuable activities, whether these be as private as reflecting silently on what they read or as public as singing a song. It helps to think of classrooms as social settings in which students engage in educationally valuable activities under the teacher's direction. From this perspective the crucial things teachers do that realize a curriculum in the classroom happen when they plan classroom activities, when they introduce students to the curriculum in the first days and weeks of class, and when they continually adjust their plans during the course of the school year.

Curriculum Realization during Class Planning

Teachers typically make some sort of plans for their classes prior to the start of each academic year and then do detailed planning of units or lessons throughout the year. For convenience, teachers' class planning will be divided into three phases, although in practice these overlap:

- identify frames that apply to the class
- outline a curriculum plan for the entire course, including:
    major units of content
    main controlling purposes
    basic structure of the curriculum
    principal types of classroom activities
- develop detailed unit plans, including for each unit:
    list of goals and objectives
    list of important content items
    schedule of activities and assignments
    curriculum materials
    plans for lessons or activities
    tests.

Identify Frames Legally and ethically, teachers must answer for their curriculum decisions to several duly constituted authorities. Both the state and the profession certify teachers' professional competence, and the local school system employs teachers on behalf of a local community. These authorities specify certain aspects of the school program that all teachers are expected to realize in their classrooms. These frames, resulting from institutional decisions, determine whether there will be a classroom, how students and teachers will be selected, grouped, and matched in classrooms, how much time and what resources they will have to work with, and what the community expects from students and teachers. The decisions that establish these frames limit and direct what teacher and students do within the classroom, and in this way shape the classroom curriculum.

At an early point in planning, teachers need to find out exactly what frames govern their work in their classroom and to acknowledge these frames as constraints on their further planning. If the school system provides approved curriculum materials such as textbooks, workbooks, or supplementary materials, teachers must either plan to use these or else prepare alternative materials and get them approved. As we saw in Chapter 7, curriculum materials exert a powerful influence on the classroom curriculum by presenting information directly to students and also by influencing other choices teachers make. Various studies (Komoski 1976; McCutcheon 1980) have revealed that a great deal of what happens in classrooms (estimates range from one-half to over ninety percent) involves published instructional materials.

Most school systems also provide local curriculum guides that specify the content, purpose, and structure teachers are expected to use in their classes. Tests provided for use in the classroom are a special case of prescribed curriculum materials, one with a particularly important influence over the criteria teachers use to judge students' progress and mastery. Standardized tests administered to students by the school are important frames for teacher class planning.

When teachers believe that the frames that govern their classroom curriculum are substandard, harmful, limiting, or otherwise professionally objectionable, they face an ethical dilemma. If they follow the duly authorized curriculum, they betray their professional obligation to offer students the best education they can. If they offer a curriculum in their classroom that violates the governing frames established by the appropriate authorities, they betray obligations to the school system, the community, and the state. Teachers should try to resolve such dilemmas by working to change the objectionable frame or, at least, by securing official exemption from it.

When teachers deviate from the prescribed materials, with or without the blessing of school authorities, they make additional work for themselves. Teachers must find ways to present nonstandard content themselves or find or create materials of their own. Teachers must assume full ethical and legal responsibility for any materials they introduce into their classroom, whereas they are protected by the authority of the institution if they use the materials provided. On the other hand, school systems incur substantial costs if they try to force teachers to comply with frames they object to, perhaps the greatest of which is the loss of initiative and independence in their teaching staff.

Outline a Curriculum for the Year Once teachers have ascertained the frames that apply to their classroom curriculum, they can then make major decisions about content, purpose, and structure for their class with confidence that their plans will conform to official frames. Teachers typically plan a rough outline of the year's work at the beginning of the school year and then make more detailed plans for each week or for units of a few weeks' duration throughout the year. Curriculum experts generally recommend that planning begin with statements of purpose, or course objectives, but research indicates that teachers typically begin with lists of content to be covered (Zahorik 1975; Taylor 1970; Peterson, Marx, and Clark 1978; Clark and Yinger 1978; Yinger 1978). In order to be clear about their classroom curriculum, teachers eventually need to decide both what content they will present and what students should be able to do with the content (recall it, apply it, or explain why it is believed to be true, for example). At this early stage of global planning, though, precision of statement is not as important as it will later become. It is more important now to decide about inclusion of major content and purposes, about the relative emphasis to be given to those included, and about the basic organizing principles relating them to each other.

The major items of content to be included can simply be listed, as can the major goals of the course. The amount of time to be devoted to each item is one rough indicator of relative emphasis. The amount of content students must master in order to understand this item and the extent to which mastery of this item will affect further study are also indicators of how central the item is to the course. A schedule specifies how the purpose and content of a course will be organized over time. Relations among items of content must generally be described in ordinary language; they are usually more difficult to depict graphically. When the content and purposes of a course are only loosely related to one another, they can be organized in many different ways, but when the separate items have definite, established relationships that must be maintained, then organizational options are more limited. In the extreme case of a tightly structured body of content such as school mathematics, each objective of a course may be prerequisite to the next, all culminating in some single course objective, such as solving algebraic equations of the first and second degree.

Content whose inherent structure is not so tightly specified can often be organized in a great variety of ways. Posner and Rudnitsky in *Course Design* identify the following principles for sequencing topics within courses.

1. *World-related sequences,* such as those based on time, space, or physical attributes such as size or complexity.
2. *Concept-related sequences,* such as more basic ideas before other ideas that depend on them or more concrete ideas before more abstract ones.
3. *Inquiry-related sequences,* such as ones that follow the order of discovery of a principle.
4. *Learning-related sequences,* such as easy before hard, familiar before strange.

5. *Utilization-related sequences,* such as the more widely useful before the less widely useful or problems encountered frequently before rarer ones.

Particular ways of organizing material for teaching become standard in a school subject. Teachers learn these in their preservice training or from professional publications and workshops.

The time students need to learn this material and the time teachers have available in the class to help students learn it are usually the critical constraints at every stage of planning. Typically, therefore, a schedule of class activities is the primary curriculum planning document teachers use.

Develop Detailed Unit Plans As they list content and purposes and begin to shape the organization of their course, teachers think about classroom activities that could be used to teach each item. When they have completed the course outline and turn to the preparation of detailed unit plans, teachers therefore already have some classroom activities in mind. Unit plans typically include:

- a list of goals and objectives for the unit,
- a list of important items of content,
- a schedule of classroom activities and homework assignments,
- references to appropriate pages in textbooks and curriculum materials,
- plans for lessons or activities,
- tests or other assessment procedures.

The heart of these detailed plans are the classroom activities. Teachers recognize that students learn from the activities they undertake, and so they devote a considerable amount of their planning time to selecting good classroom activities. Experienced teachers can recall many hundreds of activities they have tried or heard about. The teachers' guides that come with textbooks commonly suggest class activities, as do the courses of study and curriculum guides provided by the school district. These are only suggestions, and teachers feel quite free to use other activities instead. Teachers can find other activities described in teaching methods texts, professional journals, and curriculum guides from other districts. Expert teachers can generate unlimited numbers of good classroom activities by making variations on models derived from such sources.

Why does a teacher judge one activity to be better than others for a given occasion? This is one of the most fundamental questions one can ask about the classroom curriculum, yet we cannot answer it with any precision and confidence. Most professional authorities advise teachers to choose activities on the basis of their demonstrated effectiveness in helping students learn. Effectiveness, they maintain, should be determined by research and evaluation, be guided by analyses, and be informed by theories or models of learning. Apparently, though, teachers usually rely on their own judgment of how well an activity worked or would work

BOX 10-1   Tactics to Promote More Principled Activity Selection

- Identify one or two crucial ideas or skills that students seem to have difficulty mastering.
- Search in research journals and professional publications for articles that review and synthesize research on the teaching of this topic. [Use such reference materials as *Education Index, Current Index to Journals in Education, ERIC* (Educational Resources Information Centers), and the Dialogue computer database system. If necessary, seek assistance from a graduate student or faculty member in a nearby university in conducting a literature search].
- Collaborate with other teachers to review and discuss the evidence from your review and to compare it with your own pedagogical judgment.
- Seek expert advice. Ask your principal to help you locate persons in the school district, in neighboring school systems, in nearby colleges or universities or elsewhere who can assist you in making sense of what you have found and using your findings to make an informed choice.
- Collaborate with colleagues to carry out controlled field experiments in your classes.

for them, rather than on formal studies of the effectiveness of certain types of activities in many classrooms, even when such studies exist (Yinger 1978; Clark and Yinger 1987).

When they have a choice, teachers generally select activities because they are consistent with their personal teaching philosophy and style, because the teacher has tried them before and they worked, because a friend, fellow teacher, or other trusted source has recommended them, or because they are practical and convenient. This emphasis on practicality by teachers probably arises, as Doyle and Ponder (1977) suggest, from the overwhelming demands it would place on teachers' time and expertise if they were to attempt to select activities in a more principled way. Perhaps one day classrooms will be organized so that teachers have time to investigate the effectiveness of activities systematically by conducting their own field studies. In the meantime, such tactics as those in Box 10-1 may be helpful in some situations.

Introducing the Curriculum to Students

During the first few days of the school year, teachers introduce themselves and their classroom to a new group of students. It is important that they introduce the classroom curriculum, too. What students do determines what they will take away from this class. When students are told little about the content, purpose, and structure of a class, they have no sound basis for deciding which of their abilities to employ when, for how long, and in what way. Then they can only rely on their preconceived ideas for making these crucial decisions. Depending on how they perceive the class and themselves initially, students will put forth varying amounts and kinds of effort that will in turn influence how they perform in the first few weeks of the course and in turn how the teacher perceives them. Some students, believing the class will be easy and irrelevant to any of their personal goals, will decide that they do not need to work hard. If they discover after the first few examinations that they made a mistake, they may have trouble recovering. Others, fearing failure, may panic or give up, and as a result miss crucial early learnings.

Many times students enter a subject with strong prejudices based on hearsay or a chance encounter with the subject. Sometimes these prejudices interfere with their marshalling their own learning resources properly. For example, an adolescent boy may dislike poetry because he thinks it is not masculine and may devote as little time as possible to studying it. A teacher can accept such prejudices and conclude that poetry is not appropriate content for this student at this time, but a teacher can also introduce that student to poetry in ways that overcome his prejudice, perhaps by selecting as the first poems ones that could dispel his prejudice.

Students should probably be more involved in decisions about purpose, content, and structure of their educational programs. At the very least, teachers should share with students the plans for their courses and their rationales for them. Without this information students cannot make informed decisions about whether to invest and how to invest their abilities, energies, and attention. If the material is required, students should understand why those responsible for their education consider this material important enough to require them to learn it. When students have choices, they should be given information about the consequences of their curricular choices: What other topics or subjects will they be enabled to study if they succeed in learning this one and what kinds of careers will be open to them?

A good introduction to a curriculum does more than inform students about the course and the subject. It also encourages them to put forth the effort needed to learn the subject and helps them discover how to collaborate with the teacher and the curriculum to achieve the purposes of the course. Usually, teachers must work hard and give much thought to securing and maintaining students' engagement with classroom activities. A major part of this work and thought should go into finding a good way to introduce the curriculum in the first crucial days and weeks.

We know surprisingly little about how teachers actually introduce children to the classroom curriculum in any subject. Box 10-2 lists some options that seem plausible, but no one seems to have studied either the tactics that are most effective or the tactics teachers actually employ.

The ground rules and standard operating procedures teachers lay down in the first few days of school also affect the direction and extent of students' engagement with the classroom curriculum. Teachers of mathematics typically establish such ground rules as "Each person works alone," "Grades are based on tests," "There is only one right answer," and "Every answer is either right or wrong." In art classes, on the other hand, teachers generally make it clear early in the course that there are many good solutions to an art problem, that grades are based on products and

BOX 10-2   Some Options for Introducing Students to a Curriculum

- Describe the purpose, content, and structure of the course in a lecture in the first class.
- Have students speak or write their own thoughts about the course and subject; discuss their ideas; correct any misconceptions about the curriculum.
- Show students some questions or problems that they will be able to answer when they have completed the class; explain what they will need to do in order to master this material.
- Involve students in an opening activity that is prototypical of the subject and then help them to reflect on what they must do to become able to do such things themselves. For example, in a chemistry class students might view reports of chemical analyses of water samples taken from their own community and discuss how the findings were obtained, to what extent the results can be relied on, and what the findings may mean for them and their community, and then follow up with a discussion of how they can learn to do chemistry such as this.
- Read and discuss a biography of a great contributor to the subject; point out what that person did that made him or her a good learner of that subject.

effort, and that students are encouraged to help one another to improve their art. Such ground rules define for students what art and mathematics are like as well as how the good mathematics student or art student should behave.

I recall vividly how surprised I was during my freshman year in college to find problems appearing on examinations in my science and mathematics classes that were completely unlike any problems we had done as homework or in class. Prior to that point, one of the unspoken ground rules of my schooling had been that teachers would not expect you to know how to do a problem unless they had shown you how and given you a chance to practice. My college professors lived by a different set of rules. Once I realized the rules had changed, I had to figure out how to prepare for the new types of examinations. Reviewing the problems I had done as homework and those the teacher had done in class did not prepare me to solve totally new problems. It took me more than a year to find effective ways to study for these new types of examinations.

Box 10-3 shows some of the types of procedural ground rules that communicate strong messages about the classroom curriculum to students.

Teachers influence students' perceptions of the curriculum by the interpersonal relationship they establish with students, too. Students are more open to the influence of a person they like, whom they feel likes them, whom they care about and who cares about them. Most people are more eager to please a person they care about than a stranger. By their behavior teachers embody and symbolize purposes and priorities. This modelling sends a powerful message. Students naturally assume that the way their teacher thinks and acts reflects the way other specialists in this subject think and act. If they admire the teacher, they will want to learn how to think and act the same way.

BOX 10-3   Groundrules and Procedures that Shape Students' Perceptions of a Classroom's Curriculum

- **Grading**
  What really counts? Test results? Homework? Participation? Effort?
  To what extent is grading based on subjective judgment by the teacher or objective performance criteria?

- **Norms for pupil conduct**
  How assiduously must students work in class?
  How much homework is expected? How difficult?
  Are students' expected to interpret assignments in original ways or to follow instructions to the letter?

- **Norms for classroom interactions and relationships**
  Is helping forbidden or encouraged?
  Do students work alone or in groups?
  Do students cooperate or compete?
  Are students' work and teachers' evaluations of it shared in public or kept private between student and teacher?

- **Expectations about the outside world**
  What relationship will the content and goals of this class have with life outside school?

From the standpoint of the curriculum, a teacher's personal influence over students can be used for good or ill. Ideally, classroom exposure gives students a taste of the intrinsic benefits of learning the subject. The teacher whose personal charm or interpersonal skills attract students to a subject may do them a great service if the intrinsic character of the subject can then be made appealing. But if students confuse their attitude toward the teacher with their attitude toward the subject, they may make decisions they will regret later. Portraying the curriculum to students, presenting and clarifying the subject or topic so that students can decide what relationships they wish to establish with this material, is an important purpose of general education.

In order to introduce students to a curriculum teachers need to know a great deal about the students. What do they already know about the subject? What preconceived ideas do they have about it? What do they expect their experience in the class to be like? What do they hope might happen? What do they fear might happen? What sorts of school experiences do they find rewarding and what sorts punishing? Teachers need to know such things about their students in order to find good ways to introduce the curriculum to them. In addition, teachers need to know the subject in sufficient depth to help students cultivate their abilities in the subject. What kinds and amounts of knowledge teachers need to guide students is little studied and poorly understood.

Adjusting Curriculum Plans during the Year

The best laid plans for a classroom curriculum will need to be adjusted to accommodate unforeseen circumstances. Students may enter the class not knowing everything assumed in the plan or they may have already learned some of the things the plan called for teaching them. The planned pace may prove too fast or too slow for this group. An activity included for its motivating value may turn out to be uninteresting to this group, or the subject itself may prove so intrinsically interesting that a motivating activity is superfluous. Good, timely adjustments of curriculum plans can make an immense difference in what students learn from the class.

Maintaining Engagement Teachers most often adjust the curriculum so as to maintain students' engagement with it and with the class. Maintaining students' active engagement with what happens in the classroom is the teacher's most fundamental and irreplaceable contribution to realizing the curriculum. As Lortie (1975) discovered, teachers place a high value on a colleague's ability to maintain productive engagement of students with classroom activities. The several hundred elementary school teachers Lortie interviewed, asked to describe characteristics of outstanding teachers, cited the ability to sustain student motivation more frequently than anything else. Lortie commented:

> It is evident that [teachers] are impressed by teachers who establish and sustain cordial, disciplined, and work-eliciting relationships with students. (Lortie 1975, 133)

Teachers' efforts to maintain appropriate depth and quality of attentiveness and mindfulness on the part of students despite distractions and turbulence give the classroom environment its purposefulness and thus make it possible for the purposes envisioned by the makers of a curriculum to be realized there. By helping students to make sense of activities, to see them as contributing to larger long term goals, and to understand why they are doing these activities, teachers help students to internalize the purpose of the activity and thus to connect the planned purposes of the curriculum to the students' own purposes. Teachers can and do adjust curriculum plans so as to maintain students' engagement with the prescribed curricular content and purposes in spite of the multitude of mischances that constantly threaten to deflect their attention elsewhere.

Interpreting Students' Difficulties Teachers adjust their curriculum plans in light of students' responses. When they perceive signs of distress in students, such as increased incidence of worry, complaints, misbehavior, avoidance, and so on, or when the quality or quantity of students' work falls short of expectations, teachers may suspect that an adjustment in the curriculum might be appropriate. Whether a curricular adjustment is appropriate and, if so, what kind, will depend on how the teacher interprets the difficulties students are having. When teachers perceive that students are struggling to meet their expectations but falling short, they will react differently than if they perceive students to be putting forth less than full effort. Early in their school careers students become experts at presenting themselves, their efforts, and their results to the teacher in the most favorable possible light.

Learning to interpret students' responses to a curriculum accurately in spite of their determined efforts to present themselves in a particular light is one of the great arts of teaching, unfortunately little studied. Good teachers constantly have their antennae out searching for clues that may help them to adjust their curriculum so that it better serves their students. They learn from everything that happens in their classroom and from much that happens in halls, playgrounds, and outside the school. They use everything they know to help them interpret what they see. Teachers' subject matter knowledge, for instance, enables them to interpret their students' responses to the curriculum. Carlsen (1988) found that intern teachers were more responsive to students' questions and conducted more open-ended, wide-ranging discussions when they were teaching topics they knew well. It is plausible that teachers are better able to learn from students' comments in such discussion and to make appropriate adjustments to their curriculum plans in light of what they learned from the discussion.

The most direct tactic teachers can use to test a tentative interpretation of students' difficulties is to compare students' performances in various situations. If a teacher can arrange to observe students in situations in which they are clearly doing their best, then the teacher has a standard for judging effort in other situations. Similarly, teachers who are uncertain whether a concept is really too difficult for students or whether they are simply not being as resourceful as they could be in using what they already know, can challenge them by offering a special reward to the class if everyone masters it.

But when is curricular adjustment warranted? Some teachers seem eager to adjust their curriculum plans to ease any difficulties their students experience. The obvious, natural, and seemingly humane response when students are having difficulty is to ease expectations in some way—allow more time, accept lower standards of performance, delete difficult topics, or some combination of the methods listed in Box 10-4. Easing curricular demands is generally a successful tactic. It lowers anxiety, maintains effort, and achieves scaled-back, short-term results, but at the expense of long-range achievement and accurate self-image of students as learners of the subject. In extreme cases, students can graduate from high school virtually illiterate and only dimly aware of their disability because teachers consistently lowered their expectations, inflated grades, and passed the student along to the next grade.

When teachers consistently sacrifice curricular plans whenever students encounter difficulties, they communicate symbolically that mastery of the content and goals of the course is not really important. On the other hand, rigid adherence to a planned curriculum, regardless of students' responses to it, sends the message that

■
BOX 10-4   Ways Teachers May Adjust Topics or Activities

- change time allocations,
- change sequence,
- add or delete topics or activities,
- modify topics or activities,
- change grading criteria,
- raise or lower change achievement standards.

students' reactions are not important. No one benefits when students are forced to keep up a pace they cannot sustain (or a pace they could easily increase) or to learn material that is too difficult (or too easy) for them. Clearly, teachers should generally avoid the two extremes of adhering rigidly to curriculum plans or too readily adjusting those plans to ease students' apparent difficulties.

Teachers should explore several options when their students have difficulties: increase motivation, employ more effective teaching methods, study in detail the difficulties students are having and devise ways to overcome them. Abandoning difficult parts of the curriculum should be a last resort and will always be something of an admission of failure by the teacher—failure to realize the curriculum expected by the community, school officials, and colleagues. A more aggressive response is to keep pushing the mastery/coverage/affect tradeoff. Actively seek ways of helping students to succeed at difficult learning tasks. Vary the intensity and pace of the course to accustom students gradually to higher levels of performance. Use different types of activities that call on different student aptitudes and abilities. Arrange for students to help one another to overcome difficulties. Try to find ways to help students come to enjoy working hard and achieving success in spite of difficulties. Refuse to let them fail; insist on persistence and eventual success. Establish the attitude that everyone is expected to learn everything thoroughly and permanently, and let your tests and grading reflect this attitude. Do anything to avoid either watering down the curriculum or putting students in situations in which they will fail no matter what they do.

Ethical Dilemmas of Equity More than any other kind of curriculum work, adjusting curriculum plans brings teachers face to face with individual and group differences between students and confronts them with hard choices about equity. When students respond in various ways to the same curriculum, as they always do, adjustments favorable for some students may be unfavorable for others. In the simplest case, a pace that some students find comfortable will often be too fast for some and too slow for others. The public, the profession, and school officials often evade or deny the dilemmas this situation poses for teachers by mouthing such slogans as "education for all," "meeting every student's needs," or "equal educational opportunity." Everyone assumes that teachers will somehow translate these glib generalities into working principles to guide their daily decisions, but in fact there is nothing like consensus on the practical meaning of such slogans.

No matter what choices a teacher makes, some students will be less well served than they might be. Every curriculum is a compromise that leaves some students with legitimate complaints that this curriculum was not the most appropriate one for them, and leaves sensitive teachers feeling dissatisfied and constantly searching for a better curriculum. So long as everyone involved is aware of the inherent dilemmas, this bittersweet situation can be endured. But many well-intentioned idealists, perfectionists, and passionate advocates find it impossible to accept curricula that are not ideally suited to some students, so the inevitably imperfect fit between the actual curriculum and what would be ideal for particular students or groups of students provides a continuing source of contention. The struggle to distribute these inevitable injustices in a generally acceptable way is the source of much recurrent curricular conflict.

A Student's Role and Society's Role in Maintaining a Satisfactory Classroom Curriculum

Ultimately, formal education is a compact between the individual and society and between one generation and the next. Students must accept on faith that what they are asked to learn in school will be worth the personal investment it will require of them. They cannot know in advance what learning something new may mean to them. They may be changed utterly by something they learn in class, choosing an occupation undreamed of before, deciding to undertake years of further study, making new friends, altering personality, attitude, lifestyle, and becoming a significantly different person. The experience could be disastrous—they might fail, undermining confidence, weakening self-esteem, smashing treasured dreams and projects. Or, the class might be a waste of time. The price of finding out is an investment of oneself—of time, energy, effort, attention, and the courage to risk failure. If students avoid the risk of failure by keeping well within their capacities, to choose only one of the hazards they face, they will not learn what their capacities really are and may live beneath their potential.

During the years of schooling children should move gradually from complete dependence on authorities who determine what they study toward the mature adult's independent judgment. Indeed, enabling students to make better decisions about their future learning is one of the main justifications for general education. When youngsters try to learn mathematics, for example, and their efforts meet with success, their faith in the institution that told them to study mathematics is justified, and their investment of time and effort is repaid. If failure comes too often and if benefits are rare and meager, faith in either self or others or both may falter. The art lies in sustaining progress toward independence as a learner while maintaining high goals and standards. And this is a collaborative art to which students, teachers, and curricula, as well as influences from outside school, must contribute.

CHANGING A CLASSROOM'S CURRICULUM

Reform within the Conventional Classroom Pattern

Teachers realize the curriculum in their classrooms, and teachers must be the ones to change it. All others who want to bring about change in the classroom curriculum must find ways to influence teachers to make the necessary changes. Box 10-5 lists eight things teachers need in order to make a major change in their classroom curricula. These things are not just desirable; they are essential if lasting classroom curriculum change is to be achieved. Let us consider why each is essential and some of the ways each can be accomplished.

Opportunity to Study the Change Teachers need to understand the key features of a proposed curriculum change, why each feature of the change is important, and the implications of each for classroom practice. Teachers who do not fully understand the proposed change are unlikely to implement it faithfully. I recall visiting a high school chemistry class in the late 1960s in which the teacher was purportedly using an innovative, inquiry-oriented curriculum. The teacher read from the textbook, pausing every now and then to ask the class a question. Afterwards someone asked the teacher how he liked using this inquiry-oriented curriculum. The teacher replied with evident enthusiasm that he liked it very much. He found the new book to be much more interesting than the one he had used before because it explained how chemical knowledge was discovered. He said he did not use the recommended laboratory experiments because they took too much time, though. The class would not be able to finish the whole book if he took time out for the laboratories. This teacher thought he was implementing the curriculum as its developers intended, making what he considered a few minor adjustments for greater efficiency. In this case, superficial understanding of a curriculum change led to a classroom curriculum that bore little resemblance to the curriculum the textbook writers wrote or the curriculum the school district adopted.

For some teachers and some changes, reading the teachers manual, hearing a single speech, or reading a brief article may be enough to bring adequate understanding of a proposed change. In most cases, however, teachers need an opportunity to discuss the change with other teachers in order to bring to light features of the change and aspects of the rationale and its implications that are not immediately obvious on first hearing or reading. Possible negative features of a change are seldom mentioned in the professional literature, and thorough consideration of pros and cons is essential for a considered professional decision. Discussions that include opponents as well as advocates of the change, will promote more informed decisions. Consultation with appropriate experts would surely inform teachers' decisions even further.

In addition to listening, reading, and discussing, teachers generally find it extremely useful to visit a school or classroom in which the proposed change is in

---

BOX 10-5   What Teachers Need to Change the Curriculum of a Conventional Classroom

1. Teachers need an opportunity to study the change and its implications for classroom practice.
2. Teachers need a voice in the deliberations leading to a decision to undertake the change.
3. Teachers need incentives to undertake the change effort in their classrooms.
4. Teachers need an opportunity to learn what students will be expected to learn.
5. Teachers need an opportunity to master the new pedagogical skills required by the change.
6. Teachers need temporary access to the resources required for making the transition and continuing access to the resources required by the new practice.
7. Teachers need ways to check the quality of their realization of the new pattern.
8. Teachers need continuing support to work out bugs in the new pattern and to resolve conflicts between the new pattern and what remains of the former one.

---

operation. They get a great deal more information from a visit than they could from listening or reading about it. On the other hand, richness of information can be confusing or misleading, so a combination of observation, explanation of key features, and discussion has much greater potential for fostering understanding than any one used alone. Video presentations offer the possibility of artfully combining all these ingredients in a medium that can be used flexibly. When practical, teachers should try the change out on a small scale; often, however, a new practice is too complex to be tried without considerable preparation and expense.

A Voice in the Adoption Deliberations Any pretense of professionalism requires that the professional critically assess new practices and form an independent judgment of their value based on the best available evidence. If teachers are to be more than bureaucratic functionaries, they must make their independent judgments of the merits of proposed changes and make their judgments known both within the school organization and in the public media.

No principle presently stands in the way of teachers making their views about a curriculum proposed for adoption known to their employers or to the public. As individuals, they can write letters or request an audience with responsible officials. As members of local teacher organizations, they can appoint study groups, develop position papers, and negotiate formally with the school district. And as members of national professional organizations, they can see that their representatives act on their behalf in reference to a particular curriculum change. That teachers have not been more active in making their views known on curriculum issues in their schools may indicate that they feel their views are adequately considered already, that they fear to challenge local authorities, or that they put a low priority on influencing local curriculum changes in comparison to other local decisions.

In the school, teachers may well be content if the principal or sponsoring district officials offer them a chance to speak out about a proposed change and then, having made their views known, trust the decision to the professional judgment of school officials. Typically school administrators assess the extent and quality of teacher support for any change in a variety of informal settings before they commit themselves to a local change effort. School leaders may seek a public show of hands to confirm teacher support. A secret ballot would be even more convincing. A requirement that a secret ballot of teachers be taken on every major curricular initiative and publicly reported to the board before it votes would greatly strengthen teachers' voice in adoption decisions without infringing on the power of the public and its appointed school officials to make decisions.

Incentives to Undertake the Change Effort Teachers are plagued with the overcommitment typical of busy professionals. Usually, teachers believe they are working hard and doing a good job now. Every teacher can see ways to improve further, but unless the incentives to change what they are doing are strong enough to overcome the effort, cost, and risks of changing, most find it easier to continue what they are now doing. Whether the incentives are intrinsic to the task or extrinsically provided, teachers need to perceive a favorable ratio of benefits to costs for them in their professional lives before the effort to make the change will seem worthwhile.

The most satisfactory incentives, as always, are those intrinsic to the task. When teachers believe in the value of the change for students and for the society, they can see their effort on its behalf as a personal contribution to human betterment, and many teachers find this satisfying. A teacher who loves a subject and loves to teach it to young people may be thrilled at the thought of undertaking an arduous effort on behalf of an inspiring curriculum innovation, even if there are no tangible rewards. Sometimes also teachers find the process of change itself rewarding, because it brings relief from routines, contacts with different people, chances to go to new places and undertake novel personal and professional challenges. On the other hand, many teachers value their routines and resent intrusions on them.

Sometimes teachers receive tangible rewards for helping to change the curriculum in their classroom. Students, parents, colleagues, or superiors may show their appreciation by awarding gifts or public honors. The teacher's reputation may rise in the community, the school, the profession or all three. (On the other hand, if the change proves unpopular, teachers run a risk of damaged reputations.) Through their efforts in curriculum work teachers may bring themselves to the attention of persons in a position to employ them or to recommend them for professional advancement. Sometimes teachers are able to earn additional income by working on a curriculum change project during summers or on their free time. Sometimes the expertise teachers acquire brings opportunities for earning further income, as when a teacher learns a great deal about the language and culture of another country and then finds summer work as a tour guide. If teachers are to continue to work on behalf of changes, they must feel that the effort they will have to expend and the costs and risks they are likely to incur are likely to be outweighed by benefits they find personally and professionally rewarding.

Opportunity to Learn the New Content Teachers need to know what they are going to teach and know it very well. When teachers only know a few major items of knowledge in a field or when their knowledge is superficial, they can only present the subject to students as they learned it. To improvise pedagogically or to respond to students' questions opens such teachers to the frightening possibility of revealing personal ignorance of a subject they are supposed to know well enough to teach. So, teachers whose knowledge of a topic is too limited can only implement a curriculum in a rigid way (Carlsen 1988).

Major changes in the content students are expected to study and learn generally call for substantial periods of formal study by teachers. At best teachers learn only a few basic concepts from the typical one or two day in-service workshops provided by schools. They cannot learn expository writing, the Constitution, set theory, computer programming, or plate tectonics. Teachers with the best general education will have the best preparation for continuing to learn on their own, but there comes a time in every teacher's life when further progress demands sustained study. Most colleges offer courses for teachers over the summer and in evenings, but most teachers need this time for their families or need the money they can get from working. Self-study from video, audio, or print sources is more convenient, requires less time for commuting, and permits more flexibility in scheduling, but it still takes a major time commitment and it places greater demands on teachers for self-direction and self-discipline. Collaborative study groups combined with self-study can provide additional support and maintain higher participation rates. Participation in curriculum development can motivate teachers to learn more about a topic and provide an occasion for learning that enhances professional dignity and self-respect. However it happens, teachers must somehow learn, and learn well, whatever content they will be expected to teach.

Opportunity to Master New Pedagogical Skills Teaching can be thought of as requiring a combination of pedagogical skills in several areas, including classroom management, planning, presentation, and evaluation of student learning. Most teachers master a limited set of pedagogical skills so well that they can adapt them to teach in most any situation. Their personal teaching style is then built around a few focal skills. Nearly all teachers learn the pedagogical skills required to give a lecture, to conduct a discussion, to supervise students during seatwork, to administer tests, and to review the results of a test with the class. Some subjects have distinctive types of lessons. In mathematics, teachers often have students work problems at the chalkboard; in science students do experiments; in reading students may read aloud; and so on.

When teachers try a pedagogical skill they have not fully mastered, classes do not go as smoothly and teachers are likely to be dissatisfied with the results. A science teacher who tries to use guided discovery, for example, or to teach writing as part of science classes, or to use cooperative learning groups in the classroom, or to use computers feels nearly as awkward as in learning to teach in the first place. A teacher who has learned how to keep a question-and-answer session moving quickly along preset paths toward the correct answers must do a lot of relearning in order to deliver a guided discovery lesson in which they help students suggest alternative hypotheses, work out their consequences and compare the results with available data. New pedagogical skills of this order are not learned in a day.

To master a complex pedagogical skill teachers generally require a variety of learning experiences, including:

- thorough description and demonstration of the skill,
- opportunity to plan and rehearse with expert advice,
- repeated practice with feedback from a master,
- ongoing coaching until they achieve mastery,
- a continuing forum for sharing problems and discoveries with knowledgeable others.

In typical curriculum change efforts, teachers must do without these forms of assistance.

Mostly teachers develop their pedagogical skills in the early years of their career by imitating other teachers. Later, a teacher may learn a new pedagogical technique by reading a journal article or book or a conference. The teacher may rehearse alone or with a close friend and try out techniques in the classroom a little bit at a time. When something does not go well, the teacher will drop it or modify it, adapting the technique until it feels comfortable. Sometimes such informal self-teaching of pedagogical technique works beautifully. And when it works, the teacher gains a precious independence. But it has its limitations. The self-taught teacher, like the self-taught artist or ball-player, can ingrain habits that work at first but limit future performance. Also, unless a self-taught teacher is persistent and thorough, he or she will tend to jettison the most innovative features of a new pedagogical technique because these are the most likely to misfire the first time a teacher tries them, and those who do not persist and adjust intelligently will conclude prematurely that the most innovative features of the techniques do not work for them.

Not every teacher absolutely requires all of these experiences in order to learn every new pedagogical technique, but good teaching produces results that are generally superior to self-instruction for teachers as well as for students.

Access to Resources The realization of any curriculum change benefits from teachers and students having access to such resources as materials students can use to study individually or in small groups, materials for teachers to use with the entire class, materials to assist teachers in planning, and an allocation of time in the classroom free from other demands. Teachers sometimes acquire their own materials and make their own adjustments in the classroom schedule, but most teachers would consider this to be service above and beyond the call of duty and would only do it for changes they believed in deeply. When someone other than the teacher seeks to initiate classroom curriculum change, the sponsors and champions of the change must provide whatever resources teachers need if they expect teachers to make the change. Occasionally, a curriculum change requires modification of the physical environment of the classroom, for example, providing running water, storage space, or additional electrical outlets, and obviously the teacher could not be expected to make such modifications. Also, the process of change itself requires resources, especially additional time for teachers to plan new lessons and materials to inform teachers about the change and to assist them in making it.

Checking the Quality of Classroom Realization Teachers must decide whether what they are doing is a good and faithful version of the change. This is the most neglected aspect of classroom curriculum change. Teachers who have participated in developing a particular change and comprehend it fully, should have little trouble determining how faithfully their classroom curriculum realizes the plans they themselves helped to make. On the other hand, if, as is usually the case, the plans were developed by someone else and the change is complicated, and especially if the teacher's only exposure to the change has been through a brief one or two day workshop, teachers will not be able to judge reliably how well they have realized the planned change.

Teachers should be able to present a sample of their teaching to someone knowledgeable to receive their judgment of how well the sample realizes the curriculum as planned. Those who make these judgments should serve as consultants to teachers, the consultation should be confidential, and the consultant should not be able to affect the teacher's career prospects. Their purpose would be strictly to help the teacher to compare their classroom curriculum to the plans and ideals the teacher is striving to attain. The possibility of videotaping classroom sessions for viewing by others makes such a proposal feasible on a large scale.

Continuing Support The learning of any complex skill takes place in stages over an extended period of time. Only when teachers achieve a basic minimum level of competence will they put their skill to use, develop fluency and flexibility, and assimilate the newly learned techniques fully into their teaching repertoire. Teachers who need support at all will need continuing support throughout the months during which they will continue to learn and assimilate new knowledge and technique.

As teachers learn more about the change, they will find ways to improve it. The change set in motion can thus continue to be revised and adapted for years. The ability of teachers to take the change into their own hands and make continuing refinements and developments over a period of years is a valuable benefit gained by thorough implementation efforts.

Traditionally district supervisors have been assigned responsibility for providing continuing support, but their small numbers in relation to the number of schools and teachers to be served make effectiveness in this role nearly impossible in most districts. Some schools have regular staff meetings to discuss the changes being implemented. These may be called quality circles or simply faculty meetings, but in them teachers are encouraged to report on their successes and problems and to call issues to the attention of colleagues, authorities, and the sponsors and champions of the change.

Conclusion Clearly, teachers who undertake any substantial change in the curriculum of their classroom must expect to spend extra time and work on the effort and to assume significant professional risks. Others who want to see particular changes take place in classrooms must find ways to incite teachers to undertake these efforts and endure these risks on behalf of the change they advocate. It has taken three decades of disappointing results from major reform efforts to show how daunting a challenge this is.

Inadequacy of Common Approaches to Fostering Classroom Curriculum Change

The multitude of persons and organizations who seek to influence the curriculum of K–12 education must somehow foster curriculum change in many hundreds of thousands of classrooms around the nation. Even those who seek to influence the curriculum of only one school must find ways to affect dozens of teachers and classrooms. Box 10-6 shows some of the approaches most commonly employed.

Consider how many of the eight needs identified earlier are met by each of these strategies. For instance, local adoption of new curriculum materials—typically textbooks and accompanying workbooks—simply confronts teachers with a new frame that they must somehow consider in their planning. New materials that are very different from those already in use disrupt more of teachers' previous plans and therefore coerce from teachers more revision of their classroom curriculum plans. Unless other approaches are also used, materials adoption leaves teachers with only

---

BOX 10-6   Some Common Approaches to Fostering Classroom Curriculum Change

- local adoption of new curriculum materials,
- development of local curriculum guides,
- local curriculum development projects,
- in-service teacher education,
- team planning by teachers,
- national curriculum reform movements.

the teachers' edition of the textbook to help them learn new content and pedagogical skills, check the quality of their initial efforts to realize the new curriculum, and make continuing improvements. Able, dedicated teachers can accomplish these other tasks on their own, especially if the changes demanded are not extensive or radical, but only with efforts that go beyond their contractual obligations to their employers.

None of these common approaches offers a comprehensive strategy for supporting classroom curriculum change. Most of them do not even involve teachers in discussions of what happens in their classrooms. They bring the teacher into contact with some material or activity and then hope that the teacher will take appropriate action behind the classroom door. No wonder that getting curriculum innovations through the classroom door has proven so difficult. Those who think that rapid, substantial, coordinated changes in the curricula of many classrooms should be possible as a matter of routine underestimate the difficulties teachers face in maintaining and changing their classroom curriculum.

In order to make lasting and substantial changes in their classroom curriculum teachers need all of the eight items in Box 10-5. But meeting all these needs for all teachers would be impossibly expensive. If possible, we would like to be able to meet just enough of the needs for enough teachers in a few strategic situations so as to get most of the benefit without the full cost. It is not difficult to imagine ways this might be done.

Promising Approaches to Fostering Classroom Curriculum Change

Suppose, first of all, that teachers belong to a team that includes other teachers who listen, question, suggest, and stimulate ideas. This might be a departmental or grade level team within a school, a collaborative associated with some project or university, or it might simply be a voluntary group formed by interested individual teachers. Imagine that members of this group met regularly to discuss the curriculum change efforts being undertaken by individual members or teams. These efforts by teachers might be supported in any of several ways. Teachers could invest their own free time and pay their own expenses for the intrinsic satisfaction they get and possibly in anticipation of some form of public or professional recognition. Sometimes when a teacher's efforts fit within a larger project, he or she might be paid as a member of the staff of an externally funded project. Teachers could get time to work on a classroom curriculum change project by taking on an intern teacher and using any time freed up from direct work with students in the classroom to work on a curriculum change project. One could even imagine that a school system might want the results of the teacher's work enough to negotiate a separate contract that has the teacher teaching part-time and doing curriculum implementation during the other part.

The very nature of a teacher's work inhibits the development of a broad perspective on educational matters. Suppose teachers were encouraged to go out and learn more about students, community, other schools, and developments in the profession. Suppose teachers had ready access to other types of resources that they could use to extend their own limited perspectives. Imagine, for example, that these teachers have access to a database of information about innovative curricula previously developed and access to a library of curriculum materials in which these curricula can be examined. Imagine that the teacher could consult with experts to validate the content and with psychologists, instructional researchers, or social scientists to assess the promise of pedagogical innovations being considered. Imagine that the teacher can order videotaping of lessons for later study and documentation. Suppose that the teacher makes a formal presentation to colleagues and peers at critical points in the project, and gets assistance in publishing articles in professional journals or giving presentations at professional meetings. Suppose that teachers could earn formal recognition, such as advanced certification, for this type of professional work.

In an environment such as this, it would be realistic to think of teachers routinely making substantial and lasting improvements to their classroom curriculum. Still, not all teachers would want to invest so much in curriculum improvement. For them, an individualized program of in-service work on the curriculum changes adopted by their school seems the best solution. School and district specialists, perhaps other teachers who have developed expertise in this change, would talk with the teacher, learn the teacher's views and concerns about it, and work out together a program of activities designed to enable the teacher to realize this change in his or her classroom. These activities could be continued until the teacher had successfully made the changes. Such an approach would be more expensive than mass in-service workshops, but it would be much more effective.

An enlightened school system would incorporate teachers' own professional planning into curriculum planning. It would provide in-service education on teachers' terms, at convenient times and places, on an individual basis, sensitive to what each teacher needs, including the use of video and collegial deliberation. It would develop a system of flexible teacher contracts that make it possible to give teachers breadth of experience and that free teachers' time to make classroom curriculum changes. A profession dedicated to the development of teachers' professionalism would devise ways of recognizing and certifying the special curriculum skills and expertise teachers develop through such efforts. A sound national educational system would foster constructive collaboration in teacher education and in curriculum development among universities, states, districts, professional associations.

In such an environment the cost of supporting serious efforts at classroom curriculum change need not be too high. Truly determined teachers can find ways to get what they need or do without and still maintain and improve the quality of the curriculum they offer in their classroom. The more support that is available, the greater the fraction of teachers who can and will follow suit.

The favorable climate for classroom curriculum change just envisioned amounts to only a modest incremental change from the present situation. Classrooms would still operate under basically the same frames as before. Many serious educational authorities call for much more radical restructuring of classrooms: individualization of instruction, cooperative group learning, grouping the same students with a teacher for several years, paying teachers according to students' test results, allowing parents to choose their children's teachers, to mention only a few proposals that challenge the conventional classroom structure head-on. Perhaps through some such restructuring the classroom curriculum would become more amenable to change. Perhaps. But probably only if the basic limitations of limited teacher time, limited opportunity for professional communication, limited expert assistance and support, and weak incentives for teachers to improve are somehow overcome. Most of the restructurings that have actually been tried in the last half-century in American schools have increased the burdens of time and effort on teachers, and this is one of the reasons they have failed. Will the successfully restructured classroom put even more pressure on teacher time, energy, and talent?

PLANNING CLASSROOM ACTIVITIES

To change a classroom curriculum is to make different classroom activities happen, activities that present different content, intended to achieve different purposes, and structured in different ways. Planning new classroom activities is therefore one of the most fundamental steps in bringing about classroom curriculum change. Usually teachers find ideas for new classroom activities in public sources—teachers' guides, teachers' editions of textbooks, or books or articles about teaching—and adapt them for their personal use. This customizing process is an interesting one that deserves more study than it has received, but it is a special case of the development of a new activity from scratch.

Activity development is a form of pedagogical expertise possessed in some measure by all teachers, but one can be quite a good teacher with little of it simply by relying on activities developed by others. So the development of new activities is not a necessary part of classroom curriculum change for all teachers, though it is an important part for many and it is essential that *somebody* develop new activities. In this section we will examine how teachers, beginning with a teaching problem or challenge, can get ideas for activities and develop these ideas into complete activities they can use in their classroom. (We will consider how these activities may be put together to form units, courses, or complete curricula in Chapter 13.)

The Complex Nature of Educational Activities

Every human activity has the possibility to exhibit structure, meaning, and purpose on several levels simultaneously. The raising of one hand above the head is a simple action that can be described physiologically and anatomically in terms of muscles and joints, but it may also be described as a stretch, a salute, or a bid to be recognized. Each of these actions, in turn, may be described in terms of the person's motives: to answer a question, to show off, or to conform to classroom norms. The structure of an activity is a matter of its form, of relations between its parts. The meaning of an activity is a matter of relations between the activity itself and other things outside the activity. The structure of a classroom activity on *Macbeth* might consist of assigning parts and reading the play aloud in class, with pauses at intervals for discussion. The meanings of the *Macbeth* activity depend on the substance of those discussions. They might have to do with such matters as loyalty, ambition, and evil; or such matters as plot, metaphor, and literary form; or such matters as getting a good grade, impressing the teacher, and getting into college.

Every activity intended to be educational has the potential for at least three types of structure and therefore three levels of meaning: as a **task** in itself, as a **symbolic representation** of other matters, and as a **form of social interaction.** Educators may not always attend to all three levels, but they are there as resources to be used for education anyway.

Furthermore, the educational outcomes of interest in general education are always complex. Typically we expect students to come away from any educational activity with

1. **achievement** (learned ability to perform)
2. **retention** (indefinitely continued)
3. **transfer** (generalizable to new situations both similar to the learning situation [near transfer] and quite different [far transfer]
4. **understanding** (ability to provide a correct explanation and to relate to other learnings)
5. **motivation** (continuing interest and willingness to pursue the matter further)

These complex expectations for outcomes and these levels of meaning and structure apply to nearly all activities designed for inclusion in the curriculum of general education. To ignore this multidimensional complexity of activities and to proceed as if whatever happens in classrooms can be regarded as purely, simply, and definitely one thing and one thing only with simply specifiable outcomes, is to reduce the scope of human intelligence and to impoverish classroom interactions to the point where it is doubtful whether they can be said to be educative at all.

The Essential Starting Point: What the Student Does

The most important principle of classroom activity design is that **the student's actions determine what will be learned.** Curriculum materials can present information, but students only learn when they bring their attention and their abilities to bear on what is presented. Curriculum materials can influence students' actions, but they are only one influence and seldom the strongest. Ultimately, curriculum materials have an effect on students, if at all, by encouraging, directing, and assisting their own efforts to learn. The kernel of an educational activity, then, is what the student is to do.

A teacher's chief resource for generating tentative suggestions for activities is a set of *activity schemata* that are either tacitly held in memory or explicitly included in the curriculum's platform. A schema is a kind of script for creating an activity, a general form whose blanks when filled in describe a particular activity of a certain type. Everyone would be able to fill in the blanks in the activity schema *Lecture* to create a specific lecture. What the student does in a lecture is listen, take notes, try to understand, and ask questions if puzzled. The lecturer selects appropriate and important ideas, organizes them convincingly, memorably, and entertainingly, and delivers them clearly. Lectures may vary in content, length, purpose (to inform, to entertain, to persuade, . . .), and style. Someone from another culture would have to learn this schema, but it is so common in Western Civilization that everyone can be assumed to be familiar with it, though not necessarily to be able to perform well as either a lecturer or auditor. Other activity schemata likely to be familiar to teachers include:

Class Discussion
Reading Groups (Circles)
Going Over Homework
Seatwork
Testing
Field Trips

Teachers with a more progressive orientation are likely to be familiar with such activity schemata as:

Teacher-Pupil Planning
Class Projects
Individual Student Projects
Games
Independent Study

Some school subjects include specialized activity schemata, such as:

Laboratory (science)
Rehearsal (music)
Calisthenics (physical education)

And new activity schemata are invented (sometimes reinvented or rediscovered) continually.

To employ more than a handful of fundamentally different activity types within a single course or unit puts stress on teachers and students. Teachers must become fluent with many types of activities, which is not an easy task. Students must learn to play their proper part in the orderly realization of an activity and, as generations of teachers and a few recent researchers will testify, they, too, must learn how to participate productively in a new type of activity. The time needed to learn and become fluent with a new type of activity is an additional cost of employing varied activity types. For these reasons most teachers rely on a small number of basic activity types that they repeat with variations. The teacher's first response to the task of designing a new activity is therefore typically to ask which familiar type of activity is best suited to the present purpose. In some cases, a plausible activity of a familiar type springs readily to mind, but when one does not, an activity can be developed by using a kind of heuristic reasoning.

One form of heuristic reasoning begins by determining what students should do either during or at the conclusion of this activity. A plausible educational activity can be designed from this beginning by using the following line of heuristic reasoning.

> Here's something we would like students to be able to do. Call it T, for target activity. Suppose we just show them T or tell them about it and then have them do it. (If this works as a learning activity for students then use it. If not, we proceed as follows.)
>
> Supposing that just showing the target activity or telling about it will not work because of certain specific barriers, call them B_1, B_2, and B_3, can we find or devise an activity that is nearly equivalent to T but that does not present these barriers?

Usually the target activity comes from some field of human endeavor to which students are being introduced. For example, reading a novel is an activity that originates in literature as a living tradition and has a hallowed place in the English curriculum of secondary schools. Why not just select a novel and ask students to read it? Well, our students may not be able to read fluently enough (B_1), they may not know how to extract any meaning from a novel except the plot (B_2), and they may be uninterested and unwilling to give novel reading a serious try (B_3). Can we then find an alternative activity that is nearly equivalent to reading a novel, but does not have these shortcomings? We can easily devise several plausible candidates. For instance, in response to the first barrier, we can find a novel that makes relatively light demands on reading skill. Or we can write one, commission one, or adapt one. We can even create a comic book version of an existing novel. Taking a different tack, we can permit students to listen to a recording of someone reading the novel while they read along. Or, we might decide to enlist parents or volunteers as aides to help individual students with their reading. If the contortions required are too great, we might simply postpone or cancel the attempt to teach this particular target activity. Each of these courses of action has its costs and risks as well as its advantages and, depending on the situation, we might have good reason to prefer one over the others.

Adapting real-world activities to educative purposes in this way is a staple method for generating possible curriculum activities, especially in secondary schools and in higher education. Science experiments, mathematics problems, foreign language dialogues, vocational education projects, musical performances, and art projects are common examples that present opportunities for using real-world activities in very nearly their mature, fully developed forms.

For younger children it is often necessary to produce a simplified version of the target activity. Instead of novels, we offer stories written especially for children. We offer simple scientific observations and experiments, simple arithmetic problems, and other miniature, child-sized versions of adult activities. Activities adapted from serious adult endeavors for the education of children are most educative if they retain all the essential values of the original. In particular, the objects and operations of the adapted activity should ideally be genuine instances, however simplified, of the developed activity. Children's mathematics should still be recognizable as mathematics by mathematicians, children's literature still recognizable as literature by literati, and so on. The best examples of the adapted activity should stand comparison in some meaningful sense with the great exemplars of the developed activity. The adapted activity should be capable of evoking similar kinds of responses in children to those that the developed activity evokes in adults. The thought processes required to deal appropriately with the adapted activity ought to be useful when applied to real-world problems in the related adult domain. Adapting serious adult activities for use by children is a difficult challenge to our understanding of both children and subject, and requires a gifted creative imagination.

A second type of heuristic we can follow for generating activities is to create new, artificial tasks to serve as **exercises** for the development or training of some ability or aptitude. Making exercises works something like this:

> Search for small activities that are constituents of many important larger activities, or that develop abilities required in many such activities.
>
> Practice these in steadily increasing doses so that we build gradually improved performance on them.
>
> Practice on the target activities simultaneously or wait until students become capable of a sufficiently high level of performance on the exercises.

The physical exercises known as calisthenics are a clear example of using this strategy. The motions have no effect on the world and they express no idea or feeling. They are designed purely to develop strength, flexibility, and endurance for use in other physical activity. Phonics drills on meaningless letter-sound correspondences are designed to help children to learn a meaningful and useful activity—reading. Musical scales and arpeggios, multiplication table drills, flash cards, sentence diagramming, filling in blanks, connecting dots, and lists of names and dates are other familiar products of the exercise heuristic. Currently, new types of exercises modelled on intelligence test items are being recommended as a way to teach thinking skills.

Exercises are a staple activity type in all subjects and grades, but they are generally regarded as a necessary evil. Many people have painful childhood memories of working away at exercises when they would rather have been doing something else. (On the other hand, many children find great satisfaction in mastery of arbitrary but difficult tasks.) Educators with progressive leanings strive to eliminate mere exercises in favor of meaningful and intrinsically satisfying activities. Perhaps the greatest danger of using exercises is that they will acquire a life of their own and come to be considered useful or meaningful or both, in their own right. Spelling exercises, once an aid to writing, have grown into a school subject. We have spelling books, spelling tests, and spelling bees and children even receive a grade in spelling. Performance on exercises is easily measured and so people tend to compare one another on the basis of performance on exercises. Test items are a kind of exercise, and so testing tends to promote the use of exercises in the school curriculum. Exercises also appeal to us as orderly rule-bound actions and therefore lend themselves to ritualization. The military dress parade and the drills of marching bands at sporting events are exercises that have become rituals valued for their intrinsic order and precision. Exercises can clearly be carried too far, acquire an inflated importance, and become detached from their propaedeutic purpose. Nevertheless, the heuristic strategy of looking for exercises can generate valuable educational activities.

Educational activities can also be generated from children's own spontaneous activities. Children spontaneously engage in make-believe, pretending they are Mommy, Daddy, the doctor, the firefighter, the police officer, and so on. An educational activity schema—role playing—has been patterned on this intrinsically satisfying child activity. Also, children in many cultures play games with tokens, a practice that in our culture has evolved into board games of various kinds, which serve as the inspiration for any number of educational games. The activities children do in kindergarten have nearly all been designed with this play heuristic, which might be expressed this way.

- Make what you want to teach part of a game like those children play spontaneously.
- Let children play the game until they grasp the teaching intuitively and incorporate it into their actions.
- Then, and only then (and only if necessary) teach about it formally.

There are surely many more activity-generating heuristics. We have not yet considered the most staple one of all: **telling.** Tell students about it. Any school textbook, workbook, or teacher's methods book will have dozens of other activity-generating heuristics.

When an activity kernel has been developed that shows promise of working, it can be shaped, revised, and enriched to make it more educationally valuable by considering in detail various features that might be incorporated into it. This is not necessarily a process of adding on other bits of activities, making the original more complicated, but it is rather a consideration of various versions of the basic activity with different emphases and orientations. The result of this reconsideration of the activity can as easily be a simplification of the original activity kernel as a complication of it.

The heuristic reasoning employed here is deliberative—strengths and weaknesses are considered and ways are found to capitalize on the one and to compensate for the other. The essential method of reasoning is to isolate first one feature and then another of the kernel activity and to ask of each feature whether an alternative to the present one can be found that improves the activity. An unlimited number of features may be isolated from any activity. The teacher's educational ideas and commitments suggest which features are likely to be most central to the operation and success of the activity. Box 10-7 gives examples of some kinds of questions a teacher might ask in order to identify features of an activity that might need to be reconsidered.

Teachers must rely on their judgment to decide whether an activity kernel can be improved in any of these ways, to set priorities on possible improvements, and to make the improvements. For example, suppose a teacher had decided to teach *Macbeth* by assigning students to read different parts and interrupting the reading at intervals to discuss the play. This is what we have called the activity kernel. The teacher would need to consider what features of this kernel might need to be modified. Perhaps the teacher would judge that students were likely to find

---

BOX 10-7   Is the Activity Basically Sound?

> Is what is to be learned clear to students?
>
> Is it also clear why this is important to learn?
>
> Does the activity *work* in the classroom?
>
> Are students able to comprehend the presentation?
>
> Does the activity permit students to perform in ways that show (to them and to others) that they have learned what was intended?
>
> Is the activity tailorable to suit different students and classroom situations?
>
> Does the activity make good use of appropriate resources in the learning situation?
>
> Does the activity require resources not normally present in the classroom?
>
> Is there a proportionality between the results achieved and the resources consumed?
>
> Does the activity support and assist students at critical points at which they might falter?
>
> *(continued)*

■
BOX 10-7 *(Continued)*   Questions about the Content of the Activity

Can the content of the activity under review be improved and made more valid, by appropriate tests of truth and correctness?

    Responsive to the educational challenge?

    Representative of the best, most important content in that domain?

    Reflective of the inherent structure of the content domain?

    Comprehensive and more inclusive of relevant objects and operations?

    Important to the content domain?

    Important to the culture at large?

Can the content be made more appropriate to students?

    Would other forms of meaning investment and recovery be more suitable?

    Can the activity be made to take into account students' naive models and concepts?

    Can it be made more intrinsically motivating, interesting?

Can the content be presented in a better form?

    Can media and sensory qualities be improved?

    Can stimulus discriminations be made clearer?

    Can we provide more, clearer examples and non-examples?

    Can we find a better form of representation?

    Does the presentation include the full range of examples students are expected to learn to cope with: hard/easy, simple/complex, and so on?

Can standards of performance with respect to content be improved? Raised? Brought into line with student's capabilities? Made more explicit?

Is adequate attention given to common, serious content-related problems, such as content being foreign to students' experience?

Is content too complex?

Shakespeare's vocabulary and grammar so difficult that the reading would be unclear, would absorb nearly all of students' attention, and might even be embarrassing. Having reached this judgment, the teacher might consider various modifications of the activity kernel. The teacher could prepare a sheet of notes

BOX 10-7 *(Continued)*   **Question about the Tasks Students Are Asked to Perform**

Can the activities students are asked to perform be improved so that they give students greater opportunities to recall what was presented?

> Practice what they learn?

> Demonstrate the validity of what they learn?

> Apply what they learn to new situations?

> Explain what they learn?

> Integrate what they learn with other knowledge?

Can the task be modified to provide a better opportunity for students to learn the content presented?

> More powerful or wider opportunities for experiences that will make content meaningful?

> Sufficient repetition, time, variety of stimuli and responses?

> Problems for application, practice, self-testing?

> Opportunity to integrate content with other aspects of personality: perception, action, valuing, . . . ?

Can the activity be made more intrinsically motivating?

Can the activity be modified to guard against any of the following types of difficulties that students often encounter?

Inadequacies in Entering Factors:

> mistaken ideas, competing inadequate models

> study skills required (reading level, and so on)

> starting points in prior learnings that may be used as hooks either cognitively or motivationally

> prerequisite skill and knowledge

> aptitudes for learning

Insufficient Engagement with the Learning Activity:

> make evaluation cumulative

> provide rewards, incentives (intrinsic, if possible)

> make goals clear to students so they can mobilize their developed psychological resources in pursuit of them

> increase variety of task   *(continued)*

BOX 10-7   *(Continued)* **Questions about Social Aspects of the Activity**

Tasks Comprising the Activities Are Too Difficult:

    making the user's job easier by controlling the introduction of novelty, difficulty

    difficulty (variety, intricacy of skills demanded)

    complexity

    simplification techniques

    provide better and more frequent feedback

    provide supports, for example, emphasize cues

Superficial Learning:

    multiple simultaneous criteria

    criteria for success (goals)

    make sure tasks used in the activity include samples of the full variety of tasks to be learned

    make clear all standards that apply and levels of performance that are acceptable (or outstanding) for each
(continued)

on difficult passages and assign students to study these and rehearse their parts as homework. Alternatively, the teacher might divide the class into small groups and assign each small group the task of understanding both the literal meaning and possible connotations and allusions of one character's speeches. The teacher would then review each group's analysis prior to the reading for the whole class. The teacher would certainly need to give further thought to the discussions to be held at intervals in the reading of the play. When should the reading be interrupted? Which of many possible purposes should be pursued in these discussions (clarifying the dramatist's meaning, analyzing language, examining characters' motivations, discovering how the dramatist achieved his effects, or exploring students' personal associations, for example)? What questions should be posed? How long should the discussion be permitted to go on? How closely should the teacher guide the discussion? What criteria should the teacher use to judge the quality of individual contributions or of the discussion as a whole?

By considering such questions as these the teacher finds and exploits opportunities to improve the activity. The original activity design is modified, sometimes by adding features, sometimes by eliminating them, sometimes by reorganizing.

BOX 10-7   *(Continued) Questions about Social Aspects of the Activity*

Can any of the following social aspects of the activity be made more appropriate or be used to make the activity more effective?

Pre-activity:

Entry conditions (compulsory, voluntary, restricted), the occasion, the location, group size?

During Activity:

Differentiation of role or duties?

Division of responsibility for group performance?

Interdependence of tasks?

Mobility permitted?

Is evaluation public or private?

Control, choice, decision-making

to enter or not,

to continue or not,

what to do,

how to do it,

how fast, how long, how often, . . . timing,

with whom

social meaning of the tasks, the setting/occasion, and the related enterprises, and their relation to cultural context

Depending on what questions teachers ask here and how they answer them, the activity kernel could take on completely different complexions in the teacher's planbook. And depending on the skill and judgment with which the teacher carried out these plans, the developed activity could take on completely different complexions when realized in the classroom. It is this dependence of the classroom curriculum on so many judgments, some made in advance and some necessarily made on the spur of the moment, that makes the realization of plans made outside the classroom so problematic. This is also the reason why the individual teacher plays the pivotal role in shaping the classroom curriculum.

Summary

In this chapter we have considered how classroom curricula are maintained and changed. Clearly, each classroom presents unique problems that those involved must understand if they are to act sensibly. All that can be done without considering particular cases is to indicate how to think about classroom curriculum improvement and how to approach the most important problems that ordinarily arise. Different assumptions about classrooms and how they work or about curricular aims and priorities will lead to different recommendations for how best to seek classroom curricular improvement. The same problems—how to realize curriculum plans, how to bring about changes, and how to develop new activities—will probably arise in any effort at curriculum improvement and the ways we have thought about these problems should prove generally applicable, but the conclusions about how best to seek classroom curricular improvement will change. There are no infallible recipes. Therefore it is essential that teachers and others charged with fostering improvements in classroom curricula learn to think through specific situations and make their own determinations of what to do in each case.

QUESTIONS FOR STUDY

1. Reflect on your own teaching. Recall the first few days of one of your classes. Describe how you introduced the curriculum of that class to your students. Are you happy now with what you did then? How would you change it?

2. Conduct a case study of how one or more experienced teachers introduce their curriculum to students in the first few days of class. Observe the class and interview the teacher. Compare your findings with what student teachers do and how they talk about their work.

3. Examine some textbooks. How do they introduce the subject? Can you suggest ways to improve them?

4. Identify the frames in a typical elementary class, a typical secondary class, and a typical undergraduate class. How are they alike and how do they differ? How might the differences affect teachers' planning at the three levels mentioned in the chapter?

5. Examine two or more unit plans. Assess their strengths and limitations and suggest ways they might be improved.

6. Some observers maintain that teachers are powerless pawns in curriculum reform, while others maintain that teachers are the most powerful shapers of the actual curriculum students receive. Can you shed any light on this dispute using the ideas presented in this chapter?

7. Find a teacher who has recently been expected to adopt a curriculum reform that required making a substantial change in her classroom curriculum. Interview that teacher about her attempts, the support she received, how she felt about the process, and what happened as a result of it.

8. Choose one of the activity schemata mentioned in the chapter or identify an additional one. On a single sheet of paper list the slots or blanks that need to be filled in when creating a specific activity of that type.

9. Leaf through a school textbook or workbook or a teachers' methods book and see if you can identify a heuristic that would generate the kernel of each activity you find.

10. Develop an educational activity by beginning with some out-of-school activities that are not usually taken as sources of educative activities. For example, try chanting, shopping, telling jokes, writing graffiti, gossiping, arguing, travelling, and partying.

RECOMMENDED READING

It is curious how little close study has been done of what happens in classrooms between students, teachers, and curriculum materials. Until the present decade we have had only common sense and conventional wisdom to rely on in understanding such basic questions as what teachers actually do with the curriculum plans and materials they were presumed to be following, what teachers do when they implement a curriculum change, and how students, teachers, and curriculum materials interact in the classroom. Even now, the encyclopedic *Handbook of Research on Teaching* (Wittrock 1986) touches on teachers' curriculum work only indirectly as part of broader discussions of topics such as teacher planning (Clark and Peterson 1986).

In the 1970s studies of teacher planning discovered that teachers usually began their planning with the content to be presented and that they relied heavily on plans found in textbooks and curriculum materials (Peterson, Marx, and Clark 1978; Taylor 1970; Yinger 1977; Zahorik 1975). In this decade investigators have asked more penetrating questions. What role do textbooks and curriculum plans play in teachers' planning (Komoski 1976; McCutcheon 1980)? How do teachers cope with curriculum policies made outside the classroom (Schwille, et al. 1983)? What is the significance of teachers' emphasis on practicality in planning (Doyle and Ponder 1977; Elbaz 1983)? How do teachers respond when they confront curriculum materials that are in some way incompatible with their beliefs and preferences (Floden, et al. 1981; Feingold, Connelly, and Wahlstrom 1979)?

A later generation of investigators has focused specifically on how teachers think about curriculum matters in their planning (Ben-Peretz 1975; Elbaz 1983; Kremer and Ben-Peretz 1980; Ben-Peretz, Bromme, and Halkes 1986). Investigators have recently begun to look at how the curriculum enters into interactions between teachers and students in the classroom (Barr and Dreeben 1977; Carlsen 1988). It turns out that subject matter and teachers' conceptions of subject matter have a great deal of influence on those interactions (Barr 1986; Carlsen 1988; Davis and McKnight 1976; Stodolsky 1988).

I hope that the coming decade will see a similar explosion of studies of students and their interactions with curricula. Wittrock's chapter "Students' Thought Processes" (Wittrock 1986) shows that as little attention has been given to content and curriculum in these studies as was given to them in studies of teaching in the 1970s, and the topic is so fundamental that we stand to gain at least as much from studies of students as we have from studies of teachers.

REFERENCES

Barr, Rebecca. 1986. Classroom Interaction and Curricular Content. *Literacy, Language, and Schooling.* (D. Bloome, ed.) Norwood, NJ: Ablex.

Barr, Rebecca and Robert Dreeben. 1977. Instruction in Classrooms. *Review of Research in Education 5.* (Lee S. Shulman, ed.) Itasca, IL: F. E. Peacock.

Ben-Peretz, Miriam. 1975. The Concept of Curriculum Potential. *Curriculum Theory Network* 5:151–159.

Ben-Peretz, Miriam, R. Bromme, and R. Halkes. 1986. *Advances of Research on Teacher Thinking.* Berwyn, IL: Swets North America.

Carlsen, William. 1988. The Effects of Science Teacher Subject-Matter Knowledge on Teacher Questioning and Classroom Discourse. Unpublished Ph.D. Dissertation. Stanford University.

Clark, Christopher and Penelope Peterson. 1986. Teachers' Thought Processes. (See Wittrock 1986.)

Davis, Robert B. and Carolyn McKnight. 1976. Conceptual, Heuristic, and Algorithmic Approaches in Mathematics Teaching. *Journal of Children's Mathematical Behavior* 1:271–286.

Doyle, Walter and Gerald Ponder. 1977. The Practicality Ethic in Teacher Decision-Making. *Interchange* 8:1–12.

Elbaz, Freema. 1983. *Teacher Thinking: A Study of Practical Knowledge.* N.Y.: Nichols.

Feingold, Mehachem, F., Michael Connelly, and M. W. Wahlstrom. 1979. Determining the Compatibility of a Teacher's Orientation to Science Instruction with a Set of Curriculum Materials. *Studies in Educational Evaluation* 5:215–222.

Floden, Robert E., Andrew Porter, William Schmidt, D. Freeman, and Jack Schwille. 1981. Responses to Curriculum Pressure: A Policy-Capturing Study of Teacher Decisions about Content. *Journal of Educational Psychology* 73:129–141.

Komoski, Kenneth. 1976. Educational Products Information Exchange. *EPIEgram* 5:1.

Kremer, Lya and Miram Ben-Peretz. 1980. Teachers' Characteristics and Their Reflections in Curriculum Implementation. *Studies in Educational Evaluation* 6:73–82.

Lortie, Dan C. 1975. *Schoolteacher.* Chicago: University of Chicago Press.

McCutcheon, Gail. 1980. How Do Elementary Teachers Plan? The Nature of Planning and Influences on It. *Elementary School Journal* 81:4–23.

Peterson, Penelope, Robert W. Marx, and Christopher Clark. 1978. Teacher Planning, Teacher Behavior, and Student Achievement. *American Educational Research Journal* 15:417–432.

Posner, George and A. N. Rudnitsky. 1978. *Course Design.* N.Y.: Longman.

Schwille, Jack, Andrew Porter, G. Belli, Robert Floden, D. Freeman, L. Knappen, T. Kuhs, and W. Schmidt. 1983. Teachers As Policy Brokers in the Content of Elementary School

Mathematics. *Handbook of Teaching Policy*. (Lee S. Shulman and Gary Sykes, eds.) N.Y.: Longman.

Stodolsky, Susan. 1988. *The Subject Matters*. Chicago: University of Chicago Press.

Taylor, Phillip H. 1970. *How Teachers Plan Their Courses*. Slough, Berkshire, England: National Foundation for Educational Research.

Wittrock, Merlin (ed.). 1986. *Handbook of Research on Teaching* (3rd ed.). N.Y.: Macmillan.

Yinger, Robert. 1977. A Study of Teacher Planning. Unpublished Ph.D. Dissertation. East Lansing: Michigan State University.

Zahorik, J. A. 1975. Teachers' Planning Models. *Educational Leadership* 33:134–159.

chapter 11

SCHOOL CURRICULUM IMPROVEMENT

The American school seems to be almost systematically making . . . of the school experience something deadening, restricting, and limiting rather than growing. Therefore, any efforts to increase flexibility, to cut down the miseries, frustrations and internal conflicts for the teachers are worthwhile if only to encourage some change in the school's atmosphere, its feeling tone.

Gertrude McPherson
American ethnographer, 1972

PURPOSE OF THE CHAPTER

- To show the types of challenges that face those who attempt to improve the curriculum of a school

- To describe common strategies for improving a school's curriculum

- To suggest other approaches that may be more suitable for conditions commonly found in American schools

OUTLINE

IMPROVING THE SCHOOL CURRICULUM

In this chapter we consider how to improve the curriculum offered by a school. To many with no experience, making curriculum improvements seems to be a straightforward and relatively simple matter compared to making changes in teaching methods or school organization, but this apparent simplicity is an illusion. Before turning to the primary topic, we will first briefly consider some of the complexities that make the task difficult.

Most of the curriculum work of local school personnel is devoted to keeping the curriculum they already have in good working order, as we saw in Chapter 8. Curriculum improvement must be accomplished with the small but precious margin of resources, talent, and time left over from the central task. Were there world enough and time, every school could set up elaborate procedures to keep every facet of the curriculum continually renewed, but in the real world of the public schools curriculum improvement usually comes down to a question like: "What can we do this year with $2000 and six in-service days?" Sadly, many schools waste even the few precious resources they have for curriculum improvement by thoughtlessly copying unnecessarily elaborate procedures. Happily, some schools somehow manage to do a great deal of curriculum improvement with very meager resources by doing the same work in simple, direct, no-nonsense ways. Throughout this chapter keep in mind that in most schools curriculum improvement must be done on a shoestring budget.

Remember, too, that the school curriculum is the shared creation of many parties. The principal may draw up the master schedule, but it must suit the elective choices of students and their parents, the qualifications of teachers, and the requirements of many external authorities. Committees of teachers may write the curriculum plans, but administrators appoint the committees, the board accepts or rejects their products, and the community elects the board. Sustaining compatibility of purpose among so many for so long presses the limits of human ingenuity and good will. Success requires organization, discipline, shared values, hard work, and a high order of leadership. As we saw in Chapters 7 and 8, everyone except the teacher has extremely limited power to control what happens in classrooms, so that the coordination demanded by a curriculum extending over four to six years of a student's life and across a dozen or more school subjects must be attained indirectly.

The activities of individual teachers must somehow be coordinated into a coherent school curriculum by two basic modes of indirect influence: interpersonal and structural. Interpersonal influences include all the myriad forms by which one human being affects another, such as by giving orders, handing out rewards and punishments, posing a challenge, bribing, cajoling, begging, and so on. A principal or committee chair who has responsibility for implementing a new curriculum in a school and is confronted with resistance from some teachers must rely on interpersonal influence. Everything we know about American schools today indicates that educational leadership requires a great deal of skill at interpersonal influence.

Much of the coordination of individual behavior required to sustain a school curriculum comes about because those individuals all conform to the same structure. The school's daily schedule coordinates the movement of teachers and students from class to class. Its annual calendar coordinates examinations, grading, and holidays. The secondary school's master schedule coordinates teachers, students, courses, and rooms and is one of the major structural features of the school curriculum. The ability to create special courses and programs and to assign teachers and students to them is another major structural feature of the school curriculum. Others are adoption and provision of textbooks and curriculum materials, selection and administration of tests, specification of the subject matter qualifications required of teachers to be hired, and assignment of teachers to subjects, grades, and schools. Decisions about these structural matters set frames within which individual teachers and students function and thus bring a degree of order and coordination into the total school program.

Because it affects the activities of so many in the school in so fundamental a way, bringing about a lasting and substantial change in the curriculum of a school is always a major undertaking. Box 11-1 shows some of the major requirements that must somehow be met if a proposed change in a school's curriculum is to have a reasonable chance of eventual success. Such a demanding list of conditions is seldom met and this is the main reason why curriculum change efforts so often fail.

Ultimately, what we want from school curriculum improvement efforts is that students receive schooling with better content, purpose, structure, and effects. The judgment that a new curriculum represents an improvement over an existing one is as complex a judgment as any in education, and it would be foolish to expect unanimity on it among the members of any reasonably diverse school and

BOX 11-1   **Major Requirements for Curriculum Improvement in Local Schools and School Systems**

1. A working consensus in support of the change among
    a. parents and community
    b. teachers
    c. school leaders, formal and informal, lay and professional
2. Consistency of the change with given frames, including
    a. economic constraints
    b. policies of higher authorities
    c. other relatively fixed local realities
3. Good leadership for the change effort
    a. local champions with leadership ability
4. Deep, clear understanding of the change, including
    a. central features that must be present
    b. appropriate variations
    c. ideas (theories, rationales) supporting the change
5. Training and support for teachers, including
    a. explanations and demonstrations
    b. opportunity for practice with feedback
    c. continuing support to overcome difficulties
    d. incentives for the extra effort of change
6. Material and administrative support for the change effort, including
    a. provision of curriculum materials
    b. adjustment of routines to accommodate the change
    c. assistance in handling unanticipated problems
7. Provision for revising the plan to adapt it to local circumstances
8. Provision for monitoring change efforts and evaluating their effects

community. Ideally, every curriculum change would have the support of a solid consensus of affected parties. Practically, achieving lasting curriculum change requires that the change be viewed as an improvement by enough people with enough power and influence to make and defend the change. Usually, we accept uneasy, ambiguous compromises that no one finds totally unacceptable, but that few consider optimal. As a result, dissatisfaction can nearly always be found with any curriculum, and curriculum matters always threaten to break out in controversy. The feelings of those responsible for curriculum improvement are therefore generally tinged with anxiety.

Local school systems distribute the responsibility for curriculum improvement among principals, department chairs, teacher leaders, supervisors, curriculum coordinators, and other school officials. To understand any specific curriculum improvement effort it is essential to know who does what and who bears what responsibility. But for discussing the issues raised in this chapter, in most cases it is sufficient to speak simply of the school leadership or the project leadership without regard to job titles. The approaches discussed in this chapter will assume that leadership exists and that it represents and is responsive to all the school's important stakeholders. Furthermore, the discussion of procedures will assume the desirability of open communication, participation, and sharing of power among all affected persons in the process of school curriculum improvement.

Keeping these guiding principles in mind, let us turn to a consideration of the fundamental problems encountered in curriculum improvement and the main alternative strategies for responding to them. The work of improving the school curriculum can be analyzed logically into six main functions:

1. reviewing the school curriculum,
2. considering curriculum changes,
3. instituting changes in the school curriculum,
4. facilitating curriculum change in classrooms,
5. evaluating curriculum change efforts,
6. making long range plans.

In practice these six functions are blended together and combined with the other work of running a school. In this chapter we indulge ourselves with the academic fiction of treating them as distinct activities.

REVIEWING THE QUALITY OF A SCHOOL CURRICULUM

People are always making judgments about the quality of a school and of its curriculum, so in a sense the curriculum is under constant review. We will speak in this section about those rarer periods during which the curriculum receives extraordinary scrutiny. These investigations go by many names—studies, reports, surveys, evaluations, assessments, needs assessments, and so on—but in this section we will use the term *review* for any systematic effort to collect information in order to make a judgment about the quality of an educational program. Curriculum reviews may be planned, regularly recurring reviews, as in annual reports, periodic accreditation studies, or cyclic reconsideration of textbook adoptions. Or, they may be unplanned reviews precipitated by some crisis or demanded by an outside authority or required as part of a grant proposal the school wishes to make. Reviews may be comprehensive, dealing with all aspects of the entire school program, or they may be focused on a particular problem. A review may involve dozens of people from the public and the profession or it may consist of a study by a single individual. Reviewers may be empowered with nearly prosecutorial investigative authority and the funds to go with it, or constrained to use only publicly available information volunteered by those involved and very little funding. Reviews may operate in the full glare of public meetings covered by the media or in private sessions with confidential reporting to the authorizer only.

Explicit formal reviews of a school curriculum can serve many purposes. They can be used to disturb the complacency of school staffs and spur them to ambition. They can be used to explore and discover the nature and seriousness of possible problems. Reviews that focus on particular problems can be used to communicate the determination of school leaders to deal with these problems. Reviews offer a possibility of capitalizing on unique historical opportunities for curriculum improvement by creating local concern about issues where political and economic support is momentarily strong. Reviews can help schools to find an appropriate response to changes in educational beliefs and priorities of parents and community members or to correct their mistaken impressions of the school. Reviews also provide an occasion for those involved to consider possible responses to changes in objective conditions in the school or community such as growth, decline or change in the student population or changes in the local economy.

Curricular reviews may be conducted in several ways. Most reviews are self-studies, conducted by the same people who are responsible for the curriculum under review. The stimulus for the review may come from outside this circle, outsiders may participate in the review, and the results of the review may be communicated to outsiders. Outsiders may even impose conditions on how it should be conducted. But the carrying out of the review is usually the responsibility of the school staff. Almost the only exception to this are reviews of school programs carried out by staff from the district office. The most common audiences for reviews of school programs are the Superintendent and school board. Accreditation committees become a significant audience when a school is undergoing accreditation. Schools occasionally conduct voluntary reviews and needs assessments for a state or federal agency from which they seek funds or recognition. In normal times, the audience for reviews consists of central office staff, principals, teachers and local lay leaders. In times of crisis, however, the general public and others with no previous knowledge of the school and no special expertise in dealing with educational issues, such as citizen groups, legislators, or judges, become important members of the audience.

Comprehensive Program Reviews

A comprehensive review is not literally comprehensive. A truly complete review would require a study beyond the means of the wealthiest school and beyond the technical capability of the most advanced research. Selection is unavoidable. Labelling a review *comprehensive* simply signals an intention to include in the review in some way any relevant question proposed by any participant. Most of the questions considered in any review will receive only cursory attention. Still, the striving toward comprehensiveness is important politically and organizationally.

Consider by way of illustration the case of the Schenley High School Teacher Center that the Pittsburgh Public Schools created in 1981 on the recommendation of Superintendent Richard C. Wallace, Jr. When Wallace was asked how he persuaded the board of education to approve such a project, he replied

> . . . it grew out of a comprehensive needs assessment. Probably the smartest thing I ever did when I arrived in Pittsburgh in September of 1980 was to get Bill Cooley and Bill Bickel [of the University of Pittsburgh] to work with me. . . . We conducted a very broad-based needs assessment, surveying samples of public school and private school parents, community leaders, and every level of employee in the district . . . (Wallace 1987, 40)

He explained that the board members were able to use the needs assessment to focus attention on a few achievable priorities from among their diverse concerns and to unify the board on behalf of some important projects.

Cooley and Bickel describe this comprehensive needs assessment in their book, *Decision-Oriented Educational Research* (1986). They call their activities research and think of themselves as researchers serving decision-makers, but as their eleven case histories make plain, one of their major functions is to collect information that would help to identify strengths and weaknesses of the educational program of the Pittsburgh public schools. One of the case histories recounts a district-wide needs assessment. It can serve as a good introduction to outstanding contemporary practice in program review.

As they recount the events, the needs assessment was undertaken at the request of the newly appointed Superintendent, a fairly common occasion for program reviews of all types. The purpose of the review was to determine the extent to which the Pittsburgh public schools were meeting the needs of children enrolled in them and to identify priorities for program improvement. In meetings with the Superintendent, Cooley and Bickel came to understand the purposes and constraints of the review and developed a plan that relied on data from two sources: surveys of stakeholders' perceptions and existing school records. The Superintendent appointed a 30-member task force to assist with the design of the study; half of the task force members were community leaders and the rest were representatives of teachers, principals, and other employee groups. The technical staff wrote the items for questionnaires and field tested them, designed a sampling plan, and settled the practical details of distributing, collecting, and analyzing the data. The planning and instrument development occupied between two and three months, data were collected in less than one month, analyzed in less than a month, and reviewed by the board of education in less than five months from the first meeting with the Superintendent. In previous work with the district, researchers had already entered much of the district's data into a computer in a form in which it was easily retrieved and processed. Analyses were carried out to discover trends across grades, trends over time, and comparisons among schools on questions considered important by the Superintendent, task force, and technical staff, including such topics as percentages enrolled in remedial programs, enrollment trends, suspension rates, and costs per pupil in various schools. Since the data were already in computer files, analysis took only three months.

Based on these data the needs assessment identified five pressing needs: improving student achievement in basic skills, better procedures for personnel evaluation, attracting and holding students, managing enrollment decline, and improving individual schools. For each need, the study was able to deliver fairly detailed documentation of the extent and nature of the problem. For instance, they were able to discover that students assigned to several distinct remedial programs had similar profiles of academic achievement and were receiving similar remedial programs, though under quite different labels, and that the coordination between what was taught in these remedial programs and what was taught in regular classrooms was lax. Study personnel presented the results of the assessment in the form of a series of slide shows held over a period of three months for different audiences, including the Superintendent, the board president, the entire board, the central office staff, building administrators and supervisors, teachers, task force members, and the press.

On the Monday following the first presentation of results to the Superintendent and school board at a weekend retreat, the Superintendent publicly announced a push to develop an *action plan* to address two major areas: school improvement and cost-effective management. At its next meeting the board endorsed these initiatives and authorized funds to begin the planning.

This example is typical of needs assessments in several respects. It was initiated by a newly appointed Superintendent. It was jointly planned by technically trained staff, Superintendent, and a representative steering group. No facet of the school system's operation was exlcuded from consideration in the study. The study used numerical data already available in district files and also results of surveys of a representative sample of various stakeholders. The study is unusual and exemplary in several other respects. It was completed very quickly, in less than one academic year. The data were analyzed with particular care and astuteness. The results were disseminated with special thoroughness. And the relation of the review to actions based on its results were particularly close. This is an example of a district-level needs assessment, rather than a school-level program review, but in the most important respects the two are similar. Needs assessments are more often done for a school district rather than an individual school, though newly appointed principals may also conduct needs assessments for their schools. Accreditation reviews are the most common types of comprehensive reviews of school programs. They, too, cover all aspects of a school's operation, including the educational program, but also including finance, personnel, administration, and even buildings and grounds. Accreditation reviews take place on a fairly regular schedule, typically every five years or so for a school at which few problems are identified, though as often as every year or two in the case of a school with serious problems.

Just how effective are comprehensive reviews? As the case of Pittsburgh showed, comprehensive reviews can be powerfully effective in calling attention to problems, in gaining consensus on priorities, and in precipitating action on the problems identified. But they are costly and they will only repay their cost when there is a good chance something effective can be done about any major problems discovered.

Focused Selective Reviews

Obviously, comprehensive formal reviews are major undertakings. The costs and risks associated with them must be carefully weighed against the benefits that can reasonably be expected from them. There are less costly alternatives. Intentionally focused selective reviews are one kind of alternative that is preferable in many situations. Such a frankly targeted review is preferable when the existence of a particular curriculum problem is not in question, but it is necessary to define the problem better, to document its extent and seriousness, or to identify its causes. Sometimes it may be clear to school leaders that complacency has set in with some component of the curriculum, and a focused review may call the situation to everyone's attention. Sometimes it is important to look into rumors or charges being circulated in order to confirm or dispel them. Often when a change is under consideration a focused review of the present situation may help in planning the development and implementation of the change.

A focused selective review should begin with a statement of the reasons for undertaking the review of this part of the curriculum at this time. It should state the best current understandings of the processes and outcomes of this part of the curriculum extant among those involved, and the initial questions to be answered, if possible, by the review. All participants should understand that there is likely to be disagreement on these matters, and alternative positions should be welcomed as helping to guide the review. Also, everyone should understand that the chief outcome of the review is likely to be a different appreciation of the situation and therefore a redefinition of the problem and a restatement of the questions of most importance. For this reason, plans for focused selective reviews should allow the maximum possible flexibility.

Arrangements should be made to collect data that are both easy to collect and highly informative as early as possible and to compare these against existing alternative interpretations of the problem. As a result of discussions of early results with the governing body, the next phase of the study may be substantially altered from original plans. As understanding develops from the review, it is likely that questions will multiply. It will probably be necessary to spin off several sub-studies to pursue different questions. The entire review should be organized in such a way that substantial progress can be made in a matter of a few weeks and the entire study redesigned in progress, with staff redeployed, expanded, or reduced as necessary. For such an organization to work, communication lines must be short, because there is no time for results to filter through to a wide, distant audience; the governing body must be trusted, because such arrangements can be exploited by an unscrupulous person or group to protect themselves or to harm others; and the technical staff must be tolerant of compromises with prevailing standards of disciplined inquiry.

Mixed Designs

A mixed strategy is often appropriate. The initial phase of a review might include a broad and necessarily superficial look at the entire program. Two or three levels of intensity might be distinguished in this first phase, most intense scrutiny going to those components that are believed to need most attention. Since some resources will be directed toward all major components, the review would be comprehensive, but it would also be focused right from the start on some areas more than others. In later phases, the review could focus only on those areas in which those involved judge that inquiries are most likely to reveal something of importance.

On Methods for Conducting Curriculum Reviews

All studies directed toward assessing the quality of educational programs face similar problems of framing questions, collecting and analyzing data and interpreting findings. Let us look briefly at each of these types of problems.

Framing Questions Box 11-2 lists some of the questions that might guide a comprehensive review. Determining which questions are of most interest and concern should be the first and most fundamental step in any curricular review. It is critically important to insist that the review answer the questions considered most important by the steering group and not the questions that are most easily or definitively answered by standard research methods. Some scientifically acceptable form of inquiry can be found to address any empirically meaningful question. On the other hand, sometimes the best feasible study will shed little light on the most important issue, while another study much easier to conduct could make a major difference in answering another question only slightly less important. So decisions about the best questions to ask need to be informed by technical considerations, not controlled by them.

Data Collection and Analysis To answer questions such as those in Box 11-2 and to monitor the variables listed in Box 11-3, a review must generally have data not in school records and not normally included in needs assessment surveys. Surveys of graduates, of employers, of schools that graduates attend, and other groups not routinely involved with the school may need to be made. Global judgments of the overall quality of the school program can be solicited from a variety of persons likely to have different perspectives: employers of graduates,

BOX 11-2   Possible Questions for a Comprehensive Curriculum Review

How are our graduates performing in important domains by relevant standards after they leave our school?

Important domains might include academic, personal, vocational, and civic.

Possibly relevant standards include their own, their families', their community's, the school's, the state's, the nation's, and the world's.

How well are our students meeting relevant expectations at various stages of their schooling?

Possibly relevant expectations include participation and involvement in school activities (especially attendance), mastery of curricular content and objectives, satisfactory development in nonacademic domains (personal, civic, vocational, . . .).

Do curricular offerings meet appropriate standards of quality and quantity? Do the programs students actually receive meet appropriate standards?

Is the school program functioning smoothly? Are students attending, participating, engaged with school activities? Do school and classroom climate meet appropriate standards?

What resources are devoted to the school program?

Is there a clear positive relationship between the pattern of curricular inputs and the students' achievements?

How are these resources distributed among students?

Is this distribution equitable?

teachers and admissions officers in schools to which students pass on graduation, parents, teachers, and students themselves. In addition, the following kinds of rough indicators of public perceptions of school quality can be solicited: reputation of the school, ease of recruiting and retaining staff, extent to which quality of schools is a factor in local real estate transactions, and ratings of the school by college admissions offices. Data of various kinds may need to be collected from municipal, state or federal governments or from commercial sources. Additional test data or other student performance data may be needed.

Finding sound data that faithfully represent such complex matters as these and collecting them economically are the greatest technical challenges facing designers of reviews. The intellectual compromises involved in using, for example, a student's reading score on a standardized test as a measure of what the student has learned in elementary school are enormous. But the compromises involved in choosing other indicators, such as grades on teacher-made tests or grades in middle school English, are at least as great. Multiple measures can compensate for the limitations of any one, but only at additional cost. Such dilemmas haunt designers of social research in field settings. Sadly, we have few adequate measures for the global processes and outcomes of schooling. We have relatively good tests of many important specific outcomes such as mastery of arithmetic or reading comprehension, but tests of overall mathematics achievement are problematic for two fundamental reasons. First, there is no consensus on the relative weight that should be given to different kinds of mathematics learning or to different content in these tests. As a result, different tests give different results. Second, valid interpretation of the scores on

---

BOX 11-3   Important Data for a Comprehensive Curriculum Review

Inputs	Processes	Outcomes	Consequences

offerings
programs
time
allotments
	teacher
	assignments
	
	services
	provided to
	teachers
		tests:
		  teacher,
		  district,
		  standardized (SAT)
			admission to
			selective
			schools
			
			performance
			in later
			schooling,

teacher characteristics	engaged time	grades student achievements	jobs
student characteristics	attendance course	student honors	recognition, honors, awards
home, community characteristics	completion (drop-outs)		achievements (patents,
curriculum materials	critical incidents		publications)
courses of study	(discipline, failures, complaints)		perceptions of graduates
tests	reputation		
statements of purpose and philosophy	visits from other schools to study programs		
history, tradition	honors and recognition for curricular excellence		
	frequency of complaints		

such a test depends on knowledge of the curriculum to which the student was exposed. Students who missed an item they never studied must be distinguished from those who missed it after encountering it in their school program, or else the wrong conclusions will be drawn about the program's strengths and weaknesses.

So, designers of the data collection for a curricular review must carefully balance the competing demands of validity, relevance, coverage, and cost in selecting data to include in the review. Emphasizing low cost and validity at the expense of relevance and coverage, for example, yields a tough-minded, hard-nosed, quantitative review focused on those matters most readily captured by current educational measurement methods: attendance, enrollments, grades, test scores. Reversing the priorities, emphasizing relevance and wide coverage at the expense of economy and validity, yields a tender-minded, subjective, qualitative review. Needless to say, the results of two such different reviews will not necessarily agree. Therefore, the design of data collection for a curriculum review should never be left only in the hands of technically trained people. Design decisions should be made by the governing body for the review after discussion with technically trained staff.

Generally, the expertise demanded by planning and carrying out this additional data collection is beyond that normally found in school staffs. Staffs of program review committees should include experts in research methods. Traditionally, these experts are trained in psychological methods of testing, measurement, and evaluation. They tend to recommend review procedures that call for collection of numerical data in objective forms obtained under controlled conditions. These scientifically controlled data collection procedures are designed to guard against various forms of error and bias that can lead to mistaken conclusions. Qualitative methods are now a viable alternative to quantitative methods. They rely more on judgment than procedure to guard against errors. An intensive ethnographic study of students' citizenship attitudes and behavior in schools, classrooms, and community settings might yield more helpful data less expensively and with more credibility than quantitative methods that count incidents of particular civil and uncivil occurrences in these same settings, for example.

Analyzing the data in a way that leads to valid, defensible conclusions about the questions actually of interest in the review is another major technical challenge. Hundreds of thousands of individual items of data must be reduced to comprehensible patterns. The aggregated data must be reduced to summary statistics, a few numbers, graphs, or statements that represent the key patterns in the data. Answering most questions requires the analyst to discover the existence, and sometimes the size and direction, of a relationship among data representing different variables. This requires that the data be manipulated mathematically and results compared to statistical models that indicate what results one would expect to find by chance in such complicated data. The technical intricacies involved in such decisions are daunting and demand a high level of training. Decisions about data analysis are generally best left in the hands of the chief technical person on the staff of the review, but this person should be given a clear set of questions to be answered and must be involved in the planning. When the plan of the review is complete, the data analyst should be able to say which questions will be answerable with these data and with what range of uncertainty.

   Interpretation Interpretation is primarily a process of finding meaning in the data by relating it to prior beliefs and values. When the interested parties to a review begin with different beliefs and values, they will nearly always interpret the review's results differently. Reviews can raise new issues or change the salience of preexisting ones, but even the most rigorous reviews never yield definitive results, and comprehensive curriculum reviews cannot even come close. Reviews seldom resolve hot disputes because the parties can always find ways to discount or dispute unpalatable findings. To have any impact on a disputed issue, findings of a review must survive the give-and-take of public debate among all the interested parties. A written report of the study's findings is therefore only the beginning of the process of interpretation.

CONSIDERING CURRICULUM CHANGES

   Jon Schaffarzick (1975) coined the term *curriculum change consideration*. It refers to the process in which local curriculum leaders consider whether to undertake a proposed curriculum change. It can be as brief and informal as a hallway conversation or as imposing as a formal inquiry by a school-community task force. The change consideration process is important because most proposed innovations do not proceed beyond this stage. At any one time there are dozens, perhaps hundreds, of innovations being urged on schools. In any particular school several of these may find local champions who will urge their adoption in that school. Curriculum change consideration is the varied, complex, and seldom-documented process by which the proposal either fails and drops from active consideration or succeeds and becomes an official attempt at curriculum improvement. It is the death knell for most innovation proposals, and a major step toward realization for others.

   A proposal survives the change consideration process when the school leadership launches an official effort to make the proposed curriculum improvements. This decision, in turn, rests on leaders' assumptions that support for the change would eventually be widespread enough to permit it to be implemented. This means that the test that the change consideration process imposes on proposals is fundamentally political. The merits of the change proposal will only matter if they influence those who make implementation decisions.

   In many schools the process of change consideration is visible only to top school leadership, completely hidden from the sight of casual participants such as parents or outside observers, and hidden from teachers except those active in school affairs. On the other hand, some schools have an open, public change consideration process. In either case, the process must become visible when, as must happen eventually, those in control of the official school curriculum seek the collaboration of teachers and the approval of the public. Box 11-4 describes some stages through which such an open, explicit curriculum change consideration process typically passes.

It is easy enough to list the kinds of questions that should be asked in considering whether to undertake a particular curriculum change. Box 11-5 includes some of them. The hard decision is how much to invest in the effort to answer each one.

Schaffarzick (1975) studied curriculum change consideration in a stratified random sample of 188 schools in 34 school districts in six Northern California counties. His survey showed that in most cases curriculum change consideration took place in obscurity. In the rare cases when an issue became controversial, the change consideration process became more political, but it also became more public, more rational, and open to wider participation. When controversy burst out, contending parties demanded the right to state their case and to influence the decision. These opposing pressures on decision-makers mobilized rational procedures—hearings, studies, and the like—as a protective measure, if for no other reason. Thoroughgoing institutionalized rationality, giving full and systematic consideration to an issue, was rare in his sample and was associated with having a clear, simple, open set of procedures in place.

Schools varied considerably in the quality of their curriculum change consideration processes. Large, wealthy districts with well-qualified staffs entertained more options, proceeded more rationally, and experienced more conflicts than others.

BOX 11-4   Typical Stages in Curriculum Change Consideration

1. **Origination:** Some person or group comes to believe that a curriculum change of some sort is needed and suggests that a change be made.
2. **Preliminary Consideration:** Some person or group (usually different from #1) is authorized by legitimate authorities to consider whether change is needed; if so, to propose what type of change and how it should be further considered.
3. **Full Consideration and Preparation[1]:** Some authorized person or group collects additional information, defines the proposal more fully, and prepares the background for the adoption decision.
4. **Official Decision:** Some person or group decides whether the suggested change is to be adopted or rejected and, if adopted, how it is to be implemented.

[1]The main difference between preliminary and full consideration is the investment of resources required to carry them out. Preliminary consideration is quick and cheap. When it provides an insufficient basis for the commitment required by an official decision, further consideration becomes necessary.

Schools in communities with higher socio-economic status and education, higher community educational aspirations, more open politics, and less social diversity had better change consideration. Schools that had a positive attitude toward change, a history of successful innovation, and offered incentives for innovation were more likely to have better change consideration procedures.

BOX 11-5 Pivotal Questions about Curriculum Proposals

- **Is the proposal good on its own?**
  What evidence of its quality do we have? How credible is this evidence? If necessary, how could more credible evidence be collected? Should we try?

- **Is the proposal better than competing alternatives?**
  What are the closest competitors? Why is this proposal preferable to them? What would it displace, and what case can be made for the displaced? What are its advantages compared to the program in use now? Disadvantages?

- **Is it in the long-term interest of all parties. . . ?**
  including school, community, students, teachers, and leaders? If not, whose views are most important to consider in this case? Among those with a vital interest in the issue, whose views are poorly represented in the change consideration process? Who are the proposal's supporters and champions? What is their power base? Will the proposal advance their self-interest at the expense of others? Who offers resistance, opposition? What are their power bases and will defeat of the proposal advance their self-interest at the expense of others?

- **Is the proposal relevant to this school's situation now?**
  Its agenda; morale; history; staffing; budget; community relations; relations with district; and so on.

- **What will be its likely impact on classrooms and school?**
  - How will it affect what happens in classrooms?
    What are the changes required of students and teachers?
    The cost/benefit for students and teachers?
    The effect on behavior settings?
  - How will it affect what happens in the school?
    The forces tending to maintain the present situation?
    The forces supporting change?
    The cost/benefit for principal?
    The cost/benefit for community?
    School-community relations?

- **Is it worth the costs and risks of implementation?**
  - Can we afford it in money, time, and opportunity cost?
  - Are the risks of undertaking the improvement effort (conflict, implementation failure, unanticipated negative consequences) tolerable?
  - What are the costs and risks of rejecting it?

On the whole, however, these districts' change consideration procedures were not impressive.

> Valid, reliable, objective, comprehensive evidence of the effectiveness of the programs being considered was infrequently sought, rarely obtained, and rarely utilized in the cases I studied. (Schaffarzick 1975, 164)

Of 112 cases of change consideration on which he had data, 19% used no evidence at all in considering the change, while an additional 35% considered only the materials to be used in the proposed program. In 22% of the cases, evidence from observations of pilot programs was considered. Test scores and results of program evaluations were considered in only 4% of cases and available research results in only 3% (Schaffarzick 1975, 167). Even so, Schaffarzick concluded that

> The participants in the cases of curriculum change consideration that I studied were better about searching for alternative solutions to problems than they were about defining and verifying the problems to be solved. (Schaffarzick 1975, 162)

An official decision to terminate the change consideration process was not always made; often it just dwindled away or moved smoothly into implementation without any clear, official decision. When official decisions were made, they were most often made by boards of education (40%) and by miscellaneous agencies, committees, and advisory groups (32%). Unilateral decisions by principals were common in small decisions, but when official institutional action was required, the board or some committee appointed by the board were the final authority.

Teachers were nearly always involved in the curriculum change consideration process, but they seldom played central roles. Schaffarzick noted that

> The changes that teachers initiate are relatively small in scale. . . .
> The . . . activities that teachers frequently carry out . . . are often delimited by earlier . . . decisions. And, although teachers are included in more planning and review committees, the major decisions are still dominated by administrators and Board members. (Schaffarzick 1975, 117)

Members of the lay community participated in some way in 38% of cases and Schaffarzick concluded that "Laymen can be influential when they genuinely care." Lay groups were among the winning factions on 14 of 19 cases that were disputed between opposing factions, and among losers in only 6 of the 19. And in three of the cases they lost the community groups involved had developed reputations for opposing almost everything about the schools (Schaffarzick 1976, 143-44). On the other hand, lay advisory committees frequently did little more than rubber stamp professionals' plans.

INSTITUTING CURRICULUM CHANGE EFFORTS

Assume now that school leaders have made a commitment to bring about a certain kind of change in the curriculum of a school. The change itself has been defined in some detail, perhaps in the form of a set of curriculum plans and materials. And school curriculum leaders have determined from the change consideration process that the change has sufficient support from interested parties in the school and community. Now those responsible for the school must make the commitment a reality by introducing a curriculum change effort into the school.

The typical school curriculum change effort is a rather casual, almost off-hand affair, more personal than institutional. An influential person—the principal, a superintendent, or an influential teacher, say—champions an innovation. Their proposal runs a gauntlet of approval processes as part of the change consideration process and emerges with an "OK." The champion is appointed to a committee charged to bring about the change. The committee meets, some individual members work hard between meetings. The principal, if he or she is not the key figure, keeps current on developments and provides necessary institutional support. The rest is individual work. When the individuals are talented and respected, such a low-key, informal approach to institutional change may be all that is needed to bring about lasting and substantial change in the school curriculum. But in many cases, a more serious effort at institutional change is needed. Many innovations fail to spread beyond the classrooms of the teachers who championed them because the proposals are taken too lightly by the institution. They are insufficiently discussed, underplanned, underfunded, and undocumented, slighted so much that they barely have a chance to succeed. The occasional success achieved in this casual way is due to the heroic efforts of individual champions, whose talent and energy are in short supply.

To counter this tendency to slight local curriculum change efforts, I will discuss *curriculum change projects,* by which I mean identifiable efforts that have the status of temporary units within the school, with their own personnel assignments, budget, goals, deadlines, and a place within the formal organization. In practice, most curriculum change efforts are blended in with ongoing operations. If we are to learn from our change efforts, however, we must at least keep track of them. It is important, therefore, that projects be well documented. When school leadership expects a teacher to play a major role in a curriculum reform project, they should assign that teacher to work some fraction of time on the project and count the salary as a cost of the project. That way, project participants, supporters, and advocates can know what is required in order to implement their proposals, and responsible officials can estimate the benefits, costs, and risks of incorporating the experiment into the fabric of the school program.

School leadership must arrange the support necessary to establish the change project and make it work. I assume here that the school leadership creates a project team that will report to the principal, if, in fact, the principal is not included in the team. The school leadership must also arrange for staffing the change effort, scheduling it, and supplying it with the material support necessary to carry out its task. The project staff must negotiate its charge, which normally includes some targets and a timeline. School leaders must negotiate with project staff about arrangements to monitor the progress of the project.

The overwhelming number of local curriculum change efforts do not require such a curriculum change project because they fall into one of the standard types of curriculum changes for which schools have built-in provisions: curriculum materials selection, course approval, course of study development, and teacher in-service education. Schools are prepared for these standard kinds of curriculum changes. Steps have been agreed on in advance by interested parties. The expenses have been included in the budget and the necessary tasks written into job descriptions. Everyone knows what to expect and has planned for these kinds of changes. They will not disrupt established routines because they have themselves already been routinized. No wonder, then, that a school leadership's first, automatic response to any proposed curriculum change is typically to ask how it can be accomplished through the curriculum revision procedures already in place.

These built-in standard forms of local curriculum change provide an opportunity for committee members to negotiate mutually satisfactory resolutions of the major types of recurring, planned school or district curriculum decisions. As such, they are an important form of participation by teachers in decisions about the conditions of their work, and a vital step in the process of negotiated design that establishes the legitimacy of the school curriculum. They may also perform other useful functions, such as adapting commercial materials to local conditions, enabling teachers to share ideas about their craft, or securing more cooperation from teachers in making the changes decided on. But by themselves they are seldom effective vehicles for bringing about significant curriculum changes.

For instance, what schools call curriculum development rarely involves the development of original plans and materials for teachers and students to use. A typical first step in what is conventionally called local curriculum development is a search for commercially published materials and for ones created by other school systems. If anything even remotely suitable is found, it is adapted by committees of local teachers. Actual development by local schools of curriculum materials used by students and teachers is rare, as Schaffarzick discovered and numerous others have also reported.

> In only 10 of the 112 cases studied (9%) did people in the schools and districts actually develop program materials themselves. In all other cases, already available programs, including commercial programs and programs developed by other schools and districts, were suggested for adoption or adaptation. This low rate of actual development coincides with the observations of several interviewees, who pointed out that people in schools and districts rarely have the time, money, or expertise required for actual development. (Schaffarzick 1975, 102)

The curriculum changes recommended in the course of these standard procedures may seem large to teachers and administrators, who may find them difficult to implement, but, when measured against the range of curriculum change proposals discussed in the professional press and in public policy debates, or against historical changes in what is taught in schools, they are all relatively minor incremental adjustments. Only if they cumulate over decades and across subjects and grades will these incremental changes become significant for the education system as a whole. Proposals that require interdisciplinary cooperation fit poorly into standard curriculum change procedures—writing across the curriculum, environmental studies, career education, and integrated science and mathematics, for example. Still more radical proposals, such as programs in health involving weight control, stress reduction, or study skills stand even less of a chance of being considered. These standard procedures are notoriously ineffective in dealing with proposals that call for new pedagogical approaches, such as direct instruction, cooperative group learning, inquiry-oriented pedagogy, or computer-based instruction.

Serious efforts at substantial curriculum change, in contrast to negotiations over year-to-year adjustments that fall well within the normal range of school activities, require more substantial change projects. They may require more resources than the few person-months typically expended on these standard types of change efforts, expertise beyond that possessed by the local school staff, methods for influencing teachers stronger than a written guide or a 2-day workshop, and procedures that include all the major stakeholders.

Local Curriculum Change Projects

The first concern, naturally, is to staff the project. To mount a curriculum reform project in a local school is, first and foremost, to recruit time, talent, and energy from a school staff already overcommitted. Unfortunately, those who have the most talent and energy are usually the most overcommitted. And, except in very large schools, expertise vital to the project's success may exist in only one or two individuals; failing to recruit them to participate then dooms the project. For instance, the local project team must include individuals with a deep understanding of the reform, of its central defining features, and its optional variable ones, and of the rationale that supports these features. Without such knowledge and the authority to use it, the project can become a blank screen onto which participants project any image they wish. Many reforms are trivialized or distorted for lack of such deep authoritative understanding. In any given school, only a handful of individuals will have this deep understanding on any given topic, so the fate of the reform in this school hinges on recruiting these individuals to join the project.

The charge given to the local project team may be as narrow as to develop a plan for a new course, or as broad as to do whatever is necessary to bring about lasting and substantial curriculum improvements of some kind. We will consider the case where the project team has a broad mandate. The team needs to have a clear idea of what kinds of changes are needed in the school curriculum. They need to determine what would have to change about the school in order to bring about these curriculum changes and, especially, who would have to change. And they need to consider what combination of actions on their part and on the part of school leadership would facilitate those changes.

In considering the types of curriculum changes needed, the team will of course be guided by work done earlier in review and change consideration. When they inherit from earlier phases a clear and complete specification of the purposes of the reform, they can proceed to implement it. Usually, however, they inherit only a vague and general indication of rough directions and boundaries. In this case, the conventional advice is to begin by formulating objectives for students: What should students be able to do? This is sound advice if the team can answer such a question. Typically, it cannot. The team members may be able to state a few specific objectives, but they will generally not be sure that these are sound, complete, or exact enough to form a secure basis for further work. And so, they will generally need to reflect further on their intentions, and those of the other interested parties they represent. This can be done in many ways.

The basic alternatives are to ask people, informally or via surveys, interviews, or needs assessments; to collect data such as test scores, attendance rates, grades or the like; or to carry out armchair analyses by reading studies and articles, analyzing textbooks, and so on. All these procedures lead to essentially verbal statements of purpose and these are limited. If they are general enough to make sense on a survey, for example, they are probably not specific enough to help teachers in lesson planning. Also, people are not always aware of their preferences, so that they say one thing but behave differently. In general, expressions of purpose are much more adequate when they include references to concrete embodiments, such as incidents or events that indicate that students have achieved the desired changes, people who are models (current or former students, graduates, adults in the community, public figures), exemplary works (of literature, science, and so on by world figures, local figures, students, teachers), exemplary ideas, exemplary curricula or curriculum materials that embody the purposes espoused by the team, or educational programs that embody these purposes.

With purposes clearly expressed, the project team then needs to consider options for incorporating the change into the school program. Box 11-6 shows some of the more common options, arranged roughly in order of likely disruptiveness and therefore difficulty of making the change. Fitting a change of most of these types into the school program entails major changes in school routines, such as modifying the master schedule or reassigning teaching staff. Such changes always require approval of the principal and often district, community, or board review. The project team would have to recommend to school leaders the best options for the particular situation and then plan further in accordance with the decisions made.

When they have a clear idea of the new curriculum to be sought, the project team would do well to then consider what and who would have to change in order

BOX 11-6   Options for Fitting a Curriculum Change into a High School Program

1. Change the organizational framework of the entire school curriculum. For example: adopt flexible modular scheduling, from subjects to a house system with seminars
2. Institute a change across the curriculum. For example:
    teachers as counselors
    writing across the curriculum
    daily silent reading period
3. Offer a new program of study. For example:
    school within a school
    community service internship program
4. Offer a new course sequence in a subject. For example:
    aeronautics (in a vocational program)
    computer programming
    economics I, II
    accelerated mathematics sequence
5. Offer a new course. For example:
    Japanese language
    music composition
    ecology
    human biology
6. Substantially revise an existing program or course sequence. For example:
    convert to English I-IV from multiple electives
    convert to discipline-based art from studio courses
7. Revise a course. For example:
    physics to rely less on math
    English 9 to include more grammar and writing
    Typing to teach keyboarding, wordprocessing

to realize this curriculum. This is the backward mapping strategy discussed in Chapter 9. Revising a single high school course taught by only one teacher is typically a problem that would be handled by a teacher and principal, department chair, or supervisor. A new course could possibly be instituted by a single teacher without needing to change what any other teacher does—although the new course would siphon off enrollment from others and might therefore affect more people. Instituting a new course taught by a hand-picked individual is one of the quickest, most direct, and most powerful ways school leaders can make a big difference in a small part of the curriculum. On the other hand, changes that require many teachers to make major changes in their classroom routines are difficult for school leaders to bring about and control.

As the needed changes become clear, the project team must consider whether they are feasible. Can the individuals be persuaded to change their behavior? Can the money be found to buy new materials? Can other interested parties, particularly school leaders, teachers, students, and the community, be persuaded to accept the needed changes? If, as often happens, a project requires substantial changes in many classroom curricula, the team needs to consider what the avenues are through which they might influence what happens in classrooms. Some of the likely prospects are listed in Box 11-7.

Curriculum change projects are subject to the many of the same conditions and constraints that hamper the effectiveness of the standard curriculum change procedures and so are vulnerable to many of the same problems. It may be wise to take steps to forestall these by strengthening the local change effort in certain key respects.

Broadening the Base of Expertise Schools can hire scholars, scientists, artists, or local citizens with appropriate expertise as subject matter specialists to review the content of a K–12 program in their field or recruit them as volunteers to assist a curriculum planning team. Collaboration with faculty in a nearby college or university in a joint project may be possible. Collaboration might be arranged with teacher preparation institutions to offer courses and degrees that meet common needs of many schools. Recently many curriculum projects have encouraged participation by schools and teachers in a regional or national network. Joining such a network gives schools easy access to greater expertise than any school could possibly afford otherwise.

Schools might join in and even initiate joint ventures in curriculum development with many types of outside agencies—federal and state education authorities; professional associations, charitable foundations, and other nonprofit organizations; publishers of educational material and other profit-making firms, as well as other schools, even schools in other states and networks of schools covering a region, the whole nation, or even international agencies. Participating local schools might supply some of the funding, perhaps in the form of support for their staff members to allow released time for work on the project. Additional support, in money and in expertise, would come from the outside agencies in exchange for rights to the joint products (curriculum plans and materials, tests, videotapes, and so on) and for access to schools as field sites. One organization, Educational Research Corporation of America, headquartered in Cleveland, Ohio, solicits participation of school districts in developing textbooks and curriculum materials. ERCA works with the staff of local schools to develop, field test, and revise curriculum materials that it then seeks to market through contracts with commercial textbook publishers. Many local and regional philanthropic foundations might be delighted to support joint projects of interest to a number of schools in a city, state, or region, even though they may resist funding projects that benefit only a single school system.

Local schools could also put out curriculum reform projects for competitive bidding. Requests for proposals could be prepared specifying what kinds of curriculum work the school needed, when, and how much they would pay for the

■
BOX 11-7   Things a Local Project Team Might Change to Influence Classroom Curricula

Materials used by students:
    textbooks, other books
    workbooks, activity sheets
    films, videotapes, audiotapes, software

Materials used by teachers:
    teachers' guides
    resource books
    audiotapes, videotapes for teachers

Classroom environment
    equipment, supplies, facilities: computers, TV
    personnel: aides, volunteers

School organization
    team teaching instead of self-contained classroom
    collegial evaluation of teachers by teachers
    parent participation in classrooms

Classroom frames
    principal, supervisor expectations, standards

Teachers' beliefs and attitudes
    lectures, talks, workshops
    quality circles, discussion groups

Teachers' skills and knowledge
    lectures, talks, workshops, demonstrations
    viewing and discussing videotapes

work. Local school employees, or possibly also private organizations (which might include teachers supplementing their income), would be invited to submit proposals. Relevant expertise could be specified as a criterion for accepting proposals.

Of course, all use of outside expertise entails costs and carries risks, chiefly the risk of incompatibility between local thinking and the experts'. These will have to be weighed against the benefits in each particular case. Unfortunately, local school budgets are so heavily contested by other local interest groups that spending district funds on personnel not regularly employed by the school system is interpreted as a vote of no confidence in local staff and thus becomes a controversial act.

Overcoming the Domination of Commercially Published Materials The chief attractions of published materials are relatively low cost, convenience for the teacher, and high production values. If locally developed materials are to compete, they must equal or exceed these advantages or offer other compensating ones. One of the inherent advantages local development holds is the possibility of **widespread participation** by teachers in development activities and materials. Suppose, for example, that a project team only produced sample lessons and that all teachers in the school or school system were invited to submit their own lessons for inclusion in a steadily expanding teachers' guide. This would presumably act as an incentive for teachers to develop their own lessons, yet the project would retain editorial control over the teachers' guide.

Materials created by the project team for use by teachers should be as convenient and attractive as possible. Suppose the project team actually wrote alternative chapters and sections of a teachers' guide to be used instead of corresponding chapters in the adopted text. Or, suppose they created a package of supplementary materials for teachers to duplicate and use, materials more closely tailored to local conditions. Many such variations on the theme of producing a teachers' guide can be found that will encourage and support teachers in their efforts to tailor their classroom curriculum to the characteristics and needs of their students and communities.

Even more radically, suppose teachers submitted course syllabi for the board to approve, and that, after approval, teachers were permitted to select their own curriculum materials within a given budget. A project team could assist the board by developing guidelines concerning content, purpose, and structure of particular courses and programs, but the preparation of syllabi for board approval would be the responsibility of individual teachers or teacher teams.

Increasing the Impact of Local Curriculum Development on Teachers' Classroom Behavior Anything that made the products of local curriculum development more useful and attractive to teachers would increase their influence on the classroom curriculum, of course. Beyond that, suppose teachers received clearer instruction in exactly how to use locally developed materials in their teaching and continuing advice and support in trying out new teaching tactics. For example, suppose that videotapes were produced of the classrooms of teachers who were well-versed in teaching according to the new plans. Suppose these videotapes were viewed and discussed at teacher in-service meetings. Suppose teachers throughout the district were given time to meet once a week to report on their experiences as they attempted to make changes in their classrooms. In these meetings they could discuss their successes and problems in a safe collegial context, and bring issues as a group to the project team for discussion. Substantial curriculum changes amount to a professional remodelling job for teachers, and it is difficult to see how they can be expected to make them without continuing effort and support.

A Variety of Approaches Schools might well think in terms of a variety of types of projects, ranging from a multiple year project involving a substantial fraction of the school staff to a lightning strike over spring break to develop plans and materials for a specific problem in one subject or grade. It might be possible to arrange for students in one class to work more independently, thus freeing that teacher to develop teaching/learning materials. School systems can marshal the entire resources of the community for education, not just the full-time professional staff. Joint projects might be launched with museums, youth organizations, or city government. Videotapes show promise as a means of communicating curricular innovations, demonstrating their practicality, and as a training device to help teachers master new classroom techniques. It is always difficult to convey a skill, particularly an interpersonal skill, in print. Also, video can be shown at the viewer's convenience rather than at a fixed time and place. No school needs to be limited to the traditional pattern of local development by teacher committees meeting after school or over vacations and writing courses of study and teachers' guides.

An obvious limitation of all these improvements in local curriculum development procedures is that they cost more, either in real budget dollars or in time and energy diverted from other school activities. If standard practices are producing effective curriculum change in the schools and classrooms of a particular school system, then more costly procedures are not needed. But the evidence is strong that most local curriculum development is ineffective, so that the resources currently devoted to it are not being well utilized. Slight additional investment combined with substantial reforms in the local curriculum development process may yield much greater effectiveness. Alternatively, school systems that cannot afford the funds to make local curriculum development really effective may find that it would be wiser for them to limit their attempts to a single project each year and to make a really serious effort there. Also, by joining in leagues of cooperating schools, local systems may be able to spread the costs of local development more widely.

FACILITATING CURRICULUM CHANGE IN CLASSROOMS

Policy-makers and administrators have much greater control over institutional and organizational operations and structure than they do over what happens in classrooms, so they are often tempted to concentrate their energies on organizational changes and assume that a highly visible change in the school actually produces a substantial change in what students experience and learn. A new course may be instituted with much fanfare, but if the teacher is reluctant, uncomprehending of the innovative aspects of the course, or unprepared to teach it, students may experience no benefits. Much curriculum reform is purely symbolic for just this reason: titles and descriptions change, but practice and results do not. Many other attempted curriculum reforms result in trivialized classroom implementations of subtle or complex educational innovations. The obvious, surface features are implemented, but the more complex features that complete the innovation are not. Students dabble with apparatus in the name of inquiry methods or engage in simple group work in the name of cooperative group learning, but real innovation requires more. Complex or subtle reforms require that administrators and teachers know the difference between full realization of the reform in the classroom and mere adoption of a few of its obvious features.

In order to change the curriculum that students undergo, the school leadership must influence what teachers do behind their classroom doors. As we saw in Chapter 7, the typical school organization does not provide its leaders with powerful means of influencing teachers' classroom behavior. And because of their working conditions and professional traditions, teachers have very considerable capacity to resist unwanted influences on what they do in their classrooms. Clearly, then, the school leadership needs active cooperation from teachers in order to change the school curriculum. Finding ways to evoke active efforts from teachers on behalf of a particular curriculum change is usually the greatest implementation challenge the school leadership faces.

The most frequently used strategies for facilitating classroom curriculum change strive to get teachers involved in the process of curriculum planning. The near-universal popularity of teacher involvement as a strategy for implementing curriculum change in classrooms rests on the recognition by everyone with experience in schools that a) teachers need sustained, intensive contact with any innovation before they will embrace it as their own, and b) teachers need to work out their own differences of opinion about a proposed innovation before it can function as a common framework for the school or district.

Teachers' need to be immersed in the details of a proposed change springs from their image of themselves as professionals with a calling. If they are to feel good about what they do in their classrooms, they must see their actions as flowing from themselves, from the same source as the calling they felt toward the profession. Teachers believe that technique should grow from roots in philosophy, style, and, ultimately, personality. A major change in classroom technique therefore implies a major change in professional self-image for the teacher. Given this perspective, it is obvious that teachers need to develop a personally meaningful interpretation of any innovation. Teachers need to be satisfied about its meaning and value to them, if they are to cooperate in an informed and active way in incorporating the innovation into their work in their classroom.

Usually, reading about the innovation or listening to speakers talk about it does not suffice for creating the kind of personal meaning teachers need. In general, teachers need to work with the innovation, adapt it to their personal style, and discuss their personal and philosophical reactions to it with others whose opinions they value and whom they trust. This is especially so for teachers who are indifferent to a particular innovation or skeptical of its value. In the process of adaptation and discussion, teachers may discover ways to use it and reasons to use it that are consistent with their personal teaching styles and developed repertoire of professional skills. As a result of trying on the innovation in this way, some teachers may find ways to interpret the innovation so that it seems part of them, and thus come to embrace it enthusiastically. Local curriculum planning sessions in which teachers adapt curriculum plans and materials to their own classrooms amount to a negotiation of meaning, in which teachers assimilate some features of the innovation into their personal teaching styles and modify or reject others.

For example, suppose the faculty of an elementary school whose student body includes an increasing proportion of Hispanic students has been asked to make revisions in the social studies curriculum to teach more about the history and culture of Mexican-Americans. Some teachers may see this as a long-overdue response to changing community demographics. Others may see it as an opportunity to reduce the parochial ethnocentrism of the traditional social studies curriculum. Still others may view it as an unwanted intrusion of community politics into the school curriculum. Some may fear that it will interfere with the assimilation of Mexican-Americans into the mainstream culture. Each teacher's willingness to work on behalf of the proposed curriculum revision will depend on how that teacher interprets it.

Different approaches will prove attractive to different teachers. Some may prefer to add a unit here and there, for example, focusing a bit more attention on events in Mexico as part of the study of American history, Spanish colonial history and the Spanish-American War. Others may prefer to focus extra attention on Mexico as part of the study of world geography. Still others may advocate study of contemporary Mexican and Mexican-American life—food, dances, art, and holidays. If teachers followed their individual preferences, the social studies curriculum in the school would lose its coherence. Requiring teachers to agree on a common curriculum, with permissible variations, insures the necessary coherence and also provides an opportunity for teachers to discuss their differences and to negotiate acceptable resolutions of them. Some teachers' practices, styles, philosophies, perhaps even personalities, may be changed in the course of the give and take with colleagues. An effective implementation plan will find ways to involve faculty members in negotiations with advocates of the innovation about these meanings as they plan for their classrooms.

Teachers' Benefit/Cost Ratios

While involvement in curriculum planning is indispensable, it will generally not suffice to produce lasting and substantial changes in the curriculum of classrooms throughout a school. Other barriers to teachers' adoption of an innovation must also be overcome. The easy assumption that teachers who come to know an innovation will therefore implement it is naive. Students of recent social and educational reforms have come to a more Machiavellian conclusion. Their studies suggest that an innovation's success in the classroom depends on teachers' perceptions of the ratio of its benefits to its costs. Teachers must expend time and effort to make changes in their classroom curriculum and to reexamine their personal teaching styles. These changes inevitably interfere with routines that have made life in the classroom easier for the teacher, and they run risks of disrupting classroom operations, spoiling classroom climate, and reducing mastery, coverage, order, and affect in their classroom. Serious efforts to make substantial and lasting changes in the classroom curriculum are therefore major events in the professional lives of teachers. Unless teachers receive benefits commensurate with the costs and risks, they will experience a disincentive to implement the innovation. Box 11-8 lists some of the potential benefits teachers may receive from a classroom curriculum change and some of the costs they may incur. These are classified as temporary when they only occur while making the change, and permanent when they continue after the change has been made.

The project team, with the cooperation of school leadership, can and should assess the benefits and costs or risks for teachers of implementing the reform in

---

BOX 11-8   Benefits and Costs of Curriculum Change for Teachers

Benefits	Costs and Risks
Temporary	**Temporary**
excitement, enthusiasm of doing something new	trouble of rearranging routines to fit the changes
team membership, participation in a team effort	greater time and effort required
enhanced self-esteem from being a pioneer	risk of dissension among colleagues
opportunity for wider social and professional contacts	diversion of attention from ongoing social and professional activities and relationships
opportunity to make a difference in the school	risk of failure, potential embarrassment
Permanent	**Permanent**
greater self-esteem, pride, status from successful change	loss of self-esteem and status from failed change effort
improved prospects for career advancement	greater risk of revealing ignorance, incompetence
better days in class if students like it and do well	worse days in class if students dislike it and fail
less teacher time and effort required	more teacher time and effort required
classroom coverage, mastery, affect, and order may be improved	classroom coverage, mastery, affect, or order may be reduced

their classrooms **as the teachers perceive it.** Simple discussion among teachers usually suffices to reveal their perceptions. Different teachers may perceive these matters differently, of course, so the team should be prepared for considerable variation. Where benefit/cost ratios are seen as unfavorable, the project team can take actions designed to influence them. Box 11-9 lists some examples of ways school leaders might attempt to influence teachers' perceptions. Artful orchestration of such measures may transform how teachers see the change. On the other hand, clumsy efforts to fool teachers into taking actions not fundamentally in their interest are likely to backfire sooner or later.

Teachers are frequently portrayed as wanting a packaged curriculum that tells them step-by-step exactly what to do. This is the premise behind the detailed teachers' editions provided by publishers and behind the detailed courses of study

---

■
BOX 11-9   Ways Project Leaders Influence Teachers' Perceptions of Benefits and Costs of Curriculum Changes

Provide additional benefits. For example:
    pay participating teachers a bonus
    promote teachers who pioneered
    provide additional supplies to project classrooms
Increase perceived value of existing benefits. For example:
    arrange for prestigious advocates to extol the benefits of the innovation
    recognize, honor teachers for success
    play up the excitement of doing something new
    emphasize psychic value of material benefits
Decrease expectations for receiving benefits. For example:
    appeal to altruism, call for sacrifice
    emphasize need for belt-tightening
    label current performance unsatisfactory
    insist on more results for less reward
Reduce costs. For example:
    assist teachers to change routines
    release teachers from other duties to make time, energy available for changing
Reduce perceptions of costliness. For example:
    make teacher joint planning sessions fun
    make changes gradually, phase them in
Reduce risks. For example:
    provide training, coaching in new techniques
    redesign the innovation to take less time, effort
Reduce perceptions of risk. For example:
    arrange for contacts with teachers who have successfully made the change
Increase willingness to incur costs or risks. For example:
    reward risk-taking
    encourage teachers to invest in their professional growth

provided by many districts. Yet teachers also frequently complain that these documents conflict with their teaching style and constrain them too much. This ambivalence reflects one of the teacher's main dilemmas in attempting curriculum change. Developing a new set of classroom routines is hard work, so teachers naturally look for the path of least effort. If they can find existing routines and advice on how to institute and maintain them, their burdens are considerably eased. On the other hand, teachers hate having to follow uncongenial routines. The trick for those who want to foster classroom curriculum change is to facilitate changes in classroom routines flexibly enough to permit teachers to find congenial routines or ones that can be adapted to be congenial with little time and effort.

Teachers' assessments of benefits, costs, and risks change as the project proceeds. Initial enthusiasm can be dissipated by early disappointments, and initial resistance can be overcome by early successes. In the absence of first-hand information, nonparticipants form their impressions of the project mainly on the basis of reports they receive from others. New projects are a common topic of casual conversation among teachers, and rumors can spread easily. The project team can defend against potentially damaging rumors by supplying plenty of timely, accurate information before rumors have a chance to spread. If the project team includes persons adept at monitoring and influencing messages flowing in teachers' informal communication networks, their efforts on behalf of the project can be valuable in attracting more teachers to participate.

In addition to involvement in local curriculum planning and attending to benefit/cost ratios, school leaders can employ many other strategies for influencing teachers to change their classroom curriculum. Here are brief descriptions of some promising ones.

Continued Recruitment Efforts   To promote wider participation by teachers, projects can be organized to offer frequent enlistment opportunities on a recurring basis for small and large assignments. For example, all teachers should be routinely invited to attend meetings about the project, not just those who have volunteered, and requests for volunteers to carry out some project assignment should be circulated to all teachers. Opinions of all teachers about the developing project should be sought periodically. All teachers can thus be involved in the project in meaningful ways. Project participants should maintain personal contacts with nonparticipants and guard against attitudes that imply superiority over those not currently involved. Sometimes other teachers perceive project staff members' pride in their achievements as arrogance.

Tailoring Project Efforts to Individual Teachers   Local change projects can be tailored to individual teachers. Beginning teachers may be concerned about how to maintain discipline when using the unfamiliar classroom activities, while experienced teachers may be more concerned about slower rates of progress through the material. The project team could devote effort to both sets of concerns, perhaps by forming subgroups to develop techniques in collaboration with individual teachers concerned about each aspect of the innovation.

Continuing Interventions   Hall, et al. (1983) in their Principal Teacher Interaction Study found that the number of day-to-day interventions by principals with teachers on behalf of the innovation was a major predictor of implementation success. For one thing, continuing efforts demonstrate continuing commitment to making the change. For another, they respond to the changing array of difficulties that arise for teachers as they work the innovation into their routines. Making a curriculum change that calls for extensive changes in classrooms requires continuing efforts over several years, at least. Lasting and substantial change is a result of continued, cumulative efforts.

Monitor Levels of Use   Hall and Loucks (1977) developed a scale to describe levels of use of an innovation by teachers. These levels range from **Nonuse** (no knowledge, no use, and no involvement) through **Orientation** (some knowledge, exploration), **Preparation** (preparing for first use), **Mechanical use** (short-term, day-to-day, unreflective), **Routine use** (ongoing use with few changes or improvements), **Refinement** (varied use to improve effects), **Integration** (combining innovation with other efforts of self and colleagues), to the most intensive stage, **Renewal** (major modifications or alternatives, new goals and strategies). School leadership or the project team should monitor the extent and level of use of the proposed curriculum improvement periodically and redirect their efforts to respond to whatever obstacles they discover.

Presently, school systems invest nearly all of their scarce resources for curriculum improvement in a few standard procedures: curriculum materials selection, course of study writing, course approval, and in-service workshops for teachers. A careful study of just how well these standard procedures are working to foster change in classroom curricula will usually reveal better ways to spend some of the money. We have very little firm evidence on the impact of teachers' guides on the classroom curriculum, for example, but every bit of evidence we do have indicates that they have little impact on what actually happens in classrooms, and what little effect they have depends on how well they are enforced by supervisors and principals, not on the intrinsic quality of the documents. Because teachers make them, they are supposed to engender a sense of ownership and support on the part of teachers; yet teachers who do not participate in local development may feel left out, just as much as they feel left out of the publication of the textbook. School leaders intend service on the committees that produce these guides to be an honor, a reward, and an opportunity for renewal and growth, but not all teachers welcome this opportunity. In many cases it would be better if schools defined their curriculum policies in briefer statements of purpose, content, and structure and then to relied on a variety of other strategies for realizing them in classrooms. When extensive changes in pedagogy are proposed, printed materials will never suffice. Videotapes, live presentations, and ongoing support for individual teachers will be essential.

EVALUATING SCHOOL CURRICULUM CHANGE PROJECTS

The resources for evaluating school curriculum change projects come from the same meager source as the resources for realizing the change. Schools only barely able to scrape together funds for a curriculum change project are not likely to divert any to evaluation. Using scarce resources for evaluation rather than for improving the innovation itself is justified only if something is learned from the evaluation that makes greater improvement possible or helps avoid a harmful result. The purpose of evaluation in the present context is therefore to foster institutional learning. By documenting what we have attempted, what happened to our attempts, and what traces seemed to persist, and by considering carefully why these things happened and these results ensued, we can possibly learn some lessons that will help us improve this project and others to come.

Elaborate methods have been devised for evaluating the effects of educational programs. Indeed, educational evaluation is a field of study in its own right. But the fundamental principles of curriculum evaluation are not at all arcane or difficult. In my opinion, the best stance for one not trained in the methods of evaluation is to rely on fundamental principles and straightforward procedures. When this proves impossible, seek expert advice and make the expert explain the complexities in terms of fundamental principles. Complexities of design and measurement are generally out of place in school level evaluations, anyway.

An evaluation study of a school curriculum change project is essentially a field experiment—in other words, an experiment carried out under real field conditions rather than under controlled laboratory conditions. The experimental treatment is the curriculum change. The subjects are classes of students and their teachers drawn from those who will use the new curriculum if it is adopted. The outcomes of interest are those that were of interest before the change plus any new ones hoped for or feared as a result of the change. So, if standardized tests were normally used to evaluate the success of students' and teachers' efforts under the old curriculum, they would continue to be used unless something about the curriculum change made them no longer relevant. If students and teachers who use the new curriculum perform very well on a certain outcome measure, the change is a plausible explanation of their success. If they perform poorly, something went wrong—perhaps the curriculum. The standard of good performance is most naturally established by the prior performance of students in previous years or by the concurrent performance of other students not exposed to the change.

Field experiments of this kind are vulnerable to several serious threats to their validity. For example, it is possible that this particular class of students just happened to be exceptional, and that they, rather than the curriculum change, produced the observed results. We can check for this possibility by comparing the students in this class with their peers on such things as grades, ability test scores, and teacher evaluations. Or, we can field test the curriculum change with several classes; they can't *all* be exceptional. It is also possible that a good showing by students could be produced by outcome measures that are too easy. We can give the test to other groups of students to see whether they do unexpectedly well, too. It is possible that the teacher for this class was exceptional and would have produced good results no matter what curriculum was used. We can try the new curriculum with other teachers, too. And so we go, considering various alternative interpretations of the study's findings and inventing ways to check their plausibility.

This process never reaches a logical end because alternative interpretations can always be invented. What calls a halt to it is the cost of checking additional interpretations. At some point, the additional confidence in our conclusion that would come from checking another alternative interpretation is outweighed by the cost and trouble of doing the checking. In evaluating school curriculum change projects, the point at which additional checking is not worth it comes quite early. The noise in the experimental setting is so great that a well-controlled study becomes impossible to interpret. Even if we carefully assign students and teachers to a thoroughly controlled treatment and measure a great many results accurately, we cannot be sure that the findings of the controlled study would apply to normal conditions, since these are so variable and uncontrolled.

For most purposes, evaluations of school curriculum change projects need only take special pains to:

1. Document the curriculum change as it is actually presented in the classroom.
2. Elicit from those involved (teachers, students, local experts, . . .) claims of possible ways the change might impact students, teacher, and school and classroom activities.
3. Rely largely on informed judgments to assess claims about outcomes. Discipline these judgments to the extent possible, such as by having impartial judges view representative samples of students' work or by asking teachers to collect specific anecdotes to support their judgments.
4. Collect whatever data are routinely available bearing on the central claims and supplement these with additional measures that are convincing to those involved and yet practical to administer, such as teacher-made tests or experimental tests supplied by a university researcher.
5. Deeply consider possible lessons to be learned from the field trial and discuss them at length with all interested parties. Ask everyone involved "What would you change on the basis of this trial, and why?"

Questions to Study Certain questions nearly always come up in evaluations: Did the curriculum work as planned? How did students and teachers like it? Did students learn? Beyond these, the choice of question to address in the evaluation depends on the concerns of those affected. What benefits do local champions claim for the change and which of these are most valued by the interested parties? What possible negative results do opponents or skeptics fear? Identify these questions and stick with them in spite of difficulties you may encounter in finding ways to measure them. It may be that the outcomes of interest locally are too vaguely stated to define a measurable outcome. *Appreciation, understanding,* and a *good attitude* are notorious cases. Just ask for examples. Hypothetical ones will do if real ones cannot be found. Emphasize to everyone concerned that only very substantial improvements in such outcomes will be detectable by people or tests, so that unless there is a reasonable prospect of the change producing a major improvement in some outcome, a measurement effort is not worth the trouble.

The further away in time the supposed outcome manifests itself, the more difficult it will be to detect a change in it. Some outcomes are apparent in the classroom (interest, motivation, engagement, time on task, and so on). Let us call these process outcomes, since they manifest themselves while the program is in process. Other outcomes are detectable within days of completing the relevant part of the curriculum (end of unit test performance). Call these immediate outcomes. Still others are delayed, possibly becoming apparent after years have elapsed (lifelong interest in the subject, willingness to engage in further study of the subject, application to personal decisions, and so on). Conceivably, delayed outcomes could be studied by follow-ups of graduates, but it is doubtful whether results could be generalized to a new generation of students. Practically speaking, end-of-year measures and year-later follow-ups are the outer limits in evaluations of school curriculum change projects.

Similarly, the more conditions where an outcome manifests itself differ from conditions in the classroom where it was learned, the greater the difficulty of detecting it. Teach children to add a column of figures and then test them on similar columns of figures, and it should be easy to detect their learning. Test them on a list of figures read aloud to them, and some of the learning will not carry over or transfer to the new task. Test them on the playground when they encounter a problem calling for addition of several figures, and they may not even use what they learned at all.

Whatever questions you ask in your evaluation, remain alert for claims of good or bad outcomes that arise unexpectedly in the course of the field trial.

Allocating Resources to Questions Usually many more questions arise than your evaluation can begin to answer. Cronbach (1982, 225–26) offers four criteria for deciding which questions should receive more attention in the evaluation design:

1. amount of prior uncertainty about the issue,
2. anticipated information yield,
3. leverage of this information on the decision,
4. costs of the information.

Types of Data to Collect As a rule, evaluations of school curriculum change projects should rely on the kind of data that those involved find most convincing. Teachers are accustomed to using students' responses to various kinds of teacher-made paper and pencil tests, and when these are well-made, they should be quite serviceable. Tests designed by groups of teachers working collaboratively with a little advice from a measurement specialist should probably be the bread-and-butter of these evaluations. Furthermore, teachers are keen observers of classroom process and, with only a little consultation, should be able to observe one another's classrooms as keenly and objectively as anyone could ask. The products of students' work in the classroom and their homework will in many cases be persuasive. With a little practice, teachers should be able to conduct interviews with students that give valuable information.

More formal and quantitative data than this are seldom required, and, when they are, expert assistance should be sought in selecting an available instrument (test, interest inventory, attitude measure, or the like) or constructing one. When relevant standardized test data are available, they should be used. In general, several informal measures of the same outcome, although none may be acceptable as research instruments, serve as a useful check on the relevance of the standardized information in such an evaluation measure.

What to Do with the Results of the Evaluation Discuss them! The point is not just to reach a final thumbs-up or thumbs-down judgment about the curriculum change, though that may sometimes emerge as a clear result of the evaluation, but rather to learn what worked and what did not and why. Typically, the results of the evaluation will look good from some points of view and not so good from others. Advocates will attempt to explain away potentially damaging results and critics will magnify the slightest hint of a problem. Evaluations do not quell debate or take its place, but they can inform debate and enlighten negotiations among those affected by the decision. The evaluation results should ideally be a developing story. The parties to the field trial should be looking forward to periodic reports of the latest results. The worst thing is to produce a report nobody reads after everybody has lost interest in the questions.

It is not easy for institutions to learn from experience. Normal practice is already complex and the change being introduced may be lost in the noise of that complexity. Unpredictable incidents upset well laid plans, events in the world, nation, community, and school intrude as alternative explanations of both positive and negative results. People bring preconceptions that color their experience.

Partisanship impairs objectivity. Evaluations themselves become political when they are caught up in partisan struggles. In the context of school curriculum change efforts, evaluations can promise only modest improvements over the unassisted judgment of those who are intimately involved with the change. They cannot resolve disputes, but they can contribute to informed decisions when the decision-makers are enlightened enough to choose to be guided by experience as well as by beliefs.

LONG-RANGE PLANNING FOR CURRICULUM IMPROVEMENT

The case for long-range planning in curriculum is easy to make. Implementing a curriculum change takes years—years of sequential learning for students to learn how to learn many of the things the school teaches, such as algebra or American literature. And the results, for good or ill, stay with students for a lifetime. To realize cumulative, long-term curriculum improvements demands long-term planning. Although the figures are somewhat arbitrary, I suggest that schools make curriculum plans for two, five, and ten years ahead. (Planning for next year happens anyway and need not concern us here.)

Elaborate methods of strategic planning are generally out of place in schools, but a valuable form of advance planning can be carried out within the frames most schools face. The three critical types of information a school needs for long-range curriculum planning are 1) where we are now; 2) where we want to be; and 3) what human and material resources we will have to work with in getting from here to there. Chapter 8 details the key ingredients of the school curriculum; describing what the school curriculum is now is a relatively straightforward matter of documenting the school's status on these key factors.

How best to determine where we want to go is not so clear. A properly designed set of surveys may help to determine what the community wants, but it is extremely difficult to put people's dreams into questionnaire form. Interviews, either one at a time or with small groups, may be an improvement, but only if the setting is right and the interviewer is skilled. Even the best possible process assumes that the people interviewed indeed *know* what they want. What people *think* they will want and what they *will* vote or pay or work for are often quite different things.

Ideally, people would be asked to express preferences for things that have real meaning and significance to them. For example, parents of a youngster in the primary grades can easily be drawn into thinking about what they want their children to study and learn over the next ten years, and many parents of older children would welcome the chance to do their part to leave behind a better school for those who come after. Teachers, except those planning to leave or those on provisional status, clearly have a long-term interest in curriculum planning. Even students are interested in what they will study and learn later on and graduates will usually say what they wish they had done in school. Businesses and community organizations clearly have a long-term interest in good schools. Curiously, it is the school leaders who, statistically speaking, will not serve in their roles for a decade and therefore might lack the self-interest to take such planning seriously.

If the planning task is presented to everyone in meaningful terms, it should be relatively easy to engage them in serious planning. Those participating in long-range curriculum planning should have some orientation to the task: speakers who spin out alternative visions of the future, perhaps, or community forums to discuss the future of the community and of the schools. A consultant could be hired to write alternative scenarios for the community and its schools. The local newspaper could set aside space for a forum on the future of education in the community and invite local officials and citizens to contribute. Something is needed to draw people's attention to the topic and to shake them out of the lazy assumption that things will always be the way they are.

When the planning itself is ready to begin, those participating should consider how they would wish to answer the basic decisions that shape the school's curriculum, questions such as: What courses and programs should be offered and what major bodies of content and skill should be covered by them? What major bodies of learning should be required of every student and what other work should be elective? What sorts of performance will we expect of students on tests and in life? Then the professional staff will need to work out the implications of their preferences for needed resources and their deployment. How many teachers, with what qualifications, will be needed to offer the programs people say they want? What other resources will be needed? Demand nearly always exceeds supply. But this gets ahead of the story.

It is also necessary to make some assumptions about the resources available. It is possible to estimate how many teachers will leave through retirement, resignation, illness or death, but one cannot say in which subjects or grades these vacancies will occur. Similarly, there will inevitably be uncertainty about the number of students attending the school in the future and their backgrounds and aspirations. Budget amounts are also uncertain. It is customary to make favorable, unfavorable, and neutral assumptions on these uncertainties and to develop three corresponding scenarios. In that way, some thought will have been given to a range of likely eventualities.

Schools' long term curriculum plans will generally be affected by conditions in several important areas of community and cultural life including:

demographics (for example, number of students, the aging of the community)
politics (for example, votes for schools, priorities among aims)
economics (for example, funding levels, career aspirations)
religion (for example, treatment of sensitive issues)
social mores (for example, family structure, social mobility)
ideas in wide currency (for example, ecology, information)
technology (for example, electronic communication)

Widespread or large changes in any of these areas will almost certainly affect either what kinds of curriculum changes are desirable or what kinds are possible or both. Explicit guesses about possible and likely changes in such characteristics should support any long term curriculum plan.

The resulting plans will then be contingency plans. Depending on unforeseen developments, some aspects of the plans—no one can know which ones—will never come to fruition. But the school is more likely to be prepared for a crisis or unexpected opportunity. The schools can use the plans to guide their day-to-day decisions. A new planning group will consult these plans again in two to five years, measure progress, and start a new cycle. Once the cycle is established, people will save up items to propose in the next cycle.

Concluding Note on the Importance of Leadership

The very characteristics that make the curriculum so resilient in the face of change, conflict, and severe resource constraints, also make it resistant to reforms. Reform-minded leaders have an enormous task in getting those involved to seriously question the content, purpose, and organizing framework of the educational programs they participate in and thus to give new ideas a fighting chance. Yet, in view of the masses of people affected and the comprehensiveness and intimacy of

---

BOX 11-10   Some Components of Leadership in Curriculum Improvement

1. To find or create and to express vividly educational visions and goals so that they become widely shared,
2. To encourage people to work hard for the shared visions and goals,
3. To act resourcefully in pursuit of shared visions and goals; to reward resourcefulness in others,
4. To inspire feelings of competence; to make people feel strong, effective, and able to influence their fate; to stimulate them to strong, prompt action,
5. To build relationships of trust among those whose interests and perspectives differ but whose lives and fates are intertwined; to express strong, unwavering faith in people,
6. To encourage people to work together for common goals,
7. To allocate resources appropriate to achieving shared goals; to know when and when not to cut corners,
8. To confront and resolve conflicts and difficulties, not to deny them,
9. To demonstrate personal competence by such steps as: planning personal goals and steps to reach them, assessing personal weaknesses and taking steps to improve,
10. To deal effectively with interests and individuals powerful enough to defeat or deflect your purpose; to build coalitions, to balance conflicting interests, to resolve conflicts that threaten important goals.

the changes they are required to make, it is probably fortunate that making lasting and substantial curriculum changes is so difficult. Learning to consider such changes deeply and carefully is therefore all the more important.

School curriculum work is fundamental to bringing about lasting and substantial curriculum improvement. The curriculum comes to life in the classroom, but the most direct and powerful influences on the classroom are found in the school. Maintaining excellence in the curriculum of a school is a professional and civic accomplishment of the same high order as fielding a good opera, ballet, or symphony or sports team. In all these cases, many individuals and institutions must work together. For this, leadership is crucial. (See Box 11-10.) So many shifting, conflicting purposes must be reconciled and coordinated. Such consistent attention must be lavished on the work through periods of years, even decades, as individuals assume and relinquish roles in the institution. The resources provided are so constrained and variable. The obstacles to change are many and very deepseated. Only with good leadership can a school hope to maintain the quality of its curriculum.

QUESTIONS FOR STUDY

1. Interview an experienced principal or supervisor about their most successful curriculum improvement project. Try to discover how each of the functions described in this chapter were carried out in this case.

2. Examine an accreditation report produced by a local school. These reports are produced by the school for a visiting accreditation committee. They include a variety of factual information about the school. Read the report and, based on what you have learned, list the three most serious weaknesses in its curriculum. For each weakness you identify, note the facts that support your claim that it is a serious weakness.

3. Consult a book about the principalship. Scan the chapter(s) that deal with the principal's role in implementing innovations and note the recommendations given there for what principals should do to facilitate curriculum improvement. Which of these involve interpersonal influence and which involve structural change? Do you agree with the emphasis represented by this proportion?

4. Based on what you have learned about what is involved in bringing about curriculum change, suggest what personal characteristics would make principals effective at fostering curriculum improvement in their school.

5. Imagine that you are the principal of a school. Examine a recommended process for assessing teacher performance. Does it give due attention to teachers' contributions to curricular management? How could it be improved in this regard?

6.   Make a list of events in the day-to-day life of schools that, if unchecked, could adversely affect the quality of the curriculum (content, purpose, structure of the school program) offered in a school. Consider measures school leaders might take to counteract these causes of erosion of curricular quality.

7.   Examine any curriculum book or recent issues of curriculum journals to find a checklist of things to do to improve the curriculum of a school. Examine that checklist in light of the analysis of school curriculum improvement given in this chapter. What would you add or change?

8.   Choose some aspect of school curriculum work such as: reviewing texts or tests for adoption, developing curriculum guides or courses of study, planning in-service education activities for teachers, determining course offerings, developing the master schedule, setting promotion or graduation requirements, monitoring quality of classroom curriculum, or allocation of school resources. Describe how this particular task is accomplished in a school you know well. Assess this procedure in light of the ideas in this chapter. If possible, suggest ways to improve how this school accomplishes this task.

9.   Assume a friend of yours has just been appointed superintendent of a small district with two high schools, two middle schools, and twelve elementary schools. She explains that the district has only a few people on the central office staff, all of whom are very busy, and little money to carry out studies or to hire consultants. She asks for your advice on how she can assess strong and weak points of the curriculum in the schools of the district (elementary, middle school, or secondary: choose one). Suggest seven steps she can take to learn the most about the curriculum with the least expenditure.

10.   A school board member, told that the results of a review may depend upon how it is designed, asks why spend the money since the Superintendent can do a subjective study using her own staff. He says, "The only reason to spend extra money on a curriculum review is if it can yield objective findings not based on people's opinions." How would you, as Superintendent, reply?

11.   The state board of education has just mandated that every high school student study mathematics for three years in order to receive a high school diploma; the present requirement is two years. The principal of the high school at which you work has called a meeting to discuss the new requirement. He has asked you to prepare a list of ways that this new requirement might affect the school curriculum. Suggest which of these have the greatest potential for causing problems and briefly explain why.

12.   We saw in Chapter 8 that schools include many social niches that operate somewhat independently of one another in many respects. What are the implications of this fact for the implementation of innovations in the school?

RECOMMENDED READING

A great deal has been written about how to improve school curricula. For the most part this advice has been supported by the author's experience. Tankard (1974) and English (1987) are good examples. I have tried to base the procedures presented here on systematic analysis and research. The following were my main sources.

On school curriculum improvement generally: I find Fullan's *The Meaning of Educational Change* (1982) to be the most useful single reference on the overall topic. Good and Brophy's (1986) comprehensive review is a more recent review of the research literature on the effects of various kinds of school-level school improvement projects. Joyce's *The Structure of School Improvement* (1983) and *Improving America's Schools* (1986) are also valuable and deeply informed by practical experience in innovative projects as well as theory and research. Joyce is especially strong on the role of staff development in school improvement. Hopkins and Wideen (1984) is a valuable source. Hall and Loucks (1977) offer insights from the perspective of studies of the implementation of innovations. Sergiovanni's work on supervision (Sergiovanni and Starratt 1979) and on departmental leadership (Sergiovanni 1984) set the standard for those subjects. Glatthorn (1987) is also valuable on the topic of supervision. Leithwood and Montgomery (1982) review the research on the role of the principal in curriculum change in elementary schools. Austin and Garber (1985) review research on schools identified as exemplary; some of their findings bear on curriculum improvement in helpful ways, though, like most of the effective schools research, they have more to say about what quality already achieved looks like than about how to achieve it. Glatthorn's (1987) curriculum text is helpful.

On curriculum reviews: The traditional literature here is that on needs assessment, now largely discredited, though still practiced. (See the discussion of needs assessment in Chapters 8 and 12.) Cooley and Bickell (1986) offer an excellent example of what I have called a focused comprehensive review here.

On curriculum change consideration: Schaffarzick (1975) remains the only direct reference.

On instituting curriculum change efforts: The traditional literature here is that on curriculum innovation so ably synthesized by Fullan (1982). He ably reviews the research on the roles of the various people involved and the tactics they employ.

On facilitating classroom curriculum change: Hall (1987) gives a comprehensive set of recommendations based on the implementation research carried out mostly in the last decade. Joyce (1988) looks like a new standard reference on staff development.

On evaluation: The volume by Cronbach, et al. (1980) is my standard source on evaluation. I have found no better source on the design of evaluation studies than Cronbach's own *Designing Evaluations of Educational and Social Programs* (1982), though it requires careful study. The Bloom, Hastings, and Madaus *Handbook of Formative and Summative Evaluation of Student Learning* (1971) is full of useful practical advice, especially on measures of learning.

REFERENCES

Austin, Gilbert R. and Herbert Garber (eds.). 1985. *Research on Exemplary Schools.* Orlando: Academic Press.

Bloom, Benjamin, Thomas Hastings, and George Madaus. 1971. *Handbook of Formative and Summative Evaluation of Student Learning.* N.Y.: McGraw-Hill.

Cooley, William and William Bickell. 1986. *Decision-Oriented Educational Research.* Boston: Kluwer-Nijhof.

Cronbach, Lee J. et al. 1980. *Toward Reform of Program Evaluation: Aims, Methods, and Institutional Arrangements.* San Francisco: Jossey-Bass.

Cronbach, Lee J. 1982. *Designing Evaluations of Educational and Social Programs.* San Francisco: Jossey-Bass.

English, Fenwick. 1987. *Curriculum Management for Schools, Colleges, and Business.* Springfield, IL: Charles C. Thomas.

Fullan, Michael. 1982. *The Meaning of Educational Change.* N.Y.: Teachers College Press.

Glatthorn, Allan A. 1987. *Curriculum Leadership.* Glenview, IL: Scott, Foresman, and Company.

Good, Thomas L. and Jere E. Brophy. 1986. School Effects. *Handbook of Research on Teaching* (3rd Edition; Merlin Wittrock, ed.). N.Y.: Macmillan.

Hall, Gene. 1987. *Change in Schools: Facilitating the Process.* Albany: State University of New York Press.

Hall, Gene E. and Shirley F. Loucks. 1977. A Developmental Model for Determining Whether the Treatment is Actually Implemented. *American Educational Research Journal* 14: 263–276.

Hall, Gene E., Shirley Hord, L. L. Huling, W. L. Rutherford, and S. M. Stiegelbauer. 1983. Leadership Variables Associated with Successful School Improvement. Paper presented at the annual meeting of the American Educational Research Association, Montreal.

Hopkins, David and Marvin Wideen. 1984. *Alternative Perspectives on School Improvement.* Philadelphia: Falmer Press.

Joyce, Bruce R. 1983. *The Structure of School Improvement.* N.Y.: Longman.

Joyce, Bruce R. 1986. *Improving America's Schools.* N.Y.: Longman.

Joyce, Bruce R. 1988. *Student Achievement through Staff Development.* N.Y.: Longman.

Leithwood, Kenneth A., and D. J. Montgomery. Fall 1982. The Role of the Elementary School Principal in Program Improvement. *Review of Educational Research* 52: 309–339.

Schaffarzick, Jon. 1975. The Consideration of Curriculum Change at the Local Level. Unpublished Ph.D. Dissertation. Stanford University.

Sergiovanni, Thomas J. 1984. *Handbook for Effective Department Leadership* (2nd ed.) Boston: Allyn and Bacon.

Sergiovanni, Thomas J. and Robert J. Starratt. 1979. *Supervision: Human Perspectives* (2nd ed.) N.Y.: McGraw-Hill.

Tankard, George G. 1974. *Curriculum Improvement: An Administrator's Guide.* West Nyack, N.Y.: Parker Publishing Co.

Wallace, Richard. May 1987. An Interview with Dick Wallace. *Educational Leadership* 44:40.

CURRICULUM POLICY-MAKING

*P*olicy, *regardless of which level of government initiates it, ultimately affects schooling to the degree that it affects organization and practice [of schooling]. Problems of variability, adaptation, lags in implementation and performance, and the seeming unresponsiveness of the "system" to shifts in policy all find their roots in what happens in the school and classroom.*

Richard F. Elmore and Milbrey Wallin McLaughlin
Steady Work. 1988.

PURPOSE OF THE CHAPTER

- to explain the strengths and limitation of policy in curriculum
- to show how effective curriculum policy might be made in the American educational system

OUTLINE

Curriculum Policy-Making in a Decentralized System

Strategies for Curriculum Policy-Making

Building a Policy Agenda

How Useful Is Needs Assessment in Agenda-Building?

Strategies for Developing Policies

Strategies for Understanding the Problem

CURRICULUM POLICY-MAKING IN A DECENTRALIZED SYSTEM

The Case for Curriculum Policy

People turn to policy in curriculum matters when they want to make a major change in the practices of an entire education system within a briefer time than such changes normally occur. That such changes are possible seems evident. The Soviet Union, Japan, Israel, China, and India have all adopted in this century vigorous national policies to encourage education in the sciences, mathematics, and languages, and these policies have·played an important role in their economic and social development. England, Sweden, and several other European countries redesigned their secondary education systems in the 1970s to be comprehensive rather than selective. It is the potential power of curriculum policy to make such sudden, far-reaching changes that makes it such an attractive idea.

In the United States since World War II, Americans have confronted a series of situations that have led many to call for massive, rapid improvements in the education system, including concern about the nation's scientific and technological proficiency, about equality of educational opportunity, and about economic competitiveness. These concerns continue and are likely to grow as the basic trends underlying them advance—increasing global communication and transportation, worldwide economic development, economic restructuring toward a postindustrial economy in which knowledge and skill become primary forms of capital, and the continuing rapid expansion of scientific knowledge, for example. For better or worse, Americans forced to respond to such trends are likely to make greater demands on their schools in the future. Unfortunately, the ability of the education system to respond to these demands through incremental improvements seems to be eroding. As productivity increases in the rest of the economy through automation and restructuring of services, the effective per-pupil cost of a traditional education will continue to rise. As more and more able women, who, traditionally, had few other career opportunities, find other areas opening up to them, those recruited to teaching are becoming less talented. Negotiated settlements of struggles for control of the education system by teacher organizations, administrators, and the public and its representatives lock the schools into increasingly rigid stances. The net result of all these trends is likely to be increasing demand for sudden, massive reforms in the education system. The normal process of gradual cultural change will not be seen as adequate. New and more potent action will be demanded.

Conceivably, the education system could be restructured to emphasize market processes over explicit planning. Voucher systems are the most radical of many such proposals. In a market oriented system, individual *firms* (schools or teachers) competing for *customers* (students) would develop their own policies about such matters as curriculum. As some schools attracted more students, their policies would come to dominate and the complex influence system would be replaced by a market system. In reality, any issue of such public concern as the curriculum of the nation's schools would also be subject to regulation, so that a pure market system is not a realistic alternative. In a mixed system the need for curriculum policy-making in connection with regulation of the education market would still be great.

The potential benefits of policy-making seem far too tempting to be ignored. Politically, it will be much easier to rally support for a dramatic national reform, especially in a crisis, than for a sustained, systematic program of incremental improvement in each local school. The national interest will rarely be well-served by purely local action in curriculum matters. Curriculum issues are rarely considered in local school system governance, anyway, and the public feels powerless and excluded from such decisions when they do occur. In policy-making, the public at least has an opportunity to lobby the policy-makers, whereas in local school systems curriculum issues are controlled by the professionals. Policy-making offers an occasion for forging the political alliances and coalitions needed to achieve sustained, concerted action on a large scale.

Economically, policy offers the possibility of garnering additional resources for curriculum improvement. Legislatures, foundations, and taxpayers are more willing to pay a large amount for a brief time to produce a substantial immediate improvement than to invest the same amount in a longer, less dramatic, and less glamorous plan of improvement. Furthermore, economies of scale make it possible to bring larger and qualitatively better resources to bear on the development of curriculum plans and materials. Larger investments in such activities make economic sense when the products can be sold to a larger market, and a unified curriculum policy in the school of a state or nation forms a large market. Large scale policies also eliminate the need for wasteful duplication of effort in the central offices of thousands of local school districts. A reasonable degree of standardization makes scarce resources go further.

Policy gives us the opportunity to express and uphold shared values. In debating policies we bring reason to bear on public decisions, air contending views, clarify what is at stake, and engage with one another in dialogue on substantial public issues. The examined choices that result help to define public standards and public values.

Technically, policy makes a complex, diverse, and extended education system easier to manage. All aspects of curriculum design from school scheduling to curriculum materials design to test construction are simplified when more schools participate in a common curriculum pattern. Record-keeping, transfers from school to school, preparation and selection of teachers—all are made simpler when different schools follow common curriculum policies.

The attractions of policy in curriculum are so great and so responsive to the pressures of our time that it is hard to imagine a future for the American education system that does not include more curriculum policy. Yet curriculum policy is a much more limited tool than it seems. And it remains to be seen whether curriculum policy can be made to work in the American decentralized curriculum influence system.

Limitations of Policy in Curriculum

In all fields, policy disappoints in the sense that results do not live up to advocates' promises or policy-makers' expectations. Political scientists Bardach and Kagan point out that ambitious policies (*regulatory goals* in their terminology) invite disappointment and that the competitive search for solutions by policy-makers creates inflated expectations.

> When legislatures establish ambitious regulatory goals . . . , even aggressive regulators armed with specific rules and strong sanctions will not achieve them. . . . (Bardach and Kagan 1982b, 20)

In education, effects of the sort anticipated by the major curriculum reforms of the previous generation would take at least a decade to appear, and yet these initiatives were largely abandoned in less than a decade.

Bardach and Kagan argue that the most familiar form of policy, regulation, can never be sufficient for bringing about the kinds of changes its advocates seek.

> The restraints of the rule of law . . . command certain procedures, and they dictate that all statutes and regulations be applied uniformly, consistently, and fairly. The realm of human activity to which these rules are applied, however, is diverse and complex. It is not always possible to successfully connect the procedural and substantive requirements of law to the variety of experience. (Bardach and Kagan 1982b, 3)

They suggest that attitudes work in ways that rules cannot.

> By their nature, formal rules are enforceable only if they specify minimum **conditions** of performance or quality or whatever. They cannot be designed to bring about higher levels of aspiration or continuous improvement or concern about quality. . . . [Also,] formal rules usually cannot be detailed enough to cover all the diverse [situations that arise]. . . . Finally, even when rules can in principle cover all the relevant situations, compliance is problematic unless there is an underlying attitude of willing cooperation. (Bardach and Kagan 1982b, 100)

Although policy tools may be powerful, they are certainly blunt.

Extensive reliance on policy can lead to a formalism and bureaucratization that causes us to lose sight of educational issues. Bardach and Kagan give the following example from education:

> In a typical day an elementary teacher deals with sign-in sheets, lunch counts, hall passes, absence slips, rollbooks, attendance cards, class count forms, parent communications, textbook and materials requests, lesson plans, student evaluations, documentation, [and] paperwork relating to teaching students. Additionally, different levels of the bureaucracy frequently request distribution and collection of questionnaires, ethnic surveys, free lunch applications, permission slips, walking trip permits, emergency cards, class schedules, federal forms for Impact Aid, home language surveys, audio-visual surveys, needs assessments, nine-week objectives, yearly objectives, report cards, requests for special services, testing materials, program descriptions, time cards, field trip requests, and several profile cards for each student. . . . (Bardach and Kagan 1982a, 91)

Partly for this reason, and also because it allocates resources on political rather than economic criteria, policy is usually an inefficient way to allocate resources.

Because it involves public declarations, policy-making is subject to hypocritical posturing. People espouse a high-sounding position publicly, but behave differently in private. For example, they may mandate that children read classic literature in school, but read something quite different, or nothing at all, themselves. (Mark Twain defined a classic as something everybody wanted read but nobody wanted to read.) Eventually, the contrast between public piety and private vice becomes apparent to everybody and the policy loses its credibility.

In an open, democratic polity, policy-making seems at first sight to be a just way to decide public issues. Yet, in the American system, policy-making favors organized interest groups. Those who are alert, who have someone placed in or around the many arenas in which important decisions are made, and who have or can hire the knowledge, skill, and connections will usually win the struggle to shape the curriculum.

In the decentralized American system, policy-making is subject to manic-depressive cycles. Policy leaps into the American system when crises open the door. Out of the depths of public concern a bold policy emerges and gathers adherents. Advocates, carried away by their enthusiasm, overpromise, but their ambitious claims attract further support. In their heady optimism, advocate policy-makers frame ill-considered and half-baked policies whose defects are overlooked by a hopeful public. When the crisis passes or another captures the headlines, public interest lags, the policy loses steam, critics crawl out of the woodwork, the inevitable weaknesses of an immature policy are dragged into the spotlight and the reform is discredited. The experience amounts to a kind of national morality play in which our emotions are discharged—fear, action, relief, disillusion, vengeance—

but the sudden, massive changes demanded never materialize. One would think that the public would catch on sooner or later.

Clearly, policy is anything but a sure thing. Thus forewarned, let us see what can reasonably be expected.

What We Should Expect from Policy

The potential benefits of policy include economic efficiency, political unity, symbolic expression of shared cultural values, and practical benefits arising from standardization. To realize these benefits in curriculum matters, it is necessary to have policies that can be understood by those who must carry them out, policies that are widely enough supported so that serious efforts will be made to carry them out, that prove to be workable when carried out, and that achieve results that are judged to be satisfactory by the major parties involved.

No policy-making arrangements can meet this standard all the time. Although we sometimes speak of policies as being right or wrong, we can never demonstrate conclusively that any given course of action is optimal, or even define what *optimal* would mean in the case of a policy question of any complexity. We must often make do with policies that are only satisfactory. Furthermore, good policies—the best anyone could have made—can produce bad results due to unforeseeable events, and bad policies can turn out well. The appropriate criterion for judging the quality of decisions of any sort is that they be well-made given the information and resources available. This means that the decision-makers considered all the relevant factors and, in their consideration of each, used the best available information, a standard that we abbreviate with the term informed, considered decision. Adequate arrangements for curriculum policy-making ought to produce well-informed, well-considered decisions.

Workable policies meet such criteria as the following. They are compatible with the frames within which schools operate, consistent with the organizational structure of the school system. They call for actions that schools and teachers are able to take and that do not contradict or undo other valid policies already in force. Workability also implies continuity across time, space, individuals, and organizations to insure that what is accomplished at one time and place will not be undone at others. And policies should be stable enough to provide time for them to be built into the institutional routine.

Adequate policy-making arrangements also manage the institutional and individual stresses of change well enough to keep the inevitable dangers and disorders of change within acceptable bounds. The policy ought not to arouse undue anger, fear, or other negative emotions in those who must implement it, certainly not to the extent that it interferes with their ability or willingness to carry on their other duties. Other important parts of the school program should not be weakened by the adoption and implementation of a new policy. The school system's capacity for supporting further improvements should not be substantially reduced.

Conflicts will always arise in connection with significant policy decisions, but satisfactory policy-making arrangements should resolve most conflicts constructively. They should lead to accommodation of legitimate differences whenever feasible, through adjustments, compromises, negotiated settlements, and the like. When conflicts proceed to contests, satisfactory arrangements for policy-formation will channel the contention in socially constructive paths—debate, legitimate politics, nonviolent action. Resolutions, when reached, will be accepted by all parties, including the losers on this particular issue. Participants will retain their allegiance to the institutions and to the policy-making arrangements in spite of losing on particular issues. The rights of those in the minority on any issue will be respected, including rights to continue to participate in the process, to appeal, to continue their struggle, to protection from infringement of their basic rights by the majority, and so on. Ideally, over the years the process of reaching widely acceptable accommodations will achieve a widely shared appreciation of strengths and weaknesses of school programs and thus lead to reduced levels of conflict.

These arrangements and the policies they engender should embody appropriate shared values and ideals. Curriculum policy arrangements should be democratic, open to public participation and influence, fair, equitable, and representative. But they should also recognize the rights of public employees in such matters as hiring, firing, promotion, and professional judgment. In general, American traditions require considerable acknowledgment of the rights of the individual in relation to governmental agencies—rights to due process, to equal protection of the laws, to basic freedoms of speech and religion, freedom from unreasonable searches and seizures, and so on.

STRATEGIES FOR CURRICULUM POLICY-MAKING

Policy Is Fundamentally Political, Not Technical

As we begin to consider some means of making better curriculum policies we may be tempted to think of them as methods or techniques, but these words carry connotations of formality and precision that are not appropriate in the context of policy-making. Policy-making is a process in which people's ideas and feelings are implicated, a process that ultimately rests as much on values and preferences as it does on the facts of the matter. The dream that dominates some students of the subject—to solve curriculum problems by some rational analysis or scientific procedure—leads to a process in which human interaction with its values, feelings, and ideas no longer have any place except as inputs to a calculation. Yet as long as people retain the capacity to govern themselves, the people involved must accept the solution or it is no solution at all, regardless of what the calculations say. This is not to imply that calculation is out of place in human affairs or that the results of careful study should be overruled by mere whim, but only that in curriculum matters the value of the results of any technique cannot be taken for granted but must be judged by the people involved with the problem. Techniques may suggest possible solutions, but whether they are solutions or not is a matter of human judgment. This is the meaning of the claim that curriculum policy processes are fundamentally political.

All phases of the curriculum policy process call for all the arts of politics, especially including those interpersonal arts of deliberation, negotiation, and accommodation. Policy-makers, therefore, must be at least as concerned with how to keep the basically political institutions and processes functioning so that curriculum issues can be raised and resolved effectively as they are with how to find rational solutions to particular problems. Particular tools and techniques may be useful at times in the context of these political processes, but technique, at best, informs and facilitates; it does not prescribe.

In this section we will consider some strategies—formal and informal—that can often be helpful in curriculum policy-making. Different strategies are needed for different tasks that comprise the policy process. We will consider five policy challenges:

1. building a policy agenda,
2. developing individual policies,
3. implementing policies,
4. evaluating policies,
5. maintaining effective policy-making arrangements.

Each of these is fundamental to the policy process in a variety of curricular contexts: state, local, or federal; official or unofficial; crisis or routine. The present discussion will assume a context in which some designated group is assigned official responsibility for one of these tasks within a policy jurisdiction, while various unofficial groups seek to influence its official decisions. This emphasizes official policy-making somewhat at the expense of unofficial policy-making, but some corners must be cut. It is impossible to do justice to the diversity of unofficial policy-making in such a brief treatment of the subject.

BUILDING A POLICY AGENDA

A policy agenda is a set of problems or issues that a policy-making body sees as deserving its attention during some period of time. A policy agenda normally consists of several issues at various stages of work. Some policies will already have been adopted but will continue to need attention during implementation. Other agenda items consist of cases for which the need for an action is not questioned, but a decision needs to be made about which action to take. In other cases the issue may be whether a problem exists at all. An issue that is not yet on the policy agenda cannot even be discussed formally and explicitly by the group, though it may be, and usually is, discussed earlier by individuals off the record. To receive consideration as a possible area in which policy might be needed, an issue must pass this first hurdle; most do not. Only a tiny fraction of the most frequent and serious problems individuals encounter ever make it onto the agenda. And if the most important problems are not on the agenda, good work in subsequent stages of policy-making will be to no avail. Hence building a sound agenda is fundamental to good policy-making.

In view of the long time it takes to adopt and implement curriculum policies and the even longer time it takes for them to bear fruit, a serious attempt at planned curriculum change probably needs a long-time horizon. Ten years ahead is not too far to consider. In view of the vulnerability of curriculum decisions to unforeseen and uncontrollable events, it would seem wise to plan in a way that leaves considerable flexibility to respond to changing conditions. These thoughts suggest two features desirable in a sound agenda-building process: multiple time horizons and contingency planning.

An ideal agenda-building process would attempt to identify all major areas in which curriculum policy might be desirable or necessary in the coming decade; to flag some of these for immediate attention, some for attention within perhaps 4 or 5 years, and some for attention within 10 years; and then update this agenda every year or two in light of changing circumstances. Longer-range plans for any given agenda item could consist of several alternative policies designed to take advantage of different possible circumstances that might arise during the time required for the policy to come to fruition. For instance, plans for incorporating computers into the regular curriculum of the school might include an ambitious policy, in case funds are plentiful and public support strong, and a couple of less ambitious policies, including a bare-bones policy in case of no additional resources and tepid public reaction.

Ideally, any policy agenda includes all the items of vital importance to any substantial segment of its constituency. In practice, the list of such items is much too long for each to receive thorough consideration. Furthermore, contending groups often struggle to keep one another's concerns off the agenda as a way of preventing action on them. The establishment of the agenda is therefore a fundamentally political action. The agenda itself is a concrete indication of the policy-making group's priorities, and of the priorities of the constituency that supports and legitimizes it, to the extent that its recommendations are followed. Those concerns that do not make it onto the agenda must wait for next year or look elsewhere for attention to their concerns.

Anyone seeking a place for an item on the agenda of a curriculum policy-making body must accomplish at least two distinct but related tasks: making the case (to justify the item's place with convincing arguments and evidence) and showing support (to demonstrate that constituents and other influentials favor including the item on the agenda). Within the framework of official curriculum rhetoric, the traditional means of making the case has been to argue on the basis of relevant statistics that students have an educational need not being met by the existing curriculum. The traditional means of showing support has been a survey or poll, in the case of constituents, and through citations of published opinions, in the case of experts and other influentials. In practice, the case is often most effectively made through anecdotes and aphorisms and support is often shown through letter-writing campaigns or face-to-face meetings, either in casual interactions or by calling out the troops for a meeting or demonstration.

Agenda-building is therefore both a rational and a political enterprise. It is rational inasmuch as those involved strive to base their decisions on the best available facts and theories. It is political since the effective resolution of the matters under discussion comes when those involved make up their minds to act, whether or not the facts and theories reveal a clearly preferable course of action. As might be expected, more tools and techniques have been developed to assist decision-makers in building a factual basis for decisions than for validating theoretical underpinnings or convincing others to accept and act on what is known.

Needs Assessment

Needs assessment is a formal, systematic effort to document the existence and importance of educational needs among a population. Typically, questionnaires are designed and mailed to representative samples of the population or those presumed to be acquainted with their needs—usually students, parents, teachers, graduates, teachers of graduates, employers of graduates, community leaders, and citizens at large. The questions usually ask respondents to report the needs or problems they perceive (perhaps also the areas of greatest success), and to indicate in some way how serious and important they think each of a series of reputed needs actually is for themselves or for the population in question. Such surveys yield perceived needs; if there are needs respondents are unaware of, they cannot report them. Perceived needs may also be assessed through interviews with key or representative individuals or through discussion among groups of them.

Indications of need may also be found in data about students and the school, such as: achievement test scores, attitude measures, accomplishments of graduates, incidence of school problems (drop-outs, vandalism, referrals for discipline, and so on), attendance, enrollments, and the like—or from the community, such as: unemployment rates, literacy rates, levels of schooling completed, family income, occupational patterns, housing patterns, incidence of health problems, crime rates, and so on. Such data do not speak for themselves; assumptions must be made about desirable levels before data about *what is* can be used to support claims of *what ought to be*. Inferences about causes of problems are frequently required in order to establish that a need calls for an educational response. For example, unemployment might call for higher levels of education or it might also call for different tax or government spending policies, depending on the relative importance of these factors in causing the problem.

HOW USEFUL IS NEEDS ASSESSMENT IN AGENDA-BUILDING?

In principle, formal needs assessment is fairer, more objective, and more complete than informal procedures for agenda-building. Data collected according to a scientifically defensible plan are less subject to bias than casual observation and opinion. Data covering a wide range of possible problems yield a more comprehensive picture. A formal and systematic effort to identify all significant needs and to establish their relative seriousness should provide a firmer basis for agenda-building than any informal process. This is doubtlessly the reason that needs assessments are so commonly demanded in the planning of local curriculum change projects.

In practice, however, needs assessment appears to be a tool of limited usefulness for agenda-building, though it can make an important contribution in certain specific conditions. Here are some of the problems. The process of needs assessment rests on an assumption of a close and obvious connection between facts and needs: When the facts are clear, the needs will be apparent. In practice, though, facts are often subject to more than one interpretation. Achievement test scores averaging in the 90th percentile may be viewed as a triumph by one school and a failure by another. A trend of rising communicable disease rates may be interpreted as evidence for an educational need or for better public health measures. When a wide spectrum of data are collected in an effort to discover all important needs, it is unlikely that they will include the specific facts needed to decide between different interpretations of the problem, even assuming that the differences have a purely factual basis. Often, of course, different interpretations rest on different values or worldviews rather than merely on disagreements about specific facts.

Accepting people's stated needs as real carries some risks, too. They may not be aware of their true needs. With the benefit of reflection and discussions, they might identify quite different needs and priorities among them. Expressing a need can be a way of making a claim on a greater share of community resources. Needs assessment that asks people to identify their needs does not avoid politicking, it only channels it into a different form of expression (questionnaire responses rather than face-to-face encounters).

The logic of needs assessment rests on certain assumptions built into the language. Even the most scientific procedures will be subject to the limitations of the underlying logic. The language of needs is a particular form of moral or political rhetoric. It makes a moral claim on policy-makers to help the needy and hence has a redistributive, egalitarian thrust. Suppose, for contrast, that we spoke of *opportunity assessment* and searched for opportunities to strengthen the school system instead of for needs it should meet. Would the difference be mere semantics? The language of needs implies that the powerful look out for the welfare of the weak, since policy-makers are assumed to be able to meet the needs of beneficiaries who are incapable of meeting their own needs or seeing to it that others meet them. Suppose, for contrast, that we spoke of *performance assessment* of schools, a process in which powerful constituencies studied the performance of policy-makers. It also has a built-in activist orientation. By definition, all needs should be met, whereas mere wants or demands may or may not deserve to be satisfied. Having established that a certain need exists, the debate should focus on how, not whether, to meet it. Suppose, for contrast, that we spoke of *dissatisfactions*. Would we assume that all dissatisfactions should be eliminated?

The identification of even a single genuine need that fulfills all of the assumptions built into the rhetoric of needs assessment would require a comprehensive and searching examination of the situation of the school and its students both as these are now and as they might be when the students reach adulthood and take their places as full members of the community, the nation, and the world. Appropriate data is vital to such an examination, but basing the examination wholly or primarily on data from a single survey or on data collected at a single point in time is unwise. In any event, such data can only help by providing information for what should be a much deeper and more extensive process of self-examination. In most cases the deliberation that takes place within an effective policy-shaping community can be expected to bring to light potentially serious and important curriculum problems that might merit inclusion on the policy agenda. Such deliberation will in most cases be a more appropriate process for need identification and agenda-building than formal needs assessment.

Formal needs assessment is best reserved for those situations in which it can be of specific help rather than prescribed routinely for all major curriculum change efforts. Under normal conditions, a formal needs assessment is likely to reveal little that is new or surprising to those close to the situation. A review of the state of the art of needs assessment in federal projects by the Center for Social Research and Development (1974) for the Department of Health, Education, and Welfare surveyed 30 federal projects identified by federal officials as exemplary. They found that:

> [Respondents] did not expect that new problems would be discovered, although they felt that the magnitude of the need might become more apparent. As one respondent stated: Many people were expecting an analysis that would dramatically illustrate the needs of the population. In fact, the results were predictable and unspectacular. (Center for Social Research and Development 1974, 48)

Except in certain special conditions, less costly informal methods are probably as likely as more formal methods to uncover previously neglected or unknown needs.

However, in certain specific situations the normal activities of the policy-shaping community can stand to be strengthened with some more systematic procedures. For example, when some segment of the population has not been effectively represented in the agenda-building process and their needs have therefore been neglected, a formal needs assessment can call attention to their needs and make it more difficult for agenda-builders to overlook them. In this way formal needs assessment can help to make the agenda-building process fairer and more representative. When social or psychological barriers prevent policy-makers from considering a sensitive issue fairly or completely, a more systematic formal process may be useful. For example, when the ethnic composition of a community is changing, or when the economic basis of the community is threatened, policy-makers may need help in viewing the situation realistically. When these barriers are at their highest, mere data collection will be insufficient. It can take a major social movement and drastic actions such as publicity campaigns, strikes, boycotts, marches, or riots to put new items on the policy agenda.

When formal processes are used, they should be designed to strengthen and augment informal processes. For example, in informal agenda-building those most interested in a particular area of policy are usually among the first to spot a potential problem. They are closest to the situations in which the problem would first manifest itself and they have the strongest motivation to want it solved. So, the very early phases of calling attention to a potential new agenda item are usually the work of partisans and advocates. They collect the facts to document the existence, extent, and importance of the problem, and they marshall facts, arguments, and rhetoric to persuade others. When support is strong enough from within a nonpartisan policy-making agency, it may also sponsor activities designed to document the need. Occasionally an area of need for policy may be discovered through disinterested analysis of routinely collected data, but much more often committed partisans make the case and routinely collected data confirms (or does not confirm) it. Involvement of partisans in designing the data collection and interpretation process can produce much more satisfactory results than striving for a purely objective process.

Formal data collection will generally be more helpful if focused on validation of claims about the existence and importance of problems that have already attained some plausibility within the policy-making group. In a thoughtful critique of needs assessment, Wayne A. Kimmel (1977) suggests that the first step in exploring a potential policy problem be the preparation of an issue paper that lays out the structure of the problem, those probably affected by it, possible causes of the problem, an analysis of the theory of the problem, the potential appropriateness of policy for solving the problem, a review of others' experience with the problem, and the major steps necessary to understand the problem further. The data that would be most helpful in understanding and further validating the problem should be apparent after discussion of such an issue paper among policy-makers and interested members of the more extended policy shaping community.

Other Strategies Potentially Useful for Agenda-Building

Several other somewhat formal strategies would seem to be particularly useful in building a curriculum policy agenda.

Follow-Up Studies of Graduates One of the most fundamental curriculum concerns is the adequacy of students' preparation for adult life. Follow-up studies of graduates, using interviews or questionnaires, can be helpful here. Also, data from employers of graduates and from teachers and school officials in the schools to which students go after graduation can be extremely helpful. Establishing an outside review committee comprised of representatives of the agencies who receive most of the graduates to observe, review documents, and suggest needs can be helpful. In many cases articles can be found in the professional literature that identify the most common and serious difficulties young people encounter in making their transition to the next stage of their schooling or life. A systematic review of this literature can suggest potential problem areas. Case studies of particular incidents (called *critical incidents*) can help to interpret the origins and nature of problems. Students are also in a privileged position for recognizing certain types of curricular problems. Surveys, end-of-course and end-of-year evaluations, and interviews with students can yield helpful information about needs and problems.

Opinion Polling Techniques developed for opinion polling also offer great potential for discovering commonalities and differences in the views of those affected by policy. The polls of public opinion about the schools of the nation commissioned by Phi Delta Kappa and conducted by the Gallup organization show what can be done in this respect on a nationwide basis. State and community efforts are also possible. As levels of education in our communities grow, opinions of parents and taxpayers can be expected to become more informed. Also, parents and taxpayers are more likely to demand a voice in policies affecting them. Telephone polls, newspaper and television polls, and door-to-door interviewing of scientifically chosen samples of the relevant population can reduce policy-makers' uncertainties about their constituents' views.

Analysis and Projection of Trends We would really like to know what the future needs of our graduates will be. The best we can do is to attempt to forecast future conditions in and out of school. Demographic projections can help to anticipate changes in the student population. Economic projections alert policy-makers to changes in the demands placed on graduates from the world of work. Identification of social trends may suggest likely changes in life outside school with implications for what students should be taught. Unfortunately, such forecasting must be based on assumptions whose validity we cannot even estimate. As a result, projections are unreliable. Demographic forecasting would seem to be the most reliable, but different demographic models and assumptions lead to different forecasts. Demographers have failed to forecast some major shifts in school populations over recent decades, including the fall in birth rates in the 1960s, the later age of marriage in the 1970s, and the increases in immigration to the United States from southeast Asia. The wisest course of action, for those that can afford it, would seem to be to plan for alternative possible futures using the best forecasting available, and to retain enough flexibility to respond to the unexpected.

Setting Priorities The question "Whose agenda items will receive the highest priority?" tends to dominate the agenda-setting process. To the extent that people's priorities are set and cannot be changed, public priorities will be established through the exercise of political power, whether it be in the form of a vote, a decision by an authorized individual, or some other form. To the extent that people can be persuaded to change their priorities, various forms of persuasion, including formal procedures for supporting claims of relative importance with evidence, become appropriate. These familiar strategies can be supplemented with some more formal ones.

Delphi Technique A formalization of deliberation that may be helpful in priority setting is the Delphi technique. After exposure to appropriate information and arguments and participation in discussion of the issues, participants in the Delphi session are asked to rank or rate the various items contending for a place on the policy agenda. These ratings are compiled and participants are shown where they stand in relation to the others on each issue. In the original Delphi technique individuals are then invited to write arguments defending their ratings. The written arguments are circulated anonymously, so that no one knows who wrote any argument. In a looser version of the technique participants are asked to express their arguments orally, but this eliminates an important source of the technique's objectivity, since more influential individuals may sway others by who they are rather than by what they are arguing. Then the items are ranked again. The process continues so long as the distribution of responses change significantly from one rating to the next. The Delphi technique does not guarantee consensus; in fact, differences may be widened at this stage. But it does guarantee that arguments are made explicit and that all arguments are given a fair and thorough hearing. In practice, individuals whose views are initially most at odds with the majority are more able to persuade others to their views than is the case in unstructured discussions.

Curriculum Conferences Karl Frey (1986) has experimented in West Germany with holding curriculum conferences, meetings of articulate, interested representatives of the most directly concerned groups to discuss possible solutions to curriculum problems. This technique could easily be adapted to agenda-building. Participants in the conference are provided with background papers prior to the meeting. Their goal is to emerge from several days of intense discussion with a ranked list of curriculum policy issues, together with the reasons for their rankings, for presentation to the policy-making body. Even if their conclusions are not accepted, the debate among the general public can begin at a more advanced level than it would otherwise.

When Is a Curricular Response Appropriate?

A curriculum change is not an appropriate response to every educational problem. Some problems can only be solved by changing the teaching staff, their teaching methods, funding levels, or the way the school is organized or governed.

For example, if students need closer personal relationships with caring adults, it is unlikely that changes in the content, aims, and structure of the school program will meet this need. Many serious educational problems can only be addressed through curricular changes of such a magnitude that the disruption caused by the change would create problems as great as would be solved. For example, schools could potentially do much more to prepare students for the personal stresses they will experience in life outside the school—coping with violence, establishing an occupational identity, forming and sustaining relationships with others, dealing with disappointment, confronting illness and death, and so on—but to do so effectively would demand a reconsideration of schools from the ground up, questioning such givens as the primacy of literacy, the integrity of school subjects, the value of tests and grades, and so on.

Other problems are so deeply embedded in the surrounding society that a curricular response would not be permitted. For example, to reform the curriculum of elementary and secondary schools to respond effectively to the problems of racial, social, and economic inequities and injustices in our society would require that the school operate with a completely different set of values than the community it serves and that supports it. Still other problems are of too short a duration to permit an effective curricular response. For example, an explosion of racial tensions in the community would have subsided before the social studies curriculum of a local school system could be revised, even assuming the revisions could be helpful in dealing with the underlying racial tensions.

In general, for a curricular response to be effective the educational problem should be:

- capable of being significantly ameliorated through formal instruction of young people ages 5–18,
- likely to persist for at least a decade, that being the minimum time required for a curriculum change to influence enough young people to make a difference,
- important enough to justify the expense and difficulty of making the changes,
- capable of being addressed by the existing teaching staff with their present competence, or else, by a retrained teaching staff, the expense and difficulty of retraining being justified,
- regarded as a serious problem by enough of the policy-making body and its constituency so that the curricular solution has sufficient legitimacy to stand a chance of being realized.

Quite often problems that are cited as reasons to undertake curriculum change fail to meet these criteria. Since the problems are all real and important to some part of the community served by schools, it would not be appropriate, even if it were possible, to reject these problems. However, some form of response other than a curriculum change is called for in such cases. For example, a short-term problem such as an explosion of racial violence might be met by special assemblies and other temporary, extracurricular or cocurricular activities. Adjustments to changes in the ethnic composition of the student body might best be handled through in-service education of teachers and through the work of parent groups and the board of education.

The safest way to judge the appropriateness of a curricular response to a problem is to ask whether precedents exist, either locally or elsewhere in the nation or the world, for successful curricular responses to similar problems. If not, the risks of failure will be high, and these high risks must be weighed against the risks and costs of some other form of response and against doing nothing at all. This is also a timid strategy. Even when no precedent can be found, a curricular response might still be appropriate if the problem is new and therefore literally unprecedented or if there is reason to believe that a solution can be found and implemented now that was not available to be tried before. For example, perhaps the availability of videotaped teacher in-service educational materials makes it economically possible to upgrade teachers' knowledge in ways that were not possible before. Or community attitudes may have been changed by recent events. A clear and penetrating analysis of the problem and exactly how a curriculum change might solve it is an essential starting point before adding an item to a serious curriculum policy agenda.

STRATEGIES FOR DEVELOPING POLICIES

Unified and Conflicted Contexts

It is helpful to think of two contexts in which policies may be developed: unified and conflicted. In a unified context like-minded individuals strive to develop policies that they prefer and that they hope to persuade the schools to adopt. In a conflicted context individuals with opposing views strive to develop a mutually acceptable policy. In unified contexts, policy development is more like problem-solving because the criteria for a good solution are agreed on. In conflicted contexts policy development is more like negotiation. In conflicted contexts discussion centers on resolving differences among partisan groups rather than on how to attain accepted policy goals. Policies that emerge from conflicted contexts are often strange creatures of compromise whose final implemented form and results no one may be able to predict. Those involved in developing policy in unified contexts usually believe they can predict the results of their policies, but they are often wrong in that belief.

Developing policy in unified contexts involves:

- choosing appropriate policy targets,
- selecting appropriate policy instruments,
- building policies that are feasible,
- anticipating and making provision for likely causes of failure in implementation,
- providing for flexibility in adapting the policy to varied local conditions (without sacrificing its intent).

Developing policy in conflicted contexts also requires:

- determining the policy goals and priorities of the contending parties on this issue,
- establishing trade-offs the contending parties are willing to make among their various desires,
- changing features of an existing policy so that it will be possible to negotiate agreement,
- designing altogether new policies on which agreement can be negotiated.

Policy Targets and Policy Instruments

Choosing appropriate policy targets is more difficult than it seems. The same problem may be attacked by policies directed at quite different targets. For example, policies to improve writing skill might increase inputs by allocating more time to writing instruction, by increasing the pay of writing teachers, by providing more and better instructional materials, or by exhorting teachers and students to give it more attention. Alternatively, the same policy goal might be pursued by choosing processes as targets: by establishing a writing contest or competition and offering prizes, by instituting a statewide writing examination, by individualizing the teaching of writing through writing clinics to be established in all schools, or by establishing an interdepartmental faculty committee charged with improving writing across the school curriculum. Still other policies might seek to improve writing by specifying outputs such as increases in the frequency with which students write in class and have their writing criticized, the amount of improvement in standardized test scores desired by a certain date, the level of writing skill to be exhibited in writing samples.

Policy-makers may also choose among a variety of policy instruments for pursuing their curriculum policy targets (see Box 12-1).

STRATEGIES FOR UNDERSTANDING THE PROBLEM

Deciding on the best mix of policy targets and instruments for a given situation requires the policy-maker to understand the problem as profoundly and completely as possible. (See Box 12-2 for a list of curriculum policy instruments.) At a minimum, designing an effective policy for a given policy problem requires an analysis of the problem—in other words, an account that describes the problem and its symptoms, explains why the various symptoms should be regarded as part of one and the same problem, and explains the fundamental causes of the problem. To continue the example of writing, suppose our analysis of the problem indicated that the root cause of poor writing among students was simply lack of practice in writing and in revising after criticism. To eliminate this problem requires that more

BOX 12-1   Possible Curriculum Policy Targets

Inputs

Resources
     time (of students, teachers)
     talent (of students, teachers, administrators)
     things (books, equipment, facilities)
     services (technical assistance, training, consultations)
     information (how-to, where-to-find)
     funds (for curriculum materials, facilities)
Legitimacy
     authorizations (for new programs)
     charters (for organizations, institutions)
     credentials (for personnel)
     awarding of honors, diplomas

Processes

Institutional reforms
     new programs
     forms of curricular organization (subjects, tracks)
Procedures for doing curriculum work
Meta-Processes
     policy-formation processes
     policy-implementation processes
     policy-evaluation processes

Outputs

Provision of learning opportunities
     coverage
     content presented
     years of education offered, completed
Levels of achievement attained
     performance on standardized achievement tests
     number of dropouts, graduates
Performance of graduates after leaving the program
     completion of subsequent levels of education
     subsequent field of employment
     honors (representation in *Who's Who*)
Education-related indicators of community well-being
     literacy rate, mental health, hospitalization rates, government participation rates, family life, divorce rates, economics, manpower shortages, surpluses, social equity, social mobility rates
Judgments
     ratings by students, graduates, public, experts evaluations of pundits, accreditation and program review

time be spent on writing and criticism of writing in class and more time spent in homework sessions. Since the limited classroom time is already fully occupied, ways must be found to gain more time for writing. Criticizing the writing takes more teacher time; ways must also be found to secure this extra time. We assume that teachers are able to offer sound criticism and that students have the ability and will to profit from it. This analysis of the problem suggests policies that focus on allocation of time on the input side, on processes that will support and encourage criticism, and on amount and quality of actual writing as outputs. A different analysis of the problem would probably suggest other policy targets.

BOX 12-2   Curriculum Policy Instruments

Input-Focused

Generate and allocate inputs
    unconditionally
    conditionally
Establish frames for inputs
Establish standards for inputs
    student entrance requirements
    (stated standards, exams, requirements,)
    accreditation and program review
    program definition
Develop curriculum materials

Process-Focused

Create programs
    comprehensive improvement programs
    dissemination and assistance programs
    testing programs
    parent involvement or information dissemination programs
    structural organization
Promulgate rules for process, mechanism
Exhort
    articulate ideology
    enunciate goals, aims, philosophy
Publish documents
    syllabi, courses of study

Output-Focused

Establish standards for outputs
Evaluate performance
    testing and assessment of student achievement
Mandate locally designed evaluations

How do we develop and validate an analysis of the problem? In actual practice all too often we simply accept the analysis supplied with some innovation offered as a solution to the problem. Typically policy-makers follow their hunches, which are usually strongly influenced by the prevailing climate of opinion, the set of ideas in good currency. Seldom do policy-makers undertake an analysis of the problem themselves, nor do they commonly even examine alternative analyses critically. Ordinary deliberation suffices for this in many cases, but sometimes more formal strategies can be helpful. Some of the more promising ones are described below.

Theory-Mapping Simply isolating the analysis of the problem underlying a proposed policy and making it explicit can help policy-makers to gain a perspective from which to question and be constructively critical. When the case for a particular policy has been made in print, it is often possible to make the underlying theory explicit by such simple steps as: 1) underlining and numbering the important steps in the argument; 2) supplying missing steps in the argument in brackets; 3) circling important connectives, such as *and, or,* therefore, since, because, and the like, supplying missing connectives and spelling out the relationships between all the key terms; 4) arranging the statements in a parallel list in numbered order with the logical connectives highlighted in the margins; and 5) making a diagram with arrows connecting the statements about causes to the statements about effects. Dunn (1981) refers to this type of analysis as *theory-mapping*. Often theory-mapping or another form of careful analysis of the problem will reveal unstated assumptions not at all apparent; invariably it clarifies the steps in the argument and facilitates a critical assessment of the weak points in the argument as a whole.

Strategic Assumption-Making Strategic assumption-making (SAM) (Mitroff and Emshoff, 1979) is a technique for bringing hidden assumptions to light during policy deliberation. SAM begins with the identification of the assumptions underlying the rough ideas about the problem and possible ways of attempting to solve it that policy-makers hold initially. This is done in much the same way as theory-mapping. In the second stage of SAM, called the dialectic phase, each assumption is **negated** and new counter-policies built on assumptions contrary to the initial ones. This is done for each assumption, even those that seem obviously true. In each case the most plausible counter-assumptions are used to devise counter-policies. If the same policy seems called for regardless of whether the original assumption or the counter-assumption is made, then the assumption is not critical to the policy and may be safely ignored. If the best counter-assumption that can be found is not plausible to any policy-makers, the original assumption is retained. Plausible counter-assumptions go into an assumption pool. In the third phase of SAM, called the integration phase, the policy-makers negotiate the most acceptable set of assumptions, or perhaps two or three of the most acceptable sets. This is done by ordinary deliberation. The result of this integration phase is a new analysis of the problem. The fourth and final phase is the creation of a composite policy. Here the new analysis of the problem is used to develop new policies. The

SAM technique can be used to critically analyze well-developed policies, to modify a policy when circumstances change, or to secure agreement among contending groups of policy-makers, as well as to develop policies from vague initial ideas. Curriculum specialists could conduct such analyses as staff to a policy-making body.

Case Studies Detailed, documented narratives of individual occurrences of a problem can be used to check the adequacy of an analysis proposed for the problem and may also suggest more adequate analyses. Profiles of individual students complete with work samples, grades, teacher comments, and test scores, as well as appropriate background information about the student's performance in other subjects and earlier grades, personality, family background, and so on, can give a tangible reality to what may otherwise be perceived as an abstract exercise. Such details enable policy-makers to apply their knowledge, skill, and judgment more surely than if they were dealing with the same problem characterized only in abstract, general terms.

Similarly detailed histories of previous attempts to overcome the problem can be extremely informative in shaping an effective policy. Studying the strategies of other states (or local districts) that have attempted to upgrade writing skills before has obvious value. Normally this information is only available in professional publications. Commissioning a literature search would often be worthwhile. Interviews with local officials, administrators, and teachers who participated in earlier local efforts may be worthwhile, too.

Statistics Data that are already routinely collected can often be used to document the prevalence and extent of a problem. Achievement test scores have obvious application here. Other potentially useful data include attendance figures, incidence of violence or vandalism, records of prizes and honors, college-applications, college-acceptances, degree-completions, and results of surveys of parents, students, and graduates.

The Limited Role of Evidence in Settling Policy Disputes

When the assumptions underlying the problem are exposed to view, it is likely that some of them will be questioned. Disputes about the adequacy of these assumptions can seldom be settled merely by argument. Sometimes they rest on deep differences of outlook and values, in which case they can hardly be settled at all insofar as the requirements of policy-making are concerned. Better to let the contending parties negotiate a mutually acceptable policy directly or create alternative policies and give them their choice. But when minds are changeable, evidence is helpful.

The most direct and compelling evidence is the experience of others who have encountered the same or a very similar problem and have attempted to solve it using policies based on the assumptions in question. If the analysis of the problem on which a policy is based is incorrect or incomplete in some important way, the policies based on it are likely to have gone awry in some readily perceptible way. If the policies worked, the analysis of the problem on which they have been based are probably safe to use again. If the policies did not work and if other explanations for the failure cannot be found (such as that the policies were never fully implemented), then the theory is called into question.

In the case of our example of writing, we would like to know about school districts or states that have made concerted efforts to increase writing skills. Among these, we need to distinguish those that have succeeded in allocating more time to writing instruction and in providing more frequent criticism of students' writing. We should certainly search the historical record for useful precedents. If we are lucky, we might find a review of research on the teaching of writing that would tell us the results of systematic studies that may have been done on the problem. If not, we might be wise to commission such a review. We can put out a call for districts or state departments who have recently undertaken to improve writing instruction and ask for the information we need. Here again, we might want to commission a study or to apply for state or federal funds to conduct such a study.

Examining the evidence for competing analyses of the problem is not without its costs and risks. Policy can seldom wait for enough evidence to satisfy scholars; scholarly debates tend toward the never-ending. Resources spent examining analyses of the problem are not available to solve the problem. The coalition-building necessary to attain support for any policy addressing the problem may be hindered by debates about the underlying theory. There will come a time when it will be wiser to do something now than to study the problem further. But frequently a small investment in clarifying our interpretation of the problem and the theory behind the major policy options will more than repay itself in improved ability to design an effective policy.

Discovering Promising Policy Proposals

When a thorough analysis of the problem does not yield enough promising potential policies, it should at least discover enough criteria that a satisfactory solution must meet to narrow the range of policies to be explored considerably. Building concrete proposals that fit the problem's criteria is work that can require a variety of forms of judgment, knowledge, and skill. Often the most productive strategy is simply to explain the problem and the criteria any solution must meet to the staff and the public at large and to invite proposals. Experts can be consulted, too. Formal techniques are not appropriate to such a task, but policy-makers can find inspiration and guidance from two quite different quarters: precedent and theory.

Adapting policies already tried at other times and places and perhaps for other purposes is a common-sensical approach with much to recommend it. At its best it takes advantage of what has been learned from experience. It can help us avoid repeating mistakes and reinventing the wheel. The logic of applying precedents is essentially reasoning by analogy. When the analogical basis is unsound, the application of seeming precedents can be misleading. For instance, one often hears the universally successful early learning of a first language proposed as a precedent for school programs that are informal, relatively unstructured, and improvised on the spur of the moment. But in the early language learning situation the ratio of adults to children is nearly 1:1, not 1:30; the amount of incidental contact with the content to be learned typically amounts to 14 hours per day, not 6; the usefulness of what is learned is immediately obvious to the young child, whereas formal education is inherently a longer-term process of preparation; and there is even reason to believe that young children are genetically programmed to be particularly adept at language learning in their early years. With so many deviations from parallelism, the analogy is dubious and its use as a precedent for curriculum planning is questionable.

On the other hand, precedents with a sound analogical basis can provide a kernel from which new policies well adapted to the current situation can be adapted. Much of our present curriculum is grown from such adaptations. For example, the use of calisthenics in physical education was adapted from nineteenth-century Swedish school experiments. Biology books feature the dissection of a frog because American textbooks copied a best-selling Victorian English biology textbook that chose the frog because it was readily available in the wild throughout the British Isles. Other countries have adapted American innovations, too. The new math and science programs of the 1960s were translated and adapted by many countries and these adaptations are now more widely used in some countries than the American descendants of the originals. The American creation of the school subjects biology (out of botany, physiology, and zoology), English (out of rhetoric, grammar, spelling, and literature), and social studies (out of history, geography, civics, and others) have been widely followed throughout the world.

Policies can also be derived from theory. The logic of this is quite distinct from the mathematical derivation of a result from a series of axioms. It is a logic of generate and test. The theory suggests courses of action in ways that are fundamentally psychological. Once a course of action has been discovered, relevant theory can be applied in a rigorous deductive fashion to determine the consequences one would expect from the policy. Behavioral psychology has been applied systematically to early reading instruction in direct instruction materials, for example. Several attempts have been made to base a curriculum for developing thinking and problem-solving based on Piaget's psychology (Furth 1974). On the larger scale of most policy issues, however, rigorous application of theory is rare. Head Start as an intervention to equalize educational attainments of disadvantaged youngsters is loosely based on theories of Benjamin Bloom, which purport to show that some large fraction of cognitive growth is completed before the age when children typically enter school.

The theoretical basis for such major curriculum policies as requiring four years of study of English, two years of science, three of mathematics, American history, biology and the like in high schools is sadly almost nonexistent. Whenever the rationales offered for major curriculum policies have been tested, they have failed. For example, the drill and practice programs based on the faculty theory of psychology failed to produce the improvements in basic abilities for which they were designed. The claims made for generalized cognitive benefits from learning a second language continue to be elusive. The cognitive benefits claimed from learning to program computers are proving difficult to verify. To base major curriculum policy decisions on unstated—let alone unverified—theories is an admission of intellectual defeat.

ASSESSING THE MERITS OF POLICY PROPOSALS

Feasibility Analysis: Backward Mapping

All too often the policies we develop are unrealistic and therefore not feasible. The goals we seek may not be attainable at all or only attainable by procedures that are unacceptable for political, economic, or other reasons. Even if the theory behind the problem is sound and the policy targets and instruments are appropriate, the policy may still be incapable of being carried out in the situation we have in mind or the practical difficulties of implementation may be greater than the benefits. We need techniques for anticipating possible failures when attempts are made to implement the policy, so that we can build into the policy countermeasures to prevent them, minimize the damage, or, if costly failure appears likely despite our best efforts, abandon the policy.

The technique of **backward mapping** (Elmore 1982) can be used to help anticipate sources of potential policy failure. Backward mapping consists essentially of envisioning the practices you want to occur in schools and classrooms and then working backwards to identify the conditions necessary to achieve and sustain those practices. With each element found to be crucial to the change, backward mapping then asks: Who controls or influences this element? What will it take to get them to put their efforts behind the change? Any point in the analysis at which a crucial contribution might be missing or at which opponents of the policy might disrupt delivery is a potential source of failure in implementing the policy. Frequently, backward-mapping shows that curriculum policy stands or falls with the ability and support of two key actors, the classroom teacher and the school principal. Policy-makers must make delicate judgments about how well received various possible features of the policy will be to many thousands of teachers and principals. Appropriately designed surveys of teachers and principals should be able to reduce the uncertainty of such judgments and thus contribute to better estimates of the likelihood of success of curriculum policies. But even when teachers and principals are overwhelmingly enthusiastic, they may be unable to act for lack of some resource or other enabling condition. Backward-mapping should reveal the need for this crucial element and either informal or formal techniques can then be used to improve policy-makers' judgments about likelihood of failing to supply critical resources and it can then lead to the design of more effective policies. For example, many curriculum reforms have failed in part because teachers lacked the knowledge or skill to put them into practice in their classrooms. Backward-mapping should reveal the needed knowledge and skill and a few informal practical experiments attempting to teach it to representative teachers should give policy-makers an idea of how difficult and expensive the teacher training effort would need to be. In its simplest form, backward-mapping is a straightforward extension of commonsense that all policy-making bodies can and should employ regularly. It can be extended, elaborated, and made more systematic when more certainty is needed.

Scenario Writing

Another extension of commonsense techniques that can be valuable in identifying possible sources of failure and ways to overcome them, is scenario writing. In its simplest form, scenario writing consists simply of imagining what could happen when the policy under consideration is adopted. First, one must identify those who are affected by the policy, how they may perceive its impact on them, and the actions open to them in responding to the policy as they perceive it. Then, one plays out the various scenarios that arise when the actors respond in the ways open to them. Since the number of actors and the number of possible responses open to each are both large in most curriculum policies, the number of possible scenarios is huge. The value of the exercise hinges on walking a fine line between playing out only those few obvious scenarios with which everyone is already familiar and playing out too many improbable ones. It is usually helpful to ask a few individuals who know a group of actors well to offer their judgment as to "What would the A's do if . . . (a bare-bones description of only the part of the policy affecting the A's)?" A series of scenarios based on the responses considered most likely by knowledgeable persons can reveal many possible pitfalls for the policy.

In general, scenario writing about curriculum policies will reveal many potential sources of failure in carrying out the policy. The effect of the exercise, if any, will likely be to dash cold water on the optimism of policy-makers. Instead of appearing like the perfect answer to a prayer, the policy under consideration is more likely to present a mixed picture of advantages and disadvantages. It is helpful, therefore, to also include scenarios based on continuation of present policy and practice for comparison. If the potential consequences of adopting the new policy under consideration do not look much better than the consequences of continuing the present ones, then it deserves the cold water. It is probably unwise to dwell too much on the difficulties in store for the policy. It should be sufficient if the worst preventable problems can be identified and avoided. The purpose of the exercise is to develop more realistic and feasible policies, not to depress policy-makers, whose enthusiasm and optimism are scarce and important resources. Hirshman (1967) has offered an ingenious justification for a certain amount of optimistic self-deception among policy-makers.

> The only way in which we can bring our creative resources fully into play is by misjudging the nature of the task, by presenting it to ourselves as more routine, simple, undemanding of genuine creativity than it will turn out to be. Or, put differently: since we necessarily underestimate our creativity, it is desirable that we underestimate to a roughly similar extent the difficulties of the tasks we face. (Hirshman 1967, 9)

STRATEGIES FOR IMPLEMENTING POLICIES

Implementation problems are endemic to curriculum policy-making in the United States. Some of these problems should not be blamed on those responsible for implementation, however. Faults that occur earlier in the policy process—like poorly framed or unrealistic policies—may not become apparent until attempts are made to implement the policies. A bad policy may only be recognized as such when it proves to be impossible to implement! But successful implementation is difficult under the best of circumstances. As one of the foremost students of policy implementation expressed it:

> It is hard enough to design public policies and programs that look good on paper. It is harder still to formulate them in words and slogans that resonate pleasingly in the ears of political leaders and the constituencies to which they are responsive. And it is excruciatingly hard to implement them in a way that pleases anyone at all, including the supposed beneficiaries. . . . (Bardach 1977, 3)

Successful implementation requires that the following tasks be somehow accomplished:

- communicating the policy accurately and completely to all those who must cooperate in its execution in ways that help them to appreciate the need for the change,
- securing and maintaining commitments from all involved to do their part in implementing the policy,
- making long-term plans and strategies for implementation,
- encouraging constructive adaptation while realizing the intent of the policy,
- monitoring implementation activities and goal attainment,
- building the policy into the standard operating procedures of the institutions involved.

Implementation is further complicated because different agencies must manage it: the national Education Department implements acts of Congress; state departments of education and state superintendents implement policies of state legislatures and state boards, as well as federal policies binding on them; local district superintendents and central office staffs implement policies of the local school board, which also follows state and federal policies. Policy-makers, therefore, are not as much in control of implementation as of other phases of the policy process.

It might seem that communicating the policy accurately and completely to all those who must cooperate in its execution is a simple matter of good English. In fact, good policies will be straightforward and capable of being clearly described in simple English. If they are not clearly expressed, misunderstandings are sure to surface and interfere with the realization of policy-makers' intentions. The rationale for the policy must be made plain. Implementors must explain how people will benefit. Questions, charges and counter-arguments likely to be raised by skeptics and opponents should be presented and the policy defended against them in the strongest possible terms. To be both clear and persuasive can pose a serious rhetorical challenge. Airy abstractions into which everybody can read their own specific meanings can be a strong temptation, in conflicted contexts, especially. Ambiguity can be a powerful tool in rallying support for the policy, but it leaves holes in the fabric of the innovation through which resources meant for one purpose can slip to others. Judging the best trade-off between clarity and ambiguity in a particular situation is one of the arts of effective implementation.

Finding ways to get the message across to all those who must cooperate in implementation is a challenge. Written documents cannot carry the major burden of communicating the policy. Principals see hundreds of pieces of paper each day. The paper describing your policy and making the case for it will often go straight from the in-basket to the file cabinet. Few teachers have time to read anything having to do with their work—memos, journal articles, or position papers, for example. John Goodlad and his associates summarized their observations of the role of curricular documents in hundreds of schools across the country this way: "The documents produced at both [federal and state] levels do not command attention" (Goodlad 1970, 49).

The important messages in schools are communicated orally and face-to-face. Speeches will have to be made, panel discussions held, public question and answer sessions, and other personal appearances by those who sponsor and advocate the policy. The greater the authority and esteem of the speakers, the more the message will impress. The more moving the rhetoric, the more action it is likely to get from the audience.

It is impractical for policy-makers to deliver the message in person to every school. Advocates and sponsors must somehow be recruited from among those already in or near each school. A number of studies have indicated that the local school superintendent is usually the key figure in bringing an innovation to the local school system (House 1974; Fullan 1982). Professional meetings and informal contacts with other education professionals are the chief means by which the innovation comes to the superintendent's attention. Principals play the key role in determining what innovations receive most attention in their school. They, too, respond mainly to professional communication networks. An important early task of implementation, then, is to inject messages favorable to the innovation into the professional communication networks frequented by local school leaders.

When the message is strange or distasteful, it may be necessary to do things to increase the likelihood that leaders will listen and take it seriously. All kinds of histrionics can be and are used for this purpose, but the most basic and least risky technique is to show that the message, as strange or distasteful as it may be, is or is going to be important to the well-being of their schools.

Securing commitments from all involved to do their part in implementing the policy is a delicate but fundamentally important part of implementation. Persuasive communication is but a beginning. Initially, a few leaders given designated responsibility for implementation will bear the main burden of the work, together with their staffs, and, much more numerous, the volunteers they are able to recruit. Most implementation effort eventually comes from volunteers. Varied roles must be established that will attract able people. Occasions must be found at which those who have signed on can publicly demonstrate their commitment, both so that others will be moved to follow suit and because public declarations will strengthen their own commitment. Efforts should be made to recruit able and influential figures first for key roles; it will then be easier to attract others. Recruitment will always be easiest at the beginning, so it is important to develop ways to involve potential recruits early in satisfying and nonthreatening ways. One of the most powerful ways to change attitudes about people is to have people work together on a common task. Arranging for the uncommitted to work together with the committed can be a powerful recruitment device. Critics should probably be given an opportunity to express their views early and should be invited to help fix the policy, or at least to help find the first signs of the problem they predict the policy will bring. Some, perhaps most, will not volunteer. Keep the work moving forward with those who do, and keep the door open to others. [Try to avoid letting in-groups form.] If possible, find other related constructive projects for those who cannot be recruited to help with this one, but keep the groups in contact.

Arranging for person-to-person contact is always the heart of the process. Contacts must be made with all the organizations that have important roles to play and forms of interorganizational cooperation worked out. In curriculum policy this can mean dealing with organizations as diverse as the teacher education departments of universities, the state department of education, private textbook publishers, and parent and business groups. Networks and coalitions of representatives of various organizations perform a vital nurturing function for the innovation all along the way. It is important to establish such networks early and to keep them playing a vital role.

It is important to be alert to differences in the real interests and perceived interests of different groups involved in and affected by the policy. In general, those groups who stand to gain or lose the most from the policy will be its strongest supporters and opponents. Try to draw as much support as possible from benefiting groups. Try to avoid polarizing groups with differing interests. Look for ways to calm fears and reassure those less favored by the present policy that they are not forgotten, that their turn will come.

As the implementation effort develops, it is important to maintain and, if possible, strengthen the constituency for the policy. Work for early successes and arrange for good publicity. Don't tackle the hardest subtask first; save it until you have a few successes on record. The best ways to retain support of the committed are to make progress toward the goals they share and to reward individuals who contribute to this progress with recognition, responsibility, career advancement, and other incentives to continue and redouble their efforts. Organize supporters to give them a sense of group identity. The surest way to lose support is to fail to deliver promised resources and assistance. Commit resources in stages; as one task is accomplished, be sure to deliver the resources for the next. Don't hesitate to make deals with other organizations to get and retain the resources needed. Do use your own personal influence and charisma, or the influence and charisma of those you recruit. Remember that your innovation is competing with hundreds of others for the attention and loyalty of thousands of persons crucial to your project's success. To succeed you will have to attract them and hold their allegiance long enough to see your innovation to the point where it can be self-sustaining.

Severe constraints of time and resources dictate that implementation be carefully, yet flexibly, planned. Roughly speaking, implementation of a major curriculum policy succeeds or fails in a three to five year window of opportunity when enthusiasm for the reform still runs high, when the policy has not yet been eclipsed in the spotlight of public attention by other problems, and when the resources can still be obtained to implement the policy. If, as is often the case, the changes simply cannot be made in this brief a time span, then institutional mechanisms must be established in that period that permit the work of implementation to continue on a routine basis, without the need for continued attention from policy-makers and the public. Gains that are not quickly achieved and secured are easily lost to inertia, staff turnover, budget tightening, and the thousands of vicissitudes that any curriculum policy faces.

Bardach (1977) recommends that policy-makers continue their involvement with policy through to the implementation phase so that they can still influence the adaptations that inevitably take place. He urges policy-makers who particularly want to help see a policy realized to engage in fixing the policy once it has been enacted. Fixing is done by a political coalition of advocates with diverse and complementary resources. In the case of curriculum policies an implementation planning group might be established consisting of such individuals as representatives of the primary policy-making body (for example, a state legislator instrumental in passing the authorizing bill) and the primary implementing organization (a current or former official of the state department of education), along with representatives of the major professional groups (superintendent, principal, teacher, subject matter specialist), representatives of the chief lay groups supporting the policy, and the chief evaluator. All would be supporters of the policy, but since the policy has now been adopted, they would not necessarily make up a partisan group. While they would have no formal authority as a body, they would be able to inform and influence those they represented and, most important, one another. Their informal contacts might be more important than their formal meetings. When problems arise or progress bogs down, somewhere among this group a solution should be found, if one exists. With a small budget, perhaps supplied by a foundation that supports the policy, they could carry out such vital tasks as:

- develop alternative model plans for implementation under varied circumstances,
- anticipate potential problems and suggest how those involved might deal with them,
- serve as a clearinghouse to facilitate exchange of information among implementors and between implementors and other groups, such as researchers,
- assist in studying and finding solutions to unanticipated problems,
- marshall the power and resources of supporters when needed to overcome political obstacles,
- keep the public and various interested groups informed.

Such a group would work best as advisers to the responsible agencies, or even as watchdogs, rather than being charged with official responsibility for implementation. They could thus preserve their independence and pursue their advocacy role singlemindedly. The chief virtue of such a group is that they make it possible for the implemented policy to respond to "the unexpected nexus of causality that actually evolves during implementation" (Pressman and Wildavsky 1973, 217). If, as Pressman and Wildavsky claim, a little anticipation and a lot of resilience go a long way in implementation, then such a group can help to give a policy the capacity to bounce back from attacks and reversals.

Of course, it is also possible, even likely, that opposition groups that failed to block adoption of the policy will work to block implementation and will also form a similar coalition of opponents. Such opposition groups would also be entitled to try to influence the implementing agency.

Any group interested in advancing the prospects for faithful and competent implementation of policy would be well advised to carry out a careful analysis, using backward-mapping and scenario writing, of the likely impact of the implemented policy on schools and classrooms. In this way they can anticipate needs for resources, information, training, or the like, and make plans to meet them. Where this is impossible, as will often happen, the policy will have to be adapted to the actual conditions. Usually adaptation can be done in several ways, some of which are more faithful to the original policy's intent than others. Advance planning makes it possible to adopt measures to encourage the more constructive adaptations.

In staging the implementation, it is important to concentrate attention early on those schools and districts that are influential, visible, and have a tradition of being first with innovations. Others look on them as models and try to profit from their experience. Set realistic, short-term goals (ones that can be achieved in a year or less) and work for tangible, early success. Seize the initiative. Get things moving. Keep things moving. To the extent possible, let the implementation effort itself come from small organizations with few levels of review, so that minimal energy is wasted on the organization itself. Whenever possible, let activities be driven by the demand for the service, not by fixed rules and regulations; arrange the organization so that those parts that provide what implementors need and want can grow rapidly at the expense of those that do not.

A policy is insecure as long as it requires special efforts by individuals and organizations not normally involved. Real success comes only when the changes called for in the policy are built into the standard operating procedures of the institutions involved. The policy, having been handed from advocacy groups to policy-makers to implementors, must in the end be delivered to the teachers and principals who must incorporate it into their routines if it is to remain a part of the ongoing curriculum of the schools. Temporary funding must be withdrawn and base budget funds redirected to support the change. Special personnel must be reassigned and their duties taken over by regular employees. Everything must go from special status to normal, from merely a project to a standard operating procedure. This ultimate step must be taken by teachers and principals, sometimes with a strong push from officials up the line or from students and parents. Policy-makers can do little further to influence the decisions and actions of so many. If they have failed to sell the front-line service providers on the change, all their earlier work will come to nothing insofar as lasting impact on the curriculum is concerned.

STRATEGIES FOR EVALUATING POLICIES

Evaluating a curriculum policy means evaluating the curricula realized under the policy. This is a huge subject in its own right. What follows here are brief comments that apply particularly to the use of data and conclusions from curriculum evaluations to evaluate policies.

Strictly speaking, the only curricular realities that have tangible effects on students that can be evaluated directly are the programs actually delivered in schools and classrooms. Policies are merely one of the forces shaping these programs. To trace the effects of policies on these programs and hence on students logically requires a form of experiment in which representative groups of students are exposed to different policies, all else remaining constant. This form of social experiment has been attempted on a limited scale only a few times. The Planned Variation Experiments carried out as part of the Follow Through Evaluation in the 1970s (House, et al. 1978) are the only large-scale recent example in curriculum. In this series of experiments twenty models of early childhood education programs were tested on nearly 80,000 children in schools around the country. The Eight-Year Study in the early 1940s was an important precursor. In neither of these studies was it practical to assign students randomly to the various experimental treatment. In the Eight-Year Study schools volunteered and designed their own programs, while comparison schools were selected to be as like the schools finally selected as possible. In the Follow Through experiments participating schools were selected from among those who had opted for one of the planned variations. Therefore it was not possible to rule out the possibility that students were different to begin with. True experiments await a political climate in which people are willing to subject their children to controlled experimentation as part of the curriculum policy process.

In a loose sense, though, all attempts to implement policy are experiments: policies are an intervention in the on-going operations of schools and by comparing how things were before and after the intervention we may be able to increase or decrease the plausibility of some hypotheses about what might or should have happened. Policy implementation becomes a form of hypothesis-testing. When a policy is implemented we begin to see relationships and connections we never expected and we learn about new causal links we never expected. Even when, as is usually the case, the experiments are not well controlled, they are nearly always better tests of the hypotheses than what we had before.

Policy evaluation is, then, a way of learning from attempts to make policy. Formal methods of policy evaluation supplement the ways we ordinarily use to learn from such experiences: ordinary observation and informal discussion, testimony of those involved and affected, journalistic investigations, analysis of routinely collected statistics, historical studies, and so on.

But policy evaluation is also a way of establishing the public estimation of not only the policy being evaluated, but also the theories and values that support them. It is therefore a potentially powerful weapon in the struggle to gain acceptance and support for those ideas and values. Therefore, our learning, difficult enough already, must take place in a conflicted context where every shred of doubt and item of contrary evidence is sure to be trumpeted as truth by somebody—and no one can prove them wrong. And so evaluations are likely to be as controversial as policies, often even more so in the academic community.

And yet, despite the difficulties, we do learn from evaluations. Seldom are long-standing debates resolved by evaluations. Often what we learn is something neglected or altogether unanticipated in the debates that led up to the policy. For example, evaluations of the post-*Sputnik* curriculum reforms showed that the reforms that required major changes in teachers' classroom behavior—inquiry teaching, in-class laboratory experiments, open-ended critical discussion—proved more difficult to implement than changes in content only. They also focused attention on implementation issues. The Coleman Report shifted public and professional attention from a focus on inequality of resources provided for education to inequality of outcomes and called attention to the strong influence of early education in the home on later academic achievement in school. The Follow Through Planned Variation studies brought site-to-site variation to the attention of policy-makers. The concept of mutual adaptation emerged from the RAND evaluation of local responses to federally sponsored innovations (Greenwood, Mann and McLaughlin 1975). The IEA studies called attention to the importance of time and opportunity to learn.

One clear lesson from the most recent generation of curriculum policy evaluations would seem to be to commission evaluations with the broadest possible scope. Evaluations that merely measured attainment of stated policy goals would have missed some of the most important lessons we have learned from the evaluations of the 1960s and 1970s. On the whole, most major commissioned evaluations of particular curriculum policies seem to have been of substantial help in the effort to learn more about our education system and how we can and cannot improve it.

Cost/Benefit Analysis

Quantitatively oriented policy analysts are inclined to use the results of curriculum evaluations in some ways that can be misleading, however. Cost/benefit calculations based on curriculum evaluation results and used to compare the overall value of educational programs almost always give misleading conclusions. Costs are easily measured in completely comparable terms; educational outcomes are not. In a cost/benefit comparison, therefore, the cost figures usually weigh much more heavily than the benefit figures. They are, in fact, largely cost comparisons. The benefit comparisons are usually derived from scores on an hour-long multiple choice, standardized test designed to be insensitive to differences between educational programs. Scores on these tests are very crude and indifferent measures of the outcomes of the programs being compared, so that measured differences between programs are certain to be small. Therefore, more costly programs will nearly always seem less cost-effective when such measures are used. Furthermore, different curricula often have quite different goals. For example, the new math introduced new content (sets, inequalities, and so on) and new purposes (understanding proofs, careful use of formal terminology) and downplayed some traditional goals (long division, fluency at numerical calculation). How could the benefits of the new and the old math be computed numerically on a common scale? Still another problem with cost/benefit studies is that they seldom include estimates of the variability of their results. A study may tell us that one curriculum costs $110 per unit of achievement while another costs $150 per unit. If the cost/benefit ratios at schools using the first curriculum range from $50 to $180 and if the range in the schools using the second curriculum is from $80 to $210, there will probably be many schools in which the second curriculum would have a lower cost/benefit ratio, even though on the average its ratio was higher.

Carefully designed cost/benefit calculations can be extremely informative. For example, Henry Levin (1986) compared the cost/benefit ratios of three types of educational innovations all designed to improve mathematics and language skills in the elementary grades: peer tutoring, computer-assisted instruction, and reduced class size. He discovered that all produced benefits, as measured on standardized test scores, over conventional instruction, with peer tutoring being most cost-effective and reduced class size least cost-effective. He went on to analyze the cost-components of each program and discovered that hardware and software costs were only a small fraction of the total costs of the computer-assisted instruction program. Most of the costs were for personnel, training, and facilities. Comparisons of programs with similar goals done carefully in a way that helps us understand the origins of costs and benefits can be extremely instructive. Superficial calculations that compare curricula with different aims using scores on an insensitive test lend a false aura of science to what is in reality a simple calculation of cost. Great care needs to be exercised in basing policy decisions on such simple comparisons.

Limitations of Data from Standardized Tests

The Achilles' heel of all policy evaluation is the standardized achievement test. These tests are a remarkable technical invention. By sampling only a few minutes of a students' performance they can place that student's mastery of the subject relative to other students in a nationally representative norming sample accurately and reliably, even though the students studied from different books, with different teachers, for different amounts of time, and so on. There is no other way to get such good information about students' learning so quickly and therefore so cheaply. But in order to gain this accuracy and reliability with such a brief sample of students' behavior, the tests sacrifice something. Namely, they give up all possibility of measuring anything else about the students' achievement except how it stands in comparison to the norming group. Would you like to know whether Maria learned to add two digit numbers? The tests can't tell you. Whether Johnny can write a grammatically correct English sentence? The tests can't tell you. Whether Kim's improvement in math this year was greater than his improvement last year? The tests can only tell you how his improvement compared to that of the national norming sample.

Test items are carefully selected to represent a range of difficulty. Items that nearly every student answers correctly are eliminated because they are of little help in comparing students with one another—even though the item may be an important part of the curriculum and we may be very much interested in knowing whether students learn it. The tests are not designed to tell us what a given student knows and does not know, but rather how the student compares with peers.

When the results of such tests are used to compare students' performance after completing one curriculum with other students' performance after completing a different curriculum, the comparison is, at best, crude and, at worst, misleading. What is needed for a fair and accurate comparison is a test that samples from three types of items: those taught in the first curriculum but not the second; those taught in the second but not the first; and those taught in both (perhaps also those taught in neither, if one suspects some difference in transfer to new material). Here again, we are up against the problem of how to value the different outcomes against one another. Evaluations that use standardized achievement tests blithely ignore these niceties by reporting a single score for each pupil, even when the score is based on a hodge-podge of items of varying relevance to the curricula being compared.

The simple fact is that comparing the learning outcomes of two competing policies is a very challenging technical feat that would require millions of dollars to do properly. Unwilling to pay this cost, yet still desiring objective results, policy-makers make do with comparisons based on readily available tests. The result is that no innovative program looks very much better than any other or than what is being done now. Even if there were startling differences in the learning of the material taught in the two curricula, the differences would only show up on the test if it happened to faithfully measure most of the outcomes of both curricula, in which case neither would be very innovative in purpose or content. Worse yet, the programs that show up best in such a comparison are those whose content is most like the test—in other words, an assortment of isolated paper and pencil skills. If a good curriculum is one that leads to good standardized test scores, then a good curriculum will consist largely of testlike activities, for anything else diverts effort to learning not tested.

The persistent reliance of educational policy-makers on data based on such tests is the single strongest argument against official policy-making and in favor of local control of all curriculum decisions.

Routine Collection of Baseline Data

To judge the effect of introducing a policy, we need to know what results have been obtained from existing programs in recent years. If results change when a new policy is introduced, we have presumptive evidence for an effect of the policy, though other events could also have been responsible, so the interpretation is not conclusive. This means that it is highly desirable from the standpoint of getting good evaluations of policies to have a good representative sample of students' achievement collected routinely for later comparison. The National Assessment of Educational Progress (NAEP) is a program that attempts to collect baseline data for the nation as a whole and also for various regions and segments of the population. But since policies are normally implemented in states, counties, or districts, and since NAEP data are by design not analyzed according to these political units, they cannot be used for policy evaluation, except for national reforms. Good baseline data that permits year-to-year and site-to-site comparisons is absolutely essential to good policy evaluation and hence, in the long-run, to good evaluation. It will be expensive, but anything else is shooting in the dark.

STRATEGIES FOR MAINTAINING A POLICY-SHAPING COMMUNITY

The policy-shaping community (PSC) is the group of individuals and organizations whose actions and interactions, taken altogether, determine the policy actually put in practice. Members of the PSC may be members of a community in the original sense of the word: acquainted, associated, living and working together. However, in today's world most curricular PSCs include important members who are distant, faceless organizations known only through their actions or their products. The PSC for one issue may be substantially different from the PSC for another. For example, the PSC for a high school vocational program may consist of different individuals and organizations than the PSC for an elementary reading program. On the other hand, most curricular PSCs have similar composition, including parents, students, teachers, school officials, and appropriate branches of the various official and unofficial organizations at state, federal, and local levels described earlier.

The tasks involved in maintaining a policy-shaping community include:

- securing participation from those affected (either direct or representative),
- assisting the PSC to carry out its policy-shaping function effectively (securing working agreements on a policy agenda and on individual policies and implementing and evaluating them),
- maintaining a good climate and good working relationships among members of the PSC.

By definition, wherever we find effective policy, we will find a PSC of some sort.

When adequate institutional mechanisms for policy are already in place, the problem becomes one of making them work well in this particular case. When they are not, it is also necessary to establish the mechanisms. When the mechanisms in place are not adequate, it is necessary to reform or replace them. Each problem presents its own challenges, but the first-mentioned poses minimal threat to the functioning of the PSC.

Making policy machinery that has formerly functioned well do so again in the present case is largely a matter of mobilizing effort and directing it to the current problem. This entails a knowledge of the machinery—who does what, when, where, why, and how—and an ability to influence it. The formal policy machinery runs on meetings and documents. To influence it one must attend the right meetings and write or influence the writing of the right documents. Policy may also be shaped informally by influencing the right people. Obviously, one must know or be able to learn who are the right people, which are the right meetings, and which are the right documents. The need for so much specific knowledge gives an advantage in the policy process to those who are able to stay informed—in other words, insiders, largely professionals—and penalizes those who participate seldom or irregularly. The insiders' advantage can be reduced, but never eliminated, by making as much of the knowledge as possible explicit and easily available to the public.

Persuasion is only the most evident strategy for influencing the policy machinery, not necessarily the most effective. Actions that demonstrate one's commitment— willingness to spend time and energy attending meetings and doing homework, for example, or going on strike—usually speak louder than words. Those who speak for many are usually heard more than those who speak for themselves alone. Demonstrations of unity among a large group of people or coalitions of organizations tend to be even more impressive.

Maintaining an effective PSC under these conditions is largely a matter of tact and common sense. It requires such mundane, but delicate and essential functions as:

- encouraging outgroup participation without alienating ingroups,
- maintaining allegiance and avoiding alienation among those who lose on a given issue,
- maintaining an awareness of common interests (for example, concern for student and community welfare) when special interests differ,
- maintaining a sense of responsibility for good process and outcome among all participants,
- maintaining tolerance of and respect for differences,
- encouraging constructive resolution of conflicts, neither evading decisions nor subjugating minorities unnecessarily,
- providing opportunities for participation in varied roles (entrepreneur, advocate, footsoldier, loyal opposition, and so on) without over-organizing,
- maintaining enthusiasm (by communicating an inspiring image of the goal, by calling attention to progress) honestly and with integrity,
- keeping members in touch with the feelings of the other members, and yet avoiding insults.

Attempting to change entrenched policy mechanisms, even when they have not functioned well and have only weak support, is usually divisive. Sadly, it is usually less divisive and always easier to create a new element of the mechanism than to try to change an existing one. The greatest difficulty with new arrangements is to attract allegiance and support. If the new mechanism works and is effective in shaping policy, those who want to influence policy will participate, and allegiance will likely follow in time. Knowing when and how to create a new group or which existing group to approach to handle a given policy problem is one of the practical arts of policy-making. Some standard types of policy mechanisms for curriculum are:

strategic planning group (district, state)
blue ribbon public commission (district, state, federal)
in-house study group
outside review committee

Building a PSC

The institutional framework through which curriculum policy has been established in the United States has undergone some substantial evolution during this century. On the national level, the national committees, beginning with the Committee of Ten in the 1890s and continuing into the 1920s, were effective during that time. The NEA, especially its Department of Superintendence and its Educational Policies Commission, were effective during the period from 1930 to 1950 or so. The curriculum projects of the 1960s and the Great Society legislation of the 1970s were powerful galvanizing forces in their eras. But the direction of evolution here is toward institutional decentralization. Power passes from one dominant group to another unpredictably. Agenda, actors, and arenas shift and continuity is sacrificed. Institutional arrangements are needed that will permit the network of agencies actually involved in curriculum policy issues to work out constructive policies, ones that are diverse and flexible enough to encompass the nation's diversity and rate of change, but that will avoid some of the waste and futility of a chaotic situation.

Unfortunately, here techniques fail us again. We need leaders, public support, political will, and efforts sustained for years. Networks and coordinating organizations of various kinds seem most likely to demonstrate the value of curriculum policy in the short term. Experimentation with coordinated efforts in limited domains seems most promising. The Bay Area Writing Project, a network of teachers, administrators, and university professors concerned with the teaching of writing, is an example worth studying. It has now become a national organization. Another instructive model is the Joint Council on Economic Education.

For obvious reasons there are few formal techniques for building or maintaining an effective PSC. Opinion polling is sometimes used to determine the views of nonparticipating yet interested parties. Techniques from advertising and marketing such as focus groups—small groups of representative members of a population brought together to discuss and react to something in an effort to explore the views of the entire population—can also be applied.

QUESTIONS FOR STUDY

1. Consider a contemporary curriculum innovation that is receiving nationwide attention. Assume you are acting as a consultant to a national nonprofit organization formed to promote the use of this innovation in American schools. Use the ideas of this chapter to develop a strategy for the organization to follow. Make reasonable assumptions about budget, timelines, and other constraints.

2. Develop a strategy to promote the same innovation as in question 1, but this time act as a consultant to a state superintendent who is convinced of the value

of the innovation and wants to put the maximum resources of the state department of education behind it.

3. Advise the members of a state commission appointed by the state superintendent on appropriate policies to establish the teaching of foreign language in the elementary schools of the state.

4. Use backward mapping to identify the critical policy needs for implementation of the use of computers in the teaching of writing in conventional elementary school classrooms.

5. Suppose a state (or nation) wants to develop an explicit policy for their educational system, setting systemwide goals. What types of goals would be appropriate in the area of mathematics? For instance, which of the following would be appropriate: number of students enrolled in math at various grades, number passing university entrance exams; quality of the performance of the top 10% of the students?

6. Read a chapter of a book or an article that identifies trends and forecasts changes in American society. Use these trends as a basis for writing a scenario that tries to anticipate their impact on the curriculum of a state's school system.

7. Assume that a major study of American children has shown them to be abysmally ignorant of world geography. The governor of your state has appointed a blue ribbon committee to suggest what actions your state should take. You have been appointed as staff to this committee. The chair has asked you to prepare a briefing paper suggesting the kinds of questions the committee should consider at its first meeting. Draft such a briefing paper.

8. Read a report of one of the many studies of the National Assessment of Educational Progress. See what conclusions you can draw from this study that are helpful in making curriculum policy for a state education system that you know well.

9. Make or find a list of the five most pressing problems of education today. Suggest briefly how a change in curriculum policy could (or could not) alleviate each of these problems. Compare the efficacy of the curriculum policy changes you suggest to the most promising types of policies, educational and noneducational, to address the same problem. Here are some items you might consider for your list:

- high rates of functional illiteracy,
- high and rising dropout rates,
- high and rising teen pregnancy rates,
- high and rising teen suicide rates,
- low test scores in academic subjects,
- inequality of educational opportunity for poor and minority students.

10. Many authorities on the American school system criticize the attempts made to improve American schools by federal agencies such as the Department of Education and the National Science Foundation. They maintain that the millions these agencies have spent on curriculum reform projects have produced little or no improvement in the curriculum most American children receive. Use the ideas in this chapter to design a new set of policies a federal agency could establish that you think stands a good chance of achieving more improvement.

11. A relatively wealthy developing nation has many isolated settlements in regions far from its major cities. Policy-makers wish to offer children in these communities an opportunity to study what they call the modern subjects— English, mathematics, and science. They cannot find qualified teachers to staff these schools, so they are thinking about developing a program based on print, video, and computers. They have asked you to submit a proposal for a feasibility study. Costs are not your concern. Their question to you: Assuming that this can be done technically and that it would be acceptable culturally, what kinds of policies and programs would we have to enact at the National Ministry of Education to establish and maintain such a program?

RECOMMENDED READING

I have found the work in political science and sociology on the implementation of laws illuminating. In particular, Lipsky's *Street-Level Bureaucracy: Dilemmas of the Individual in Public Services* (1980), Weatherley's (1979) study of the vagaries of implementing special education legislation (also Weatherley and Lipsky 1979), Bardach and Kagan's (1982a) study of government regulation, George C. Edwards' textbook on implementation (1980), and Pressman and Wildavsky's authoritative *Implementation* (1973), all of which offer helpful insights into curriculum policy-making.

As might be expected, the literature suggesting ways to improve policy-making is not as extensive as that studying or criticizing current practice. Bardach (1977) and Bardach and Kagan (1982a, 1982b) offer useful suggestions. I found Richard Elmore's (1982) concept of backward-mapping very useful. Ingram and Mann's book of readings (1980) contained useful tips. Mitroff and Emshoff (1979) and Mason and Mitroff (1981) suggest the promising technique of systematically challenging the strategic assumptions on which a policy is based.

REFERENCES

Bardach, Eugene. 1977. *The Implementation Game: What Happens After a Bill Becomes Law.* Cambridge, MA:MIT Press.

Bardach, Eugene and Robert A. Kagan. 1982a. *Going By the Book.* Philadelphia: Temple University Press.

Bardach, Eugene and Robert A. Kagan (eds.). 1982b. *Social Regulation, Strategies for Reform.* San Francisco: Institute for Contemporary Studies.

Boyd, William L. Fall 1978. The Changing Politics of Curriculum Policy-Making for American Schools. *Review of Educational Research* 48:577–628.

Dunn, William H. 1981. *An Introduction to Public Policy Analysis.* Englewood Cliffs, NJ: Prentice-Hall.

Edwards, George C., III. 1980. *Implementing Public Policy.* Washington, D.C.: Congressional Quarterly Press.

Elmore, Richard F. 1982. Backward Mapping: Implementation Research and Policy Decisions. *Studying Implementation.* (Walter William et al., eds.) Chatham, NJ: Chatham House Publishers.

Frey, Karl. 1983. Curriculum Konferenz. Unpublished paper. Institut Pedagogische Naturwissenshaften. Kiel, West Germany.

Fullan, Michael. 1982. *The Meaning of Educational Change.* N.Y.: Teachers College Press.

Furth, Hans G. and Harry Wachs. 1974. *Thinking Goes to School.* N.Y.: Oxford University Press.

Goodlad, John I., Frances Klein, and Associates. 1982. *Behind the Classroom Door.* Worthington, Oh: Jones.

Greenwood, Peter W., Dale Mann, and Milbrey W. McLaughlin. 1975. *Federal Programs Supporting Educational Change, Vol. III: The Process of Change.* Santa Monica: Rand.

Hirshman, Alberto. 1967. *Development Projects Observed.* Washington, D.C.: Brookings.

House, Ernest R. 1974. *The Politics of Innovation.* Berkeley: McCutchan.

Ingram, Helen M. and Dean F. Mann (eds). 1980. *Why Policies Succeed or Fail.* Beverly Hills: Sage.

Kirst, Michael and Decker F. Walker. December 1971. An Analysis of Curriculum Policy-Making. *Review of Educational Research* 41:538–568.

Lipsky, Marvin. 1980. *Street Level Bureaucracy: Dilemmas of the Individual in Public Services.* NY: Russell Sage Foundation.

Mason, Richard O. and Ian I. Mitroff. 1981. *Challenging Strategic Planning Assumptions.* N.Y.: John Wiley.

McLaughlin, Milbrey W. 1978. Implementation as Mutual Adaptation: Change in Classroom Organization. *Making Change Happen?* (Dale S. Mann, ed.) N.Y.: Teachers College Press.

Mitroff, Ian I. and James R. Emshoff. 1979. On Strategic Assumption-Making: A Dialectical Approach to Policy and Planning. *Academy of Management Review* 4: 1–12.

Pressman, Jeffrey and Aaron Wildavsky. 1973. *Implementation.* Berkeley: University of California Press.

Ravitch, Diane. 1983. *The Troubled Crusade: American Education, 1945–1980.* N.Y.: Basic Books.

Tyack, David, Robert Lowe, and Elizabeth Hansot. 1984. *Public Schools in Hard Times.* Cambridge, MA: Harvard University Press.

Weatherley, Richard A. 1979. *Reforming Special Education: Policy Implementation from State Level to Street Level.* Cambridge, MA: MIT Press.

Weatherley, Richard A. and Michael Lipsky. 1979. Street Level Bureaucrats and Institutional Innovation: Implementing Special Education Reform. *Making Change Happen?* (Dale Mann, ed.) N.Y.: Teachers College Press.

DEVELOPING CURRICULUM PLANS AND MATERIALS *chapter* **13**

*C*urriculum planning can be seen as a matter more of the intuitions and immediate matching of images rather than the logical and sequential weighing of propositions.

Reynolds, John and Malcolm Skilbeck. *Culture and the Classroom.*

PURPOSE OF THE CHAPTER

- to explain the similarities and differences between informal planning, planning by objectives, and deliberative planning
- to describe in detail how deliberative planning may be used to develop curriculum plans and materials, including: the role of platforms of ideas; the creation of plans and materials that embody the platform fully and well; and designing field trials

OUTLINE

Introduction to Developing Curriculum Materials

Deliberative Approaches to Curriculum Development

Conclusion: The Craft of Curriculum Design

INTRODUCTION TO DEVELOPING CURRICULUM MATERIALS

Some of the most creative and influential work in the history of curriculum improvement efforts is associated with the design of curriculum plans and materials. The work is one of the most distinctive and important tasks of curriculum specialists. Think of the influence of Maria Montessori's manipulative materials, John Dewey's activities organized around basic human occupations, Harold Rugg's social studies textbook series, and Carleton Washburne's workbooks. The design of plans and materials is only part of the story of curriculum improvement, but it is an important part, especially so when the improvement involves introducing content not previously taught or restructuring traditional content, or when, for whatever reason, teachers need special assistance in improving the curriculum offered in their classroom.

Curriculum materials design is not the whole story of curriculum improvement. Launching a materials development project should certainly not be the automatic response to every need for curriculum improvement, but materials can almost always lend important support to curriculum change efforts of any kind, and sometimes new curriculum materials are exactly what is most needed to bring about curriculum improvement.

Indeed, curriculum development is such a central activity that it has been impossible to avoid the subject for twelve chapters in this book. We have considered the history of some major curriculum development projects in Chapter 2, the ideas that have guided such projects in Chapters 3 and 4, the process of deliberative design in Chapter 5, and the design of activities by teachers in Chapter 10. In this chapter we consider directly the problems that arise when people set out to develop curriculum plans and materials for widespread use in schools. These types of materials potentially are called *generic* to distinguish them from *site-specific* materials—those made for use in a particular school or school system. Generic materials must contend in a national marketplace with materials produced and distributed by commercial firms and by a variety of nonprofit, public interest organizations. The textbook industry, the largest segment of this industry, is big business. Any given textbook project requires a major capital investment and its results noticeably affect the balance sheet of even the largest publishing company. Commercial success is not the only indicator of achievement in curriculum development, however. Sometimes a project that never captures a major share of its market sets an example, calls attention to an idea or approach and, over the long run, changes teachers' preferences in ways that affect all subsequent products. In this chapter we will be concerned with substantial projects to develop new and innovative curriculum plans and materials for this nationwide market.

Informal and Systematic Approaches to Curriculum Development

Teaching and learning materials are designed and produced routinely by commercial publishers, official education agencies, and public service organizations, as well as by classroom teachers. Most of these curriculum development efforts proceed informally, following no set, systematic procedure. Materials are typically developed by individual authors, editorial teams, or committees of teachers who make design decisions intuitively, acting on their personal and professional beliefs and following their professional judgment. Developers are usually familiar with curricular and pedagogical traditions in their subject, and they borrow freely from earlier designs, adapting as necessary and inventing new features as they go. Some members of the development team will surely be experienced teachers who can gauge roughly how students and teachers may react to various features contemplated for the materials. Sometimes subject matter specialists are involved in the development effort and bring a deep and current knowledge of the subject. Sometimes a psychologist or social scientist is involved when their special expertise is deemed necessary. Sometimes an evaluator also participates in the development team.

Regardless of who makes up the development team, informal curriculum materials development is an art rather than a science, an unpredictable and idiosyncratic creation that depends critically on the artfulness and judgment of the people involved. Some people find this kind of uncertainty, this *ad hoc* quality, unacceptable and strive to put the enterprise on a more systematic footing. They argue that we ought to be able to discover the essential logic of the process of development and systematize it.

The supposed shortcomings of informal approaches have prompted thoughtful observers to devise more systematic methods of curriculum development. The most widely taught systematic method is planning by objectives. Planning by objectives arose as part of efforts in the late nineteenth century to rationalize public institutions along the lines followed in rationalizing industrial production. In designing factories and offices, practitioners of scientific management had systematized the informal methods of production and had thereby improved efficiency. The most visible symbol of their triumph was the automated assembly line. Compared to the informal methods of the mechanic's shop, a modern assembly line can produce many more units in a given time with lower cost per unit. The resulting lower prices increased demand and ultimately resulted in a more productive economy and a higher standard of living. These industrial successes were widely admired, and therefore the scientific methods that were believed to be the secret of their success were applied to whatever areas of life seemed in need of improved efficiency—the military, offices, government, and eventually schools. Just as mechanical engineers had designed a more efficient system of production, so engineers of education would redesign the classroom, and especially the teaching and learning materials used there, in order to improve the efficiency of education.

One of the pioneers of this approach to curriculum planning, Franklin W. Bobbitt, was a disciple of Frederick W. Taylor, the father of scientific management. Bobbitt referred to himself as an *educational engineer* (Bobbitt 1924, 2). He recommended that educational engineers rebuild the curriculum from the ground up, beginning with a general survey of the entire field of man's life in order to discover general goals and broad strategies for achieving them. Specifically, he suggested that the broad range of human experience be divided into major fields and each field studied to discover the main activities that it required, just as industrial engineers analyzed the essential activities required of workers in producing a wagon. The ability to perform these activities then constituted the objectives of education, just as the ability to perform the essential tasks of producing a wagon determined the skills required of a workman. These objectives were to be stated in specific, definite terms, as things students should be able to do. "When so stated, it is possible for educationists to know with certainty at what they are aiming" (Bobbitt 1924, 32). Then, the curriculum-maker would take the objectives and figure out what the pupils should do and experience to achieve the objectives (Bobbitt 1924, 44). Curriculum plans and materials would be designed that enabled pupils to reach these objectives, and the effectiveness of these materials would be judged by the extent to which students achieved the objectives. This, in outline, is planning by objectives.

Since Bobbitt's day, planning by objectives (PBO) has developed into a family of widely used approaches to curriculum improvement. As a method of curriculum materials design, PBO focuses early attention on developing precise statements of the objectives to be sought. If the process is to be fully scientific, the selection of objectives must be rationally justifiable and not arbitrary. In one very broad form of PBO identified with Ralph Tyler, objectives should be derived from studies of a variety of sources and then screened for consistency with the values and educational philosophy of the school. Studies of the life activities students are being prepared to carry out can reveal objectives. Studies of the students themselves and their current problems and difficulties can reveal needs that suggest objectives. Various categories of people—parents, teachers, subject experts, child psychologists, even the students themselves—can be surveyed for their opinions as to the most important objectives. However selected, all objectives should be consistent with the educational philosophy and values of those affected and those responsible. Objectives should be checked to be certain that they are realistic under typical conditions—in other words, neither too difficult nor too easy. Finally, the school staff, working together and subject to the approval of the school board and parents, should decide on the objectives.

In another more hard-edged version of PBO identified with industrial and military training and with behavioral psychology, objectives should be derived from a thorough psychological analysis of the task to be performed and of the demands these tasks place on students, including cognitive processes and skills that must be employed as well as psychomotor skills and affective or socio-emotional capabilities.

However they are selected, in all forms of PBO objectives should be stated precisely and unambiguously so that curriculum materials designers can know exactly what they are trying to help students achieve and so that evaluations can be conducted to determine if the materials are effective. Behavioral objectives (or performance objectives) specify exactly what students should be expected to do at the end of the unit that they could not do at the beginning. These objectives constitute criteria to be applied in all subsequent phases of the materials design process.

Once objectives have been determined, curriculum materials development is largely a search for effective and efficient means to achieve the objectives. One version of PBO encourages designers to seek inspiration widely and to draw eclectically from a variety of sources of principles and precedents for creating materials and activities that will achieve the given objectives. Another version insists that activities be designed on the basis of rigorous theoretical analysis of the task (what Gagne and Briggs call the *conditions of learning*) and of the learning process. In both versions, it is often helpful to study competent performers as they demonstrate how they accomplish what is specified in the objective. Also, it is often helpful to study novices as they attempt the criterion performance in order to discover the source of their errors or difficulties. Frequently an armchair analysis of the psychological processes the task demands will suffice to reveal appropriate instructional means, but sometimes a formal study will be required.

When analysis and theory have been taken as far as possible, and when the studies of actual performers that still seem to be required are completed, then prototypes of teaching and learning activities that are likely to lead to attainment of the objective may be produced. These prototypes are checked for their consistency with the underlying theory and then they are evaluated by laboratory or field trials on the extent to which they lead to the attainment of the stated behavioral objectives. Evaluations should be rigorous experimental tests that confirm as unequivocally as possible that the materials led to attainment of the objectives. This means evaluation studies—carefully controlled experiments in which the criterion measures call for students to demonstrate their ability to execute the performance called for in the objectives. When objectives are not achieved, the materials are revised and the process repeated. If the objective is judged unattainable or if superior objectives are discovered in the course of the design, the objectives may be revised, but any substantial adjustment in objectives is rare in actual practice of curriculum planning by objectives.

The main strengths and limitations of planning by objectives as an approach to curriculum materials development are mentioned in Box 13-1. The limitations are minimized when planning by objectives is interpreted loosely. For example, if developers state their main objectives for a unit, but continue to make intuitive judgments about secondary objectives, then the possibility of narrowing our objectives is much reduced. But such compromises undermine the case for planning by objectives. If judgment can be used for some decisions, then why not for all? How can we claim scientific rigor if some decisions are still based on subjective judgments? With enough compromises on central points of doctrine, there may be little difference remaining between planning by objectives and informal approaches.

Planning by objectives can be a powerful technique in many situations. It is the method of choice in developing training programs. Here the goals are clear and

BOX 13-1   Strengths and Limitations of Planning by Objectives

Strengths

- It focuses developers' attention sharply on exactly what they want students to learn from using the materials; it forces them to be clear and explicit about this and therefore to think long and hard about it.
- It insists that developers verify that students learned what the materials were designed to teach.
- It guards against vague, wishful thinking. Often in informal development we create materials that we believe are rich in educative possibilities, but from which students may in fact learn little or nothing. Planning by objectives, properly done, prevents this from happening.

Limitations

- It requires more time and money than informal development. Cutting corners to reduce costs may cause us to narrow our objectives or to base decisions on shoddy evidence.
- We may abandon important objectives that we find difficult to state or to measure.
- We may focus too much attention on purely verbal, semantic issues in defining objectives when moving on to developing measures and activities would be more productive.
- Something may be lost in treating an extended educational program as a set of simply-related small-scale objectives. Perhaps many objectives can be attained at once. Maybe students would be better in the long run if they took away different things from a single activity rich in educative possibilities.
- Selecting objectives in advance and shaping the materials to achieve just these objectives leaves teachers and students with little remaining discretion, and thus promotes an authoritarian learning situation.

undebatable and only the means of achieving them most effectively and efficiently remain to be discovered. Looser forms of PBO can be useful in general education, especially when the contending parties make vague claims for, mysterious benefits coming from the options they favor.

But there is another less widely known way of approaching curriculum development systematically. We saw in Chapter 5 how practical reasoning can be used to make design decisions. It is deliberative approaches to development that we will develop in more detail in this chapter. Deliberative approaches are featured here because they are widely useful, similar enough to the informal methods developers commonly employ to make them relatively easy to learn and to use, and not as well or widely understood as planning by objectives. Deliberative approaches have their own limitations, of course, and no claim is made for their absolute superiority to other ways of doing curriculum development, only that they have their place along with other methods.

DELIBERATIVE APPROACHES TO CURRICULUM DEVELOPMENT

The logic of deliberative design has already been presented in Chapter 5. In this chapter we proceed to study how curriculum developers use practical reasoning to design curriculum plans and materials based on their ideas. In broad outline the process is one of formulating a platform of ideas, using these ideas to conceptualize the problem and to generate promising preliminary versions of materials, assessing the merits of promising early versions, and revising them until they cannot be improved further.

Launching the Development Project

The process of development begins officially when a development team is assembled and ordered to produce a set of curriculum plans and materials of a certain type. In order to secure the necessary funds and approval, the project team must convince powerful or influential persons and agencies to sponsor them in this work. They do this typically by presenting their criticisms of existing curricula, their vision of a better curriculum, the ideas that lead them to think that a curriculum of the sort they envision is both possible and desirable, and a plan for translating those ideas into actual materials that can be used by students and teachers. This is their platform of ideas on which they will base their project. The ideas in the platform will guide them as they make the many millions of decisions that shape successive versions of their materials. The ideas in a project's platform usually undergo some development during the course of the project, but the basic concepts and principles seldom change. They give the project its coherence and its identity.

In a very real sense, the new curriculum to be developed must nearly exist already when the project is launched. Only the actual shape of the materials to realize the vision remain to be determined. Much of the thought that shapes a curriculum development project is thus done before the project even begins. It is done by the project's initiators on their own prior to the project's officially coming into existence.

The first problem would-be curriculum developers face is obtaining funds to launch the project. The pragmatic test of whether some people's ideas about a new curriculum become a curriculum development project is whether they can garner the support needed to create first versions of their curriculum plans and materials. Curriculum materials development projects are large enterprises, requiring on the order of two to five years, perhaps 10 to 100 person-years of effort, and from $2 million to $50 million for materials to accompany a full year's course. Few organizations are in a position to invest the sums required with no anticipation of a return. Generally speaking, government agencies charged with improving the quality of education and philanthropic organizations dedicated to the improvement of education are the main sources of funds for curriculum development in these amounts. Before a promising idea becomes a curriculum project, someone must convince a sponsor to advance the necessary funds.

This process of sponsorship is a type of negotiation between the would-be developers and their patrons. The developers explain their platform and try to convince the sponsor that it would further the sponsor's interests to have the proposed curriculum materials developed. The sponsor typically likes some of the developer's ideas but has questions about others and would like to sell the developer on one or two other ideas, also. Developers and the sponsor try to work out an agreement that goes something like this: "We, the developers, promise to develop prototype curriculum plans and materials of the following general description using roughly these methods within this specified period of time. By that time we expect that we will have developed materials that show promise of making the kind of improvements to the curriculum that both we and you, the sponsor, want. You, the sponsor, will be publicly recognized for supporting this project. If, by the specified time we have succeeded in developing materials that you, the sponsor, consider to be worthy, we, the developers, will cooperate in further efforts to make the fruits of our project widely available in schools so as to attain the sponsor's philanthropic goals. If we do not succeed by the specified time, you, the sponsor, will discontinue your support for the project." This type of agreement is called the project's charter. The charter often takes the form of a written proposal submitted by the developers to the sponsor and subsequent correspondence culminating in an award of funds. A curriculum project now officially exists.

Curriculum materials development projects thus come into existence with an organizational sponsor, a charge, key personnel, and an implicit assignment to solve some serious curriculum problem that has persisted despite the normal operations of informal curriculum design. They are not given an open license to study adult life, children, and the state of organized knowledge and invent whatever curriculum materials seem necessary, nor are they given the task of designing materials to achieve clearly defined objectives. We might say that curriculum development projects are temporary social agencies that have a charter from permanent agencies to carry out a task that is loosely framed.

Before work ever begins on any organized project, developers have some idea of what a curriculum dealing with the topic in question might be like—in other words, they begin with an answer, but an answer lacking details and an answer in which they do not yet have great confidence. As the project develops, the answer takes shape. It may change radically or the initial outlines may remain valid, but, if the effort is successful, the developers will have a more detailed and specific curriculum to show by the end of their work and will be much more confident about its value. The process that leads to this clarity and confidence is essentially a dialectic between ideas and design decisions. Ideas are used to define curriculum problems and to explore designs for curriculum plans and materials that might resolve them. In the process, ideas may be changed or abandoned, and new ones adopted. Early in the project's life preliminary versions of materials are planned and shaped through deliberation to the point where more can be learned from trying out a preliminary version in the field than from further deliberation based on ideas alone. Developers then incorporate results of field tests into their discussions of the merits of the preliminary materials, and deliberation is resumed on a firmer, broader basis, leading to revised versions. Cycles of designing, field testing, and revision continue throughout the project. To describe this process in more depth it will be necessary to break into this cycle. The obvious beginning point is the set of ideas that usually precedes the project's founding. In what follows, this set of ideas will be treated as if it were amassed self-consciously early in the project. You must keep in mind that, in fact, assembling these ideas is usually the work of a career, if not a lifetime.

Once the project is launched, the chief problems developers face are 1) to extend, refine, and elaborate their platform of ideas so that they can 2) generate promising provisional plans and materials; 3) assess the merits of these preliminary products; and 4) revise them in light of ideas and evidence until they are as good as the team can make them within the practical limitations of the project. We will consider in turn some of the ways the development team can address each of these four fundamental types of problems.

Formulating a Platform of Ideas

A curriculum development team must make thousands of decisions as they shape the plans and materials for a course or unit. They lack the time and resources to investigate all the relevant arguments for and against every plausible proposed feature of the materials. The overwhelming majority of their decisions must be based on knowledge and beliefs to which they are already committed when the work begins. The process of materials design, then, is largely a working-out of the implications of these prior commitments. The platform of ideas provides the terms and concepts the group uses to pose issues, describe alternatives, and frame arguments. The platform also provides principles, theories, and models that explain how these terms and concepts and the phenomena they represent are presumed to be related. These relationships assist the development team in identifying issues, generating alternative courses of action to respond to them, generating arguments for and against proposals, and weighing the various considerations to reach a decision. Platforms thus serve as both factual and logical bases for design decisions, and, in so doing, they are an essential ingredient in all curriculum materials design and a fundamental ingredient of deliberative design.

The developer's platform of ideas usually includes:

- a conception of the educational problem at issue, including its origins, causes, and the potential contributions of curriculum materials to its resolution,
- a recognition of the constraints to which the materials and the process of development are subject, including, in the case of the materials themselves, the

client group that the materials must satisfy, limitations on cost of the materials when marketed, and the circumstances in which the materials are to be used; constraints to which the process of development is often subject include time to completion, funds, and institutional affiliations,

- fundamental educational and curricular conceptions and values to be embodied in the design, including priorities among purposes of general education, conceptions of the subject to be taught, models of the learner and the teaching/learning process, and social ideals to be pursued through education,
- a repertoire of models (good, positive models or bad, negative models) for the kinds of things that they might design, and a repertoire of strategies (again, positive and negative) for going about the process of design.

With these ideas as starting points, the developers formulate a series of specific design problems that, when solved, will resolve the fundamental educational problem addressed by their project. The merits of various proposed problem formulations are discussed in light of the platform ideas. Problems chosen for sustained group attention are pursued in classic deliberative fashion: various solutions are proposed, their merits are discussed, and eventually resolutions are reached. Prototype designs emerging from these deliberations are tried in the field and reports of these trials are used to determine if the performance of the prototypes was adequate. The standards for this judgment are the same platform commitments used throughout the deliberations. Appropriate revisions are proposed, their merits debated, and subsequent versions of the materials produced. The cycle of production, trial, and revision continues until the group's standards are met or until some constraint forces a halt.

Platforms also serve a socio-political function within the development team and beyond. The platform expresses the shared beliefs that unite the team and are the reason for its continued existence. The social strains of either constantly voicing unpopular views or else keeping silent in spite of one's opposition are great. Also, everyone realizes that the dissenting member can no longer be depended on to make decisions that represent the team consensus, and this undermines trust among team members. Members who find themselves unable to embrace a key platform principle, and unable to persuade the others to adopt an alternative, usually leave the team. To the outside world, the team's platform is an emblem signifying commitments that onlookers may or may not share. Those who share these views can support the effort in various ways, while those who oppose them can counter it. So, platforms also serve as a focus for social identity and for social support and conflict.

Examples of Platforms In *Children and Number* Martin Hughes develops an innovative set of ideas about the teaching of beginning arithmetic that could easily serve as a platform for the development of curriculum materials. Hughes describes dozens of experiments in which he and his co-workers attempt to teach young children beginning arithmetic, experiments designed to test some new ideas about the source of children's difficulties in learning to add and subtract small whole numbers. Hughes and his colleagues began with the observation that preschool children typically have developed considerable facility with simple mathematics in informal contexts. They can, for example, count on their fingers, judge which of two sets of objects contains the greater number, and remove objects from the larger set until the two sets are equal. They can, as Hughes verifies experimentally, solve problems with objects that they cannot solve when expressed in the formalism of school mathematics, such as $3 + 7 = 10$ or $10 - 7 = 3$. Hughes begins with experiments in which children guess how many blocks are in a box after the experimenter adds or takes away a few. He discovers that most of the children he works with can do this task, but when given the equivalent problems in the usual school representation, very few can solve them. He describes a series of investigations in which the source of children's difficulties is narrowed down and various kinds of cures tried. From this ingenious series of experiments, Hughes reaches the conclusion that the most difficult part of mastering formal arithmetic is forming the links between the concrete and the formal. He proposes that these links can be fostered by discovering what each child can already do, concretely and formally, and then building on children's own spontaneous strategies, the ones they use in solving simple number problems informally. He proposes to encourage children to invent their own formalisms and to respect these in teaching. He suggests discussing with children the merits of various representations, including the accepted adult representation as well as those of other children. He suggests that we explain the history and purpose of the conventional representation, in order to give children the background and rationale for it. Hughes encourages explicit teaching of the relationship between written representations and concrete ones. He proposes using games, such as those based on dice, spinners, or playing cards, and computers to provide practice in basic skills. You can easily see how these ideas would suggest teaching activities and enable a team of developers to argue their merits. This is an excellent example of a platform of ideas based on research and theory, but the theoretical basis is narrow. It has, for example, nothing to say about the social arrangements that most foster the learning of arithmetic, little to say about how to sustain children's motivation, and little to say about how to handle individual differences. But the platform he provides is soundly based in experimentally tested principles that, as far as they go, constitute an excellent basis for materials development.

In **How We Learn to Read,** Seymour Itzkoff develops a balanced, sensible platform of ideas that is deeply rooted in two generations of research on the teaching of reading. It is easily intelligible by teachers in preparation—no technical language, graphs, statistics, or the like—yet it is deeply informed by a substantial body of literature. He argues that the polarization of the debate about beginning reading instruction between advocates of phonics and advocates of the look-say method has been detrimental to theory and practice. Advocates of phonics have an important part of the truth: children need to catch on that the letters stand for words and that sound is the key to the correspondence. On the other hand, sounding out words is much too slow and cumbersome a process to permit the fluency needed for mature reading. Studies of mature readers show that they process huge chunks of material—phrases, sentences, paragraphs, even pages—in single gulps. They use the shapes of the letters and words as cues for a guessing game in which they are constantly making inferences in advance about what the text will say and using their scanning mostly to confirm hypotheses and to guide the formation of further hypotheses. This inferential reading process is what all mature, fluent readers do, called *predicting one's way* through the text. To keep children fixated on letter-sound correspondences inhibits the development of these visual abilities. He recommends a model of reading as involving three systems: a sensory system, an integrational system, and a semantic system. Most of the problems children encounter that are specific to reading occur in the integrational system (for example, dyslexia). The training of the sensory system is normally accomplished by preschool or kindergarten. The training of the integrational system should be fairly complete by third grade. Itzkoff speaks of the training of this system as *mediated reading*. Using phonics, and perhaps also a special teaching alphabet, the student slowly learns to extract spoken equivalents from written language. With much experience the process gradually becomes automatic, the child's attention shifts from sound to a direct association of letter and word shapes with meaning. "Then we will see a flexibility and naturalness of attention, much quicker completion of the reading assignments, even a general relaxation of the breathing muscles, perhaps finally a smile at the outcome of a story" (Itzkoff 1986, 95). At this point, the child should be able to read with sufficient fluency for school work and enough to provide continuing satisfaction with reading. The role of the school then is to assist in the development of fluency. "The reading process now is skill building in the areas in which the mind becomes competent in careful, systematic discursive or logical thought" (Itzkoff 1986, 113). "The key is steady day-by-day . . . instruction that will expose the child to a variety of challenges and thus expand horizons and fluency with the thinking demands of the written word" (Itzkoff 1986, 113). Students may need help with specific skills, such as keeping the eyes moving—a finger works well for this purpose. Other types of exercises can also train the scanning system to higher levels of accuracy and fluency. Students can also be taught strategies, such as quick scanning followed by selective study of the more difficult passages, rather than sentence-by-sentence plowing through from beginning to end. It should be obvious how such a set of ideas provides a vital starting point for the design of materials and activities.

Sources of Ideas for Platforms Developers are not always so fortunate as to find a fully worked out platform for development in print, and when they do, they seldom find the ideas complete or totally satisfactory. The two examples just described, although they are excellent, are hardly complete. Hughes has little to say about classroom instruction as contrasted with teaching individual children, for example, and Itzkoff says little about what kinds of material children should read or about what kinds of classroom social interaction best promotes reading. Developers relying on these works would probably want to supplement them to cover these other vital aspects of the educational situation. Where may developers look to find ideas to constitute or complete their platform? Developers generally start with their own preexisting commitments and those of their sponsors. After that, common sense or conventional wisdom, analysis of the educational problem, and surveys of relevant theory and research can be helpful.

Personal Commitments Their own theoretical and educational commitments are obvious starting points for developers looking to generate or strengthen a platform. The process of developers consulting their own commitments is straightforward except for two problems: 1) members of the team may not agree, and 2) when examined, belief systems generally exhibit imperfections that call out for revision.

Disagreements can be forestalled by judicious selection of team members with similar philosophies and by early familiarization of new recruits with the group's or the leader's ideas. The latter process ranges from indoctrination of team members by their authoritative leader to collaborative group learning in which all contribute to the group's mutual education. In all cases, the chief method for reaching agreement is to read and discuss position papers, working papers, and background books and articles and to apply these ideas to concrete examples of materials and activities. The early weeks of most curriculum development projects are spent in just such reading and discussion.

The most apparent shortcomings of belief systems are gaps—relevant and important topics that the group is unable to consider or important questions it is unable to resolve for lack of appropriate shared ideas. Problems also arise because platform principles are too vague or ambiguous, leading to controversies within the group about their implications for the design. Platform principles may be naive, oversimplified, or simply wrong. Platforms may be unbalanced in various ways— one-sided or one-dimensional, for example, though this will usually be more apparent to outside observers than to team members. Sensitivity to possible defects in the group's initial platform and willingness and ability to reconsider it are important indicators of the project's ability to adjust and adapt. Too much of it, though, can immobilize a project, for there are always other defensible assumptions on which development might be based.

Examining the Project's Charter The project's charter—the contract, written and understood, between the project team and the project's sponsors— generally refers in some way to most of the project's guiding principles, but sometimes people forget some of them. Project teams often find themselves rereading and discussing funding proposals and other founding documents. But nearly always, the sponsor's expectations go beyond what is explicitly written out in the proposal. For example, in discussing legislation that ultimately funded Sesame Street, the Congress clearly intended that the television program would narrow the gap in school achievement between disadvantaged and mainstream children, although the agreement between the Children's Television Workshop and the Department of Education did not spell out this goal, but rather specified the achievement gains to be produced for disadvantaged children. Later, in evaluating Sesame Street, it would be found that, although both disadvantaged and mainstream children benefited, mainstream children watched more often and benefited more, thus increasing the achievement gap further. Maintaining a dialogue with clients and sponsors can forestall such misunderstandings and strengthen and enrich the project's platform of ideas.

Common Sense and Conventional Wisdom Most design decisions rest on principles so familiar that we are hardly conscious of them. This is what we mean by common sense and conventional wisdom. For example, consider the following common sense principles.

- To determine what activities to present to students, let students participate in the various activities that make up the subject, the real-life activities in which the subject originates and enters into people's lives outside of school.
- If it is not practical to let students participate in activities drawn directly from these enterprises, then simplify or adapt these activities so that they are suited to the students' capabilities and interests. To the extent possible, these should be activities that are actually a part of the enterprise in its out-of-school forms.
- An activity must first engage students' attention and energies in appropriate ways before it can have any impact at all.
- The educative effect is greater when students do something than when something is done to them.
- Engagement should be maintained with a minimum of restrictive or aversive conditions.
- Real activities always require some prior skills or knowledge (prerequisites). All activities, for example, require prior facility in some expressive medium, usually language, but also sometimes visual media, and very occasionally media using other senses.
- Activities should be designed to take advantage of students' already existing capabilities.
- The level or quality of performance students demand of themselves in an educational activity determines the level of accomplishment they will reach. Curriculum materials can influence students' standards.
- Normally we want students to be able to use what they have learned in the widest possible variety of circumstances—in other words, we want their learning to generalize. This requires practice on varied applications of important principles.

Boxes 13-2, 13-3, and 13-4 offer some statements of principles from three twentieth-century writers that seem to be common sense today. Developers could

BOX 13-2   Principles of Curriculum Development Now Common Sense (from William Kilpatrick)

- Each learner should work reasonably near to the limit of his power and resources at enterprises which he feels in maximal feasible degree to be his own and for which he accepts responsibility.
- Regard should always be had for the fact that learning is never single and due attention must be paid to making the attendant learnings as wholesome as possible.
- As far as feasible, learning should take place in a situation of 'natural' connectedness. . . .

SOURCE: (From the orator and pamphleteer of Progressive Education, William H. Kilpatrick 1926)

do a great deal worse than to build platforms entirely from such ordinary-sounding principles. If all school activities were designed consistently with these principles, schools would probably be a great deal more effective.

Theory and Research Through research and theory we hope to improve on common sense. Scholars and researchers who have made a special study of a subject will often have a better understanding of it than the consensus of educated people that constitutes the conventional wisdom of the time. Most curriculum developers, therefore, look to theory and research for deeper insights and more powerful principles. Research and theory can validate the developer's choice of

BOX 13-3   Principles of Curriculum Development Now Common Sense (from Edward Thorndike and Arthur Gates)

- Other things being equal, introduce a fact or skill at the time or just before the time when it can be used. . . .
- Other things being equal, introduce a fact or skill at the time when the learner is conscious of the need for it. . . .
- Other things being equal, introduce a fact or skill when it is most suited in difficulty to the ability of the learner. The optimum degree of difficulty is one which challenges the learner to enlist his best efforts but which is not so hard as to lead to failure or serious errors. . . .
- Other things being equal, introduce a fact or skill when it will harmonize most fully with the level and type of emotions, tastes, instinctive and volitional dispositions most active [in the students] at that time. . . .
- Other things being equal, introduce a fact or skill when it is most fully facilitated by immediately preceding learnings and when it will most fully facilitate learnings which are to follow shortly. . . .

SOURCE: (From educational psychologists Edward L. Thorndike and Arthur I. Gates 1929)

BOX 13-4   Principles of Curriculum Development Now Common Sense (Ralph Tyler)

- A student must have experiences that give him an opportunity to practice the kind of behavior implied by the objective.
- The learning experiences must be such that the student obtains satisfactions from carrying on the kind of behavior implied by the objectives.
- The reactions desired in the experience [must be] within the range of possibility for the students involved.
- There are many particular experiences that can be used to attain the same educational objectives.
- The same learning experience will usually bring about several outcomes.

SOURCE: (From Ralph Tyler 1949)

fundamental assumptions about how learning takes place, assumptions that often enter into virtually every other platform principle and every design decision. For example, a developer might insist on the importance of social interaction in learning, in contrast to the conventional emphasis among educational psychologists on interactions with the inanimate world of books and apparatus. In justifying such a stance, the developer might invoke the authority of the Russian psychologist Vygotsky or the work of students of the psychology of language. In first language learning, for example, contemporary researchers have reached a virtual consensus that interactions with real people are essential.

> It appears that in order to learn a language a child must . . . be able to interact with real people in that language. A television set does not suffice. . . . A child . . . can develop language only if there is language in her environment and if she can employ that language to communicate with other people in her immediate environment. (Moskowitz 1978, 943)

Commitment by developers to such a theory would lead them to ask of any learning situation "What are the crucial social interactions in which this learning plays or will play a part?" It would lead them to arrange for significant social interactions in which the intended learning can play a role: social arrangements in which youngsters, even those whose families and neighborhoods include few college graduates, can discuss *Macbeth* or design an experiment. With ingenuity many apparently dry topics seeming to require solitary study can be taught in lively, highly motivating social situations. For example, a high school English teacher taught grammar by requiring that all communication within her classroom be in writing.

Martin E. P. Seligman (1975) presents a theory of motivation that curriculum designers can use to help them think about how motivation for learning can be developed and sustained. He cites hundreds of studies of animals, as well as humans, showing that when an organism comes to expect that nothing it can do will change its unsatisfactory situation, it gives up responding altogether, to the point at which, in extreme cases, death may result. In one dramatic set of experiments, rats were clutched tightly until they gave up struggling to free themselves, then placed in a tank of water where they had to swim to survive. They swam only a half hour on the average before they gave up and drowned. Rats not given the prior experience of complete helplessness swam for up to 60 *hours* before succumbing in exhaustion. When dogs were administered electric shocks that they could in no way avoid they lapsed into complete lethargy. Even when a way of escape was then opened, the dogs who had been experimentally induced to expect that they were helpless to avoid the shock did not move to take advantage of the escape. Eventually they had to be physically dragged across the boundary several times and coaxed across for dozens more before they finally learned that they could escape on their own. On the basis of such experiments Seligman maintains that helplessness—the expectation that nothing one can do will alleviate an undesirable situation—saps the motivation to initiate responses of all kinds, disrupts the ability to learn that one's responses are effective, and produces emotional disturbances. Seligman argues that learned helplessness is the primary origin of depression in human beings. The belief that one is powerless to improve one's situation in some important respect leads to the classic symptoms of depression: reduced initiation of voluntary responses, negative thoughts, lowered aggression, loss of appetite, and certain physiological changes characteristic of depression disorders.

For the designer of learning activities, Seligman's ideas provide a way to think about how to foster high motivation to participate in the learning activity. In dealing with students who have already developed expectations of ineffectuality with learning, the lesson is that they may have to be forcibly guided to successful responses so that they can learn that success is possible, that they are not really helpless. To prevent the development of helplessness, the designer will want to build opportunities for students to control their situation and also to build in safeguards against repeated experience of failure. More subtly, Seligman's theory suggests that it may be important to challenge students. Overcoming temporary minor failure, partial failure, intermittent failure, or threatened failure demonstrates to the student that effort leads to success. In this way students can become immunized against learned helplessness. They learn that they can control their academic satisfactions and successes.

> To reverse classroom helplessness, it is necessary to experience some failure and to develop a way to cope with it. . . . If a young adult has no experience of coping with anxiety and frustration, if he never fails and then overcomes, he will not be able to cope with failure, boredom, or frustration when it becomes crucial. . . . If we remove the obstacles, difficulties, anxiety, and competition from the lives of our young people, we may no longer see generations of young people who have a sense of dignity, power, and worth. (Seligman 1975, 157–159)

The various branches of educational theory and research and the various behavioral and social sciences offer a tremendous wealth of ideas, many of which have been critically analyzed and tested. Some ideas that seem to hold promise as a basis for curriculum development are described in Chapter 5. You may wish to look back and reflect on how these ideas could help a curriculum developer make vital decisions about plans, materials, and activities.

Judging Quality in Platforms Platforms are better when they are complete and internally consistent and when the principles that comprise them are **valid, meaningful, important,** and **relevant.** A platform is complete to the extent that it provides a sufficient basis for any and all curriculum design decisions that arise. An incomplete platform forces a design team to postpone decisions, to interrupt design work to debate "philosophy," or to base decisions on some less satisfactory grounds, such as convenience, personal preferences, or custom. A platform is internally consistent when application of its various principles to assorted decisions yields compatible results. It is quite common and completely normal for an argument based on one platform principle to count favorably for a proposed course of action while an argument based on another principle counts against it; this simply means that pros and cons must be weighed. But when one principle always counts in the opposite direction of another in every decision of a certain type, the two principles are in conflict and the platform contains an inconsistency. If the inconsistency is not eliminated, the team may waste time in arguing repeatedly over recurrences of the conflict or may make decisions that favor one principle or the other erratically.

Invalid principles are simply mistaken ideas. The problem is to identify invalid principles and to find valid ones. In the complex, poorly understood world of human conduct, the most valid principles can only claim a rough sort of statistical truth. Platform principles for curriculum materials design range from those fairly well accepted by experts to the purely speculative. Plausibility is the most that can be claimed for the majority of them. More often than not, an impartial judge would declare several competing principles to be equally plausible. Since these different principles may have quite different implications for the design decisions, it will usually be quite important which principle a design team chooses for its platform. In these cases, the choice may quite properly be made on faith, on philosophical predilections, or even temperamental preferences. It is only when a clearly less valid alternative is chosen that we can justly criticize. We are hampered even then because one principle may receive the greater support from systematic research while another receives more support from school and classroom practice. Or, one school of thought or one methodological camp may endorse one principle and another a different one. Still, in spite of the difficulties, we must make the best judgments we can of the validity of platform principles, for the consequences of acting on a false or misleading principle can be as serious as anything that can befall a curriculum materials design effort.

Meaningful principles relate ideas and phenomena in substantial and significant ways, whereas vacuous slogans sound good but either cannot be applied consistently or, when applied, do not advance the decision-making process. Such principles cannot be said to be either valid or invalid because their import is so ill-defined that validity cannot be judged. Often, lack of meaning arises from unclear or ambiguous terms, but it may also result from confusion about actualities—mistaken assumptions about how phenomena behave, for example.

Valid and meaningful platform principles may differ in importance. A trivial or obvious principle provides little help in decision-making. One that deals with a vital, central topic is more valuable than one that deals with a peripheral issue. One that is original and nonintuitive provides a more valuable addition to our preexisting ideas than one that we would probably have guessed correctly anyway. Stale, commonplace ideas lead to conventional and repetitive designs, whereas fresh ideas at least have a chance of leading to new designs with superior features.

More relevant platform principles are applicable to many decisions, whereas less relevant ones are applicable in only a few special situations.

Using Platform Ideas to Generate Plans and Materials

In Chapter 10 we discussed how teachers can use heuristic reasoning and activity schemata to develop classroom activities. This same process works for the development of curriculum plans and materials designed for wider use. In generic development, however, ideas play a larger role in the process, larger structures than classroom activities must be designed, and designers more frequently need to derive designs from ideas directly rather than to adapt previous designs. Therefore, in this section we will concentrate on using platform ideas to generate original designs for curriculum plans and materials. The first and most fundamental step in this process is using platform ideas to reach an understanding or appreciation of the educational problem to which the plans and materials are being addressed.

Using Platform Ideas to Understand the Problem Curriculum materials development efforts always begin with some sense of an educational problem or challenge they are facing and striving to overcome.[1] Nearly everyone involved—developers, sponsors, educational leaders, the public—believes that they understand the problem completely, whereas in fact they usually have accepted a prevailing view that defines the problem in a partial way. This conventional understanding of the problem is seldom adequate to guide the developers' efforts. *Everyone knows* that American youth have a drug problem, but if a project to

---

[1]In this section I use the word *problem* which connotes something wrong. For most purposes I prefer the term *challenge*, which can be something that is okay as it is or even very good, but that could still be better. Here I stick to the more familiar term.

develop curriculum materials to prevent teenage drug abuse were launched, the developers would need a detailed and accurate understanding of the nature of that problem. How many students are affected? At what ages? Does the incidence of the problem vary with such factors as gender, age, socioeconomic status, geographical region, population of community, or school achievement? Is the problem one of lack of information about the harmful consequences of drugs, or lack of alternative outlets for adolescent rebellion, of poor social adjustment, or something else, or some complex combination of ingredients? To make the decisions about what kinds of materials to develop requires developers to have answers to such questions. Developers bear a continuing responsibility to refine and confirm their understanding of the problem. Usually this means that the task of understanding the problem becomes a focus of the developers' efforts early in the project.

Careful study of the research and scholarship on any curriculum problem nearly always reveals that several plausible alternative ways of defining the problem exist and, for each definition, several plausible conjectures about what causes the problem. A logical starting point for developers' efforts to understand the problem is, therefore, to study existing definitions and interpretations, including such features as:

- concepts used to describe the problem,
- values asserted in describing the problem,
- instances cited as exemplifying the problem,
- documentation provided for its existence/importance,
- alleged causes of the problem.

To go beyond what its definers tell us about a problem requires that we probe more actively, undertaking such interpretive activities as:

- constructing a full network of major causes,
- identifying stakeholders whose interests are affected, and their interests and views,
- learning the history of the problem,
- studying the problem at various scales, from its manifestations in individuals to its global manifestations,
- exploring the limits of the problem, such as situations in which it is and is not found, and in which it is and is not serious.

To achieve the most profound understanding of the problem it is necessary to compare the most promising alternative formulations in light of the best available evidence. This entails such critically evaluative activities as:

- constructing alternative causal models,
- expressing the problem in alternative concepts,
- recasting the problem in light of other values,
- challenging strategic assumptions underlying this definition of the problem,
- collecting additional evidence from library or field research.

A thoughtful developer who has been associated with education in a special field for some years will ordinarily have carried out such analyses informally or as part of the background work for the project. Gaining such a deep understanding of the problem and its various manifestations and interpretations is an enormous help in making crucial early design decisions. Less experienced developers or developers in projects in which team members disagree about what the problem *really* is would do well to invest time in a thorough, explicit, written analysis.

The problem must be understood in terms of some ideas, and naturally the ideas that play a prominent role in the platform tend to figure prominently in whatever formulation of the problem is eventually adopted. Difficulty in construing the problem adequately using platform ideas is a sign that the platform may need to be strengthened. Success in construing the problem in terms of the ideas that make up the platform tends to confirm the platform's soundness. Obviously there is a fundamental circularity here. If our ideas influence how we construe the problem then we may notice only those difficulties our ideas permit us to notice. Closed-minded, dogmatic adherence to platform ideas leads to relatively quick, easy, and unequivocal interpretations of the problem that, if correct and complete, constitute a firm, reliable basis for future design decisions. Open-minded, inquiring attitudes toward platform principles may lead developers to revise their ideas in order to make better sense of the problem, but only at some cost in time and effort.

Problems are not visible or tangible the way objects and events are. They require an act of interpretation by the problem analyst. In the simplest case they require a valuation of some state of affairs as good or bad and a characterization, a judgment that a particular situation fits the description of this state of affairs. For example, one analyst might identify as a problem in a particular class the students' apparent lack of interest in the class. Other analysts might think it not important that students show evident interest in their schoolwork, thus challenging the valuation implicit in that characterization of the problem. Still others might question whether the evident level of interest was really low compared to other classes or to realistically attainable levels of interest in school work, a line of reasoning that challenges the judgment that this particular situation fits the general description of the problem. Neither the valuation nor the judgment that characterizes the particular situation is an objective fact found in the situation itself. They must be brought to the situation by the analyst. Finding or creating new valuations and characterizations that will survive more than superficial criticism is an extremely challenging intellectual task. Conscientious problem analysts are aware of their own contributions to the problem identification and strive to make all the bases for their interpretations—valuations, characterizations, directly observed facts, inferences, assumptions, and more—public. When the bases for the judgment are made public, others may question the analysis and propose alternatives. These alternatives can compete openly for the hearts and minds of those involved.

Analyzing existing materials and activities can be helpful in checking the adequacy of your problem definition. Why haven't existing materials sufficed to solve the problem that the proposed project is designed to solve? If designers can pinpoint what is wrong with existing materials, they may find strong clues about the nature of their design problem. For instance, if existing elementary school science textbooks introduce new vocabulary at a much higher rate than other reading materials, then the development team may want to consider whether the high demand for verbal learning that these books make on children is desirable. Even if the project team did not initially see this as an important part of their problem, they would do well to reconsider their understanding of the problem in light of such a discovery about existing materials. Inspection of existing curriculum materials can also reveal that they already make some attempts to solve the problem, and thus lead the team to inquire why these earlier attempts have not succeeded. If inspection of existing materials reveals nothing of interest or if the team is divided or confused about how to interpret what they see, then the platform probably needs attention.

Analyzing typical educational situations is another instructive test of the adequacy of our platform. Surveys of classrooms where the subject is being taught should reveal places where there is room for improvement. The platform of ideas should offer explanations for both why these problems exist and why they need to be solved, and it should suggest directions for solving them. If not, the platform may need to be strengthened. Accounts and opinions of those who are in regular contact with a wide variety of schools and classrooms—supervisors and principals, for example—can yield further documentation of the nature of the problem and of the fate of earlier attempts to resolve it. Students may have something helpful to offer. Again, studies may be helpful. In particular, studies of the National Assessment of Educational Progress regularly provide extensive data on the performance of a representative sample of children at three ages from all regions of the country. Studies are also available that compare achievement of students cross-nationally. Understanding the current educational situation and exactly how and why it does not meet our expectations is a powerful help in planning curricula to improve the situation.

Using Platform Ideas to Generate and Test Activities Chapter 10 already described the essential process of reasoning by which platform ideas are used to generate and test possible classroom activities. Materials developers must use this same process skillfully and intelligently. Much of the skill is subject-specific and age-specific, but some idea of the detail and sophistication of the considerations normally arising in such work can be gained by entertaining some general questions. Boxes 13-5 through 13-7 give examples of some kinds of questions a materials developer might ask in order to identify appropriate features for an activity.

Using Platform Ideas to Design Larger Features Programs, courses, units, and activities must all be designed, and each of them is a somewhat different design problem. In designing programs, for example, one must think in terms of years of

■
BOX 13-5   Questions Helpful in Shaping Classroom Activities

A. Questions about the content of the activity

Is the content of the activity sound?

(valid? educative? important? comprehensive)

How can the content be made appropriate to students?

(to how they perceive meaning? to their pre-existing ideas? to their interests?)

How can the content best be presented?

(media? sensory qualities? stimulus discriminations? examples and non-examples? form of representation? full range of examples: hard/easy, simple, complex, and so on?)

How can standards of performance with respect to content be improved? Brought into line with student's capabilities? With larger society's expectations? Made more explicit?

How to give adequate attention to common, serious content-related problems?

(foreign to students' experience? too complex? too many unrelated items?)

time to complete the program and of lifetimes of impact on individuals, and of possible effects of the program on fields of study and work, on knowledge, and on society itself. Designing programs is the work of major figures in the field, as much a matter of statesmanship as of scholarship. Program design is a major institutional decision; it has been touched on in Chapter 12 on Curriculum Policy. The design

■
BOX 13-6   Questions Helpful in Shaping Classroom Activities

B. Questions about the tasks students are asked to perform

How can activities be designed so that they give students opportunities to do appropriate things with what they learn?

(recall, practice, demonstrate validity, apply, explain, integrate with other knowledge?)

How can the task be designed to provide students with a better opportunity to learn the content presented?

(powerful experiences, meaningful presentation, repetition, time, variety of stimuli and responses, chances to apply, practice, test mastery, integrate content with other aspects of personality)

How can the activity be made intrinsically motivating?

How can the activity be designed to guard against any of the following types of difficulties that students often encounter?

(mistaken ideas, inadequate study skills, lack of experience, missing prerequisite skill and knowledge, low aptitudes, lack of rewards, unclear goals, monotonous activity, progress not satisfactory.)

(pace, complexity, novelty, difficulty not controlled, not enough feedback, cues, supports, oversimplifying by leaving out important standards or constraints, neglecting vital complications, restricting the variety of problems, lowering levels of acceptable or outstanding performance.)

BOX 13-7   Questions Helpful in Shaping Classroom Activities

C. Questions about social aspects of the activity

- How can social aspects of an activity be designed to foster curricular purposes?

Before the activity:
Should entry be compulsory, voluntary, restricted? What should be the occasion for the activity? location? Group size?

During the activity:
Should roles be differentiated? Responsibility divided? Tasks interdependent? Should mobility be permitted? Should evaluation be public or private? Can students choose to enter or not, to continue or not, what to do, how to do it, how fast, how long, how often, with whom? What is the social meaning of the task, setting, occasion, and so on for participants? How is this task related to the cultural context?

problems for courses and units, however, are an integral part of curriculum development projects.

The design of courses or units rests directly on the conception of the educational problem(s) to be addressed and the choice of an approach to be followed in addressing the problems. These are central features of the project's platform, as we have just seen. Course and unit planning must also take into consideration the various frames within which the materials must function.

From this beginning, the developers need to produce a specification of the major items of content to be covered, the most important purposes to be achieved, the overall structure of the unit, and the main features of the pedagogical strategies to be followed in meeting the challenge.

Purpose If developers know their objectives with precision and certainty, then they should state them, but in most cases developers just beginning their work do not know exactly what their expectations should be for students' accomplishments. They can devote time early in their work to reaching clarity on their precise objectives through extensive discussion, as many authorities recommend. Alternatively, they can begin by stating objectives roughly, as they first leap to mind, planning to revise them later as they go along. Devoting much time early to reaching agreement among the developers on statements of precise objectives can be distracting and divisive. Often there is little basis for a decision yet, since the consequences for the project of choosing one objective over another can seldom be anticipated. Care must be exercised to keep disputes about wording within reasonable bounds. Even when they go as well as possible, early discussions of precise objectives are generally frustrating and unsatisfying for team members eager to grapple with materials design issues. To seek precisely stated objectives hurriedly and arbitrarily with the thought in mind of revising them later is self-defeating. If developers are uncertain whether the precisely stated objectives are really the ones they should pursue, why insist on precision in stating them?

An alternative procedure that is usually superior is to begin with rough statements of general aims. Early discussion of these should focus on the importance of each aim relative to others and deemphasize wording. It may help to think of broad categories of accomplishments you would expect of truly outstanding performers or to imagine the kinds of questions a good student might be able to answer in an interview with a knowledgeable expert in the subject. But concern for precision of statement in your aims can be postponed until agreement is attained on the importance of the general direction roughly indicated by the aim statements. These rough directions are usually sufficient as a basis for early decisions about content, approach, and key activities. Then, alongside the development of other aspects of the unit, the generally stated aims can be elaborated and made more precise in working papers that treat the issues more fully and carefully. Selection of performance indicators and precise statements of them come last. This process of refinement of purpose is interwoven with other design tasks, taking center stage when necessary or appropriate.

Either way, a sufficiently clear statement of purposes and their relative importance is an important milestone in the development of courses or units.

Content When the project proposes to cover the same content as that normally included in existing courses or units on the topic, the main items to be included can simply be listed. More often, curriculum development projects propose major changes in content inclusion and emphasis. Then it is usually important to spell out the new content in working papers, diagrams, and extensive lists. Most important of all is to spell out the rationale for all major changes in content. Will it bring the curriculum more in line with current knowledge? Is it simpler and easier for students to grasp? Does it reflect a reorientation of priorities among educational aims in the society? A development team would do well to write out the case for every major proposed change in content and discuss them with representatives of all the major interest groups concerned with the curriculum in their subject.

Structure The problem of structure can be taken up in several ways. The simplest approach is to find a single **organizing focus** or **theme** around which the unit will be built. It is still necessary to determine how the content and purposes of the unit will be deployed around this focus. For this, it is necessary to find an organizing principle to follow, such as chronological order, from simple to complex, from familiar to strange, from whole to part, or from concrete to abstract.

Riley (1984) found that the course developers at the Open University in England started work on a course by collecting sources, original and secondary. They located sources by examining published writing on the subject of the course, by corresponding with appropriate authorities, and through personal contacts. With a body of potential content for their course literally in hand, they then faced a fundamental choice: to attempt to cover the ground (in other words, to present *all* important material found in the sources) or to support an argument and select and arrange source materials accordingly. A decision to cover the ground commits the developer to a search for the structure that best represents the content. A decision to build the course around an argument commits the developer to using the argument as a focus and its key steps as organizing principles. In sequencing the topics to be included in their courses, the Open University course developers sometimes chose to begin with the sources and work toward conclusions and at other times they chose to present the argument first and then to develop it, with references to the sources when needed. Elementary and secondary course developers probably use a greater variety of starting points and strategies, but they, too, must select an organizing focus and organizing principles for their units.

Much of the material presented in school curricula is too complex to be presented in terms of a single focus and organizing principle. When several main themes are interwoven, as often happens in the teaching of literature, for example, more complex structures are needed. These are often best represented with a diagram. For example, a unit in which subgroups pursue different purposes for awhile and then report back to the whole class might be represented as a branched structure such as that in Figure 13-1. Other common forms of curricular structure best represented with a diagram include parallel structures, in which different aspects of a subject are presented simultaneously; cyclical and spiral structures, in which the same material is presented more than once; and hierarchical structures, in which prerequisite learnings are presented before those for which they are needed.

In addition to these formal structures, units may also be designed according to more organic principles. A history unit for elementary grades on the settling of the American west, for example, might be built around the experiences of one family of emigrants. There is no limit to the subtlety and sophistication of curricular structures.

In many cases some arbitrary form of organization will be suitable. Materials intended for supplementary use at the teacher's discretion may be most accessible if organized alphabetically by topic or according to the conventional order of

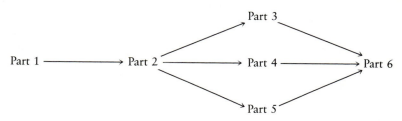

Fig. 13-1: Diagram representing the structure of a unit of six main parts in which three of the parts (3, 4, and 5) are presented simultaneously to subgroups of students (branched structure).

textbook topics. For example, a supplementary unit on strategies for mathematical discovery for high school algebra might be designed according to the topics covered in most algebra books, so that teachers could select appropriate supplementary activities for each portion of their course.

Posner and Strike (1976) present a useful categorization of principles that may be followed in sequencing items of content within a course or unit. They distinguish among sequencing principles as **world-related**—structures based on realities in the world as we perceive it, such as ordering a geography course by continents, or a chemistry course by the periodic table; **concept-related**—structures based on ideas, such as ordering a biology unit around natural selection; **inquiry-related**—structures based on the method or process that produces knowledge, such as ordering a geometry course around the idea of proof or a history unit around interpreting historical evidence; **learning-related**—structures based on how students learn the material, such as ordering a unit to begin with simple, familiar topics and proceed to more complex and novel ones; and **utilization-related**—structures based on how one may use what is learned, such as ordering a physical science course around familiar devices and situations to which physical principles can be applied.

Units may be ordered so as to reflect the inherent structure of the content being presented. Geometry courses, for example, usually follow a logical order, beginning with the most basic axioms and building theorem-by-theorem through triangles and circles to the more complex figures. Units may also be ordered so as to exhibit qualities important to those who value the subject. For example, science courses often follow a roughly historical ordering of subject matter, a practice that projects an image of science as a cumulative body of knowledge in which later contributions build on earlier ones. History courses are usually organized according to periods, a practice that reflects the importance to historians of seeking meaning in the patterns of the past.

Units may be ordered so as to facilitate students' learning of the subject. Developers commonly presume that an organization that seems clear and intelligible to them will prove to be so for students, too, and will therefore facilitate their learning the subject. But this is not always the case. As Dewey pointed out in **The Child and the Curriculum,** the logical order preferred by mature individuals acquainted with the whole subject may not be the best order for children encountering it for the first time. In particular, the logical ordering may be abstract and more difficult for students to grasp than the concepts presumably ordered. For example, the representation of numbers in terms of sets and set theory is a theoretically powerful way to order arithmetic, but it complicates learning for beginners. Also, the logical ordering of subject matter seldom takes into consideration the naive ideas students bring to the study of the subject that may, if not taken into account, interfere with learning the logical structure. For example, students' naive ideas about motion often interfere with their learning the standard Newtonian ideas presented in physics classes. In addition, logical ordering neglects motivational factors; students, unlike specialists in the subject, may not have a high intrinsic interest in the subject and therefore may need to be introduced to it in a way that makes its value and attractions apparent. A logical progression from concept to concept also obscures the psychological origins of the ideas, leaving students wondering how they or anyone else could ever have discovered such ideas. For many reasons, then, the intrinsic order of subject matter in its mature form may not be the best order to present it to students.

The structure of a unit may be described in ordinary English in the form of a unit overview, in an outline, or in a diagram. The best form of representation for the structure of a unit will depend on the relations to be emphasized among items of content and among purposes, and hence will differ for different units. One indispensable form for representing the structure of any unit is a schedule that tells how the major parts of the unit are to be distributed over the available time. Content, aims, parts of units, and even activities to be included in the unit will eventually need to be scheduled, but it is usually sufficient to begin with scheduling only the major parts of the unit. Like specifications of purpose and content, schedules are best developed through a process of successive refinement of a rough initial schedule. It is wise to schedule all available time, not just in-class time. It is wise to leave at least a twenty percent allowance for variations in time. That is, your unit should be viable if things take ten percent more time than you anticipate or ten percent less time.

Pedagogical Strategy Another important part of designing a curricular unit is to describe the **main elements of the pedagogical strategy** you plan to employ. Such a description should describe such factors as the **learning setting**—usually a classroom, but it could be a laboratory, playing field, or other setting; the **social climate** desired for that setting—including such aspects as degree and kind of student involvement, degree and kind of teacher control, and amount of competition or cooperation; the style of teaching—didactic, inquiry-oriented, activity-centered, and so on; the **mode and medium of presentation**—usually printed materials or live presentation by the teacher, but also video or film, audio or computer; and the **main activity types** planned for students—lecture, discussion, reading, writing, laboratories, and so on. It is important to give your **rationale for choosing these elements,** in other words, why you believe that these elements will meet the challenge addressed by your unit better than the most plausible alternatives. Reference to key sources (books and articles) of pedagogical ideas is often helpful in describing the approach in more detail.

Box 13-8 summarizes the main points about unit design presented in this section.

Field Testing Materials under Development

Field tests of preliminary versions of curriculum materials are so important that we ought to call materials that have not yet been tried with students something different—maybe something like "fledgling" materials, or "armchair version," or

BOX 13-8   Creating a Unit Design

Preliminary Considerations

Consider the Educational Problem
  Describe the educational problem addressed by the unit.
Consider Your Approach
  Describe methods and principles you will use.
Consider the Frames
    Student frames
    Teacher frames
    Time frames
    Facility and equipment frames

Elements of a Unit Design

Purpose
    List of the most important aims to be pursued
    Indications of relative emphasis among them
    Examples of broad categories of student accomplishments
    Working papers on most important aims (as needed)
Content
    List of the main items of content to be included
    Indications of relative emphasis among them
    Working papers on main items of content (as needed)
Structure
    Organizing focus (theme)
    Organizing principles
    Schedule (relations of unit parts in time)
Pedagogical strategy
    Learning setting
    Social climate
    Teaching style
    Mode and medium of presentation
    Main activity types
    Rationale for the above
    Working papers on approach (as needed)

"raw materials"—something to indicate that they are not *really* curriculum materials yet, only guesses about the form materials should eventually take.

The main reasons to conduct field tests of curriculum materials are to answer these basic questions: Do the materials work as expected? How can they be improved?

Working includes such mundane but vital matters as:

- Does what happens in the classroom resemble what the developers had in mind?
- Can teachers and students use the materials without too much difficulty?
- Do teachers and students find use of the materials rewarding enough to continue to use them spontaneously?
- Is the project realistic in its demands on time, effort, facilities, teacher and student ability, and so on?

Box 13-9 suggests more detailed questions of this same sort. If curriculum materials do not pass such tests as these, they are not really viable and must be revised or replaced.

When materials flop, the first step in revision is to develop hypotheses about what went wrong. Evidence collected in the field test is the factual basis for narrowing the list of hypotheses. The most essential distinction is whether the basic theory of the activity is flawed or whether it was poorly executed. A basic flaw requires a complete redesign of the activity, whereas an implementation defect may be eliminated with relatively minor revisions.

Even if the prototype materials worked, they can often be improved. Even the best draft curriculum will involve many educated guesses, not all of which will pan out. The field trial gives some indication of which guesses did not work out and should be reconsidered. Often, too, problems are encountered that were not even imagined. Finding unexpected problems is the most valuable result that can come from any field trial because an expected result shows that something important has been left out of account in the platform ideas or that we are not applying them properly. The field test may even suggest new platform ideas. In Peter Dow's account of the field testing of preliminary versions of *Man: A Course of Study* (1975) he reports that the developers discovered, much to their surprise, that

---

BOX 13-9   Basic Questions for Field Tests of Curriculum Activities

Is what is to be learned clear to students?
Is it also clear why this is important to learn?
Does the activity work in the classroom?
Are students able to comprehend the presentation?
Does the activity permit students to perform in ways that show (to them and to others) that they have learned what was intended?
Is the activity tailorable to suit different students and different classroom situations?
Does the activity make good use of appropriate resources in the learning situation?
Does the activity require resources not normally present in the classroom?
Is there a proportionality between the results achieved and the resources consumed?
Does the activity support and assist students at critical points at which they might falter?

children identified with the baboons presented to them in films to such an extent that they imputed human characteristics to them. The children believed, for example, that the baboons had a language just as complex as human language; they believed that humans just could not yet understand baboon language. Since the developers had introduced the unit on baboons to contrast animal behavior with human behavior, this finding of the field test forced major revisions. As a result, subsequent versions of the materials included units on lower animals as well as baboons.

To answer these "simple" questions is not always so simple. We must decide what to observe, what questions to ask of students and teachers, and what other sorts of instruments (tests, questionnaires, and so on) to use. And we must make inferences from data we collect in the field about whether things are alright as they are and whether they could be improved. These inferences are generally hazardous. Two observers of the same field trial might well reach different conclusions on whether the materials worked and what revisions were most needed. Worse, it often happens that neither observer can conclude anything with confidence, both coming away confused and uncertain about the significance of what they have seen.

There is no way to guarantee that field trials will be informative, but there are ways to guard against an uninformative trial. One of the most basic and important of these is to keep your eye on the ball in designing and carrying out the field test. Your purpose is to reduce **uncertainty** (your own and that of other reasonable people who support and are affected by your project) about the most troubling aspects of the project. A fundamental early step in planning field tests is therefore to identify the most troubling aspects and to find or develop simple, economical ways of reducing uncertainty about them. What would be signs that the project was or was not working? What things do members of the development team think might need improving, and what are the signs that they would look for to confirm or disconfirm their hunches?

Field tests stand an improved chance of finding serious trouble if they check whether the materials behave acceptably in the most essential and important respects. Look at the project's platform in order to identify the claimed benefits the developers and their sponsors value most. Examine the key activities and ask yourself: What data could I collect in a field test that would help me determine if the basic theory behind this activity is sound? Make sure the field trial collects these data. Make sure, too, that the outcomes you or the project's critics most fear do not come about. Keep a keen eye open for any signs of difficulties in classroom operations or in students' learning. Leave yourself enough flexibility to pursue such signs further, because anything you learn about problems is likely to be helpful in revision. If you are covered in these most central areas, you can safely depend on serendipity to single out other important good or bad effects.

So much will be going on in the classroom where materials are being tried out that there will be no hope of noticing everything, let alone recording it. You need more than observations; you need data, observations selected and organized to speak to a question. You've got the questions, so what are the data? It is convenient to distinguish types of data by the way they are collected. The most common and easiest form of data collection is informal observation—you simply look and listen. As a precaution, you might get a disinterested observer to look and listen and report to you. Another common, easy source of data is interviews with teacher and students. Both interview and observation can be strengthened in some respects by using structured lists of things to look for and questions to ask and standardized methods of recording and analyzing data.

Often some sort of test instrument is created that presents an appropriate stimulus to your subject and records the response. In this way you can introduce some types of tasks that you know have special relevance to what you are attempting to teach; you don't have to wait for them to occur naturally. This type of instrument can also be structured and standardized, but it need not be; you can simply present your subjects with the task and ask them to think aloud or give an oral or written response in their own words. In fact, if the topic is not especially verbal, you can simply watch and see if they do it and how. At the other extreme, you can select published, standardized instruments. Test instruments include interest inventories, attitude measures, and other nonachievement measures, as well as the academic tests we usually associate with the term.

These three types of data—observations, interviews, and test instruments—are the mainstay of field testing. They are versatile enough that you can probably get useful evidence on just about any question you will want to ask by using them.

Controlling for Threats to Validity Remember that your purpose is to answer the questions: Does it work as expected? How can it be improved? In order to answer these questions you will need to make inferences from observations, interviews, and test results. These inferences can easily lead you astray. For example, if a developer's ego is too heavily involved in the materials, he may be so anxious at the thought of negative findings that he overlooks signs that the curriculum is not working. A bias against some aspect of the curriculum may predispose an observer to record negative evidence about it. A field trial may go swimmingly because especially talented students and teacher make brilliant creative adjustments to the curriculum's weaknesses. A curriculum may work well on the surface but fail to teach anything of lasting value. And so on. The list of potential threats is very long.

There are standard ways of controlling the possible contaminating effect of nearly every potential threat to the validity of one's data. But these controls are not without cost in time and effort. For example, we can try out the materials in more than one classroom to control for the possiblity of an especially talented group. We can hire an observer who doesn't know anything about the experiment and has no stake in any outcome. We can compare observations of the class using the trial curriculum with another class studying from other curriculum materials. But we can't possibly control for *every* threat to validity, and in most curriculum evaluation studies we cannot realistically spend much time at all on controlling our inferences. We should, however, control any that are so blatant that they cast serious doubt on the results.

An alternative to controlling potential threats to validity is to let them operate unchecked and to estimate their contribution to the contaminated results and correct for it. There are techniques, for example, for correcting in this way classes of unequal initial ability, by lowering the final scores of the abler group an amount based on the extent of their initial differences. This is known as analysis of covariance. A more common application of this technique is in testing, where the average effect of guessing is estimated and scores are corrected for this source of error. Observing another class of similar composition is often helpful in making a qualitative estimate of the confounding effect of the particular circumstances of the field test.

CONCLUSION: THE CRAFT OF CURRICULUM DESIGN

Curriculum materials design is, finally, the building of intricate layers of order—program, course, unit, activity; content, purpose, structure, approach. The many hundreds of decisions embodied in each layer are each subject to many disparate considerations. The materials that result are woven from these simpler decisions as a tapestry is woven from single-colored threads. In curriculum materials the quality of the final product depends on the total configuration of decisions and on how well they are carried out in creating the actual materials.

Generally speaking, good orchestration of the many elements is a more critical skill for the developer than the ability to make any single category of decisions, because whether the curriculum works at all depends critically on how well the various details fit together to perform the essential work of curriculum materials. The only way to learn to recognize good orchestration, let alone to do it, is to study examples. The more examples, the better the examples, the more intensively they are studied, and the more they are discussed with others of varied backgrounds, the more you will learn.

The execution of curriculum materials design decisions requires mastery of a number of crafts. If materials are printed, the quality of the writing and the graphic design will be critical. Each medium—audio, video, computers, and so on—has its own associated crafts. In addition, the design of activities demands mastery of certain skills of managing children in a learning setting. If we add these skill demands to those of working with the content itself, it becomes easy to understand why curriculum materials design is nearly always carried out by a team.

The design of curriculum materials is a craft that benefits from the use of many arts and sciences skillfully and systematically combined. Excellence in curriculum materials design requires an immense fund of knowledge and skill on the part of the development team and considerable resources (libraries, classrooms, studios for prototype development). It requires the integration of practical judgment with theoretical insight. It demands both rationality and emotional and interpersonal sensitivity. It benefits from subtlety and sophistication in the discriminations of better and worse in things educational. To portray it as an art fails to give due consideration to the facts and relationships it must respect and to the need for its results to be objectively defensible. To portray it as a technology narrows and trivializes the many subtle and important considerations crucial to important stakeholders in the educative process. Whatever may be gained by such technicizing in reliability and validity of individual decisions must be weighed against what is lost in breadth and subtlety of the considerations brought to bear on the whole body of decisions. What we want are decisions that have received a deeper, fuller consideration. Results will then be as scientific as the state of science permits and as artful as artists' imagination can conceive. Anything more scientific than this is scientism and anything more arty is self-indulgence.

QUESTIONS FOR STUDY

1. Select an historically important curriculum project about which to read. Identify the project's sponsors and study the process by which the founders negotiated a charter with the sponsors. If possible, examine materials created by the project. In what ways are they consistent and inconsistent with the project's charter?

2. Write a briefing paper to the new executive director of a foundation who wants to improve the curriculum in a particular subject. Assume she is knowledgeable about the subject but not about curriculum development. Explain what can and cannot be accomplished by curriculum materials development projects. Explain what is involved in sponsoring a curriculum materials development project.

3. If you can find a curriculum development group at work in your area, ask them to let you sit in on their meetings. Tape record and study their deliberations. Try to see how they rely on ideas from their platform in making decisions. See if you can locate weaknesses in the platform by studying instances in which the team is unable to resolve questions or where controversies persist.

4. Read a book or article from psychology, philosophy, or a social science that you think might provide the same kind of platform support as Hughes' or Seligman's works. Abstract the ideas useful for a curriculum development platform. Apply those ideas to existing materials in some school subject and suggest how the materials should be revised to be consistent with these ideas.

5. Write a critical assessment of the comparative merits of two or three competing ideas as alternative platform elements—for example, Seligman's learned helplessness and Bandura's social modeling theory.

6. One of the weaknesses of curriculum development projects is that perspectives of the clients and users of the materials (teachers and students especially) sometimes get lost. Suggest how this weakness might be mitigated.

7. Check a convenient textbook or course of study to see how many violations you find of one or more of these commonsense principles discussed earlier in the chapter. You may be surprised to discover how commonly even such time-honored and basic principles as these are violated.

8. Choose a particular educational problem that you feel familiar with, such as teaching science or foreign language to elementary school children. Identify two or three educational programs designed to resolve this problem. Critically and comparatively assess these two programs on the criteria suggested in this chapter. If you can, suggest design features that would improve on both.

9. Analyze existing curriculum materials in an area you are familiar with. Ask questions such as those included in Boxes 13-4 through 13-6. Does the entertaining of these questions generate ideas for improving the materials?

10. Choose an educational activity that you find intrinsically interesting. Analyze this activity and identify its basic schema. Develop a theory that explains what the activity does and why it works. Assess the strengths and limitations of the activity for various educational uses. Find a better alternative, if you can.

11. Observe teachers using curriculum materials. Note kinds and degrees of adaptation and variation in how they use the materials.

12. Choose a unit from a curriculum development project, preferably a real one, but possibly a hypothetical one. Prepare an evaluation plan for it. Make up a set of questions specific to your project that would help determine if the curriculum worked and how it can be improved. Outline observations, interview questions, and test instruments that would provide the best evidence on each of the questions you raise. List what you consider to be the three most serious threats to the validity of the answers you would get from the data you mentioned earlier. Suggest low-cost methods for controlling them or accounting for their contribution to the results.

13. Find or develop a measure for a given outcome of some sophistication. Criticize what you find and suggest ways to improve.

RECOMMENDED READING

Ralph Tyler's classic *Basic Principles of Curriculum and Instruction* (1949) is seminal. Tyler's blend of practicality, rationality, science, and values has suited American education extremely well and has been enormously influential. Although it is brief, it is rich and will reward repeated reading. Gagne and Briggs (1979) show how the rational and scientific strains in Tyler have been developed by applied psychologists into the procedures of instructional design. Rowntree (1981) uses the same approach in a broader and more flexible way. Romiszowski (1981) gives the same approach a systems analysis twist.

The basic reference on deliberative design is my *School Review* article (Walker 1971a). Further details can be found in Walker (1971b, 1974). Riley (1984a,b,c) studied course development teams at the Open University and discovered some intriguing patterns and generated some interesting hypotheses. Taba (1972) recommended and followed a strategy of curriculum development essentially deliberative. Schwab's series of practical papers (Schwab 1969, 1971, 1973) are vital to further investigation on deliberation, on conceptualizing problems, and on virtually all aspects of deliberative design. Houle (1972) offers an approach to the design of educational programs for adults that is an excellent illustration of deliberative design.

Posner and Rudnitsky (1982) offer many helpful tips on course design. Cronbach, et al. (1980), Cronbach (1982), and Bloom, Hastings, and Madaus (1971) are the references I find continually helpful on field testing and evaluation.

Several exciting theoretical ideas have emerged over the past few years that call out to be used in curriculum development platforms. My favorites are schema theory (Anderson 1978), naive models (Case 1978), reciprocal teaching (Palincsar and Brown 1984), informal reasoning (Perkins 1985), cognitive analyses of problem-solving strategies (Perkins 1981; Whimbey and Lochhead 1982), and computer-based modeling (White 1984).

Development of curriculum materials also requires skills in the medium used. Some references I find myself continuing to consult on commonly used media are: on self-instructional materials (Rowntree 1986), on test items (Bloom, Hastings, and Madaus 1971), on graphics (Herdeg 1979; Tufte 1983), on computer software (Walker and Hess 1982), on video (Swain 1976).

REFERENCES

Anderson, Richard C. 1978. Schemata as Scaffolding for the Representation of Information in Connected Discourse. *American Educational Research Journal* 15:433–440.

Bloom, Benjamin, J. Thomas Hastings, and George Madaus. 1971. *Handbook on Formative and Summative Evaluation of Student Learning*. N.Y.: McGraw-Hill.

Bobbitt, Franklin. 1924. *How to Make a Curriculum*. Boston: Houghton Mifflin.

Case, Robbie. Summer 1978. A Developmentally Based Theory and Technology of Instruction. *Review of Educational Research* 48:439–463.

Cronbach, Lee J. et al, 1980. *Toward Reform of Program Evaluation*. San Francisco: Jossey Bass.

Cronbach, Lee J. 1982. *Designing Evaluations of Educational and Social Programs*. San Francisco: Jossey Bass.

Dewey, John. 1902. *The Child and the Curriculum*. Chicago: University of Chicago Press.

Gagne, Robert M. and Leslie Briggs. 1979. *Principles of Instructional Design* (2nd ed.) N.Y.: Holt, Rinehart, and Winston.

Herdeg, Walter. 1979. *Diagrams: The Graphic Visualization of Abstract Data*. Zurich: The Graphis Press.

Houle, Cyril O. 1972. *The Design of Education*. San Francisco: Jossey-Bass.

Hughes, Martin. 1986. *Children and Number*. London: Basil Blackwell.

Itzkoff, Seymour. 1986. *How We Learn to Read*. Ashfield, MA: Paideia Press.

Kilpatrick, William H. 1927. Statement of Position. *Foundations and Technique of Curriculum-Construction.* Twenty-Sixth Yearbook of the National Society for the Study of Education. Bloomington, IL: Public School Publishing Company.

Moskowitz, Breyna Arlene. November 1978. The Acquisition of Language. *Scientific American* 239:92–109.

Palincsar, A. S., and A. L. Brown. 1984. Reciprocal Teaching of Comprehension-Fostering and Comprehension-Monitoring Activities. *Cognition and Instruction* 1:117–175.

Perkins, David N. 1981. *The Mind's Best Work.* Cambridge, MA: Harvard University Press.

Perkins, David N. 1985. Postprimary Education Has Little Impact on Informal Reasoning. *Journal of Educational Psychology* 77:562–571.

Posner, George and Alan Rudnitsky. 1982. *Course Design.* N.Y.: Longman's.

Reynolds, John and Malcolm Skilbeck. 1976. *Culture and the Classroom.* London: Open Books Publishing.

Riley, Judith. October 1984a. An Explanation of Drafting Behaviors In the Production of Distance Education Materials. *British Journal of Educational Technology* 15:226–238.

Riley, Judith. October 1984b. The Problems of Revising Drafts of Distance Education Materials. *British Journal of Educational Technology* 15:205–226.

Riley, Judith. October 1984c. The Problems of Drafting Distance Education Materials. *British Journal of Educational Technology* 15:192–204.

Romiszowski, Alexander. 1981. Another Look at Instructional Design. *British Journal of Educational Technology,* 12:19–49.

Rowntree, Derek. 1981. *Developing Courses for Students.* London: McGraw-Hill.

Rowntree, Derek. 1986. *Teaching through Self-Instruction: A Practical Handbook for Course Developers.* N.Y.: Nichols.

Schwab, Joseph. November 1969. The Practical: A Language for Curriculum. *School Review* 78:1–39.

Schwab, Joseph. August 1971. The Practical: Arts of Eclectic. *School Review* 80:461–89.

Schwab, Joseph. August 1973. The Practical 3: Translation into Curriculum, *School Review* 81:501–522.

Seligman, Martin E. P. 1975. *Helplessness.* San Francisco: W. H. Freeman.

Swain, Dwight. 1976. *Film Scriptwriting.* N.Y.: Hastings House.

Taba, Hilda. 1962. *Curriculum Development: Theory and Practice.* N.Y.: Harcourt Brace Jovanovich.

Thorndike, Edward L. and Arthur Gates. 1929. *Elementary Principles of Education.* N.Y.: Macmillan.

Tufte, Edward R. 1983. *The Visual Display of Quantitative Information.* Cheshire, CT: Graphics Press.

Tyler, Ralph. 1949. *Basic Principles of Curriculum and Instruction.* Chicago: University of Chicago Press.

Walker, Decker. November 1971a. A Naturalistic Model for Curriculum Development. *School Review* 80:51–65.

Walker, Decker F. 1971b. A Study of Deliberation in Three Curriculum Projects, *Curriculum Theory Network* 7:118–134.

Walker, Decker and Robert Hess. 1982. *Instructional Software.* Belmont, CA: Wadsworth.

Walker, Decker and William Reid. 1974. Curriculum Development in an Art Project. *Case Studies in Curriculum Change.* London: Routledge and Kegan Paul.

Whimbey, A., and Lochhead, J. (1982). *Problem-Solving and Comprehension.* Hillsdale, NJ: Lawrence Erlbaum.

White, Barbara. 1984. Designing Computer Games to Help Physics Students Understand Newton's Laws of Motion. *Cognition and Instruction* 1:69–108.

INDEX